The Jews of the Republic

Stanford Studies in Jewish History and Culture
Edited by Aron Rodrigue and Steven J. Zipperstein

The Jews of the Republic

A Political History of
State Jews in France
from Gambetta to Vichy

Pierre Birnbaum
Translated by Jane Marie Todd

Stanford University Press
Stanford, California 1996

The Jews of the Republic: A Political History of State Jews in France from Gambetta to Vichy was originally published as *Les Fous de la République: Histoire politique des Juifs d'État. de Gambetta à Vichy.* © 1992 Librairie Arthème Fayard.

Stanford University Press
Stanford, California
© 1996 by the Board of Trustees of the
Leland Stanford Junior University
Printed in the United States of America

CIP data appear at the end of the book

Stanford University Press publications are distributed exclusively by Stanford University Press within the United States, Canada, Mexico, and Central America; they are distributed exclusively by Cambridge University Press throughout the rest of the world.

To my children,
heirs to the republican dream

Contents

The Jews of the Republic

Introduction:
The King's Fools and the Republic's Fools

In their glory days during the Renaissance, the king's fools occupied a privileged place at court: dressed in sumptuous garments comparable in every detail to those of the kingdom's great, in scarlet cloaks and ermine-lined capes, their magnificence was in keeping with the power they seemed to command, symbolized by the bauble they brandished, the absurd equivalent of the scepter. That was because "the fool is the king's ridiculous double,"[1] his deformed, amplified mirror image at the limits of the grotesque; the fool was such a fool for love of the king that in truth he could only appear foolish. And yet, little by little, he became the king's privileged confidant through the confidence he inspired and was metamorphosed into a true agent of the state endowed with responsibilities, into an unofficial official of the kingdom, a respectable, dignified, and competent person. As the king's power was imposed on all through relentless centralization and the legitimacy of order, the fool in the absolutist state abandoned the aspect of a foolish and imaginative buffoon.

In many ways, the administrative France of the nineteenth century continued and reinforced the institutions of the ancien régime. From the French Revolution to the Third Republic, through many fits and starts, a political class came into being that had been recruited according to meritocratic criteria. But things had changed radically, at least in one crucial aspect: the proclamation of equality among all citizens led little by little to the de-institutionalization of religion, the elimination of state denominations. It took time for these changes to actually take root, and advances and setbacks were endless: it was the so-called Republic of the Jules that finally assured the triumph of the new principles. At that time, the status of minority denominations was transformed: Protestants and Jews now became part of the state with the same qualifications as their Catholic colleagues. Things were less clear in reality, of course, and influence and solidarity still determined careers in part. But the essential had been set in place. From that point on, a phenomenon almost unique for its time came about: Jews attained high government posts without converting to Catholicism and led a public existence as high officials even though, in their heart of hearts and in their private lives, they remained faithful to their own traditions, to one degree or another.

We propose to call these men state Jews, to distinguish them from their predecessors, court Jews, who were more oriented toward the world of business or banking.[2] From the beginning, they were truly impassioned by their new roles in public service. They gave their hearts and souls to their jobs, stripping off their former costumes to take on the noble livery of grave and responsible state dignitaries. They intended to serve with all their might this emancipatory, rationalist Republic that was so concerned with progress. In that sense, the 171 state Jews who reached the heights of politico-administrative power under the Third Republic—the *préfets*, generals, *conseillers d'Etat*, and magistrates, but also the *députés* and senators who sometimes became ministers—proved to be indisputably the Republic's fools, fools for love of the Republic.

They loved it with devotion, propagated its values, rushed to its protective arms, even going so far as to constitute true administrative families, anxious to ensure the proper functioning of public service. They were the new heroes whose slightest acts and gestures were honored in Jewish circles, whose promotions within the state were all endlessly commented upon. The newspaper *Archives Israélites* periodically made up an "Honor Roll of French Jews," celebrating those who "have obtained advancement in the various administrations of the country or who have been admitted to government schools. This record of Jewish progress has no other goal than to justify the great act of emancipation of 1791, which, in breaking the age-old chains of Jews, has given useful citizens to France, each working to the best of his abilities for the happiness and greatness of the Nation."[3]

And yet, even though the republican state, at least in its administration, carried on the traditions of the absolutist state of earlier times, these modern fools for the Republic were not in the least bit foolish, as the king's fools had been at the beginning. As the products of universities and, more and more, of the *grandes écoles*, their expertise was unimpeachable. They no longer waved a bauble, but possessed the various attributes of powerful public servants; if they still wore ermine, it was now on their magistrate's cap; their costumes were no longer bright, gaudy, and provocative, but somber and respectable, stripped of all caprice, as befitted their role.

And yet, if we look more closely, does not the history of these state Jews, these fools for love of the Republic, repeat the destiny of their predecessors, but in reverse? Whereas the kings's fools, fools for love of the king, began by eliciting derision, only to later assert themselves with the seriousness of their new roles, state Jews unwittingly acted as lightning rods, attracting laughter and imprecations. In this particularly agitated period of France's history, when crises and internecine wars threatened, these devout followers of the republican state, these men whose existence we will attempt to retrace, often had a cathartic effect, purging passions, attracting rejection and hatred onto themselves. As officials who were unlike the others, they may even have served to exonerate the republican state itself in the eyes of its enemies. Such is the object of this book: to seek out those state Jews, sons of the Republic, most of whom have fallen into oblivion, in order to retrace their passionate and tragic history from Gambetta to Vichy.[4]

PART I

Family Portraits

CHAPTER ONE

At the Heart of Republican Polity: The Reinachs

On 29 January 1891, a violent debate destined to remain famous in the history of contemporary France suddenly erupted in the Chamber of Deputies: Joseph Reinach, friend and close collaborator of Gambetta, took the floor to protest the banning of *Thermidor*, a play by Victorien Sardou, which had been playing for some time at the Comédie Française. The play dared to sharply criticize Robespierre and the Reign of Terror as a whole, at the very moment of the Republic's triumph. To the applause of the monarchist right and the approving gaze of the very reactionary Count Albert de Mun, who had always opposed the French Revolution in the name of intransigent Catholicism, Reinach attacked "that political Tartuffe named Robespierre" and refused to consider "the men who made the most noble and pure republicans perish on the scaffold as the very incarnation of the Republic." Whereas he, more than anyone, venerated "the founders of the Republic," and denounced with equal vigor "the hideous law of 22 Prairial."

As he was attacking the person of Robespierre, a *député* called out to him in outrage, "You would not be a Frenchman without him!" Reinach returned tit for tat: "If there is anyone who worships the French Revolution deep in his heart, it is the man who stands before you. He worships the French Revolution, honors it, respects it, is filled with recognition and gratitude for it. He loves it." With these words, he confirmed his unshakable attachment to the achievements of 1789: like all state Jews, of whom he was one of the most famous, he was dedicating all his efforts to strengthening the Republic, which was being attacked by Boulangism and by certain currents such as socialism, which he considered too radical, and which had emerged, precisely, out of a Robespierrist tendency carried to excess.

Like many French Jews, for almost two years he had been enthusiastically celebrating the centennial of the French Revolution, and he knew better than anyone the significance of Robespierre's role in the emancipation of his coreligionists. As a French citizen who incarnated the Republic's new political personnel, he could only be shocked to have the already distant origin of his access to citizenship recalled to him: it was as if criticizing Robespierre inevitably placed the blasphemer in the camp of the counter-revolutionaries! The time of the Reign of Terror nevertheless seemed past to him; in his view, republican concord was about to be installed permanently, according to the wishes of his closest friends, Gambetta and, later, Jules Ferry.

But that was not the end of the matter: Clemenceau seized the floor and pronounced sentence before Reinach, who stood by silently: "The French Revolution is all of a piece!" Then Clemenceau adopted an ironic tone: "Here is M. Joseph Reinach, standing before us to undertake the enormous task of sifting through the French Revolution in his own way: I accept this, I reject that! I admire such ingenuity. Gentlemen, whether we like it or not, whether it pleases or shocks us, the French Revolution is all of a piece."[1]

Ironically enough, Gambetta's former *chef du cabinet* found himself mixed up in that violent altercation about which so many contemporary historians have written: this Opportunist state Jew was thus taken to task by the leader of Radicalism, thus becoming the unwilling ally of the aristocratic right, which would mercilessly pounce on Clemenceau. Clemenceau concluded in a threatening manner. "This admirable Revolution which has made us what we are is not over," he emphasized. "It still endures, we are still actors in it, the same men are still grappling with the same enemies." "You are still the same!" he cried out at another point. "We have not changed. The struggle must therefore continue until victory is assured." Called upon to join one camp or the other, Reinach and most state Jews took upon themselves the role of faithful supporters of the republican order, yet still opposed the new extremists, those who found inspiration in Robespierre and justified their radical and soon-to-be socialist struggle by calling into question the republican order on which they had founded all their hopes.

A little more than forty years later, excluded from public office by the Statute on Jews of October 1940 just as he was about to be named *conseiller d'Etat*, Julien Reinach was called in by R. Alibert, his former colleague, who had become one of the drafters of the Statute and an enthusiastic supporter of the new antisemitic policy. Alibert expressed his regret that given the circumstances, Reinach could become only an "honorary" *conseiller d'Etat*! Julien Reinach, son of Théodore Reinach (the famous brother of Joseph), who had earned first place in the general examination for graduating high school students, a great scientist who was also a *député*, withdrew to the south of France to finish his translation of *Gallus* in quiet isolation, or so he believed. Recipient of the Croix de Guerre in 1914 during a deadly battle in which he was grievously wounded, an officer of the reserve, a state Jew and son of the Republic, who remained ever confident of its protection, he devoted his time to working on his translation, experiencing little worry.

The police came for him in September 1943 and interned him in Drancy, where his wife Rita, also Jewish, joined him voluntarily. There he found other state Jews: Jean Cahen-Salvador, Pierre Pontrémoli, and Jacques Helbronner. An astonishing scene took shape: four *conseillers d'Etat* bearing the yellow star of David sewn to their clothes, trying to survive in the antechamber of death, guarded by the French police! At this particularly tragic moment, the revolutionary emancipation of Jews, desired by Abbé Grégoire and realized in 1791 with Robespierre's help, had come to an end: especially when one considers that it was the French police who kept such close watch on Julien and his companions in misfortune, who, like him, were members of the most prestigious of state institutions.[2] In Drancy, the son of Théodore Reinach even spent a long period of time in solitary confinement. Then, the *conseiller d'Etat*, the illustrious descendant of the Reinachs, traveled the road to Bergen-Belsen in a cattle car; he was liberated by Allied troops in May 1945.[3] His brother, Léon Reinach, met an even more tragic fate: he was deported to Auschwitz with his wife and children. None of them returned. Their father, Théodore Reinach, the foremost supporter of assimilation and of the most militant Franco-Judaism, had celebrated the "religion of the fatherland" and, even in 1927, had made every effort

to break down all barriers, eliminate all misunderstandings that could still separate the enlightened Jew and the patriotic Frenchman of the twentieth century, to finally reconcile our two attachments and strengthen one by means of the other: first, the touching attachment that links us to the great and painful past of Israel; and second, the no less filial attachment to this regained fatherland, which for French Jewry is the mutilated France of 1871, France, the soldier for justice, the martyr to freedom.[4]

And yet, two of his sons were turned over to the Nazi enemy by the new authoritarian regime that this same France adopted, turning its back on emancipation. These two great-nephews of Joseph Reinach (a man who had enthusiastically celebrated Pétain's military merits in his time, during World War I) were turned over to the enemy by the marshal's regime. And, in contrast, Julien Reinach's son — Théodore's grandson — Fabrice Reinach, in the name of the France of liberty and against the France identified with Vichy, joined the Free French Forces in Spain and fought in the air war. Fabrice would later attend the École Nationale d'Administration, and in 1960, would become prime minister in Michel Debré's cabinet. It is as if, from Gambetta to de Gaulle, state Jews maintained an absolute faith in the Republic in spite of everything, joining with those who defended it.

The long Reinach saga, from the 1880s to contemporary times, in itself epitomized the birth of a Jewish political class that, under the Third Republic, reached the top state posts. The influence of these Jews and their prestige seemed boundless for a time, as if they naturally accompanied the daily political life of the Third Republic, performing duties that granted them great public visibility on several occasions, whether in Gambetta's entourage, during the episode of Boulangism, the crisis in Panama, or the Dreyfus affair, that is, during a number of Franco-French wars. In their closest family ties, they also appeared as state Jews who were still part of the dominant socioeconomic world: their personal history was thus perfectly identified with the history that affected French Jews more generally and led them from an essentially economic role to a series of more strictly politico-administrative duties. By themselves, then, they were emblematic of a specific moment in the history of the Jewish elite, the moment marked by the move from economic circles, to which they gained access at the beginning of the century, to the world of politics, which was truly opened to them only with the Third Republic. Other Jews — as we will find later on — more certain of their status, joined the parties and movements on the left, especially between the two world wars, at times abandoning the framework of republican consensus in favor of revolutionary ideals. This shift horrified the Reinachs and all those state Jews who were still identified with them.

The history of the Reinachs begins with the arrival in France of the dynasty's founder, Hermann Reinach. Naturalized in 1870, this major banker was in love with the France of the Enlightenment — that of Voltaire and Rousseau — which had been the first to make Jews full citizens. From the July Monarchy to the Second Empire, Hermann Reinach was successful in business affairs, moved into the best neighborhoods, and became part of the dominant circles. A committed Orleanist, he also associated with Thiers before committing himself resolutely to the defense of the Republic in 1848. At his death in 1899, he left behind a fortune of 14 million francs, one of the largest of the time. Unlike many court Jews, bankers, and industrialists of his day—the Pereires and the Foulds, for example—Hermann Reinach remained faithful to his Judaism. He had a Jewish wedding, gave his children religious educations, and was generous toward the Jewish community: at the time of his death in 1899, the *Univers Israélite* considered him "one of our most worthy and charitable coreligionists."[5] In the middle of the Dreyfus affair, his sons took it upon themselves to give him a religious funeral, a courageous and almost provocative act. The creation of a "Reinach endowment" at the consistory, to be given to a Jewish woman born in France who married a French Jewish worker, emphasized the importance Hermann Reinach placed on the indispensability of the "regeneration" of his coreligionists, understood almost in Abbé Grégoire's sense, the sign, in his view, of true assimilation into French society at large.[6]

His three sons, nicknamed "the know-it-all brothers" by a cabaret singer in Montmartre, quickly achieved celebrity through their scholastic success, winning the awards at the *concours général*. Salomon became an eminent scholar, and Théodore and Joseph both later became *députés*; for a time, Joseph even held the crucial post of Gambetta's *directeur du cabinet* in the "Grand Ministère." Scholarly success thus allowed for a transition from the economic world to the political and cultural world: the sons, with countless degrees among them, came to serve the state.[7] But, as Julien Benda judiciously observed,

The triumph of the Reinachs at the *concours général* appears to me as one of the essential sources of the antisemitism that broke out some fifteen years later. . . . Justice no doubt required that the Reinachs get all the awards if their exams were the best; but political interest, and that of Jews in the first place, required that they be given only a few.[8]

They became involved in politics through Gambetta's intervention. Gambetta had begun his own career in law with Adolphe Crémieux, the great orchestrator of Franco-Judaism, the key personality in the formation of a politico-administrative elite of state Jews. In a kind of historical continuity, Joseph Reinach succeeded Crémieux, becoming the close confidant of Gambetta, his spokesperson and later his official biographer, responsible for spreading the thinking of the old Opportunist leader by publishing eleven volumes of his speeches. In his view, as he noted as late as 1906, Gambetta was "the incarnation of French patriotism. . . . He not only tenderly cherished "sweet France"—its lovely sky, its beautiful countryside where the living is good—he also and especially loved the moral France, the France nourished on the ideas of the world at large."[9] The link between Gambetta and many state Jews was brought about through just such a conception of the nation, oriented more toward morality and universal values than toward land and soil.

Joseph Reinach's entire career was spent beside Gambetta or in his shadow: in 1876, he became editor of the newspaper *La République Française*, which had been created by the Opportunist leader to reinforce the regime, which was still threatened by rightists. In 1881, at the time of the Grand Ministère, when Reinach was directing the government team, this daily paper became almost its official representative. In 1883, he served briefly as general secretary to the Ligue des Patriotes (league of patriots), which was founded to defend the Republic and Gambetta's ideals. He hastily quit a few months later, when it took a purely nationalist and aggressive turn. He threw himself into battle against Boulanger, vigorously denounced the threat of the "black horse" and his authoritarian inclinations, and struggled relentlessly for his defeat and conviction. Opposed to this "circus general," he maintained that with him "the history of Brumaire and December in all its imbecility is starting all over again."[10] In the face of this new attempt at a takeover, Reinach joined forces with those defending the gains of the Republic.[11]

In 1889 he was elected *député* of Basses-Alpes, beginning a long parliamentary career that brought him from the confrontations concerning the Panama affair to the battle for Dreyfus, to World War I. In an almost caricatured manner, he defended the Republic tooth and nail, vehemently opposing "modern collectivism," the revolutionary projects of Marat, and the social confrontation strategies of Marx and his spokesperson in France, Jules Guesde. He also denounced the "Commune assassins";[12] for him, "socialism is the enemy. . . . Collectivism is despicable, unjust, grotesque, backward, barbarous: the sons of the Revolution reject it as the destruction of the essential achievements of 1789."[13]

Like most state Jews of the time, Joseph Reinach was a fierce supporter of law and order in all its forms, which he saw as the only means possible for reinforcing the power of the Republic in a way that would make it indestructible. For that reason, he approved without reservation the colonial conquests in Indochina and Africa, effectively supported Jules Ferry in his policy of conquest, proposed the creation of a *ministère des colonies* and of a colonial army (one of his books was even titled *Armée coloniale*). Always looking for the most appropriate instrument for mobilizing the energies of citizens who were naturally devoted to the Republic, he also came out in favor of extending the length of military service and, in a report to the Chamber of Deputies, expressed the desire for a "reorganization of the army," so that it would be capable of facing both external enemies and the internal threats embodied by various seditious extremist groups. Later, he enthusiastically chronicled the exploits of French soldiers during World

War I, singing the praises of the army, its leaders, and its heroic soldiers, relating their military feats day by day under the pseudonym "Polybe." "From Flanders to Argonne, from the Condé camp to the Dumouriez camp, the same glorious names of old appeared in the communiqués of King Albert, of Haig, and of Pétain. . . . How lovely to be French and republican!"[14] In his last work, symbolically titled *Francia*, he once more forthrightly proclaimed his love of Frenchness, of the nation whose revolutionary inspiration was definitively assured by the triumph of a generous Republic, a Republic that showed itself open to Jews, even as it involuntarily elicited, as a reaction, a constant strain of antisemitism.

In fact, Joseph Reinach's exceptional political career proved more ambiguous: although its outward aspect consisted in an indisputable power that for several decades granted him great influence within the political class, its hidden aspect had him constantly grappling with the most extreme antisemitism. During this entire turbulent period, he was without question the most violently and systematically attacked Jew in the national and local press, during election meetings, in caricatures, songs, and lampoons. Beginning with his first election campaign in Digne in June 1889, he had to admit in the *Écho des Alpes* that "he was criticized for having been born into a religion that is not the Catholic religion"; the slander and insults continued to fly.[15] During the 1893 election campaign, the local conservative camp's rejection was absolute: according to the *Journal des Basses-Alpes*, nothing "justifies the election of a candidate of German origin, of the Jewish religion, who knows nothing of our ways, our habits, and our needs." A few days later, the same paper published an open letter from two peasants addressed to the minister of the interior:

No doubt, sir, you know that we are represented by a Jewish *député* named Joseph Reinach. He is not from around here. . . . Although we are not pillars of the Church, we do have our children baptized, we send them to mass and catechism, we have them take their first communion, we marry them in the church, and we bury our dead in blessed ground, with a priest in attendance. We did not like the idea of being represented by a Jew.[16]

Even though the French Republic, in the name of its universalist principles and as a function of its very conception of citizenship, fully legitimated the presence of Jewish *députés* and senators within its political class, the resistance of a society that had remained Catholic nevertheless made itself felt. In a single movement of rejection, that society often dismissed both the Republic and its non-Catholic servants. And, from the Third Republic to the present, one theory of representation has been invoked to justify this rejection: namely, respect for a particular cultural code, that of a society whose values remained shaped by the Catholic Church.[17]

As a consequence, *députés* had the duty to act in conformity with the Catholic particularism of deepest France. In many districts, voters saw to it that their *député* represented the local cultural traditions, from religious values to the various dialects in use, even including ways of acting and feeling, cooking habits or traditions belonging to wine-producing regions; in that sense, the *député* no longer represented the national will but rather the manners and customs of the land. The rejection of a Republic conceived as too universalist and detached from the "real country" inevitably implied rejecting Jews, since they almost always lacked roots to the land. In the eyes of many, their presence in politics immediately appeared just as artificial as the Republic that opened its doors to them. A violent political antisemitism arose against Joseph Reinach, but also against most Jewish *députés* and senators. Openly, in the most official election proclamations, Joseph Reinach's opponents denounced his Jewish or supposedly foreign origin; their platform statements, posted on school walls, were filled with hate. "He's a Jew, the son-in-law of one of the despoilers, and he expects your vote," proclaimed an election poster in Digne supporting one of his opponents.[18] At the national level, political antisemitism increased in violence, all the more so since Joseph Reinach, the most illustrious of state Jews, found himself in the middle of every one of the famous "Franco-French wars," which, from Panama to the Dreyfus affair, shook the period.

As early as Boulanger's time, opponents such as Déroulède called him the "little Jew who is enough to make you sick of Jews,"[19] while Rochefort saw him as "a microbe";[20] others nicknamed him "Jewball" (*Boule de Juif*). With the Panama scandal, Joseph Reinach was suddenly thrust into the eye of the storm. He found himself mixed up in the scandal against his will, because of his father-in-law — who, following the ferocious campaign conducted by *La Libre Parole*, finally committed suicide. Joseph Reinach's opponent warned voters: "Do not forget that it was a Jewish gang that ruined the Panama Company. He's a Jew, the son-in-law of one of the despoilers, and he expects your vote." In the face of these accusations, Reinach lost his seat. "To the rubbish heap," demanded Morès.[21] *La Diane* invented an astonishing character, Youssouf, who was supposed to incarnate Joseph Reinach, and endlessly recounted in great detail his formidable misdeeds.[22] *La Croix* (The cross), which believed it could announce his demise in April 1888, calmly maintained that "M. Reinach does not deserve the French nation's mourning."[23]

When Joseph Reinach later resolutely joined the Dreyfusard camp and became one of its principal actors, Édouard Drumont's antisemitic prose reached its heights: "Take a look at this little Jew from Hamburg. While his monkey face and deformed body bear all the stigmata, all the defects of the race, his hateful soul swollen with venom sums up even better all its maleficence, all its deadly and perverse genius. . . . Reinach has become master once more. It is he who reigns and governs in France."[24] The caricatures representing him at that time in *La Libre Parole* and *Le Pilori* deserve to find their place in the pantheon of antisemitism: almost daily, he was portrayed as an ape or some other animal. The man who adored the Republic, the close friend of all the supporters of that rationalist regime, appeared as a perverse and feeble being, a little Jew straight out of the bazaar, a prominently Semitic type who was betraying the interests of France and its army.[25]

La Croix denounced his role in the effort to rehabilitate Captain Dreyfus;[26] *La Libre Parole*, in turn, elicited an "appeal to decent folk" in response to the lawsuit initiated by the widow of Colonel Henry, whom Reinach had accused of complicity in Esterhazy's acts of treason. The newspaper called for a contribution that would allow her to carry out her plan. The famous "Henry monument," erected with the help of fifteen thousand contributors, is a memorial to hatred, poured out primarily on Joseph Reinach. One donor "would like to chock off his wheels with Reinach's brains," while another "expects to see Reinach in the gutter." Seven officers from Brittany sent money to show their anger "at the Jewish pig Reinach," and a butcher boy "would happily carve out Reinach's guts and those of his filthy gang of Jews."[27] Drumont erupted in anger against this defender of Dreyfus: "This Reinach appears as the personification of the counterfeit Frenchman. . . . He's really the German Jewish type, a Jew of the invasion that stupefied humanity."[28] On several occasions, during the many stages of the Affair, Joseph Reinach found himself obliged to defend his honor in a duel, weapons in hand. He was physically assaulted by a mob shouting, "Death to the Jews! Down with Reinach!"[29]

For a long time, antisemitic anger continued to take Joseph Reinach as the ideal scapegoat. In 1908, Léon Daudet wrote: "What is curious about Reinach is that juxtaposition of Jewish beast of prey ravaging for Jewry's benefit, and the liberated jurist decked out in all that Republican nonsense. The beast of prey leads in the direction of the Talmud, against the Christians; then the jurist projects a mantle of false common sense over the ethnic hatred."[30] And, true to himself, Léon Daudet still maintained in 1913 that "Alfred Dreyfus's treason, put into operation by Joseph Reinach . . . was the sign that our country had been turned over to the Germans by an Oriental horde."[31]

Of the three Reinach brothers, Joseph was, however, the one who most kept his distance from Judaism. He certainly belonged to the Jewish social milieu, like his wife and many of his friends, as his personal correspondence, for example, demonstrates; and when an antisemitic author turned to him in his effort to formulate a "registry" of Jewish notables, he responded:

I belong to the Jewish race and have never hidden that fact; but I could not allow myself to be part of compiling, even through tacit acquiescence, a list of proscribed persons. . . . I am completely indifferent to the prospect of being denounced as Jewish and of being once more slandered and libeled. But I am not at all indifferent to your abusing my silence so as to believe you are authorized to pursue your undertaking with impunity against the thousands of small and modest workers whose existence you are seeking to compromise.[32]

A politician in his outlook, he was certainly in solidarity with other Jews and fought measures that could affect them as such: his public activity, however, was almost entirely devoted to the nation alone and to the future of the Republic. Although he was elected in 1883 to the central committee of the Alliance Israélite Universelle, he resigned in the same year;[33] and in his speech and actions, he addressed national political life above all and not the problems proper to French Jews.

He favored secularization and intended to broaden that policy to cemeteries, which provoked the anger of *Archives Israélites*: "Oh, excuse me, M. Reinach," exclaimed the newspaper, "Ask a good Catholic, question a practicing Jew. Both of them will tell you that forcing them to go to their final resting place side by side with people they were raised to consider heretics is attacking their conscience, doing violence to their religious freedom."[34] Furthermore, he was completely opposed to the nascent Zionist movement, which he considered "idiocy." At the time of his death, the *Univers Israélite* emphasized the fact that

on the Jewish question, Joseph had very fixed ideas, which made him the very model of the assimilationist Jew. He believed that ever since the emancipation of the Jews, Judaism has been only a religious denomination, and, since he was not a believer, he stopped claiming he was a Jew. . . . We must combat tendencies that are so deadly to religion and to Judaism; we can be sorry that such a distinguished man kept his distance from the community; but we must recognize the logic in his attitude and the probity of his mind.[35]

Criticized by advocates of consistorial Judaism and by Jews who were tempted by a new kind of collective and national organization of their destiny, Joseph Reinach, like all the advocates of Franco-Judaism, nevertheless was *the* man to bring down for antisemites. In their view, he had become too much like other Frenchmen and thus threatened to abolish all difference; even before Maurice Barrès calmly asserted that no Jew could understand *Bérénice*, Drumont had written: "Speaking French is something else again. . . . You can't turn to some Leven or Reinach and naturalize his style as you naturalize his person; you must have been suckled on the nation's wine from birth, you must truly have come out of its earth. Only then . . . does your phrasing have a taste of the soil, drawn from a common bedrock of feelings and ideas."[36]

His brother, Théodore Reinach, was also a state Jew, a scholar who had accumulated university degrees and titles, and who also played a significant political role. This foremost theorist of assimilationist Franco-Judaism was also the object of an outburst of antisemitic anger. For Léon Daudet, Théodore Reinach "is almost as hideous as his brother Joseph, dyed in the same wool, with the same self-conceit. He has the aggressive pedantry of the Kraut. From his feet to his spectacles, he stinks of German Semitism."[37] Daudet continually made fun of the two brothers, whom he nicknamed "Orang" and "Outang." The man who received the largest number of awards in his generation at the *concours général*, the brilliant numismatist who published several academic works on ancient Greece and was eventually elected to the Académie des Inscriptions et Belles-Lettres, ran for office in 1906 in Savoy; he was elected and then reelected in 1910. In the Chamber of Deputies, he was particularly attentive to the problems of artistic and literary creation, and to the classification of artistic monuments. He was defeated in 1914 and completely abandoned political life. His political career was thus much shorter than Joseph's; furthermore, he never matched the prominence of his brother, the confidant and close friend of Gambetta.

The fact that he was more marginal in the public space and more preoccupied with research and history could only incite Théodore to focus more attention on the meaning of the Jews' destiny. That is why, if Joseph exemplified Jews' entry into the Republic under the leadership of Gambetta, Jules Ferry, and Waldeck-Rousseau, Théodore incarnated the ideological creation of Franco-Judaism. Joseph's writings rarely dealt with the Jews, whereas those of the *député* of Savoy very often concerned the Jews' history, mores, religion, or even their future within French society. The author of an imposing work, *Histoire des Israélites depuis l'époque de leur dispersion jusqu'à nos jours* (The history of the Jews from the time of their dispersion until our day), Théodore Reinach knew everything about Jewish history, from the most remote times to the contemporary period. For him, the fall of the Second Temple marked the end of "the history of the Jewish state, of Jewish nationality; but the history of Jews is not ended." At the end of his book, he emphasized the fact that "Judaism thus owes the breaking of its age-old chains to the Revolution . . . and we can say that any Jew today with memory and heart has a second fatherland, his oral fatherland, the France of 1791." He observed how "the secret affinity between the Jewish spirit and the French spirit hastened the moral assimilation of the two races," which allowed a true "moral fusion" in spite of the Jews' religious particularism.[38] The conclusion was obvious: "Judaism, ceasing to be a nation, has resigned itself to being only a religious community." If there was still solidarity among Jews throughout the world, it was simply a "moral tie," a "feeling of charitable obligation," which, for example, legitimated the educational and philanthropic role of the Alliance Israélite Universelle. In that sense, Jews were not working "for the good of Israel, but rather for the good of civilization in general. . . . Israel will cease to be a family only when humanity as a whole has in its turn become one great family."[39] Thus, Théodore Reinach devoted a large part of his energy to defining this Jewish morality in ethical and aesthetic terms, challenging, like his brother, any purely political dimension.

He founded the Union Israélite Libérale, the Reform Jewish institution in France, and attempted to define a Judaism oriented toward the beautiful and the true, proposing a great number of reforms that distanced it from orthodoxy and linked it to Catholic ceremonial practices. He did not hesitate to propose moving the *Shabbat* to Sunday and also wished to introduce into French synagogues the music and beauty he felt were lacking in German and Polish synagogues, so "sordid" in appearance, their "services without beauty." Seeking his inspiration in the Acropolis and the "muses of pagan antiquity,"[40] he exclaimed: "Judaism, once it has become detached from its original connection to the land and to nationality, aspires to become a truly universal belief." Far from the "outdated" imperatives of the Torah, Jews now found the foundation of their faith in humanity itself.[41]

Again like his brother, Théodore Reinach proclaimed his faith in the nation of Joan of Arc and displayed toward France a devotion close to worship.[42] He understood better than his brother that Russian and Polish Jews "are turning an anxious gaze, their needs unsatisfied by a filial heart, toward an earthly Zion, toward a Palestinian homeland." Nevertheless, for him the French Jew, who during the World War I, "fertilized with his blood . . . a hospitable land that had become his own," felt "forever indissociably linked to the destinies of his country of birth and of choice."[43] Whereas his own son would be turned over to the Gestapo by the French police a few years later and deported to Auschwitz, he remained at the time confident in the imminent disappearance of any trace of antisemitism within French society, greatly underestimating, like his brother and many other state Jews, the properly antisemitic dimension of the Franco-French wars.[44] For Théodore Reinach—and his words would become famous among Jews—one had only to oppose "the silence of disdain" to the schemings of Drumont and his acolytes, for the outbursts of antisemitism could only be "short-lived."[45]

For many historians, the Reinach brothers, including Salomon, the illustrious member of the Institut who did not number among state Jews strictly defined, incarnated an assimilationist Franco-Judaism that in the end implied the entire negation of Jewish particularism in the public space, its pure and simple dissolution into a Frenchness understood universally.[46] As a result, the Reinachs' extreme patriotism led them to blend into the national entity, marking a definitive end to Jewish history from that time on. In such a nation-state, assimilation obeys a logic of centralization that destroys particularism: the Reinachs, like Gambetta, were preoccupied with French centralization and clung to the unification of norms and values that would definitively ground the legitimacy of the universalist Republic, which the Church, for example, was still disputing. In the public space, they thus came out in favor of full integration into the French nation and the eradication of all particularism, but also in favor of the most steadfast rejection of all antisemitic scheming. In the private domain, they turned toward rationalism and faith in progress, without, however denying certain affinities or breaking the intense ties of internal sociability to Jewish circles, which were maintained from one generation to the next, though in our time they have had a tendency to weaken.[47]

CHAPTER TWO

From Generation to Generation:
The préfets Hendlé

In the department of Seine-Inférieure, in the month of February 1900, flags were at half-staff everywhere: the *conseil général* wanted to pay "a last tribute to the distinguished administrator who had devoted eighteen years of labor and dedication to the department." The *préfet* Ernest Hendlé had just died: an immense procession formed, unifying in sorrow agricultural associations, the Société Libre d'Émulation du Commerce et de l'Industrie (The society for the encouragement of commerce and industry), gymnastic societies, the Freemasons of Rouen, and even patriotic societies. Through the main arteries of Rouen, from the boulevard to Rue Jeanne-d'Arc, cavalry and infantry troops also paraded. As they did so, they passed before the *président* of the *conseil général*; numerous *préfets*; Waddington, senator and former *président du conseil*; the general in command of the Third Army Corps; the *président* of the *cour d'appel*; Zadoc-Kahn, chief rabbi of France and president of the central consistory; the clergy; the consistory of the Reformed (Protestant) Church; academic bodies; and so forth. The different municipal councils also joined in mourning: the mayor's office in La Bouille, for example, emphasized the fact that M. Hendlé "will leave behind the memory of an administration that was both active and firm, welcoming. We will all miss this man of courage and high intelligence."[1] *Le Figaro* maintained that he was "a *préfet* of the good old school that is disappearing,"[2] while *Le Temps* felt that he "led by his example an entire generation of functionaries."[3] In contrast, *La Libre Parole*, Drumont's anti-semitic journal, took one last stab at that "Hebrew" turned *préfet* by dint of the "Panamist and Jewish Republic . . . absolutely foreign in its ancestors and interests to old France, which is on its deathbed."[4]

A few years earlier, on 1 March 1893, a grand wedding had taken place at the Rue de la Victoire synagogue: *sous-préfet* Albert Hendlé, who would later become *conseiller d'Etat*, son of Ernest Hendlé, married Marthe Riqlès, the daughter of an industrialist, in the presence of *président du Conseil* Ribot, several ministers—for example, Siegfried, minister of commerce—Jules Simon, the police *préfet*, and numerous *préfets* and notables from the political world.[5] The politico-administrative class was thus assembled to pay tribute to the son of Ernest Hendlé, but also to a *sous-préfet* whose last administrative personnel report, dated 1892, had emphasized: "Belonging to a family of administrators, he was raised in matters of the administration, living in its midst; he has a consciousness of professional duty." *La Libre Parole* used other words to comment on the event: "A few weeks ago, Albert Hendlé was to be married and had to be set up in business. . . . Among the Jews, family feeling is highly developed. A family runs a police station like a hotel or a foreign exchange office. . . . He's a drab little insignificant Jew who's already been granted a high position."[6] From then on, Drumont's newspaper wouldn't leave them alone, those "yids as powerful as the Hendlés, father and son,"[7] whose slightest acts and gestures it reported.

Albert Hendlé conducted himself with great bravery during World War I, at the end of which he was named *conseiller d'Etat*, then director of the departmental and communal administration for the Ministry of the Interior.[8]

Later, in 1938, Henri Hendlé, son of Albert and grandson of Ernest, also died. He too was a member of the prefect civil service, and then general secretary of the department of Lot-et-Garonne. His death was the direct result of wounds received during World War I. He had volunteered for duty and was wounded three times, then trepanned. Awarded the Croix du Combattant and the Croix de Guerre, he also received the Médaille Interalliée and the Médaille de la Victoire for his acts of bravery during four years of conflict, which he ended with the rank of lieutenant. One of his citations was worded: "A young, observant officer, very energetic and very brave. On 6 August 1918, during a surveillance mission, was attacked by eight enemy monoplanes, turned on them with splendid courage, continuing to fire even though grievously wounded by a bullet."[9] In his personnel file dated 1925, the *préfet* noted: "The son of M. Hendlé, *conseiller d'Etat*, former *préfet* . . . has a solid administrative tradition to which he willingly conforms. . . . Should become *préfet*."[10]

From one generation to the next, from the foundation of the Third

Republic to its last years, the Hendlés incarnated in a remarkable way those state Jews who found in the principles of 1789, as they were definitively applied with the victory of the republican regime, the very foundation for an existence devoted to public service. The long-term result of the state's emancipation of Jews during the Revolution consisted in the formation of that elite of high Jewish officials attached to public service and anxious to appear as the firm defenders of the republican order. France was thus one of the rare countries where Jews could gain access to the state without converting to Christianity; in the Western world, countries as different as Germany and Great Britain, the former endowed with a strong and bureaucratized state, the latter, in contrast, limiting the growth of the state to a closed Establishment, both remained almost entirely hostile to Jews' entry into politico-administrative structures. For a long time, Christian affiliation remained an indispensable precondition for holding posts of authority in those countries.

In France, in contrast, the Jews became citizens in 1791 and were quickly granted access to positions of prestige in universities and the Collège de France. They had to wait several decades, however, before they could become part of the state, understood in terms of its public power. If we consider the particular case of the prefect civil service, the first Jewish *préfet* was named under the Second Empire: Emmanuel Lambert does not seem to have converted, though in 1858, he did modify his name, abandoning "Caïn."[11] In reality, it was only with the institutionalization of the Republic that certain Jews were to join the "new strata" that Gambetta devised to replace the ancient elite, which had remained opposed to the Republic.[12]

In the end, there were about forty Jewish *préfets, sous-préfets*, or *présidents* of *conseils de préfecture* under the Third Republic: of them, the Hendlés represented the archetype of state Jews who were *préfets*, and their history is inextricably linked to the fortunes and misfortunes of the Republic itself. Hence, Ernest Hendlé, who founded the administrative family, earned a law degree, and became a practicing lawyer, like many *préfets* of the time, before becoming private secretary to Jules Favre, at the time minister of foreign affairs, in September 1870. *Préfet* of Nord as of 1871, he became *préfet* of Loir-et-Cher until 1873, at which time he resigned to avoid serving "the dukes' Republic." With the crisis of January 1877, we find him occupying a post in Yonne: replaced on 19 May, like so many other republican *préfets* who rejected the triumph of the "reaction," he was reinstated on 18 December.[13] The republican press represented him as "full of both steadfastness and moderation, uniting all the qualities appropriate to a *préfet* of the Republic, and, through his wise, enlightened, and benevolent administration, contributing to the progress of the republican idea in Saône-et-Loire."[14] He was then transferred to Seine-Inférieure, where he remained for more than ten years: in his letter of introduction, he straightforwardly asserted: "You will find in me a republican of yesterday and before yesterday, whose every action will have as its goal to inspire love for the Republic." Upon taking his post in Rouen, Hendlé hosted a reception; he then wrote the following letter to the minister of the interior: "I have the honor of informing you that yesterday I officially received the civil, religious, and military authorities, who all came to the reception with great eagerness." In a handwritten note, he added: "The magistracy, the army, and the clergy of different religions were also invited."[15]

For everyone, Ernest Hendlé became the very symbol of the republican *préfet* capable of maintaining amicable ties with the archbishop of Rouen, and with the different local elites—civil, administrative, and military—capable too of enlivening social life (the balls given by his wife were in such demand that "ball tickets" were requested through the *députés*). In 1892, for example, a huge reception took place on the occasion of the regional agricultural competition, attended by the eight *députés* of the region and by Waddington and *député* Jules Siegfried (father of one of the founders of French political science, André Siegfried).[16] In the guise of the *préfet* Worms-Clavelin, one of the protagonists of his novel *L'orme du Mail* (The elm of Mail), Anatole France portrayed Hendlé as a kind of prudent Homais (A. France had met Hendlé in Paris in the salon of Mme Arman de Caillavet, a Jewish society woman with whom the novelist had a long affair). For Anatole France, Hendlé represented a "student of Gambetta," the Opportunist politician par excellence, who attracted to himself "the congratulations of a grateful society," through his opposition to an income tax, for example.

The colorful portrait drawn by Anatole France was not, however, free from prejudice: "His vast and fleshy nose, his thick lips, appeared as powerful tools to suck and absorb, while his receding forehead above large pale eyes betrayed his resistance to any moral delicacy. Against Christian dogmas, he insistently put forward arguments from Masonic lodges."[17] Written during a period of rising antisemitism, this description by an author as open-minded as Anatole France is startling; it would not have surprised us to find it written by Barrès, Drumont, or Maurras. Commenting on the close ties knitted between Worms-Clavelin and Abbé Guitrel, Anatole France wrote that Worms-Clavelin

vaguely felt that beside this ecclesiastic of peasant stock, as French in his priestly character and type as the black stones of Saint-Exupère and the old trees of Mail, he was himself becoming French, was being naturalized, was sloughing off the weighty remains of his Germany and Asia. A priest's intimacy flattered the Jewish functionary. Without really being aware of it, he was tasting the pride of revenge. To subjugate and protect one of these tonsured heads, who for eighteen centuries had been committed by heaven and earth to the excommunication and extermination of the circumcised, was a keenly felt and flattering success for the Jew. . . . The *préfet* claimed to be more Christian than the Christians.

Again making fun of Worms-Clavelin, France evokes his "zeal to appear Christian," adding: "He considered religion only from the administrative point of view. He had not inherited any belief from his parents, who were strangers to all superstitions as to all lands. His mind had not drawn ancient nourishment from any soil. . . . He professed positivism."[18] A functionary in authority for a rationalist Republic, Worms-Clavelin moved away from his mission by maintaining equivocal relations with the Church in order to better resolve his own contradictions as a nonassimilated Jew. In brief, that is the thesis of *L'Orme du Mail*.

Accordingly, Anatole France, still drawing inspiration from Ernest Hendlé, presented the *préfet* Worms-Clavelin — in a rather caricatured manner — as a Freemason who still displayed a conciliatory attitude toward the author's own bête noire, the Catholics. At the heart of Anatole France's condemnation was the supposed link between the republican state and the Church, a link leading to all sorts of compromises, all sorts of rallying points. Like Hendlé, the *préfet* Worms-Clavelin maintained good relations with the Church; like Mrs. Hendlé, Noémie Worms-Clavelin had her daughter raised in a convent. That was enough for them to be suspected of a lukewarm attitude in the struggle against the Church, to be suspected of abandoning the struggle for a rationalism of progress! Paradoxically, even though all the antisemitic media accused the Jews and Protestants of being primarily responsible for installing secularism, which threatened the identity of French Catholic society, Anatole France portrayed a *préfet* inclined toward all sorts of accommodations with parochial schools and the Church. This underscores how blurred Hendlé's image had become: as a *préfet* of the republican state, he was assumed to be the enemy of the Church and its institutions for some, and for others a traitor drifting away from the pure and hard ideology of the Republic. Since, in addition, E. Hendlé was Jewish, his repudiations were taken to stem from the pursuit of his own interests.

In the famous notebooks of the Sandre family, a teacher, forced into early retirement by order of the *préfet* Hendlé for having welcomed a Jesuit priest from Paray-le-Monial into his classroom, protested: "As the worthy disciple of Voltaire, who said, 'Lie, lie, something will always come of it,' the Jew Hendlé told two lies. . . . The Jew Hendlé's order was one of the first acts of persecution against religious teachers and so attracted a great deal of attention. It was carried by the newspapers as far away as America."[19] Attacked by the republican left, Hendlé was assailed even more by Catholic teachers and the extreme rightist press that defended them. Reporting his actions in Rouen, *La Libre Parole* wrote: "To provoke phenomena of social dissolution in a department, one has only to name a Jewish *préfet*. Compare the departments administered for ten years by a Jew to those administered by a skeptic, an atheist, an agnostic, and you will see the notion of social disorder caused by prefectoral Jewry take shape. . . . The orgy is becoming the most powerful means of government."[20] For Drumont's newspaper, "Hendlé associates only with archbishops. . . . That yid too often forgets the Judengasse where his ancestors crouched."[21] Even though we do not find any antisemitic attacks on Ernest Hendlé in the Seine-Maritime department where he remained in office for so long,[22] he became a national figure for popular persecution, explicitly singled out by Drumont in his *La France juive* (Jewish France);[23] for him, Hendlé incarnated all the vices of the money-grubbing, secular Republic that threatened the Christian soul.

Thus, Drumont and many others continually attacked Hendlé for reasons that were the exact opposite of those expressed by Anatole France: he was now accused of forever accelerating the secularization of education and of persecuting parochial schools. What was the true situation? Hendlé presented himself as a state Jew loyal to the French Revolution, to which he continually laid claim to justify his action in favor of public schools. For example, in a circular for teachers, the *préfet* wrote: "This circular, which you will be kind enough to take to heart, is addressed to the sons of 1789, men of freedom and progress, citizens devoted to the Republic. . . . As citizens and educators of the people, you have the right to openly assert your attachment to the principles of 1789 and to republican institutions."[24] In the direct line of the emancipatory discourse of the Revolution, Hendlé, like so many other Jews, took on the task of delivering his message of progress founded on Reason. Under the Third Republic, other Jews ardently joined with him in the defense of the gains of the Revolution, which had been consolidated by the new regime: *député* Camille Dreyfus, one of the very first, proposed the separation of Church and state in the 1890s; Camille Sée, former *préfet* and *conseiller d'Etat*, established public education for girls; *conseiller d'Etat* Grunebaum-Ballin later drafted the law of separation between Church and state. All these measures could be linked, it seems, to the work of Émile Durkheim, whose sociology was presented as the true cornerstone on which the ideological construction of secularism rested, and whose work, oriented entirely toward the civic arena, was propagated by the teachers of the Republic throughout the French countryside. These state Jews' commitment to a strict application of secularism was also linked to that of a number of Protestants, a commitment that led both groups to take on a fiercely hostile Catholic Church.

Like *La Libre Parole* and in the purest counterrevolutionary tradition inaugurated by Maistre or Bonald and continued by Veuillot and all the supporters of intransigent Catholicism,[25] *La Croix* literally went to war against those Jews and Protestants who were the builders of republican secularism. For Fénélon Gibon, for example, "Freemasons, politicians, Protestants, and Jews are all vying with one another for handy sayings that mask the odious enterprise of de-Christianization."[26] According to Léon Daudet, little by little "the crucifix is being replaced by the portrait of Dreyfus."[27] In this context, a man like Ernest Hendlé, along with so many other *préfets*, found himself quite simply given the responsibility of applying the policy of school secularization to his department: for *La Vigie de Dieppe* (The Dieppe watchtower), for example, in his conflict with the municipality, "M. Hendlé claims for himself absolute omnipotence in the matter of public education. . . . Is this a *préfet* or a tyrant speaking? You have not met my expectations, he said—in other words, my secularizing tendency—and from now on, I will no longer consult you. And so he doesn't."[28]

Ernest Hendlé found himself confronted with numerous local crises provoked by government instructions aimed at removing crucifixes from the public schools. He encountered resistance on the part of teachers as well as some parents.[29] Commenting on the refusal of the municipality to remove one crucifix, Drumont exclaimed: "Hendlé became furious when he saw before him the crucifix he hates so much. . . . He ran into the cafés, blaspheming throughout the city, pouring out his rage at being unable to get his hands on Christ."[30] On 16 October 1882, the archbishop of Rouen addressed the *préfet* to protest his circular authorizing the removal of crucifixes from the schools:

Crucifixes, the sacred sign of our religion, have been taken away. Yet the law that excludes religious education from school premises is silent regarding religious emblems. . . . It is therefore before you that I must act as interpreter for the Christian families who have been deeply grieved in their Christian faith and in their solicitude for their children's piety. Under these circumstances, I wish to appeal to the desires and resolutions of justice that you expressed to me upon your arrival in this lovely department.

On 20 October, Hendlé responded:

The minister of public education has no doubt about the importance of the law that proclaimed the complete neutrality of public primary schools in religious matters, and it is impossible for us to understand how anyone's conscience could be wounded by the absence of religious emblems in the public schools, where fathers of all beliefs and all opinions can send their children. . . . The application of the law is a matter of tact. . . . I could not have brought more moderation and reserve than I did to my circular. . . . I very loyally declare to Your Eminence that I shall remain faithful to moderation, which is in my character, my temperament, and my habits, a moderation that does not preclude steadfastness when certain resistance arises in the application of the Law.

To prevent any new incident, Hendlé immediately sent several letters to the minister to warn him of the "danger" of allowing the municipalities such as Le Havre to behave as they intended to do, even though, according to him, it was appropriate not to accept the introduction of religious emblems into newly constructed schools, despite the protests of the "clerical press."[31] He also did not hesitate to attract the minister's attention to the direct and unacceptable pressures exerted by the archbishop on teachers, who should have received instructions only from their superior, the school inspector.[32] As we have seen, Ernest Hendlé laid himself open to the criticism of both Anatole France, who found him cowardly in his actions against the Church, and the Catholic and extreme rightist press, influenced by Drumont, which, in contrast, saw him as a *préfet* steadfastly and deliberately hostile to Catholicism. Being a state Jew was no great advantage: for the author of *L'Orme du Mail*, he became the very incarnation of the Jew who favored any compromise at all that would better ground his own power, while, for Drumont and his acolytes, he represented the dictatorship of Jews under a republican regime that was destroying the Christian soul.

Assigned to Calvados, his son, *préfet* Albert Hendlé, was also the object of a violent campaign denouncing his role in the application of laws secularizing school premises. Again in 1911, a question was raised regarding the crucifixes removed in 1906 and later reinstalled: Albert Hendlé proposed that the minister take advantage of the Easter vacation to remove them, in order to assure the neutrality of the schools.[33] He also pointed to the demonstrations provoked by the bishop of Bayeux with the support of the Association catholique des pères et mères de famille du Calvados (Catholic association of fathers and mothers of Calvados), "organized, like the earlier ones, to combat both the public school and the Republic with a perseverance, a single-mindedness, and a means of action that we need to watch out for and whose development we need to follow attentively." And he added: "An entire section of the lecture by Senator Gaudin de Vilaine was nothing more than a violent attack on the government and on Protestants and Jews."[34]

The report Hendlé received from the *commissariat central de police* (central police bureau) in Caen was, in fact, alarmist; explicitly approved by the bishop of Bayeux, the senator was heard to declare:

The war is surrounding the school even though those who have declared war know beyond a doubt that it is the cradle and the future of the race. In the past, the university was not what it is today, it was independent, free; now it has been handed over, tied hand and foot, to a few renegades, poorly laundered Jews and sectarian

Protestants. There exists today a twofold plot against the university (one is two thousand years old, that's the Jewish plot, it hates Christianity; the other, the Protestant plot, is younger, only a few centuries old). . . .

In the name of French dignity, I must add that these men are not French. They show little concern for forming citizens, they think only of forming voters.

The school today is nothing more than an electoral stud farm. . . . The crucifix has been thrown out of the schools, and yet the law did not prescribe that this be done. . . . The instructors and members of the faculty are in revolt against the law. The mayors and *préfets* as well, since they are protecting them.

Your duty, fathers, is to resist, for it is you who are on the right side of the law. We are Normans: let us not be sheep, and let us avenge the soul of our children. . . . Only two parties shall remain face to face. The men of faith and hope on one hand, and on the other the Jews, the Masons, the Huguenots, in a word, all the lepers. . . .

Be men of character, and be like the Gauls, who feared only that heaven would fall down upon their heads: be like them and fear only one thing, the Jew and the Protestant.[35]

Even in 1911, then, anti-Protestantism and antisemitism were joined into a single rejection of the laws of the secular Republic. At the deepest level of French society, the battle against the neutrality of the schools was always waged by denouncing the supposedly omnipotent role of Jews and Protestants anxious to tear to pieces the Christian identity of French society. Beyond Gambetta and Jules Ferry, who, contrary to the legend spread for many years, were neither Jews nor Protestants, everyone always pointed the finger at those two groups: from one Hendlé to the next, and from the 1890s to the 1910s, these *préfets*, state Jews, saw actual antisemitic campaigns mounted against them, even though they were only applying the laws of the Republic.

In addition, Albert Hendlé had to face the problem of the new school textbooks, which Catholics had mobilized against.[36] On several occasions, he wrote to the minister of public education to defend school principals who were protecting teachers against the criticism of the parents opposed to the new textbooks. With the approval of bishops, certain of them even withdrew their children from school; demonstrations were organized, and Albert Hendlé warned the minister that "the clerical party is vigorously organizing itself in Normandy, in Calvados in particular. In the face of this party, it is indispensable that the friends of secular schools commit themselves to creating effective youth clubs that are materially and morally aided by those in power."[37] The *préfet* sent out report after report in which he described the growing strength of the clerical party, organized around the Association catholique des pères et mères du Calvados and guided by the Church and certain local aristocrats, who glorified Joan of Arc and incited students to burn the new public textbooks. The Church even refused to grant absolution to those who agreed to use the books.[38]

Hence, Albert Hendlé was particularly active in his official role in the republican battle for secularism. Like his father, he was subject to the condemnation of the antisemitic press. *La Libre Parole*, which had relentlessly assailed Ernest, also violently attacked Albert, "the young yid," whose post proved that "France is being preyed upon by Jews."[39] From one generation to the next, the same loyalty to the secular and universalist Republic was repeated, each time eliciting similar reactions from Catholic milieus. They felt threatened by the "Jewish Republic"[40] being served by certain Jewish or Protestant *préfets*, who attracted the most ferocious hatred. These high officials were, in reality, fundamentally attached to the republican order above all, which they blindly served; in their role as high officials, their respect for public service was a kind of lifetime ministry.

The administrative reports attest to this: constituting true administrative families, these officials internalized the family's norms. In their administrative personnel dossiers, they were clearly considered "republicans" from a political point of view, and their superiors praised their administrative competence: hence, in 1895, Albert Hendlé, "thanks to his affability and the steadfastness of his convictions, and also the administrative education he received from his father and uncle, M. Cohn, has quickly managed to assert himself" in the arrondissement. Again in 1901, the *préfet* of Loire recognized "the reliability of his judgment, the quality of tact, his methods of work, and the extent of his administrative knowledge."[41] The *préfet* of Lot-et-Garonne made the following evaluation of Henri Hendlé in 1935: "Has a solid administrative tradition to which he willingly conforms." The next year, he unreservedly considered him a "good coworker, very loyal, courteous, who takes his professional obligations to heart, and who, with more experience in these positions, should make a good *sous-préfet*."[42] Like other, non-Jewish administrative families that formed within the *grands corps* of the state,[43] the Hendlés appeared deeply devoted to the mission of public service, to which they remained faithful. For example, they refused all posts in the private sector, and any direct exercise of a political mandate. From one generation to the next, they did not leave the state and preferred to ignore the temptations of the private sector, which were already quite strong in the nineteenth century, and those of political power itself, toward which so many former government administrators were led.[44] Hence, in October 1894, Albert Hendlé wrote to his uncle, the *préfet* Léon Cohn: "Since my return, I am doing as much administration and as little politics as possible. In our time, in fact, many things are designed to turn our stomachs. When, then, will we see better days, more honest men, a less listless Chamber, a more intelligent universal suffrage? Before any of that, we may see dictatorship."[45] Note, by the way, that not only did three Hendlés succeed one another from father to son within the prefect civil service, but Rachel Hendlé, sister of Ernest (the founder of the administrative dynasty), married Léon Cohn, who himself had a brilliant career as a *préfet*. Cohn, the uncle of Albert Hendlé, on whom he exercised a real influence, was also the friend of Jules Simon and one of the founders of the Third Republic; in his personal papers, we find a voluminous correspondence with Arago, Casimir-Perier, Clemenceau, Jules Ferry, Jules Simon, Jules Méline, Léon Say, Freycinet, etc.[46] Long in office in Toulouse, Cohn, like Ernest Hendlé, maintained the best of relations with the Church: the archbishop of Toulouse wrote him at the time of the cathedral's completion to thank him for his help, signing the letter "with my highest consideration." In 1888, he also helped the director of the Frères des Écoles chrétiennes de Haute-Garonne (Brothers of Christian schools of Haute-Garonne) to find a meeting place, for which the director thanked him warmly.[47]

He nonetheless also played an important role in the secularization of the schools, to such an extent that in January 1882, *L'Avenir du Loir-et-Cher* (The future of Loir-et-Cher) asserted that "having secularized the schools under particularly iniquitous conditions, he was led to secularize the welfare office, and his name was linked to all the violent and anti-liberal measures of recent times."[48] Note also that Léon Cohn and Ernest Hendlé both participated in the commission organized by the Société pour l'instruction élémentaire (society for elementary education), which in 1876 proposed that "religious education not be provided in the public schools. It is to come exclusively from the family."[49] Whereas the republican press in the departments where he held his post often celebrated his qualities as a loyal administrator for the Republic, newspapers such as the *Journal du Loir-et-Cher* and *La France Libre* of Lyon, denounced him for being "the Jew of Toulouse,"[50] and Drumont made violent attacks on him (and on Ernest Hendlé) in *La France juive*.[51] Drumont kept after Léon Cohn in particular, whom he called "the eternal Jew. Like all belonging to his race, he is a born cheapjack, a player of shell games, a trickster."[52] In contrast, for Louis Lépine, the famous police prefect and republican strongman, "Hendlé's and Cohn's careers can be summed up in a single phrase: they were great *préfets*."[53]

In that sense, these state Jews who maintained very close and warm family ties among themselves, going on vacation together and maintaining constant and very intimate correspondence, wanted to be worthy representatives of the republican order stemming from the revolutionary tradition. They all embraced the battles of the Third Republic and in their professional lives were dragged into numerous conflicts with the Church and the Catholic world, provoking in turn an endless antisemitic campaign. And, though they were the scrupulous functionaries of a republican and interventionist state, they still remained attached to a minimal form of Judaism in their private lives, such as endogamous marriages in the synagogue, the presence of a rabbi at funeral services, and participation in Jewish organizations.

It is true, however, that Mrs. Hendlé placed her daughters in a convent, and Mrs. Crémieux, at almost the same time, converted to Catholicism along with her children. Fidelity to a certain idea of Judaism seems nevertheless to have remained the norm: witness the intensity of internal social relations within the Jewish milieu between the Hendlés or Léon Cohn and Jewish deputies such as Bamberger, Ferdinand Dreyfus, David Raynal, Joseph Reinach, and other functionaries in authority—Isaïe Levaillant, for example, who belonged to the prefect civil service and became director of Sûreté Générale—as well as intellectuals such as A. Franck, member of the Institut.[54] Léon Cohn was registered in the *Annuaire de la Société des études juives* (Yearbook for the society of Jewish studies), and Albert Cohn, his father,[55] played a crucial role in transferring the rabbinical school from Metz to Paris and in transforming Parisian Judaism, which he and others urged to take its distance from a certain conservatism. Albert Cohn also directed the welfare society and, in terms of community action, appeared as the "minister of Jewish questions for the Rothschilds"; he later laid the foundations for the *Alliance Israélite Universelle*.[56] The Hendlés and their relations thus illustrate, this time within the state itself, the ambiguities of a Franco-Judaism that was supposed to be purely universalist and to destroy all particularism: as servants of the Republic in the public space, they remained Jews in the private sphere. And, rather surprisingly, the state to which they were so devoted sometimes had a tendency to underscore their particularism. For example, in their administrative dossiers, well into the twentieth century, their "Jewish" origin or their status as "Israelites" was continually emphasized, sometimes even with the addendum, "freethinker of Israelite origin." Such a notation is astonishing in the dossier of high officials who had proved so well their devotion to the Republic. Why did the Republic, in documents in the public domain, cling to the tendency to emphasize religion, at a time when religion, in accordance with the new pact that these high officials respected in every detail, was being limited to the private sphere? This troubling question arises for state Jews as a whole and will require a clear answer.

CHAPTER THREE

A Judicial Dynasty:
The Bédarridès

In October 1899, the Cour de Cassation (supreme court of appeals) held its solemn opening session: before the attentive and moved assembly, final tribute was paid to Gustave Emmanuel Bédarridès, who had just died after twenty-eight years as *avocat général* on the highest court in the judicial order and fifteen years as *président* of the Chambre des Requêtes (chamber of petitions). In 1891, Gustave Bédarridès had become doyen of all magistrates in France. In this farewell speech, he was presented as "the example of what a man can give to his country, the model of the virtues with which he can honor it."[1]

Let us go back a few years and focus one by one on the traits of that emblematic personality in the judicial order. In 1862, as imperial *procureur général*, he gave a speech on the occasion of being named to the imperial court of Bastia: "It is a great mission, and I consider it a privileged honor to be on this island where Heaven has placed the glorious cradle of the imperial dynasty. . . . Justice and religion, though separate missions, are united in their common goal of assuring order here on earth and of providing mutual aid for the happiness of humanity." As a magistrate entirely devoted to the emperor, Bédarridès intended to defend the social order in the name of religion, since "all justice comes from God."[2]

On 4 November 1867, in the Église de la Sainte-Chapelle, the opening session of the Cour de Cassation was held:

At precisely eleven o'clock, the Court, alerted to the arrival of the archbishop, began its procession, with the *premier président*, the *conseillers*, the *procureur général*,
and the *avocats généraux* at its head. It met at the Sainte-Chapelle to attend the mass
of the Holy Spirit from the Grand Gallery, where a detachment of the municipal
guard formed a line all the way to the door of the Sainte-Chapelle, beating their
drums in a call for action. At its arrival, the different judicial bodies, which had already entered, rose to their feet. The Court took its place in the first seats, on the
right of the altar; the imperial Court already occupied the left side. When the religious ceremony ended, the Court withdrew first, moving to the courtroom where
its session was to take place, receiving as it passed the same honors as at its arrival.
Avocat général Bédarridès then took the floor.[3]

Bédarridès, in accordance with tradition, gave a speech in praise of one
jurist. At first glance, his choice may seem surprising: it was Duperier, a
Protestant jurisconsul venerated by Provence, who had initially joined the
Ligue before rallying behind Henry IV, and whose "truly national and
French party," according to Bédarridès's commentary, "was the only means
for preventing local usurpations, the tyranny of the Ligue, and the dissipa-
tion of the state." Bédarridès added that "today, however, political centralization is safe from all attack. . . . The reawakening of local life should be
applauded as a happy event. . . . All the nation's forces are indissolubly
linked; Provençal patriotism is the same as French patriotism."[4] Respectful
of the religion celebrated by the Empire, participating in his official capacity in the ceremonies of Saint-Chapelle, which were commonly called "the
red mass" or the *messe des révérences* because there was so much bowing,[5]
Bédarridès decided to sing the praises of a Protestant attached to the state
and, in the name of respect for particularism, to underscore the fact that
the present force of that same state was finally making possible a reawakening of local cultures, henceforth compatible with French patriotism. Was
the Jewish and Provençal judge, without saying so explicitly, identifying
with the Provençal and Protestant magistrate of the past who had accepted
the legitimacy of the state even as he wished to safeguard that of his own
cultural particularism? Did not his defense of the place of Protestantism in
a state that had become strong implicitly suggest that the place of Judaism
should also be accepted by all in a society where the most eminent members of the state still owed all due respect to Catholicism?

Who was he to proffer such a complex discourse, where respect for the
Empire and for its official religion, Catholicism, was wed to the recognition of the legitimacy of particularism? In his administrative personnel dossier, he appeared explicitly as an "Israelite" born in 1817 in Aix-en-Provence,
whose father, Joseph Haïm Bédarridès, was a banker by profession. His
mother was born Anna Crémieux:[6] through her, he was the cousin of
Adolphe Crémieux (the pivotal man in French Jewry), through whose

intervention Bédarridès entered public life. Bédarridès married Joséphine Crémieux, and in so doing, chose to link his personal fate to that of the Jews of the Southeast. The history of the Bédarridès was rooted in the distant past of Provence, and a great number of family members, linked to such names as Vidal-Naquet, Laroque, Milhaud, and d'Alphandéry also enlivened the political and cultural life of Hérault throughout the nineteenth century.[7] The man who would found a true judicial dynasty of magistrates, considered "Jews" or "Israelites," depending on the whim of administrative dossiers, thus issued from the very history of the Jews of Comtat Venaissin and Provence as a whole, whose ghettos they had only recently left, at the time of the French Revolution. He was obviously—at least we may believe so—"the regenerated man" dreamt of by Grégoire, and one of the very first Jews that the Revolution and Napoleon succeeded in "linking to the state." Having given up his "prejudices," he was able to attain the post of *procureur*, which the famous abbé would still have wanted to refuse him, since Grégoire felt that such posts implied full integration into the national political order.[8]

By a kind of irony, then, it was the Second Empire, and not the Republic and the revolutionary tradition, that consecrated this Jewish *procureur* and elevated him to the highest offices of the state! But, contrary to the desires most dear to Grégoire, not only did Bédarridès refrain from joining the ranks of Catholics but, in addition, and in opposition this time to a republican Franco-Judaism conceived as purely assimilationist, he proved to be particularly active in the Marseilles consistory. Later, he held a seat for many years on the central consistory of French Jews, even becoming vice president in 1873! He was, in fact, reelected in 1881, 1885, and 1889. Paradoxically, when Bédarridès was delivering this imposing opening speech, just after the "red mass," he already belonged to the central consistory, to which he had been elected from the Marseilles consistory.[9] He exercised a predominant influence there until his death, and, as the archives of the central consistory attest, year after year he regularly attended its meetings, aiding in the juridical interpretation of legislation, drafting proposed declarations, and so on.[10] When, a few days after his death, the Cour de Cassation judged that he had incarnated "the example of what a man can give to his country," it was eulogizing a state Jew who had taken on the interests of his particularist community as well. Soon after this last official tribute, the Marseilles court met to elect the famous magistrate's successor: Bernard Lazare, the famous writer, edged out Fernand Alphandéry,[11] G. Bédarridès's cousin. In 1892, the latter succeeded him, not at the consistory, but as *premier président de chambre* in the Cour de Cassation. Beginning in 1872, Bédarridès was also elected to the central committee of the Alliance Israélite Universelle and was continually reelected up until his death.[12] As a result, he accumulated multiple posts in the key places where the collective life of French Jewry in its many forms took shape.

Gustave Emmanuel Bédarridès inhabited all these contradictions, and he assumed them forthrightly: appointed in 1840 under the July Monarchy, he was to pursue his career throughout the events of 1848, under the Second Empire, and finally, during the Third Republic; each time, he was considered loyal to the forces in power. He was named *avocat général* in 1848 by Crémieux, at the time acting minister of justice; in the view of the *procureur général*, that constituted "an enormous advancement when so many others are being dismissed, but, since G. Bédariddès is deserving, he forgave him for it."[13] All the more so since, as a report of February 1854 underscored, "his political position is very clear: he has given unequivocal signs of his energy and devotion to the government.[14] As this same *procureur général* observed, however, he belonged to "the Jewish nation," and, even though he was "well mannered," he had, like his "Jewish coreligionists, a mind for business and a certain smoothness in his behavior."[15] In other words, negotiating between assimilation and particularism, Bédarridès did not pursue his career without difficulties. Hence, in his report of March 1849, the *président de chambre* of the Aix court noted that his new *avocat général* "belongs to the Jewish religion. He has the manners and ideas of Christian society."[16] In 1854, we again find in his dossier that

the religion of this magistrate (he belongs to the Jewish religion), might have created difficulties for him of more than one kind in this region. I must note that any apprehension on this matter could not persist: M. Bédarridès is loved and respected by all; the clergy itself and the archbishop of Aix at its head profess feelings of the highest regard for him and applaud his appointment like everyone else.[17]

Thus, we find, in the administrative dossier of this exceptional magistrate, remarks that come close to extreme antisemitism as well as many observations about how well he fit into Christian society, a quality that greatly facilitated his acceptance and may have been responsible for his astonishing career in a society and a state that still officially professed its Catholicism. Although, in the eyes of his superiors, he had "the manners and ideas of Christian society," he was still faithful to the Jewish community and greatly contributed to its life. Here was a state Jew capable of joining universalist and particularist perspectives without any difficulty; yet, in other ways, he was still almost a court Jew, since his attachment to the world of banking and commerce was very strong.

Like most magistrates of that era, he was part of a very wealthy family, a crucial element that at the time almost determined one's prospects for promotion and a brilliant career.[18] In fact, his father was a rich banker and his brother was still practicing that profession in Aix when the distinguished magistrate was dispensing justice. The banking firm of Bédarridès and Crémieux, which enjoyed the confidence of all, nevertheless went bankrupt in 1862. Gustave Bédarridès had taken the precaution of not being in any way associated with the business affairs of his brother, but, as the *procureur général* wrote in his report to the *garde des Sceaux*,

political opinion was not satisfied; the banking firm of Bédarridès and Crémieux was believed to have at its disposal the fortune of various members of the two families. . . . If Judge Bédarridès's fortune was not affected by the disaster of his family, he was at least morally affected, and I am convinced that, probing the difficulties of the situation, he will not fail to solicit your benevolence for a change that has become necessary.[19]

Let us retain this: the founder of this dynasty of the judicial order still found himself, at the beginning of the nineteenth century, at the confluence of numerous social identities. A court Jew by origin, he was already a state Jew attached to the public order, anxious to assure his role as a high official representing that powerful state. And as a court Jew, he was linked by ties of sociability to Catholic networks; but, unlike court Jews in Bordeaux or Bayonne who were in the same situation, he remained faithful to his own community. Even while keeping his private and public roles separate, he was to play a significant role in his community, owing to his knowledge as a state Jew.

In this sense, he amply contributed to the creation of that new category of public servants, all the more so since he founded a veritable dynasty of officials in the judicial order, whose personal histories can be followed through the interwar period, that is, for more than a century after his own entry into the service of Louis-Philippe. His own son, Albert, did not succeed in following the same royal road, however: assigned to the magistracy in 1870 in Chaumont as *substitut* (deputy public prosecutor), he finally resigned in 1879 after a career with few highlights; this "outstanding subject" was nonetheless "hard-working and expeditious."[20] But the exact replication of profession from father to son failed. In contrast, although certain relatives and in-laws pursued merely respectable careers, others reached the summit of theirs.

Albert Abraham Alphandéry, for example, the cousin of Gustave Bédarridès (who openly intervened with the *garde des Sceaux* to facilitate his cousin's career, using letterhead paper from the Cour de Cassation),[21] strangely enough also began his life course in 1870, as a *juge suppléant* (surrogate judge) in Chaumont. Considered by the hierarchy as likely to have a brilliant career, he preferred to remain in that city for family reasons, and became *juge d'instruction* (examining magistrate) there: this judge "without peer, who has a long and excellent service record," preferred to keep that post, "despite the flattering and kindly proposals for advancement by his superiors," until the eve of World War I. Married to a Jewish woman from the wealthiest bourgeoisie—her father, in addition, was mayor of Chaumont—Albert Abraham Alphandéry, whose own father was a banker, preferred to become part of the local Jewish milieu while keeping his position as *juge d'instruction*. In the administrative report of 1900 written about him by the head of the Court, for example, we read: "This magistrate belongs to the Jewish religion but shows extreme reserve in maintaining his distance from religious questions that could stir up public opinion."[22] Like his brilliant cousin, this state Jew, still intimately linked to the world of finance, wished to remain faithful throughout his life to a very narrow social milieu. But, as several administrative reports observe, in the exercise of his duties, he also had no other desire than to meet his obligations as an official by maintaining relations of great confidence with his immediate Catholic surroundings. Despite letters of denunciation of an antisemitic nature—for example, a certain M. Belloret attacked the "rich but little-esteemed Jew named Alphandéry" in a letter to the minister on 17 October 1887[23]—this magistrate pursued his career within the peaceful context of the city of Chaumont.

In contrast, Fernand Abraham Alphandéry, his first cousin, had a long career, at the end of which he became *procureur général* attached to the Cour d'Appel (appeals court) in Bordeaux, before succeeding Gustave Bédarridès himself as *conseiller* to the Cour de Cassation. In 1864, Bédarridès explicitly recommended him to those in power: thus, in 1892, when Bédarridès retired, he had the satisfaction of seeing a member of his own family replace him at the Cour de Cassation, in one of the highest positions in the judicial order.[24] In a social process oft repeated, this magistrate also married a coreligionist whose father was a banker, epitomizing thus the fusion between court Jews and state Jews, which was destined to weaken with the eventual legitimation of the Republic. And, like the different magistrates linked by family ties, he also took part in a rather homogeneous Jewish circle where mutual aid was the rule, as it was in all the milieus of the time. In his dossier we find numerous letters of recommendation from former minister David Raynal and from Senator E. Millaud; in addition, of course, Freycinet, H. Brisson, Boissy d'Anglas, and various other non-Jewish generals supported his candidacy for various promotions, but the properly Jewish dimension of his social identity was no less patent. It simply proved to be compatible with broader political and social affinities.

Like Gustave Bédarridès, Fernand Alphandéry navigated the various political regimes without difficulty since, perceived as "absolutely devoted to the imperial government" in various administrative reports from 1861 to 1869, he went on to attain his highest posts under the Republic. According to the local *préfet*, ever "animated by very conservative feelings," he was nevertheless labeled "republican." He was, in fact, the first to proclaim the Republic in Sisteron.[25] *La Libre Parole* attacked "the Jew Alphandéry, who has put his rifle on the other shoulder. He served the Empire with zeal. He served the Republic with ardor. With such examples, what do you expect to become of the morality of a country and its faith in certain institutions?"[26] Like the Bédarrides and his cousin Albert Alphandéry, he was born in that Provence, republican from the Salon to the Aix; like them, he spoke Provençal fluently: his descendants, not far removed from papal Jews, thus managed to bring about rapid integration into French society by achieving important positions of authority, without, however, denying their specific culture and ties; outside their "careers," they could, in what may have been the exception, maintain real solidarity among themselves, even as they integrated into the society as a whole and its institutions.

Let us also note, to conclude our study of these relatively close dynastic ties, that the daughter of Fernand Alphandéry married René Isaac Abram, born in Tarascon, who professed the most radical republican ideas. In 1923, at the end of his career, he became a judge in Nîmes. The *procureur général* said of him in 1818, "in repressive measures, [he] displayed great severity, a quality that has become quite rare, and that can therefore be invoked in his favor."[27] In 1902, he found himself at the center of a violent antisemitic campaign, with the newspaper *L'Autorité* pointing to "the base soul of the Jew. . . . The Semite winks, scratches himself, and threatens to speak. . . . So let the Jew judge speak, never could the occasion be more propitious for him and for his race. The government clique is on its knees, the press waits on them hand and foot."[28]

Day after day, *L'Intransigeant* denounced "the Jew Abram, the judge with powerful friends in the ministry"; in his report, the *commissaire* (police superintendent) emphasized "the antisemitic campaign directed by *La Libre Parole* against M. Abram, a judge of the Jewish religion. . . . This campaign appears unjustified to me."[29] It had come about, he added, after another magistrate, a Protestant, had concerned himself with the same affair, provoking a rejection campaign against him that was just as extreme. Anonymous letters arrived continually at the minister's office, accusing Judge Abram of acting on behalf of the "synagogue."[30] In other words, these Jewish magistrates often provoked antisemitic passions against their person similar to those reigning in society as a whole at that time.

We also find, in that extended family of magistrates founded by G. Bédarrides, Benjamin Abram, sixth cousin to René Abram, also born in Provence; he ended his career as *président de chambre* of the Aix court just before World War I, where he was warmly supported by the *procureur général*, Eliacin Naquet, who also belonged to this milieu of ex-papal Jews loyal to Provence.[31] Another daughter of Fernand Alphandéry married Abraham Delvaille, thus forming an alliance with a Jew belonging to the Bordeaux business milieu; supported by his father-in-law at the beginning his career, he became *procureur* in Auxerre in 1906.[32] To finish off the description of the family network, let us also note that Eugène Lisbonne, named by Gambetta as *préfet* for Hérault in 1870, who later became senator and *président* of the *conseil général* of that department, belonged to the same family of unrepentant jurists, and further strengthened that widespread dynasty of state Jews who were socially privileged and most often republican in their opinions.

But, even beyond family members — however distant — this dynasty, which temporarily brought into being something approaching an osmosis between administrative, political, and socioeconomic powers, succeeded in exerting more influence, by making certain recommendations for official posts that proved to be decisive. Together, Adolphe Crémieux and Gustave Bédarridès supported the appointing of Charles Berr to the magistracy in 1870. Bédarridès was the close friend of that Sarreguemines family in Moselle: in that sense, the family ties and the network of mutual acquaintances brought Jews of Provence, the Bordelais, and now the East into the judicial milieu. As an administrative report indicates, Berr presented himself at the outset as a sincere republican but also as a law-and-order man: as a *substitut* in Marseilles, he "showed the force of his character during the insurrection in the commune of Marseilles, where he was held hostage." In 1903, he became *président de chambre* at the Paris Cour d'Appel and was made dean of *présidents de chambre*. He was supported, but in vain, by the *premier président* of the Paris *cour d'appel* as a candidate for *conseiller* to the Cour de Cassation. In practice, he should have succeeded Fernand Alphandéry in that post after Alphandéry replaced Gustave Bédarridès.[33] But he did not attain this most prestigious of posts, thus failing to maintain the highest level within this important dynasty of magistrates. Although attached to public order and to the law, he was, like Gustave Bédarridès, also elected to the central committee of the Alliance Israélite Universelle, on which he served for more than thirty years, from 1889 to 1920, the year of his death.[34]

Knowing that others would do likewise, and in the interest of perpetuating this system of recommendations characteristic of the whole of the judicial order at the time, Charles Berr, at the height of his power, supported Maurice Gros, his own son-in-law. Gros also received the support of the republican political class, several ministers, numerous *députés*, Édouard Herriot, but also Ernest Hendlé, the powerful *préfet* of Seine-Inférieure. His career was brilliant: he became *procureur général* in Lyon in 1926, then *premier président honoraire* of that same court in 1935. Gros was born in

Nancy and united in his person various regional Jewries, bringing them even closer together into a single socioprofessional category attached to identical values, those of the republican state. In the image of Gustave Bédarridès, his already distant founder, and like most of his predecessors, he belonged to that restricted group where strong internal solidarity was maintained. His superiors considered him a republican and one inclined to use his authority, both during World War I and in the daily management of various courts for which he was responsible. In 1920, the *premier président* of the Bourges court underscored the fact that he was part of "those who know how to assert themselves with keen awareness of their duties and authority . . . in regard to his subordinates as well as ordinary individuals."[35] Named *premier président honoraire* to the Lyon court on the eve of World War II, his career ended only a few months at most before the infamous statute of October 1940 suddenly expelled Jews as a whole from public duty. This also marked the end of a long line of magistrates, unique in its longevity and scope. For almost a century, from 1840 to 1939, from the wake of the French Revolution to Vichy, they had their hearts set on proving that contrary to the "regenerative" logic of Abbé Grégoire, they could remain loyal to their specific culture. In addition, and still in opposition to the cri de coeur of the priest of Embermesnil, they were able to take on the burdens of authority at the highest level of the judicial order.

In a broad sense, in its success in establishing its longevity, this dynasty conformed to the models set in place by numerous families of magistrates who rose within particularly favorable milieus, but also as a function of religious Catholic or Protestant solidarities that were often just as marked.[36] In their image, the Bédarridès dynasty managed to last from one regime to the next, throughout the nineteenth century and almost to the middle of the twentieth, but only by conforming to a system of political clientelism. It alone offered an indispensable protection from frequent purges, and from time to time gave an indispensable hand up to accelerate the career of someone who was languishing in a distant province. In all or almost all the magistrates' dossiers, we find without fail numerous letters of recommendation from *députés*, senators, and even *préfets*.[37] It is therefore indisputable that "under the most favorable circumstances, the promotion of magistrates throughout the nineteenth century appears as a capricious process subject to favoritism, nepotism, and political patronage."[38] In this sense, successive political ideologies shaped careers: and yet, like other dynasties of magistrates, the one founded by Gustave Bédarridès necessarily owed its success to the spirit of the Opportunist Republic attached to law and order.

In actuality, this dynasty displays a certain peculiarity that may attest to the specific place still occupied by Jews in French society. It has been noted that the great dynasties in the provinces were recruited from among the nobles, property owners, or upper bourgeois, who all reigned as the masters of their own jurisdictions and effortlessly installed their own sons, few of whom

aspired to "rise" to Paris, even to sit on the Cour de Cassation. Their ambition was limited to departmental or regional jurisdictions, their only hope to serve as presiding judge there. . . . Since, parallel to their judicial activities, they had to manage large patrimonies, to oversee the cultivation of their agricultural domains, and were often mayors of their communes, and at times *conseillers généraux*, they did not want to leave their land.[39]

Jewish magistrates, on the other hand, almost always shared with their coreligionists the quality of landlessness,[40] and thus had no domain to survey. Although culturally linked to a region such as Provence or Alsace-Lorraine, speaking its idiom and respecting its customs, they rarely owned land there. Furthermore, during that period at least, they were only very exceptionally found in the mayor's office. At the same time, their greatest desire was to "rise" to Paris, to enter the holy of holies constituted by the Cour de Cassation, the site of integration par excellence for state Jews, who, because of conditions proper to their own history, were stripped of roots to the land. From this perspective, let us note that in the Bédarridès dynasty only Albert Abraham Alphandéry found it preferable to remain in Chaumont throughout his career, refusing the promotions to Parisian heights, which were constantly being offered him. Through his family, he became an integral part of the dominant social stratum, especially since his father-in-law occupied a preponderant position there, accumulating great economic power in his role as, precisely, the mayor of Chaumont. As a result, this example *a contrario* emphasizes even more the relatively atypical character of Jewish magistrates, who almost never had solid roots in distant provincial soil.

Under such circumstances, constructing a true dynasty was a real tour de force and depended on the chance events of history; only Gustave Bédarridès truly succeeded. The only comparable example was Philippe Anspach, who, born in 1801, sixteen years before Bédarridès, reached the magistracy in 1830, ten years before him. Anspach then rushed ahead, ending his career as *conseiller* to the Cour de Cassation, where he served from 1864 to 1873.[41] Gustave Bédarridès, on the other hand, was named *avocat général* at the Cour de Cassation in 1864: that is, the two founders of lines with unequal fates enjoyed relatively similar careers. Furthermore, although Philippe Anspach remained apart from the Alliance Israélite Universelle and, unlike Bédarridès, did not hold a seat on its central committee, he was present beside Bédarridès at the consistory, where for a long period of time he carried out responsibilities of the very first order. In

December 1845, he was elected to the central consistory from Paris:[42] he replaced Adolphe Crémieux, who had resigned (recall that Crémieux played a decisive role in the career of Gustave Bédarridès). Anspach was reelected to the central consistory in 1850, 1858, 1863, and again in 1874: for many years, he worked there in the company of Bédarridès, while they both belonged to the Cour de Cassation. They were both particularly active in the deliberations of the central consistory, attending almost all its meetings, placing their competence as jurists at the service of interpreting the texts of laws or regulations, personally drafting letters to the minister of religion, and so on.[43] By a strange historical irony, the two most famous state Jews in the judicial institution served together on the central consistory! This fact did not escape Édouard Drumont, who attacked Bédarridès and his relatives such as Alphandéry and Berr, as well as Anspach: "Christian magistrates are replaced by Jews like Berr, Alphandéry, Naquet, Bloch, Anspach, and others."[44]

Pierre Anspach was born in Metz into a modest milieu; Bédarridès, in contrast, originally from Aix, belonged to a family of rich bankers. Does this difference in geographical and sociocultural origin — ex-papal Jews rose more quickly in society as a whole than did their coreligionists from the East — explain the unequal power held by the only two dynasties of the judicial order, whose history we have presented here? Does it symbolize the delays encountered by Jews from the East, who did not really have access to "modernity" and to Paris until after the war of 1870 and the migration of Jews it provoked? Needless to say, Philippe Anspach rapidly overcame his initial handicap, since in 1859, his daughter married Baron Gustave de Rothschild with great pomp, while Rothschild was serving as president of the Seine consistory.[45] Anspach's posterity was nevertheless quite different and, in this sense, may reveal something about the comparative rate of integration of Jews into state structures, with those from the lost provinces becoming the majority only toward the end of the century. If Anspach's posterity was less brilliant than that of Bédarridès, it may also be because the first, born in Metz into a modest milieu, attempted to integrate in a solitary way, through marriage, into the milieu of court Jews. The second, on the contrary, was completely in synch with those wealthy court Jews, indeed was one himself by birth. His ascension in the state apparatus may have been dependent on a solid network of mutual acquaintances that generation after generation, he led to an altogether rare form of glory that joined administrative power, economic power, and social prestige. Finally, thanks to Adolphe Crémieux, the Bédarridès were able to become part of the republican political class beyond the world of court Jews, a milieu that was to become preponderant and whose help would be continually indispensable to him in preserving his role in the judicial post. The Anspachs, in contrast, would remain faithful to a conservative world and would disappear with it in the face of the progressive triumph of the Republic.

Tony Dreyfus, grandson of Philippe Anspach, failed his entrance exam for the Cour des Comptes (chamber of accounts); made *juge suppléant* in Seine, he resigned a few years later, permanently abandoned public service, and broke his cultural ties by marrying a Catholic woman, ties that the Bédarridès and their relations had preserved.[46] Maurice Anspach, the great-nephew of Philippe and *substitut* in Dreux, was unable to pursue his career beyond that point. A bachelor, he was portrayed in his administrative dossier of 1881 as a "pleasure-loving man of the world." To crown it all, he found himself violently attacked in the *L'Opinion*, which held that "this young Judaic *substitut*, this gentleman, is not one of us, either by race or by education." The *procureur* took up the defense of "this young, active, intelligent magistrate, devoted to his duties, who belongs to an honorable family originally from Metz. . . . I can only regret the gross and violent attacks of which he has been the object in carrying out his professional duties."[47] His career was nonetheless abruptly ended.

Philippe Anspach also oversaw the education of Julien Félix, his nephew born in Metz into a milieu that was also modest, and who became an orphan. His subsequent career was more than respectable, though it never reached the levels attained by the successors of Gustave Bédarridès, Philippe Anspach's colleague at the Cour de Cassation. A *substitut* in Charleville in 1857, he became *avocat général* in Caen in 1867, then *conseiller* in that same city before resigning in 1896. He was supported by Philippe Anspach, who, throughout his nephew's career, addressed more than twenty letters to the *garde des Sceaux*, by Gustave de Rothschild, his father-in-law, and by Ernest Hendlé, the *préfet* of Seine-Inférieure. According to the *procureur général*, Julien Félix was "of Jewish origin but without the Jewish mind. He devotes his leisure time to the study of archaeology and local histories. He is the author of a number of literary studies that display a cultivated mind."[48] From then on, even though Philippe Anspach and Ernest Hendlé proposed his candidacy as *président de chambre* in the Rouen court, his career reached a dead end. This was partly because he was the laughingstock of the press, which made fun of this provincially minded bourgeois, "infinitely nil in the minds of his colleagues." Finally, considered by the hierarchy as belonging "to the reactionary party," he had to leave the judicial institution, brutally bringing to an end the hopes of Philippe Anspach, who was disappointed to witness the failure of his nascent dynasty. The striking success of Gustave Bédarridès and his relatives for almost a century mercilessly underscored the fall of the dynasty to which Anspach had wished to give birth. In that sense, the Bédarridès line within the judicial institution is all the more exceptional. Its uniqueness in a structure where dynasties were so frequent may also indicate the extreme fragility of those state Jews who, because of a lack of territorial power, were most often incapable of ensuring the longevity of their authority in the nineteenth century.

CHAPTER FOUR

The Armed Services: The Generals Brisac

Through armed service and by shedding their own blood, Jews showed their attachment to their country. From one war to the next, many of them were killed in action. Military careers attracted them and were largely open to them after emancipation: when they graduated from the École Polytechnique, countless young Jews went into the army, hundreds of them becoming over the years captains, majors, and even colonels. In that sense, the notorious Captain Dreyfus was in no way an isolated case: a number of his coreligionists occupied similar or higher posts in the different army corps. Furthermore, at the time when he was so violently hated by a large portion of the nation and of the army itself, during the crisis that rent society and operated almost as a paradigm for the Franco-French wars to follow, other captains, numerous colonels, and even several Jewish generals were pursuing their careers, without necessarily encountering insurmountable obstacles. Local tensions burst out in various garrisons, internal polemics were aired, and duels frequently settled the most violent of these; nonetheless, the armed services, traversed by so many passions, also held to the notion of reinforcing the solidarity of the corps.

In that institution so proud of its traditions, the burning desire to serve was often passed from one generation to the next; at the beginning of the nineteenth century, it was primarily the great noble property owners and civil servants who offered their sons to the army, often continuing veritable military dynasties that sometimes went back to the ancien régime. Nonetheless, in the middle of the century, a real democratization came about, due to the Revolutions of 1789, 1830, and 1848: the sons of the great notables or military men lost their predominance in favor of young men from the middle and working classes. The institution underwent great upheaval and a number of officers became relatively detached from Catholicism and any form of religious practice. Side by side with their Protestant comrades, a number of Jewish officers, recruited according to meritocratic criteria, made their entrance into the army beginning in the first half of the nineteenth century, rarely encountering manifestations of antisemitism in the course of their careers.[1]

Anxious to demonstrate the extent of their "regeneration" by embracing a hard and virile career in the armed services, Jewish officers — most often from Alsace-Lorraine, a region where a meticulous patriotism reigned — frequently came from very modest circles, almost always separated from the military world, which did not predispose them to reap the benefits of an enviable family tradition, as had many of their comrades-in-arms. In reality, from the nineteenth century until our own time, a single Jewish family numbered a general within its ranks in almost every generation: the Brisacs. And, symbolically, the founder of that unique military dynasty, General Gabriel Gustave Brisac, was born in Lunéville, in the heart of Lorraine.

It all began with a document dated 25 February 1839, signed in Metz at the École d'application d'artillerie et du génie (school of artillery and engineering) by Second Lieutenant Gabriel Gustave Brisac, who wrote: "I swear fidelity to the king of the French, obedience to the Constitutional Charter and to the Laws of the kingdom."[2] Born in 1817 in that city, the son of Salomon Brisac, a merchant in Lunéville, he was accepted to the École Polytechnique. In 1876, after numerous campaigns, Second Lieutenant Gabriel Brisac became a brigadier general. He had served every regime: the July Monarchy, the Second Empire — during which he was assigned to the mounted artillery regiment of the imperial guard — and finally the Third Republic, which made him a general. He was wounded in June 1849 during the siege of Rome and, like other Jewish and non-Jewish generals, during the Franco-German war of 1870; having participated in the battles of Mouzon and Sedan, he was taken prisoner and interned in Koblenz, and then in Bonn.

Throughout the history of that long military dynasty, the bellicose relations with Germany (where Jews served in the army but could not become senior officers) often shaped the personal destiny of the Brisacs as well as the destiny of the Jews of France generally. Gabriel Brisac was interned in

Germany in 1870; Lieutenant Samuel Paul Naquet-Laroque was wounded by an exploding shell on 16 August 1870 at the battle of Gravelotte.[3] Having graduated from the École Polytechnique, he became brigadier general in 1900 and the fifth Jewish division general in the French army in 1903 (his son, Élie, went to Saint-Cyr military academy). In some cases, facing the German enemy could even prove fatal: Captain Louis Naquet, the younger brother of Samuel Paul Naquet-Laroque, died in combat during World War I: "In night battle in Issoncourt on 10 September 1914, displayed the greatest energy, brought down a German officer who was ordering him to turn over his weapon. Was killed at his post."[4] In the footsteps of the young *sous-préfet* Henri Hendlé, himself heir to a great family of *préfets*, who confronted several German airplanes and later died as a result of his wounds, Captain Louis David Naquet was "killed by the enemy."

Let us add, taking into account the in-laws, that the mother of Louis Naquet and Samuel Naquet-Laroque, maiden name Valabrègue, was closely related to Mardochée Georges Valabrègue, another graduate of the École Polytechnique, who served as division general against that same Germany, during the entire length of World War I.[5] Georges Bloch, named division general on 21 May 1914, a short time before France became involved in the conflict, also belonged to that vast family network where military service predominated.[6]

In the next generation, Pierre Salomon Isaac Brisac, whose father was born in Metz and whose uncles were Samuel Naquet-Laroque and Louis David Naquet (his mother was born Noémie Naquet), also participated in World War I: he joined up in February 1915 at the age of seventeen and a half. At the end of that long conflict, during which he was wounded, he received four citations. During World War II, now a colonel, he found himself surrounded in Vosges with the general staff of the Fifth Army; he escaped and reached the free zone on foot. He formed a *maquis* in Grenoble, barely escaped the Gestapo, which had come looking for him at his home, then continued the combat in Paris as chief of staff to General Revers, before going to Algiers on a liaison mission with General de Gaulle. He was named brigadier general in 1944.

In reality, this line of Jewish generals whose careers follow the trajectory of the very history of contemporary France, were also engaged in other conflicts besides those that pitted France against Germany. But from the war of 1870 to World War II, these particular conflicts held a very special meaning for the whole of the Jewish population in France. We also find that nearly all of them were campaigns of pacification in the wake of colonization and took place just as these new state Jews achieved the highest ranks. For more than six months, Louis Naquet participated in the campaigns in Tonkin and Annam and received the Médaille du Tonkin for his actions, becoming *chevalier* of the Ordre Royal du Cambodge. The future general Samuel Laroque-Naquet was part of an expeditionary force in Tunisia for more than two years, where he participated in the taking of Sfax: for his military deeds he received the colonial medal with the "Tunisia" clasp. In 1905, having made general, he left for an inspection mission in Algeria. Colonel Bloch also served in Algeria and was awarded the "Algeria" colonial medal; Mardochée Valabrègue became an officer in the Ordre Royal du Cambodge. Closer to our own time, during the interwar period, the future general Pierre Brisac was named to head the second group of the Sixty-Fourth Artillery Regiment in Morocco and was responsible for constituting and leading the mounted battery of the Foreign Legion there. At one time or another, the various generals of the Brisac line all played a very active role in Indochina or North Africa. While none of them participated in the military columns that crossed black Africa, other Jewish generals did participate there.

During these different conflicts and in peacetime, these generals stood out as proud soldiers of indisputable bravery: Colonel Gabriel Brisac, the illustrious ancestor, was "firm and conciliatory"; he "rode well," and his superiors were pleased to underscore his "fine build" and "fine bearing." Samuel Naquet-Laroque was described as "serving well," "distinguished," "a remarkable leader," "a disciplined mind who commands with force and benevolence the artillery of the Third Army Corps." The notorious General André (who became famous during the *affaire des Fiches* when he facilitated the promotion of officers who were considered republicans at the expense of Catholic officers thought to be hostile) judged in his report of 1898 that he displayed the best military qualities; he wrote that Brisac "knows the terrain at a glance and knows how to command with calm and precision. Deserves in all respects to have his petition for rank of brigadier general approved." Without going into too much detail, André underscored the fact that Samuel Naquet-Laroque, who headed his regiment "under delicate and difficult conditions . . . knew how to assure his command in the most satisfactory manner."[7] Perhaps we are to understand that this colonel destined to become a general was not only a good soldier but also a good republican.

Captain Mardochée Valabrègue also "rode well" and was singled out by General Boulanger, who in 1887 ordered that his name be added to the advancement lists. Later, in the administrative report devoted to him in 1910, he was presented as "one of the most distinguished general officers, to be placed at the head of an army corps as soon as possible."[8] While Captain Bloch had "an unattractive physique . . . he has a vigorous constitution. Intelligent, serves with zeal." In the 1898 report, we read that "he possesses a very high degree of all the qualities necessary for a good chief of staff. He requires a great deal of his subordinates but leads by example."[9] The brav-ery of Louis David Naquet needs no further proof, since he fell in battle in 1914: "very good officer, vigorous and zealous."[10] Finally, General Pierre Brisac was presented by his comrades-in-arms as a soldier having "that spark, that internal fire called vocation." At the time of Brisac's death, Gen-eral Blanc gave the following assessment, reproduced in the journal of the École Polytechnique:

He had Lorrainian blood in his veins, the source of good sense, balance, finesse, order, and will. The influence of the family milieu and his upbringing were equally certain. The cult of honor and of the nation, stirred up by the presence of two un-cles, generals of great renown, reigned in the family milieu, which also numbered four other general officers. Hence his taste for this kind of apostolate, which has the same origins in the military man, the physician, the servant of God, and all the other callings that demand a fundamental sense of humanity and of sacrifice and faith in a mission.[11]

The careers of these Jewish generals, so gifted in the military vocation, seem to have run their course without encountering any great difficulties. As we have already noted, the institution functioned according to its own laws and was usually careful to assure equitable promotions to all individu-als, whatever their particularist identity.[12] Certain historians have even ad-vanced the claim that at a time when French society was experiencing a vio-lent upsurge in antisemitism, the army remained relatively immune and, except in unusual circumstances, did not tolerate manifestations of anti-semitism. In contrast, such manifestations were unleashed in numerous newspapers and often targeted Jewish senior officers. The newspapers claimed that by their presence, these officers were perverting an army that according to the press, symbolized the defense of a purely Catholic France. *La Libre Parole* violently denounced the peril:

What are the yids doing in the ranks of the army? Drawing bills of exchange is bet-ter than drawing weapons. Outside of any religious consideration, there exists among the vast majority of military men a feeling of instinctive revulsion for the sons of Israel. . . . Already masters of finance and of administration, pronouncing sentence in court, the Jews will finally be the masters of France on the day they command the army. Fortunately, we are not yet to that point. The Semitic invasion is like a microbe culture; when the environment is not favorable, the culture does not fare well. The army has shown a remarkable force of resistance.[13]

La Libre Parole attacked Jewish senior officers by name: not surprisingly, we find on numerous lists of denunciation several generals of the Brisac dy-nasty. Captain Bloch was accused of climbing the ranks too quickly, "step-ping over the backs of a mass of very deserving officers."[14] Major Naquet and Captain Valabrègue were exposed to public condemnation on many occasions, with *La Libre Parole* expressing astonishment at the favors General Boulanger granted them "despite considerations that should have disqualified them."[15] *La Libre Parole* also criticized appointments made by General André, the persecutor of Catholic officers, and noted that he had favored Colonel Valabrègue and General Naquet-Laroque, among others.[16] The career of Mardochée Valabrègue was carefully scrutinized by Drumont's newspaper: named general in command of the Nancy fortress, he was said to owe his rapid career to his kinship ties to Captain Dreyfus, supposedly his cousin. For that reason, and out of hostility for the Catholic traditions of the army, André supposedly pushed him even more quickly toward the highest ranks of the army.[17]

In looking closely at the dossiers of that single dynasty of generals, we detect hardly a trace of explicit antisemitism internal to the administration itself. In 1899, when the Dreyfus affair was on everyone's mind, we do read, in the general inspection report on Major Bloch: "Extremely intelligent, very hard-working, Major Bloch is appreciated by those who employ him. In addition to the good qualities, he also has the faults of his race. He is rather common, full of self-confidence, and shows off a bit too much."[18] Such a deliberately antisemitic judgment is altogether rare, however, and we find but few examples in the administrative dossiers of Jewish generals. They nevertheless existed from time to time, attesting to the fact that even within this institution so proud of its traditions and its code of honor, antisemitic practices could manifest themselves. These practices may even have influenced the course of careers, contrary to what army historians have maintained. Of course, Bloch later became a brigadier general and even a division general; this "officer of valor, intelligent and hard-working, to be advanced," who "possessed all the qualities necessary for a chief of staff," thus reached the highest ranks of the army despite the openly "racist" judgment formulated against him.

In the dossiers of the other generals of that dynasty, dossiers that, however, were rarely long-winded and may have concealed part of the truth, no other antisemitic observations appear; in this case, the archives remain silent. In the contemporary period, General Pierre Brisac does not seem to have encountered any manifestation of hostility of an antisemitic nature throughout his career in the army. Furthermore, in 1941, when an officer demanded to Colonel Noiret that he be expelled from the regiment in conformity with the spirit of the age, the officer was immediately arrested. Pierre Brisac, in contrast, was closely protected.[19] The threat weighing upon him came rather from the political powers: under the October 1940 Statute of Jews, Colonel Brisac lost his position. In that case too, the army proved to be somewhat in solidarity with him, since he was one of the rare senior officers to retain his post for a time after the statute took effect.[20]

Pierre Brisac, like so many state Jews, was embittered by this iniquitous statute, the negation of universalist integration. When authorized to remain in the army without having requested it, Brisac chose provocation but also solidarity; he went to get his identity card stamped with the designation "Jew" dressed in his military uniform. Like other ministers, *conseillers d'Etat*, and Jewish *préfets*,[21] he also addressed letters of protest to Marshal Pétain.

During the same period, Lieutenant-Colonel Roger Dreyfuss, grand-nephew to Captain Louis Naquet and General Paul Naquet-Laroque, wrote Pétain a long, ironic letter, expressing his astonishment at seeing the rank of officer of the Legion of Honor conferred upon him in June 1942:

I have the honor of asking you, Monsieur le Maréchal, to kindly rescind this ministerial order that can only be due to a regrettable error.

In fact, I belong to that category of Frenchmen who have recently been given the label "Jew," which is meant to be pejorative, men whom various laws of the French state have in practice rejected from the French community. . . .

No thank you!

I have too clear a conception of honor to accept under such auspices a declaration that in my view, would remain marked by an indelible stain.

If some day, following in the traditions of my family, I am destined to enter the order of the Legion of Honor, it shall be on a perfectly equal footing with my comrades in war. Before that day, I will have to have become once more a Frenchman among Frenchmen.

To spell it out, I must be able to receive the cross in uniform during a taking of arms.[22]

Thus, symbolically, Vichy also played a crucial role in the destiny of that dynasty, since it brutally interrupted a century of state service. This break was not final, however, since the dynasty has continued to the present time, thus perpetuating in a striking way that line of generals whose distant ancestors go back to the fifteenth century on the Naquet side and to the seventeenth century on the Brisac side. The line also includes several nonmilitary relatives: for example, Alphonse Bloch, brother-in-law by marriage to Samuel Naquet-Laroque, who, in 1897, ended his career as *président de chambre* of the Paris Cour d'Appel;[23] and Jules David Valabrègue, also born in Carpentras, related to the mother of Louis and Samuel Naquet, and who became *conseiller d'Etat* at the turn of the century.[24]

Devoted public servants from one regime to the next, the generals who formed the backbone of that family nevertheless remained Jewish. Generation after generation, they all married Jewish women; Louis David Naquet married Laure Juzabeth Vidal-Naquet, whose father, Mardochée Vidal-Naquet, attorney, was also president of the Jewish consistory in Marseilles. Laure's mother was named Noémie; her maiden name was Carcasonne.

This means that Louis Naquet, born in Carpentras, remained faithful to his milieu of origin, that of papal Jews. His brother Samuel married Annette Laroque and obtained permission for himself and his son Élie to officially change their name to Naquet-Laroque. Annette Laroque, born in Aix-en-Provence, was the daughter of Moïse Laroque and Myriam Milhaud. Here again, endogamy was reinforced by shared membership in the milieu of Provençal Jews. It was even strengthened through similarity in professional origin, since the father of Louis and Samuel Naquet was a merchant, like Annette Laroque's father, while Laure Vidal-Naquet's father was a lawyer.

Similarly, Georges Bloch, before becoming the object of the severe anti-semitic attacks evoked earlier, married Léa Baze, who belonged to a bourgeois Jewish family from Avignon. Marriages between Provençal Jews and Jews from the East also occurred in both the judicial milieu discussed earlier and in other sectors of high government posts: hence, Mardochée Valabrègue, also a native of Carpentras where so many members of this prodigious line of Jewish soldiers originated, married Anne Katz, a native of Mulhouse. And, conversely, Pierre Brisac, whose father was born in Metz, became the husband of Édith Crémieux, a native of Marseilles. The rate of endogamy was thus exceptionally high, as if the exceptional destiny of that line of military state Jews could rest only on a shared cultural base propitious for producing similar values.

Unfortunately, the military archives indicate nothing about religious practices themselves. We have noted that Louis Naquet's father-in-law was president of the Jewish consistory in Marseilles, and we may suppose, though without any certainty, that his son-in-law displayed a minimal attention to religion. His brother, Samuel Naquet-Laroque, was elected as a member of the central consistory in 1912, where he concerned himself specifically with commissioning military chaplains and introducing rabbis into the army.[25] Similarly, Alphonse Bloch, his brother-in-law through marriage, who at the time was *substitut* to the *procureur* in Paris, was part of the Paris consistory beginning in 1817, where he held a seat for many years;[26] we find him still in that position in 1890, when he became *président de chambre* to the Paris court.[27] The relations that Pierre Brisac later maintained with the synagogue are equally clear: his wife, Édith Crémieux, whom he married in the synagogue, was very traditionalist and regularly sang during services.[28] General Brisac, who apparently had a certain acquaintance with the Talmud,[29] became a member of the Paris consistory after 1946 while heading the École Polytechnique. He took care to raise his children in the Jewish religion. His Jewish identity is illustrated as much by his religious practices as by his activities in the consistory and close friendships with, for example, Chief Rabbi Kaplan. General Pierre Brisac, a true hero of World War II, who ended his career as *sécrétaire général adjoint* (assistant general secretary) to the Union d'Europe Occidentale (union of western Europe)[30]—the highest post held by a Frenchman within that international organization—died in 1975, attended in his last moments by Chief Rabbi Bauer.

The high level of endogamy was mirrored, for certain of these generals at least, by a certain participation in the community institutions and by religious practice, which full integration into the state, or more simply, time, do not appear to have diminished. This cultural attachment was also marked by the permanence of Jewish-sounding first names. In that enduring military dynasty, there were countless Hebrew names: in the first place, those of the mothers and fathers of generals, such as Isaac, father of Louis and Samuel Naquet, whose fathers-in-law were named, respectively, Mardochée and Moïse; those of the parents of Mardochée Valabrègue, Isaac and Debora; and that of the mother of Pierre Brisac, Noémie. Often, the wives also bore such names: Myriam, Léa, Juzabeth, and so on. The generals almost always possessed Hebrew first names, from Samuel Naquet-Laroque to Mardochée Valabrègue and Gabriel Brisac. Thus, three of the seven Jewish generals composing that line did not hide their particularist identity. Two others, Louis David Naquet and Pierre Salomon Isaac Brisac, bore Hebrew middle names. Thus, five senior officers out of seven had suggestive names whose symbolic character for everyone, and in particular for their colleagues, could only be reinforced by the endogamic ties and the religious and consistorial practices we have already noted. In this sense, these generals emblematic of Franco-Judaism, like the *préfets*, magistrates, and even politicians, usually reconciled without difficulty integration into the state leading to the highest careers and the maintenance of their own religious loyalties in the private domain.

Are these different family portraits of *députés*, *préfets*, magistrates, and generals representative of state Jews as a whole during the various periods under consideration? Or, on the contrary, are these privileged and atypical examples? And to what degree did the 171 persons on whom we have focused our research and who reached the heights of state power, remain, in their private lives, and even at times in the public space, faithful to their cultural origin and to certain particularist values? Did they ever manage to form their own administrative micro-milieus where relations of profound sociability and of close mutual acquaintance shaped specific professional relations?

PART II

Culture and Sociability

CHAPTER FIVE

The Sons of Abraham: From Cradle to Grave

In July 1911, the Paris courthouse was in an uproar, with security agents watching every door, municipal guards tripled, tensions running high. Violent fights were expected following the sentencing in court of the *Camelots du Roi*, a royalist group arrested during the 14 July demonstrations. It was then that an unbelievable thing took place, something that seemed inconceivable to all the magistrates: Judge Pontrémoli, who was to pronounce the widely anticipated verdict, refused to preside over the affair, invoking problems of conscience. Emotion was at its height: the republican press latched onto the affair and called for a severe purge of reactionary judges. *L'Humanité*, in contrast, congratulated the magistrate for his "impartiality" and his sense of "honor"; *La Lanterne* saluted "this honest antirepublican judge who does not dissimulate his feelings," like so many "clericals" who were still wreaking havoc. *La Bataille syndicaliste* regretted the fact that "striking workers, less fortunate than the royalists, have never found themselves facing a magistrate who felt scruples of conscience in striking a blow against them." Finally, *Action Française* rejoiced to see a magistrate who preferred to risk dismissal rather than hastily judge the devoted militants. The Parisian and provincial press, then, had eyes only for the magistrate, eager to know what personal fate awaited him, what sanction the Cour de Cassation would apply. Acquitted out of respect for his personal convictions, Judge Élisée Pontrémoli went on to pursue his career, which he ended very honorably in 1925, as *vice-président* of the Seine tribunal.

As it happens, this judge Pontremoli, suddenly thrust into the limelight of current events, happened to be one of the rare state Jews who had converted to Catholicism. As his administrative personnel dossier indicates, he converted when he married Mary Abbott,[1] a fact that seems to have gone unnoticed by all. Only *La Libre Parole* of 24 July, always vigilant on this point, for once congratulated "the Jew Pontremoli" for his force of character, ignoring, deliberately or not, his conversion to Catholicism. In contrast, the administrative superior of this judge of extraordinary conduct underscored the conversion in internal documents on several occasions. It would, of course, be forcing the point to so closely link the refusal to hand down a verdict, which probably indicated a certain degree of sympathy for the extreme right, and the conversion to Catholicism. Nevertheless, inasmuch as most state Jews professed boundless admiration for the Republic while remaining Jews, the example of Judge Pontremoli's conduct is all the more striking.

Conversions by state Jews during the Third Republic were in fact very rare. Under the July Monarchy and the Second Empire, the Pereires, the Foulds, and some others did sometimes turn to Christianity; still close to the status of court Jews, linked to the upper classes and to the business world, they became assimilated by changing their given names, family names, or even religion. They often came from the Sephardic circles of the Southwest and took the process of assimilation, often begun toward the end of the eighteenth century, to its extreme.[2] During that same period, however, those who turned to the state remained faithful to their religious convictions, even though some of them did not hesitate to modify a too conspicuous first name. Hence, in 1838 Judge Philippe Anspach obtained a name change for one of his given names, from "Lion" to "Léon," while the magistrate born Salomon Édouard Welhof reversed the order of his given names in his administrative dossiers. Similarly, *sous-préfet* Lambert asked for authorization from the imperial administration to drop his given name Caïn from the civil registry, and General Bernard Abraham obtained permission in 1857 to replace his first name, Moyse, with Abraham.[3]

Even more so under the Third Republic, almost all state Jews succeeded, most often without difficulty, in becoming integrated into the highest levels of the state, even while remaining true to their faith in private life: Judge Pontremoli's conversion takes on exceptional importance for that reason and may explain in part his political values, which were so unfavorable toward the Republic. Other cases of conversion were almost nonexistent: there was, of course, *sous-préfet* Salvador, who was of Jewish origin but was baptized a Protestant at birth;[4] and General Aimé Lambert, who asked to be buried in a Catholic cemetery,[5] but without converting beforehand. In reality, a deliberate break with the cultural milieu of origin, leading to conversion, more often affected the wives of state Jews, those of Adolphe Crémieux, *préfet* E. Hendlé, and *député* Louis-Louis Dreyfus, for example. As the former *préfet* Isaïe Levaillant pointed out in *L'Univers Israélite*, a periodical for which he served as editor-in-chief, "the Jews in France who desert the religion of their fathers when they no longer believe in it have become rare. And that is all to the honor of France."[6]

At most, a few state Jews modified or abandoned certain of their too obvious given names, like their infinitely more numerous colleagues who took that route under the July Monarchy and the Second Empire: Judge Georges Weill purely and simply erased his given name Baruch from the registry,[7] while *député* Ferdinand Dreyfus, in the midst of the Dreyfus affair, obtained permission in 1896 to join his given name to his family name. During the interwar period, the Socialist *député* Charles Lussy abandoned his family name, Rueff, in order to be elected under his pen name, which he kept forever afterward. But these are only trifles, after all, since we are dealing with examples that by then had become extremely rare. Of course, certain state Jews later explicitly proposed the obligatory abandonment of Jewish-sounding given names, imagining that such a radical measure would make their assimilation definitive and instantaneously produce the disappearance of antisemitism: Paul Grunebaum-Ballin distinguished himself in this area by seriously imagining, during the interwar period, the application of such reforms. Pushing that idea to its logical extreme, this *conseiller d'Etat*, partly responsible for the drafting of the laws of separation between Church and state, a high official who idolized Abbé Grégoire, furthered the ideas of the emancipator of Jews by attempting to abolish all of Jews' distinctive signs and in that way make them vanish from the public eye. Before Vichy, Grunebaum-Ballin drafted bills imposing "the gallicization of family names, with the exception of Corsican or Italian sounding names"; in his view, "maintaining such elements in the nation in their former state, maintaining their segregation, is profoundly destructive to national unity."[8] When he proposed to rabbis that they move the Sabbath to Sunday, this high official, in the very name of an extreme secular republican ideal, called into question the foundation of Jewish identity. In becoming, like his Conseil d'Etat colleague Paul Cahen-Salvador,[9] the apostle for abandoning Jewish-sounding names and surnames, he actually praised the effacement of Jews' public presence. Confronted with the antisemitic legislation of Vichy—which, against his will, labeled him a Jew—this diehard advocate of secularism and of the absolute homogenization of the republican nation, wrote on 6 February 1942:

I refuse categorically to consider myself a French Israelite, a French Jew. I am a Frenchman who is not of the Jewish race because there is no Jewish race. . . . Nor am I Jewish by religion, for I am detached from any religious belief or practice, Jewish or otherwise. My marriage in 1903 was the occasion for a purely civil "ceremony." For a good deal more than half a century, the death of a member of my family was followed by no religious display. It will be the same, of course, when my own death and that of my wife come about.[10]

In an astonishing letter to André Siegfried dated 7 December 1941, he harshly accused Siegfried of having called for, in an article in *Le Temps*, a minimum of three generations for immigrants to demonstrate their perfect assimilation into France. This particularly severe condition almost justified the general philosophy of Vichy:

It was not enough for you to develop the thesis of complete assimilation occurring only in the third generation, a thesis that meets with so many reservations even in the United States, and even more so in countries of very ancient culture, in our France in particular, whose assimilating genius has produced miracles for nearly two thousand years. No, to show yourself a conformist in relation to the notorious myth, you also had to permanently deny full assimilation, citing Nietzsche and applying to the immigrant what he says of the foreigner.[11]

The former *président de section* of the Conseil d'Etat, who did so much to make public Abbé Grégoire's merits, rose up against the viewpoint expressed by André Siegfried in the name, precisely, of full integration, which would have made particularist values disappear. He persisted in seeing full integration as easily realizable even in the Vichy period.

These positions taken against the spirit of Franco-Judaism, which negotiated the relation between public and private differently, are perhaps especially valuable for their exceptionality: within the republican framework that was now solidly established, state Jews more openly took on the roles of sons of Abraham; most often, their own first names and those of their fathers evoked their particularist origins. More than a third of their fathers bore biblical given names; it is true that that proportion diminished in the following generation, the focus of this study, with somewhat fewer than one-quarter of state Jews so named. Further accentuating that slide, these civil servants, much like their fellow citizens, used a less obvious first name before their biblical middle name much more frequently than had their fathers. In a sense, from one generation to the next, these modifications revealed the effectiveness of a uniformizing assimilation. But, to the extent that last names were almost always transmitted unchanged, this strong representation of Jewish given names, whether first or second in order, attests to an indisputable visibility of the Jewish presence in the French public space.

"Abraham" was the first name of several state Jews, and almost one-fourth of the fathers of Jewish generals were so named; among the fathers of state Jews as a whole, there were also countless Salomons, Jacobs, Isaacs, Moïses, and Samuels, with mothers bearing the names, though slightly less frequently, of Sarah, Esther, and Noémie. Of course, the sons of the following generation, the one that concerns us, born around the middle of the nineteenth century or slightly later, were more frequently called Pierre, Paul, Jules, Albert, or Léon, pushing the biblical first name to the second position. Nevertheless, General Samuel Naquet-Laroque and Mardochée Valabrègue — his father was named Isaac and his mother Deborah — both had shining military careers. So too did *préfet* Isaïe Levaillant, the future director of Sûreté Générale; *préfet* Abraham Schrameck, future minister of the interior (his father was named Moïse); *préfet* Abraham Pinède; and *sous-préfet* Isaïe Valabrègue, whose father was named Joseph and whose mother was called Esther. In addition, there were the two judges, Abraham Fernand and Abraham Albert Alphandéry; the two Abram judges, sons of Joshuah and Isaac; and Judge Abraham Delvaille, son of Isaac and Esther and husband of Noémie Alphandéry, who was thus the son-in-law of Abraham Albert. Although they were undeniably in the minority within the ranks of high civil servants as a whole, their occasional presence at prominent posts in public service was highly symbolic of the French exceptionalism that alone made possible that type of state integration. In Heine's famous expression, the "ticket" for admission into public life was neither conversion, nor a name change, nor even full gallicization of given names.

We need, however, to nuance this portrait: the reader has no doubt noticed that except for Abraham Schrameck, who became a minister and senator for Bouches-du-Rhône, there has been no mention of any member of the political elite; and this sole example must be used with caution, since Schrameck began his career not as a politician but as a *préfet*. In fact, *députés* and senators bearing first names that revealed their particularist identity were very rare; furthermore, their fathers for the most part already had French first names. It is true that this population lagged behind government appointees, who were more numerous in their access to the state under the Second Empire and the very beginning of the Third Republic. *Députés* and, especially, senators were elected later, between 1890 and 1920; they thus belong almost to a different generation, which experienced an increase in the process of assimilation. This explanation, however, is hardly adequate since the near absence of Jewish first names also included Camille Dreyfus, *député* of Seine; Ferdinand Dreyfus, *député* of Seine-et-Oise; Eugène Lisbonne, senator of Hérault; Adrien Léon, *député* of Gironde; Alfred Naquet, *député* of Vaucluse; Léopold Javal, *député* of Yonne; Édouard Millaud, *député* of Rhône; and Camille Sée, *député* of Seine. That is, it included those who were elected in the 1870s and the beginning of the 1880s. In truth, from Gambetta to the Popular Front, with the exception of

David Raynal, *député* of Gironde; Raphaël Bischoffsheim, *député* of Alpes-Maritimes; Joseph Reinach, *député* of Basses-Alpes (who all bore the least noticeable Jewish given names); Moïse Lévy, senator of Haute-Saône; and *député* of Haut-Rhin Salomon Grumbach (who seems at times to have hidden his first name somewhat in his platform statements), none of them attained the striking visibility in the public eye that so marked the identity of numerous government appointees. And among their fathers, we find only Sémé-David Naquet, whose son was Alfred Naquet; Abraham Blum, whose son, Léon, nevertheless became *président du Conseil*; and Feiste Uhry, whose son, Jules Haïm Uhry, was the Socialist *député* of Oise. It is as if submitting to universal suffrage, presenting oneself before one's fellow citizens to solicit their votes, involved greater discretion, less obvious visibility, a mitigation, inasmuch as that was possible, of one's difference. The agents of the state, recruited in a more meritocratic manner and protected in the exercise of their profession by the general rules of the administrative bureaucracy, could more easily ignore such imperatives.

Identified to varying degrees by a family name or first name, these state Jews did not convert to Catholicism; moreover, at various stages of their lives, from cradle to grave and including their marriages, most of them remained faithful to their ancestral traditions. As we have already briefly noted, these symbolic moments of life were often marked by the presence of a rabbi. The immense majority of state Jews continued to bow to the rules of endogamic marriage, taking coreligionists as their spouses and almost always in the traditional manner. The statistics speak for themselves and reveal a social and cultural phenomenon that was astonishingly widespread: 95 percent of the Jewish members of the prefect civil service, 83 percent of generals, 78.3 percent of magistrates, and 72.8 percent of *députés* and senators married women who shared their specific culture and values.[12] These high percentages are particularly surprising since they lasted well into the interwar period.

Contrary to many hasty interpretations bearing on the inevitable consequences of rapid assimilation, endogamy as a practice did not die out among state Jews. It probably remained stronger there than elsewhere, in commercial or business circles, for instance, because of different logics prevailing among former court Jews and the new state Jews.[13] It is as if the republican state contract better protected the values of private life once they were clearly separated from the public space. Let us also note that elected officials participated to a greater degree in exogamic marriages: not only did they bear less marked given names, they were also more likely to plan their married lives in accordance with the overall society, which they wished to represent in the Chamber of Deputies or the Senate. In such places, they often remained more discreet concerning their particular cultural origins. Here again, contradictory logics were at work: that of the state, which was purely administrative, and most often, except in periods of crisis such as the *affaire des Fiches* concerning Catholic officers, almost indifferent to the values of its agents; and that of civil society, whose Catholic values still exercised great power, to such a point that Jewish *députés* and senators who intended to represent it were sometimes led to move closer to those values. Therefore, it was those most closely attached to the state who proved to be most protected in their particularist identity, precisely because the public and private domains were so clearly distinguished and respected. In that sense, within leading milieus in general, and contrary to all expectation, the maintenance of particular cultural traditions and social practices was more difficult among the private business elite than among the public elite. High civil servants also succeeded more easily, if they wished, in strengthening specific ties of sociability than did elected officials, who remained more attentive to the values of the overall society and less anxious to display a particularist dimension that might engender hostile reactions from a fairly broad cross-section of the electorate.

The family portraits traced in the preceding section are the indisputable proof: the *préfets* Hendlé, the judges of the Bédarridès family and their relations, the Generals Brisac, and a fortiori the two *députés* Reinach and their immediate descendants passed through the different stages of life while remaining faithful to a narrow circle of sociability; their marriage ceremonies are indisputable illustrations of this. They openly displayed the reality of their attachment to the ancestral tradition to their colleagues from the leading political and administrative circles. We could cite numerous examples, describe in detail the wedding of one or another *sous-préfet* or magistrate. To better grasp the almost unprecedented character of such practices, let us simply place side by side various ceremonies taking place in the milieu of court Jews and that of state Jews.

On 1 March 1905, the marriage of Baron Édouard de Rothschild to Miss Germaine Halphen took place at the Rue de la Victoire synagogue:

The carriages arrived through Rue Lafitte, let off guests under the porch decorated with greenery, and left by Rue de la Victoire. . . . When, to the sounds of Mendelssohn's march *A Midsummer Night's Dream*, the imposing procession made its entrance, the hallways and even the stairways were crowded with the most elegant people. . . . The orchestra and choirs were beyond all praise. M. Jean Reder, from Colonne Concerts, interpreted with great skill Rossini's *Moses' Prayer*. . . . The nuptial benediction was offered by Chief Rabbi Zadoc-Kahn.

No one could miss such an event: The wedding of the only son of Baron Alphonse de Rothschild, president of the consistory, where he had held a seat for almost half a century, regent of the Banque de France and member of the Institut. The bride came from a family of major refiners on her father's side and was related through her mother to Paul Fould of the Conseil d'Etat. This was a privileged moment in the life of the community and of Parisian society as a whole. As the *Archives Israélites* emphasized, "All that Paris and its two suburbs count among their most illustrious in the arts, sciences, finance, and the diplomatic corps were in attendance at this event, which also displayed our consistories and our different religious and charitable administrations."[14]

Among the important personalities present, we find both the *directeur du cabinet* to the *président du Conseil* and the *préfet* of Seine; what is striking, however, in running over the quite precise lists given by the Jewish press, which covered the event extensively, was the near absence of the upper echelons of government, members of the *grands corps*, and of state Jews themselves. In contrast, the business world was definitely on hand: the governors of the Banque de France and of the Crédit Foncier were present, as were the council of administration, high staff, and delegations of employees from the Compagnie du Nord; the nobility, represented by Prince Radziwill; the Gramont, Guiche, and Castallane families; and ambassadors from Germany, England, Italy, the United States, Switzerland, Brazil, and so on. Even in 1905, a wedding among the most important court Jews was an event where "the two quarters" were essentially represented by the nobility, and ambassadors, who were often themselves noble, and by the great industrial and business elite. The cosmopolitan touch obviously gave a particular dimension to the ceremony, all the more so since a number of Rothschilds, from London, Vienna, and Frankfurt, made the trip.

When Alphonse de Rothschild died soon afterward, in June 1905, the funeral services for this regent of the Banque de France, president of the famous Compagnie des Chemins de Fer du Nord, husband of Léonore de Rothschild (the daughter of Baron de Rothschild of London), and president of the central consistory, whose own daughter became Baroness Albert, took on a character of truly public mourning. The Lafitte hotel was protected by more than four hundred agents under the direction of a *commissaire divisionnaire* (division superintendent), and more than four thousand people paraded past the coffin. After the ritual prayers, the chief rabbi of France gave a short speech, then the procession moved off, led by members of the rabbinate; delegations from the Compagnie des Chemins de Fer du Nord and the Banque de France; students from the Jewish schools and the Rothschild orphanage; the "baron's men," gameskeepers and grooms. They were followed by representatives of the president of the Republic; Lieutenant-Colonel Chabaud; Paul Doumer, president of the Chamber of Deputies; Rouvier, *président du Conseil*; Delcassé, minister of foreign affairs; Thomson, minister of the navy; Selves, *préfet* of Seine; Lépine, *préfet* of Paris; members of the consistory, and so on. The representatives of the state thus participated at this ceremony; in fact, the minister of the interior and a number of generals were also part of the procession. The regent of the Banque de France, the president of the Compagnie des Chemins de Fer du Nord was, in fact, an important personality who had played a vital role in the industrial development of the nation, acquiring at the same time a truly public dimension. The imposing presence of the business world, which was burying one of its own, was equally striking: the governor of the regents of the Banque de France; the governor of the Crédit Foncier; the president of the Comptoir d'Escompte; members of the council of administration of the Compagnie des Chemins de Fers du Nord and of a great number of other industrial and banking firms all came to pay their last respects to the deceased. As had been the case at his son's marriage, they stood beside the prince of Arenberg, Prince Karageorgewitch, M. de Vogué, the prince of Monaco, and other members of the French and foreign aristocracy. As at the wedding, a Fould was present, this time Achille, the former minister of finance. Significantly, like *conseiller d'Etat* Paul Fould — the deceased's father-in-law — he belonged to the milieu of state Jews closely tied to the business world, the famous dynasty whose members had almost all converted beginning with the Second Empire and even before. It seems that no state Jew attended either the wedding of Édouard de Rothschild or the funeral of his father, Alphonse.[15]

At present, let us consider the case of another wedding which was closely related to the preceding one, since it also concerned personalities from the consistory, but which differed from it in every respect. It was the marriage of the daughter of a state Jew, not a court Jew. In fact, it involved one of the most famous state Jews, *trésorier-payeur général* (chief treasurer and paymaster) Isaïe Levaillant, the former *préfet* and director of Sûreté Générale. Levaillant also actively participated in community life within the framework of the central consistory and, in a sense, almost by himself incarnated the state Jew, just as Baron Alphonse de Rothschild symbolized the court Jew. He was marrying off his daughter Berthe. Isaïe Levaillant, as his administrative dossier emphasized, "has no fortune. He is married to a Jewish woman, Pauline Segal. The household is financially strained."[16] The future son-in-law did not belong to the business world as in the earlier example, but, like his father, to the prefect civil service. This was *sous-préfet* Fernand Torrès.

Their son would be none other than *député* Henry Torrès, who recounted with humor the dissensions born of that union between Midi Jews and Alsatian Jews, quarrels that took a violent turn on the death of Berthe Levaillant, with the grandfather and father bitterly fighting over custody of the child, with spectacular court battles in defense of the distinct values

that Henry Torrès himself considered "ethnic" at their base.[17] Later, as a famous lawyer and soon-to-be *député*, the younger Torrès married Jeanne
Levylier, who also belonged to a family of state Jews from the East with a
strong reputation (their founder, Paul Levylier, had entered the *administration préfectorale* under Napoleon III, ending his career as *sous-préfet* under
the Third Republic).[18] After Henry Torrès and his wife divorced, she became the second wife of Léon Blum.

From the outset, we note that Fernand Torrès's marriage was endogamic in two ways: within Jewish milieus and also within the politico-
administrative world. As the Third Republic became more and more institutionalized, the politico-administrative world associated less and less with
the business world, becoming as autonomous as the state it was serving.

The wedding ceremony took place at Saint-Étienne, where Isaïe Levaillant had been named *trésorier-payeur général*. Among the witnesses, we find
the *préfet* of Loire for the bride and the *préfet* of Isère for the groom. The reception took place at the synagogue, and we note in attendance the *préfet* of
Gard, the *préfet* of Somme, the *préfet* of Savoy, several generals, the *président*
of the civil tribunal, the mayor of Lyon, the secretary general of Rhône,
and numerous high officials. As *La Loire Républicaine* reported, "the ceremony was interesting especially for those who have never attended a Jewish
wedding. . . . The groom broke the traditional glass, the officiating priest
sang, the rabbi gave a remarkable speech."[19] We see right away that we are
dealing with a completely different ceremony, stripped of ostentation, at
which no representative of the business world or of banking was present:
only civil servants assisted *préfet* Levaillant during a wedding where his
own daughter was marrying a member of the same corps, another state
Jew. The cultural endogamy was mirrored in this case by a strict professional endogamy, protective of the republican and meritocratic values. We
can better gauge the unprecedented character of such socioprofessional
practices in the history of Jews in France when we compare this wedding,
which took place in 1890, to the one evoked above, which in 1859 united
the daughter of Philippe Anspach, prestigious member of the consistory
who also sat on the Cour d'Appel, and Gustave de Rothschild, in the large
synagogue of Rue de la Victoire. This was a more traditional alliance between court Jews and the high servants of the state, who were of modest
means. For the marriage of his daughter to a Rothschild, the high official in
authority within the imperial regime was surrounded by members of the
aristocracy and of French and international finance; needless to say, Guizot
and Villemain were also present, as was Adolphe Crémieux. But the representatives of the civil service moved to the background, for the Rothschilds
were intimately involved with the dominant socioeconomic circles and

were still successful in attracting magistrates of modest origin but of growing prestige, such as the Anspachs.[20]

When Philippe Anspach passed away, the chief mourner was Gustave de
Rothschild, followed by a number of French nobles (the viscount of Har-
court, Saint-Georges, and so on) and foreign nobility, such as the ambassadors of Spain, Italy, and Portugal, and by several representatives of finance. Chief Rabbi Isidor uttered the final ritual prayers.[21]

The funeral of Isaïe Levaillant, like the wedding of his daughter, was
poles apart from the extreme represented by the weddings of Philippe
Anspach or Baron Alphonse de Rothschild. Levaillant died in 1909, just a
few years after Rothschild. But there was no similarity in the funeral services. Needless to say, both men were accompanied in their last journey by
the chief rabbi of France and by the members of the central consistory, of
which they were both faithful servants. But no representative of the business world or banking, no French or foreign prince figured at the grave of
Levaillant: this time, there were only members of the high administration,
of the civil service, officials in the *grands corps*, *députés*, and so on.[22]

A few years later, in January 1915, Camille Lyon, a personality in many
ways similar to Levaillant, also passed away. This *président de section* of the
Conseil d'Etat held a seat on the central consistory, even serving as its vice
president. His funeral service was very similar to that of the former director of Sûreté Générale. Military honors were rendered with music from a
batallion of the republican guard and the six pallbearers were dignitaries of
the Conseil d'Etat; before the beginning of the procession, Chief Rabbi Israël Levi said the final prayers, and more prayers were pronounced at the
Père-Lachaise cemetery in the presence of public officials, members of the
central consistory, and of the Alliance Israélite Universelle, of which the deceased had also been a member.[23] The progressive strengthening throughout the Third Republic of circles of sociability proper to state Jews facilitated both professional and religious endogamy within a republican
administrative milieu where corps solidarity was at stake.

A high proportion of state Jews solidified their specific identity during
one of the rites of passage marking the crucial stages of existence. Death is
the inevitable end of life, but it can also define that life: the funeral ceremony that follows, often planned in advance, can take on an entirely symbolic importance. Certain state Jews, though few in number, conferred a
sense of definitive break on that event. Such was the case for General Aimé
Lambert: as the *Archives Israélites* noted, "General Lambert has always lived
far from his native religion. And he arranged to be buried in an entirely
Catholic cemetery in Auteuil."[24] Similarly, Senator Alfred Naquet and his
brother, *procureur général* Eliacin Naquet, gave their father a strictly civil

burial: the *Archives Israélites*, attentive as always, noted that "although Jewish, M. Naquet was buried without religious ceremony in Carpentras, his native city. . . . The Naquet brothers, with their well-known opinions, must not have been disturbed to make such a statement with the burial and to give satisfaction to their *political* coreligionists."[25] Other state Jews, among them the most brilliant, remained faithful to their convictions to the very end: Georges Cahen-Salvador, for example, had advocated the homogenization of the republican nation and had become "antireligious," even though he married in the synagogue. This former *président de section* of the Conseil d'Etat was led to his final resting place without a rabbi in attendance.[26]

In contrast, most of the sons of Abraham took care to be buried with a rabbi present, as if to bear witness to a final faithfulness and hence to a possible final reconciliation between public commitment and private practice. Like General Lambert, General Abraham, a military man from a pious family in Lorraine, was buried in the presence of a rabbi,[27] as was General Léopold Sée, who "never ceased to claim that he belonged to Judaism and greatly honored that religion." As the *Archives Israélites* once more observed, "A crowd of friends, comrades-in-arms, and notabilities from the army were at the gathering. Military honors were given by a batallion of the 103rd Artillery, an artillery section, and two platoons of cuirassiers under the orders of a general. The burial took place in the Montmartre cemetery. The rabbinate and the Jewish administration were present in great numbers."[28] At their weddings or at the time of their deaths, these state Jews were surrounded almost exclusively by members of the state administrations and by representatives of the synagogue, one last illustration of the force of Franco-Judaism even beyond death. General Léopold Sée belonged to a family of state Jews, to a social milieu confined to the narrow sphere of the administration: this former *sous-préfet* who became *conseiller d'Etat* and then a famous *député*, the cousin of Germain Sée (a professor at the medical school), was, like Camille Sée, buried surrounded by members of the Academy, the Institut, and an infantry battalion with flag, which all paid honors while the chief rabbi of France, Zadoc-Kahn, pronounced the final words over his grave.[29]

We could multiply indefinitely the descriptions of funeral ceremonies of state Jews: they illustrate to what degree both religious and professional endogamy was respected. Let us return briefly to the death of *préfet* Ernest Hendlé as it was apprehended through the Jewish press of the period. The *Archives Israélites* noted that he was the senior *préfet* of the Republic, and observed that "with him the last Jewish *préfet* of the Republic has disappeared, and our adversaries, who have not spared him from their attacks, will no longer be able to say that France is administered by Jews, will no longer be able to repeat the grotesque fable of the forty-three Jewish *préfets.*" The newspaper added that "M. Zadoc-Kahn, chief rabbi of France, recited prayers before all the authorities of Seine-Inférieure, brought together at the *préfecture.* . . . The chief rabbi praised his patriotism and his administrative expertise." In a single phrase, every aspect of these state Jews' Franco-Judaism was brought together: a chief rabbi praised the administrative knowledge of a Jewish *préfet* who had married the daughter of Albert Cohn, one of the most eminent men in the Jewish community and its institutions! Yet before whom, under these circumstances, did he pronounce this strange praise of state law? Essentially before an assembly of high officials: the *président* of the Conseil d'Etat, the *premier président* of the Cour d'Appel, the *préfet* from Indre-et-Loire, among others. The burial in Paris at the Montmartre cemetery also took place in the presence of the *président du Conseil* and a great number of *préfets,* members of the Conseil d'Etat, *préfets* of Seine and police prefects, including his own son, *préfet* Albert Hendlé, and his brother-in-law Léon Cohn. Once more, Chief Rabbi Zadoc-Kahn uttered praise for the deceased, emphasizing that "the country knows how to pay homage without distinction of religion to those who have served it well."[30]

Let us rapidly evoke the deaths of other famous state Jews and of those who remained more anonymous. When Léopold Javal, the founder of the Javal dynasty, which from father to son, represented the department of Yonne for many years, died in March 1872, Jules Grévy paid homage before the Chamber to "that excellent friend, that good and upright man whose loss will bring sorrow to the entire Assembly." And his funeral procession was led by a large delegation of *députés,* among them the founders of the Republic themselves, from Jules Simon to Jules Favre and Jules Ferry; behind them were the members of the central consistory and the Paris consistory, representatives of the rabbinical seminary and of the Alliance Israélite. Chief Rabbis Zadoc-Kahn and Isidor both gave speeches over his grave. As Zadoc-Kahn put it,

Other voices will speak of his role as a public man, of how he understood his duties as a citizen, the steadfastness and loyalty of his political principles, the purity of his patriotic feelings. . . . For myself, a religious minister, I limit myself to paying a sincere and moved tribute to one of our coreligionists who did honor to his sect by his character as well as his position. . . . On one hand, he showed that Judaism and agriculture are not incongruous, as false appearances have made us believe; on the other, he deserved the praise that the Bible accorded to the illustrious Mordecai: he was "great among his brothers."[31]

Rabbi Isidor emphasized how "the annexation of his native country by Germany profoundly affected him; he felt grief for the fatherland all the more keenly since his situation at the central consistory of the Jews directly reminded him of it." As the *Archives Israélites* noted, Rabbi Isidor's speech struck a chord among those in attendance: "These words, spoken with profound feeling, and to which the orator's Alsatian accent gave a very particular expression, so impressed those attending that most of them shed tears."[32] And when, in March 1893, Léopold Javal's widow also died, the same newspaper observed that "without taking undue pride in orthodoxy, she was absolutely faithful to the spirit of our Law."[33] Léopold Javal thus met his end, surrounded, like most state Jews, by representatives both of the Republic and of the synagogue.

Adrien Léon, former *député* of Gironde, whose father was the long-time president of the Bordeaux consistory before he himself became an eminent member of it, passed away in October 1896. He was led to his final resting place by several generals, officials, and *députés*, but also by the chief rabbi of Bordeaux. The *Archives Israélites* noted that "he never ceased to honor and respect his religion under the inspiration of his fine wife, who did honor to her home, and through his own inclinations. . . . It is therefore to the memory of a coreligionist, truly proud of this name and worthy of bearing it, that we address our final farewells."[34] When a carriage accident caused the sudden death of the *conseiller* to the Cour d'Appel in Riom, Isaïe Berr de Turique (his father, Michel Berr, had defended the cause of the Jews' emancipation), his funeral, again at the Jewish cemetery in Montmartre, was presided over by Chief Rabbi Zadoc-Kahn and attended by a certain number of magistrates.[35] The chief rabbi declared:

I come in the name of the Jewish community of Paris and of French Jewry to salute with a word of respect and farewell your venerated brother Isaïe Berr de Turique. . . . There are few names so honored in our faith as the names of his father Michel Berr and grandfather Berr Isaac Berr. They were valiant champions of Jewish emancipation in France. . . . At the bar, in the public ministry, and later, in magistrate's robes as *conseiller* to the Cour d'Appel in Besançon, he did honor to his forefathers and continued the traditions they had begun, to the magistracy to which he was proud to belong, and to French Jewry, which was so well represented by his person. . . . It was within our community that he came to spend the last years of his life.[36]

At the end of the century, two of the highest Jewish magistrates passed away, one right after the other. First, in March 1897, there was Alphonse Bloch, *président de chambre* of the Cour d'Appel in Paris and member of the Jewish consistory, where he held a seat beginning in 1876. *L'Univers Israélite* noted that "he was very devoted to Judaism, which he honored to the utmost by his character and his life, and when need be, he did not fear to take up its defense. His loss will be keenly felt by the community." The chief mourners were his son, Raoul Bloch, *juge suppléant* at the Seine tribunal; his son-in-law, X. Léon, director of the *Revue de la Métaphysique et de Morale* (Review of metaphysics and morals); and his brother-in-law, Paul Naquet, artillery colonel, whom we have already encountered as part of the Brisac military dynasty. Most appropriate, the pallbearers were Baron Gustave de Rothschild, president of the Paris consistory, and the *présidents de chambre* of the Cour d'Appel, wearing their robes. In the procession were to be found the *premier président* of the Paris court, delegations from that court and the civil tribunal, members of the central consistory, members of the Paris consistory, and so on. At the Montparnasse cemetery, Chief Rabbis Zadoc-Kahn and Dreyfuss, surrounded by all the members of the Paris rabbinate, "one by one retraced the sterling career of our eminent coreligionist and brought out the qualities that distinguished the magistrate, the private man, and the Jew," while choirs from the Rue de la Victoire synagogue performed a number of songs.[37] We note in passing that even in the midst of the Dreyfus affair, a ceremony of this type could take place in Paris, bringing together, elbow to elbow, some of the highest magistrates, chief rabbis, and consistorial notables, without provoking any outcry. Soon afterward, in February 1899, when the captain's cause was eliciting so much passion, Gustave Bédarriddès died: he had been *premier président honoraire* of the Cour de Cassation, the highest French magistrate (we have already traced his career but without reporting the context of his funeral), and also held the post of vice president to the central consistory. His funeral, even during so troubled a period, was once again the occasion for an impressive union, however brief, bringing together the high magistracy and the rabbinate in full force. The description given by the *Archives Israélites* is particularly revealing of the destiny of state Jews:

The Cour de Cassation was in attendance in their robes. An infantry battalion with music and flag displayed military honors. The pallbearers were the *premier président* of the Cour de Cassation, the *procureur général*, the *président doyen* of the Chambre des Requêtes, the *président de l'ordre*, the lawyers to the Cour de Cassation, Abraham Sée, member of the central consistory, and Vidal-Naquet, president of the Jewish consistory in Marseilles. At the Montmartre cemetery where the burial took place, Chief Rabbi Dreyfuss paid an eloquent tribute to the memory of the eminent magistrate.[38]

From one era to the next, numerous funeral ceremonies revealed the constancy, up to the last moments, of this double religious and professional fidelity. The true founder in deeds of Franco-Judaism, Adolphe Crémieux, as well as *député* of Savoy Théodore Reinach,[39] *député* of Gironde David Raynal (who would also become a minister),[40] and Eugène Lisbonne, Gambetta's *préfet*, then a senator, and long-time *président* of the *conseil général* of Hérault, were all buried during ceremonies where both members of the civil service and the rabbinate praised their character. For example, when Lisbonne passed away, the former *préfet*, a personality of truly national scope, was buried by a rabbi who recited several prayers in Hebrew before numerous members of the civil service; *L'Univers Israélite* expressed sorrow at the loss "of one of the most beautiful jewels of French Jewry."[41] Much later, at the very end of the Third Republic, when former *député* and minister of the interior Georges Mandel, assassinated by the French *milice* toward the end of World War II, was buried near his parents in the Montmartre cemetery, the chief rabbi uttered the final prayers according to his wishes, as he had done for his mother.[42] At the death of Max Hymans, *député*, then Socialist minister of commerce and industry and president of Air France after World War II, a military detachment paid honor to him before an assembly of high officials and politicians; Robert Buron, minister of transportation at the time, paid one last tribute before Chief Rabbi Kaplan recited the ritual words.[43] This shows how exceptional the burial of General Aimé Lambert in a Catholic cemetery seems to have been. Just as exceptional was Maurice Bloch's funeral: the first magistrate of Jewish origin to be named to the Cour des Comptes in 1912, he became its *premier président* shortly thereafter, in 1926; this high official, whose Jewish origins went back to the most remote Alsatian Jewry, was without a doubt the only one to have been a member of the Conseil d'Etat, of the Inspection des Finances, and of the Cour des Comptes! He was also one of the rare Jews to have turned entirely to Catholicism, letting his wife and children convert as well.[44] And Alfred Wallach, longtime *député* of Haut-Rhin in the interwar period, who married a Catholic woman and, it seems, never in the course of his career gave any sign of his Jewish identity, wrote among his last wishes: "I have never denied the religion into which I was born and in which I was raised, but I have not practiced it for a long time. I have always considered that all religions are equal and are a human need. . . . My wife and I, though belonging to different denominations, have never had the slightest disagreement on this subject."[45]

In some cases, the sons of Abraham, and even more so, their children, who sometimes became high officials in their own right, distanced themselves from Judaism to the point of forgetting it altogether: in certain cases, in three generations of high officials, those of the first generation still went to synagogue and practiced endogamy, those of the second considered themselves agnostic and became involved in exogamic marriages, and those of the third were baptized and married in the Church, sometimes to children of other Catholic high officials, without even rejecting a specific past. In the Conseil d'Etat, for example, we often come across such life profiles in which many upheavals came about within a single professional milieu, that of high civil servants. One of the central hypotheses of the present work, however, is that such assimilation remained fairly atypical, for the republican state was very successful in establishing a distinction between the public space and the private space, which proved to be propitious for values and traditions, ways of life, and forms of sociability. Integration into the state did not in any way impose assimilation to the dominant religion: to various degrees, most of the sons of Abraham at one time or another in this long and almost immobile Third Republic, dedicated themselves with passion to state service, even while marking their fidelity to the traditions that had been handed down to them during the various phases of their personal lives.

CHAPTER SIX

Dimensions of Judaism

No question about it: *Préfet* Isaïe Levaillant would not let himself be for-gotten. This high official whose parents had intended him for the rabbinate and who had almost entered the Jewish seminary, this strongman who be-came director of Sûreté Générale and then *trésorier-payeur général*, without a doubt one of the most active state Jews, installed at the heart of the ad-ministrative apparatus, was the close friend of countless high officials. And then, as often occurs, he is brutally rejected from the state after a dark cabal; we suddenly find him not only at the head of the prestigious news-paper *L'Univers Israélite*, which he edited for more than a decade beginning in 1896, but also on the central consistory. Elected on 27 June 1905 to this supreme organ of French Jewry, he rubbed shoulders with Vice President Camille Lyon, *conseiller d'Etat* and longtime *directeur de cabinet* to the min-ister of the interior; Jacques Helbronner, another *conseiller d'Etat*, who, as president of the consistory, later confronted Vichy and German domina-tion; the *préfet* Eugène Sée; Major Levylier, and others.[1] In other words, a good portion of the leading members of the central consistory came there directly from high government posts: created by Napoleon to control the community and better integrate it into the French nation, the institution was being led less and less by notables from socioeconomic milieus, such as, among others, the Rothschilds. Rothschilds still regularly held a seat on the consistory but, increasingly, the institution was made up of state Jews, who sometimes acquired their administrative and religious offices concomitantly. In that sense, this sharing of staff members implied that state Jews, who placed their administrative competence at the service of the community, were also taking charge of religion.[2]

Before the advent of the Third Republic, an unconverted state Jew such as Michel Goudchaux had served as vice president of the central consistory beginning in 1827; he became minister of finance in 1848 and soon after took over the vice presidency of the Assemblé Nationale.[3] This double duty, however, became more frequent after the republican regime became a fait accompli. The arrival of Isaïe Levaillant to the consistory was saluted by the president of that assembly in the following terms: "He has created a place for himself within Jewry and his entry into the Jewish administration at this time is very precious, since the consistory is preparing for actions relating to the legislation in the Senate and the Assembly separating Church and state." The very active Isaïe Levaillant, present at every work meeting week after week, was involved in a close working relationship with the vice president and *conseiller d'Etat* Camille Lyon, helping to define the consistory's position on the new legislation. On 9 July 1906, when the discussion at the national level was very keen, the consistory even addressed a document to *député* Théodore Reinach dealing with the conditions for a weekly day of rest, asking him to act as spokesperson for the consistory at the Chamber of Deputies. On 20 July, Théodore Reinach, who was also vice president of the Société des études juives (society for Jewish studies), revealed that he had set forth his theses in a commission, but that it seemed to him impossible to modify the already-written legislation. Under such conditions, Levaillant claimed that "there is urgency in making provisions to hasten the reconstitution of the Jewish community in France under the conditions presented in the law of 9 December 1905." He was later congratulated by the president for his "zeal and activity."[4]

This vital question of the separation of Church and state, to which several state Jews of the active administration or members of the assemblies were greatly attached, directly targeted the very status of the consistory; we shall return later to the outcome of that affair, but we already perceive to what extent its internal management within the milieu of the Jewish community was taken in hand by other state Jews, whether or not they were still active within their own corps. Their administrative knowledge, their familiarity with the milieu, and their practice of the arcana of power placed them in a most favorable position for attempting to confront state legislation they wished to modify. As *L'Univers Israélite* would note at the time of Levaillant's death, "The experience he gained from his past as a government official, his competence in questions of interest to French Jewry, his love for our community and our institutions very naturally designated

Levaillant to occupy a seat on the central consistory."[5] In such a context, we better understand the scope of the tasks realized by the former *préfet*. In October 1911, at the time of his funeral — which we have already evoked as particularly representative of the funerals of sons of Abraham, surrounded to the very end by so many high officials — the president of the consistory expressed his "sorrowful emotion in learning of the death of Isaïe Levaillant, whose role in the work of the central consistory was considerable."[6]

At both the beginning and the end of the Third Republic, state Jews were at the heart of the consistorial institution. The most famous of them were named in the first years, between 1870 and 1880: the minutes of many meetings held during that period attest to the constant activity of Gustave Bédarridès and Philippe Anspach, two judges on the Cour de Cassation whom we have already encountered. As distinguished jurists, they focused on the regulations affecting French Jewry as a community. At their side were also General Sée, the first Jew to have attained that rank in the French army. Gustave Bédarridès, for example, drafted the proposal to the minister of religion regarding the *more judaico* oath.[7] And, at the end of the Third Republic, during the dramatic period that preceded Vichy and under an authoritarian regime hostile to the Republic (and consequently to state Jews), two *conseillers d'Etat* — Jacques Helbronner, its *président*, and René Mayer — again figured among the members of the consistory, as did a high-ranking military man, General Pierre Boris. At that time, when the fate of all Jews in France was at stake, it was again high Jewish officials, among others, who tried to defend their coreligionists by using their juridical competency and the friendships they had forged within their administration or the corps they belonged to, to try to have thrown out one or another of the legislative texts calling into question the process of emancipation as a whole.[8]

Préfets, *députés*, and senators were elected to local consistories, and a fortiori to the central consistory, less often than were magistrates, *conseillers d'Etat*, and generals, unquestionably a sign of nonelected officials' intense involvement in Jewish communal life. Elected officials, as we have observed, bore biblical given names less often than did appointees and were also less concerned with respecting traditional endogamy. Similarly, they seem to have taken care not to appear too linked to a minority community, since they depended so much on the goodwill of an electorate that was very remote from the Jewish religion; thus, it was only under exceptional circumstances that they held seats on purely religious bodies. It is true that Adolphe Crémieux, long the jack of all trades of republican state Jews, seems to belie this hypothesis, for he was almost always very involved in the activities of the consistory. Named to the central consistory in 1830, he attended all its meetings regularly, was personally responsible for a great number of foreign missions, to the Middle East in particular, and rapidly became its president. He remained in that post until his wife's surprise conversion, which led him to resign temporarily. Among elected officials at the very beginning of the Third Republic, perhaps only Adrien Léon, *député* of Gironde elected in 1871, Eugène Lisbonne, senator of Hérault, and Léopold Javal, *député* of Yonne elected during the Empire, really played an important role in the central consistory for a number of years. Léopold Javal, elected during the Empire, also held a seat there for nearly twenty years, from 1853 until his death in 1872; in the company of a still-active Crémieux, he intervened in 1867 with the minister of foreign affairs regarding threats made against Serbian Jews.[9]

This rather unusual presence deserves to be noted since, when consistorial voters proposed the candidacy of *député* Fernand Crémieux, who was then elected against his will, the *député* of Gard protested and challenged any possible appointment. He wrote that "I have not accepted any candidacy . . . and I especially want you to know that although my mandate as *député* may give me a small amount of influence, that influence belongs exclusively to the voters of my district."[10]

Later, during the interwar period, Raphaël-Georges Lévy, senator of Seine, did join that highest institution of French Jewry; and Pierre Masse, *député* of Hérault, became a legal adviser to the Paris consistory, without, however, officially being part of it. Similarly, with the exception of Adolphe Crémieux and Léopold Javal (who were among its founding members and president and vice president respectively), and then Pierre Masse, who had agreed to become involved in the internal life of the consistory—only Joseph Reinach, from 1883 to 1885, and Jules Moch, in 1960, were members of the Alliance Israélite Universelle, placing their administrative competence and their political ties at its service.[11] The notoriety of Crémieux and Reinach predestined them to this type of role turned toward the external world.[12] With a few notable exceptions, then, *députés* and senators more or less studiously avoided displaying a too visible participation in the various official institutions of French Jewry. Perhaps the fluctuations of their political careers were too subject to the opinions of their fellow citizens as a whole.

As officials in authority, living representatives of the state in its executive dimension, *préfets* and *sous-préfets* in and of themselves incarnated the power of the administration. As it turns out, few of them entered simultaneously into the service of community organizations such as the consistory and the Alliance Israélite Universelle. As we know, the ousted *préfet* Isaïe Levaillant was one of them: a crucial person at the consistory, he was also co-opted by the central committee of the Alliance and thereafter dedicated himself wholeheartedly to its activities. At the time of his death, Salomon

Reinach claimed that the Alliance "is losing one of its devoted friends, the most heeded, most informed councillor, the most certain guide: when Levaillant spoke, you could hear a pin drop."[13] It seems that, outside of his example, only the *préfet honoraire* Eugène Sée sat on both the consistory and the Alliance at almost the same time, from 1902 until his death in 1934. He was very active and also put to use his administrative competence and his access to the state: for example, in 1912 he came to the aid of threatened Moroccan Jews in the name of the Alliance. After intervening, he noted that "General Lyautey is well disposed toward us and will do what is necessary with respect to the sultan."[14] In each case, however, these high officials were no longer part of the active administration. Certain active *préfets*, such as Ernest Hendlé and Léon Cohn, did participate indirectly in the affairs of the community, by writing, for example, for the *Revue des études juives*; nevertheless, that activity remained altogether discreet, for the public character of their positions seems to have required that their loyalty be exclusively to the state.

In contrast, generals and magistrates, who like the *préfets* frequently bore biblical first names and displayed high rates of endogamy, did not draw back from the potential consequences of very visible membership in community institutions. At one time or another during the Third Republic, numerous generals were elected to the central consistory or the Paris consistory: that was the case for General Léopold Sée; General Abraham, said to be "from a pious family";[15] Naquet-Laroque, who also participated in founding the Alliance Israélite Universelle; Weiller, who was very active somewhat later in the struggle against antisemitism; Dennery, who in 1913 wrote numerous articles on Jewish officers in the French army for *L'Univers Israélite*; Geismar, who, as a young adolescent, attended a Jewish school and was a very devout officer throughout his career, participating in all religious services[16] and becoming actively involved in Zionist organizations; Boris, who played an essential role within the consistory during the Vichy period; and finally, Brisac. That is, from the very beginning of the Third Republic to the beginning of the Fifth Republic, almost a third of Jewish generals in the French army, indisputably the highest proportion of all state Jews, were so involved; at their side, we find several colonels and majors with a military past that was just as glorious. It is as if, proud of their indisputable patriotism, of their bravery recognized by so many decorations, these generals and officers were seen as the ideal spokespersons for French Jews. The indisputable legitimacy acquired in the eyes of the nation as a whole and the truly symbolic preponderance they enjoyed among their coreligionists, automatically assured them of a place of choice within consistorial organizations.

Next to generals, it was primarily *conseillers d'Etat* and magistrates who played a vital role in the community, with their knowledge of law and their perfect familiarity with procedure allowing them better to defend the interests of Judaism when legislative and regulatory reforms dealing with religious matters were being set in place. *Conseillers d'Etat* occupied a very visible position: in 1902, at the turn of the century, Camille Lyon, *président de section* at the Conseil d'Etat, moved to the central consistory, after serving on the Lyon consistory; in 1906, he became its vice president, serving in that capacity for many years. His almost daily contribution to the functioning of the consistory was such that when he was promoted to the rank of officer of the Legion of Honor in 1913, that assembly voted in a particularly laudatory text for him.[17] This former *directeur du cabinet* of Waldeck-Rousseau (at the time minister of the interior), this high official who had also been *chef de cabinet* to the minister of justice, rose almost to the level of Isaïe Levaillant within Jewish institutions. When he died in January 1915, *Le Figaro* wrote that "he was, in the most noble sense of the word, the quintessence of the civil servant, one of the most eminent civil servants that the government of the Republic has known for thirty-eight years."[18]

During the same period, *conseiller d'Etat* Jacques Helbronner served that institution by concerning himself with the duties of military chaplains. Later, he presided over the consistory; in that role and aided by René Mayer, another *conseiller d'Etat*, he personally confronted the Vichy regime. We could cite many other persons belonging to that great state body. More unexpectedly, the sociologist René Worms, author of numerous works, who became a *conseiller d'Etat*, also attempted to become part of the institution representing Judaism: considered by the *Archives Israélites* as "belonging to a fundamentally Jewish family, and never forgetting that fact,"[19] he was continually present at consistorial assemblies and even attempted, but in vain, to be elected to the consistory. It is as if being a famous sociologist, doctor of science and letters, graduate of the law faculty, and Bergson's replacement at the Collège de France, did not prevent him from wishing to participate in the life of a purely religious organization (on the other hand, another sociologist, Durkheim, was never interested in such a post: he wanted to be the theorist of secularism and positivism). That august assembly seems to have wanted nothing to do with a *conseiller d'Etat* who was mainly preoccupied with sociological questions.

These *conseillers d'Etat*, members of one of the most prestigious state corps, were also often elected to the central committee of the Alliance Israélite Universelle: Camille Lyon held a seat there from 1898 to 1915; Jacques Helbronner was appointed in 1934 and remained there until his deportation in 1943. Others took up the mantle: René Cassin, vice president of the Conseil d'Etat and president of the Alliance after the war; Georges Huisman, appointed in 1952; and many others.

At various periods during the Third Republic, judges joined jurists on the consistory. We have already noted the essential role played by Gustave

Bédarridès and Philippe Anspach up until the end of the century, at a time when they were at the summit of the judicial hierarchy. They accumulated posts within both institutions without anyone taking offense. Bédarridès remained on the consistory from 1867 until his death in 1899, displaying "within the foremost administration of the community, a great and intelligent devotion to the interests of Jews."[20] Alphonse Bloch, *président de chambre* at the Paris Cour d'Appel, was also part of the consistory beginning in 1876; at his death in 1897, *L'Univers Israélite* underscored the fact that "thanks to his enlightenment and experience, he was able to render precious services within that assembly to his coreligionists. He was very devoted to Judaism, which he honored to the utmost by his character and his life, and which he did not hesitate to defend when necessary. His loss will be keenly felt by the Community, of which he was one of the most eminent members."[21] Let us spend more time with the example of the Masses: *président de chambre honoraire* to the Cour d'Appel court in Besançon, Édouard Masse succeeded his own father in 1904 (the elder Masse was the *bâtonnier de l'ordre des avocats*) as vice president of the consistory; his son, *député* Pierre Masse, who would eventually be deported by Vichy, became an active *conseiller* soon afterward. For nearly sixteen years, Édouard Masse played such an important role in that community institution that at the time of his death Chief Rabbi Israël Levi paid tribute to him in the presence of the Paris rabbinate as a whole and members of the consistories, in terms that could be applied to most state Jews:

Édouard Masse was the quintessence of the modern Jew, who knew how to join respect for religious traditions and the feeling for progress. He learned of Judaism in his father's home and did honor to it throughout his entire life of dignity and probity, just as he did honor to the magistracy through the uprightness and nobility of his character. He served Judaism in devoting himself to his religion and his coreligionists. Fifteen years ago, when the separation of Church and state obliged the Jewish community to reconstitute itself on new foundations, we appealed to his enlightenment and devotion; his authority asserted itself, as a result of which he was the most heeded craftsman of our new organization. He gave his heart to the consistory.[22]

We cannot multiply the examples forever; but let us note the altogether exceptional case of Judge Raphaël Job, who, before embarking on his judicial career, was himself a student of the Jewish seminary in Paris and a rabbi.[23] As the final illustration, let us point out that even in the contemporary period, the *président de chambre honoraire* of the Paris Cour d'Appel court, Louis Guthmann, was serving as president of the Jewish community of Fontainebleau at the time of his death.[24] These magistrates, wanting to participate in the operation of Jewish religious institutions, did not for all that neglect the Alliance Israélite Universelle: Gustave Bédarridès, *président de chambre* at the Cour de Cassation and member of the consistory, was very active in the Alliance beginning in 1872, when he was elected, until his death in 1899; at the time of his election, he assured the president of his "absolute devotion to the work of the Alliance."[25] The *président de chambre* of the Paris Cour d'Appel, Charles Berr, also became part of the central committee in 1889 and remained there until his death in 1920; on that same date, taking up the baton as it were, the new *président de chambre* of the Paris *cour d'appel*, Eugène Dreyfus, took a seat on the Alliance, where he remained until his own death in 1936, once more ensuring a kind of temporary fusion of the positions. Upon obtaining a promotion within the judicial institution, he received the congratulations of the president of the Alliance, and responded: "These congratulations are touching, for they come to me from eminent coreligionists; I am proud to be their colleague and have long admired their devotion to a cause that is as dear to me as it is to them."[26] Other magistrates were also part of the central committee of the Alliance: Édouard Masse, *président de chambre honoraire* from 1905 to 1920; and Raoul Bloch-Laroque, *avocat général* to the Cour d'Appel, who in 1920 participated in the activities of the Alliance and was continually reelected to it until his death in 1958.

Hence, a fairly impressive proportion of state Jews, most often those in public service, did not hesitate to openly display their participation in various essential communal positions in French Jewry: each time, they brought to it the use of their profound juridical competence. This astonishing application of Franco-Judaism reinforced once more the ties of sociability binding this very small group of actors in a thousand ways, all the more so since a number of them came from various institutional Jewish circles by virtue of their immediate families. Surprisingly, several state Jews, almost always distinct from those already mentioned, had fathers who were rabbis or consistorial leaders: hence, the father of *conseiller d'Etat* Georges Saint-Paul was elected to the Paris consistory;[27] Judge Eugène Salomon Cahen's father was chief rabbi of Oran, and then of Algiers;[28] Judge Lucien Salomon Levy's father was chief rabbi of Bordeaux and then of Paris;[29] and Judge Edgar Marx's father was also chief rabbi of Bordeaux.[30] The father of *sous-préfet* Oury was also a rabbi; the father of *préfet* Myrthild Caen presided over the Metz consistory; and the father of *sous-préfet* Paul Levylier performed the same role in Nancy.[31]

One of the most representative *préfets* at the foundation of the Third Republic, Léon Cohn, brother-in-law to Ernest Hendlé, was also the son of one of the most visible and longstanding personalities of French Jewry, Albert Cohn, member of the central consistory and the central committee of the Alliance Israélite Universelle and president of the welfare committee, the Société du Patronage des Apprentis et Ouvriers Israélites (society for

the patronage of Jewish apprentices and workers), and the Société Terre
Promise (promised land society). For *L'Univers Israélite*, he was quite
simply "the soul and mainspring of our lovely institutions. . . . All his time
is entirely, exclusively devoted to the Jewish cause to which he has given —
sacrificed — his strength and health."[32] He was very devout and regularly
went to synagogue; he visited Jerusalem numerous times, his first journey
taking place in 1854, that is, two years after the birth of his son Léon, the
future *préfet*. As a result, Léon was raised in an atmosphere profoundly
concerned with the various facets of Judaism.[33] Let us note in passing that
like state Jews, many Protestant politicians and high officials also had fathers who were pastors,[34] as if strong religious traditions favored the socialization of minority groups in the direction of the strong state, which
protected all its citizens, whatever their particularism.

Among the generals, there also figured several sons of leaders of the
Jewish community: the father of General Lucien Levy was a rabbi in
Meurthe-et-Moselle,[35] while General Julien Carvallo's father was one of
the founders of the Alliance Israélite Universelle.[36] To conclude this significant enumeration, let us note that the father of *député* Adrien Léon was
president of the Bordeaux consistory; the grandfather of *député* Pierre
Masse was vice president of the central consistory and his father also had a
seat on the consistory for a long time; Baron Edmond de Rothschild, father of *député* Maurice de Rothschild, was president of the central consistory; the father of *député* Max Hymans was a member, but at a more modest level; and the brother of *député* David Raynal was also an important
member of the Paris consistory. Let us also observe that the father of L.-L.
Klotz, former minister of finance, was vice president of the Administration
des Temples Israélites de Paris; the *député* of Charente, Lazare Weiller, was
a close relative of the chief rabbi of the consistory; and the senator from
Seine, Paul Strauss, was the nephew of the rabbi of Belfort.[37] Finally, other
state Jews also participated, more indirectly however, in this small milieu
where administrative posts and various posts within Jewish institutions
were intimately combined. For example, several of them had fathers-in-law
who were leaders of the consistory: that was the case for General Adolphe
Hinstin, whose father-in-law was president of the Lyon consistory;[38] Captain Louis Naquet, whose father-in-law, Mardochée Vidal-Naquet, was
president of the Marseilles consistory;[39] and Colonel Jules Moch, whose
father-in-law was a rabbi.[40]

These seemingly interminable lists allow us to bring to light a completely unknown phenomenon, namely, the surprising degree of imbri-
cation and social proximity of state Jews within consistorial or other Jewish institutional milieus. This strong presence, whether direct or indirect
(through their fathers or fathers-in-law), added to the dimensions of their

Jewish personality, which has already been apprehended through their first names, their choice not to convert, and their primarily endogamic marriages. This maintenance of a Jewish identity, visible through several variables, thus proved compatible with full integration into the norms of the state and absolute devotion to the general interest, as if, precisely, what was proper to Franco-Judaism was its ability to allow values oriented toward the public to coexist with traditions stemming from private life, for these citizens and state Jews. It is nonetheless true, however, that their presence within the consistory or the Alliance necessarily took on a public dimension, appearing as an action directed toward the state or even toward foreign countries where other Jews were living (the Alliance's concern): as a result, it presupposed a certain public visibility that could at times trouble the boundaries between these two domains.

There was a risk of just such an ambiguity arising when state Jews resolutely fought against any sign of antisemitism and were prompt to react against any racist threats in France or abroad that targeted their coreligionists. Let us take the example of Alfred Naquet, anarchist, revolutionary, deist defender of all religions, critic of marriage and the social order, and rebel against capitalism, who did not hesitate to temporarily ally himself with Boulangism in order to hasten the calling into question of society's framework. The *député* of Vaucluse, whom we shall often discuss later on, married a Catholic woman and buried his father in a deliberately areligious ceremony; yet he did not hesitate to move to the front lines during any manifestation of antisemitism. He wrote: "I am myself of the Jewish race and, far from being ashamed of it, I glory in it, for it is always glorious to have ancestors who struggled. . . . I would not return there [to the synagogue] except out of a feeling of protest and to join with the oppressed against the oppressors." In response to this attitude, unexpected from an internationalist and atheistic revolutionary, the *Archives Israélites* did not conceal its satisfaction:

The war against the Jewish race has taken such a form that even those who have definitively broken with Judaism, thrown religious practices overboard, tumbling from freethinking to the most typical and crimson atheism, have been moved by these violent and unjust attacks. Even in spite of themselves, the Jewish blood that flows in their veins has revolted against such insults continually thrown in the face of that great family to which they belong. . . . Among these Jews by birth, which the chance events of the times lead to take up the cause of their coreligionists, we must mention in particular Alfred Naquet.[41]

In his childhood, the chemist and theorist of materialism "learned to read Hebrew on my own; I devoutly said my prayers morning and evening. I hid myself to pray. . . . At thirteen, I wanted a Bar Mitzvah and I fasted on Yom Kippur. My father had forbidden me to do so out of his antireligious spirit . . . but I managed to disregard the prohibition."[42] Later, as a revolutionary socialist and a republican militant oriented toward the universal, Naquet seemed to have become entirely distanced from Judaism. But the detour of Boulangism, in which he played an essential role,[43] opened his eyes. Under pressure from Drumont, antisemitism was in the process of overwhelming that movement, which Naquet had thought would bring about greater democracy; he then battled the national-populist ideology of Drumont and his friends, dedicated himself to denouncing antisemitism, which was gaining in the French population and even in the socialist camp (which was "flirting" with it in the guise of anticapitalism), and called for respect for the emancipatory traditions set up by the French Revolution, which had made Jews citizens. He defended those emancipatory traditions continuously, for he felt that antisemitism was "the best weapon that the reaction could have forged to beat down the revolutionary spirit."[44] Frequently denounced at the national level and in his department of Vaucluse as a Jew,[45] Naquet came to combat antisemitism[46] more and more openly, yet appeared almost embarrassed to be personally involved in that task: "If I were not a Jew," he remarked, "if I could not be suspected of pleading my own cause, I would conduct a campaign against antisemites like the one I conducted in the past regarding divorce."[47] Even though, at the time, the *Archives Israélites* still claimed that "in the true sense of the word, M. Naquet is only slightly Jewish, perhaps not at all,"[48] he solemnly took the floor at the Chamber of Deputies, in the fiery context of the Dreyfus affair, and for long hours, continually interrupted by jeers from *députés* on the right, he identified himself as Jewish and attempted to demonstrate the unacceptable nature of antisemitism in a republican France made up of equal citizens.[49] "I belong to no religion," he wrote in a letter published by *L'Univers Israélite*, "I was married in a civil ceremony to a Catholic woman. . . . My one remaining child was raised (without my consent, it is true, and in spite of me, but without my using my legal rights to oppose it) in the Catholic religion. But I shall never deny my race."[50] Late in life, attending a large protest banquet against the Yom Kippur fast, which as an adolescent he had imposed upon himself, he once more declared himself against all religion, but he added: "We feel Jewish when Jews are attacked, and we declare it proudly."[51]

Even the Jewish *députés* most reserved in their allegiance to any particularist community suddenly manifested a completely different attitude when they were confronted with antisemitism. The case of *député* Camille Dreyfus was very revealing from this point of view: even though the organs of the Jewish community press continually made fun of him,[52] even though he was an ardent advocate of secularism and was particularly hostile to religion, he did an about-face when confronted with the Dreyfus affair.

"Bazaine, who handed over France," he exclaimed, "was not a Jew, and Dumouriez, who went over to the enemy, professed a profound horror of Jews. . . . We would like to believe that French consciences will see to it that the campaign they are being drawn into does not go unchallenged. Traitors who have no nation also have no religion." *L'Univers Israélite* celebrated these lines "of a praiseworthy impartiality," inasmuch as they came from "a Jew who long ago broke with the practices and even the beliefs of Judaism."[53] Furthermore, personally taken to task by the protagonists in the antisemitic campaign linked to the Affair, Camille Dreyfus went so far as to fight a pistol duel with the Marquis de Morès, one of the leaders of the antisemitic movement. *L'Univers Israélite* applauded him: "Dreyfus and Naquet, bravo! Jews by birth but not by religion, you have kept the Jewish fiber, or at least the human fiber."[54] In the same way, Ferdinand Crémieux—who, we recall, refused to endorse his own involuntary election to the consistory, and who would be buried in a purely civil manner[55]—intervened with the government to defend Tunisian Jews threatened by a particularly violent outburst of antisemitism. When the Marseilles consistory congratulated him on this behavior, he replied: "My attitude should not surprise you. . . . Whatever my way of seeing things in the question of external worship, I am not among those who are ashamed of his origin, but am always happy to bear witness publicly to my family solidarity to coreligionists who are worthy of it."[56]

Confronted with antisemitic negation, the *députés* and senators who were least prompt to acknowledge they were Jews did not hesitate to respond firmly to their adversaries. For example, there were countless surprisingly open antisemitic interruptions at the Chamber of Deputies and the Senate, which were immediately challenged: in 1884, at the most intense point in discussions on the separation of Church and state, *député* Ferdinand Dreyfus was virtually denied the floor simply because he was not Catholic. "M. de la Rochefoucauld," he responded, "there are none but French *députés* here. You have no right to make religious distinctions." To which Paul de Cassagnac mockingly replied: "We are not attacking the rabbis, M. Dreyfus!"[57] A bit later, in 1902 in the Senate, after an attack by the count of Pontbriand against "the great Jewish and cosmopolitan fortunes," Paul Strauss hastened to cry out: "Gentlemen, I shall not let pass without protest a statement before the Senate that establishes a division between Frenchmen, distinguishing them according to their origins and religious denomination." *L'Univers Israélite*, under the authorship of its editor-in-chief Isaïe Levaillant, congratulated Senator Strauss, since "under the pretext of showing reserve, which most often dissimulates a less easily admitted feeling, the Jewish members have until now most often refrained from raising their voices in favor of their threatened or violated coreligionists."[58]

In this regard, many other state Jews showed great vigilance, especially those who already belonged to the various community institutions; fortified by that first Jewish dimension, they were less hesitant to publicly cross swords with the leaders of antisemitic campaigns. Among the very first ranks of these men figured once more the former *préfet* Isaïe Levaillant, a central character we will encounter several more times in the course of this saga of state Jews. Having become editor-in-chief of *L'Univers Israélite*, the former *préfet* and director of Sûreté Générale, who knew the power of the extremist movements of the radical right because he had followed their trail, continually sent up cries of alarm, appealing in all or almost all his editorials for the most active vigilance. "It seems impossible to believe," he wrote in August 1897,

that on the eve of undergoing a decisive assault, the Jews of France have not thought to arm themselves for the struggle and to organize their defense. What have they done to prepare themselves for tomorrow's battle? What organizations have they created? Who are the allies whose cooperation they have ensured? . . . The French Jews are incapable of protecting themselves: no coming together has even been attempted; no committee or association has been founded; in short, there exists not even the shadow of an organization. . . . Never have a herd of sheep consented to be slaughtered with a more docile and stupid resignation.[59]

The former *préfet* sounded the alarm since, for him, the Dreyfus affair was threatening the very existence of French Jews:

Antisemitism is in full bloom. . . . It has found allies in every party, it has taken on the most varied hues. We shall have clerical antisemites and socialist antisemites, Boulangist antisemites and even republican antisemites. . . . In the presence of the formidable outcry expected, what will the Jews of France do? Are they in any condition to stand face to face with the enemy and push back the assault that threatens them? . . . It seems the moment is come for preparing ourselves for battle.

Levaillant relentlessly proclaimed that "in the presence of the formidable coalition that threatens them, it is time for Jews to prepare for combat."[60] In order to take concrete action before it was too late, a Comité de Défense contre l'Antisémitisme was finally created in 1902; Isaïe Levaillant naturally became its secretary. By his side figured Narcisse Leven, president of the Alliance Israélite Universelle and vice president of the consistory; and Salomon Reinach, vice president of the central committee of the Alliance, member of the Institut, and the brother of Joseph and Théodore Reinach. The plan was clear: take all measures necessary to confront antisemitic movements. In a long communiqué, the committee declared that

the necessity has arisen to defend ourselves against incitements that are as evil as they are criminal. And it is from this belief that the work we have undertaken for legitimate self-preservation has sprung. . . . Devoting ourselves above all to the triumph of the cause of equality of all Frenchmen before the law, we distinguish only between the opponents and advocates of the principles of the Revolution. We have battled the former, whatever label they might have used. And we have made every effort to support the latter.[61]

Following these precepts, which favored actual mobilization, several state Jews prepared themselves on an individual basis to wage battle: Jules Moch, for example, recalled how, as a high school student in Janson-de-Sailly in 1904, he hastened to acquire the rudiments of boxing so as to be able to confront his antisemitic fellow students.[62]

Fortunately, in 1906 the reasons for alarm disappeared, the Dreyfus affair ended, and the captain was rehabilitated. The Republic triumphed, and the extreme right agitation waned. Law and justice finally prevailed and the threat abated without even the need for any real organizing, let alone fighting. Isaïe Levaillant was overjoyed to see the antisemitic candidates defeated at the legislative elections, proof of "the collapse of a transformed and perverted antisemitism that calls itself nationalism"; henceforth optimistic, he announced the disappearance of that nationalism that was so hostile to the Republic and to Jews.[63] And, in an important lecture given to the Society of Jewish Studies in April 1907, he focused one last time on the Drumont case, discussed the links between Boulangism and antisemitism, turned again to Panama and the Dreyfus affair, the negation of the republican tradition, and ended, the inveterate optimist, with this final forceful observation: "It is precisely through the Dreyfus affair that antisemitism was finally killed off. . . . The scales have fallen from the country's eyes, and it has seen clearly that antisemitism not only threatened a religious minority but also placed in peril all the gains of modern France. As a result, it was inevitable that it should be vanquished and driven back."[64]

The former director of Sûreté Générale was wrong, however. After diminishing during the national unity of World War I, the same threats rapidly reappeared on the horizon, probably even more grave than at the time of the Dreyfus affair. From all sides and in an explosive international context, antisemitism was oozing forth. This time, the Jew hunt would be pursued to the end and would culminate in the state antisemitism set in place by Vichy. Other state Jews during the interwar period, following Isaïe Levaillant's lead, rapidly moved into action: Léon Blum and Jean Pierre-Bloch were among the first members of the Ligue Internationale contre l'Antisémitisme (LICA), founded by Bernard Lecache in early 1928, which was very active in the streets of Paris. The organization included a vigilante-type force capable of physically confronting the *Camelots du Roi* or members of fascist organizations. Jean Pierre-Bloch was to become its president in 1968.[65] Still others launched various concrete forms of defense: according to *L'Univers Israélite*, General A. Weiller "has proved to be a worthy servant of his country, a worthy son of Israel, to which, he declares, he is proud to have remained faithful. As a Jew, he is profoundly so, and that youthful ardor that shines in his eyes is revealed at its most brilliant when he speaks of Judaism."[66]

He placed this passion in the service of the struggle against antisemitism: in July 1925 he became president of the Association Sportive Juive (Jewish sports association), an athletic version of the "Jewish reawakening."[67] Very active against the extreme right, he also participated in meetings of LICA: in April 1933 he took the floor beside Bernard Lecache, Jewish *député* Théodore Valensi, and several personalities, including Marc Sangnier, in support of an economic boycott of Germany. He openly appealed for military action, later provoking the disapproval of the community's pacifist current.[68]

In August 1938 General Weiller also became president of the Union et Sauvegarde Juives (Jewish union and protection force) for the Paris region. His vice president was none other than *député* Henry Torrès: that organization had as its goal, in cooperation with the Centre de Vigilance linked to the consistory and other associations, to organize the counterattack by calling on public authorities if necessary; for example, in late 1938 General Weiller himself organized the rapid destruction of antisemitic posters displayed in various Parisian neighborhoods. Disappointed by the wait-and-see policy of the Jewish authorities and as resolute to act as Levaillant had been in his time, Weiller desired the implementation of more immediate, less restrained actions, determined actions that would remain "within the framework of legality as far as possible" but would also step outside the law in emergencies. He shared these plans with the president of the central consistory, Jacques Helbronner, *président de section* at the Conseil d'Etat.[69] And almost symbolically, when a vigilance committee was set in place at the end of the 1930s to keep a close eye on the antisemitic movement, of the three commissions created, two were directed by state Jews, Jacques Helbronner and General Weiller. In this same vigilance committee inaugurated in early 1936, there was also a magistrate, Bloch-Laroque. Linked to the consistory, he was given the mission of following the evolution of antisemitism and combating it by every means; quickly, this committee moved closer to the Union et Sauvegarde Juives created by Weiller throughout France; their propaganda actions in the most diverse forms quickly became widespread.[70] As during the period of the Dreyfus affair, it was once more state Jews who played a crucial role in the community institutions that took the initiative against antisemitism.[71] Therefore, we cannot entirely go along with the *Archives Israélites* in its claim that "we have not seen Jewish parliamentarians stand up against the enemies of Israel or courageously take the defense of their vilified coreligionists, Jewish officers, and functionaries who are blacklisted or blocked in their advancement," or when it concluded without comment that "when they step over the threshold of the two assemblies, Jewish senators and *députés* check at the door every sign that might awaken the idea that they belong to the family of Israel."[72] We are more in agreement with the interpretation of Isaïe Levaillant, who maintained that beyond the profound political differences that led them toward Opportunism, Radicalism, Bonapartism, socialism, and later even communism, all wished "spontaneously, naturally, and in some sense instinctively [to be] republicans," and showed their attachment to defending "the place that is legitimately due them in this Republic, which they have contributed toward establishing."[73] At the same time, all rallied around the flag of "freedom of conscience" and the rejection of antisemitism, a common denominator in their political commitments, distinct from and sometimes antagonistic to their religion.

One last dimension that emerged among state Jews was Zionism, which, contrary to all expectations, sometimes held their attention. Anxious to ensure their integration into the state, to make their entry into the public space definitive, to legitimate as much as possible a Republic that had proved to be emancipatory and meritocratic, state Jews most often turned away from the Zionist solution, the absolute antithesis of their destiny.[74] Théodore Reinach, who, through his celebrated academic success, incarnated French-style meritocracy, a scholar turned *député* and theorist of a radical transformation of Judaism, which he envisioned as organized in many of its aspects like Catholicism, took a position sharply opposed to Zionism. In a lecture given in February 1927, he maintained that Judaism had become "a great spiritual fact"; as a result, "the Zionist undertaking is deadly if it fails and even more deadly if the impossible happens and it succeeds. . . . Drumont will have won his case. . . . If Judaism officially becomes a nationality, the Jews of France will have to choose between Judaism and France."[75] This declaration provoked a huge debate in which a number of Jewish newspapers participated. For *Ménorah*, "M. Reinach's fears are not well founded. The Jewish state, should it be founded in fifty or a hundred years . . . would be for Jews of other countries what France is for French Canadians, what Ireland is for the Irish in the United States"; *La Tribune juive de Strasbourg* maintained that "Théodore Reinach's liberalism would like to establish a Judaism without material basis or ritual law."[76]

His brother Joseph, Gambetta's right-hand man, who best symbolized the new political elite of republican Jews close to the Opportunist camp, rarely expressed himself on this subject, which, in fact, was hardly the object of heated discussions in Paris within politico-administrative circles at the end of the nineteenth century. His passion, like that of many state Jews, was solely for the French Republic and its tradition of instituting equality among all citizens, whatever their individual religions and values. Under these conditions, Zionism seemed preposterous and dangerous, since it threatened the status of Franco-Judaism and openly called into question the Jews' integration into French society. In a little-known text dating from after World War I, when national concord increased appreciably, Joseph Reinach unambiguously declared:

> If we mean by Zionism the constitution of a Jewish state in Palestine, I say clearly, resolutely: No. . . . 1) The very idea of a state having religion at its base is contrary to all the principles of the modern world . . . 2) There was a Jewish nation at the time of the kingdom of Israel. There has been no Jewish nation for twenty centuries . . . 3) Just because there existed in very ancient times a kingdom of Israel in Jerusalem does not mean that the Jews have a special right to Jerusalem . . . 4) To speak of a Jewish race, you have to be either ignorant or acting in bad faith . . . 5) Since the Revolution decreed, through Mirabeau and Abbé Grégoire, the equality of all sects, it is no longer permitted to speak of French Jews. There are Frenchmen who are Jewish and there are other Frenchmen who are Catholic or Protestant. Does the blood of Jewish Frenchmen that flowed freely on the battlefields of 1914–18 differ from the blood of Catholic or Protestant or freethinking Frenchmen? Since, therefore, there is neither a Jewish race nor a Jewish nation, since there is only a Jewish religion, Zionism is quite simply idiocy, a triple error: historical, archaeological, and ethnic.[77]

The judgment was clear and definitive: within the French Republic, the Jewish religion was legitimate and antisemitism had to be combated, as Reinach himself had combated it at the time of the Dreyfus affair. Reacting in great part to this fissure, to this Franco-French war, Theodore Herzl concluded that assimilation was impossible, and hence, that the creation of a Jewish state was indispensable. In contrast, Joseph Reinach, who contributed greatly toward the final acknowledgment of the captain's innocence, had his confidence in the Republic restored and could only reject categorically any Zionist perspective. His adversary, socialist sympathizer Alfred Naquet, the hot-headed atheist *député* from Vaucluse, shared without dispute this fundamentally negative interpretation of Zionism: on several occasions, in the name of the successful integration of Jews into the French nation, he explained "the chimera of a nationality of their own pursued by the Jews" solely as the result of the persecution provoked by the Affair, which had dissociated them from the nation and temporarily prevented their fusion with the community as a whole.[78] As we recall, Naquet too was hostile to antisemitism and denounced "the noble but absurd utopia of Zionism that would resuscitate an oppressive clericalism."[79] State Jews, who often confronted one another during great national debates — Naquet, for example, was the spokesperson for Boulangism, which Reinach strongly opposed — nonetheless easily reached an agreement on this point, since both were greatly attached to the primacy of the republican framework.

During the same period, Isaïe Levaillant also took care to underscore the fact that "it is above all our excellent antisemites who are thrilled by the meeting of the Zionist Congress." He did not pull his punches in condemning the "utopia," the "puerile dream" that the project of a Jewish state defended by Herzl represented to him. For him, Zionism was simply a consequence of antisemitism, and one had only to remove the latter, return full citizenship to Jewish Frenchmen, and they would definitively turn away from Zionism, which was not otherwise attractive to them.[80] This man, who was long at the center of the administrative apparatus and who at the time was playing a crucial role within Jewish institutions, did not hide his opinions: Zionism was "an adventure with no way out," whose "inanity" was patent and which could only lead to "a miserable abortion"; he pressed the Zionist leaders to abandon their "phantasmagorical dreams" and to join with the more modest efforts to develop agricultural colonies, which the Alliance Israélite Universelle was already setting up in Palestine, to help Jews living there improve their way of life.[81] Somewhat less skeptical later on, Levaillant wrote:

We are not Zionists, not in the slightest; but we regret not being so. If we imagine Zionism solely as a movement of protest against intolerance and persecution, how could we not associate ourselves with it? It is precisely because Zionism has legitimate causes that despite its utter impossibility, its incoherence and puerility, it has awakened such keen sympathies and attracted so many followers. And that is also why we do not feel we have the right to disapprove of it or ridicule it.[82]

What we have here is a clear change of direction, the abandonment of a purely negative position. Even though the immense majority of Jews in France remained indifferent and often hostile toward Zionism, the path was nevertheless opened by one of their most illustrious spokespersons toward a certain acceptance and later even an openly favorable approach to it. In 1927, a Ligue des Amis du Sionisme was constituted, with André Spire, former member of the Conseil d'Etat and poet, at its center. In late 1917 and early 1918, Georges Wormser, member of Clemenceau's cabinet, played an important role in France's recognition of a Jewish settlement in Palestine, which followed England's similar recognition, thus indirectly ratifying the notorious Balfour Declaration.[83] In 1919 Spire also intervened with the French minister of foreign affairs to plead the Zionist cause.[84] In 1925 a France-Palestine committee was created that included Poincaré, Herriot, Briand, and Painlevé as well as André Spire and Léon Blum: its goal was to link France to the enterprise of Palestine's renewal. Blum very quickly became interested in Zionism, which he supported as of the end of World War I. Convinced by Weizmann, he aided the Zionist leaders with his knowledge of the politico-administrative circles. In 1929 he was among the French representatives at the conference constituting the expanded Jewish

Agency, as a delegate of the Ligue des Amis de la Palestine Ouvrière (league of the friends of the workers' Palestine). "I am a Zionist," he declared, "because I am a Frenchman, because I am Jewish, and because I am a socialist, because modern Jewish Palestine is the unprecedented and unique encounter of the oldest traditions of humanity with its newest and most daring search for liberty and social justice."[85] He added that "in this respect as well, unlike many French Jews," he was passionately interested in the Zionist cause.[86] At the time of the Front Populaire and in May 1948, he intervened to hasten the birth of Israel: during the *Exodus* affair, he noted: "I was born Jewish; for twenty-five years, I have done my best to help in constituting the 'Jewish national homeland' in Palestine, and I have never thought of leaving France."[87] In his honor, a kibbutz called Kfar Blum was founded in Israel.[88]

Somewhat later, other state Jews played an even more prominent role in the Zionist movement: hence, General Geismar became honorary president of the Keren Kayemeth Leisrael of France, an organization designed to raise funds for the Zionist movement. In a series of articles published in *La Terre Retrouvée*, he maintained that "the Jews of the Diaspora, Zionist or non-Zionist, are called upon to support those who are doing constructive work in Palestine. To take no interest simply because the task is difficult would be an act touching on cowardice and would cover us all with shame."[89] In the company of André Spire, former member of the Conseil d'Etat, and R. R. Lambert, a member of several ministerial offices under the Third Republic and head of the UGIF under Vichy, Geismar was elected in February 1927 to the council of the Fédération Sioniste de France.[90] Many *députés* such as Jean Pierre-Bloch, Pierre Mendès France, and Henry Torrès also participated in meetings in support of Zionism and protested against the violence suffered by the Jews of Palestine.[91] Even later, in 1947, Jules Moch, minister of public works at the time, took measures to facilitate the transfer of arms from Czechoslovakia to Israel: every night, an airplane landed at the Ajaccio airfield, before taking off again toward Lydda with all its lights turned off.[92] He openly expressed his admiration for "the audacious rebirth of the state of Israel."[93] After independence, *député* Jean Pierre-Bloch organized the first dinner in honor of the official representative of the state of Israel: among the participants were *député* Salomon Grumbach, member of the World Jewish Congress, as well as Léon Blum, René Cassin, and Paul Cahen-Salvador from the Conseil d'Etat.[94]

What are we to conclude, except that a very large proportion of state Jews showed an awareness of their Judaism in one way or another? Their integration into the public space as a whole and into the state, which had been so successful, was not accompanied by an assimilation that eliminated all their own values. Not only did they frequently bear biblical first names like their fathers, marry Jewish women, and have themselves buried in the presence of rabbis, but, in addition, and more consequentially in terms of public visibility, a very large number of them, like their fathers, belonged to one or another of the community institutions, in which they proved to be very active. The most alienated of them discovered their Judaism and even proclaimed their identity when confronted by an outburst of antisemitism at one time or another during the Third Republic; and, however attached they were to the republican identity of the nation, which they all understood in almost Jacobin terms, a small number did not hide the sympathy they felt for the Zionist project, though others resolutely fought it. These diverse dimensions of Judaism form something like a cluster of indexes of the way certain state Jews — and they were probably in the majority — lived out their Jewishness. The claim is simple: at the highest levels of the state, holding office and adhering to the norms and values of the nation as a whole rarely weakened the intimate feeling of difference experienced as compatible with full adherence to administrative or political roles: the most complete integration did not imply pure and simple assimilation.

CHAPTER SEVEN

The Birth of a Milieu

This was still the era of family networks, the reign of clientelism, the "word" put in for someone with the knowledge it would be heeded. Recommendations were still the royal road to the most prestigious state careers. Meritocracy was slowly triumphing, however: the administration was setting its own rules for recruitment and operation, limiting government high-handedness and the almost complete arbitrariness that had earlier guided careers. Hence, the state was imposing its administrative order by reducing to an ever greater extent the traditional omnipotence of dynasties and other notables: in the second half of the nineteenth century, examinations more and more supplanted pure and simple co-optation, and merit continually gained strength over the many forms of social collusion. One after another, the state corps adopted specific examinations whose avowed goal was to ensure a certain equality among all citizens.

In looking more closely, however, we quickly have to change our tune. For at the turn of the century, those holding high administrative posts managed to conserve the privileges held by the state's most senior servants by permitting them to keep in operation informal processes of co-optation, considerably restraining the possible intrusion of anyone who originated elsewhere, outside the state, in the many social and cultural groups of the overall society. Fathers always knew how to protect and promote their sons' careers within the state; administrative dossiers were filled almost to bursting with letters of recommendation written in confidence and complicity. Social collusion reinforced networks of sociability; and mountains of hand-written letters, each harboring a precise request for intervention capable of unblocking or promoting a career, were legion. An analysis of these letters leads us to a veritable web spun among a limited number of actors holding positions of importance.[1] In the end, in that intermediate period, the leading milieus of the past preserved their predominance and often succeeded, by any means necessary, in passing it on to their heirs, in particular by conducting well-orchestrated strategies of alliance.

Under these conditions of almost complete socioprofessional closure, what could be the place accorded the new arrivals within the leadership, the place of all those whom the Republic had called to its side, and in particular, that of state Jews? On the whole, they remained unlike the others in many respects: their recent past was not the same, and the most stunning meritocratic virtues couldn't do anything about that. What, then, were the characteristics that distinguished state Jews from their colleagues in high public office? First of all, and this fact still counted for a great deal, none of them belonged to the landed aristocracy or the nobility in the most general sense of the term: in the army in particular, where the offspring of the different aristocracies remained very numerous, that difference acted as a social marker. Furthermore, none of them chose their future spouses from within noble circles, which were still strongly represented within the state; inasmuch as most of them preferred to respect endogamic practices, they differed from the leading group and further excluded themselves from it. Even though, at the turn of the century, literary narratives often recounted the history of alliances between court Jews and the children of great aristocratic families, who lent them their names from the ancien régime and received their new relations in their salons, state Jews in fact remained apart from such social strategies. Similarly, the number of state Jews who emerged from the École Libre des Sciences Politiques (the school of political science), where the new leadership elite had been formed beginning with the defeat of 1870, can be counted on the fingers of one hand. A certain osmosis between the aristocracy and the upper bourgeoisie was coming about; and for a long time, this shaped the profile of the new leaders united through networks of sociability, which were reinforced by the values identical to those acquired at that prestigious school. While Protestants had access to the leading milieus through the mediation of that establishment, state Jews remained all the more excluded.

State Jews, then, were a new elite still excluded from the establishment where the upper bourgeoisie and the old aristocracy were intermingling more and more; other than in exceptional cases, they did not attend the same private — and often Catholic — schools or the all-powerful École Libre des Sciences Politiques, through which so many future executives of the state and nation passed. They also differed in many other ways from their colleagues in government.[2] Without pausing too long on comparisons that for lack of information, would not be very satisfactory, we may note that among the fathers of state Jews, there were no nobles and no peasants, no workers, and in fact, almost no representatives of the popular classes. Even more striking is the near absence of fathers who were lawyers, journalists, physicians, or minor officials, all groups from which, at different periods during the Third Republic, nearly half of judges and *conseillers d'Etat* and a large proportion of *préfets* and generals were recruited. The emancipation of Jews was still too recent: only in exceptional cases had the fathers of state Jews benefited from schooling that allowed them to move into such professions. Of course, beginning in the first decades of the nineteenth century, there were already a few Jewish students in most of the classes of the École Normale and the École Polytechnique; nevertheless, they remained very rare overall, as were lawyers and journalists during that period—perhaps until the first years of the Third Republic. Thus, even though these socio-professional groups were amply represented among state Jews who were beginning their careers during the 1870s and 1880s, their fathers only rarely practiced such professions.

Similarly, although the fathers of high officials in the prefect civil service, the Conseil d'Etat, or, in the judicial domain, the Cour de Cassation, had frequently also held high public office, this was not the case for most state Jews. Here again, the fact that Jews were named later to executive positions in the state accounts for this highly consequential anomaly. It distinguished them greatly from their colleagues as a whole, who had often spent their adolescence years in the shadow of the state and its power. Of course, some state Jews who embarked on their careers later, at the turn of the century or slightly before, were sons of high officials. In that sense, a certain administrative legacy came about, but, at the time, it remained incomparably weaker than within administrative positions as a whole, where it reached very high proportions in certain corps. Here, such a direct legacy, extended somewhat unfairly to the political administration, was still almost always a result of schooling. A few examples come to mind, however, most of which have already been evoked in our family portraits—this simply emphasizes how rare they were. The *préfets* and *sous-préfets* of the Hendlé family succeeded one another for three generations, as did the three *députés* Javal, to which we may add the *préfet* Léopold Javal, another son of the first Javal, who was elected *député* of Yonne. The dynasty of Bédarridès magistrates lasted only two generations, and this was also the case for judges Seligmann and Bloch, *conseiller d'Etat* Cahen-Salvador, the *conseillers de préfecture* Caen, and, if we agree to go beyond the period strictly in question, the Generals Brisac. Other cases, however small in number, also stem from the politico-administrative legacy, but this time involve a career change from one generation to the next. Hence, the fathers of *conseiller d'Etat* Pierre Laroque and *député* Pierre Masse were high magistrates, and the father of *conseiller d'Etat* Henri Weil was the *préfet* Eugène Weill. In an even broader sense, the father of *sous-préfet* Jules Franck was none other than A. Franck, professor at the Collège de France and member of the Institut; the father of Judge Léopold Berr was *ingénieur en chef des Mines* (chief mining engineer); General Léon Francfort's father was *ingénieur des Ponts et Chaussées* (engineer of bridges and roads); and the *préfet* Albert Heumann's father had been a colonel. Let us also note that only two generals belonged to this category: Georges Bloch, the son of a military man who occupied the subaltern position of *officier comptable* for military subsidies; and Jules Heymann, whose father was a mere *adjudant* (warrant officer). In this corps, however, high-ranking military men were frequently the children of senior officers, a phenomenon that sometimes occurred over several generations. Can we then understand why sixteen out of twenty-five Jewish generals had been students at the École Polytechnique, an extremely high proportion, which may perhaps be explained by the choice of a school where the sons of officers and nobles were less well represented?[3] Overall, administrative legacies remained very limited. Far from nonexistent, this was generally because state Jews, except in unusual circumstances, reached the different public posts rather late, becoming in turn — but much more than other elites — part of the process of self-recruitment, an undeniable sign of integration.

A final difference in their social recruitment, which logically resulted from those already mentioned: nearly two-thirds of them came from commercial milieus, their fathers almost always exercising one of the many trades associated with the cycle of financial exchange. That may be what made them most atypical and different from other high officials. Unlike most of their colleagues, the economic pole predominated to a large degree in the social origin of state Jews. An important precision is called for, however: with very rare exceptions, their fathers did not belong to the leading circles of business or major banking. That was the case, however, for the Reinachs and the Javals; for a few magistrates such as Gustave Bédarridès, Abraham Albert Alphandéry, and Léon Levylier; and for a few members of the prefect civil service such as *sous-préfet* Georges Simon, whose father was a former banker (at the time, Simon was considered "the son of a good family" whose "family possesses a great fortune and subsidizes his needs," a remark not often encountered in these dossiers).[4] But these cases seem to be the exception and point back to the Second Empire and the July Monarchy; hence, the banker Jacob Javal, father of Léopold Javal (founder of the political dynasty of Javal *députés*), retired from the business world in 1835 with a fortune of over three million francs.[5] Much nearer to our own time, during the interwar period, *député* Maurice de Rothschild also belonged to this milieu through his father. But this was an even more marginal case.

Far from being court Jews, most of the fathers of state Jews were modest garment workers or tailors, small provincial merchants, salesmen, trade representatives, vendors of livestock, goods, furniture, iron, or canvas, or merchants who had succeeded in making their businesses prosper and had in the end acquired a certain material comfort—a sum of capital that was not always easy to measure precisely. Nonetheless, and this is significant, there was not a true industrialist among them. From this point of view as well, their fortunes only very rarely reached the level of the parents of the high officials' colleagues, who were proportionally less well represented in such milieus but infinitely better provided with capital. In the administrative dossier of several state Jews, the "very modest" character of the family fortune was emphasized. The father of the *préfet* Eugène Sée, an iron merchant from Colmar, succeeded in building a more than comfortable fortune of 800,000 francs, and Judge Achille Katz's father was "a very rich Alsatian grain salesman," while his father-in-law, a banker, had a fortune of more than 250,000 francs.[6] But the father of *préfet* and future minister of the interior Abraham Schrameck was only a "modest ribbon salesman," while the father of *préfet* and future director of Sûreté Générale Isaïe Levaillant had "no fortune." Judge Raphaël Job's father, like so many others, "had no fortune." Nor did the fathers of *préfet* Abraham Pinède, *sous-préfet* Georges Mossé, a small businessman from Marseilles, and many other members of the prefect civil service: their revenues were in the neighborhood of 3,000 to 8,000 francs, at the most 15,000 to 20,000 francs. That was the sum, at the very most, that the father of *conseiller de préfecture* Lucien Aaron, a tapestry maker, and the father of Judge Charles Berr, a fabric maker, had at their disposal.[7]

In fact, it was often marriage that provided them with fortunes. This observation can be verified in particular for the generals, who almost always came from modest economic milieus, but who were the recipients, as seemed to be the custom among senior officers, of very comfortable dowries, which immediately conferred the good life on them. Hence, the future general Samuel-Laroque received 100,000 francs in cash at the time of his marriage, with the expectation of an inheritance of another 150,000 francs; the future general Mardochée Valabrègue was given 225,000 francs by his in-laws, payable at the time of his marriage to their daughter; the future general Léon Francfort received 140,000 francs from his father-in-law, a banker, as did Captain Louis Naquet when he married the daughter of an attorney; the future General Carvallo received 50,000 francs, with the hope of receiving a sum equal to that later on.[8] *Sous-préfet* Edmond Cahen also married the daughter of a banker with a very impressive dowry, as did Georges Beaucaire, one of the very rare state Jews to attend the École Libre des Sciences Politiques, whose father was also a banker.[9] These cases, however, were altogether the exception. In the magistracy, the father-in-law of Judge Adolphe Seligmann was a major banker from Metz; the father-in-law of Judge Abraham Alphandéry had a fortune of more than 300,000 francs; and Judge Katz's father possessed a fortune estimated at about 250,000 francs.[10] But these examples were still very rare and in almost every instance concerned officials whose fathers already belonged to the favored milieus. A high proportion of state Jews, in contrast, preferred to marry the daughters of other high officials of the same denomination, thus extending the administrative legacy in the broad sense, to the point of favoring the birth of a true social milieu.

This milieu took shape bit by bit, uniting state Jews not only through endogamic ties or an administrative legacy understood in the strict sense but also through structures of mutual acquaintance fashioned by the extended family of uncles, cousins, nephews, and so on. As a result of being atypical and original, a true administrative milieu with social and cultural connotations was formed, reinforced in many ways by the most unexpected alliances. On a foundation of shared base values that were both republican and particularist, and through all kinds of Jewish practices, there was created a sort of constellation, a mobile group that almost became autonomous within the French Jewish population as it brought state Jews closer together. Family circles within the administrative world overlapped again and again, establishing professional ties propitious for the appearance of the most diverse forms of sociability between relatives distant in time and space. The family portraits have attracted attention to the most patent circles of family networks, with the example of the judicial dynasties founded by Gustave Bédarridès and Philippe Anspach perhaps the most impressive of all, since they brought together, generation after generation, numerous magistrates and *sous-préfets* — as sons, brothers-in-law, fathers-in-law, brothers, uncles, cousins, nephews, and so on. Many other family networks on a smaller scale can be cited, which were sometimes even connected through a shared member. Hence, it happened that one of the sons of *député* Léopold Javal, Ernest Léopold, married Marie Seligmann, the daughter of Adolphe Seligmann, *président* of the *tribunal de grande instance* of Nice, whose mother was an Anspach linked to the magistrate Philippe Anspach, and whose son in turn became a magistrate; furthermore, the nephew of Philippe Anspach was none other than Judge Julien Félix, who in turn became the uncle of Judge Oscar Kinsbourg, whose daughter married Judge Émile Worms. At various times, several state Jews thus found they had distant kinship ties.

In reality, it is often difficult to unravel the skein of ties linking so many Valabrègues, Naquets, Bédarridèses, Lisbonnes, and the Lions. Let us go over some of these family networks, which were at times very closely linked, at other times only loosely connected. After those we have just mentioned, the most intimate ties were undeniably those between brothers, such as Judge Eliacin Naquet and *député* Alfred Naquet, or *sous-préfet* Paul Levylier and his brother, *trésorier-payeur général* of Indre. Beyond this, any connections could appear. Hence, the son of Judge Raoul Bloch became a magistrate in turn and married the daughter of R. Laroque, *président du tribunal* at the Aix-en-Provence court. R. Laroque was in turn the father-in-law of *député* Édouard Millaud. The daughter of *préfet* Isaïe Levaillant married *sous-préfet* Torrès and their son later became a *député*. And, as we have seen, *préfet* Léon Cohn married the daughter of *préfet* Ernest Hendlé, just as, through the same kind of marriage, General Valabrègue became the brother-in-law of Judge Achille Katz. Through his marriage, *député* Lazare Weiller became part of the Javal family of *députés*. Furthermore, *conseiller de préfecture* Lucien Aaron found himself the nephew of *conseiller d'Etat* Jules Valabrègue, and Senator Paul Strauss became the uncle of *préfet* René Strauss. *Député* David Raynal was also the uncle of *sous-préfet* Georges Beaucaire, and *député* Fernand Crémieux's nephew was *conseiller de préfecture* Jules Levi. *Préfet* Albert Heumann was the close relative of *conseiller d'Etat* René Mayer.

The proximity of all these state Jews is revealed in the repetitive nature of their names, which at times is the sign of a close-knit family, but at other times merely points to individuals bearing the same patronymic who are not necessarily part of the same family. Hence, in the population we are considering, there were seven Levys, five Naquets, four Javals, four Weills, four Sées, four Blochs, four Dreyfuses, three Brisacs, three Lisbonnes, three Hendlés, three Arons, three Valabrègues, three Reinachs, three Bédarridèses, three Worms, three Laroques, three Crémieux, three Masses, three Strausses, three Seligmanns, two Anspachs, two Grunebaum-Ballins, two Torrèses, two Abrams, two Alphandérys, two Berrs, two Caens, two Levyliers, two Lamberts, two Grumbachs, two Francks, and two Weillers. This means that 94 of a total 171 persons shared a patronymic once or several times within this small milieu of state Jews, which was also traversed by family ties linking them to other persons of that same overall population! When, in addition, we learn that a number of state Jews worked together in different political currents, in administrative commissions, or in particularist community structures of various kinds, we begin to understand the intensity of the multiple networks that united them.

These innumerable ties of sociability draw our attention to one last difference that distinguishes state Jews from their colleagues as a whole: proportionally, they did not come from the same regions in France. In fact, almost all of them were from the East, from Paris (where so many of their families had headed after the 1870 disaster), or from the Southeast, regions where, along with Alsace and Lorraine, they were well established from time immemorial. The Sephardic Southwest had been lost; the particularly successful assimilation realized since the seventeenth century had overcome particularist values, especially since it had been accomplished through the economic world; virtually none of the descendants of that community figure among the state Jews of the contemporary period. Very few of the 171 high officials were born in that region or came from it originally, even distantly: the only key man from the region was *député* and minister of the interior David Raynal, closely associated with the Gambettists at the national level, and powerful enough to advance the careers of others. For example, in December 1879, he wrote a letter to the minister in support of Joseph Léon, originally from Bordeaux. A few months later, Léon was named *sous-préfet* in Castellane; his career, however, ended there that same year.[11] In 1890, David Raynal also sent five letters to the minister supporting Edgar Marx's reinstatement in the magistracy. Marx had also been born in Bordeaux, had a law degree, and had been awarded prizes five times by the Bordeaux faculty. Moreover, he was the son of the chief rabbi of that city; nevertheless, like the missives sent by Jules Steeg, also *député* of Bordeaux, these letters were without effect.[12] Raynal also intervened in support of the son of the new chief rabbi of Bordeaux, Isaac Levy, who would later become chief rabbi of Paris: Lucien Levy proved to be a judge without peer, with each of his superiors portraying him as beyond praise, applauding his competence, his sense of authority, and so on. Since, in addition, he showed proof of extreme courage during World War I, where he was wounded several times and awarded the Croix de Guerre, his career course was not one of fits and starts. Even though we also find a letter in his administrative dossier from Georges Mandel, future *député* of Gironde, dating from 1909, and another from Charles Berr, *premier président* in Paris, these interventions from other state Jews counted less than his own merit. Named a *juge suppléant* in Bazas in 1889, he became *premier président* of Seine in 1931.[13] Outside of these rare high officials, only *sous-préfet* Fernand Torrès and Pierre Mendès France, who turned to another chief rabbi of Bordeaux in 1938 to better understand his own history,[14] could claim a distant identity with the Southwest, which in the past had been one of the cradles of French Jewry. Interventions by a key man such as David Raynal, who was also a full-fledged member of the national political class, more often concerned state Jews from the East or Southeast.

As we begin to sense, two vast family networks are taking shape before our eyes, bringing together in a purely analytic way Jews from the East on the one hand and those from the Southeast on the other, with both groups linked in many ways to their Paris colleagues. It is to these two vast family systems that we will now turn our attention, ready to focus as well on the alliances that might also unite them, or, in contrast, to the rare cases of full exclusion, absolute marginality of one of the two groups from the other, or from their respective extensions in Paris. The first system was indisputably formed in the Southeast, where papal Jews more quickly left the ghetto and entered modernity, leaving their earlier jobs, opening themselves to external sociability, and emancipating themselves in every sense of the term, but almost always without completely breaking with the past, as had happened in Bordeaux and Bayonne. Just as quickly as the Sephardim of the Southwest, but without abandoning all of their specific culture, they moved into the many professions of modern society, while their Ashkenazic coreligionists, more aloof and turned in upon themselves, their own practices and traditions, continued in traditional professions. From then on, in Carpentras, Avignon, Aix-en-Provence, Nîmes, and Montpellier, but also in Nyons, Tarascon, and Salon-de-Provence, a new Jewish milieu blossomed, far from the *carrières* (the Jewish ghettos) and in touch with society. There were countless lawyers, as in Provence as a whole, as well as physicians, merchants, and bankers oriented toward openness and exchange. A local banking network formed, which Bédarridès and Alphandéry would inherit; but, unlike the Pereires or Mirèses in the Southwest, they remained faithful to their own values, fashioned and supported, as it were, by a truly local milieu. That was how the move from court Jews to state Jews, the mingling of the two categories, came about in a most intense way. We could cite as evidence the successive appearances of the Emperor's Jews and of Gambetta's men, all of whom we will encounter later on, the one group more conservative, the others full-fledged republicans. In the end, the birth of a certain radicalism, which was of course limited to personalities such as Alfred Naquet and Gaston Crémieux, also anticipated future political battles between utopianism and socialism.

Thus, it was in this vast Provence marked by conviviality and republican ideas, but also open to external markets and trade networks, that the first family network was constituted, linking together most state Jews from the area in a thousand ways, in an intermingling that no one could really untangle. Endogamy also had a strong effect in structuring vast but intimate networks of mutual acquaintance; yet in itself, it no more explains the flourishing of epistolary exchanges we find in administrative dossiers — through which so many deliberations and coordinations increasingly linked these sons of Provence in a vast system of mutual favors — than does the narrow circle of the family.

To speak of a network inevitably implies the presence of an animator, a relay man, a jack of all trades through whom interactions are delivered:

someone who assures the overall regulation of the network and, through his authority, establishes the link between the center—the state institutions concentrated in Paris—and the local peripheries, lending a helping hand, judiciously intervening wherever necessary. The entire system of government administration buzzed with such messages in the nineteenth century and certainly even later; in this restricted place, groups, clans, and networks fought for jobs, grabbed the most envied posts, or suddenly accelerated or rescued careers, breaking with the strict monotony of promotion based on seniority. At first glance, the administrative dossiers of all the high officials are astonishing, disorienting for the way they overflow with letters of recommendation. No systematic analysis attentive both to the circles of sociability they reveal and, beyond that, to the literary qualities they indicate, has ever been produced. Yet these dossiers hold treasures of information, shedding a completely different light on the world of the bureaucracy, at a time when it was slowly rejecting the former notables who had been assigned there and opening itself to new talent, to elites who were anxious to demonstrate their competence in the service of the Republic. In fact, it is a rude shock to realize that the setting up of these structures of mutual acquaintance, these mechanisms approaching complicity proper to each political, religious, or social clientele, was in every case organized around one of several key men.

One miracle man was undeniably Adolphe Crémieux, who played that role in Provence and in the Southeast generally. He was from that region originally and practiced law, having also held a seat on the local consistory. He controlled that milieu with such ease that in 1848 and 1870, he held preeminent responsibilities in the government, in the ministry of justice, and in the ministry of the interior. The careers of numerous high officials assigned to those ministries depended on him. As we have already noted, he was directly responsible for the career of his cousin Gustave Bédarridès, thus making possible the birth of that long and complex judicial dynasty. He suggested to Gambetta that Eugène Lisbonne—whose actions on behalf of the Republic will be discussed later—be named to the Hérault *préfecture*, and that Charles Berr be made a *substitut* in Marseilles in 1870. As the report from the *procureur* emphasized, Berr "worked in the office of Adolphe Crémeiux, his coreligionist. *Avocat général* Bédarridès, a close friend of the family, shows a keen interest in him and is soliciting a post in the magistracy for him." Crémieux followed Berr's career closely, writing to the minister of justice again in 1879. At the time of his nomination, because of the presence of another Jewish magistrate, namely, Alphandéry, it was judged "that we mustn't have two Jewish judges. A Christian was named and Mr. Berr was completely abandoned. I beg of you, give a promotion to this magistrate worthy of advancement."[15] Originally from Moselle, Charles Berr thus moved into the other network, which ran through Provence; with this support, he rapidly attained a more important Parisian post and later found himself publicly mixed up in the scandalous lawsuit brought against his friend, the *préfet* Isaïe Levaillant. He was thus among those who moved without difficulty from one network to the other. Like all magistrates, he in turn took advantage of the recommendation system, for example, on behalf of Judge Maurice Gros, his son-in-law.[16] Others besides Berr also participated in several networks: Édouard Bloch, who was also born in Moselle, was named by Crémieux in 1870 to be a *substitut* in Bordeaux, where he was taken in hand by *député* and minister David Raynal, who considered him a "magistrate without peer," and who wrote five letters of recommendation for him. In one of them, addressed to the minister of justice, we read the following surprising statement: "I most profoundly recommend one of my friends and coreligionists."[17] Just as Bédarridès took Charles Berr in hand, David Raynal looked after Édouard Bloch, as did Senator Édouard Millaud, a member of the Provençal network. Both of these magistrates had been named by Adolphe Crémieux. As a result, there existed between the various circles of this milieu in formation personalities of national scope, ministers such as Adolphe Crémieux and David Raynal. Others besides Raynal were nonetheless capable, by means of their national scope, to structure the milieu in the Southeast: Senator Fernand Crémieux, who was related to Adolphe, intervened on several occasions through handwritten letters in support of Jules Levi, born in Nîmes. The *chef du cabinet* to the *président du Conseil* observed in October 1913 that "Mr. Levi is the nephew of Mr. Crémieux, senator of Gard, who is very close to him, it seems";[18] he also wrote the minister eight letters in support of Judge René Abram, born in Tarascon, the son-in-law of Fernand Alphandéry, *vice-président* of the *conseil général* of Bouches-du-Rhône, and related to the magistrates of the same name and to G. Bédarridès. He believed that his career had been deliberately stalled. This judge also received the support of Eugène Lisbonne, who wrote two letters to the court *procureur* on his behalf.[19] One final example: in 1927, Senator Fernand Crémieux and *député* Albert Milhaud attempted without success to give a more favorable turn to the career of *conseiller de préfecture* Édouard Aron, born in Nice and considered by the administration to be a "free-thinking Jew," a view, we recall, shared by the senator from Gard.[20]

Alfred Naquet, antiestablishment by nature, preoccupied with socialism and the revolutionary struggle, nonetheless did not hesitate to lend a hand to another Crémieux, originally from Avignon. In support of an earlier recommendation supplied by Fernand Crémieux, the senator from Gard, Naquet wrote to the minister in 1888 that "the administrative work of Joseph Crémieux and his devotion to the Republic have resulted in qualifications that you in particular will appreciate." A few months later, Crémieux was named *conseiller de préfecture* in Var.[21] In 1870, while working at the Ministry of Justice, Alfred Naquet very effectively intervened on behalf of his nephew Jules Valabrègue, born in Carpentras, who began his career as a *substitut* in Nîmes that same year, and later became part of the Conseil d'Etat.[22] Along with *préfet* turned *député* Eugène Lisbonne, Naquet also supported Isaïe Valabrègue's beginnings in a prefectoral career in numerous letters. Valabrègue, also born in Carpentras, became a *sous-préfet*.[23] Ever loyal, he tried in vain, once more in the company of Jules Valabrègue, to obtain a promotion for *conseiller de préfecture* Lucien Aaron. Aaron was born in Nancy but was related through his wife to the Valabrègues and also, less directly, to Captain Dreyfus himself.[24] But Naquet also could not neglect more intimate concerns: on several occasions, he wrote to the *garde des Sceaux* to point out with humor that "*procureur général* Eliacin Naquet," that is, his own brother, "is as anti-Boulangist as can be, and it would be unfair for him to bear the burden of the attitude taken by the senator" — that is, by himself! He tried without success to free up his brother's career in that way. In 1892, he also wrote to the minister to ask for "reparation," since his brother was "one of the most distinguished jurists, an excellent republican, who had to resign before attacks from clericals, which were absolutely unfair but relentless."[25]

For his part and in an almost circular manner, Eliacin Naquet successfully recommended Alexandre Abram in 1884, a man who had been born in Bouches-du-Rhône, as sole candidate for a job as *vice-président* in Marseilles. Abram then worked in Aix-en-Provence under his orders; in 1897, Naquet again vainly tried to obtain through several letters the removal of obstacles in the career of that magistrate, who still held the same position.[26]

Thus, men of Provence in the broad sense did not conceal the solidarity that linked them to one another: yet their actions were rarely crowned with success. Of course, as we have seen, they also acted on behalf of a state Jew from distant Alsace or Lorraine on some occasions, to help him find a post in those southern regions. Sometimes, for reasons not possible to grasp, they even came to the aid of someone who had no link to their region: Alfred Naquet and Eugène Lisbonne failed to obtain the reinstatement of *sous-préfet* Alfred Beer, born in Lunéville, despite warm letters sent to *conseiller d'Etat* Camille Lyon, who was at the time *directeur du cabinet et du personnel* of the minister of the interior and a far-reaching personality, whose strong presence in community structures we have already noted.[27] This circle of sociability that solidified professional relations within the administration was to all evidence, by its longevity and intensity, attributable to a community of soil and destiny. It was the most solid of all ties that attached state Jews to one another. It also attests to the astonishing persistence of papal Jews, many of whose heirs managed to move into careers offered by the state.

High officials from the regions in the East experienced a more tormented past, beginning with the era of the French Revolution and lasting until the disaster of 1870, which nearly always obliged their families to leave their "little fatherland" for the capital, where they themselves were often born. The leadership role in that other milieu, henceforth almost entirely transplanted to Paris, indisputably fell to the two *préfets* Hendlé, and messages were relayed less through members of their own family as in the Southeast than through a few personalities with whom at one moment or another they shared a destiny. These associates had the same geographical origin as they did, but were entirely independent from the Hendlés. Furthermore, they managed to become virtual jacks of all trades through the administrative posts they occupied: these were Isaïe Levaillant, Camille Lyon, and Abraham Schrameck. Only Léon Cohn, whose close ties to the community world we have already noted, belonged to Hendlé's immediate family, since he had married the sister of Ernest, the founder of the dynasty. His private papers are a gold mine of information on that circle of sociability proper to eastern Jews and their allies.

The correspondence of Léon Cohn, *préfet* from Toulouse, who ended his career as *trésorier-payeur général*, is unique in this respect, and allows us to trace the outer limits of that other great circle, which is distinct from the first. His brother-in-law, Ernest Hendlé, sent him thirty-one letters, and their collaboration remained very close. "Have you thought," he asked him, "of getting information on my future *chef de cabinet*? I'm especially concerned that he be a man of the world and from an excellent family." On another occasion, he wrote: "Write me about your projects and impressions so that our efforts, our actions, and our views are in absolute agreement." Very affectionate toward each other, they continually shared news of their wives and children. Beyond that, Cohn received letters from a great number of state Jews who came from the East or had families who did. Bamberger, *député* of Seine, wrote him in 1876 while he was working at the Ministry of the Interior, to recommend "his friend Eugène Sée, young, active, devoted; he shares our opinions." Born in Colmar, Sée later had a long career as a *préfet*. Similarly, Isaïe Levaillant, born in Alsace, sent him several letters and assured him of his friendship, as did *député* Ferdinand Dreyfus, who addressed him with the familiar "tu" form and frequently had lunch in his company. Cohn also maintained a long correspondence with *députés* Joseph Reinach, Camille Dreyfus, and Ernest Javal, *conseillers d'Etat* Camille Sée (born in Colmar), Camille Lyon, and E. Meyer, and magistrate Charles Berr (born in Moselle). Of course, at the periphery of the circle, farther to the south, he also received letters from Gustave Bédarridès, David Raynal, and Édouard Millaud, but he was more immersed in this milieu of state Jews from the East and was even involved with their Ashkenazic coreligionists from Eastern Europe who had immigrated to Paris.[28]

Like a formless nebula around the nucleus represented by Ernest Hendlé, Albert Hendlé, and Léon Cohn, many interactions, which often intersected, were organized in this eastern milieu and its extension in the capital. Like *député* Camille Sée, Ernest Hendlé attracted the minister's attention to the career of Judge Oscar Dalmbert, born in Alsace.[29] And in 1884 Ernest supported Judge Julien Félix's assignment to an important post. Félix was born in Metz and was the nephew of Judge Philippe Anspach, himself born in Metz and the founder of the quasi dynasty of magistrates we focused on above; this dynasty included Judges Seligmann and Worms, who wrote eighteen letters to the ministry on Félix's behalf. Hendlé maintained that "Mr. Félix can be considered sincerely behind the republican government and our institutions; I do not hesitate to support the candidacy of the honorable Mr. Félix to you, inasmuch as I am permitted to give an unofficial opinion and to contribute toward enlightening and informing the government."[30] Ernest Hendlé also recommended that Joseph Léon, born in Bordeaux, embark on a prefectoral career. Léon was the son of David Raynal, *président* of the *conseil général* and *député* of Gironde, who supported him in several letters. This recommendation came from outside the circle only in appearance, since Joseph Léon had been his *chef de cabinet* when he held a post in Macon in 1877.[31] Much later, in 1917, as if to demonstrate the permanence of the ties favoring the integration of members outside the circle, Henri Dadoun wrote to Albert Hendlé, director of the staff at the Ministry of the Interior, in a letter whose words allude to the links that were knit across time from within that circle. "Under the auspices of Mr. Schrameck, *préfet* of Bouches-du-Rhône, I have the honor of requesting an audience."[32]

In reality, to follow the topography of that circle, we would have to be attentive to all the collateral relations that were extended by other friendships. Without undertaking such an inquiry, we prefer, to conclude the examination of this second network, to return to the nucleus. Ernest Hendlé and Léon Cohn collaborated on a work on civic education, and Léon Cohn published a book on election polls with *député* Ferdinand Dreyfus, also from Alsace, whom we shall later meet on several occasions. Dreyfus's personal papers and those of Léon Cohn allow us to uncover the scope of his social contacts. While he received letters from Albert Hendlé, his work relations with the *préfet* of Toulouse proved to be just as close as those that Cohn maintained with his brother-in-law Ernest. But it was Joseph Reinach who was his closest friend. A central character in national politics, owing to his essential role among the Opportunists, Reinach wrote on numerous occasions to "his old friend" Ferdinand Dreyfus. After his electoral defeat, the circumstances of which we shall later have the occasion to examine, he protested against "the abjection of the antisemitic conduct, the insults and lies, the only weapons" of his opponent.[33] Furthermore, Joseph

Reinach and Ferdinand Dreyfus figured among the closest friends and collaborators of Gambetta, a former collaborator in Adolphe Crémieux's law office, his friend and, for a brief time in 1870, his colleague in the government. Eugène Lisbonne and Alfred Naquet from the first circle—like Ernest Hendlé and Camille Sée from the second—became part of the Gambettist coterie, like many state Jews.

As a result, we realize that at the top of each of these two circles, at least in the beginning, eyes and expectations were turned toward Gambetta as founder of the Third Republic, but also, as so many letters of recommendation contained in their administrative dossiers show, toward Jules Ferry, Jules Simon, Buisson, Arago, Méline, Rouvier, Loubet, Freycinet, Casimir-Perier, Clemenceau, Poincaré, Gaston Doumergue, and so on. Of course, the state Jews in each of the two networks often maintained both social and professional relations among themselves, but it would be greatly distorting reality not to see that the Jewish administrative milieu in formation was also blending into the larger field of the republican political class, the "new talent" destined to lead French society from then on. And this was all the more true since, as we have often emphasized, the recommendation of a state Jew on behalf of another very often failed and was far from facilitating the course of a career.

Such recommendations failed even more surely when they claimed to invoke properly religious ties. Before such manifestations of a religious particularism stemming solely from the private sphere, state Jews lent a deaf ear, draped themselves in their dignity as agents of the state, and barely deigned to respond to letters stripped of all legitimacy (in fact, in certain dossiers of Catholic high officials, we also note, just as surprisingly, the occasional presence of a letter written to the minister by a bishop or archbishop, a real attack, here again, on the secularization of the state). Of the 171 cases analyzed, we were able to document five intercessions of this type. There were first of all the altogether exceptional letters from three chief rabbis: one from Bordeaux who, we recall, closely followed the career of his magistrate son and sometimes wrote to the *député* of Gironde, David Raynal, even as late as 1897, addressing him "Dear Coreligionist" and even once, "Dear Compatriot."[34] Then there was the case of the chief rabbi of Paris, Zadoc-Kahn, who, even more astonishingly, wrote to Camille Lyon, *conseiller d'Etat* and *directeur du cabinet* to the minister of the interior, who would later hold a seat on the central consistory. In 1884, Zadoc-Kahn asked him, "at the risk of appearing inopportune," whether he could look kindly on the career of *conseiller de préfecture* Jules Kahn. Camille Lyon's negative response could not have been more reserved: "Mr. Kahn is not in a position to obtain a promotion. I could therefore not propose to the minister that he be raised to the *2ᵉ classe*." But the affair was not over: the next year, the new chief rabbi of Paris, Isidore, also took up his pen to address the same matter: Invoking his "affectionate relations with his family," he expressed the hope that Camille Lyon would pardon "the liberty taken in this act" destined to right the wrongs that, according to him, had been done to *conseiller de préfecture* Jules Kahn, who believed he had been "forgotten." Once more, nothing was done, no one wanted to hear about it, and Kahn's career ended.[35] Let us quickly touch on three other intercessions on the same note. First, there was that of David Raynal, already mentioned, who confided to the minister his interest in magistrate Édouard Bloch, "his coreligionist."[36] Second, there was the case, which was truly unique for its kind, of *sous-préfet* Édouard Cahen, who in 1883 wrote Camille Lyon at the Ministry of the Interior in the following terms: "I realize it is not really hierarchical, but, I am convinced that the coreligionist will excuse, if necessary, this action taken before the *directeur du cabinet.* . . . I long to leave a region like Saint-Jean-de-Maurienne, and it would be painful for us, my mother and myself, to spend a fifth winter here." Apparently, this *sous-préfet* did not obtain satisfaction since he remained not one but two more winters at his post![37] A final example of an intervention considered inopportune: in May 1883, Alfred Naquet and Édouard Lisbonne wrote to Camille Lyon to urge him to reinstate *sous-préfet* Alfred Berr to the prefectoral corps, from which he had been removed in 1881. They did not succeed either.[38] As an official holding a role of authority in the name of the state, Camille Lyon, who was nonetheless an influential member of Jewish circles, was inflexible in every instance; uncompromising, he turned a deaf ear to any demand formulated in the name of a particularist sociability. In that, he mirrored state Jews who had become ministers, who "seek to bury their Jewish origins in oblivion," as the *Archives Israélites* bitterly noted.

They are only Jews by birth and in no other way. Not only do they show no favor toward their coreligionists, but the advancement of Jewish officials in their departments is slowed, with the Jewish minister showing a displaced coquetry in not seeming to acknowledge the services of said officials. There has been much talk in the press of the Republic of "comrades" where someone was given a leg up. We could never reproach our Jewish ministers for practicing the policy of "Jewish camaraderie." Needless to say, they are only the representatives, in the executive branch as in Parliament, of France above all. . . . But is that a reason for Jews who are part of a public administration to find themselves deprived of their right to regular advancement, because one of their coreligionists has become a minister? . . . For the most part, these are ashamed Jews.[39]

Such judgments were common in the *Archives Israélites*: accentuating the "pusillanimity" of Jewish *députés*, "little disposed to publicly support the most just demands of their coreligionists,"[40] they maintained that "Jewish representation" did not "care in the slightest about the interests of Jewry"[41] and sometimes even openly wished for its disappearance.[42] Such an evaluation was obviously excessive and inexact, for a number of Jewish *députés*, as we have just seen, hardly hesitated to concern themselves with the careers of certain state Jews who were part of their circle of sociability, or to protest against antisemitic schemes. But, in addition, even though state Jews with a real power of decision, such as Albert Hendlé, Camille Lyon, and Isaïe Levaillant, most often opposed any letter of recommendation that referred to a dimension stemming solely from private life, it was not out of self-loathing. Far from denying their origin, they were often very active within community structures. Their attitude is better explained by the administrative posts they occupied, which were oriented as much as possible toward uniquely universalist and meritocratic values.

The solidarities internal to this milieu, organized into vast subsets, are certainly undeniable, but they are not for all that decisive. To reach the top of the state, one had to be helped by the great orchestrators of national politics and by their local allies. To understand this, we need only note the presence in every state Jew's administrative dossier of numerous letters of recommendation not only from the great republican leaders but also from an infinite number of non-Jewish *députés* and senators who told the forces in power the esteem in which they were held. It reached such a point that certain administrative dossiers—such as those of *préfet* Isaïe Levaillant himself, or *préfet* Eugène Weill, whose son became part of the Conseil d'Etat, or *conseiller* Oscar Kinsbourg, supported by, among others, the Protestant Jules Steeg, Judge Julien Sée, and *préfet* Abraham Pinède—contained only such letters. Their careers were thus initiated entirely outside the Jewish milieu, supported solely by non-Jewish and republican *députés*, senators, or high officials.[43]

The more time passed the more the new regime took root. Letters of recommendation from state Jews among themselves were proportionally less frequent; those coming from the non-Jewish politicians and administrators came to greatly outnumber them. Let us consider the single example of Eugène Dreyfus, whom we shall have the opportunity to consider later on: born in Mulhouse, he began his judicial career in 1893 and became *premier président* of the Paris court in 1936. In his very thick administrative dossier, there appears only a single letter from a state Jew, from the modest *député* of Vosges Camille Picard. In contrast, we find recommendations from Gaston Doumergue, F. Buisson, Waldeck-Rousseau, Jules Siegfried, the director of *Le Temps*, and from several *députés* and senators.[44] The Jewish milieu thus seems to have been dislocated, to have lost its uniqueness in diversity. In time, dispersion within French society increased, breaking the old structures of sociability. Like Provence, Alsace and Lorraine receded further and further and, as we move into the twentieth century, while state Jews preserved their endogamic practices and often still participated in the diverse activities linked to their particularism, they constituted a shared administrative milieu less and less. At present, we need to describe in detail the political values and practices of these fools for the Republic, from the time of Gambetta to about the middle of the twentieth century.

PART III

Love for the Republic

CHAPTER EIGHT

The Republic's Ideologues: The Secularization of Society

The time had come to celebrate with dignity the moment of emancipation. At the Rue de la Victoire synagogue on 11 May 1889, a considerable crowd assembled to praise the benefits of the Revolution. The honorable chief rabbi of Paris rose to the podium, comparing the events of 1789 to "a new social Passover," then underscoring how "the Jews, through their devotion to the French nation and their eagerness to take on all careers, have justified the enlightened generosity of the men of 1789."[1] In reality, during the revolutionary period, even the most resolute advocates of the emancipation of the Jews, such as Abbé Grégoire, were not at all in favor of opening the most prestigious state careers to them, careers through which the state exercised the force of its public power. But these reservations and delays were now forgotten; in 1889, the Third Republic was assured in its foundations and values, and state Jews, who sometimes constituted true administrative families, constructing their own destiny within the state and at its exclusive service, and respecting the legitimate gulf between the public and the private spheres, were also making an effort to reconcile their love for 1789 with continued religious fidelity. At the forefront of this exceptional ceremony marking the first centenary of the events of 1789, thronged several of the most representative state Jews: G. Bédarridès, *président de chambre* of the Cour de Cassation, also active in the consistory at the time, and General

Sée, the first Jew to have attained that rank in the French army, who also played an important role in the central consistory.

That same day in Bordeaux, Chief Rabbi Isaac Levy recalled how the French Revolution had made the Jews citizens, adding: "It is not only as Jews but also as Frenchmen that we should bless the Revolution." After paying homage to Gambetta, he recited traditional prayers for the Republic and for France.[2] At the same moment in the Marseilles synagogue, the chief rabbi there was beginning a patriotic speech in which he paid homage "to our illustrious dead, two children of the Midi, Mirabeau and Crémieux."[3] In Saint-Étienne, Isaïe Levaillant was playing his part in a "patriotic ceremony," where the happy events of 1789 were also celebrated.[4] Among the men close to Gambetta whom we have already encountered, E. Lisbonne, the *préfet* turned *président* of the Hérault *conseil général*, was at that very moment opening the session of that assembly with a speech in which he emphasized how 1789 symbolized the birth of a "new era." He then appealed to the union of republicans and recommended "an absolute devotion to the interests of the country as the best means to make the Republic last."[5] Not to be left out, Théodore Reinach, also close to the Gambettists, *député* and member of the Institut, remitted a sum of five thousand francs to the office of public assistance on the occasion of the centenary, to go to the poor.

Later and more lyrically, on the occasion of the centennial of the meeting of the États-Généraux in Versailles, Camille Dreyfus wrote in *La Nation*, a newspaper he published:

The men of the États-Généraux annihilated the ancient law and founded the new. They reestablished the consonance between the conscience of citizens and the written law. It seems that on the anniversary of that day, all those who lay claim to the French Revolution, all those who are its heirs, all those who would have remained artisans in corporations, Jews in the ghetto, or soldiers in the ranks, all those who lowered the barriers of social inequality should take a new vow of loyalty to the spirit of that Revolution. May the memory of you, our ancestors who, a hundred years ago, struggled for us, be forever respected! As long as the French name shall live, may the memory of your struggles, your suffering, and your conquests remain engraved in the spirit of our children. You were the Christs [*sic*] of that new Passion and the authors of a new humanity.[6]

For *député* Camille Dreyfus, everything was combined in that messianic movement that embraced both the Jewish hope and the Passion of Christ, embraced even the emancipatory morality instituting equality among men before the law and in the professions. Republican France was continuing the new redemption begun in 1789, liberating men from all forms of slavery. Jews and Catholics were uniting to share the hopes of the revolutionary Christ in a single, reconciled humanity. A few months later, when

Hoche and Carnot's ashes were transferred to the Pantheon, Camille Dreyfus asked: "Is not the Arch of Triumph, where the names of our victories and the names of the generals who led them are inscribed, the natural catafalque for the soldiers of the first Republic?"[7] As the champion of revolutionary military glory, Camille Dreyfus returned to the question and sounded one last note: on 10 March 1892, he defended a bill before the Chamber of Deputies, taking shelter behind the indisputable intellectual authority of Aulard, historian of the Revolution. That bill fixed 22 September as the celebration of the centennial of the proclamation of the Republic. For him, it was not a question of

using this centennial that we are asking from you to celebrate something like a victory of certain citizens over other citizens. . . . Rather, we are asking you to unite in a shared and exclusive feeling of patriotism, to remember that on 20 September 1793, in Valmy, the French army held off the invader that had come over the eastern border. . . . It is these memories that we ask you to celebrate in common, by linking them to the Republic that is today the constitutional and undisputed form of the French nation.[8]

Camille Dreyfus justified the presentation of this legislation in the name "of a country that wants to remain free and master of its destiny, which has placed national defense above all other concerns." Valmy symbolized in striking miniature the will to reconquer the provinces lost in 1870. Among those who voted in favor of the motion, made in the name of one hundred and fifty *députés*, we find Maurice Barrès and Paul Deroulède as well as Georges Clemenceau, Léon Bourgeois, Casimir-Perier, Joseph Reinach, and Alfred Naquet, all brought together for a single instant to sing the praises of the military deeds of revolutionary France. Across from them, all the counts, barons, marquis, and princes, still very present in the Chamber, did not conceal their hostility.

It was from within this same conciliatory perspective that Joseph Reinach intervened in January 1891 regarding the banning of *Thermidor*, the play in which Victorien Sardou had criticized Robespierre. Let us return briefly to that affair, which was particularly revealing of the importance of the Revolution in the political imaginary of state Jews: "If there is anyone," noted Reinach, "who worships the French Revolution deep in his heart, it is the man who stands before you." The orator then rose up against "the men who made the most appalling and odious of tyrannies weigh down upon this country for many long months" and saluted the friends of Danton who "erected at their own peril the great road of sympathy against the hideous law of 22 Prairial, against the Reign of Terror."[9] We know that, when *député* Moreau observed that without Robespierre and his friends "you would not be a Frenchman," Reinach did not respond to the direct address and engaged in a general defense of the Revolution, to the great displeasure of *Archives Israélites*. They reproached him for not having picked up on that "historical blunder"; since the Jews were emancipated on 27 September 1791 by the men of the Constituante, they owed nothing to the "sinister characters who two years later made the guillotine a permanent fixture."[10]

Against Clemenceau, who retorted with the infamous "the French Revolution is all of a piece," Joseph Reinach, the Gambettist par excellence, praised the unity of the nation and its universalist foundation, challenging all that divided it, then as now. The point of view held by state Jews who honored the French Revolution just when France was moving into a period of violent strikes, harsh social conflicts, and contradictory extremist movements was thus clearly explained: for Joseph Reinach, "the link between modern collectivism and the Middle Ages is Marat; reread Marat's articles of the period, and you will think you are reading the Workers Party or the *Revue libertaire* of today."[11] Against Robespierre and Marat, most state Jews wanted to retain from 1789 only the announcement of restored national unity. Coming to the defense of Danton in the middle of the Dreyfus affair, Reinach denounced the use of secret documents by the Reign of Terror, which had unjustly accused the revolutionary chief, drawing highly suggestive parallels between the manipulatory practices of the two eras, and calling Robespierrists "madmen"[12] whose direct heirs were overjoyed at the new Franco-French war that was threatening and devastating the republican order.

At the end of that same year, a violent incident that is rarely remembered exploded in the Chamber of Deputies. On 29 October 1891, before an assembly overheated by the last repercussions of Boulangism, already almost numbed by the anathema, the sarcasm, and the insults flying every time advocates and opponents of the Republic confronted one another, a brief but violent squabble took place. Occurring five years after the publication of *La France juive*, it allows us to measure the importance that inflammatory book still had, weakening the project of the Republic's founders, who found themselves suspected of wanting quite simply to de-Christianize France. In the view of Drumont, who was the true founder of modern French nationalism, the desire for secularization displayed by Gambetta and Jules Ferry was part of a covert plot set in place by the obscure forces whose schemes he relentlessly denounced. There were Protestants and above all Jews, hiding behind the Opportunist leaders. In the name of Reason and beyond the noisy celebrations of 1789, state Jews close to Gambetta wished to deal a fatal blow to the Catholic identity of France. Such was the accusation made day after day by the entire counterrevolutionary tradition beginning with Abbé Barruel.

On that day, catching everyone unaware, just as the meeting was about to end because of the late hour, Camille Dreyfus, *député* of Seine, proposed a bill whose aim was nothing less than the separation of Church and state. The idea had been in the air for several years; legislation had already been proposed, but real discussion of it had always been avoided. This time, in the name of several dozen *députés* — among them, Pelletan and Millerand — Dreyfus stunned the Chamber, which could no longer retreat: with his colleagues, he even called for a state of emergency so that the *députés* would have to grapple with the question without waiting any longer. He thereby avoided the possibility that the bill would be rejected again and handily sent back to a parliamentary committee. Paul Déroulède, who was perhaps not to be expected in this role, instantly reacted and, along with Camille Dreyfus, opened a debate that we need to reproduce here. Through him, in a symbolic and almost caricatured manner, before the representatives of the nation, a redoubtable thesis was expressed for perhaps the first time: state Jews were threatening to de-Christianize France by intervening every time one of the "thresholds of secularization" was crossed. From then on, their actions as ideologues of the Republic marked them with suspicion and stripped them of any legitimacy.

Eagerly, Déroulède mounted the assault and took the floor:

That's it! You are declaring war! Well, then, so be it. Let's have war! as you said to M. de Mun the other day. All those of us who are believers, Christian republicans as well as Christians on the right, we are all ready to accept combat. Yes! If you want to de-Christianize France, we shall struggle against you to prevent this abasement of our country (*Very good, very good, from the right*).

Yes, even if I have to part ways with many of my friends on this point, I will energetically reject your proposal, which attempts nothing less than to close the Church to the nation.

And I add, gentlemen, that I am surprised that such a debate has been opened not by one of the 36 million Catholics in question but rather by one of the 500,000 or 600,000 Jews (*Lively interruptions from the left*).

I am a Christian republican, and I protest whenever I see that someone wants to de-Christianize France, perhaps in order to Judaize it. . . . That is why my vote as a Christian republican is about to fall into the ballot box with those on the right, for the defense of the Christian faith. For, in pursuing the disappearance of any spiritualist idea, in working to weed out any faith, we are disparaging beliefs, dividing minds, and dispersing the treasure of moral forces that, sooner or later, we will need to raise up the nation once again!

This long interruption deserved to be cited almost in full: it is as if, through it, Drumont were expressing himself before the Chamber. Next to Alfred Naquet, Déroulède led the battle for Boulanger in one of the Franco-French wars we shall discuss later on: and beginning in 1889, hatred for Jews had become more patent every day in the general's entourage.

Barely a year earlier, the campaign for the reelection of Francis Laur in Neuilly marked the advent of extreme antisemitism, with which Déroulède and the Boulangist leaders had been personally associated. They had not hesitated to draw attention to themselves in the company of Drumont. Against Camille Dreyfus and through Déroulède, it was thus Drumont who was holding forth; Déroulède used the same clichés and fell into the same errors, publicly denouncing the harmful role of 600,000 French Jews (who in reality numbered barely 80,000 at the time!). This time, the words were uttered: a war without mercy would be unleashed against them. In the name of the Catholic faith, political barriers had to give way: Republicans and monarchists were all united against the Judaization of France! The almost socialist populism of the Boulangists was forgotten. Confronted with the demonic plans of the Jews, they immediately threw themselves into the arms of the most reactionary right, led by Count de Mun. It was now out of the question to "separate the Church from the nation," which was in fact the project imagined for a long time not by the Jews but rather by the founders of the Republic, who had every intention of pursuing their systematic undertaking and secularizing the state in the name of Reason. Hence, separation figured at the head of the Programme de Belleville formulated in 1869 by Gambetta. For the creators of the Republic, the new citizen had to give up, at the very least in the public space, religious values that turned him away from progress. He had to escape the authority of the Church so as to adhere fully to the universalist values of the Republic. At that time, however, the project of separation had not come about because of reservations and prudence among the different groups. Camille Dreyfus and the *députés* who supported him had surprised their own people and caused quite the scandal; hence the outbursts.

Publicly assaulted within this solemn enclosure, Camille Dreyfus, radical *député*, who was even close for a certain time to the Boulangist movement, protested in terms that also deserve to be quoted:

I am not a Jew. . . . I am neither Jew nor Catholic: I am a freethinker and I have proved it my whole life. . . . I am a freethinker of the English school and of the eighteenth-century French school and I do not allow anyone to apply any other term to me. I might add that, as such, and as a politician having to concern myself with the ties that exist between the state and a certain number of special organizations that hold to a certain conception of the world, I have the right to concern myself with them, whatever my origin and whatever your origin might be. It is the right of freethinking that I am defending, and I defend it energetically (*Very good, very good, on the left*).[13]

As a republican celebrating with pomp the glory of 1789, a law-and-order man not hesitating to launch into quasi-nationalist speeches praising the profound Frenchness of a Republic supposedly with Latin origins, Camille Dreyfus proclaimed himself the spokesperson for all those for whom, in the famous expression of Gambetta, "clericalism is the enemy." To make his cause more viable, he laid claim to freethinking, refusing to consider himself a Jew. This public confession, this denial almost unique in the annals of Parliament, went largely against the grain of the Franco-Judaic pact. In response to the accusation made by Déroulède insinuating that Dreyfus was undertaking to Judaize France, Dreyfus was constrained to deny his own origins. Here we are touching on the final consequence of the enterprise led systematically by Drumont and his stooges to delegitimate a Republic they called Jewish, simply because a few Jewish *députés* close to Gambetta and Jules Ferry contributed to making it work by entering the administration or by acting as its ideologues.

In thus surrendering his arms, Camille Dreyfus did not succeed in guarding against a new antisemitic attack. The press let loose, for the incident was rife with symbols: for *Le Soleil du Midi*, "a Jew asking for the separation of Church and state is certainly not lacking in interest! It was M. Déroulède, thought to be fairly indifferent, who took the floor to defend the Church. He affirmed he was a Christian as well as a republican; he put poor Dreyfus in his place and set him packing back to the synagogue." Another newspaper made fun of the "Freemason Jew" guilty of such a sacrilegious proposal, crying out: "Catholic sheep, get a little enraged, won't you?"[14] The Jewish *députés* reacted in a disorganized manner, as if to avoid any equivocal interpretation of their vote: whereas Alfred Naquet supported the Dreyfus proposal beside Clemenceau and Millerand, friends of Gambetta such as Joseph Reinach and David Raynal—more favorable to a gradual and prudent approach—as well as all the marquis and barons in the Chamber opposed it. The *Archives Israélites* also protested against the initiative taken by Camille Dreyfus: for them,

reasons of propriety go against the idea that such questions be raised by Jews, however slight their identification, and even if they work like the devil not to be Jews or are only so by chance of birth. . . . The proof of such a gaffe, the danger of the intervention, was immediately provided, and yet, if there is one Jew whom Judaism would be unable to acknowledge as its own, it is the *député* of Seine, who has always represented himself as an atheist. . . . Whatever M. Dreyfus may do, they will always persist in seeing the Jew in him, and his opponents will shut their eyes to his split personality. . . . Our enemies, in the interest of their cause, have created a Jewish solidarity. Those who try to except themselves from it do so in vain.[15]

In fact, a profound break between the Jewish *députés* and the more traditionalist *Archives Israélites* followed, for the newspaper was not in the least enthusiastic about the proposal for secularizing religion. For example, it sought out a quarrel with Joseph Reinach, guilty of voting in favor of secularizing cemeteries: "Jews and Christians live on earth in absolute dissidence, clearly divided in the field of religion. They have neither the same dogmas nor the same worship. . . . You must respect the wishes of Christians and Jews who want to have their final rest beside their coreligionists and who find repugnant a promiscuity that the dogmas of religion disapprove."[16] In the same way, the Jewish press protested against the votes of the four elected Jews who spoke against the reestablishment of tax credits favoring the Jewish seminary, even though some of them had accepted the proposal of bestowing new tax credits on Protestant seminaries: "That is an incredible iniquity on the part of the French Chamber with which Jews should never have been associated."[17] The attitude of state Jews toward secularism, which may have been more ambiguous than it often appeared, was also revealed among the Protestants, who, as we know, were very active in that enterprise. In that sense, the long letter sent in December 1880 to Jules Ferry by "a state Protestant," A. Monod, *conseiller* to the Cour de Cassation, takes on even more interest. He began: "As a Protestant, I accept with gratitude the principle of secularizing the primary schools, precisely because I find in it a precious guarantee for my coreligionists." He added, however, that he hoped it would be permitted, "where there are no temples, for religious instruction to be given to the children of Protestants by their pastors, outside of classroom hours, outside the teaching of the school, which must remain absolutely secular."[18] Certain Jews and Protestants thus came out in favor of secularism, even while wishing to maintain religious education one way or another—within a private religious structure or, lacking that, at school.

In accordance with a desire expressed by Gambetta, the republicans of the period began by "undoing or breaking one after the other all the ties that unite the two powers," the state and the Church. From the beginning of the 1880s, obligatory Sunday rest was eliminated, the dissolution and expulsion of the Jesuits was declared, monasteries were harassed, cemeteries and then hospitals were secularized, religious emblems removed, and so on.[19] With reluctance and willingness varying from group to another—notable differences became visible on this point among the founders of the Republic—the secularization of the state was relentlessly pursued. Its most extreme version was presented by Ferdinand Buisson, with secularism becoming itself a true religion. "We are the country," he maintained,

that has resolutely undertaken the secularization of all public services. Our forefathers of '89, who began it, could not accomplish it with all desired purity. Today, we have become familiar with the idea that a people can live without religion. . . . The nation wished all its establishments to be exclusively secular because it is itself secular. Legally and officially, the country has no god and no master.[20]

This maximalist perspective implied a homogenization of society, a disappearance of all religions, complete victory of militant atheism, a view that even Jules Ferry did not share, since he took such care to distinguish between religious beliefs, which were to dwell in the soul, and churches, which he wished to see disappear from the public space.

In banning churches from the public sphere, secularization affected education first. The founders of the Republic were immediately aware of what was at stake and applied themselves to bringing the schools into the bosom of the republican state. In their view, the secularization of the world, which bore with it progress, implied the birth of a new citizen oriented toward Reason and no longer held captive to ancient beliefs and prejudices. For the citizen to become free, a school system had to be set in place where he could acquire such emancipatory norms. For Jules Ferry, "It behooves the Republic and civil society, it behooves all those who have taken to heart the tradition of 1789, that those who direct and oversee the schools not be ministers of religion who, concerning these things that are dear to us and upon which society rests, have opinions that are separated from our own by such a wide abyss."[21] Anticlericalism thus required changing the status of schools, making them the place of political socialization for new citizens. Most often, it was not so much a question of battling religion as such but rather of separating it from the public space by imposing religious neutrality on the schools of the Republic.[22] In that sense, secularism was presented as a truly political ideology legitimating the Republic. It stemmed from the tradition of '89 and, before that, of the Enlightenment itself: it was the equivalent of a moral system encompassing the state and its citizens.

As one of the new manuals destined for the public schools proclaimed, "Catholics, Protestants, Jews, and freethinkers all have the same rights; all can enter government schools, provided they pass the exams; all have access to all jobs, can become *préfets*, generals, *députés*, senators. Their opinions are their own business only, and no one is allowed to harass them for these opinions."[23] This meritocracy laid the foundations for equality among all citizens and also favored the arrival to power of the famous "new strata" that Gambetta had called for: the meritocracy gave birth to elites by competition rather than by birth, dismantling the ancient categories of leadership that resulted from inheritance and not knowledge. It was nevertheless true that with such reforms in the school system the former Catholic elites lost their near monopoly of public life, since they too were required to submit to the examinations. In contrast, those who had been more or less excluded in the past celebrated the triumph of the republican school set in place by the founders of the Republic, men of Catholic origin who had become the proponents of Reason, and often even of freethinking.

Protestants participated actively in setting up the new system, drafting regulations and holding crucial posts at the heads of ministries: around Ferry, men such as J. Steeg, Ferdinand Buisson, and Félix Pécaux, all three former pastors, spent a great deal of energy establishing a secular school policy.[24] In contrast, the many state Jews who were Gambettists remained in the background in this particular context and did not become at all active. Needless to say, in their platform statements, they expressed unqualified support for this policy of secularization: in 1881, David Raynal explicitly linked "the struggle against clericalism" to "the energetic defense of the principles of '89," and Ferdinand Dreyfus expressed his desire "to establish in a definitive way the free, compulsory, and secular school." In the 1885 elections, Raynal declared himself in favor of "a policy of secularization tending to resist energetically the designs of clericalism and to prepare for the separation of Church and state." And during each of the elections, Camille Dreyfus defended his aborted project for separation.[25]

Nevertheless, only Camille Sée participated in a visible way in the secularization of the school system, taking the initiative to extend it to girls, a highly symbolic decision inasmuch as it ran the risk of shaking up the status of women in modern France in the short run; as a consequence, it also risked transforming the family order, to which a conservative France, often obedient to Catholicism, was so attached. This was an altogether vital measure, for it struck full force at the strong influence the Church exercised over women. Although it is true that Ferry "warmly" supported it, the introduction of the bill resulted from the personal initiative of Camille Sée. The matter was habitually called "delicate," and therefore prudence was the rule in the Chamber as in the government and the administration of public education itself.[26] In an 1870 speech, Jules Ferry naturally pointed the way: "Bishops know very well that whoever holds woman holds everything, first because he holds the child, second because he holds the husband. . . . That is why the Church wants to hold on to woman, and that is also why democracy takes her away from the Church. We must choose, citizens: either woman belongs to science or she belongs to the Church." Camille Sée claimed that a girl left the convent "with an almost nonexistent education, and an upbringing that has placed in her heart hatred for all the principles, all the ideas, that govern the France of 1789 and our institutions." From the outset, he was touching on the most sensitive point: the principles of 1789 were at stake. It was a matter of applying them in their essence, at the risk of going head to head with those who rejected them, in particular the Catholic world that demanded continued control over woman's soul, the guarantee of the Christian identity of French society.

In thus abruptly posing the question of secularization of the girls' school system, Sée set off a storm that was long in passing over: his initiative was interpreted as the final proof of the reality of a Judeo-Masonic plot that since 1789, had supposedly aimed at the systematic destruction of the Catholic identity of French society. For Fénélon Gibon, "the genealogy of the law can be summed up in one line — Jewry has imposed this reform on the lodges, the lodges on the Chamber, and the Chamber on the country." Many attacked Camille Sée, "Jew and Freemason." Father Lescoeur declared to the Catholic Congress of 1883: "In adding the name of F. Gréard to those of J. Ferry and Camille Sée, we realize that the three men who have exerted a considerable practical influence on public teaching during these last years are the right-hand men of Freemasonry."[27]

Camille Salomon Sée was a Gambettist: born in Colmar in 1847, he became secretary general at the Ministry of the Interior on 10 September 1870, became a *sous-préfet* in 1876,[28] and reached the Conseil d'Etat in 1881.[29] After his law was voted in, he sat on the administrative commissions of the École Normale Supérieure of Sèvres and of girls' high schools, devoting his energy to the application of the law. He thereby ran the risk of disturbing social relations. This role earned him a place of choice in antisemitic literature; Drumont (again!) devoted many fine pages to him in *La France juive*: "Camille Sée is a Jew who is organizing high schools for girls, in such a way as to exclude all religious education." In his view, Sée and his *conseillers d'Etat* were persecuting the mother superior of the Sisters of Saint-Vincent-de-Paul: "In their hatred for these holy daughters of charity whom the savages themselves venerate, these wretched men have not stopped at the idea of robbing the poor."[30] Note that *L'Univers Israélite* also seems not to have appreciated his policy, but for opposite reasons: "Adolphe Crémieux should not have committed the blunder of taking the floor on questions that concern only the Catholic religion. . . . His friends looked on with pain as he, a Jew, attacked what only a Christian has the right to attack."[31] In general, we note certain reservations with regard to the project of secularizing the school, which in fact also concerned Jewish children: whereas the *Archives Israélites* came out in favor of the idea of free and compulsory education, they nevertheless felt that "morality needs to be sanctioned: we would be very distressed if, under the pretext of secularism, the idea of God were banished from the schools."[32]

Faithful to the Republic's values, the few state Jews in office at the time applied the laws secularizing the schools in all their rigor. They especially found themselves confronted with the delicate problem of religious symbols; like their colleagues, they were obliged to remove such symbols from the schools. Let us mention a few of the crises that resulted in the various departments. In 1881 in Nièvre, *préfet* Isaïe Levaillant declared with a touch of malice:

I know that the bishop does not complain very much about my procedures in his regard, and when he has the occasion to speak of my person, he is far from using the disobliging terms that he used in regard to my two predecessors. That stems no doubt from a fairly frequent oddity, the fact that I was born into the Jewish religion and that expecting less from me, he does not believe he has the right to be demanding.[33]

It seems, in fact, that most Jewish *préfets* and *sous-préfets* managed to maintain cordial relations with the bishops during this period of confrontation. That was the case for Abraham Schrameck in Montauban, Abraham Pinède in Saint-Claude,[34] and Léon Cohn in Toulouse.[35] Nevertheless, in many cases, when the question of the schools provoked too much tension, the relations of conviviality rapidly degenerated into serious confrontations. Hence, in Montpellier, even though Eugène Lisbonne was linked amicably to Monsignor François, who supported his firm republican policy, when the problem of secularizing the schools was raised, it was too much: the bishop rose up against "the obligation forced on the family patriarch to give up his children to such schools exclusively—this is communism violating the sanctuary of the home," and abruptly broke off with Lisbonne. A. Schrameck, though the friend of the bishop of Montauban, remained very firm concerning the removal of symbols, eliciting the opposition of the *conseil général* of Tarn-et-Garonne, which "disapproved highly of the removal of crucifixes from auditoriums. It claimed that nothing obligated the government to take the odious measure that reverberated so painfully in Christian hearts, weakening the value of the judicial oath."[36] Schrameck was just as inflexible toward monastery schools: "The *préfet* from Tarn-et-Garonne, both very firm and very prudent, thwarted the clerical maneuvering and assured the inventory of all churches within a few days."

The *préfets* Hendlé were also in office during that period of secularizing the schools, and *La Libre Parole* angrily noted that Ernest Hendlé "frequents only archbishops,"[37] a fact that also provoked the amusement and irony of Anatole France, as we recall. It fell to the Hendlés to oversee the removal of religious symbols: relations with the cardinal-archbishop of Rouen immediately turned venomous, with the cardinal writing an indignant letter to Ernest Hendlé. It seemed unacceptable to him that "crucifixes, the sacred signs of our religion," should be removed from the schools, since "Christian families are deeply saddened out of concern for the piety of their children."[38] Ernest's son Albert, *préfet* of Calvados, in a letter to the minister, wrote that he felt that

we should take advantage of the coming Easter vacation to ensure that the law and principle of the school's neutrality be applied in all schools whose religious symbols are only mobile objects placed on pedestals or simply fastened to classroom walls. In the rare schools where religious symbols are carved into the stone of the walls themselves and upon which neither public attention nor that of the academic authority has as yet been drawn, perhaps it would be better not to introduce any modification, awaiting new orders, and to take advantage of the appropriate circumstances to make them disappear, for example, repairs to be made on the buildings concerned.[39]

The Hendlés were particularly vigilant in everything concerning the diffusion of new civic teaching manuals: Albert Hendlé very carefully oversaw the reception of these books and met any refusal with vigorous sanctions.[40] Ernest Hendlé and his brother-in-law Léon Cohn were also vigilant as part of the commission organized by the Société pour l'Instruction Élémentaire (society for elementary education). In 1876, the commission proposed a bill whose first article stipulated that "religious education is not given in public schools."[41] In a speech at the awards ceremony for the Lycée Corneille, he maintained that "we can inscribe on the frontispiece of each of our high schools: here is a sacred sanctuary for every conscience, a school of patriotism, a home of light and liberty."[42] This militant *préfet* remained faithful to the choices he had made: in 1869, he wrote a book titled *La séparation de l'église et de l'état* (The separation of Church and state) and called for the exclusion of the Church from educational institutions in the name of freethinking and the French Revolution. In his view, "it [the Church] abuses the passions and weaknesses of minors to bring about their religious conversion with or without their consent."[43]

This deliberate action inevitably provoked a violent antisemitic reaction against "the Hendlé yids," who became one of the favorite targets of *La Libre Parole* and of the many admirers of Drumont. Drumont himself recounted the actions of *préfet* Hendlé in his own way: "In Dieppe, he was distressed for a moment. There existed a school there maintained by nuns who enjoyed the esteem and affection of the entire population. The municipality was resolutely opposed to sending the sisters away. . . . Hendlé picked the lock of the school doors and threw the nuns out into the street." Elsewhere, in the face of the resistance of a mayor who "replaced the crucifix that had been removed,"

Hendlé and his agents fumed, threatened to close the school; the mayor looked at them and said calmly:

"This Christ is in our school and will remain there. If you touch it, I'll sound the alarm, and then watch out." As you might guess, nothing more was needed to give Jews a dreadful panic, and *préfet* Hendlé went away venting his spleen, blaspheming his rage in the cafés of the city, at not having been able to get his hands on Christ.[44]

The Hendlés were not the only ones to elicit the anger of antisemites through their policy of secularization. *Le Réveil du Loir-et-Cher* wrote, for example:

As for M. Brisac, *préfet* of Loir-et-Cher, not satisfied to preside over this Masonic celebration against freedom of education, he felt he ought to make his position public by taking the floor at the banquet. Perhaps, in the interest of his administrative future, he would have been more prudent had he not so openly counted himself among the sectarians, enemies of freedom of education. Perhaps as well, M. Brisac, who belongs to the Jewish denomination, would have been better advised to refrain from underscoring the excessive influence that Jews exercise in our public affairs, especially in questions that affect consciences and the Catholic faith.[45]

The war between the two Frances was to be waged to the very end: the nation had to return to the general problem of the separation of Church and state, which, so often begun, had not yet been carried out. Despite local and national difficulties, all the founders of the Republic and the men who succeeded them a generation later, in the 1890s — when so many secular measures were passed, leading little by little to the turning point of 1904–5 — were agreed on the henceforth ineluctable and irreversible character of that properly French form of secularization. The advocates of secularism depended on a resolved and constant parliamentary majority composed almost entirely of *députés* of Catholic origin with very diverse personal and political values, who were above all decided on making this specific form of access to modernity their own. *L'Univers Israélite* made fun of Drumont's theses, which were received with enthusiasm and spread by so many of his faithful, theses maintaining that secularization was a cover for the Judaization of French society. "In the Chambers that voted on these measures," the newspaper noted ironically,

there were Jews — thus the Jews are responsible for all the evil. . . . It's the Jews who, after 4 September, continued the resistance, since the government of Défense Nationale included one Jew. . . . Would you say that the four or five Jewish *députés* of the Chamber were the heads of the republican party that initiated the legislation in question? That would be giving them too much credit. Neither Jules Ferry nor Paul Bert nor M. Brisson, nor M. Clemenceau are Jewish, as far as we know. Or would you have us believe that the three or four hundred *députés* on the left have been terrorized by their four or five Jewish colleagues, to the point of being forced to vote against their will for laws they disapprove of ? Let a Catholic *député* stand up in the Chamber and dare to declare it was the Jews who instigated these "persecutions." Success is assured: he will be welcomed by an immense roar of laughter.[46]

A few state Jews did sometimes act as ideologues, theorizing or drafting plans for secularization: each time, however, they were men who had little sense of being part of Judaism. Some even went so far as to attempt to transform the foundation of Franco-Judaism through their militant atheism. They were certainly the ones who went the furthest in distancing themselves from their religion, regularly eliciting a final judgment from the institutional spokespersons of Jewry. This observation applies both to the man who, among the very first, proposed the separation of Church and state, namely, Camille Dreyfus, and to the man who finally drafted the definitive measure in 1904, Paul Grunebaum-Ballin. With time, however, the disapproval of the Jewish press attenuated a great deal. The leaders of the consistory were also devoted republicans and did not want to strengthen the camp of those who, under cover of hostility to secularism, were far from truly rallying behind the tradition of 1789. In 1904, when the eventuality of that capital decision was on everyone's tongues and was provoking strong polemics, the *Archives Israélites* began by emphasizing the strong reservations expressed by the chief rabbi and by the bishops themselves. Nevertheless, this newspaper added immediately:

We have the conviction that this will be only a difficult moment to get through and that Judaism will triumph and will come out of the trial greater than ever. . . . In becoming autonomous, the Synagogue as a whole will know how to make good use of the emancipation acquired. . . . The Jews, knowing they can no longer count on anyone but themselves to survive, to ensure the regular operations of the organs of the religion, will become energized by that and will find in their hearts the means to achieve the plans destined to support holy emulation within Israel.[47]

Thus, French Jewry no longer feared the separation it had earlier condemned: the new law would not attack the republican feelings of Jews in France. For the *Archives*, Jews still had a "deferential and loyal attitude" toward the state, unlike Catholics, and "no disaffection with the Republic is to be feared."[48] Instead of condemning the reform being prepared, as they had earlier opposed Camille Dreyfus's proposals, the *Archives* considered favorably the legislation presented to the Chamber: even if it penalized smaller denominations disproportionately, "this is a blessing in disguise" that would "reawaken dormant zeal."[49] An argument was even drawn from this to invalidate Drumont's thesis on Jewish domination: "We need acts such as the vote on the law of Separation to reduce to dust the legends woven about the so-called omnipotence of the Jewish race."[50] The entire text of the law penalized religious minorities the most, even though they were very much in favor of the Republic. It was particularly unfavorable to Jews, for it called into question the statist and centralized status of the consistory, at a time when the Jews, unlike the Catholics, could not depend on a powerful Church with numerous resources. The Protestants, also concerned by this unequal treatment, vigorously rose up in the Chamber against this aspect of the law. Jews, in contrast, remained silent and did not dare plead their case. Hence the irony of the *Archives Israélites*:

But when they come to talk to us again about the *Jewish conquest*, about *Jewish France*, about *the Jews our masters*, to show that these assertions, these flashy words, which have made fortunes for shameless pamphleteers, add up to nothing, it will be enough to place before them the pusillanimity of our consistories, which did not even raise their voices in this concert of recriminations that welcomed a plan that sacrifices without pity the future of our communities.[51]

Without worrying about these reservations, as they had in the 1880s, most Jewish *députés* turned the plan to their own account in their platform statements. During the legislative elections of 1906, Joseph Reinach maintained that "the law that separated the state from the Churches was conceived in a spirit of liberty and equity"; L. L. Klotz judged that "the separation of the Churches and the state has become a living reality." And again during the 1910 elections, Joseph Reinach represented himself as "the resolute defender of the secular school, where patriotism will always be taught as the first of the civic virtues." In a police report, Camille Picard in Vosges declared that "he is not animated by an antireligious spirit but rather by the secular spirit that the founders of the Third Republic possessed to such a high degree, men whose esteemed names are on all lips and in all hearts."[52]

Let us return to the debate itself. The discussion held in the Chamber was influenced by the writings of Paul Grunebaum-Ballin, at the time a young *auditeur* for the Counseil d'Etat, who had just published a book titled *La séparation des églises et de l'état. Étude juridique* (The separation of Churches and the state: Juridical study),[53] which presented itself as a commentary on the proposals of the commission created in 1903, which Aristide Briand chaired. Grunebaum-Ballin had become one of Briand's principal collaborators; even though he seems not to have played a decisive role, rumor, as before, eagerly latched onto this name to attack the plan.[54] It is true that his book allowed the juridical terrain to be cleared and that his contribution was far from negligible. That is why Monsignor Montagnini warned the Vatican: "[Its] author, as his name would indicate, must be Jewish, and is seeking to justify the Jacobin provisions of the separation plan. . . . He praises the rigor of the plan and tries to push for even more rigor. The author justifies all the unjust and arbitrary provisions under the pretext that we have to face a new politico-religious situation."[55] Grunebaum-Ballin and others were responsible for overseeing the application of that law to Briand's staff and also became mixed up in the inventory battle.

His name, as had been the case for Camille Dreyfus, thus provoked the anger of nationalist groups, especially since Rome was lending its support to the legitimist camp. Suddenly, antisemitism was reborn in force against this Jew guilty of attacking the Catholic identity of France. Even though, in reality, he played only a secondary role, he rapidly came to occupy a central place in the antisemitic imaginary, a place he would hold for a long time, eclipsing the name of Louis Méjean, a Protestant high official and a crucial actor in determining the final focus of the law. As at the beginning of the Third Republic, the situation was nonetheless exemplary: a Protestant and a Jew at the origin of the law separating Church and state! What a godsend for the nationalist right, which throughout the last years of the century, joined to political antisemitism a no less aggressive political anti-Protestantism, which it also directed against the few *préfets* who were charged locally with applying the law! [56] Times had changed, however, since only Paul Grunebaum-Ballin was singled out for popular condemnation, with his Protestant colleague escaping the nationalists' wrath. [57]

Like Dreyfus, Grunebaum-Ballin claimed to be a freethinker; he was raised in a family detached from any religious practices, and he himself kept apart from Jewish milieus; socialist and anticlerical, he wanted to take into consideration only the finalities of human emancipation and ignored the reservations and uneasiness that the plan elicited in the Jewish world. He displayed "great obstinacy in denying his place within the Jewish community," [58] an obstinacy that inevitably recalls the behavior of Camille Dreyfus, which was identical in every respect. Dreyfus, as we recall, refused to recognize his status as a Jew and considered himself a freethinker. Similarly, Paul Grunebaum-Ballin wrote in 1940: "We refuse to declare ourselves 'Jewish.' . . . We refuse to see ourselves as belonging to the Jewish religious community, for the only community to which we belong is the French nation. We have always lived as freethinkers, detached from any religious belief." Like Camille Dreyfus, the hot-headed editor of the newspaper *La Nation*, he was attacked all the more by antisemitic hatred, which until Vichy named him as an essential actor — which he was not — in this law of separation. At the origin of this fabrication we find Charles Benoist and Louis Capéran, both conservative theorists hostile to the process of secularization: for Benoist, Grunebaum-Ballin "was sitting in the office next to A. Briand" while the plan of separation was being elaborated by the commission, "listening in profound silence . . . [Briand] had a bailiff remit an appeal to his Egeria" before making his decision known. [59] Without hesitation, *La Libre Parole* claimed that "this Jew is the true author of the law of Separation, since Briand did nothing but put his signature on the Yid's wild imaginings." [60]

As we did for Camille Dreyfus, let us give a few examples of the antisemitic hatred that through Grunebaum-Ballin, attacked the Republic itself. Whereas Maurras pointed a vengeful finger at secularism, and against freethinking on which it rested, [61] Léon Daudet, always vigilant, denounced with more precision "the domination of the Kraut Grunebaum-Ballin, responsible for the separation of Church and state." [62] Relentless, the tribune of Action Française saw in him "the aptitude among the circumcised to transform into a combat post whatever position they improperly occupy.

Hardly was he in his place and the Jew of the Conseil d'Etat, Grunebaum-Ballin, had but one idea: set up a Talmudic law called the law of separation that will dispossess the Catholics, that will make them pariahs in their own country."[63] He also invented the following sketch:

"Oh, the devil with it," said Aristide Briand, scratching his head, "now there's something. Israel is taking arms against Rome, that's obvious. Israel wants to move the population again against the Catholic clergy. If I don't act, what will they think of me? What will my *conseiller* and supervisor Grunebaum think?"[64]

Those close to Drumont, such as Urbain Gohier, saw in Combes and Jaurès "puppets whose strings are pulled by the Synagogue"; and *La Libre Parole* used the same clichés against Grunebaum-Ballin that it had used against Camille Dreyfus.[65] Monsignor Jouin, who became famous by distributing *The Protocols of the Elders of Zion* in France, also attacked the "anti-clericalism that is the central core of the Judeo-Masonic action 'and denounced' the law of separation of Grunebaum-Ballin, the secular policy of the Blums, and so on."[66]

After World War I, everything seemed to be settled, separation became part of the mores, the republican state seemed to have succeeded in imposing full neutrality in the political-administrative institutions and a universalist conception of citizenship within public life as a whole. Of course, in 1924, during the legislative elections, André Fribourg still appeared to fear "an offensive return of clericalism that is strong enough to destroy the gains of secularism," and Albert Milhaud was still counting on Ferdinand Buisson of all people to defend the secular school.[67] In reality, however, with the 1924 elections and those that followed, socioeconomic preoccupations were what mattered most: the social question, the rise of socialism and the conflict with the dominant powers pushed the eternal questions of separation and secularism to the background. It was, however, at that time that the last quarrel erupted: should the laws of the Republic be extended to the regained provinces of the East, which had not been affected by that legislation in 1904–5? Could the undertaking initiated by Gambetta and Ferry tolerate these particularisms which prevented full secularization of national territory? With the aftermath of World War I, the controversy erupted, brutally ending the *Union Sacrée*. Georges Weill, leader of Alsatian socialism and the *député* of Strasbourg, ardently defended the introduction of secular laws into the three departments: he played an important role in working out the Herriot Declaration in June 1924, which announced the introduction of secular laws. On that occasion, during a large meeting held in the Palais des Sports in Strasbourg, he admitted that he was obsessed by the question of secularism, and added: "We have the firm will to end this regime of exceptions, which is humiliating for us, and to resist the clerical party, which is subordinating the national interest to party interest, and has not hesitated to push our populations of Alsace toward a particularism, if not a neutralism, that is at the very least moral in nature."[68] Soon after, he was defeated in the legislative elections and the *préfet* noted that "the defeat of Georges Weill could only be explained by the [need to] satisfy clerical spite."[69] As the *Journal d'Alsace et de Lorraine* noted on that occasion, "the clergy led a campaign of hatred, lies, and slander" against the Socialist candidate. The *préfecture* was even more explicit:

The clericals' hatred . . . in order to take revenge on Georges Weill's too-French attitude, impelled them to not retreat before any alliance whatsoever. . . . It was by order of the priest that the peasant voted, it was under the influence of the Catholic clergy that the election of the autonomists came about, and the campaign was led from within the confessional, especially at Easter. A single argument was at stake: religion and the state are always threatened by atheist France.[70]

Here and there, there was an uprising against "Jewish money," which had supposedly manipulated the elections.[71] Even in 1932, *Der Elsässer* (The Alsatian), the clerical newspaper of Strasbourg, attacked Weill, "this fanatic of assimilation, this most hateful enemy of the Church."[72] The newspaper pursued a long polemic, year after year, against the separation of Church and state.

Alsace seems to have experienced a Franco-French war in miniature: on its own scale, the same passions came to light. As the *préfet* again observed, "the autonomist milieus depend upon the Catholic and Protestant clergy, which, with rare exceptions, are more hostile than ever to the republican regime and any national assimilation." In another *préfet's* report in Bas-Rhin, remarkable for its almost sociological vocabulary, we read: "The elections were distorted by the passion exercised by the Catholic and Protestant clergy on the majority of voters whose civic culture is underdeveloped. The clergy is hostile to our secular conception of the state. Hence the support it brings to regionalist candidates." Foreign policy was mixed in, since Georges Weill, in a public meeting, maintained that the autonomists were turning toward Hitler and were doing "everything to prevent French citizens from accommodating themselves to the French idea."[73] The rejection by Alsatian Catholics was total, as another police report attests. It dealt with the campaign against Georges Weill: "I have the honor of informing you that forty-eight out of fifty voters who were part of the Capuchin monasteries in Strasbourg took part in the vote. Almost all the ecclesiastics had their voting ballots up their sleeves." In the churches, tracts were distributed appealing to Catholics to vote against Weill—in favor of the Communists! The priests themselves distributed Communist bulletins to better combat the candidate and divide the left: in the end, it was the Communist Party that triumphed. It is true that the Party expressed itself in high German and supported Alsatian autonomism, which Léon Blum and Georges Weill resolutely opposed. Anxious to respond in the same vein, Weill, addressing a Socialist audience, began by speaking in Alsatian to his Communist opponent and then, met by boos from the hall, returned to French.[74]

Lazare Weiller was also associated with this polemic: this Jewish senator from Bas-Rhin, however, was on the side of the national wing of the Republican Popular Union in matters that concerned him: from a political faction that opposed Weill, whom he himself fought, he also approved Édouard Herriot's declaration, which, except for a few nuances, was satisfactory to local autonomists, whom he refused to antagonize. Elected with the Bloc National in company of the canon Muller, one of the heads of the Heimatbund, he received the support of Catholics, who appreciated his great moderation. Even the *Elsässer*, the most radical organ of a Catholic and autonomist Alsace, supported Lazare Weiller, whom Georges Weill himself had personally confronted while locally supporting the Socialist slate![75] Salomon Grumbach, Socialist *député* heading the current most hostile to Alsatian autonomism, was also anxious to apply all the laws of the Republic as quickly as possible, including those concerning secularism. He was beaten in Mulhouse in the legislative elections of 1932 by another Jewish *député*, Alfred Wallach, who was seated among the Alliance Démocratique but declared himself in favor of extending the separation between Church and state to Alsace: nuanced on this question, he also received the support of Catholics who identified with this "ardent patriot, this veteran" and did not conceal their profound hostility toward Grumbach. *La Voix d'Alsace* went hammer and tongs at "the Jewish trio of G. Weill, Salomon Grumbach, and Israel" and called for a Catholic candidate.[76] At the same moment, however, another Jewish *député* on the right, Camille Simonin, representative of Bas-Rhin, came out in favor of maintaining the status quo in the matter of religion and education. As we have noted, in this region, so long the cradle of French Jewry, the few Jewish *députés* who participated in the electoral jousting matches took very diverse positions on local political and cultural issues. Might we advance the hypothesis that from the two lost and then regained provinces came profoundly nationalist and revanchist state Jews, politicians, and generals, who were, for a time at least, recognized as such and accepted by the enemies of the Republic, those turned toward autonomism and Catholicism? They were confronting a new category of state Jews, who, beyond law and order, were preoccupied with social justice, to which Gambettists remained largely indifferent.

Soon after, the Front Populaire again envisioned prudent measures to extend national legislation to the East: that was enough to immediately make the fantasies of the past resurface. In the place of Camille Dreyfus and Paul Grunebaum-Ballin, Georges Weill and Salomon Grumbach, this time it was Léon Blum who was accused of relentlessly pursuing the Judaization of France under cover of secularism. Charles Maurras, as usual, sounded the charge. "Blum," he said, "is a messianist who believes in the secularized mission of Israel."[77] Immediately, the canon Hincky, director of diocesan works in Strasbourg, wrote to the *Tribune Juive*: "Catholics are not anti-semitic . . . but we note with indignation that every time our religious status has been attacked, beginning in 1918, an atheist Jew like Georges Weill, Grumbach, and so on was in the wings. Today, it is Mssrs. Blum, Zay, Moch, and Blumel. We shall never bow down to the dictatorship of a minority, namely, of atheist Jews."[78] Anger mounted, as expressed, for example, in *Les Jeunes d'Alsace* (The youth of Alsace): "It fell to the *premier président* of the Jewish and atheist *conseil* of the French Republic to propose to Alsace a stinking Jew deal. The devout people will oppose with the most ferocious energy any atheist Jew who removes the crucifixes from our schools."[79] *La Nouvelle Voix d'Alsace et de Lorraine* (The new voice of Alsace and Lorraine), "the organ of militant Christians," one of the most important newspapers of the region, ran the headline: "The Talmud in Its Worst Applications. . . . Blum Government Shows Its Jewish Hand."[80]

This new question of Alsace and Lorraine[81] resurrected the debate about the finalities of secular education: the Opportunists, then the Radicals, and finally the Socialists joined forces to further the secularization of French society, most often without calling into question the legitimacy of religious beliefs, which survived deep in the population. Between the Programme de Belleville and the end of the Third Republic, several hundred parliamentarians of the two assemblies voted in measures of separation and secularization. Majorities were arrived at and universal suffrage was pronounced. The whole of the republican political staff took a stand in this direction, and the leading lights of the Republic gave it their continuous support. Nevertheless, beyond the Republic and its defenders, from Gambetta to Vichy, there were many who considered the Jews — and at times the Protestants — as solely responsible for this attack on the Catholic identity of French society. This quasi-diabolization was repeated on numerous occasions, in particular at the most difficult times in French history, the successive Franco-French wars.

CHAPTER NINE

Inside the Franco-French Wars: From Boulangism to the Popular Front

Historians have shown how the "Franco-French wars" punctuated the political life of contemporary France, how their rhythm and recurrence imposed itself in an almost cyclical fashion: they disturbed national unity and weakened the consensus and agreement on the rules of the game, threatening to fracture that sense of belonging to the public sphere shared by all citizens. On each occasion, these great quarrels put into play ideologies and visions of the world that were so antagonistic that those who held them were resolved to defend them to the end. These quarrels put in question the very definition of citizenship in a social group that was understood at times as an organic community and at times, on the contrary, as simply a collection of individuals who had decided to live together in the name of a common moral system. The Franco-French wars[1] rent the social fabric to this degree largely because, quite simply, they illustrated French exceptionalism and extended to the modern period a violence that had been a part of the nation's construction since the most remote times. Their properly religious dimension simply referred back to the many conflicts and intolerances by means of which national unity had been formed.

As we have already suggested, under the Third Republic these Franco-French wars took a particular turn: in opposition to the universalism of the republicans, who intended to build a society resting on all citizens and oriented toward Reason, there was now an organic vision that rooted nationalism in a land, a religion, and at times, even a race. The builders of the Republic imposed measures aimed at restoring this universalism through secularism, the schools, and so on; the new nationalists, in contrast, almost always depended on Catholicism to justify their resistance. Protestants and Jews were called upon to choose between the two camps: in fact, however, the nationalist camp placed them among the opposition from the beginning; and true to the counterrevolutionary tradition, Protestants and Jews became the object of hatred and rejection.[2] Traditional anti-Protestantism and antisemitism were accompanied by a properly political rejection: set apart, separated from all other citizens, they appeared as political stakes. In some ways, their destiny prefigured the final destiny of the Republic to which they were to be assimilated. Reciprocally, many of them lent their cooperation to the republicans, who for the most part had come from a Catholic cultural tradition. In truth, there existed something like a graduated scale of hatred whose victims were these two religious minorities: throughout the Third Republic and, except for a few periods of calm (for example, the *Union Sacrée* of World War I), Jews were of the utmost importance. Their centrality in the political debate and in cultural life was only all the more striking. As the *Archives Israélites* observed:

Caesarism, Boulangism, nationalism, in a word, all the movements hostile to the Republic and against which it had to defend itself found in the enemies of Israel ardent thurifers and precious instruments. . . . We find militant antisemitism mixed up in all the conspiracies that had as their goal to sneak off with the regime of freedom that France bestowed upon itself. . . . The line is very clear, clearly delimited, between those who want to set our country back by five centuries and those who are resolved to follow the path of freedom, progress, and social justice opened by the movement of 1789. And the Jewish question is the infallible criterion by which one can recognize one's own.[3]

In fact, the Jewish question obliged everyone to join one camp or another, and the camps were becoming all the more clear-cut. Every time a break occurred, the Jews were, as it were, sent off to one of the two camps and enclosed there, whatever their wish might be; and it was only rarely that particular Jews — we will meet some of them later — would make an effort to cross the boundaries in order to join a camp that hardly opened its doors willingly. Indelibly allied with the builders of the Republic, they were labeled as such and combated precisely because of that identification. For the *Archives Israélites*, suddenly "there is a party or rather a jumble of parties that could never win Jewish votes; namely, the party that has put on the garish mask, but with indistinct features, of nationalism."[4] Full of bitterness at the rise of the extreme right, former *préfet* Isaïe Levaillant admitted his distress when confronted with currents that rejected with growing intransigence universalist citizenship. These currents were giving rise to the preeminence of a Catholicism of exclusion that pushed for the return of irrationalism by contesting the very foundations of a rationalist and open Republic. Following a virulent campaign that was antisemitic in tone, he was obliged to step down from his post as *trésorier-payeur général*; it was as editor of the *Univers Israélite* that he spoke out, outlining another political morality that the Jews were to rally behind:

There were Jews among the Opportunists, there were Jews among the Radicals, among the Socialists, and a mark of the infinite diversity of their tendencies, there were even some among the Boulangists. But there had never been a Jewish policy or a Jewish program or a Jewish party or a Jewish committee or a Jewish grouping of any kind. . . . It is that situation which the criminals who crafted the civil war have succeeded in changing. What is agitating us in the elections about to take place is no longer, as in the past, the question of what direction the Republic must follow and in whose hands leadership will be entrusted . . . but rather whether we Jews will keep our place, the place that is legitimately due us, in this Republic that we have contributed to establishing.[5]

The rise in power of nationalism, then, obliged all state Jews to join the same camp, thus involuntarily facilitating the identification of Jews with the Republic, an identification the antisemites proclaimed endlessly in order to weaken all those who rallied behind Marianne. Certain Jews, however, balked for a long time before rejoining the party of the Republic: Alfred Naquet, whom we will discuss at length later on,[6] was perhaps the most famous of them. His name is forever associated with the rise in power of the Boulangist movement. He was, perhaps contrary to all expectation, one of its undisputed leaders. He was to live this adventure with passion, engaging body and soul for the general. He was often considered Boulanger's close collaborator, the one who, in any case, was to focus the attention of the press and the public at large on Boulanger himself, and the one whose features would be the object of an incalculable number of caricatures.

On 15 March 1888, the *Journal Officiel* published a report removing General Boulanger, at the time in full ascendancy on the political stage, from active duty. This expulsion stunned his followers, who immediately organized a response: on 16 March, Alfred Naquet, "vice emperor of Boulanger,"[7] the man who could be considered almost the "political head of the undertaking," its "brain,"[8] announced the creation of a "Comité de Protestation Nationale" (committee of national protest).[9] In April, a large meeting was held at the Café Riche, Boulevard des Italiens, to which guests rushed, wearing white carnations (the general's favorite flower) in their buttonholes. Boulanger and Naquet then revealed the fundamental objective of the movement they had decided to establish: a revision of the constitution. Taking the floor, Naquet asserted that "General Boulanger is the greatest force that we could now place in the service of the nation and the Republic"; in his view, he was not "a Caesar, a dictator. Ever since the French Revolution, France has known only party governments. . . . Creating a national government . . . has been the dream of all politicians. . . . Gambetta failed, but you, General, will succeed, such is my firm hope." At these words, Boulanger took the floor: "I thank my fine friend," he said, "the honorable senator of Vaucluse, for such kind words."[10]

Naquet was "the first of the principal Boulangists to appear on the political stage";[11] it was he who theorized the rejection of the parliamentary system and called for universal suffrage: for him, thanks to a revision of the constitution, the "parliamentary caste" would meet its end, giving full legitimacy to the executive power, which would then be the direct emanation of the people. His socialist vision was now colored by an authoritarian populist dimension in the name of the supremacy of the people alone. He encouraged Boulanger to resort to a coup d'état to prevent the definitive slippage of the Opportunist political class toward the right: in so doing, he clearly set his reflections within the framework of the nationalist current to which Barrès, in his Nancy program, would give a final push, by combining socialism, nationalism, antiparliamentarianism, but also — antisemitism. The Lorrainian writer accentuated the antisemitism that was already present at the beginnings of Boulangism, depending on Rochefort and allying himself with Drumont, who had shown himself very critical of the general.[12] Paradoxically, his search led Naquet to a strategy from which everything was to be feared; he, the radical who had linked Boulangism to a leftist base, involuntarily gave weapons to the Boulangists on the right, who had been present from the beginning of the adventure and who did not always hide their antisemitic feelings, as events would soon demonstrate.

A year later, on 17 March 1889, a major event took place, the Banquet of Tours: in a speech prepared by Naquet and revised by Monsignor Freppel, the conservative and antisemitic bishop of Angers, Boulanger proclaimed his intention to end the war against clericalism, since for him, freedom of conscience had to be unqualified. It was time for Catholics to participate with full rights in national political life. Seeking to gain the goodwill of that electorate, the general declared: "The Republic as I conceive it must consecrate all liberties; it must repudiate the Jacobin heritage of the present Republic; it must bring religious peace to the country through absolute respect for all beliefs."[13] Alfred Naquet, a radical oriented toward materialism and a great advocate of science who had fought against the compromises of the Opportunists, had made a turnaround for strategic reasons; it was he who had suggested this fundamental shift to the general.

Like the declaration made at the Café Riche, this Banquet of Tours was an essential intellectual stage for Boulangism. In both cases, Alfred Naquet was for everyone an essential personality influencing the strategy of the movement. In Tours, he made the following declaration: [14]

Citizens, I believe that the principle of the secularization of society that has been brought to the world by the French Revolution is a salutary principle, because it is a principle of freedom. But if such are my personal convictions as a citizen, here is what I think as a statesman: This great social transformation must be brought about not as an act of war, as an act consecrating the victory of one party over another, but rather as a shared agreement among the interested parties. . . . Absolute respect for all philosophical and religious convictions, condemnation . . . of the hatred and religious struggles of another age, aimed at Catholics today, at freethinkers tomorrow, and day after tomorrow, bringing with it from Germany that antisemitism which dishonors civilization and which the French, a century after the French Revolution, should be ashamed to borrow from their rivals.

These words were met by vigorous cries from participants: "Down with the Jews!" One faction of the Boulangist militants openly displayed their feelings before an orator who was something like "the prolix and at times ingenious . . . mentor" of the general.[15] Mercilessly, the *Archives Israélites* reported in great detail the lecture and the antisemitic reactions it provoked:

Has not the leader himself, General Boulanger, under whose banner M. Naquet has assumed his place, has not that general today at the head of an army, half of which is ultramontane, on many occasions been accused of using insulting language toward "Jewry"? What safeguard does this protest against antisemitism offer to religious minorities, coming from an army where the sons of crusaders constitute a formidable contingent? [16]

And this periodical went on to denounce "that day of dupes in Tours" during which "a Jew, but only by birth, an admitted materialist by his works, speaking at a meeting convoked and patronized by the most typical clerical element, did not really feel at ease." [17] There were many who were astonished by the surprising presence of Alfred Naquet in a place where, according to the *commissaire de police* (police superintendent), the royalists vigorously applauded Boulanger, often breaking into cheers. The *commissaire* added: "The republicans judged the speeches severely, especially M. Naquet's. They didn't expect that a senator, despite the fact that he had rallied behind Boulangism, would abandon his political past to make overtures toward the reactionaries." [18] The newspaper *Le Progrès* sneered at the "harangue of the Jew Naquet," who "flattered the clergy," whereas *Le Ralliement* openly made fun of Boulanger and Naquet "taking their inspiration from the sacristies." [19]

Sometimes, frank hilarity reigned at this reversal in the situation: in Naquet's dear Provence, in Mormoiron, very close to the cherished city of Carpentras, the populace couldn't get over it. And they made him know it with humor. The newspaper *Le Mont-Ventoux* of Carpentras, addressed "the honorable abbé Naquet," begging him, when he returned to the region, "not to forget his cassock, for otherwise he would run the risk of not being recognized." And the reporter added:

Allow me to beg you to be kind enough to come to Mormoiron, today Sunday, the day of the votive celebration, to attend your apotheosis. We will praise God, who in his infinite goodness, inspired in a republican of Bédoin the idea of offering you a cassock, the distinctive mark of His chosen people; we will celebrate the holy and admirable virtues that earned you the grace of conversion and ordination. And then, isn't it true, my dear abbé Naquet, that you will do the honor of saying your first mass for your faithful of Mormoiron and of blessing with your pure hands the new banner that the Conservatives and Catholics of the country have adopted since the last election? . . . We will have the pleasure of contemplating our great Saint Naquet carried triumphant by those most steeped in devotion. And the students of the monks and sisters will sing at the top of their voices a canticle, which a secret admirer has dedicated to you:

(*Sung to the tune of: "Je suis chrétien"*
[I am a Christian]):
He is a Christian
He is a holy brother
Yes, that is certain,
He is a Christian
Let us sing it loud, let us sing, comrades
The Jew Naquet is a great saint.[20]

For their part, the *Archives Israélites* attempted to compose a dossier on "M. Boulanger" and "Jewry," a dossier constructed from a declaration that the general had subsequently rushed to deny, but which had been confirmed on several occasions by the man to whom it was made. In it, Boulanger maintained: "We will have to get rid of Jewry." The *Archives* added an important element to this dossier, in the form of a pamphlet distributed by the Boulangist committees and asserting that the general would be elected "because Reinach the Jew and Spuller have been linked to hatred for the infamous."[21] In truth, the debate has not ended even in our own day: was Boulanger an antisemite, did the man who gave birth to the first real Franco-French war that almost called into question the republican order already profess sentiments that would then reappear again and again? This question concerns, in the first place, Alfred Naquet himself; the man represented as the brains behind Boulangism could not avoid facing it. He was still actively involved beside Déroulède and appeared at his side during a tumultuous, highly publicized trial.[22] He signed various proclamations with that same Déroulède in the name of the Comité National, and concluded: "Long live the national Republic."[23]

Everyone seems to agree implicitly that the general himself was not antisemitic; he sometimes intervened to make it known, and Naquet could take comfort in that. Nevertheless, in Boulanger's immediate entourage, among the candidates who claimed him as their own during the 1889 elections, the hatred of Jews was patent; it grew with the arrival of the Marquis de Morès and indisputably erupted the following year at the time of Francis Laur's campaign for reelection in Neuilly. That campaign unfolded entirely under the banner of the most virulent antisemitism; and Drumont presided over meetings where most of the Boulangist leaders were present, including Déroulède. Naquet was almost the only one to stay away: the Nancy program of 1898, when populist Boulangism found in the most official antisemitism the foundation for its own legitimacy, was not far off. It stemmed from a logic with which Alfred Naquet could no longer be associated.

In reality, the question of the relations between Boulangism and antisemitism was raised at the end of the 1880s: the moment the Marquis de Morès joined corresponded to the resignation of Eugène Meyer, the editor of *La Lanterne*, for it was already nearly impossible to be both Jewish and Boulangist.[24] A little later, the editors of the *Archives Israélites* themselves stated as much: "We do not believe," they underscored, "that Boulangism of defunct memory, despite the presence of several Jews in the general staff of the good general, numbered many followers among us. However much it protested, it had a clerical appearance that made it suspect to many of our coreligionists."[25] Hence the dilemma of Alfred Naquet, a central character in the Boulangist crisis, hurt by an orientation that he could not really prevent. For a long time, however, he tried to exonerate the "true" Boulangism by distinguishing it from other currents that had supposedly perverted it. In a long, little-known letter, he detailed his position:

I belong to no religion, I am married to a Catholic woman . . . but I shall never deny my race. . . . The antisemitic campaign is not the work of the Boulangist party. . . . From the time of M. Drumont's first book, a faction, and unfortunately a large faction, of the Socialists allowed themselves to be led into antisemitism. . . . Boulangism did not create antisemitism; it confined itself to accepting antisemites among its followers, just as it accepted Jews. . . . We must refrain from saying that Boulangism is antisemitic, since its leader proscribes antisemitism and I occupy one of the most important positions in the party, after the leader.[26]

Through the words of Isaïe Levaillant, its editor-in-chief, *L'Univers Israélite* focused on that question on numerous occasions: for the former *préfet* exercising the duties of director of Sûreté Générale, and as a result, an expert in the matter, there is nothing more natural than this alliance between Boulangism and anti-semitism in a shared work of hatred and denigration. Boulangism and antisemitism were born during the same period; they proceed from the same passions and the same desires; they employ the same means; they are two phenomena of the same order, two plants that grew from the same manure. They are distinguished from each other in that the first is demagogy tied to Caesarism, and the second demagogy allied with clericalism, but they are indistinguishable in their equal horror of any idea of tolerance, freedom, and justice.[27]

The faithful Naquet, who went to Brussels and to Jersey to find the ousted general, and to whom this same Boulanger addressed a letter from London to support him during the 1889 legislative campaign, telling him: "You are a Boulangist *avant la lettre*,"[28] who became vice chairman of the Comité National for Boulanger, could only be devastated by the irresistible rise of antisemitism within his own movement. For close to a decade, he took care to personally clip almost all the hateful articles that *La Libre Parole* devoted to him. Nevertheless, he had to take a position: in a long interview with *L'Éclair* (The thunderbolt), he declared in July 1892:

I became part of Boulangism with high ideas and generous hopes . . . but it is certain that Boulangism rapidly took a direction that would have prevented me from joining it if I had not already done so. Antisemitism, which is an abominable movement, was not caused by Boulangism, but it grafted itself onto it and drew life from it. This makes me regret the contribution I made to Boulangism.[29]

Again in 1893, he tried to convince voters in Carpentras of the sincerity of his commitment: he had acted in the sole interest of the Republic; confessing his "error," he wished to persuade voters of the sincerity of his republicanism.[30]

More and more, he felt implicated by the Jewish question, and attentively followed the unfolding of the Dreyfus affair, again clipping innumerable articles, and delivering a vast speech in May 1895, where he retraced the history of Jews before his open-mouthed colleagues, from time immemorial to the contemporary period. Finally, in 1900 he published a book, which he called a "testament," in which he made one last evaluation of his life and of Boulangism. In *Temps futurs. Socialisme. Anarchie*, he admitted his disappointment from the first lines:

My participation in the Boulangist movement was certainly the phase of my entire political life that I regret the most. It ruined me morally. . . . When I see to what point parliamentarism has justified my warnings against it, I cannot blame myself for having participated in a movement that failed. . . . But in contrast, I am inclined to blame myself when I evaluate the men in whose hands I placed my own, the Déroulèdes, Thiébauds, and Rocheforts whom I believed to be republicans of the old school and whose deep wickedness the Dreyfus affair has shed light on.[31]

The situation of Alfred Naquet, a central character in Boulangism, had thus become untenable: despite his total commitment and his duties, a Jew had no place in a populist movement that was hostile to parliamentarism and depended on certain socialist currents. He immediately found himself confronted by an antisemitism that had its origin both in the extreme right and in the extreme left, in the Proudhon movement and, at times, in the Guesdist movement as well. Later, during the interwar period, other state Jews experienced the same disillusions elicited by antisemitic reactions coming from within the Socialist or Communist parties themselves. In contrast, Alfred Naquet appeared as an almost unique state Jew in his commitment toward socialism, anarchism, and Boulangism, in his radicalism, and in his opposition to the parliamentary regime of the Third Republic. Through his crucial position in the movement and his exceptionality, he became the ideal scapegoat for all antisemitic pamphleteers.

Nonetheless, Naquet was not the only Jew among the various protagonists in this parody of a civil war. Others played a significant role, which contributed even more to crystallizing a certain resentment toward them. On 29 November 1887, the "second historic night," the final political orientation of the movement was decided, faced with the possibility that Ferry, from whom everything was to be feared, would come to power. That night, Boulanger dined peacefully with his general staff at the home of his mistress, Marguerite Duran. At his side were Déroulède, Naquet, Laisant, Rochefort, Clemenceau, Eugène Meyer, and Camille Dreyfus, editor of *La Nation*.[32] Eugène Meyer, editor of *La Lanterne*, left the Comité National when de Morès became a notorious figure of Boulangism, and Clemenceau also turned against his friends when it became impossible for him to identify with their new authoritarian orientation. Among these allies of a moment there also figured Arthur Meyer, the flamboyant editor of *Le Gaulois*. He was a highly colorful character, one of the rare Jewish converts to Catholicism of the time, a thundering monarchist who had allied himself with Boulangism in hopes of turning it to his own advantage.[33]

Almost at the same moment, in the opponent's camp, there was an attempt being made to organize the resistance: in May 1888, a Société des Droits des Hommes (society for the rights of man)[34] was created during a private meeting in the hall of the Grand Orient of France, a society joined by Radicals, possibilist Socialists, and Opportunists, among them Paul Strauss, a Gambettist who would later become a minister, and would attach his name to the application of a social policy through which the Republic could prevent populist excesses. The most determined enemies of Boulangism, as we have noted, also included Camille Dreyfus, who resolutely attacked the objectives of a general who, according to him, was eager to "reestablish his personal power."[35] For his part, Lazare Weiller led one of the most followed electoral campaigns of that period: in Charente in June 1888, he opposed Déroulède as an Opportunist, with Déroulède wearing Boulanger's colors: the leading lights spoke out or published innumerable articles on this by-election, which served as a barometer for Boulangism, and which ended with the defeat of Déroulède. In Seine-et-Oise, Ferdinand Dreyfus, who had been defeated in 1885 after a particularly virulent antisemitic campaign, attempted to regain his seat by defending the Republic;[36] in Gironde, David Raynal, like Dreyfus one of Gambetta's loyalists, ran for election by committing himself to vote for the "postponement of any plan for revision." Thus, most of these men, either from the outset or after a few hesitations, sought to stem the Boulangist tide, whose authoritarian inclinations they feared, and contested the alliances that privileged the extreme right. Alfred Naquet found himself almost alone in persevering in his Boulangist commitment, and still he postponed the final break. At the 1889 elections, he ran in Paris on the following platform: "I have nothing to add to the general's words." He still denounced "the parliamentary regime that is bringing down our country."

In contrast, Joseph Reinach, a famous Gambettist like David Raynal, Paul Strauss, and Camille Dreyfus, passionately committed himself to the anti-Boulangist crusade, in which he rapidly became a leading figure. In his platform statement in the 1889 election in Digne, he opposed what he called "the odious threat of dictatorship": "Contemptuous of the insults and base slander with which one faction has pushed me to the wall, I shall continue until the end to battle the coalition of cynical and masked Boulangists of the reaction."[37] Gambetta's former collaborator at the time of the Grand Ministère thus stepped forward as one of the figures of anti-Boulangism. In 1886, Jules Ferry and Joseph Reinach came together to attempt to limit the Boulangist thrust, and their correspondence deals with that question almost exclusively.[38] In 1889, Reinach published *La foire boulangiste* (The Boulangist fair), in which he asserted his hostility toward the "circus general" and combated this new version of Brumaire and of 2 December. He was astonished to find Naquet on the side of the general: "This is no longer the same Naquet."[39] For Drumont, everything was clear from then on; the defeat of 1889 was simply due to the coordinated actions of Jews, whether within or outside the Boulangist movement. Lumping together men who in fact were doing battle with each other, the pamphleteer maintained that "the two Hebrews [Arthur Meyer and Alfred Naquet] are as thick as thieves with Reinach and, in reality, it was they rather than Constans who decided the elections."[40]

The team at *La Libre Parole* very quickly took Joseph Reinach as a favorite target and refused to let go. It is hardly forcing the point to maintain that French nationalism, from Drumont to Barrès to Maurras, was constructed as an antithesis to Joseph Reinach, who as we have seen, represented the quintessence of the emancipated and republican state Jew. A little later, in the middle of the Dreyfus affair, when, with the suicide of Henry, everything was about to topple, allowing the truth to finally burst forth, *La Libre Parole* devoted an entire illustrated supplement to the Reinachs. In it Drumont wrote, "On the one hand, there is Henry. . . . He had only one love, only one passion, only one religion: the flag, the army. . . . On the other, there is Reinach, who forms the most striking antithesis to Henry. This Reinach appears as the personification of the counterfeit Frenchman." He continued by developing a formidable logic that has resurfaced from one period to the next across the entire recent history of France:

Everyone today can understand that the principal leaders of the Dreyfus affair have figured in one way or another (1) in Boulangism, on the Reinach side; (2) in Panama, also on the Reinach side; (3) in the Southern Railroad, again on the Reinach side. . . . For fifteen years, the same operation has continued; and it's the same gang operating. . . . At the time of Boulangism, the people were crying: Down with the thieves! At the time of Panama, they cried: Down with the *chéquards*! The scandals of the Dreyfus affair erupted and the people today cry: Down with the Jews! That is, down with the corrupters! Down with the cosmopolitans! Down with the foreigner![41]

When the Waldeck-Rousseau staff took power, it was decisive on the question of doing justice to Dreyfus, and Drumont conceded that now "Reinach has become master again. He is more powerful than ever. It is he who reigns and governs in France. Why didn't he want to be *président du Conseil*? Out of disdain and out of prudence. He knows that the truly strong leaders are those that lead from the wings. But he holds the ministry as a whole in his hands."[42] Thus, Joseph Reinach unwillingly occupied a central place in the nationalist imaginary, which the close-knit and determined team at *La Libre Parole* successfully contributed to fashioning: stone upon stone, it carefully built the foundations. From then on, the potential and still hesitant antisemitism of Boulangism, often socialist in origin, was erected into an explanation for the mishaps of French history. The few state Jews who played an essential role in the many Franco-French wars, in one camp or the other, served as perfect scapegoats whose presumed responsibility also exonerated the people as a whole: populism could rise up by joyfully attacking the big Jews and bringing together millions of little French people against them, people who managed to remain clean by remaining faithful to the French identity sanctified in Reims. Reinach was the ideal scapegoat, even more than Dreyfus perhaps. It was against him and those like him, Gambettist state Jews and all those who, like Naquet, were assimilated to them, that the nation-community reconstructed itself.

Later, other state Jews such as Léon Blum and Pierre Mendès France would take Joseph Reinach's place in an antisemitic logic that would consistently fashion French nationalism, even to our own time.

These state Jews situated in the eye of the storm were thus the object of all opprobrium; in addition, their position in relation to politico-administrative power was made more vulnerable by an atmosphere of scandal favoring the emergence and blossoming of a tired economic antisemitism. The crash of the Union Générale in 1882 had already led to the return of the most fantastical antisemitic mythologies: it did not, however, directly target state Jews.[43] Soon after, however, in 1883, David Raynal signed the notorious agreements with the railroad companies, which for a long time symbolized the too-close ties between the state and private enterprise; it was at that time that he definitively became "the man of wicked agreements." Numa Gilly devoted a pamphlet to him, *Mes dossiers* (My dossiers), which created quite a scandal, in which he accused Raynal of professional misconduct. Numerous, highly publicized trials followed. The press of all leanings also had a great time with Gambetta's friend: for example, in Gironde, his political fief, *L'homme gris* led a ferocious campaign, publishing a number of caricatures praising "the crushing defeat of the Jew Raynal by all the uncircumcised groups," a campaign supported by the Girondin federation of the Workers Party, which proclaimed: "Citizens, in the greater interest of the democratic and social Republic, it is indispensable that we overthrow the Jew Raynal at any price, for he is the author of the wicked agreements. You will all vote against the Jew Raynal to deliver this country from the Opportunists' regime, which is ruining and dishonoring it."[44] This incident, which acquired a symbolic dimension to be discussed later, involved one of the most famous state Jews of the time: it reinforced antisemitism despite the proven innocence of Raynal, but it still did not unleash a full-fledged Franco-French war.

With the Panama scandal, which erupted in 1892 after the revelations of *La Libre Parole*, it was Joseph Reinach who was singled out: his father-in-law, Jacques de Reinach, in tandem with Cornélius Herz, was the principal actor in this new affair of parliamentary corruption by the "chéquards." Herz probably blackmailed Jacques de Reinach, who was also taking exorbitant commissions from the Panama company. The press blasted Jacques de Reinach, and an indictment was about to be handed down; after a very lively discussion with Joseph Reinach, the father-in-law committed suicide. As usual, a discreet silence was extended to the big banks, which, from the Crédit Lyonnais to the Crédit Industriel et Commercial,[45] had reaped enormous benefits from this misconduct; also prudently passed over were the almost unlimited list of newspapers that had been bought and an even longer list of political personalities of all kinds—from Floquet to Rouvier,

Freycinet, Clemenceau, and Léon Daudet himself—who had cashed their checks to contribute to the operation. Drumont took advantage of this stroke of luck both to revive the Boulangist agitation and to take his revenge on one of the general's principal detractors. He directly attacked Joseph Reinach:

O Youssouf, nephew and son-in-law of a swindler and a spy, do you remember our just laws? You called for these just laws in the case of a heroic soldier who, though a mediocre party leader, nevertheless had received six wounds fighting for France. What do you think of your estimable father-in-law, von Reinach, that thief, German agent, and corrupter of politicians?[46]

L'Intransigeant, the newspaper headed by Rochefort, the firebrand of Boulangism, day after day published incendiary articles against Joseph Reinach, "the horrid yid of *La République Française*" who was supposedly in cahoots with the baron.[47] Barrès, who had also gone head to head with Joseph Reinach during the Boulangist episode, could now settle the score: in *Leurs Figures* (Their faces), he theatrically recounted the baron's suicide, "that cynical sensualist, that boulevard swine" and evoked "Joseph, in his frock coat of the Molé Conference, concealing the obstinacy of a prophet of Israel."

In playing with identities and the similarity of names, the press managed to more or less voluntarily implicate the Gambettist leader, by attributing to him the misdeeds of his father-in-law: for *La Croix*, "like his fellow Jew Dreyfus, Reinach has committed treason";[48] the Catholic newspaper targeted the Baron de Reinach by linking his name to Dreyfus, of whom Joseph Reinach was one of the most ardent defenders. This allowed for confusion, which prejudiced people against the younger Reinach. The man who occupied this position in all the Franco-French wars at the turn of the century was not at all mixed up in the scandal, however: but for public opinion heated up by the extreme rightist press, that mattered little. It was too good an opportunity for finally destroying Gambetta's man, who had managed to oppose Boulanger with such courage and foresight. The traditional antisemitism hostile to the Jewish bank, magnified by Drumont, now stirred up political antisemitism directed against the state Jew. But Joseph Reinach refused to hide and ran for the 1893 elections in Digne. His opponent, who declared himself a liberal republican, did not hesitate to write in his platform statement: "Do not forget that it was a Jewish gang that ruined the Panama Company. He's a Jew, the son-in-law of one of the despoilers, and he expects your vote."[49] Nevertheless, Joseph Reinach was reelected in this extremely troubled atmosphere. It would take the Dreyfus affair to bring him down.

From the outbreak of that affair, *La Libre Parole* (once more!) advanced the idea that the captain had been named to the general staff because he was "Reinach's protégé."[50] The same scene would now be played out again, but infinitely magnified.[51] Joseph Reinach, very quickly persuaded of Alfred Dreyfus's innocence, committed himself in his behavior toward politicians. In August 1896, Bernard Lazare wrote to him: "We are not in agreement in our political ideas, and our social ideas differ a great deal. . . . As it happens, a thousand things separate men, but a single thing can unite them. We are both attacked as Jews. Sir, that is why we can forget our economic and philosophical divergences and agree on the continuing struggle against antisemitism."[52] Like Bernard Lazare, but as a famous state Jew rather than an anarchical intellectual, Reinach once more became an essential protagonist toward whom severe blows were directed, as he had during that other profound crisis. In his enormous *Histoire de l'affaire Dreyfus*, he recounted in detail the unfolding of the affair and his own successive interpretations.[53]

Above all, in a manner that almost anticipated the reactions of other state Jews when, under Vichy, injustice extended to Jews as a whole in France, Joseph Reinach committed himself by intervening within the leading milieus of the state. Long familiar with the politico-administrative staff, he had easy access to the highest institutions, unlike Bernard Lazare or Lucien Herr. In conjunction with Senator Scheurer-Kestner, one of the rare political leaders who led the Dreyfusard camp and found himself center stage in the Parliament, he went to see the ministers one after the other. As at the time of Boulangism, other state Jews took public positions, most often opposing Joseph Reinach's voluntarist actions, just as most of them had rejected Alfred Naquet's commitment to Boulanger. In both cases, what they feared above all was singling themselves out as Jews and appearing (in very different contexts, of course) as troublemakers threatening the Republic in the first place and a certain nationalist conception of France's identity in the second. Curiously, even Alfred Naquet, ardent defender of justice and liberty, was very reserved and prudent this time, to the great astonishment of his friend Clemenceau, who publicly criticized him.[54] Similarly, Fernand Crémieux, who also almost always leaned toward the militant left, appears to have displayed the following poster at the time of the 1898 elections in his arrondissement of Uzès:

Voters,
　　To cut short all the slander and all the lies, I declare upon my honor that, as a patriot above all, from the very first moment I branded odious the campaign directed against the army of the Republic and that, as I have always said, I officially commit myself to voting against a reconsideration of the Dreyfus trial.

Faced with the commotion caused by this text, Fernand Crémieux wrote to Clemenceau, asserting it did not come from him: Clemenceau was satisfied by the explanation of his "old comrade of the extreme left," but the local press persisted in its accusation.

To win the reactionary votes of the arrondissement of Uzès, the Socialist Crémieux committed himself to letting his coreligionist, the innocent Dreyfus, die on Devil's Island. This executioner has had a certificate of Dreyfusism delivered to him today by *L'Aurore*. Too late![55]

Ferdinand Dreyfus, though close to the Gambettist movement, proved to be almost hostile to the captain who shared his name: "Antisemitism," he wrote,

has become a parliamentary party . . . thanks to the Dreyfus affair and the capital crimes committed by certain Jews such as that unfortunate J. Reinach, who is in the process of ruining himself by losing his cause and who, out of simple tact, as everyone admits, ought to have decided to remain in the shadows.[56]

On this matter, L.-L. Klotz took a pointed position, since he declared in his platform statement in 1898: "As a patriot above all, from the very first moments I branded odious the campaign directed against the army of the Republic, and I formally commit myself to voting against the reconsideration of the Dreyfus trial."[57] Nevertheless, unlike the Boulangist period when the confrontation between various state Jews had been patent and had made them more visible, this time divergences remained more discreet. Later, Léon Blum justifiably observed that

the Jews of the Dreyfus era, those who belonged to the same social stratum, and who, like him, had passed the difficult examinations and moved into the roles of general staff officers or into the most sought-out corps of civil administration, were exasperated at the idea that hostile prejudice would come to place an obstacle in the way of their irreproachable careers. . . . Rich Jews, Jews of the middle bourgeoisie, Jews who were functionaries, were afraid of the struggle engaged for Dreyfus just as they are today afraid of the struggle engaged against fascism.[58]

Léon Blum rightly noted the prudence of most Jews of the time, whether they were — to put it briefly — court Jews or state Jews. But he underestimated the very great combativeness of certain Gambettist state Jews devoted to the Republic and anxious for justice; on the other hand, he may have implicitly overestimated certain state Jews, who, like him, belonged in many respects to currents of critical ideas turned more toward revolution than toward money or the meaning of the social and institutional hierarchy. It is in fact significant from this perspective that Bernard Lazare the anarchist turned to Joseph Reinach and not to Alfred Naquet or Fernand Crémieux: he sought help from the Gambettist leader and not from the militant socialist anarchist, who was closer to his own values.

As a result, among the Jewish politicians of the Chamber, Joseph Reinach became virtually the sole object of a tenacious hatred: once, he even confronted several hundred *députés* giving an ovation to Count de Mun. Similarly, when he brought a suit against Rochefort, he was booed by the crowd as he left: "Lawyers in their robes," he recounted, "men of society, and Catholic *députés* were crying at the top of their lungs: 'Death to the Jews! Down with the traitors! Down with Reinach!'"[59] And, while leaving Émile Zola's trial, which was unfolding in 1898 in an electric atmosphere, Reinach was assaulted by Jules Guérin's antisemites while the traditional slogans reverberated: "Death to the Jews! Death to the traitors!"[60] His unqualified support of Captain Dreyfus was bought at a high price: in the May 1898 elections, he openly and almost provocatively ran as "the candidate for the Republic of the rights of man and of the citizen," and loudly exclaimed his actions on behalf of justice, which he placed in the tradition of Gambetta. While Drumont was elected in Algeria, Reinach was beaten in his Dignes district in the first round. *La Libre Parole*, which had wanted to get rid of him for so long, wrote triumphantly: "With Reinach beaten, Jewry is dead; with Drumont elected, France is reborn. Long live France for the French! Long live Algeria! Long live the Republic! Down with the Jews!"[61]

Even then, his misfortunes were not over. After the suicide of Colonel Henry, Drumont started a fund "for the widow of the affair and the orphan of Colonel Henry, against the Jew Reinach."[62] This fund, to which so many generals, *députés*, academicians, and intellectuals contributed kept Reinach center stage. He was the Jew against whom anger was raised by the nationalist camp, the one you could insult by making a small offering. He was the most often targeted, with "929 exhortations to hatred and assassination." "For hanging Reinach"; "Seven francs for the ignoble Orang"; "Give me Reinach's skin"; "Throw Reinach down the sewer"; "Bleed that pig Reinach"; "Skin him alive": These are some of the comments that accompanied the sums of money sent to the Widow Henry. In addition to a very high number of *députés*—often well-known Catholics—both professors of Catholic schools and 350 priests sent small amounts of money to the Widow Henry. For example, the "three French priests from France (Mauriennais) who would like to apply their thirty fingers to the obscene face of the Jew Reinach" (three francs); or "a poor priest, sickened to realize that no bishop in France would send his widow's mite to avenge the French widow and orphan from the insults of the German bandit Reinach" (one franc). While some recalled the drownings of the Chouans in Nantes and called for expeditious methods (for example, vivisection or the application of acid to Reinach's private parts), we find, among the anonymous notes, this premonitory and tragic announcement: "For renting an export wagon." As if, forty years in advance, the intellectual conditions for the tragedy that the Jews under Vichy would experience had already come together, their destiny already sealed in the consciousness of a large portion of their fellow citizens. The prediction was all the more sinister in that certain of the Reinachs would perish as a result of collaboration and Joseph's own nephew Julien Reinach, *conseiller d'Etat*, would actually suffer the fate promised his uncle: imprisoned in Drancy, he was in fact put in an "export wagon" for deportation.

Until the end of the Dreyfus affair and the proclamation of the captain's innocence, hatred was poured relentlessly on Joseph Reinach, who found himself mixed up in numerous incidents that punctuated this interminable procedure. In fact, following the advice of Mathieu Dreyfus, he himself participated as a witness in certain hearings. In spite of everything, he remained faithful to the ideals of 1789 and showed himself an optimist: France could not deny the traditions of the Great Revolution. The *Archives Israélites* underscored his "civic courage":[63] as a convinced patriot, he could only reject the extreme nationalism that identified France with a race or a religion, turning it away from its universalist mission. In 1899, after the Cour de Cassation decided to rehear the Dreyfus trial, Reinach believed his patience had paid off: It was not in vain that he had awaited the triumph of the universalist French tradition over all temptations toward nationalist isolation justified in the name of a particularist identity. Of course, he had been battered by the many base actions directed against him, and his political career was permanently affected: although he regained the confidence of his Digne voters, he was still always distanced from national political life. But, as he now proclaimed,

A cry for freedom in London does not cross the Channel; the same cry in Paris shakes the earth. An iniquity committed in Berlin or Rome frightens a few German or Italian consciences: the same iniquity, if committed in Paris, grieves the universal conscience. Why? Because more than one innocent man has died in the Russian prisons or the Prussian fortresses; we hardly know their names. But Calas and Dreyfus belonged to humanity as a whole.[64]

It was in the name of that moral vision of France that Reinach had proved to be so steadfast in his Dreyfusard convictions: his personal actions as a state Jew had been determined by it, even though these actions elicited certain ambiguities regarding the logic of his own motivations. Hence, for Charles Péguy,

In the Dreyfus affair itself . . . in the general staff of Dreyfusism and of the Dreyfus affair, it is very noteworthy that it was the Jews, the important Jews, who have flagged the least. The example of M. Joseph Reinach is characteristic. We can say that he . . . represented in a certain sense, and even so to say officially, what has been called the Jewish party. In the Dreyfusist political party, he represented, as it were, the Jewish political party. . . . Of all our general staff, he was the only one who did not flag before the Dreyfusist demagogies, before the political demagogies stemming from our Dreyfusist mystique.[65]

Needless to say, Reinach could only enjoy such words, which recognized in him a militant acting in the name solely of moral ideals and not for political reasons: in Péguy's view, therefore, he was the only one for whom the mystique had not degenerated into politics. He had even more merit, we might add, in that he found himself at the heart of the political system and knew all its pitfalls; as the principal state Jew to be totally invested in the drama, it was precisely his sense of the state that may have preserved him from that degeneration. Did he, in fact, act in the name of a "Jewish party," as Péguy inferred? Joseph Reinach would have only challenged such a restriction in the meaning of his actions, since he, like most state Jews, took such care to separate the public space from private happiness, where particularist convictions and values were expressed.

A number of state Jews—from Naquet to Reinach, Raynal to Schrameck, Blum to Mandel, and including so many less famous judges, *préfets*, and *sous-préfets* to whom we shall return—had to confront such calls for murder during the contemporary history of France. The violence that threatened them was equal to the scandal their presence within state institutions represented for the nationalist right. The violence that rose up against Joseph Reinach is only all the more emblematic: its scope, the phantasms on which it rested, the threatening words that were pronounced, in effect anticipating the blacker periods yet to come, also focused attention on this right-hand man to Gambetta, this friend of Jules Ferry and of so many other politicians of the Third Republic. Through the very nature of his commitment, he contributed to weakening that Republic in spite of himself. This paradox was repeated several times: anxious to preserve the revolutionary gains of 1789, state Jews rushed to the aid of the Republic every time it found itself threatened, especially by the extreme right, on the occasion of one or another of the Franco-French wars. The civic courage evidenced by Joseph Reinach, for example, turned against them, to the extent that it involuntarily delegitimated this very Republic in the eyes of all its detractors, who were able to influence a significant portion of public opinion. This better explains the concern by state Jews not to appear to act in the name of some Jewish party, as a function of some Jewish solidarity, but only from the essential values related to universalist citizenship.

After Boulangism and the Dreyfus affair, the Front Populaire also played an important role in the Franco-French war that rent the social fabric through the depth of the anger and resentment it provoked and the scope of the contradictory commitments it elicited. Yet, in this time of real social and cultural change, as in other similar periods, a state Jew was responsible for decision making: Léon Blum was its indisputable inspiration. He was no longer Boulanger's second, as Naquet had been, or even the principal adversary of Drumont and the anti-Dreyfusards, as Reinach had been. For the first time, a state Jew had become head of the government, and this upheaval occurred in a context of profound dissensus, as would also be the case later for Pierre Mendès France. It was a period during which many reform measures in the social order were carried out, finally making possible the integration of the working class into the nation.

Let us emphasize the ambiguity of that situation. When Léon Blum became head of government, he was in many ways prolonging the viewpoint not of Reinach but of Naquet: that is, he was effectively playing the part less of a state Jew attached to law and order like the Opportunists or those who belonged to the great state corps or the judicial apparatus, than that of a socialist or anarchistic Jew, critical of the social hierarchy and of dominant values. In fact, the times were no longer the same: the Republic, more sure of its foundations, was now confronting social questions above all, represented by a working class galvanized by the Bolshevik revolution and by the confrontation strategy set in place by the Communist Party, which demanded total participation in the life of the commonwealth and a redistribution of national wealth. Léon Blum was a state Jew attached to the values of public service and a perfect specialist in administrative law, someone with whom Reinach and state Jews could identify. But state Jews had never understood the working class, judging severely strikes and condemning outright any socialist vision of questions they wished to settle through a solidarist policy close to philanthropy; Léon Blum, in contrast, appeared as a state Jew identified with Jean Jaurès, at a time when the Bolshevik solution was imposing brutal choices within a context of the rise of fascisms in Europe. Thus, everything threatened to become even more dramatic than before. On the extreme right, Action Française and the leagues were still honing their weapons and training their militants in putschist strategies. They were no longer alone since beside them—and sometimes with them—fascism was advancing with its groups financed by Nazi Germany. On the extreme left, the anarchists and radicals had given way to the communists, organized into a centralized party depending on the Soviet Union. In the extremism of values and ideologies, Boulanger's or Dreyfus's France had seemed on the brink of civil war: at present, the breaks were already there, and under their impact the Republic itself seemed almost obsolete. For both groups, the conception of a universalist republican citizenship was really no longer current.

Although a socialist convinced of the urgent necessity of remedying the injustice of social relations, Léon Blum was closer to Reinach than to

Naquet in his relation to Jewry, since he also found himself part of networks of particularist sociability. He was faithful to a Jewish culture and milieu. Like Naquet, he spoke about Judaism before stunned deputies, but he did so in a completely different way, since he claimed his Judaism independent of any antisemitism. In the Chamber of Deputies, he declared in January 1923: "I am Jewish. . . . That is a fact. It is no insult to me to be reminded that I belong to the Jewish race, a race I have never denied, and toward which I feel only gratitude and pride."[66] Like the Reinachs, who had been through republican school and graduate school exams, he had become the very essence of the state Jew through the École Normale Supérieure and the Conseil d'Etat. And, like Reinach, he was at the very heart of the political system, with socialism simply replacing in his mind the Opportunist government of an earlier time. Furthermore, instead of building political majorities, he activated and led them, remaining faithful to his milieu of origin without it interfering with his public activity. In that sense, at a time when that balance was becoming rare, he, like Joseph Reinach, incarnated the state Jew in harmony with Franco-Judaism: "I was born in France," he said, "I was brought up in French schools. My friends were French. . . . I have the right to consider myself perfectly assimilated. . . . And yet, I have no less the feeling of being Jewish. And never have I noticed, between these two phases of my consciousness, the slightest contradiction, the slightest opposition."[67] Between Naquet and Reinach, between contesting and remaining faithful to a Republic that respected law and order, but also between universalism and particularism: Blum found himself at the crossroads of all these contradictions. Having reached the summit of the state, incarnating the legitimate power that France as a whole had bestowed upon itself, he would be rapidly drawn into the uninterrupted flood of slander. From this perspective, let us once more underline the presence of a state Jew at this instant when the clash between the two Frances had reached its paroxysm, accentuating the contradictions and multiplying the uncertainties.

Even while there were rumblings of intolerance from every corner, he did not hesitate to assert, in his famous Luna Park speech of 6 September 1936: "I am a Frenchman who is proud of his country, proud of his history, nourished as much as anyone else on its tradition despite my race."[68] While Naquet and Reinach, despite their deep divergences, both fought the Zionist movement, Blum relentlessly lent it his fraternal and open aid. On this point, he was close to Bernard Lazare, during at least a certain period of his life, sharing with that anarchistic intellectual, who was in no way a state Jew, his interest in a movement[69] that many state Jews could only reject absolutely, tied as they were body and soul to the meritocratic republican state.

But, in wishing to take on all these dimensions of his being, Blum exposed himself even more than Alfred Naquet or Joseph Reinach to an antisemitic hatred that was all the more boundless in that this time it was targeting the head of the government, the man who, through the popular will and universal suffrage, led a society that some considered ever more estranged from its identity, which had been properly fashioned by Catholicism. As we know, Naquet, Reinach, and most Jewish *députés* and senators had already run up against this sort of argument, which posed the problem of national representation in different terms. But, as head of government, Léon Blum was the only one to provoke a reactionary rejection that even Drumont in his most optimistic days could not have foreseen. Let us give a small sampling.[70] As was often the case, Pierre Gaxotte particularly distinguished himself in this matter: in a text entitled "L'homme maudit" (The cursed man), which is still striking for its virulence, he declared:

First, he is ugly. On the body of a disjointed puppet, he carries about the sorry head of a Palestinian mare. . . . How he hates us! He begrudges us for everything and for nothing at all, for the fact that our sky is blue, that our air is caressing, he begrudges the peasants for walking in wooden shoes, the French soil for not having had camel-driving ancestors wandering in the Syrian desert with his pals from Palestine. . . . Socialism reigns like those nomads of old, who swarmed into the southern Algerian oases, plundering the sedentary and, gorged, left again for other raids. . . . We must choose between France and the cursed man. He incarnates everything that revolts our blood and flesh. He is evil itself. He is death.[71]

Eternal France could only break with a Franco-Judaism "degenerating" into socialism: its land, its soul, its blood rejected a socialist Blum even more perhaps than a Gambettist Reinach.

Let us return to a particularly symbolic moment in this rejection. On Saturday 6 June, in the parliamentary debate that followed the swearing in, Xavier Vallat, a new version of Drumont and Maurras combined, took the floor: "Your arrival, M. President, is indisputably a historic date. For the first time, this old Gallo-Roman country will be governed . . . by a Jew. . . . I say that to govern this peasant nation of France, it is better to have someone whose origins, however modest, disappear into the bowels of our soil, rather than a subtle Talmudist."[72] Before the assembled representatives of the nation, it was, in fact, the ultimate consequences of the emancipation of 1791 that were being disputed: Barrès-style nationalism, hungry for rootedness, reached its paroxysm, proclaiming the urgency of another theory of representation and citizenship. The direct heirs to Drumont—some of whom had collaborated on *La Libre Parole* with the master—joyfully returned to service. Endowed with exceptional longevity, they simply replaced Reinach with Blum in their antisemitic tirades. The leading lights of the radical right such as Maurras and Léon Daudet—who, in the past, at the turn of the century, were already directing their attacks against Joseph Reinach—cheerfully changed targets and now attacked "Blum-Karfunkelstein," the foreigner who imposed his law on the French while violating their Catholic identity. Let us simply quote this little passage by Maurras, which deserves to appear in all the anthologies:

For forty years, a hundred times, we have described the life course of the little Carpathian, Balkan, or Rhineland Jew, who arrived in the Saint-Antoine neighborhood like a filthy Levite, making his living from second-hand clothing, then from speculation, and finally, shaved, washed, togged out, even a little bilingual by now, adding to his natural Yiddish something resembling French: he sent his boy to high school, through law school, and then pushed him to the Palais with the help of all the little Jews, into administration and then politics, and the boy became a candidate in various elections, finally ending up in the Chamber, the Senate, the *présidence du Conseil*. . . . That is the story of Léon Blum.[73]

This text could have been taken from *La France juive*: that is the extent to which it borrows the same vocabulary and a similar logic. The denunciation of socialist state Jews replaced the systematic enumeration of Gambettist state Jews: in each case, there was a condemnation—explicitly in the case of Drumont, who accepted the Republic, and Maurras, who fought against it—of the "Jewish Republic," the "state within the state" whose power was exaggerated endlessly. Just as Drumont had infinitely exaggerated the number of state Jews under Gambetta and Jules Ferry and their place in the high administration in order to justify his thesis of a plot and of "Jewish conquest," in the 1930s, day after day the press published long fantastical lists. Louis-Ferdinand Céline proclaimed, as had Drumont, his rejection of the "Blum occupation" and declared he was ready to make instead "an alliance with Hitler." Marcel Jouhandeau rejected with horror "Blum and all his Jewish hangers-on in power. Léon Blum is the true successor to Louis XVI. That is what the Revolution did for Israel."[74] The Barruel-style counterrevolutionary thesis, strengthened by de Mun, Barrès, Maurras, and Drumont, bore fruit: for them, the Franco-French wars and the division of the French would end with the ever so disgraceful "Jewish Republic" founded by 1789 and institutionalized by Gambetta's men.

As at the time of the Dreyfus affair, the usual imagery was used; caricatures that were identical in every detail to those depicting Naquet and Reinach now presented Léon Blum, Jules Moch, and Pierre Mendès France to the public as Semites, foreigners, extremely effeminate, often endowed with animal attributes, and oversexed neurotics. As had been the case with David Raynal, Camille Dreyfus, Alfred Naquet, and Joseph Reinach, under the expert pen of Charles Maurras, Henri Béraud, Henri Massis, and so many others, the eternal fear of castration was revived with the coming to power of "Blum-Flower, baptized with pruning shears."[75] Like their Gambettist predecessors, Léon Blum and Jules Moch were also perceived as foreigners linked to the cosmopolitan capital, but also as revolutionaries destroying French and Christian mores. Like Naquet and, even more, like Reinach, Blum and the state Jews linked to the Front Populaire very often ran up against threatening crowds who yelled out the traditional "Death to the Jews!" The France of the Henry Monument exulted and let loose. Léon Blum would finally be "exported" to Germany, to the great satisfaction of all those still alive who had been frustrated to see Joseph Reinach die in his bed when they had wished a similar destiny for him.

CHAPTER TEN

Maintaining Order:
From the Fourmies Shooting to the
Ambush on Rue Hermel

The first of May 1891 was a fateful day that would long remain engraved in the memories of French workers. At a time of joy and celebration, blood flowed. Army troops fired and the brand-new Lebel rifles[1] spat out their hail of bullets on the impatient and hostile working-class crowd. The use of force answered the stones and various projectiles that were wounding soldiers and their officers. There were nine dead, including two children and four young women. A young flag-bearer's innocent companion, Maria Blondeau, collapsed, mortally wounded, still holding in her hand the hawthorn branch given her by her fiancé. The priest Margerin rushed to the side of the dying. Everything was about to topple, the government was being challenged, and the press — Catholic, Boulangist, and socialist — lashed out at a money-grubbing Republic accused of murdering with impunity the children of a working class that had been struck full force by the local economic crisis. Emotions were running high, and the leaders of the workers, including Lafargue, the son-in-law of Karl Marx, were arrested and imprisoned. The elderly Engels, Marx's longtime companion, followed the affair with attention and exchanged numerous letters with Lafargue: he helped defray Lafargue's legal expenses (at his trial Lafargue was defended by Millerand). The Guesdists mobilized the workers. All of France followed the events with great anxiety, all the more so since, when a legislative seat opened unexpectedly at the local level, Lafargue was elected and came triumphantly to take his place in the Chamber. In the language of the time, Lafargue led a campaign hostile to the "bourgeois Republic": "It's up to you," he proclaimed to his voters, "to say if the Republic of the Union Générale, of Panama and other Rothschildian economic crashes is the Republic of our dreams." He also attacked the Church, which he believed had been won over by the work bosses' arguments. In that way, he was already pointing out the importance of that cultural variable in the region.[2] All the ingredients were present to transform this affair into a highly symbolic moment of class confrontation that would gravely affect the legitimacy of the Republic. That republic, we must recognize, had done very little to facilitate the integration of the working class. As Paul Leroy-Beaulieu noted, "We consider this election a capital act, perhaps the most important act that has occurred in France since 1871. With M. Lafargue, the son-in-law of Karl Marx, collectivism is entering Parliament."[3]

If Fourmies immediately took shape as an important moment in the Third Republic, it was because the context and the place lent themselves admirably to dramatization at its most extreme: the first social "slip-up" of the Republic took place within a very particular setting. The department of Nord, a region where traditional Catholicism was very much alive,[4] was also one of the areas where the Guesdists had made major inroads, since the textile workers, who had particularly harsh working conditions, willingly turned to the intransigent revolutionary party that was leading strikes and often forceful actions. The historical context was itself altogether unique: for the last six months, the question had been raised whether the Church would join the Republic, an issue decisive for the Republic's future. Most bishops, who rejected such a development, passionately denounced the "anti-Christian sects"; in Nord, the rebels took a very extreme position and refused to reach a compromise with republican institutions. Three years earlier in that same region, Boulanger had twice been triumphantly reelected.[5] In other words, the positions of both sides were so rigid and antagonistic that, at the slightest spark, anything could happen.

Yet history might not have remembered that dramatic event (there were others that were comparable in various worker localities) had not another ingredient been added to give it an almost mythic dimension. As in most of the Franco-French wars, the presence of a Jewish participant played a central role and suddenly radicalized the behavior of all, plunging it into the irrational, the phantasmagoric. *Sous-préfet* Isaac was on the scene, representing the highest administrative authority responsible for maintaining public order; this young Jew born in Algeria became everyone's target. Without losing a moment's time, Drumont rushed in, took advantage of this stroke of luck, conducted his own inquiry, and inevitably found what he was looking for to nourish his antisemitic gall. From then on, the die was cast and everyone had a predetermined role to play. The sociopolitical reality was theatricalized, its character distorted to illustrate concretely the "truths" proffered five years earlier in *La France juive*. To this day,[6] everyone has fallen into the trap set by Drumont's delirium.

Let us consider the affair from the beginning. We can start by evoking the protagonists in this drama, which historians have neglected.[7] Who, then, was this *sous-préfet* Isaac, who, three years before Captain Dreyfus, plunged France into a moment of madness that, however, did not degenerate into a true Franco-French war because the issues were so confused? Charles Ferdinand Isaac was born 22 September 1860 in Constantine, Algeria; his father was a successful businessman and a devoted and militant republican. At the height of the controversy, a man banished in 1851 after the coup d'etat insisted on taking his defense, recalling that in 1852 the elder Isaac had been secretary of the committee that formed in Constantine to come to the aid of the exiles: "More than one of those who risked escape owed a debt to him for being able to continue on his way."[8] The young Isaac did his military service in the artillery, occupied his first post in the administrative office of the governor of Cochinchine, was then named *chef du cabinet* to the *préfet* of Dordogne, and then, in 1887, *sous-préfet* of Puget-Théniers. In 1889, he took a post in Avesnes, to which the city of Fourmies belonged. The administrative reports portray him as a man with a "firm character," "fine, very considered judgment"; "very sagacious and practical." There was nothing irascible, warmongering, or belligerent about him; as the *préfet* of Dordogne put it, "He will later be a candidate for the high posts in the administration." In his 1886 administrative report, we also find the following observation: "M. Isaac will be a good *sous-préfet* on whom the republican government can always count; we could entrust a *préfecture* in a reactionary department to him, he would certainly succeed there."[9] His destiny may have been sealed in this judgment, which recognizes Isaac's full devotion to the Republic and his aptitude for confronting the most hardened enemy. In Fourmies, where his fate awaited him, there reigned one of the most reactionary groups of work bosses; wishing to do battle with the working class, it had adopted the most openly provocative attitudes. *Sous-préfet* Isaac was committed to strengthening the Republic through numerous visits to mayors, and attempted to limit the influence of Boulangism, which, in his own words, had "strong attachments" in certain parts of the district. In a report to the *préfet* in July 1889, however, he claimed he had also noted "that a true anti-Boulangist current has established itself."[10]

In 1888, while he was *sous-préfet* in Puget-Théniers (Alpes-Maritimes), his superior noted in his administrative report: "M. Isaac is a Jew, an Algerian; there will be reason to take these circumstances into account in the choice of the post that may be assigned to him." A little later, in November 1890, a few months before the Fourmies affair, his superior, the *préfet* Vel-Durand, added one last element: "His religion," he wrote, "is in itself an obstacle to his being sent into a clerical Catholic department like Nord." And he observed lucidly: "He is too young in age and character for a district where those he must deal with are, if not aged men, at least very serious leaders of major industries, having at times, and justifiably, a high opinion of their situation."[11] Thus, the *sous-préfet* was in an impossible situation from the beginning: a republican Jew, he was thrown into the middle of a violent class conflict, charged with maintaining order just when an employer-oriented and clerical bourgeoisie, fundamentally reactionary, was seeking to use the conflict to advance its own interests. His position was the one wished for by the *préfet* of Dordogne: he was certainly at the heart of a reactionary and even clerical region. But, in opposition to all the optimistic predictions, he was simply incapable of mastering the situation, which he nevertheless did everything to defuse.

The activities scheduled for 1 May 1891 were to culminate in a popular ball to close a day of strikes. The meticulous report of Sûreté Générale tells us in detail the tragic history of that city in Nord, where workers represented more than 75 percent of the population; industrial concentration was high; and the principal activity, weaving, had recently experienced a grave crisis that compromised worker solidarity. Salaries were falling, the unions were weakly organized: the presence of Guesdist militants, including Paul Lafargue—who delivered speeches in the region and in particular led a meeting in Fourmies on 12 April—channeled agitation against the "industrial vampires" and the Church. According to Marx's son-in-law, a new 1789 of the workers was about to erupt, and May Day was to mark the workers' resolution to reject any form of paternalism. The Boulangist militants were also present, seeking to use any sign of discontent toward the Republic. The Sûreté Générale report describes better than any sociological work the narrow circles of sociability connecting the people and recounts in great detail the songs of the workers, their walks in the woods, and the dances planned for the evening. In the region, May Day also corresponded "to the Feast of Flowers that each year provides the pretext for popular festivities."[12]

On the other side, the mayor and *conseillers municipaux* were almost all hostile to the presence of any union; to provoke the workers, they decided to prohibit the day off from work on May Day. Thus, the workers came together singing protest songs: "We need war, we need blood, oh, oh, oh"; they had devoured the incendiary articles from *L'Intransigeant* and *Père Peinard*. *Sous-préfet* Isaac, who was there with the *procureur de la République*, wanted the cavalry to come rather than infantry troops, whose excesses he feared. He tried to attend to the most urgent matters first, but did not succeed in avoiding the drama that unfolded while he was meeting with the mayor in his office. According to the *préfet*, things were clear: one might reproach him for "an error of inattention. Would another have been able to do any better? I am not sure of that." Stones were flying, the forces of law and order charged and took prisoners, whom the workers tried to rescue. Suddenly, the troop commander, wounded by a stone, fell, calling on his men to fire. On the day of the victims' funeral, the population showed its support for the *sous-préfet*; for them, "the principal accused is the mayor, whom we criticize for calling in the troops."

Thus, everything was clear enough; and yet, it was *sous-préfet* Isaac who would be singled out for popular condemnation: demonized to an absurd degree, he served as a true scapegoat in a Catholic region where anti-semitism was common. Two years before the shooting, Isaac's predecessor, Georges Mossé, had been the object of antisemitic slander: anonymous letters from Fourmies denounced "one of the circumcised" from the *sous-préfecture* of Avesnes.[13] In the same vein, on 2 May 1891, *Le Courrier de l'Est* (Courier of the east) jumped at the opportunity and called for "vengeance for the martyrs of Fourmies," who had been murdered on the orders of "one of the circumcised."[14] The stage was now set to make Drumont's task easy: "Perhaps Isaac simply wanted to celebrate the centennial of the Jews' emancipation in 1791 in his own way. Certain newspapers, with no sense of shame, had the nerve to recall it as a glorious date."[15] The man who consistently saw the Revolution and the installation of the Third Republic as a Jewish plot handily connected these events by endlessly suggesting that the Jews were the real beneficiaries of a social upheaval that had allowed them to ensure their domination first over the Jacobin populace and then over the working populace, by force of arms if need be. According to Drumont, the people were innocent, as were the bourgeoisie, and a fortiori the army; no one — except the Jews — wanted confrontation or class war. The author of *La France juive*, a veritable Bible for provincial priests — who, as we know, avidly read the inflammatory book — contrasted to his heart's content the murderous and Jewish *sous-préfet* and the priest who had come to help the dying. *La Croix* also staged this confrontation between the Jewish *sous-préfet* and the "heroic priest who gave absolution in extremis; the workers who no longer had heaven as their horizon and who asked to take their pleasures immediately were answered with bullets. The soldiers would never have had to point their rifles at the people if the people had not been alienated from the priest for a long time."[16] A legend was created, giving the best role to the priest, who was supposed to have courageously exposed himself to rifle bullets. This was sheer fabrication, since the priest did not arrive on the scene until the shooting was over.

The separation of Church and state, the secularization of society, Gambetta's struggle against clericalism — to which, as we have seen, the Protestants and Jews were linked in a phantasmic way — were presented as the true causes of the Fourmies shooting ordered by a Jew. The mayor and *conseillers municipaux*, all Catholics, who knowingly provoked this massacre for socioeconomic reasons, were thus largely absent from this new Last Supper, where the innocent people appeared as the eternally betrayed victim. For *La Croix*, Isaac represented the anti-Margerin, the freethinker who, following the policy of secularizing the regime and pushing its excesses to the extreme, remained forever distanced from the properly Catholic values of French society. According to the daily paper,

The Jew has the hatred, the suppleness, the hypocrisy, and the tenacious perseverance to go straight for the goal. A mere freethinker often has a devout wife, a pull from his Christian education, friendships, relatives he dares not cross, Catholic parents he holds in affection, or uncles with an inheritance whom he must not upset. The Jew has none of all that. He is the master.[17]

Nothing could hold him back, for he remained entirely outside simple French sociability, which, whether he liked it or not, was shaped by properly Catholic values and cooperative relationships.

Drumont stopped at nothing in feeding hatred and awakening fear; in his depiction, Maria Blondeau became the heroine of popular and Christian France, pitilessly brutalized by the Jews. He attracted his readers' attention to the fate of her blond and pure hair: "Legend claims," he wrote in a text of unbridled imagination, "that her hair was stolen and sold; it probably went to adorn the bald head of some old Jewish baroness, and some ruined gentleman, playing the comedy of love to the woman so that the husband would lend him money, perhaps covered the blonde remains of the murdered worker with kisses in some boudoir in the Monceau quarter."[18] He also hastened to include *sous-préfet* Isaac on the list of members of the prefect civil service whose presence within the state he relentlessly denounced: Isaac thus joined Hendlé, Levaillant, and Cohn, Drumont's favorite whipping boys, and was transformed into an active instrument of the "Jewish Republic." Truncating Isaac's career to demonstrate more easily the favoritism reigning in the state to the advantage of Jews alone, Drumont went after the young "twenty-five-year old *préfet*" even though, after almost ten years of service, Isaac was thirty-one. It is clear, added the hack writer, that "from such functionaries as Isaac, recruited in degenerate families, sons of Jews who are recently naturalized citizens, strangers to all the ideas that inspired the French of old, we cannot require a cool head, courage. . . . The Jew, who has become our master by making Frenchmen fight among themselves, will one day see all Frenchmen reconciled over his dead body."[19] To justify his thesis, Drumont presented an idyllic image of

Fourmies, where a "true cordiality" reigned between employers and workers: think of it, "bosses and workers playing bowls together on Sunday, sharing a friendly beer. . . . In Fourmies, the bosses were at work at five o'clock in the morning, and their existence differed little from that of their workers. . . . Christian feelings, so hardy in Nord, had long been maintained among the honest population of Fourmies." The mayor, "a child of the region," managed his city "in a leisurely way, as everything is done in Fourmies."[20] This veritable paradise of a France of old miraculously preserved from capitalism, where human relations gave off the sweet aroma of friendship, this Christian region sheltered from Panama-type scandals and practices of forced secularization imposed by a brutal and anticlerical Republic, remained an island of conviviality: the arrival of the Jew set off the storm. Social conflict, socialist agitation, threats of strike, the prohibition of a day off from work on May Day, all that was not very serious, and Frenchmen could always settle things among themselves: "There was little malice in all that, and, if there had not been a Jew there to organize from the shadows the murder of Frenchmen by Frenchmen, it would have been limited to a few scuffles."

Drumont then launched into an astonishing purple passage that set the good and the just face to face with the criminal concerned with his own interests: the priest and the Jew. The priest went to the aid of the workers, took care of everything, carried the victims into his modest presbytery, rang the bells in honor of the murdered martyrs; the Jew showed himself indifferent, cold, pitiless in his repression. The "antithesis of Fourmies" would become famous:

The one who ordered shots fired against the workers was the Jew who ought to have thanked the people for having founded this Republic at the cost of so many sacrifices, which the Jew exploits in every manner possible. The man who rushed through the bullets to lift up and bless the workers fired upon on the Jew's orders was the poor priest toward whom the people, deceived by ghetto newspapers, were so often unjust in these last few years.[21]

The priest Margerin, congratulated by the pope, would acquire enormous fame, even though his real role, according to police reports, seems to have been quite modest. The martyrdom of these supposed Catholics, the workers of Fourmies, allowed Drumont to sketch out the French-style national socialism theorized later by Maurice Barrès. Within its framework, Catholic workers and bosses would come together through the land and form a solid community, rejecting capitalism and the secular Republic, the two instruments that Jews used to impose their power on the French as a whole. In this department of Nord, where, as Drumont drummed it in, "the population has remained almost entirely Catholic," the presence of a Jewish administrator was presented as a real provocation: "How feeble and flabby Christians must be to bear such an ignominious yoke, to admit this downfall!" "How did it happen," he asked, "that a Hebrew on one day in May made poor baptized living souls disappear from the world, souls for whom the sun seemed sweet to behold?"[22]

Against all historical evidence, Drumont, as he often did, constructed an exemplary fable that, beginning from an authentic fact — the presence of a Jewish *sous-préfet* — completely transfigured and biased the account, plastering over the socialist will of the workers, the Boulangist agitation, the repressive character of an employer system attached to its privileges, the decisive role of the mayor (himself a work boss), the call for troops who were prompt to fire, and the responsibility of Major Chapus who ordered his men to shoot. Nineteenth-century France, with its long tradition of anti-worker repression, disappeared from the tale; the significance of the Franco-French wars was overturned. The demonization of the Jewish functionary charged with public order was to have great success and would even influence a part of the socialist press, which was always ready to adhere to the myth of great Jewish exploiters using the state as an instrument for maintaining order. The antisemitism proper to the socialist tradition from Proudhon to Toussenel resurfaced; later, it would lead to a solid anti-Dreyfusism that was not devoid of all antisemitism. Reductionist and schematic Guesde-type Marxism, whose militants were present in the field, sometimes leaned in the same direction.

The Fourmies affair was thus also situated within a tense national context where capitalism and socialism, secularism and Catholicism, were going head-to-head. Naturally, Drumont sent a telegram to Albert de Mun, the leader of intransigent Catholicism, who would attempt a Catholic reconquest of the working class: "The *sous-préfet* Isaac, one of those naturalized by Crémieux," he wrote, "tried out the Lebel on French workers. Those who love you still hope that you will pronounce the words of vengeance that will do away with the murderer. The *préfet* Veil-Durand is also Jewish; they are all Jewish out there." As always, Drumont was being approximate at best and shaped the facts to fit his thesis. On the one hand, the *préfet* Vel-Durand, whose name was intentionally deformed by Drumont, was not Jewish.[23] On the other, although Isaac had been born in Algeria, he did not owe his nationality to the infamous Crémieux decree; that decree, which conferred French nationality on Algerian Jews, regularly provoked the anger of the antisemitic journalist, who used it handily on this occasion. He then had an easy time developing his redoubtable logic by establishing a perfect continuity between 1789, the Third Republic, the role of Adolphe Crémieux at Gambetta's side, Fourmies, and soon, the Dreyfus affair. The reality, however, was entirely different: although he was born in Algeria, Isaac was of Lorrainian origin! Underscoring this fact, the *Archives Israélites* established Drumont's bad faith:

We do not have to defend here the *sous-préfet* of Avesnes, who seems to have become the scapegoat for the sins of the administration and whom M. Constans threw overboard with an offhandedness that provoked this fine rejoinder on the part of a deputy: it was *the sacrifice of Isaac*. . . . One sees only the Jew Isaac and not at all the mayor, who is a perfect Christian. . . . It is fortunate that the commander who ordered gunfire was not a Jew.[24]

Albert de Mun, to whom Drumont sent his plea, had not yet officially declared his intention to join the Republic, and he incarnated the resistance of a Catholic France hostile both to the Republic and to capitalism. Along with La Tour du Pin, he would attempt to set backfires in the associative structures in order to reconquer the working class. The Fourmies shooting was no doubt the only time Drumont and de Mun found themselves close to each other, when a conservative and monarchist right fused with a radical right that intended to commit itself resolutely in the construction of an aggressive nationalism intent on reshaping French identity. For the space of an instant, these two forces came together to denounce the Republic and capitalism, which was also perceived as Jewish. Since the two forces shared the vision of a world founded on the idea of a plot, expressed for the first time by Abbé Barruel at the beginning of the nineteenth century, they could easily agree on a strategy aimed at bringing down the disgraced Republic. All the more so since, in Fourmies itself, as if on purpose, the priest Margerin was at the same time secretary of the mixed union of corporatist inspiration, set in place, in conformity with the social philosophy of De Mun and La Tour du Pin, to unite once more social classes that had been artificially divided.

Once more, *sous-préfet* Isaac was at the center of a drama that to a great extent went beyond him. De Mun appealed to the government and supported the creation of an investigating commission in the Chamber to identify those responsible for the tragedy. For him, of course, "the army is exonerated." It was therefore necessary to turn to the administrative authorities who alone were capable of accounting for the conduct of a state that had wrongly named so many Protestants and Jews to positions of responsibility (as he so often put it in his writings). In such a tense context, even though he continually challenged the minister of the interior by shouting, "What about the *sous-préfet?*" he did not make any allusion to Isaac's Jewish origins. Neither he nor any other interlocutor, in fact, made any remarks of an antisemitic nature, even though outside the Chamber Drumont and Rochefort were exciting passions. Everyone, on the left and on the right, wished to absolve the army in advance, and Constans, the minister of the interior, firmly defended his subordinate, underscoring the fact that the *sous-préfet* "was on the site at the same time as the honorable priest of Fourmies — he must therefore not be accused."[25] After long debates, a majority took shape against the creation of an investigating commission. Among those who voted against that initiative were Poincaré, Deschanel, Henri Brisson, and Léon Bourgeois, as well as Joseph Reinach. This defeat raised Drumont's ire and he renewed his campaign against Isaac, who under those conditions could hardly escape dismissal. Even though the local population supported him and a few republican deputies of the region publicly proclaimed his innocence and highlighted his merits, it was no use.

Fourmies, forgotten by theorists of the Franco-French wars, deserves in every way to figure in that representation of the moments of break in national unity. The constant traits that recurred from one era to another reappeared at the time of that dramatic event, and the antisemitism it reignited left a long-lasting mark on national consciousness generally as well as on working-class consciousness in particular. Let us give a few more examples, among dozens that exist, of the hatred expressed on that occasion. For *Le Constitutionnel*,

Once more, we have noted the base and ferocious hatred that animates the sons of Jews against Christian workers; once more, we have seen the cruel greed of the goats of Israel and the barbarous fear of the rich Semites before the starving masses. . . . Then, before the savage yid, the door of the presbytery opened, and three priests emerged. But the shooting continued; the view of the priests of the Man his forefathers had crucified exasperated the descendant of Iscariot, and terrible bullets went through the bellies of poor little girls, crushed the jaws of their mothers, and shattered the members of boys who had barely reached adolescence. . . . Jewry defends money over poverty to spite Catholicism; one of the circumcised has murdered workers to defend capital at the price of their distress, scorning the supplications of the Christian priests! . . . The sinister victory of the Jews over our race and our religion has been finally elucidated; the dogs lying about in the Ghetto have in turn put the collar of servitude around our necks.

In *Le Courrier du Pas-de-Calais*, the focus was on the role of "a certain Isaac, a pure-blooded Jew"; along with the *préfet* Vel-Durand, "they appear as two great sacrificers to the ancient law." *La Vendée* accused "the Jewish *préfet* Vel-Durant" of having had his orders carried out by "another Jew, a nigger Jew, the *sous-préfet* Isaac"; *Le Combat Périgourdin* placed the emphasis "on the few 'liddle' services" rendered by "the filthy Jew Isaac" to explain his career.[26]

A caricature published in *Le Lillois* deserves to be presented in detail:

Our engraving represents the sacrifice of Isaac. Raising his arm with a gesture full of majesty, Abraham-Constans, tears in his eyes, brandishes the fatal knife over the head of the young Isaac, his little *sous-préfet* from Avesnes. The sacrifice will be carried out, the god of the day, public opinion, indignant about the scandalous conduct of this Jew in Fourmies, demands a victim, and nothing can delay any longer that inevitable sacrifice. But then an angel (of darkness), Jewry, rises up and cries to Abraham-Constans: "Stop! Stop! Do not lower your sacrilegious arm on one of our own!" In saying this, with one hand the angel seizes the arm ready to strike and with the other slips a sack full of coins into the minister's left hand. What can be done? Greed counsels clemency; but fear is stronger, fear prevents him from seeing the sparkle of gold; and, remorseful, lost, he strikes a fatal blow: Isaac is no longer *sous-préfet*.[27]

This text is emblematic of the Drumont period, when traditional anti-semitism found in money the sole explanation for why (and how) Jews went into government. This was the Rothschild myth in all its power: gold attracted the greedy minister of the interior and incited him not to sacrifice Isaac. Constans had not hesitated to take his distance from his *sous-préfet* out of administrative solidarity, but out of the lure of gain. And if Constans dismissed Isaac anyway, it was simply because the indignant people demanded it.

The *sous-préfet* Isaac thus became a permanent part of the legend of the extreme right, but also of a large part of the radical left: all the more so since, there again, things were to end in a duel that never actually took place. From London where he had taken refuge, Rochefort had insulted Isaac's father, and the younger Isaac demanded satisfaction: the sword was selected as the weapon, the seconds were chosen, a place and time fixed, but the presence of the police finally ended this battle, part of a solid tradition since the radical rights' frequent attacks on the Jews. The national and local press related in detail various aspects of this aborted duel: for *L'Autorité* (The authority), for example, "the Jew Isaac was trying to rehabilitate himself. . . . He should have risked his life in Fourmies. The blood he might have spilled on the ground could not efface the blood that was spilled through his criminal negligence. There is no pardon possible."[28] Subsequently, Isaac confronted Philippe Dubois, editor of *L'Intransigeant*, and this time the duel was quite real; it took place on the outskirts of Paris and was within an inch of ending tragically before the doctors put an end to it. According to the *Archives Israélites*,

After two duels in less than a month, M. Isaac will no longer have to worry about the attacks of professional antisemites. . . . With the current polemical proceedings, our coreligionists are morally forced to prove, with sword in hand, that their personal honor is as heartfelt to them as it is to the most violent of their detractors. Blood washes away the offense of the private citizen: for the functionary, the court of law is there, with equality and justice for all.[29]

Everything was coming together in an extreme theatricalization of the Fourmies affair, projecting the young *sous-préfet*, who couldn't do anything about it, to the epicenter of the crisis. The figure of Isaac would remain fresh in the memories of various factions of the extreme right: in 1936, for example, when France went through the conflicts of the Front Populaire, Léon Daudet was still evoking the famous shooting: "The name of the Jewish *sous-préfet* Isaac was mixed up in the affair. My father told the author of *La France juive*: 'Every time you lift up a rock, there is one or several circumcised bugs underneath.' The line became famous."[30]

The Fourmies tragedy was clearly rooted in myth. As in a fairy tale that ends too neatly, every detail reinforced the phantasmagoric dimension of the event: the *sous-préfet* was Jewish and born in Algeria; the priest Margerin displayed social concern; Maria Blondeau was an innocent fiancée cut down while holding her hawthorn spray in her hand; and the only soldier, according to the legend, who refused to fire was named . . . Lebon (The good). In contrast, in some antisemitic caricatures, the Devil appeared as Isaac's inspiration and savior. To crown it all, Lafargue — the revolutionary and internationalist theorist, son-in-law of the Jew Marx, who was actively militating at the site — was himself Creole! History will probably never again succeed in bringing together in a single place dominated by a profoundly Catholic bourgeoisie, so many marked actors, actors who were fixed in roles already cut out for them.

In reality, Isaac, the convinced republican, the administrator with qualifications constantly underscored by his superiors, did everything to prevent the spilling of blood: as the report of 15 June 1891 sent by the *procureur* of Douai to the *garde des Sceaux* confirms, the use of force had been justified by the "insurrectional" nature of a situation, which had already attracted the attention of this same public prosecutor, who had emphasized in April "the workers' turmoil in Fourmies." According to the magistrate, the *sous-préfet* was in no way responsible, and, in Fourmies, the population did not direct any of its anger toward him.[31] His status as a Jew nevertheless made him the ideal object, transforming a banal class confrontation into a true legend of the fortunes good and bad of Catholic France. Francisque Sarcey underscored how,

> during the entire day of 1 May, Isaac did his duty as *sous-préfet*. . . . An entire party and a very restless one, the clerical party, had a keen interest in showing that a priest had demonstrated the most heroic devotion. Isaac's misfortune was that he disappeared behind the shadow of a cassock. To elevate the glory of the Lord's anointed, they had to put down the Republic. The religious leaflets did not fail to do so. . . . The revolutionaries, glad to explain the adventure at the expense of the ministry, joined with the Catholic newspapers.

As an anonymous republican deputy noted in the *Courrier de l'Ain*, "We may have been too hasty in making the priest of Fourmies into a hero. . . . It's a pretty little morsel to tell children in catechism for their edification. At the same time, we chose a scapegoat that we charged with all the sins of

Israel, all the more easily since he happened in fact to be a Jew."[32] This explains how Drumont's worst fabrications could so easily spread throughout France: even in the faraway *Réveil du Var*, it was maintained without batting an eye that Isaac had ordered the shooting in order to try out the Lebel rifle so as to be able to communicate the results of his observations to the Prussians! The *Marseillaise fourmisienne* expresses this theme much more lyrically:

> Onward, prisoners of the mill,
> The first of May we'll celebrate.
> Finally tired of all travail
> Rise up to demonstrate.
>
> Cain in his most hateful wrath
> Has produced a great bloodbath.
> He turned the soldiers on poor Abel
> To test the mighty Lebel.

Another song, *Les martyres de Fourmies*, shaped the "ballad" this way:

> In floods the blood reddened the earth.
> But good fortune shone, for soon
> From the presbytery
> Came the good priest, crucifix in hand.
> Mercy! There have been enough victims!
> Cried out the trembling priest.
> Striking your brother is a great sin
> Put down your arms, my children.
>
> Frenchmen, we are all brothers
> Let us learn to love one another,
> Let us save the deadly lead
> To protect our sacred borders.
> When the sons of Germania
> Sneak over like wolves
> To threaten Champagne
> Then we will have our revenge.[33]

These were simply so many *Marseillaises* turned on their heads and reversed in their meaning, quite certainly inspired by the community-based nationalism of Drumont, who was seeking to deflect 1789 away from its universal dimension to finally make the Revolution truly French, that is, Catholic. A new political formula came into being, of which Fourmies was the best illustration: if only all Frenchmen, Catholic and socialist, bourgeois and working class, would become aware of the foreign and oppressive character of a regime stemming directly from 1789, if only they would form a once-more united nation, as in the past, then France, rid both of republican institutions and of Jews who had access to them with impunity, would finally rediscover the sense of its own identity. The true people, socialists and Catholics mixed together, had to stand up against the Jew who maintained order in the name of the Republic.

The state Jews of the period were most often very reserved toward social struggles, because they feared the disorganization that could result: the most famous among them, Joseph Reinach, judged without mincing words that "socialism is the enemy"; he engaged in a polemic with Guesde and even Juarès, disputed Marx's theories, carried on against "the swarming socialist microbes" and "the tyranny of the unions," which, according to him, were committed solely to exciting "social hatred." Like his brother Théodore, who believed it urgent to "to set aside this ragtag civil war called class struggle," he was more open to solidarist ideas and shared the philanthropic theories of his times.[34]

Within the administration, the *sous-préfet* Isaac was not the only one who had to confront more or less violent social movements in regions with a strong Catholic tradition; other Jews maintained public order under identical circumstances, as did their non-Jewish colleagues in the prefect civil service. Hence, in 1849, *sous-préfet* Emmanuel Lambert was sent to Toul to attempt to control a strike that had broken out on the railroads.[35] As *préfet* in 1877, Ernest Hendlé also faced the miners' strikes of Montceau-les-Mines, which won him the confidence of Waldeck-Rousseau and, in contrast, attracted the hatred of *La Libre Parole*, which attacked the Opportunists, of whom he was purportedly the instrument: "Back then, he was thinking more of having the socialists shot than of joining with them, as he has done today." A trial then took place in Riom to judge socialist miners; Hendlé, who reportedly declared: "I opened eyes, and the government did what it had to do," was violently taken to task by the press hostile to the Republic.[36]

The *sous-préfet* Georges Simon also behaved in a manner that, under dramatic circumstances, came close to heroism during the workers' struggles during the Decazeville strikes. Simon, according to the *préfet*'s report, played "a very honorable role in the actions taken against the strikers"; later, during the trial, he even served as a witness for the prosecution against five miners whom he had recognized.[37] And in 1891, all the *députés*, senators, *conseillers généraux*, and *conseillers municipaux* of the district of Valenciennes wrote a long letter to the minister to praise the "administrative and political qualities" of Georges Mossé and to express their wish that he be named *préfet* as quickly as possible, since his intervention in the strikes of Pas-de-Calais and Nord had had the most felicitous results. A little later, in 1893, this same *sous-préfet* received a thank-you letter from the director of the Compagnie des Mines d'Anzin: "In 1891, you enforced respect for the freedom of work in our operations; this time, the situation was much more difficult, and required all the experience you had acquired during the last strike to succeed as completely as you have done these last few days." [38]

In carrying out their roles as *préfets* or *sous-préfets*, the Jewish high officials were thrown into the middle of social conflicts that, in the name of the Republic, they had to master as best they could, while remaining faithful to the political vision of a regime that was most often hostile to the strikes and actions of various socialist groups. The republican order was quite conservative from the social viewpoint and, in its battle against the Church, was especially committed to changing the values of the population in order to definitively ensure the institutions of the Republic. Social conflicts placed that strategy in danger, for they introduced another source of division, and the Republic ordered all its *préfets* to rapidly put down that source of dissension.

Members of the prefect civil service were all required to limit the impact of the strikes, since they also had to dedicate themselves to defending the state against all those who were threatening its stability. The key person at the time was the minister of the interior: he was the strong man to whom the task fell to pursue the enemies of the state by every means. It happened that several state Jews who were not *préfets* occupied that crucial post at moments of extreme crisis. In September 1870, Camille Sée was secretary to the minister of the interior and invested with full powers; Adolphe Crémieux became minister of the interior for a time in the provisional government and vigorously dedicated himself to maintaining public order. He was succeeded by David Raynal in 1893, L.-L. Klotz in 1913, Abraham Schrameck in 1925, and Georges Mandel in 1940; in the wake of World War II, Jules Moch also proved to be a forceful minister of the interior. Let us not forget as well that Alexandre Israël was named undersecretary of state at the Ministry of the Interior in 1932.

In this respect, David Raynal was indisputably one of the most despised figures on the extreme left and right: minister of the interior in the Casimir-Perier cabinet in 1893, he successfully led impressive police operations against the anarchists in close collaboration with his friend, the *préfet* Lépine. In a very strong reaction to the anarchist attacks, he personally led a large operation with searches and arrests, not hesitating to risk his own life. His friendship with Lépine says a great deal about his determination: [39] in admiration, Lépine represented him as "the image of Henri IV." [40] Since Raynal had prohibited the red flag in cemeteries and public demonstrations, Henri Rochefort proposed that the socialists who met at the graves of their confederates should exchange their black ties for red: "However brazen the turnkey Raynal might be, he will probably not dare seek a quarrel that would repeat the murders of Fourmies."[41] Hence, the journalist himself established a link between *sous-préfet* Isaac and David Raynal, at the time minister of the interior. *L'Intransigeant* denounced what it considered the unlawful force used by "Vidocq and eighty-nine police *préfets* created by the Hebrew Raynal," while *La Lanterne* and *La Libre Parole* rose up against his police procedures, the control he exercised over the mail service and over individuals, by attacking his ties to the *préfets* Hendlé and Cohn: "Is Raynal cynical enough to place Jews at the head of all our administrations? . . . You will see that one day we'll have a Jew with the ambition to be president of the Republic, unless by then the people's good sense has won out and Jews have been sent back to the ghettos."[42] Let us note, finally, that slightly before the end of the Third Republic, Minister of the Interior Georges Mandel fought with equal determination the movements on the extreme right, in particular, Action Française; as a result, he became its privileged target.

At a slightly lower but still highly symbolic level, the *préfet* Isaïe Levaillant also crystallized all hatred and suspicion. An ardent republican linked to Gambetta, in 1885 he became director of Sûreté Générale at the Ministry of the Interior, "an important post," according to *La Libre Parole*, "in terms of espionage, and one that Jews are enormously interested in seeing occupied by one of their own." Drumont's newspaper did not hesitate to establish a link between the shooting of Fourmies that had occurred four years earlier, with Levaillant behaving in the same manner as the *sous-préfet* Isaac toward the forces of law and order, by imposing measures on them against their will.[43] These law-and-order men, all friends of *préfet* Lépine and Jews[44] on top of it, did not hesitate to use every means possible, as their position required, to defend the Republic, and in this way provoked Drumont's ire. Fourmies served as a founding event and was endlessly evoked as well to judge Raynal's and Levaillant's actions. Let us repeat, these few men represented only a tiny proportion of all those who, during the Third Republic, held vital posts in the Ministry of the Interior. The presence of a few state Jews in these dramatic circumstances — in 1870 and 1940 (and even, we might add, in 1958, when Jules Moch was charged with defending the Republic against General de Gaulle, who was threatening to take power by illegal means) — at moments when a change of political regime was due to military defeats at the hands of the German armies (or later, following the Algerian war), could only reinforce the antisemitic fantasies of the friends and heirs to Drumont. In fact, these men had a strong inclination toward mislabeling as Jews the many law-and-order men who dared oppose the schemes of the seditious right.[45]

Let us spend a bit more time with the example of Abraham Schrameck, who before briefly occupying a preeminent place in the political imaginary of his time, long performed the duties of *préfet*. Like all his colleagues, he acted very firmly in Marseilles when faced with social conflicts. In 1897, as secretary general of Bouches-du-Rhône, he succeeded in putting an end to strikes, which were threatening to get completely out of hand, without brutality and without bloodshed: his management of this difficult social conflict attracted the attention of Waldeck-Rousseau, who had previously also focused on E. Hendlé. Schrameck then found himself facing the strike of construction workers in Aix-en-Provence, which erupted in 1913, and which placed him in a delicate situation: in Aix, a violent campaign, not lacking in antisemitism, held him responsible for police brutality, despite the legal autonomy of the Aix police, which had intervened on its own. Nevertheless, a *député* accused the *préfet* of joining "the side of employers whenever it is a question of manhandling the working class."[46]

If Abraham Schrameck's name was suddenly thrown into the middle of the Franco-French wars and became, like Isaac's name, the object of all opprobrium, it was particularly on account of the operations for maintaining order carried out against the machinations of the leagues and of Action Française. He had entered the new staff formed by Painlevé as minister of the interior in April 1925, and he endured the escalating violence of campaigns by Action Française, which was intoxicated by the incendiary speeches of Maurras and Daudet. In one fell swoop, he saw the heirs to Drumont standing against him. As in the period of the Fourmies shooting, they launched an extremely harsh antisemitic campaign of disruption. By a curious conjuncture of circumstances, Schrameck and Drumont almost confronted each other personally: in 1897, as secretary general of Bouches-du-Rhône, Schrameck was the first to organize methods for maintaining order; then, coming from Algeria, the antisemitic deputies Drumont, Firmin Faure, Marchal, and Morineaud arrived. Incidents erupted, the police charged, blows were struck once more; the press on the extreme right found in this situation reason enough to carry on about the Jewish *préfet*. The press hounded him until Vichy, when it finally obtained his imprisonment. By a strange twist of history, through the person of Schrameck, Drumont and Maurras were linked and the two extremes of the Third Republic came together in him: the Dreyfus affair, in which Schrameck participated, and Vichy, which convicted him.

Abraham Schrameck, who had a long and brilliant career as a *préfet* — director of the Administration Pénitentiare in the Ministry of the Interior, *gouverneur* of Madagascar, senator, and minister of the interior before being interned in 1940 — was a particularly emblematic figure for all state Jews. His father, a small manufacturer of ribbons and silk, who had been a national guardsman during the war of 1870, was named Moïse; his mother's maiden name was Bloch; he himself married a woman named

Bernheim, originally from Alsace, whose father had fought as an artillery officer in 1870.[47] Thus, Abraham Schrameck came from a milieu that was both Jewish and oriented toward the Republic: in his letter dating from 1940, addressed, almost at the end of his life, to Marshal Pétain, he acknowledged without reservations that he was of the Jewish religion. Like the Hendlés or Isaïe Levaillant, he incarnated the Jewish *préfet* in particular, placing all his energy in service of law enforcement to defend the values and institutions of the Republic.

In a few months, as minister of the interior, Schrameck would run up against Action Française. On 24 April 1925, shooting broke out on Rue Damrémont and militants from Action Française were killed by police: Maurras and Daudet denounced the actions of the "entrapment specialist," the man the movement designated every day as a "Gallophobic Jew." A few days later, the minister prohibited the May Day demonstrations and those in honor of Joan of Arc; Action Française judged that "the circumcised Schrameck must regret not being able to burn a second time that impertinent reactionary, symbol of the saber and the aspergillum. The tradition of the Jewish nation is to spit on France and its glories. Léon Blum's watchword, 'I hate you' can only be received with enthusiasm by Abraham Schrameck."[48] Léon Daudet attacked that "dirty yid" and showed he was determined to demonstrate: a veritable battle took place between the police and members of Action Française, aided by Jeunesses Patriotes. There were several hundred wounded. The events rushed headlong: Ernest Berger, *trésorier* for the Ligue d'Action Française, was murdered in the Saint-Lazare metro, and the extreme right immediately suspected the police.

Finally, on 5 June, an incident took place that caused immediate national reverberations: the incident on Rue Hermel, a confrontation between Schrameck and Maurras that almost took a tragic turn. As with the shooting at Fourmies, it happens that the archives have preserved a very large number of documents about that event.[49] On 5 June, Action Française organized a meeting on Rue Hermel, and the minister ordered a careful search of the participants. As a result, the police discovered about fifty revolvers on various individuals, who were arrested. To protest against their being charged, Charles Maurras sent an open letter to Abraham Schrameck, designating him as "the instigator, the initiator of the ambush on Rue Hermel"; the theorist of Action Française, judging the persecutions against his movement unacceptable, explicitly accused the minister. He added:

Your race, a degenerate Jewish race, since there are well-born Jews who are ashamed of it, the race of Trotsky, Kurt Eisner, and Bela Kuhn, has now charged you with organizing revolution in our nation. You symbolize for us in an all too visible way the Foreigner who has taken the government by surprise and who makes it serve antigovernmental and antinational ends. . . . It is without hatred and without fear that I shall give the order to spill your dog blood if you should happen to misuse public force to open the tide gates of French blood under the bullets and daggers from your dear bandits in Moscow.[50]

Maurras was charged with "death threats under special circumstances." For several months, a great and highly scandalous trial unfolded, which the public followed eagerly and passionately. Among the witnesses for the defense who brought their unreserved support to Maurras, we find a certain number of crucial figures from the period. First, there was Xavier Vallat (a little later, he would lead a violent antisemitic campaign against Léon Blum before putting his talents to use under Vichy), who accused Schrameck of being responsible for the deliberate massacre of the Catholics of Marseilles in February 1925. There was naturally Jérôme Tharaud, the author of *Quand Israël est roi* (When Israel is king), who maintained that with his letter, Maurras had intended to protect France from a Bolshevik revolution. There was also Henri Massis, as well as Léon Daudet, who invoked Drumont's spirit, which "demands, in the name of Frenchmen, that Maurras, rather than being convicted, be given a civic award by the court." There was, finally, among so many others, Jacques Maritain, who proclaimed that it was necessary to reject an unjust law: "The initiative in such a case falls to a legitimate social authority . . . in whom for a moment the common good would be incarnated and who would act not as the head of a party but as an organ of the supreme interest and vital necessities of the community whose consent is thus presumed." The attacker of Luther and Rousseau, the great theorist of Catholicism, close at that time to Action Française, the man to whom many other currents of Catholicism, such as that represented by *Esprit*, would later lay claim, did not hesitate to join this concert of justifications for the letter from Maurras, whose vehement antisemitism here reached rare heights.

Day after day, the newspaper *Action Française* launched violent diatribes: according to Maurras, "Blum and Schrameck were dreaming of reverse pogroms," and the minister of the interior, "like his coreligionist Cain will always find the eye of Action Française everywhere."[51] A portion of the press of all leanings also drew the comparison: on the right, *Liberté* denounced Schrameck, "plague-ridden rat from the politician's sewer. A rodent head with something of the tapir about him. Blinking eyes like a nocturnal beast caught in a net and dragged into the sunlight. A dark and vile soul that nothing could move but fear." On the extreme left, *Le Libertaire* warned: "We will not lift a finger to prevent that act (the murder of Schrameck), which we would consider a professional accident . . . but at the first gesture made by the royalist riffraff on one of our own, we must respond vigorously." *Charivari* evoked the man "come from Judaea to be minister. . . . Abraham has sunken eyes, a dried-out body, and the lean face of an idiot."

The death threats against the minister of the interior accumulated. He received numerous anonymous letters: "Old Abraham," declared one of these mysterious correspondents, who attacked his "race" and the "government of orgies, feasts, and carnivals," "I'm the one, not Maurras, who will tear your guts out."[52] In the provinces, in Charente-Maritime, for example, police reports noted preparations being made: a minor country squire of very dubious nobility, Perrier des Brousses, a great admirer of Maurras and Daudet, "of a very hot-headed temperament," according to the police, declared he was "determined to immediately take the train to go and carry out the order" of the head of Action Française. The *préfet* warned Schrameck and went to the site to see that close surveillance was kept on the suspect. Another anonymous correspondent addressed a long handwritten letter to the minister of the interior: "You gang of bastards, you stuff yourselves and have illuminations every night with your little dancing girls, paid for by the proletariat. I used to like the Jews, I had respect for them, but I am beginning to see that you are louts. . . . I don't fear anyone, not even the devil."[53] Like *sous-préfet* Isaac or *préfet* Ernest Hendlé, Abraham Schrameck, as *préfet* and then as minister of the interior, got involved in the long saga of political antisemitism that denounced the Jews' hand behind the repressive actions of the republican state. And, under Vichy, *Au Pilori* and many other organs of the collaborationist press again displayed vitriolic portraits of him.[54] The defense of the republican order, like the defense of the nation itself, relentlessly attracted antisemitic hatred.

CHAPTER ELEVEN

The Defense of the Nation from 1870 to 1940

Jewish French senior officers were introduced to German prison camps, with their stalags and concentration camps, well before World War II, and even before that of 1914–18. Without going any further back, we note that the war of 1870 already found them on the outposts of the nation's defense, ready for the supreme sacrifice, confronting the enemy, or captured like so many others at the end of difficult battles. Colonel Gabriel Brisac, for example, commanding the reserve artillery of the Twelfth Army Corps of the Rhine, was interned as a prisoner from 1870 to 1871 in Koblenz, and then in Bonn. On 19 October 1870, Captains Abraham Samuel and Adolphe Hinstin, captured after the fall of Metz, were interned in Hamburg. Colonel Jules Moch, taken prisoner on 2 September, was locked up in a military camp in Germany. Second Lieutenant Samuel Naquet-Laroque had better luck: he was wounded in Gravelotte and taken by the German forces, but on 28 December 1870, he succeeded in escaping and returned to France. Lieutenant Justin Dennery served in the Eighth Foot Regiment; Colonel Bernard Abraham was assistant to the general staff of the artillery in the Rhine Army; Lieutenant-Colonel Abraham Lévy participated in the battles of Châtillon and Meudon and played an important role in the defense of Paris. He fought beside Captain Victor Mannheim, who during the siege, commanded the artillery battery of the École Polytechnique. Certain Jewish lieutenants and colonels fought in 1870, as they would also do in 1914:

for example, Colonel Isidore Ausher, whose son, a lieutenant in the 304th Infantry, was killed by the enemy in Meuse. Lieutenant Léon Francfort, a prisoner in 1870, succeeded in escaping: he fought again in 1914, as a general. Lieutenant Jules Heymann, captured in 1840, also fought during World War I as a division general.

We could multiply the examples: as citizens integrated into the armies, Jews participated in defending their nation. Entering the army was, in fact, one of the royal roads to their integration into the state, the ultimate proof of their final "regeneration." By becoming soldiers, they proved their courage and vigor, belying the antisemitic stereotypes: from the beginning of the century, for example, they entered the École Polytechnique and slowly climbed the career ladder. In truth, the army was a profoundly Catholic and conservative institution, and Jews reached the highest ranks, those which interest us here, only rather late. When, in November 1870, Léopold Sée was named brigadier general—after being named to the Order of the Army on 27 August 1870 for his conduct during the battles of Gravelotte and Saint-Privat, where he was wounded—he was the first Jew to attain that rank. Thus, during this first conflict with Germany, Jews defended their nation while occupying the intermediate ranks. Furthermore, that war did not lend itself to heroics, since defeat was swift. The hour of glory and tragedy would come later, during World War I, when, with the strengthening of the Republic, state Jews serving in the army, like their colleagues in administration, reached positions of high responsibility.

The loss of Alsace-Lorraine, as we know, elicited a cult of revenge and the rise of a nationalism aimed at recovering those two provinces: the mutilation of the Hexagon galvanized the sense of identity. In October 1876, Senator Adolphe Crémieux and *député* Eugène Lisbonne, in the company of Jewish soldiers from the contingent, participated in Yom Kippur services in Montpellier. During that ceremony, Crémieux gave a speech that said a great deal about the patriotic feelings of Jewish soldiers:

Now you are soldiers, my dear children, soldiers of our beloved France. Will you fight? Will we go to war? If you fight, fight like your ancestors fought, fight like the people of God defending the nation. . . . You have long been forced to bow under the yoke of slavery, under religious hatred; today you are free, you can hold your head up high, you are French soldiers. Now you are among your fellow citizens, and are citizens like them. . . . Love this French Republic that has made you French and given you rights and duties equal to those of her other children. Love those who have become your comrades; establish fraternal ties with them. Children, long live France! Long live the Republic![1]

Alsatian Jewry was particularly affected by this loss of the eastern provinces: out of gratitude toward the nation that had been the first to emancipate them, a great number of Jews left the occupied departments and chose to remain French. Careful to appear fundamentally faithful to their nation and their fellow citizens, they took their distance from German Jews, to whom they were in fact quite close: without question, national identity overruled religious affinity.[2] They often headed to Paris, and their children were even more attracted to military careers: obsessed by the amputation of the nation, they demonstrated a haughty nationalism and placed their own lives in the service of revenge. They were not alone: the state Jews close to Gambetta and then to Clemenceau were also in the forefront in patriotic organizations. For the most part, they challenged the chauvinistic nationalism propagated by the leagues, and most often took care not to fall into the error of basing their identity on race or organic community. But as citizens horrified by the loss of two eastern provinces, their nationalism was very keen. Sons of the French Revolution, they perpetuated military traditions placed in the service of a nation of citizens moved by an ethics of Reason. In their eyes, the defense of the nation was the logical perpetuation of the ideals of the soldiers of Valmy.

State Jews originally from regions in the East were obviously not the only ones to react vigorously: in 1870, Édouard Millaud in Lyon became a very steadfast *procureur général*, and the next year published a brochure titled *Le Soufflet. Devons-nous signer la paix?* (The slap: Must we sign the peace agreement?); in 1872, he, along with Alfred Naquet, introduced a bill that named Napoleon III responsible for the war and called for his personal wealth to be seized and sold to pay war indemnities. Édouard Lisbonne, *préfet* in Hérault, was truly at the head of the struggle against the Prussians, and his declarations bore witness to his passion. But those who came from the East occupied a preeminent place. In the opinion of all the nationalists, Édouard Bamberger, a liberal *député* hostile to Napoleon III, became one of the most fervent spokespersons for the lost provinces. He went to Bordeaux as the head of a delegation of Jews from Alsace-Lorraine to protest annexation before the Assemblé Nationale. Denouncing the Frankfurt Treaty, he presented a petition signed by two hundred thousand inhabitants of Moselle. Once the treaty was ratified, he resigned along with all the other deputies representing those provinces.[3] In this context, Bamberger took the initiative for two actions with wide repercussions. In an energetic speech, he exclaimed: "The planned treaty with Prussia constitutes one of the greatest iniquities that the history of peoples and the diplomatic annals will ever record. A single man, and I declare it out loud, a single man should have signed it, and that is Napoleon III." At those words, a great tumult arose in the Chamber, and the dynasty fell in an almost unanimous vote, making it "responsible for the ruin and dismemberment of France." Returning to Versailles so as not to "commit desertion," he was also responsible for a proposal aimed directly at Marshal Bazaine, whose arrest and sentence were almost immediately decided on.[4]

In Paris, Catholics, Protestants, and Jews from the annexed region passed over their differences to unite in an effort to arouse and sustain a national desire for revenge. Within the Masonic lodge of Alsace-Lorraine, considered the most patriotic in Paris, Bamberger, Crémieux, and the Opportunist *député* Edmond Goudchaux (who, like Bamberger, had chosen to leave the lost provinces) led the battle as French citizens. Next to a very great number of their coreligionists, these state Jews also participated in leading the Association Générale d'Alsace-Lorraine, which among other acts, came to the aid of young people who had decided to do their military service in the Foreign Legion rather than serve in the German army.[5] Among all the Jewish adolescents who made up their minds to cross the border, we find Lazare Weiller, future senator for Bas-Rhin, later elected with the Bloc National, who liked to call himself the "senator from Alsace." His mother had sent him to Angoulême and had instilled in him a patriotism that would burst forth in the book he published after World War I, *Pro Alsatia*.[6] At his side, Édouard Millaud the Gambettist exclaimed at and against everything:

No, France is not conquered. The lioness is awakening, she is still beautiful, she is still strong, and imprudent is he who makes her roar. . . . Although Alsace has been ravished away from us, we will seize her back some day, we give our word as republicans. Like the old Don Diego, we shall say to our sons: "Die or kill." Woe to Prussia. . . . The ancient Druids in our forests will tremble with delight. The Teuton will find flames and famine before him.[7]

Camille Dreyfus, who volunteered to serve during the conflict, demonstrated a very meticulous patriotism: like Édouard Millaud, he even sometimes spouted an ambiguous metaphorical language, foreign in any case to the republican ideology and the tradition of the Enlightenment from which it stemmed. "The moment is come," he wrote, "to make war with Germany. . . . On the flanks of the nation, like an ever open wound, what were once the departments of Haut-Rhin, Bas-Rhin, Meurthe, and Moselle are bleeding. To put an end to this mutilation, it was indispensable, by virtue of the "laws of history," to take up again "the struggle between the Teutons and the Gauls," with the hope of receiving help from Italy, "the Latin sister," which had with France "shared races" in this combat. "O war," he exclaimed, "despite the corpses and ruins you sow along your route with open hand, I call upon you with desire, because I have the conviction that, under the folds of the tricolor flag, the French will forget their pitiful internal quarrels."[8]

Not shy of any temporary alliance, Dreyfus conducted patriotic lectures in favor of war, even surrounded in the early days by Boulangist militants.

During one of these lectures held in Paris, Avenue Kléber, in November 1892, numerous incidents occurred: he himself shook a fist at insulters and — as the *commissaire de police* reported — "when participants reproached him for not being French, he responded that in 1870, he had defended France, which was his nation, whereas Drumont had not done so."[9] He occupied the post of secretary of the army commission on the composition of permanent war councils. He also introduced numerous bills between 1890 and 1893 in favor of reorganizing the army to accelerate mobilization; drafted legislation on voluntary service; reported on a plan modifying the length of military service; and concerned himself with the struggle against espionage, for which he demanded the death penalty. Swept away by national feeling, he wrote: "Patriotic feeling is developed enough in France that one may without fear lay the burden of defending the country on each of its children. We wish no other guarantee than the deep emotion raised by a recent trial, and we can be certain that, if the jury had evaluated the facts to which we are alluding, it would have imposed its severity to the fullest extent of the law."[10]

As for Joseph Reinach, he also became the spokesperson for Alsace-Lorraine and dedicated a large part of his energy to building a military force capable of bringing France a victory. In 1908 and 1910, he delivered reports on the artillery and the 75mm cannon to the Chamber, and discussed six-piece batteries and shooting strategies in extremely precise terms; he intervened in the careers of officers who had displayed discipline and endurance, and engaged in a polemic with Jaurès on the military strategy of the Convention and the lessons to be drawn from it. According to him, "Jaurès misunderstands the teachings of the Revolution," which, he believed, implied adopting an offensive strategy. He defended the law of three years of military service, to face the German army: hence his peroration. "Gentlemen, you are the heirs to the men of 1792, for whom republican and patriot were synonymous. Your political ancestors are Carnot, Danton, Gambetta, and Ferry. They have bequeathed this ideal to you: the Republic safeguarding France, the soil, tradition."[11]

Far from the nationalist flights of fancy à la Barrès familiar to Camille Dreyfus, the Gambettist leader steered clear of any organicist or racial metaphor and supported the cause of Alsace-Lorraine in the name of a conception of the nation drawn straight from Michelet and Renan. In 1916, when violence was breaking out, he challenged "that false German historical science" that reasoned according to racial determinism, and underscored, in the very terms of Renan, that "'nation' means having lived, struggled, worked, hoped, and suffered together." In this view, History rested not in geography or ethnology, but in the soul. For Reinach, "France is something besides a geological being or a geographical being; it is a person, according to the ever admirable expression of Michelet." Alsace and Lorraine had "preserved their French soul." And, he concluded, "We must conquer and we shall conquer."[12] During the same period, his old adversary Alfred Naquet was compiling several little-known texts on the comparative virtues of the cruiser and the armored ship in ensuring "the defense of the country." After much reflection, he gravely pronounced himself in favor of the cruiser, "mobile, difficult to seize," while the armored ship was said to lack "autonomy because of the paucity of coal."[13] Just imagine: in this context, Alfred Naquet, anarchist and social protester, was taking on the guise of a military strategist!

The French army of the 1880s remained dominated by the advocates of uniting the saber and the aspergillum and was structured by a ruddy-faced conservatism. Anticlericalism had a fragile existence in the army, and the traditional elites were hardly unseated in their prejudices and privileges: The processes that affected the political class did not extend to the army. Gambetta made an effort to modify voluntarily that situation by favoring republican officers, with the general staff and the high hierarchy supposedly remaining hostile to the regime. According to Gambetta's secret records, nine out of ten generals were conservative, Bonapartist, or royalist, often aristocratic in origin, and profoundly clerical.[14] As Raoul Girardet observed, "Quickly spotted, even more quickly catalogued, clericals and Freemasons, reactionaries and republicans, lived in relation to one another in a state of perpetual constraint. In the mess halls, in public places, sometimes even in the barracks, the incidents multiplied."[15] The systematic and at times concealed actions of Generals de Galiffet and André, however indirect the means they used to achieve their ends, shattered military isolationism. Later, in 1906, Picquart himself, the defender of Dreyfus, would be named minister of war by Clemenceau. In certain sectors and for certain ranks, a new equilibrium was progressively being instituted in favor of republicans: the Ark of the Covenant was opening itself to society thanks to the recruitment of officers based on a final exam at the graduate schools. This certainly favored the old families, but also made meritocratic competition possible. Thus, after an intense struggle, the "new strata" also penetrated the military hierarchy.

Like the state Jews close to Gambetta, the Jewish officers stemming in a much higher proportion from the École Polytechnique, in a game of social "catch-up," smitten with science and oriented toward positivist Reason, also pursued their careers within an institution that was closed upon itself, but without encountering any insurmountable barriers. They climbed the ladder of the hierarchy, and more than twenty of them would become generals under the Third Republic, with colonels and a fortiori captains numbering in the hundreds or more.[16] As in the administration, their values were identical to those of the founders of the Republic: they adhered without reservation to the "moral reform" that the founders meant to impose on France. The Dreyfus affair once more slowed Jews' access to duties of command and revived antisemitism in an army that was, however, often able to remain neutral and ensure equal protection to members of its own corps.[17]

Antisemitism was no less revived by the determined campaigns of Drumont and *La Libre Parole*, which relentlessly denounced the presence of Jewish officers in the army.[18] In *La France juive*, several senior officers were covered with insults. As always, Drumont's fantasies depended on half-truths that had been exaggerated to the extreme and endlessly deformed in their interpretation. Jews were climbing the ladder of the hierarchy but they were doing so as French officers anxious to serve their country: as Ferdinand Dreyfus noted, "by a peculiar fanaticism, this obvious sign of adaptation has been denounced as a kind of takeover, an effort to gain hold of the army."[19]

The frequent duels, which set journalists of the extreme right or officers sharing their feelings against Jewish military men or politicians, provide an interesting path for measuring the conflicts within the army. With time, as the possibilities for rising in careers based on their own merit increased, certain Jews, unlike what had happened in 1870, and in spite of a particularly tense ideological context, reached the very first ranks of the army. They displayed a keen nationalism, which they wished to place at the service of retaking the lost provinces and, more generally, in the service of revenge. However, we have few memoirs of senior officers to bear witness to their values and beliefs in this moment of truth for Franco-Judaism, where assimilation was threatened by the turmoil of the Dreyfus affair, while state Jews — in whose front ranks the famous captain was to be found[20] — were entirely oriented toward defending their country.

World War I was almost welcomed, since it ended harsh internal confrontations, inspired a sense of national unity that, as it were, threw a veil over the most recent past. It took on a kind of messianic dimension and appeared as a transfiguration of the exodus from Egypt: the time of oppression was ended, the hour for revenge had arrived, and all citizens, become once more brothers, would participate. Jews sacrificed themselves in great numbers on the altar of the nation and were killed in action, faithful to the tradition of the French Revolution: as the *Archives Israélites* expressed it, "the holy patriotic ardor whose glorious blaze was offered us in 1792 has set the French people of 1914 on fire, all of them mixed up together, without distinction of origin, class, or religion. . . . In this patriotic duty, our coreligionists have not faltered."[21] In the chauvinistic context of the era, other notions were also bandied about to justify the sacrifice. On 14 July 1916, the *Archives Israélites*, which were publishing the names and military feats of Jewish soldiers in every issue, wrote:

A people of Latin origin like the French, who react so courageously that the final and decisive victory cannot escape them, deserve that victory. . . . For the Jews, the commemoration of this date, doubly unforgettable, has allowed them once more to commune (in the Latin sense of the word, of course) intimately with their Christian and freethinking fellow citizens in the eternal cult of national glory. . . . The blood shed in such appalling quantities since 1 August 1914 will germinate in extraordinary fashion for the glory of our country.[22]

The numbers give an idea of the enthusiasm of these men, who were expressing this same love for the Republic of the Enlightenment: 32,000 Jewish soldiers were mobilized, and 6,500 of them fell in battle; 12,000 foreign Jews volunteered, and 2,000 of them were killed; at the École Polytechnique, of 148 Jewish alumni (classes of 1895–1914), 24 were killed, that is, 15.4 percent, compared to the average of 14.3 percent.[23] In general, the proportion of Jewish soldiers killed in battle was 3.5 percent, while the proportion among French soldiers generally was 3.4 percent.[24] Numerous Jewish noncommissioned officers perished: hence Colonel Salmon Lévy, described in all the reports as "very vigorous," "firm and devoted," died for France in 1915;[25] Captain Louis Naquet was killed in September 1914.[26] Oscar Kahn was wounded twenty-three times during the long conflict; each time he "asked to return to the front despite the state of his wounds" in the head, arms, and legs.[27]

Many of them went to war moved by this patriotism of revenge, wanting to efface the humiliation of 1870 and, for some of them, to recover the provinces to which they were linked by their own history. Captain Raoul Bloch wrote: "With what joy I shall go to Alsace, and what memories I shall have upon entering in uniform this country of our dreams! Our poor papas shall leap up from their graves!"[28] The state Jews who were originally from the lost eastern provinces, whether civilians or soldiers, went to the outposts of the war effort. Alfred Wallach, for example, who would later become *député* of Mulhouse, the native city he had secretly left to join the French army, fought for the entire duration of the war and received three citations; when peace returned, he presided over the Association des Engagés Volontaires du Haut-Rhin (volunteer soldiers association of Haut-Rhin) and the Fédération des Engagés Volontaires d'Alsace et de Lorraine (federation for volunteer soldiers of Alsace and Lorraine) for many years.[29] Georges Weill, representative for Metz at the Reichstag, contributor to *L'Humanité*, and no doubt the most important personality for Alsatian socialism, who was seated at table next to Jaurès when the latter was murdered, did not hesitate: he joined the French army, was sentenced to death by the Germans for high treason, and addressed the Alsace-Lorrainians in these terms: "There are no longer reservations in our hopes and patriotic will. In joining the army of the Republic, in thus pursuing the struggle against a military and Prussianized Germany, oppressor of the freedom of all peoples, I am aware that I have fulfilled my contract as a Socialist *député* and as a *député* of Alsace-Lorraine." Promoted to the rank of captain, he then participated in the Alsace-Lorraine conference whose goal was to prepare for the return of the lost provinces.[30] Édouard Ignace, who left Metz with his father in 1870 in order to remain French, was elected *député* of Seine in 1914, proclaimed he was, "like all Lorrainians from Lorraine and like all Metzians from Metz, twice French."[31] He was named by Clemenceau in November 1917 to the post of undersecretary of state at the Department of Military Justice, where, until the end of hostilities, he operated a ministry of public security: with a patriotism that was quick to take offense, he was associated with initiating very public trials for consorting with the enemy or for defeatism.[32]

In reality, most state Jews who were members of the political class were involved in national defense in one capacity or another. Joseph Reinach, still active, became a commentator on the conflict, retracing its striking events for the public. For that figure emblematic of Franco-Judaism, mixed up in all the Franco-French wars, "the soldiers of year II, Sambre and Meuse, Rhine and Alpes, were the precursors, the pioneers" of patriotic sacrifice: "How wonderful it is to be French, and how wonderful to be republican."[33] They shared the same ideal: Camille Picard, *député* of Vosges, wrote in his platform statement drafted for the 1914 elections: "As a patriot, I made my contribution without hesitation to the work of national defense. . . . I place duty toward country above all else."[34] Like other *députés*, he left for the front even though he was exempted from taking up arms, and received a citation in 1917. At different levels in the military hierarchy, we find Moïse Lévy, future *député* of Haute-Savoie, attached, at his request, to a foot battalion; André Fribourg, future *député* of Ain in 1919, grievously wounded on the front line, who received the Médaille Militaire and the Croix de Guerre; Jean Ehrlich, *député* of Seine in 1919, who fought for three years; and Achille Fould, later *député* and minister, who, at the head of his platoon, was wounded and received seven citations. Maurice Bokanowski, *député* of Seine beginning in 1914, participated as an infantry second lieutenant in the battles of Argonne and then, as member of the general staff, in the offensive of Champagne: he was cited as a "model of duty understood in its highest sense." Let us also cite Henry Torrès, grandson of the prefect Isaïe Levaillant, who helped out on several occasions: grievously wounded during the attack on the Laffaux mill, he received the Croix de Guerre with palm leaf and the Médaille Militaire. Jules Moch, who fought during the entire war, received his fourth medal from Marshal Pétain personally: "Proved his remarkable courage, which never flagged for a moment, giving a shining example of abnegation and absolute devotion."[35] Pierre Masse, *député* of Hérault, left for the front in 1914 as an officer, was wounded, was awarded laudatory citations, received the Croix de Guerre, then became undersecretary of state at the Ministry of War in 1917. He exhibited remarkable energy in that post, signing the execution order for the spy Mata Hari, for example.[36] Klotz, the future minister of finance under Clemenceau, who had already been chairman of the war budget beginning in 1906, fought Jaurès on this matter: Jaurès had declared that "when a government is attacked, the duty of the working class is to refuse it the means necessary for making war." Klotz retorted: "I do not allow in any case disobedience, insubordination, or desertion," and called Jaurès a "demagogue." He concluded: "We are forced as the good patriots that we are to make all the sacrifices required for safeguarding our society in order to pave the way for the victory of our soldiers."[37] Anti-Dreyfusard and nationalist, Klotz received a visit from Barrès in 1914, who declared he wanted to join him: "You know the deep respect I have for you," he said; a major during the war, he paid a visit to Pétain on 24 April 1916, who spoke to him "in noble language."[38]

Among a number of Jewish officers, the theme of revenge and of the necessary liberation of the lost provinces was omnipresent. André Fribourg stood up for the martyrs of Alsace and Lorraine: "When this war is over, the Alsace-Lorrainians will have once more taken their place within the French family" by finally rediscovering "the French land."[39] France was perpetuating the tradition of revolutionary armies confronting Prussia, now and in the past.[40]

Fribourg did not neglect to send each of his books with a warm and respectful dedication to Maurice Barrès, champion of French nationalism.[41] In 1938, he dedicated his last book, *La victoire des vaincus* (The victory of the vanquished), to Maurice Barrès's son, Philippe: "In memory of the generous friendship his father was kind enough to show me." Without in any way evoking the antisemitism of Nazi Germany, he wrote: "We allowed ourselves to no longer think French. . . . Evil overtook us, penetrated our blood; let us react against that intoxication that has made us feeble, that has made us lose our national meaning. Let us think French first of all."[42] As the height of irony, this work contained a preface signed by Marshal Pétain himself, who underscored "the tremor of patriotism that animates the author and with which his whole person is permeated. . . . He has contributed to forming the generation of Saint-Cyr cadets who will mount the assault in plumes and white gloves, and he deserves the Médaille Militaire and the Croix de Guerre on the battlefield, at their sides."[43] At that date, André Fribourg and probably Klotz and many others were still acknowledged by Barrès and Pétain as forming an integral part of the great French families: they shared the nationalism of the worst adversaries of republican state Jews.

With the exception of the political staff, the members of the prefect civil service were among the first to support the nation's war effort. Albert Hendlé dedicated himself wholeheartedly to the proper operation of his department of Calvados: he led the spirit of resistance and wrote to the colonel of the Thirty-sixth Artillery Regiment to speak of his hope that "permanent victory will one day, and as soon as possible, bring back the great regiment of the Thirty-sixth, which, under your orders, has earned the most glorious citations through so many stunning actions." He saw that packages were sent to the soldiers and joined the association called "A Nos Braves. La Tirelire de la Jeune Fille" (To our brave men. The young ladies' piggy bank), supported by Raymond Poincaré, which came to the aid of soldiers.[44] Soon his excessive activities for the population exhausted him and he fell ill; for the *Journal de Caen*, "M. Hendlé has made considerable efforts since 2 August 1914, and especially during the mobilization; although very ill, he refused to take the necessary rest; it was because he was always on the go that he became ill while on an inspection tour. We are as glad of his return as we would be of a friend's."[45] On 6 January 1918, he wrote to the minister: "The morale of the population has remained healthy, despite some sagging, and we may, I believe, remain confident in the good sense and the spirit of patriotism among the inhabitants." On 6 April, he acknowledged that "the steadfastness and decisiveness of the honorable premier have had the most felicitous influence."[46]

Let us evoke another figure: during nearly the entire length of the war, Abraham Schrameck was at the head of Bouches-du-Rhône; like all *préfets*, he oversaw everything—the price of commodities, the supply of coal, labor, and the recruitment of soldiers. The *conseil général* expressed "its gratitude for the many services rendered to the national defense and the many works of assistance created since the mobilization of the department." In response, he paid tribute to the fallen soldiers: "They are ensuring the freedom of the world with their blood." The *président* of the *conseil général* was happy about "the definitive crushing of the Teutonic race, that enemy of Latin genius," and Schrameck spoke at length of "the justice of our cause."[47] Others who later joined the prefect civil service also behaved valiantly under fire: the son of Albert Hendlé joined up and wore the uniform for four years, during which period he was wounded three times and received the Croix de Guerre and the Croix du Combattant. He also received several citations, including the following: "On 6 August 1918, during a surveillance mission, was attacked by eight enemy monoplanes, turned on them with splendid courage, continuing to fire even though grievously wounded by a bullet." Trepanned, he continued to suffer from the aftereffects; he joined the *préfectorale*, but died after a few years in that career.[48] Pierre Aron also joined up at the age of seventeen and ended the war as a young captain, with several wounds and decorations: a *sous-préfet*, he died young, at thirty-four, from the effects of his war wounds.[49] André Caen, *vice-président* of the *conseil de préfecture*, also fought during the entire war, as did the future *préfet* Henri Dadoun.[50] Other older *sous-préfets* sat on war councils.[51]

More than forty years after the creation of the Third Republic, certain state Jews who joined the armed services reached the highest levels of the hierarchy. This time, in that war of unprecedented dimensions, they had a certain visibility, just as they had had during the Franco-French wars. Even though the last vicissitudes of the Dreyfus affair were still recent, eight of them served as generals during the conflict. Let us spend some time with their military dossiers, which in themselves bear witness to the definitive setting in place of a true republican meritocracy in a corps that was closed on itself and whose hierarchy had until then been attached to conservative and Catholic values. Four state Jews, of whom three were originally from the lost provinces, began the war as generals: Justin Dennery, mobilized as a lieutenant in 1870; Mardochée Valabrègue, who owed his advancement in part to the personal intervention of General Boulanger; Georges Bloch; and Jules Heymann. Bloch was one of the rare Jewish division generals linked to the Brisac dynasty and to numerous magistrates: in many ways, he represented those who belonged to the leading milieus of the state.[52] Brigadier general Jules Heymann, also a veteran of 1870, was promoted to division general in 1916. When his son, an officer, died on the battlefield, the *Archives Israélites* noted: "Suffering, far from destroying the energy of these admirable Frenchmen, only augmented their desire to avenge their children, who sacrificed themselves with such heroism for the triumph of the nation, on their odious enemy." The *Archives* underscored that, at the same time, a young Jewish boy had covered himself with glory in the Russian army, receiving the Cross of St. George, and concluded: "Can we imagine any more noble and beautiful symbol than this old Jewish man in his kepi wreathed with gold, coming out of retirement to lead a French army to victory, holding out his arms beyond the enemy lines to a brave, heroic Jewish corporal of fourteen from the allied and friendly army?"[53]

Four other Jews became generals during the conflict, often winning that rank in stunning actions that earned them many citations. Colonel Georges Alexandre, brought into the general staff of General Joffre in 1915, became brigadier general and commanded the artillery of the Eighth Army. Joffre signed this citation in person: "General officer of high valor. . . . Succeeded in organizing numerous artillery operations that had a vital influence on the final result of the war."[54] Colonel Lucien Lévy, born in Meurthe, son of Salomon Lévy, the rabbi of Meurthe-et-Moselle, was able to attend the École Polytechnique thanks to a scholarship offered him by the city of Blamont; he became brigadier general in 1917 after numerous citations from the army.[55] Colonel Camille Baruch Lévi, born in Bas-Rhin, was also a scholarship student and became famous for declaring to his officers: "Pronounce the word *boche* and you will sense all it contains that is abject; it's more than pejorative, it's more than a nickname, it's a mark of infamy."[56] Made general in April 1916 after impressive military deeds, he fought on numerous occasions, at the battle of the Marne, of Aisne, of Champagne, and of Verdun, including the battle of Douamont. As a general, he intervened in the Somme, in the battles of hill 108, at the Chemin des Dames, in the battle of Flanders, Champagne, and Picardy; his citations are too long to cite in full here. "Shows exceptional qualities under fire"; "advanced to the foot of the enemy's entrenchments, and led a victorious counterattack"; "resisted for five days the furious attacks of the enemy, prepared by a deluge of high-caliber missiles, and did not lose an inch of ground despite considerable losses," and so on. This brilliant soldier was congratulated by Pétain: "Under your command, the Forty-sixth Infantry Division has written some of the most glorious pages in the history of the army, pages that have earned you the gratitude of France. You can be proud of your success." He died in 1932, before the marshal had become part of a movement with a completely different policy toward Jewish officers.[57] Colonel Paul Grumbach, twice wounded, also displayed "a great energy in leading repeated attacks with felicitous results"; he became a division general in April 1918. Colonel Gédéon Geismar, also born in the East, was described in one of the citations he received as "full of ardor, energetic activity during pursuit of the enemy."[58]

Lieutenant Colonel Albert Frank, born in Nancy, was also a

senior officer of the highest valor. Took command of the Champagne regiment during a difficult period and particularly distinguished himself in this command. Selflessly exerted himself organizing the artillery, at the constant risk to his person, in front line reconnaissance, and showing in all circumstances the greatest contempt for danger.

Made a division general in 1926, he was "passionate about a military calling"; he died in 1936, a few years before everything began to fall apart.[59] Lieutenant Julien Carvallo, son of Jules Carvallo (one of the leaders of the Alliance Israélite Universelle), considered in 1916 to be "a senior officer whose professional value is equal to his ardor and love for action," "successfully proving excellent mobility on the field, completed all missions entrusted to him" in Verdun, Champagne, and Lorraine: he was named brigadier general in 1923 before dying peacefully the next year.[60] Colonel de Mazenod then eulogized the deceased:

My general, permit one of those who had the distinguished honor of serving under your orders from the first hours of the war to offer you the tribute of his constant devotion even in death. . . . I saw men cry when your passing was announced, and soldier's tears, my general, do not lie. That is because each of us perceived that you were a leader in the highest sense of that term. You obtained everything, because you struck at the heart. Brave to the point of temerity, you inspired boundless confidence in everyone, and in the grave moments that sometimes happen in a war, your presence sufficed to galvanize energy. My general, it is in the name of that group in mourning and in tears, that group you loved so much, that I come today to give you a final farewell. We will ever keep within our hearts the memory of the great solider and venerated leader that you were.[61]

These Jewish generals knew nothing of the fate that awaited their comrades in arms a few years later, with Vichy's about-face. In fact, they would have been quite incapable of imagining this disavowal that turned its back on the republican contract. We shall need to return to this matter later to evoke the reactions of the ousted generals. These soldiers, almost all born in the East, some of whom had already fought in 1870, earned their rank under fire, devoting all their force to driving the enemy from national territory. They often died before World War II. Younger men participated in these same battles and achieved the rank of general in the interwar period: unlike their elders, whose patriotism triumphed with no unfortunate aftermath, almost all of them experienced a particularly difficult fate in 1940. Present together on the battlefields of World War I, the two groups form a military chain linking together as it were the three conflicts that opposed France and Germany, and little by little brought Franco-Judaism in its military version to its triumph, and then to its repudiation. Some of the Jewish generals whose destinies were reversed with Vichy had in fact been intrepid soldiers during World War I. That was the case, for example, for Lieutenant Colonel Albert Baumann, born in Alsace, who participated in the battles of the Marne, the attacks of Champagne and Verdun, and the battle of the Somme. He was wounded and received numerous citations, including the following: "Always displayed great bravery and a cool head"; "despite heavy bombing of tear gas, powerfully contributed to pushing back the German attacks." He became a brigadier general in 1927, but was stripped of his commission by the Vichy government, under the provisions the Statut des Juifs of June 1941.[62] Captain Pierre Boris was an officer "of great valor, rendered the greatest services during the offensive of Flanders." On 4 August 1915, Marshal Joffre himself bestowed the Croix de Guerre with palm leaf on him, accompanied by the following citation: "Since the beginning of the campaigns shows activity, initiative, and a contempt for danger beyond all praise." In the interwar period, he contributed to reorganizing the armed forces to endow them with greater speed of execution and insisted that tanks be linked to air power. He fought in World War II as a general of the army corps before he too was stripped of his commission.[63] Captain Léon Rheims, according to one of his citations received in 1917, was a "senior officer of great merit through his knowledge, his zeal, and his relentless devotion. . . . Particularly distinguished himself between 6 and 16 July 1916 in the command of an attack sector during rough days." He became a brigadier general in 1930, but he too was stripped of his commission by the Statut des Juifs.[64] In 1917, Colonel Louis Rueff was considered "a model of bravery and reflective courage. Exercises considerable moral ascendancy over all those around him." The next year, with his regiment, he "conquered, at the cost of an all-day relentless struggle, a series of formidably organized positions. Then pursued the enemy with tenacity and indomitable energy." Wounded three times, he received five citations, was promoted to division general in 1929, but was stripped of his commission in 1942.[65]

The life of Lieutenant Colonel Alphonse Weiller was not very different; born in Bas-Rhin, he was wounded on nine separate occasions and was given eight citations during World War I: "Through his personal bravery and the intelligent energy of his command, obtained a great deal from his troops"; "in the trenches of the Souain sector for eleven months, played an active role in all actions"; "corps leader of the first order who made his regiment an elite corps"; "wondrous regiment, bringing together daring, fire, and heroism. Engaged in very difficult battles under the orders of Colonel Weiller, from 1 to 15 September 1918. Stormed the strong positions that were his objectives, renewing, with the assault on the Crouy plateau, the glorious exploit that on 22 May 1916 made him master of the powerfully defended Douaumont fort in eleven minutes. Relentlessly pursued the enemy with remarkable tenacity and courage." Brigadier general in 1926, he met the same fate as his comrades and was expelled from the army in 1942.[66] We shall encounter him again on numerous occasions, for like General Boris, he became very active in the battle against antisemitism, both before and after the outbreak of World War II: thus, in Verdun in June 1938, he inaugurated the national memorial raised to the memory of the Jews who had fallen during World War I, in the company of M. Campinchi, minister of the navy, and the chief rabbi of Nancy. He was elected chair of the committee to erect this monument, which was raised with the participation of the city of Verdun and of regional and national authorities.[67]

This presentation of the military deeds of these state Jews who all became generals may appear tiresome and repetitive, and this frozen memorial may seem too systematic. There are so many examples: nevertheless, the presence of a significant number of Jewish generals in the army during the Third Republic is one more proof of the meritocratic character of the republican state. To this end and to underscore this exceptional fact, compared to the situation in most other countries[68] (in Italy and Hungary, this phenomenon also appeared but to a lesser degree), it is perhaps appropriate to evoke the career of those defenders of the nation who, through the force of their patriotism and beside Captain Dreyfus himself, who rejoined the service at the beginning of World War I, belied the stereotypes that were often current in the army. Their shining actions even earned them the gratitude of the champions of the extreme right: Barrès, for example, at the end of the war, could do nothing less than integrate Jews into the great French family. To symbolize that definitive integration, a monument to the memory of the Jews who died for France was inaugurated in June 1938 in Douaumont. The Tablets of the Law, engraved on the wall, were here added to the cross that dominated the charnel house in the Lorraine sky. That ceremony took place in the presence of the minister of the navy, the bishop of Verdun, Chief Rabbi Israël Levi, Senators Louis-Louis Dreyfus and Moïse Lévy, *député* Henry Torrès, General Geismar, and numerous personalities of the political, administrative, and military world. Also present were many Jewish officers: generals, colonels, majors, and so on. *L'Univers Israélite* maintained that "those of our own who wore the uniform were so numerous at that pious ceremony that they could have formed the general staff of an army corps." General A. Weiller, chair of the monument committee, recalled that "all citizens of every condition, of every denomination, and of every party have courageously done their duty, Jews along with the others, no more, no less. . . . If circumstances demanded, Jews would join up tomorrow in legions under the folds of the tricolor, to ensure respect and victory. . . . The Union Sacrée must be maintained among all the children of our great Nation." After these words, the bishop of Verdun gave an accolade to General Weiller, and his violet-gloved hand thanked the Jewish crowd, declaring: "This is the reconciliation of the Old and New Testaments."[69]

But the wound was not healed and antisemitism would burst forth again a few years later. Drumont's heritage was not lost and was again used to denounce the presence of Jews in the army. Moreover, before the possibility of a confrontation with Nazi Germany, it quickly renewed the refrain about bellicose Jews agitating to defend and further their own interests to the detriment of France. General Weiller once more had quite a task attempting to preserve the unity of all the former fighters, imploring all recipients of the Croix de Guerre, in a great speech given in Nantes in June 1939, to remain united, in solidarity, in the face of those who wished "to sow hatred against members of certain denominations, who are better servants of the Nation than they are. . . . Let us vow to remain forever men of honor and duty, for the French Nation first, the Human Nation second."[70] Even so, the "Jewish war" was forcefully rejected: Maurras daily attacked "Blum-la-Guerre"; he was fairly quickly joined by certain pacifist currents within the socialist movement led by Paul Faure, whose hostility toward Blum, oddly enough, was expressed in similar terms. For the *Revue Hebdomadaire*, "Blum-la-Guerre is the true belle of the ball. Will France be the soldier of Israel and the instrument of Yahweh's vengeance against Nations?"[71] "Frenchmen," asked Léon Daudet, "young and old, of every milieu and every category, of every province, of every profession, are you ready to leave to avenge Israel for the persecutions inflicted on it by Hitler and the swastika? Are you joining the new crusade, this one beginning in Jerusalem, to which the ethnic half-breed and hermaphrodite Léon Blum invites us?"[72] And, to perpetuate traditions established a half-century earlier, the new *Libre Parole* also asked: "Frenchmen who read me, are you ready to die and to sacrifice your children for the Crusade of the Jew Blum against the impious anti-Semite Hitler?"[73]

The Jews were thus trapped: patriots wanting to defend France as they had done since emancipation, in all the wars of the nineteenth and twentieth centuries, they now found themselves accused of hiding other, properly particularistic goals behind their military ardor. In a word, instead of battling for the nation and the Republic, their desire to fight against Hitler's Germany supposedly corresponded merely to the concern to come to the aid of Jews who were being persecuted there. The accusation of treason was often made against career military Jews beginning at the end of the nineteenth century, and it also touched numerous *députés*, such as Joseph Reinach himself. Nevertheless, this was indisputably the first time that France confronted, not the Reich with its own interests, but a Germany justifying its aggressions through an antisemitic ideology. The place of Jews in the defense of the nation was set on its head because they were accused of acting in a partisan manner: fearing that insinuation, even Georges Mandel cooled his ardor and refused the most conspicuous roles. As if to justify his fears, Pierre-Étienne Flandin expressed his regret that "he let his personal interests take precedence over those of the country." In the meantime, an independent socialist, former *président du Conseil* Ferdinand Buisson, asserted that Mandel was in favor of the war "because, like all Jews, he is pursuing Hitler with his hatred."[74] Beyond their deep opposition, Léon Blum and Georges Mandel were objects of the same opprobrium: their Jewish origin attracted suspicion to them. Both nonetheless committed themselves to defending the nation threatened by Hitler, to the point that, for Winston Churchill, Georges Mandel incarnated the last hope of seeing France remain in the war. As for Léon Blum, the arguments advanced at the Riom trial took up the same refrain, once more condemning "Jewish bellicosity."

State Jews who had the opportunity once more leapt into action. René Cassin, Pierre Mendès France, and Pierre Laroque joined General de Gaulle in London;[75] Georges Weill rejoined the service as a captain, as in 1914, then went to Algiers to sit on the Comité de la France Combattante (committee for fighting France), denouncing "Hitler's philosophy of blood and race."[76] Jules Moch also went to battle, as during World War I, but this time in an attack submarine. He participated in the Norway campaign, then in many missions in 1943, aboard submarine cruisers: in between, in Bordeaux, where the government was hiding out, he led a meeting of ministers in the resistance with Reynaud, Louis Marin, Mandel, and Blum.[77] In the summer of 1940, *député* Max Hymans, alias Grandpré, set in place one of the first *maquis* of the Resistance in Indre and with Jean Pierre-Bloch organized the first allied paratroopers in the *maquis* in Dordogne.[78] Sentenced to death by a military tribunal in Lyon, Hymans ended the war with three citations and the Croix de Guerre. His companion Jean Pierre-Bloch, arrested in Marseilles by the Vichy police, escaped from the Mauzac camp and returned to London where he became chief of political services of the BCRA. *Député* André Wallach, like Jules Moch, had already fought in 1914–18 and presided over the Rhine and Danube organization and various organizations of Alsatian volunteers; as a refugee in Roanne, he gave information to the Resistance. A German tribunal sentenced him to death but the French policeman charged with his arrest allowed him to cross over to Switzerland. The deputy mayor of Havre, Léon Meyer, took the lead in his defense of his city, then entered the Resistance in Grenoble: denounced, he was deported with his wife to Bergen-Belsen. The Socialist *député* Salomon Grumbach escaped from Bourassol where he was imprisoned with Mandel and Moch and joined the Resistance in Cévennes.[79] Some were too old to serve: others, like Mandel and Levy-Alphandéry, left on the *Massilia* in the hope of continuing the war effort from North Africa, only to be arrested. Except for them, almost all the deputies and Jewish senators, like a number of their coreligionists of all social and regional origins,[80] physically took up arms to defend republican France and renew forever and once more the pact of Franco-Judaism.[81]

PART IV

On the Left and the Right

CHAPTER TWELVE

The Emperor's Faithful

In its edition of 12 June 1875, the *Courrier de la Moselle* shared with its readers the keen emotion gripping it: "The naming of M. Lambert to the *sous-préfecture* of Lunéville has stunned men of all parties in Nancy, except of course the Bonapartist party; M. Lambert was *sous-préfet* all during the Empire and distinguished himself by deploying a most unscrupulous political zeal, and by his prudence during the siege." We can easily understand the astonishment that seized the newspaper before this truly unique event: a *sous-préfet*, and a Jew on top of it, who didn't give a damn about the political upheaval that had just taken place, had immediately succeeded in winning the confidence of the new masters after having long served the old ones! The Republic thus seemed to be extraordinarily obliging toward one of the Emperor's faithful, who had always displayed complete loyalty toward the fallen regime.

This faithfulness was beyond doubt: in his report of 14 November 1866, the *préfet* of Meurthe took care to emphasize "his ardent and sincere devotion to the government of the Emperor, his constant preoccupation being to round up those who opposed it. He belongs to the Jewish religion but his extreme tolerance and impartiality have earned him the confidence and the esteem of the clergy."[1] Two years later, "in recognition of the government's satisfaction," Napoleon III "personally" decided to promote him to the first class of *sous-préfets*.[2] The war of 1870 found him at his post: he remained in Toul and participated to the end in the defense of the city, where "he conducted himself nobly." Lambert then rallied behind the Republic; and as the *préfet* of Marne noted in 1872, "after the capitulation of the palace, wishing to cooperate with the resistance, he offered his services to the government of national defense. . . . He was a former *sous-préfet* of the Emperor. But truly, M. Lambert is an exception." It is true that, as a servant of the Emperor, he nonetheless began to equivocate in the face of the 2 December coup d'état, which found him "hesitating"; while he joined the regime, he remained attached to liberalism, and the administration took him for a "constitutional opponent." His own values singled him out quite naturally to later serve the Republic.

Who, then, was this *sous-préfet* Emmanuel Lambert, the only Jewish functionary to hold such a post all during the Empire?[3] Born in Lyon in 1814, the son of Lambert-Caïn, a peddler and hence of extremely modest means, he did not pursue his studies, but instead went into business: he became director of the Société Forestière et Agricole de Belgique (forestry and agricultural society of Belgium), whose seat was in Paris, and which belonged to the Rothschilds; his own brother was director of the Rothschild firm in Brussels. Lacking any real fortune, he married Sophie Enthoven, who as often happened at the time, brought him a significant dowry; according to the *préfet*, she was "a society lady, a bit cool, but conducting her salon, where the society of Toul came together, to perfection. Of an uncommon talent as singer and pianist, she attracts a large crowd to the *préfecture*, exercises a certain influence, and helpfully seconds the actions of her husband. She is a member of the Jewish sect."[4] Through the milieu he was born into and through his marriage, Emmanuel Lambert illustrated the slow shift from court Jew to state Jew that has so often been at issue in this book: like the vast majority of his colleagues in high public office during the Second Empire—and even more, perhaps, during the July Monarchy—he became part of the state through the mediation of privileged milieus. We thus note without any real surprise several letters on his behalf signed by the Baron de Rothschild himself, an altogether common practice at the time, when the dominant circles benefited from a strong influence with the forces in power.

The Second Empire not only represented an opportunity for "promotion" for a group of Jews who were following the general movement of society's industrialization and urbanization; it was also the period when several of them succeeded in rising to the summit of economic power: the Rothschilds, the Foulds, the Pereires, among others. They played a significant role in setting up a banking system at the national level, participated in launching the railroads, and maintained permanent relations with the Court. They were similar to court Jews in Central Europe in that they had succeeded in knitting close ties with the political powers owing to their economic power; they knew how to make themselves indispensable and attain recognition and prestige. Nonetheless, unlike the Bleichröders and other of Bismarck's bankers, they had been emancipated citizens for almost a century, voters and eligible for office. Some of them even became *députés*. Nonetheless, the state, closely tied to the Church, accepted them only with extreme parsimony in the areas where its own legitimacy was at stake. Jules Azevedo,[5] a long-time convert before being named director of general police in the Ministry of the Interior, was made *préfet* of Basses-Pyrénées in 1842; in February 1848, he preferred to resign to remain "faithful to the oath he took to M. Louis-Philippe, king of the French." With that exception, the prefect civil service in general, through which public power was actually exercised, remained hermetically sealed against Jews. As Arthur Meyer, one of the rare royalist Jews of the Third Republic, recalled,

I once more found myself, a modest secretary and the sole survivor of the great plebiscite committee, accompanying its vice president, the duke of Albuféra, and his private secretary, M. Janvier de La Motte, to the Tuileries. They were going to bring the first results of the 1870 poll to the Emperor. . . . The imperial administration had only one Jewish *sous-préfet*, from Toul if memory serves. If 4 September had not happened, there would have been two. After my collaboration with the great plebiscite committee, I had in fact been promised the Yvetot *sous-préfeture*.[6]

This assertion is inaccurate: before *préfet* Lambert, Édouard Salvador had been named *sous-préfet* during the events of 1848; even though the Empire recognized that he was "deeply attached to the Emperor's government," his career stagnated. He was named *conseiller de préfecture* in Lyon, a position he kept for thirteen years! He moved without much damage into the service of the Republic, but his hardly brilliant career then rapidly took another direction.[7] It is therefore true that, under the Empire, Lambert remained the sole Jewish *préfet*, although Édouard Salvador was *conseiller de préfecture* in Nîmes, and Myrthild Caen, who began his career in 1865, was *vice-président* of the *conseil de préfecture* of Haute-Saône in 1870. He moved into that position after his father wrote to the Emperor:

Sire, in 1864 and in April 1858, Your Majesty deigned grant me an audience where I explained that His Excellency the minister of the interior thought he should not name my son, because he is of the Jewish religion or because his name is too Jewish; Your Majesty was kind enough to respond that such a reason did not exist, that He allowed all Frenchmen, without distinction of religion, to participate in public office.[8]

This document is unique in every respect, for it affirms the reality of the equality of all citizens with regard to the highest public employment. The career of Myrthild Caen, however, was not very satisfying.

Given these conditions, Emmanuel Lambert was an altogether exceptional person; is that the reason his administrative dossier is so rich and voluminous? In any case, in Paris and in Nancy, impressive archives describe in detail the life of this Jewish *sous-préfet*, who in what was a unique case, managed to cross the threshold of this place where the state defended its own power and extended its control over society; and, due to his equally rare prowess, he was able to move without great difficulty from the Empire to the Republic and to join for a time all of Gambetta's men. His destiny, in fact, was played out during the events of 1848: as all his superiors noted, "He distinguished himself in June 1848 among all the national guard troops that defended order and security in Paris." In another report, it was observed that "he always devoted himself to the defense of law and order and, during the days of June 1848 in Paris, according to reliable witnesses, he maintained a conduct worthy of praise: this earned him the honor of being named to the duties of *sous-préfet*." His candidacy for this job had been supported by numerous *conseillers municipaux*, with Arago himself at the top of the list. Lambert was thus above all a man of law and order: during the Republic, like other state Jews later, he fought any attack on the legitimacy of the state, even if it came from a popular movement. The sudden events took him away from a career in business; the Bonapartist order made him a high official; and it was all the easier because he "sincerely loves the Emperor; we can therefore count on him absolutely."[9]

The imperial administration continued to show confidence in him even though it regretted the fact that he belonged to the Jewish religion: in 1860, his superior observed that "his religion may make the situation difficult for him in several places in the Empire." For him, "the Toul arrondissement is composed almost exclusively of very religious Catholics, which makes me think that a first magistrate should not be of a dissident religion." Nonetheless, every report was glad to underscore the "remarkable," "astonishing" character of the ties he was able to establish with the clergy. In 1850, his superior indicated one of his exploits to the minister: "The *conseil municipal* had voted against an allocation for repairs at the cathedral. M. Lambert made it reconsider its negative decision, and the sum of twenty thousand francs requested has just been unanimously approved. He is on very good terms with the clergy." He added: "In what concerns his position as a public employee, as a Jew, I think it would be good to keep him in a region where his coreligionists are fairly numerous, which is an advantage in theory, and which, in practice in Toul, has up until this time offered no disadvantage."[10]

Nevertheless, letters of denunciation flooded the minister's office. In one of them we read:

He is a pure-blooded red. His best friends are reds. . . . He is a Jew and that is a reason for not being liked in our region, even in our city, where they are extraordinarily numerous. He is not well looked upon for that reason by the upper class, since our great ladies, to make fun of him, spread the rumor that he was going to be baptized. He is a priestophobe, a priest hater like no other. . . . How do you expect him to support the Christian religion when he is Jewish?

For another correspondent with the minister, this one anonymous, Lambert was "a sower of disorder, a friend of reds, a rampant traitor." And all of them accused him: "He's a red! A Jew attached to the cause of socialism. . . . He reinstated the red mayors who should have been dismissed on 2 December, as happened in the other arrondissement." After the minister's investigation and a favorable report from the *préfet*, who defended Lambert and removed all suspicion from him, he succeeded in quietly pursuing his career, moving throughout the Empire without any problems. He even played the hero in 1854, during a terrible cholera epidemic, personally coming to the aid of the ill: present on the field, he took personal risks that earned him the admiration of all. He received the Legion of Honor, accompanied by a personal note of congratulations from the Emperor. Despite his heroism, history has paid little attention to the personal destiny of Emmanuel Lambert.

Practically excluded from the prefect civil service under the Second Empire, Jews nevertheless reached the highest levels of the magistracy without difficulty during that period. More than any other institution, the field of justice proved to be the most propitious for their entry into state service. The example that comes immediately to mind is, of course, that of Philippe Anspach: having begun his career under the July Monarchy, he became *président de chambre* in Paris in 1862, then *conseiller* to the Cour de Cassation in 1864.[11] Without going into detail on the veritable judicial dynasty he founded, let us simply recall with what determination the Empire placed him at the top of the judicial hierarchy. He was the first Jew to reach that post. A real notable, he married his daughter to a Rothschild in a sumptuous event that, we recall, attracted a great deal of attention at the time. His nephew, Julien Félix, was named *procureur* in Montpellier in 1860 and then *avocat général* in Caen in 1867, as a result of Anspach's and the Baron de Rothschild's intervention. Like Lambert, he then served the Republic without difficulty even though his superiors were no dupes: "He has not always been a republican," wrote one of them in 1887. "Despite a certain liberalism of spirit, he belonged to the reactionary party."[12] In that "dynasty," we also find Adolphe Seligmann, whose mother was an Anspach.

His father and father-in-law were also bankers, and he himself enjoyed great wealth. He began his career in 1851 and pursued it under the Third Republic: in 1878, he was named *président* of Nice.[13]

In the Justice Department of the imperial era, the Bédarridès dynasty also imposed itself from the outset. The career of Gustave Emmanuel Bédarridès amply shows that before the Republic, in certain sectors at the very least, the Empire was open to state Jews: *président de chambre* in Aix in 1854, he was made *procureur général* in Bastia in 1862, then *avocat général* to the Cour de Cassation in 1864. "His political position is very clear," noted the *procureur général*. "He has given unequivocal signs of his energy and devotion to the imperial government."[14] We recall that, with great pomp and in the presence of the Emperor and all the corps assembled, he pronounced the great opening speech of the Court at the infamous "red mass"! Like Anspach, he belonged to a family of wealthy bankers and maintained extremely amicable ties with the clergy and archbishop. In the image of our only *sous-préfet* and of most of the judges already cited, he pursued his career under the Republic, rose to the very top of the profession by becoming *président de chambre* of the Cour de Cassation and *doyen* of all magistrates in France. More than Lambert or even Anspach, Bédarridès could depend on a powerful and close-knit social milieu, that of papal Jews: his own promotion in reality had a collective dimension, illustrated by the veritable judicial dynasty he founded. He was far from being a unique and isolated Jewish magistrate, and his career, like that of other judges who shared his origin, bore witness to the birth of an elite of state Jews that was the first to constitute itself within the judicial corps, well before the Third Republic.

Among the Emperor's faithful who gave signs of loyalty, let us also mention Abraham Alphandéry: a member of the "Bédarridès dynasty," he was named *substitut* in Castellane in 1864, then *procureur* in Barcelonnette in 1867, and occupied the same post in various cities until the end of the Empire, before being promoted by the new Republic to the position of *procureur* in Bordeaux. He finally succeeded Gustave Bédarridès in 1892 upon the latter's retirement. Here again, relations were formal:

Under the Empire, M. Alphandéry was singled out as absolutely devoted to the imperial government. At the time of the plebiscite, he was *procureur impérial* in Sisteron, and distinguished himself through his zeal. According to the *procureur général* of Aix, "he takes care to keep me apprised of everything happening in the arrondissement." He shows great activity and displays intelligence and tact. Assured of the cooperation of the mayor of Sisteron, he impressed an excellent direction on the plebiscite movement.

Again according to his superior, "In politics, M. Abraham Alphandéry professes very clearly drawn conservative and dynastic sentiments." He was nonetheless the first to proclaim the Republic in his city. But his reputation for conservatism pursued him; in 1873, for example, those in Toulon ardently wished for his arrival to hasten "the reestablishment of the moral order, which presents many difficulties."[15]

Many other judges of Jewish origin began their careers under the Empire. That was the case, for example, for Berr Isaïe (de Turique), who in 1858 became *avocat général* in Douai, before being named *président* of the *cour d'assises* in Besançon. "This magistrate," noted his superior in his report of 1857, "devoted to the government of His Majesty, belongs to the Jewish religion, but that circumstance has never created an obstacle in the exercise of his duties. . . . He is attached to law and order and the sworn enemy of all excess."[16] Similarly, Alphonse Bloch wrote in 1865 to the minister of justice: "I have the honor of soliciting the kind support of Your Excellency with His Majesty in order to attain the post of *substitut* within the jurisdiction of the imperial court of Paris." He succeeded and, "having loyally joined the republicans beginning 16 May," he ended his career in 1891 as *président de chambre* in Paris.[17] Let us complete our discussion of this level of the judicial hierarchy with the example of Alexandre May, who entered the magistracy under the July Monarchy, became *procureur* in Verdun in 1854, then *président* in Nancy in 1860. He "belongs to one of the best families in Nancy. . . . He has the ways of a rich man," declared one of the reports contained in his administrative dossier. As his superior indicated in 1865, "M. May is a *président* whose sense of honor and devoted cooperation are helpful in the actions that the administration must exercise in the interest of the government of the Emperor." The task was nevertheless arduous in that part of France: in fact, "M. May is a Jew and in this respect, he would be better placed somewhere besides a city where Jews are numerous, tricky, and full of intrigue: owing to a great deal of agility, M. May has succeeded in avoiding difficulties, and today there are good relations between him and the bishop."[18] These judges loyal to the Emperor belonged for the most part to the most well-to-do milieus: many of them even came from banking families. In this regard, let us reiterate that several maintained visibly close relations with the Rothschilds, to whom some were even related. In that sense, these loyalists of the Emperor, who, like *sous-préfet* Lambert, often managed to negotiate the transition to the Third Republic, represented an intermediate stage between court Jews and the state Jews of the Third Republic, whose origins were far more modest, and who often had to successfully cross the barriers of a meritocratic institution that was more demanding than it had been in the past. The Emperor's loyalists participated regularly in the organizations of the Jewish world, the most important of which was the consistory: Anspach and Bédarridès, we recall, held seats there for a long time. In all points, they presented themselves as notables who were assured of their social role; [19] nevertheless, beyond their socioeconomic status, it was their position within the state that assured them of this preeminence within the religious structures. Politically conservative and strongly attached to the social order, they proved hostile to any idea of reform and in favor of religious orthodoxy. Let us emphasize that it was without a doubt under the Second Empire that these relations between the state and the consistory, made all the more evident in the fact that they shared some of the same positions, were truly knitted together for the first time.

In addition to certain high magistrates, numerous Jewish military men pursued their careers under Napoleon III, though they did not succeed in rising to the apex of the hierarchy (none of them became generals). Although we find several colonels during this very propitious period for Jews entering the army, it is not until the fall of that regime that we see a Jew named general for the first time. Although Anspach and Bédarridès sat on the Cour de Cassation, the army was less tolerant and blocked the ascension of Jewish colonels. As William Serman remarked, "Even though we cannot rule out the hypothesis that the government before 1870 had hesitated for political reasons in naming a Jew to the rank of general because of the duties of representation assigned to generals invested with a territorial command, there is no doubt that the government on the whole respected freedom of conscience and the principle of the equality among religions."[20] In a systematic study of Jewish senior officers of the Empire, David Cohen underscores how their access to the highest ranks was always blocked: Lieutenant Colonel Abraham Lévy, named colonel of the First Regiment of the First Foreign Legion in June 1855, was at the time forty-five years old and should have become general five years later, according to the conventional system of promotions. Nonetheless, he did not reach that rank, proof if there is any, of the limits that the regime imposed even then on the careers of its servants.[21]

These servants of the Emperor, more modest in their origins than Jewish magistrates, almost always from the eastern provinces and not from the more comfortable milieus of Provence or Bordeaux, graduated from military schools such as the Polytechnique or Saint-Cyr, the royal road to the meritocracy of arms, more often than did their non-Jewish comrades. They had few ties with court Jews or, as a result, with the world of the high magistrates. The relative fragility of their social position and their place in a milieu that was attached to the traditions of eternal France were factors that makes the uneasiness they sometimes felt toward their particularism easy to understand. This is true to such an extent that, under the Empire, the father of the future general Bernard Abraham abandoned his Hebrew given name (Moyse) while the future general Aimé Lambert, in a post in Sidi-

Bel-Abbès in 1861, explicitly concealed his origins by altering his father's given names, to Adhémar-Samuel from Abraham-Samuel. In his administrative dossier, the great loyalty of this soldier of the Second Empire was emphasized on several occasions: in 1868, the *inspecteur général des armées* (inspector general of the armies) noted that he was "very devoted to the Emperor and to his dynasty." The next year, the judgment was no different: Lambert was still considered "extremely devoted to the government of the Emperor." This "officer animated by a sacred fire" participated in all the Empire's campaigns, in Africa and in the Orient, Italy, Mexico, Martinique, and finally with great courage against Prussia, before commanding the Versailles fortress and struggling against the insurrection of the Commune. This law-and-order man, who had already fought the 1848 insurrection, had fully identified with the Emperor's authoritarian regime.[22]

The situation for Louis-Napoléon Bonaparte's loyalists was nonetheless far from being comfortable at all times: well before the Dreyfus affair, difficulties arose. Witness, for example, the letter from General Raoult in October 1868 from the Papal States, where the French army was quartered in the wake of its campaign:

The position of colonel of the Thirty-fifth has become vacant. Lieutenant Colonel Sée of this regiment is, I believe, next in line to move to the next rank. Perhaps there might be, in the current situation of the Thirty-fifth, some disadvantage to placing him at the head of this corps.

We go to mass, a demonstration that is much more political than religious. The colonel of the Forty-second used to come to mass with me every Sunday. Lieutenant Colonel Sée, to whom I proposed the same thing, objected for reasons of freedom of conscience, refusing to make such a demonstration, which I consider entirely political. He is a Jew and believes that as such he could not agree to my request.

The Jews are execrated here; and it could happen that Sée, were he named colonel of the Thirty-fifth, might become commanding officer of Viterbe in my absence. The position, with a cardinal and a delegate who is a priest, could become embarrassing and difficult. The population itself, which has extremely deep-rooted prejudices, would not look kindly on a Jew at the head of the armed forces. Perhaps, in contrast, the Mazzinians would be amused and would publish this fact in the newspapers in Italy. That would be an unfortunate result, I believe, and, if possible, we must avoid causing it.[23]

The man who would become the first Jewish general of the French army the very year that the imperial regime fell, and who simultaneously played an altogether important role in the central consistory, thus saw his career openly opposed for the moment because of his religious origins. In reality, apart from the magistrates, most of the Jewish servants of the Emperor seem to have encountered, at one time or another, antisemitism more or less openly expressed. In that way, the Second Empire seems to have been an intermediate period between the Restoration, openly identified with Catholicism, and the secular Third Republic, with the former excluding de facto state Jews, and the latter welcoming them almost everywhere. Yet even during the Republic, prejudice was far from having disappeared, and it still slowed the progress of their careers. The strong state set in place under the Second Empire favored the growth of the administration on which its power rested: this administration was transformed, as Tocqueville and Marx both noted, into an immense machine that meant to extend its control to the whole of society, impose its modernizing inspiration on it, inciting it in an authoritarian manner to turn toward industrial progress. After the advent of the Third Republic, which, in the name of other values, pushed to make the French national and France secular, state Jews started being promoted in public life and no longer only within the private domain. But this moment of transition was still opposed to the idea of secularism: hence the somewhat paradoxical idea of state promotion coming about in a state that remained close to the Church.

As a result, there were many loyal to the Emperor who proved to be extremely timorous as Jews. Some of them changed or disguised too-explicit given names; others actually converted to Catholicism, a practice that was nonetheless very rare in France. As we have seen, the *préfet* Jules Azevedo converted under the July Monarchy. General Wolff, who had volunteered, was wounded several times, became Louis Bonaparte's aide-de-camp in 1803, and ended his career as brigadier general of the cavalry. He was made baron of the Empire by Napoleon I, "through the grace of God and the constitutions of the Empire, the emperor of the French." He participated in the retreat from Russia under the orders of Napoleon and, in his presence, succeeded in crossing the Elbe, commanded the rear guard of Marshal Ney, received a bullet wound, and had a horse killed while he was riding it, a misadventure that was repeated at the battle of Waterloo. Wolff, whose mother's maiden name was Cerfberr, abandoned his first given name, Moïse (which in fact had become "Marx" on certain administrative documents) and only retained "François-Jérôme": it is those names that are engraved on the Arch of Triumph. The career of General Rottembourg, to whom the Emperor also conferred the title of baron, and whose name is also engraved on the Arch of Triumph, was quite similar; he also converted to Catholicism.[24]

Like them, certain members of the Conseil d'Etat converted: Alfred Vieyra-Molina, for example, whose uncle actively participated in the coup d'état of 2 December as chief of staff of the Paris national guard. Morny, the minister of the interior under Napoleon III, brought the younger man into the Conseil d'Etat after he had apparently abjured his faith.[25] His cousin Henri Gradis could not disguise his confusion:

I have just learned some news that has caused me deep sadness. They claim you are preparing to abjure the faith of our fathers, the religion of your mother! in order to be baptized. I can hardly believe such a decision on your part. The act by which one voluntarily renounces the beliefs of one's childhood and family, a religion we didn't choose and that was in some way imposed on us by Providence, in order to assume the responsibility of a change in religion is very rash, and even the most artificial mind must retreat before it. . . . In our century, ambition does not require the sacrifice of conscience.

His uncle Benjamin Gradis also sent him a particularly moving letter:

I learned with pleasure of your nomination to the Conseil d'Etat. . . . But today I want to discuss a graver matter with you, one that, if I am to believe the reports reaching me, is a cause of distress for your family. They claim you intend to change religions. Such a move could only have been suggested to you by the advice of confused friends or by a poorly contained ambition. To abjure one's religion for any human reason is an action that is not honorable in any instance. How, then, should it be judged on the part of a young man who brings together all the advantages one could wish for, who occupies your position, your shining place, and who is doing so only out of vanity or personal interest? . . . Your apostasy would cause despair among a part of your family and might make your poor grandmother die of grief; it would be an insult to the memory of your mother. . . . You would lose the esteem and consideration of most of your relatives. . . . One might think you are forgetting that we live under a regime where all religions are equal before the law, where religious prejudices are much weakened, where the difference of religion does not destroy anyone's consideration or celebrity. The resolution they say you are considering thus has no excuse and no pretext. It will weigh eternally on your conscience.[26]

The legal equality of religions was not enough to dissuade Alfred Vieyra-Molina. Like many state Jews of the July Monarchy and the Second Empire, he converted to Catholicism, and at the end of his career, conducted entirely under Napoleon III, he became *maître des requêtes* (master of petitions) at the Conseil d'Etat in 1865. For a time during that period, conversion appeared to be the condition for access to the state, just as it was in Germany: in France, which had gone through the events of 1789, such a bargain did not go without saying. Nevertheless, several Jewish *députés* also resolved to convert. During the elections of 1863, Achille Fould, minister of state, was elected in Hautes-Pyrénées, and his son Édouard in Allier: they had probably both already converted to Protestantism. Others converted just before elections without, however, successfully convincing the electorate: Henry Avigdor loudly proclaimed his "devotion to the Emperor" and renounced his Judaism just before the 1860 elections.[27] Félix Worms de Romilly clearly committed himself in his platform statement: "I will loyally aid and support with all my efforts the government France has given itself and the dynasty it wants to maintain." As a candidate in Seine-et-Oise in 1869, he did not renounce his Judaism but, as

La Concorde observed, "nevertheless abandoned the synagogue for the circumstances, in favor of the Catholic church. . . . A seat at the Palais-Bourbon is surely worth a mass . . . with music." He was nevertheless defeated.[28]

Apart from Adolphe Crémieux, elected just before the fall of the Empire in December 1869, most Jewish *députés* came out more or less openly in favor of the regime: almost all appeared as something approaching court Jews in that they were still closely linked to the business world. Hence, the banker Maximilien Koenigswarter, elected in Seine, could be considered "governmental" and his loyalty was total. The Pereires, also from banking and credit institutions, who played a leading role in the development of the railroads in France, were also openly supported by the administration and appeared in many ways as official candidates: Eugène Pereire was elected in Tarn in 1863 (he lost in 1869 to an opponent who did not hesitate to continually point out he belonged to the Church). In spite of considerable "administrative pressures," the election of Isaac Pereire in Aude was invalidated, and he was permanently defeated in 1870. The scandal of the Crédit Mobilier, whose creation was favored by the highest authorities, cast a shadow over his candidacy, which was denounced in antisemitic terms: as *La Fraternité* put it, "M. Pereire is the financier of the Empire, the accomplice of all the great guilty parties who made an immense killing at the expense of France's fortune. The orgy is over. He is the incarnation of the Empire." It was in the name of Catholicism that a governmental *député*, who was nonetheless from the same camp as Pereire, supported the necessity of invalidating the election to respond to the demands of the clergy. The bishop of Carcassonne, it seems, preferred to elect someone in the image "of an essentially Catholic country." Before the Chamber, the former director of the Crédit Mobilier let his bitterness show through in terms that bear repeating, for they foreshadow many other debates that broke out during the Republic:

The anathema was such that all the priests of the district became overexcited and preached against me from the pulpit in the most passionate terms. The priests are citizens, and in this respect they have the right to have an opinion on the choice of the nation's representatives. But what does not seem permissible to me is that the pulpit be transformed so that it serves as a forum for speaking—for preaching—against a candidate. In this enclosure, there are neither Jews nor Protestants nor Catholics; there are citizens permeated with the great principles of '89, which are nothing but the political translation of Christian brotherhood. In this respect, I am a Christian.

At the site, there nevertheless erupted numerous demonstrations where, as always, the traditional cry was heard: "Down with Pereire! Down with the Jews!"[29] The commentary of *Archives Israélites* was serene and ironic:

M. Isaac Pereire was born a Jew, but we can say, without broaching personal questions, that he does not cling to that description; it is rather the description that clings to him. . . . As an official candidate, he had the democratic party against him, which is natural, and he did not have the government party for him, for it is in too great a majority the clerical party.[30]

That says it all.

The fact that Isaac Pereire, the great banker so close to Napoleon III, should lay claim to a Catholicism turned toward universalism, at the very moment when his election was invalidated by an assembly that shared his political values, says a great deal about the nature of the Second Empire! His own political friends were sensitive to the identity argument conceived in terms of religion, believing that France could not give itself representatives who were not Catholic. Most state Jews, however loyal they might have been to the Emperor, lived in a similar contradictory and almost intolerable situation, which pointed toward the past and exclusion, even though they already had access to power and the state. To varying degrees, the *conseiller de préfecture* Myrthild Aroncaen, who changed his name to Caen; *conseiller de préfecture* Benjamin; Édouard Lévy-Salvador, who conducted his career under the name Édouard Salvador; *sous-préfet* Lambert, who legally dropped a too-obvious part of his name, Caïn; the future general Lambert, who wisely modified the too-explicit given name of his own father; the *auditeur* at the Conseil d'Etat Alfred Vieyra-Molina; and one or another *député*, all shared the same uncertainty regarding their true status in a society organized around a strong and relatively open state that was still in a more or less obvious symbiosis with the values of an intransigent Catholicism. With the exception of the magistrates, anchored in their solid, almost communitarian milieu, the temptation to leave Judaism, as a way of resolving the contradiction, proved to be strong. This tendency was almost unique in the history of Jews in France. Even Philippe Anspach, who was the first to rise to the highest level in the judicial order while fully performing his role in the consistory, nevertheless felt obliged to modify one of his given names, transforming "Lion" into "Léon."

To finish this portrait gallery of the Emperor's loyalists, whose destinies were more or less tortuous, let us spend a little time with the example of Léopold Javal, the only Jewish *député* who actually founded a political dynasty in the strict sense of the term, since two other Javals, his son and grandson, would succeed him in Yonne. Here again, fortuitous finds in the archives and the long duration of the successive mandates greatly facilitated the researcher's task. Léopold Javal was also an opulent banker, who, despite his liberal positions, was not radically hostile to the Empire. Like the Pereires and Maximilien Koenigswarter, his name symbolized a kind of tacit alliance between the regime and certain state Jews close to the status of court Jews. The Javals also experienced an exceptional economic success, which further integrated them into that small milieu of court Jews. Beginning at the turn of the century, they participated in a number of economic adventures, from textiles to railroads, and established close ties with business milieus: the father and uncle of Léopold had a true calling as general entrepreneurs. Members of the Conseil Général des Manufactures (general council of manufacturers) in the heart of the industrial network, which was open to foreign markets, they launched financial operations of great scope beginning during the July Monarchy, thus amassing a considerable fortune that placed them at the forefront of the socioeconomic elite.[31]

Opposed by the imperial power because of his political liberalism, Léopold Javal succeeded in spite of everything in establishing roots in Yonne, to the point of becoming undefeatable. A person of great scope from many points of view, he was one of the great misunderstood men in the history of Jews in France and in the history of France itself. Close to the Saint-Simonians, an industrialist and a banker, he participated in the creation of the railroad lines. He married Ana de Laemel, the daughter of a Jewish banker from Prague with numerous rabbis in her family. She became a disciple of Rousseau, to the point that she and her husband chose to name their first son Émile (he later became *député* of Yonne as well). Like Anspach and Bédarridès, Léopold Javal belonged to the Paris consistory beginning in 1841 and was elected to the central consistory in 1853, to the great satisfaction of the *Univers Israélite*, which judged that "it would be difficult to make a better choice, to find a better, more worthy Jew in the capital, or one more distinguished by his position, more honorable by his character, or more devoted to his coreligionists."[32] This meant that when he became *député* for the first time, his inclusion in the Jewish community structures was extremely visible. Subsequently, in 1868 — still following the example of Bédarridès and Koenigswarter — he became vice president of the Alliance Israélite Universelle, thus showing the great interest he was taking in Jewish matters. Court Jew by his fortune, state Jew by his popular legitimacy, he nevertheless refrained from alluding to his origins in the public space, during political meetings or in his speeches.

With the 1857 elections, Léopold Javal signed his platform statement as a farmer-landowner in Vauluisant, to signify his deep integration into rural France. This brave soldier, the first to enter Blida in November 1830 where he planted the national flag on the highest minaret — an act that earned him the Legion of Honor — also managed to become rich in business by perpetuating the family tradition, and to establish roots. He organized with great success the agricultural fairs that attracted to Sens, according to the *sous-préfet's* testimony, "a people that, like the Romans, are laborers no less than soldiers . . . at the initiative of a generous citizen, an intelligent and zealous landowner, M. Javal, who created this fair."[33] Javal was one of the rare state Jews to have become a landowner, a particularly competent cultivator of farmland, intending, according to his ideals, to apply rational techniques made possible by progress to the land, for the greater well-being of collective wealth. Thus, he established in Vauluisant a great domain that was displayed as a model farm, and he organized national agricultural contests. He extended that ardor into Landes in Gascogny, favoring the repopulation of those regions in accordance with the policies of the Empire.[34] *Conseil général* of Gironde in 1851, he finally settled in Yonne and became, in great part because of his land holdings, a true political notable.

Nevertheless, in 1857 the imperial administration fought Javal's candidacy, actually calling back the ballots bearing his name; he was denounced as a "demagogue" and a "vulture," and the *sous-préfet* called him a "dangerous" candidate.[35] During the next elections, in 1863, things had changed a great deal: at the instigation of the *sous-préfet*, the ballots for Javal were clearly displayed by the mayors on a separate table, giving voters a view of them alone. The *sous-préfet* nonetheless wished to "avoid giving that candidacy too much acclaim, leaving it in the shadows as much as possible" in order not to harm its chances.[36] More explicitly, the *procureur impérial* noted the fact that "the sympathies of the government have been won over by the candidacy of M. Javal, the *député* from Yonne"; the *préfet*, in an official proclamation, declared that "the government of the Emperor, in not fighting the candidacy of M. Javal, has done justice to liberal opinion, which was sympathetic to him, and, by spontaneously designating him by virtue of its right of initiative to the will of the voters, has proven that it did not consider him an adversary."[37] But Javal publicly refused this "official patronage and the unfortunate interpretations that have been the consequence. . . . I have always thought and I still think that, to serve one's country well, it is important above all to be free of all party commitments." In the electoral struggle that followed between this candidate of the Empire who did not wish to be so officially and his adversaries, the Church once more aligned itself with the opponent's camp: "The conduct of the clergy revolts everyone and brings in many votes for M. Javal."[38] As in the case of Isaac Pereire, the Church fought a candidate who was supported by the Emperor, at least unofficially: there again, his Judaism, however little touted in the public space, confused the matter. The Javal dynasty, however, could not be uprooted. All the more so since Léopold knew both how to support the Empire when it was taking liberal measures and to combat it when it was tempted by authoritarianism. In 1864, he thus declared before the legislative body: "The imperial government should not be preoccupied exclusively with the situation of industrialists but rather with French citizens as a whole. I should say I am addressing my sincere thanks to the

Emperor for the noble initiative he took by inaugurating freedom in commerce, taking the first step toward the great and fertile road to freedom."[39]
A little later, in contrast, he publicly pronounced his opposition to the
plebiscite.

Émile, the son of Léopold, succeeded his father without difficulty. A
law-and-order man also, he entered Paris with the army of Versailles, where
he had served as a doctor-major. A recognized scientist (he was a specialist
in strabismus, an ailment on which he wrote several treatises), he was
named director of the ophthalmology laboratory of the Sorbonne. In 1871,
he was elected *conseiller général* of Yonne, then *député* in 1885, a seat he kept
until 1895, devoting his time to improving hygiene in the schools, spreading education, and struggling against depopulation. Modest, always wearing a black tie, getting around on a bicycle, he became a fervent devotee
of Esperanto, a language in the service of humanity as a whole. He was
solidly rooted in the family district, and never again in his public or private
life did he appear to evoke even a distant identity with Judaism.[40] Having
enormous local legitimacy at his disposal, he provoked practically no antisemitic reaction. *La Croix* cites his views and comments very favorably on
his theses on the dramatic consequences of the fall in the French birthrate,
concluding: "It is because France is being de-Christianized that, physically
and morally, it is threatened with death."[41] Locally, as a study of the ballots
shows, when his name was crossed out, it was only very rarely accompanied by insinuations of an antisemitic nature.[42]

Thus at one with his district, a devoted man of science who was apparently distanced from Judaism, he elicited a curious polemic in the *Univers
Israélite* concerning his scientific interpretations, which were taken for arbitrary or even wrong: in a speech given before the Académie de Médecine,
he tried to link certain traits of Jewish religious thought to the visual disturbances of astigmatism, of which he was one of the recognized special-
ists. "M. Émile Javal is a great doctor," retorted the *Univers Israélite*, "an
oculist of the first order and a very expert optician, but — even though he is
a Jew and even though his late father sat on the central consistory — he is
perfectly ignorant of Judaic matters. He proved this well at the last meeting
of the Académie de Médecine, where he advanced outrageous claims about
us that we would hardly pardon from a Christian."[43] And yet — as his
daughter recalled, evoking the time of the Dreyfus affair — "he was a Jew.
With all his force as a sociologist and a scientist, he set out in pursuit of
truth. Bent over his oculist's lens, he continually scrutinized the facsimile
of the trial documents, the Esterhazy *bordereau*, the counterfeit Henry, to
uncover the subterfuge. He went to the trial of Rennes in 1889."[44] For a
long time afterward, under the Third Republic, this son of loyalists to
Napoleon III maintained within his heart the ambiguities of the status of

state Jew during the time of the Emperor. His own son, Jean Javal, who succeeded him in Yonne—he was elected in 1909—seems to have been even more rooted in the region, to the point of entirely forgetting his by now distant particularist origin. Only *La Libre Parole*, after so many years, seemed to still remember his Jewish origin, when it knowingly opposed the measures praised by Jean Javal to "the spirit of labor and thrift in the men in whose veins flows the old blood of France."[45]

CHAPTER THIRTEEN

Gambetta's Men: The Republic of Southerners

Bismarck's armies were drawing dangerously close to Paris; the situation seemed so desperate that, to prolong the combat and avoid a devastating surrender, the government was forced to organize emergency national defense measures from the provinces. On 12 September 1870, a decree declared that "M. Crémieux, member of the government of Défense Nationale, *garde des Sceaux*, minister of justice, is delegated to represent the government and to exercise its powers." Having thus provisionally become the leader responsible for the resistance in Tours, Crémieux had to take a back seat to Gambetta at the beginning of October; Gambetta, at the time minister of the interior, flew to Tours by hot air balloon to take things in hand.[1] A civil instruction manual distributed by the Republic to strengthen citizens' convictions presented that historic moment: Gambetta descends from his balloon; among those waiting for him, in the very first row, is Crémieux.[2] The two men knew each other well, respected each other, were both deeply devoted to the Republic; in addition, Gambetta had begun his career as a lawyer with Crémieux and had even pleaded cases beside him.

In that dramatic context, Gambetta also wrote to his friend, the future *député* Ferdinand Dreyfus, and begged Dreyfus to join him at the Ministry of the Interior. But Dreyfus preferred to continue in armed combat. Camille Sée was named general secretary to the Ministry of the Interior. Alfred Naquet decided to accompany the government delegation to Tours as secretary of the Commission d'étude des Moyens de Défense (study commission on means of defense).[3] Under these circumstances of extreme emergency, Édouard Millaud was named *premier avocat général* in Lyon and performed the duties of *procureur général* before becoming a parliamentarian and close friend of Gambetta and Jules Ferry.[4] Among the numerous *préfets* named at the same time by Gambetta, Eugène Lisbonne was installed at the head of Hérault:[5] he would become *président* of the *conseil général* and senator there, incarnating the new republican regime in that region. Named a *préfet*, he proclaimed on 7 September: "Citizens, let us all to our post! The nation is making the supreme appeal to all its children. Let us close ranks and go forward, for what we must save is everyone's home, everyone's France."

While Crémieux, Millaud, and Lisbonne could be considered Gambettists, the ties between Naquet and Gambetta were more intermittent and stormy: as Naquet himself told it, after he had given a speech at a meeting of the Union Républicaine, "Gambetta shook his hand and said: 'If you continue to talk like that, you will be not only a useful man but a necessary man.'" They parted ways when Naquet refused to consider the Constitution definitive; he gave hostile speeches regarding Gambetta's supporters and even opposed him in Marseilles during the legislative elections of 1876. In 1878, they once more came together; in the words of Naquet, "he had not had any personal animosity toward Gambetta. He had distanced himself from him for tactical reasons, and now it was time for the policy of concord, which alone could be fruitful."[6] Their rediscovered friendship was beyond dispute, as the tone of their private correspondence bears witness.[7] It is nonetheless clear that, subsequently, through his Boulangist and then anarchistic positions, Naquet once more distanced himself from Gambetta's Opportunist vision. But they were still close for a time during the consolidation of the Republic.

With Crémieux, Millaud, and David Raynal, Gambetta's ties were truly very close. In 1865, Gambetta underscored: "I am winning a real place of confidence in M. Crémieux's mind and heart. . . . I can no longer leave their home. I am attached to them. The discussions with M. Crémieux are for me the most penetrating lessons I've ever received in my life, and I most ardently vow to hold on to such a great, amiable, generous teacher for a long time."[8] He owed him a great deal, in particular, his professional career. Often, he evoked with tenderness the occasions when the Crémieux welcomed him into their home: "I could have cried with joy, the son of the house would not have been given a greater welcome."[9] He shared that intimacy with Millaud as well, who participated in the founding of the Union Républicaine. The two often dined together.[10] In addition to Joseph Reinach, who was long one of his closest collaborators and friends, he also established ties of friendship with David Raynal. Raynal was elected in Bordeaux after Gambetta himself had publicly declared: "Bordeaux could not choose a better interpreter of my political ideas." Gambetta was Raynal's "teacher and friend" owing to whom "the Girondin populations have come to the Republic."[11] He in fact presented himself explicitly as a Gambetta loyalist; his presence on the political staff was something like the sign of the irreversible character of republican commitment. In 1883, the *préfet* of Basses-Pyrénées observed, in his report to the minister of the interior, that "the population is reassured by the naming of Gambetta's friends, such as David Raynal" to the Ferry cabinet.[12] He occupied the position of minister of transportation in the Grand Ministère led by Gambetta in 1881, whose office was managed by Joseph Reinach; in 1893 he became minister of the interior in the Casimir-Perier government. His family played a fundamental role at the Bordeaux consistory; upon his death in 1903, a battalion of the Fifth Infantry Regiment paid him honors, and, in a long funeral procession of more than a thousand persons, there figured Casimir-Perier, Waldeck-Rousseau, Combes, Freycinet, Loubet, Caillaux, the *préfet* Lépine (with whom he had worked closely), General Mercier, the *président* of the Cour de Cassation, a great number of *députés*, senators, and high officials as well as Chief Rabbi Zadoc-Kahn. Combes and Fallières, among others, were the pallbearers; on his grave, after many speeches celebrating the services rendered by the deceased to the republican cause and to France, it was Rabbi Israël Lévi who pronounced the final prayers.[13]

Like Gambetta, son of an Italian father and of a mother whose ancestry could be traced back several generations to Quercy,[14] the majority of Gambettist Jews were from the South: they were for the most part papal Jews, the first to have been involved in the great movement of emancipation leading to full assimilation into French society. They were almost always part of one of the two family networks that composed the milieu proper to republican State Jews: Crémieux was born in Nîmes, and that is where he first practiced the legal profession; Lisbonne was from Nyons; Millaud was born in Tarascon; Naquet in Carpentras; and Raynal in Paris, though his family was firmly rooted in Bordeaux. From these two regions with relatively dissimilar structures of sociability and more particularly from the Southeast, there thus emerged a considerable proportion of state Jews: they were the first to be admitted without reservation into public life, to benefit from promotions in the administrations, especially in the magistracy. They were also the first—with the Pereires, the Foulds, and the Léons, politically rooted in the Southeast—to be elected *députés* by their fellow citizens, with whom they maintained real relations of sociability and confidence. Later, other Jewish *députés*, also from the Midi, were elected there: Fernand Crémieux in Gard, Albert Milhaud and Pierre Masse, both in Hérault, a department that would later elect Jules Moch, originally from the East, and his neighbor Léon Blum, elected in Sète. However different, these two regions were accustomed to cultural and linguistic particularisms and attentive to multiple cultures; they lent themselves less to uniformization.[15] "The Republic of the village" that took root in the regions of tolerance and pluralism, where Protestants often lived harmoniously with Catholics, was considered legitimately represented by these Jews who had left their *carrières* — that is, the Provençal ghetto where they had earlier been confined — and who were the first to abandon traditional clothing, a mark of their submission, to participate in local political life, almost always joining the ranks of the democracy.

To these southern republicans of an almost Girondin tradition on whom Gambetta depended,[16] were added, in his more immediate entourage, two Jews from the East, members of the other large family network, Joseph Reinach and Ferdinand Dreyfus; as if, between Adolphe Crémieux, in whose shadow Gambetta began his professional life, and Reinach, his close collaborator while in power (he also entrusted him with the task of publishing his speeches), the founder of the Republic did not hesitate to call on particularly assimilated Jews to help him impose the republican order. Beside the many Protestants and Catholics who joined him, these Jews entered on equal footing in the famous "new strata" whose emergence he so strongly desired. Confronted with the resignation and opposition of the former elites, the "Moses of the republican Land"[17] was naturally forced to call to his side not only a large number of atheist or deist Catholics but also members of minority denominations: their status as the formerly oppressed elicited obvious affinities with the values of a Republic founded on the equality of all citizens. These men helped Gambetta in his undertaking to legitimate the Republic at a crucial moment in its history: although active in that process, they constituted only a minuscule part of the republican staff.

Let us spend some time with the destiny of two of them, Adolphe Crémieux and Eugène Lisbonne, and try to describe through them this "southern" character of Gambettist Jews, who associated with one another and who, in spite of their ideological differences, made their political plans together: Crémieux defended Naquet in court; Millaud mounted a legal defense for David Raynal; Lisbonne and Naquet introduced several bills together, as did Millaud and Naquet (the bills proposing to the Assemblé the sale of Louis Bonaparte's wealth failed, however). A real republican milieu had been constituted, made of political and ideological collusion, linking southern Jews first to Gambetta and then to Ferry. Take, for example, the hunting expedition that took place on 26 December 1886 at the home of the Pereires: Édouard Millaud, David Raynal, and Joseph Reinach all feasted in the company of Jules Ferry.[18] Millaud also dined on several occasions at the home of Victor Hugo, who had been a war buddy of Adolphe Crémieux.[19] The author of *Les châtiments* wrote him in 1872: "You are one of the founders of the 1848 Republic, you are one of the founders of the 1870 Republic, and you are my friend."[20]

Crémieux was a real jack of all trades, inasmuch as he was the linchpin of Provence Jewry, where the Republic was so compatible with maintaining all cultural particularisms; he was also at the origin of a certain number of nominations to the judicial apparatus, including Millaud's. Gustave Bédarridès, originally from Aix-en-Provence, also saw his career greatly facilitated in 1848 by an intervention on the part of Crémieux, his cousin; like Lisbonne and Crémieux, the entire Bédarridès dynasty expressed itself fluently in Provençal. This southern Jewry, deeply anchored in the land, loved all its traditions and happily expressed itself in the local idiom: Crémieux sent out many letters in Provençal,[21] while the *préfet* Lisbonne did not hesitate to respond with a quatrain written in that language — and with what fervor! — to a letter hostile to the Prussians that had been sent by someone in his district:

> Quatrefés grameci, Roch, dé ta dédicaço
> Téi vaïan vers man tout ésmougut dé plési;
> Sentoun poudr'é mitraï é dirien qué la raço
> Dés Prussien s'espantis aou bru dé toun fusi.[22]

> [Many and sincere thanks, Roch, for your dedication,
> Your valiant verses moved and pleased me
> They smell of gunpowder — it's as if the race
> Of Prussians were taking fright at the sound of your gun.][23]

Far from the antisemitic caricatures of wandering Jews, poor creatures stripped of any local roots, the southern Jews and their relatives who became magistrates or part of the prefect civil service were tied body and soul to their land: they shared its values and its customs, as their superiors observed in their administrative dossiers; and like Naquet, they spoke Provençal. Finding it improper for Naquet to have such familiarity with a language from the deepest culture of the soil, Léon Daudet accused him of "usurping the southern accent."[24] Eugène Lisbonne belonged entirely to the Midi of France, and in Montpellier, where he was named *préfet*, we find among his fellow citizens several Crémieux and Vidal-Naquets. "These southern Jews, through their civic spirit, have managed to incorporate themselves intimately into the life of the Christian masses, all the while keeping their religious beliefs intact."[25] Thrown into the center of struggles for the Republic during the events of 1848, Lisbonne became *procureur* for Béziers before being deported to Algeria after the 1851 coup d'état. Like

Adolphe Crémieux, who played an important role in the 1848 revolution before becoming minister of the Second Republic, Lisbonne was a southern Jew, a lifelong republican. At different levels of French society, their acts were, as it were, emblematic of the Jews' love affair with the Republic. Let us also emphasize that Crémieux and Lisbonne were both practicing attorneys, as were Millaud, F. Crémieux, and later Pierre Masse, all elected from these same southern regions. They could not but integrate easily into that "republic of lawyers" that was set in place under the leadership of Gambetta, who had in fact learned his craft beside Adolphe Crémieux.

Their funeral services attest to that symbiosis instituted between certain Jews and the Republic. In February 1880, the government decided to organize a national funeral for Adolphe Crémieux, "a reward reserved for citizens who have rendered great service to their nation." Adolphe Crémieux, minister of justice in 1848 and 1870, soldier for freedom and the Republic, defender of oppressed Jews throughout the world, the man who made French citizenship accessible to the Jews in Algeria, senator, former president of the central consistory, and acting president of the Alliance Israélite Universelle, had just died: in the streets, two squadrons of dragoons under the command of a colonel were waiting in full regalia. The pallbearers were Gambetta, president of the Chamber; Cazot, minister of justice; Jules Ferry, minister of public education; Pelletan, vice president of the Senate; E. Arago, senator; and A. de Rothschild, president of the central consistory. On the coffin could be seen the senatorial sash, the attorney's robe and wig, and the insignia of Freemasonry, of which the deceased had been a grand master. Among the wreaths that adorned the hearse drawn by four horses, there was one from the "members of the Jewish community of Nîmes, to their illustrious compatriot"; in the crowd, walking in procession beside the delegation from the bar association—*députés*, senators, and functionaries—were the representatives of the central consistory, the Alliance Israélite, the students of the Jewish seminary, and the Masonic lodges. The dragoons stood in line with children from the consistorial schools and the Talmud-Torah. In this endless procession that crossed the streets of Paris the police prefect, the *premier président* of the Cour de Cassation, Freycinet, Sadi Carnot, Jules Simon, Ernest Renan, *député* Bamberger, General Sée, and others walked together.[26] At the Montparnasse cemetery, after tributes from Camille Pelletan and Arago, the chief rabbi of France paid homage to the man who in and of himself symbolized the fulfillment of Franco-Judaism.[27] In his memory, the consistory had hired an artist to engrave a commemorative medal:

On the right of the bust is represented the Daughter of Zion crying and joining in mourning for the French nation; a long mantle of black crepe covers her robe of golden brocade as a sign of mourning.

With her right hand, she is placing a laurel wreath at Crémieux's feet; with her left, she is wiping away her tears, which are falling in memory of her most illustrious son, protector of art and science, the most valiant guardian of the Commonwealth.

To the left of the bust, History is preparing to inscribe on her tablets the imperishable achievements of the immortal orator.[28]

A little later, in 1891, Eugène Lisbonne, senator and *président* of the *conseil général* of Hérault for almost two decades, also died. His funeral too had the character of public mourning: on the grand balcony of the building housing the Montpellier *préfecture*, the tricolor flag was furled and craped, and the gas lanterns of the *préfecture* grill were covered with a black veil. In addition to numerous *préfets*, *sous-préfets*, generals, and magistrates, there followed a considerable crowd, which walked the entire length of the procession, crossing the city. As *Le Petit Méridional* emphasized, "he was given a truly popular funeral." Many speeches from the administrative and political authorities highlighted the patriotism of "citizen Lisbonne," while a delegate from the workers exclaimed: "In the name of the working class, I have come to bid you a final farewell—M. Lisbonne, farewell." The arrondissement council, the delegation of the Académie des Sciences et des Lettres of Montpellier, the mayors and municipal delegations, but also the service staff from the hospitals, students, the Masonic lodge of Montpellier, and many others moved off while the military honors were rendered by a rank of the 122d line troops. At the front of this imposing procession, we find the rabbi of Nîmes, the president of the Marseilles consistory, Vidal-Naquet (a relative of the deceased), and numerous representatives of the Montpellier Jewish community. After speeches from politicians, the rabbi celebrated Lisbonne's virtues, his love for all men, and his ardent patriotism.[29]

In Paris and Montpellier, funeral ceremonies symbolized the deep symbiosis existing between state Jews and the political class of the Republic, in the name of a conception of citizenship oriented toward the cult of universalism, and compatible with beliefs understood in an almost messianic way. The love of country mingled with full devotion to the Republic, conceived almost as the realization of the rationalist ideas of Freemasonry, but also as the incarnation of secularized hopes in keeping with the utopian dimension that marked Freemasonry's vision of the world.[30]

These two southern Jews brought together all the characteristics of the founders of the Republic: like most of them, they were lawyers; they fought for freedom of the press and for the defense of democracy; they were close to Gambetta and Jules Ferry, and supported the battle for secularism; and finally, like numerous republicans, they were Freemasons. We know that Freemasons played a significant role in the founding of the regime and that a number of the regime's leaders were members of lodges: Gambetta, Jules Grévy, Jules Ferry, Jules Méline, Paul Doumer, Jules Simon, Émile Combes, Émile Loubet, and Félix Faure, among others.[31] In the government of Défense Nationale, in addition to Adolphe Crémieux, there were several Freemasons: Eugène Pelletan, Garnier-Pagès, Ernest Picard, and Gambetta. As early as 1869, Gambetta belonged to the lodge of the Grand Orient in Marseilles, beside Gaston Crémieux, the future communard, and the journalist Gustave Naquet, who in 1870 was part of the committee that proclaimed the Republic in Marseilles. The next year, he became *préfet* of Corsica for a short time. A little later, in 1875, Gambetta gave a great speech before the Grand Orient on the occasion of the admission of Jules Ferry and Émile Littré.[32] More generally, it is estimated that 40 percent of ministers between 1877 and the outbreak of World War I belonged to Freemasonry.[33] For all that, the Republic did not result from mysterious, clandestine acts by Freemasons involved in a conspiracy: they had many different political opinions, opposed one another, and did not in any way act in a coordinated matter. The lodges in France were very decentralized.[34]

The membership in Freemasonry of certain southern Jews such as Crémieux, Lisbonne, and Millaud[35] simply reinforced their integration into the republican milieu. Once more, Adolphe Crémieux is the best illustration. His career in the lodges of Scottish rites propelled him to the top since he was unanimously elected grand commander by the supreme council and, in this capacity, had at his disposal all privileges related to the magnificence of that high position.[36] As he forcefully expressed it at the end of his life, at a celebration organized by the supreme council at the palace of Trocadéro in 1878,

The Masonic religion is not religion as we know it: Freemasonry accepts all religions, it rejects none. I who am speaking to you am the great proof of that truth. Whether you are Catholic, Protestant, Jewish, or Muslim, Masonry will not inquire. Spiritualism is thus the real ground of Masonry. . . . The force that will maintain that institution is the attachment it has for sane doctrines, and at their head the most beautiful, the most worthy of enthusiasm, the one we place above all: love of country."[37]

Gambetta's men, who for the most part rallied behind Jules Ferry, were convinced patriots inspired by a transcendent ethos compatible with the ideals of Freemasonry. Like the founders of the regime, they presented themselves as fierce supporters of universalist citizenship, which assured the preeminence of "French centrality" owing to the voluntarism of a "state with its great protection, its perfected police force, and the endless procession of its functionaries." They were also especially concerned with establishing a Republic on solid ground, with Reason as its foundation, which would, by the same token, be a guarantor of equality among all men, beyond their particular cultures. Like republican leaders, they intended to battle for the construction of a "secular state" that drove all churches from the public space.[38] They therefore enthusiastically rallied behind Gambetta's famous slogan: "Clericalism, this is the enemy!" and supported his struggle for the separation of Church and state. They also took on the task of secularizing the school system, and of extending education to girls, a task to which Camille Sée later attached his name.

As a result, republican Jews shared the ideals of the founders of the Republic. In the 1870s, Adolphe Crémieux was too old to participate actively in building the new democratic order: always excited by political struggles — under the July Monarchy, in 1848, and in 1870 — he was more a passionate man than a statesman capable of investing his energy in everyday administrative tasks, which were indispensable for anchoring the Republic in reality.[39] In contrast, Gustave Naquet, *préfet* of Corsica, described himself as "the Robinson Crusoe of *préfets*, capable of republicanizing the island";[40] he nevertheless remained more revolutionary than Gambettist, and his career in public office was extremely short. In spite of marked differences in ideology, let us note his justification of "the Republic, firm as a rock, which attracts all hearts and all intelligences to it."[41]

At that time, Eugène Lisbonne appeared definitively as the only Jewish *préfet* from the South, entirely loyal to realizing republican ideas, and belonging body and soul to the new political leadership of the Third Republic. Elected in 1849 as secretary of the republican committee of Montpellier, arrested and deported in 1851, head of that same party at the end of the Second Empire, *préfet* in 1870, and member of the *conseil général* of Hérault, he almost immediately became its *président*. He was then made *député* in 1876 and 1877, and senator from 1888 until the end of his life: we can hardly imagine a more exemplary career for a local republican notable. He was a decisive and ardent man: he was given the honor of proclaiming the Republic in Montpellier before a considerable crowd that had rushed to receive Gambetta's envoy.[42] Among all the *préfets*, it was he who galvanized his fellow citizens when confronted with the enemy. On 26 October 1870, he exclaimed: "In its heroic resistance, Paris calls the departments to itself. . . . France, recovering its sense of itself, will speak its language of freedom. We will become ourselves once more: the sons of '92. The hour is come, we must vanquish Prussia or become Prussians."[43] Made in September 1870, his proclamations offer a striking historical tableau of France at war: "Paying taxes," he said, "is an act of patriotism, an act of public safety"; "To be a national guardsman is not only a duty, it is an honor. . . . Do not be deaf to the alarm the nation is sounding. On your feet, national guardsmen of Montpellier, on your feet!"; "The only commitment the state is asking of you is to run toward danger. . . . Thus, first to the elections, then to maneuvers, and finally to the enemy!!!" He painted the portrait of the perfect citizen joyfully fulfilling his civic and military duties at the hour of the nation's danger, not flinching at any contribution to serve the new mass uprising, identical to the one in 1792 through which the republican people had proclaimed its political identity. "Under our First Republic," he exclaimed, "the children of Hérault almost by themselves formed the Thirty-second Half-brigade whose heroism has remained notorious in history. The sons, do not doubt, will know to march in the footsteps of their fathers and to rise to their height." The reference to revolutionary France formed the matrix for his publications: it was the nation of freedom and emancipation for which citizens had to risk their lives. No hesitation was allowed in aiding "the Republic in chasing off the foreigner." The rebels were "traitors," who should be punished "with all the severity of military laws." "The pennant that every district offers you is a remembrance of the region. The children of Cévennes are strong, they will not falter. Let this flag guide you into combat." Lisbonne co-signed the declarations of the government of National Defense approved by the members of the delegation, such as Gambetta and Adolphe Crémieux, and increased his vengeful tone: "To work, everyone, and let us save the Republic! Only it has the virility of supreme moments; Prussia has only it to fear because despots fear only free men."

This decisive action in favor of the Republic was not in the least sectarian. Lisbonne had near unanimity on his side, to the point that the bishop of Montpellier, in these uncertain and troubled times, sang his praises. In response to a request for financial aid for the war effort, Monsignor François wrote to him:

I wish with all my heart to respond more fully to your honorable confidence and to the gratitude that your wise administration has the right to expect from the clergy of the diocese and of all. . . . Since on the day of the nation's perils, sacrifice must go beyond ordinary boundaries, I am wholeheartedly putting my name down for a sum of one thousand francs for work at the Hérault artillery. . . . And since we are dealing with a *préfet* such as M. Lisbonne, I will offer the round figure of fifteen hundred francs as my part of the patriotic work.

Monsignor François thus agreed to "serve the true interest of a just and honest Republic" and, in an episcopal pastoral of 6 March 1871, emphasized that "at the head of the department we have a magistrate full of wisdom, of moderation, and consideration, a conciliatory spirit whose high intelligence has understood that the true and healthy Republic is based on justice, the law, and honest methods based on rights." The prelate did not hold back his praise of *préfet* Lisbonne, and shared with Adolphe

Crémieux, minister of justice, the great esteem he had for him. Crémieux responded:

Your letter contained praise of my friend M. Lisbonne, which touched me very deeply; the example of the primary administrator of the department and the primary pastor of a vast diocese getting along so well with each other in the interest of a just and honest Republic, as you call it, must arouse the sympathies and loyalty of everyone to the government of National Defense.[44]

The relations between Monsignor François and Lisbonne were so straightforward that François, on chilly terms with the Protestant mayor, Pagezy, wrote: "It is easier to get along with one's ancestry than with one's collaterals."[45]

Glory did not last, however: suddenly, on 23 April 1871, Eugène Lisbonne, who refused to exchange posts with the *préfet* of Isère, put on his lawyer's robes once more; thereupon, he denounced "the scheming, the intrigues, the slander of those who brought about his replacement." Thiers paid tribute to the ousted *préfet*: "Among all the *préfets* we have named," he noted, "M. Lisbonne is without dispute number one."[46] In a personal letter to the minister, Monsignor François asked that the civil servant be retained. But the legitimist *député* wanted him to leave: "M. Lisbonne is an honest Jew, an agile lawyer who wishes above all to maintain and even increase his clientele." A mayor exclaimed: "Long live the Republic! For pity's sake, citizen Gambetta, give us a *préfet* of the Republic who speaks less well and who commands a bit better. . . . The Prussian prisoners in Montpellier are ten times better than that useless Frenchman."[47] Southern conviviality had its limits: the local political struggles were translated into a few rare antisemitic outbreaks coming from the more conservative France, or into the rejection of a representative of Opportunism, considered to be inadequately reformist.

The dismissed *préfet* would rapidly extract his revenge by moving into the local republican political class, where he remained for a long time. In October 1871, he was elected to the *conseil général* of Hérault; to celebrate the event, "a fraternal banquet organized by a few workers" brought together citizens from various districts of Montpellier. Lisbonne was invited to be their president: "Four hundred citizens were present at the meeting: workers, bourgeois, lawyers, doctors, all distinctions had disappeared to make way for the patriot; the keenest joy, the frankest gaiety, and the deepest cordiality animated that family celebration." At the end of the celebration, a baritone, "dear child of the Montpellier public," offered a bouquet to the former *préfet* in the name of republicans. While balloons rose in the air and firecrackers popped, a ball began: women displayed their republican sentiments by wearing a symbolic ribbon."[48] The republican sociability characteristic of southern regions pushed social differences to the background: a kind of ideological unanimity came forth, taking root in solid revolutionary traditions.

From that point on, Lisbonne confronted the government and for the first time embraced the defense of effigies of a patriotic nature, with which the population identified. On 30 October 1871, the new *préfet* wrote him a letter to protest the presence, in the meeting room of the *conseil général*, of a bust of the Republic topped with a Phrygian cap, an emblem that was "more that of the Commune than of the Republic," that "of demagogy" or "sedition, which recalls the bad old days of 1793," and that could "put off many good citizens." Thiers asked the *préfet* to have the bust removed: "The Phrygian cap is not the emblem of the Republic of 1871 and must disappear." The *préfet* protested:

> Since voters in Montpellier have offered the *conseil général* a white plaster bust of the Republic, a Dupré copy with a Phrygian cap, also white, the great majority of the *conseil* has accepted it with its thanks. Injunction from the *préfet* to have it removed as a demagogic emblem. That measure would provoke a very regrettable protest on the part of the *conseil* and of the population devoted to you, at a time when the most perfect calm reigns.[49]

Eugène Lisbonne was thus confronted with the ideological drift of a new republican order uncertain of its referents and symbols. When Marianne took power, her revolutionary attributes frightened some; at a time when it was indispensable to avoid a slowdown in the rallying of public opinion behind the Republic, it was better to play down its effigies.[50]

A convinced republican who did not hesitate to express himself in Guesde's newspaper, *La Liberté*, Lisbonne played a crucial role in one of the most striking local ideological conflicts of that period, when a fragile Republic seeking to set itself off from excessively revolutionary traditions was being installed. However, let us retain the fact that the southern Jewish *préfet* with the tough militant past could only balk at such shillyshallying. He actively battled for the Republic on all fronts, vigorously defended freedom of the press through a law that bore his name, and militated in favor of public schools. Witness the superb speech given on 2 August 1890 at the awards ceremony of the boys' Grand Lycée of Montpellier: he underscored his loyalty to the "government we love and serve with all our devotion. . . . No one here, in our patriotic and republican commonwealth, has forfeited its solicitude and justice. . . . I call for everyone to emulate these teachers and students of which our school is so proud — our school, one of the most beautiful jewels in the region's crown!"[51] In the same way, Lisbonne devoted all his energy to creating a public law school because "under laws that authorize free schools and universities, the government must look favorably on provisions tending to propagate state universities." A jurist and *bâtonnier* under the Second Empire — confronted with authoritarianism, he had already proclaimed he was a "soldier of law" — Lisbonne, after repeated efforts before the minister of public education, finally obtained satisfaction.[52] Although the Church hardly seemed moved by that demand, this was not the case in the matter of the diehard struggle for obligatory, free, and secular public schools. This time, Monsignor François raged against "the obligation forced on the family patriarch to give up his children to such schools exclusively — this is communism violating the sanctuary of the home"; secularism appeared as "an attack on the freedom of the family, the first and most sacred of freedoms." According to the bishop, an admirer and friend of Lisbonne at the time of struggle and war, "Evil has never required that the Protestant teacher be a stranger in his temple, that the Jewish teacher be a stranger in his synagogue, while it has always vehemently required that the Catholic teacher be entirely separated from the Church and its ministers, and it is in the name of freedom and equal rights that such an unjust partiality is professed."[53] In a local context where Protestants and Jews had a real presence, such a declaration signified a break: it was an echo of the struggles that the advocates of secularism were waging at the national level, on whose front lines we find, in addition to numerous Catholics who had turned to atheism or to freethinking, several Protestants and a few Jews. Had the time of local concord passed, a time of the symbiosis of cultures and religions in a southern sociability oriented toward tolerance?

We might think so, as the local flare-up of political anti-Protestantism that came to light during these years also confirms. It was then that the Franco-French wars crystallized.[54] Antisemitism, it seems, still remained relatively rare in that region where Jews had for so long blended into the population. During his local political career, Lisbonne does not appear to have elicited any violent animosity of an antisemitic nature, with rare exceptions. At the time of his defeat in the senatorial elections of 1876, the *Archives Israélites* emphasized that "the religion to which this honorable candidate belongs was inconsequential in his defeat. For the first time, the status of Jew was not invoked against those of us who canvassed for votes. M. Lisbonne failed in Hérault along with the slate on which he appeared."[55] This fact must be given even more emphasis in that the candidate never concealed the fact that he was Jewish: not only was he a member of the local consistory, but he always demonstrated, in the words of *Archives Israélites*, "proof of his attachment and devotion to Judaism. We have not forgotten the speech given by Lisbonne the first time he took the floor as *président* of the *conseil général* and in which he reminded everyone he was a Jew."[56] This republican notable with strong local roots, this powerful man, proved to be knowledgeable in Judaism: paying last respects to Israël Bédaridde, former *bâtonnier* of the Montpellier bar, a local Jewish personality of great scope, he noted that Bédaridde, a colleague of Adolphe Crémieux and "deeply attached to his beliefs" had recently written a study on the Talmud. He went on to exclaim: "It is unprecedented in its simplicity, its synthetic clarity. . . . Nothing is missing. The author methodically separates the Mishnah, or doctrine, from the Gemara, or commentary, and from the book of legends."[57] Even though he was not a practicing Jew, Lisbonne showed a real loyalty toward Judaism, which the *Archives Israélites*, so prompt to condemn the rapid distancing of Jewish elected officials, celebrated. And, as we have seen, a rabbi officiated at services the day of his funeral, while the *Univers Israélite* deplored the loss of "one of the best jewels in the crown of French Jewry."[58]

Édouard Lisbonne, a Gambettist par excellence, a southern republican Jew, a man of the land who was continually reelected, true "patron" of Hérault for almost two decades, also appears as the archetype of a Republic's fool. His rootedness in the land, his use of the local language, and his insertion into the particularly dense networks of sociability gave him a threefold aspect as it were: a *préfet* concerned with law and order, a notable mingling in clientelist structures, and a loyal Jew managing to maintain, parallel to his commitments in the public space, an institutional membership in organized Jewry. Strikingly, in 1873 he was elected to the Marseilles consistory by the voters who returned Adolphe Crémieux to the central consistory.[59] His case is all the more exemplary in that it would rapidly become the exception among Jewish politicians from the nineteenth century to our time: he expressed the force of a Provençal Judaism that was ancient and rich in traditions. This Gambettist, this friend of Adolphe Crémieux, shared with him a rare aptitude for uniting dimensions that were often perceived as contradictory.[60] Abbé Grégoire could only have shown disappointment in these loyalties, which he conceived as antithetical: state Jews, now accepted by the nation, were reaching posts of authority without converting to Catholicism, as Grégoire had wished. In addition, Grégoire—who had attacked the use of patois and, in his report on the politics of language,[61] had ardently wished for the abrupt disappearance of all anachronistic idioms—would have been displeased that Jews, though "regenerated," persisted in using these patois, showing by that their keen attachment to provincial cultures. In that sense, their entry into the republican state did not abrogate any of the characteristics related to their membership in civil society.

Adolphe Crémieux, teacher but also faithful admirer of Gambetta, was, for an even longer time, at the head of the central consistory, to which he had belonged since 1831, before moving to the presidency of the Alliance

Israélite Universelle and relentlessly intervening in favor of persecuted Jews throughout the world, in Romania and Russia and Syria: the minister, jack of all trades in the republican political and judicial staff, held that post on two occasions, in 1848 and 1870, and, during a brief period, virtually presided over the national government. That political figure, which France repaid with a national funeral ceremony, was, even more than Lisbonne, involved in the internal life of French Jewry. As the *Archives Israélites* observed, Crémieux and most southern Jews — Eugène Lisbonne, Adrien Léon, David Raynal, and even Alfred Naquet — "belonged to a generation of Jews who, even though they stopped practicing their religion, still remembered that they bore Jewish names."[62] He perfectly incarnated the symbiosis between the Republic and the Jews. In May 1872 he declared at a meeting: "To the God of Abraham, of Isaac, and of Jacob, to the God of David and of Solomon, our adoration as believers; to our France of 1789, our worship as sons; to the Republic of 1870, our absolute devotion. That is our great Trinity."[63]

Crémieux ensured the link between the beginning of the nineteenth century, a period where the debate on the conditions for Jews' emancipation was still going on, and the period when Jews were being integrated into the "new strata," assigned by Gambetta to the task of constructing the Republic. In his *Histoires des sectes religieuses*, Abbé Grégoire, who knew Crémieux personally, took him as the very model for the new generation of emancipated and "regenerated" Jews. For the famous defender of the Jewish cause, Crémieux symbolized a particularly striking success: upon Grégoire's death, the honor fell to Crémieux to pronounce the eulogy of the author of *Essai sur la régénération physique, morale et politique des Juifs* (Essay on the physical, moral, and political regeneration of the Jews). And yet, Adolphe Crémieux, this regenerated Jew who entered the legal profession so rapidly, remained attentive throughout his life to reinforcing Jewish cultural and institutional specificity; in contrast to the explicit wishes of Abbé Grégoire, he remained faithful to the Jewish world, even as he filled the post of minister of justice on two different occasions. For Grégoire, not only was it strongly desirable that Jews ultimately convert in order to reach the final level of regeneration, it was also inconceivable that one of them could before long fill a post of authority — such as that of *procureur*. No one could imagine a Jew holding a measure of authority over a Catholic people. Yet Crémieux, whom Grégoire considered the fulfillment of his own prophecies, devoted a large part of his energy to reinforcing the community structures and also held high government posts on two occasions. Even worse, it was he who, during a brief period, named the *procureurs*![64]

In that sense, Crémieux was closer to Mirabeau, who accepted without difficulty the idea of maintaining multiple cultural particularisms in revolutionary France; note, in fact, that in 1789, the Provençal orator demonstrated his respect for religious specificities in the *Courrier de Provence*, in a region attached to tolerance and conviviality. And again, from this perspective, Crémieux, like Ferdinand Dreyfus,[65] shared with Gambetta an admiration for Mirabeau: "Mirabeau is one of the figures of history that Gambetta admires the most," observed Joseph Reinach. "He exerts a real fascination over him. Long ago, the resemblance between the great man of the first revolution and the great man of the Third Republic was pointed out."[66] Unlike Grégoire, both men intended to maintain the cultural diversity of republican France; and Crémieux, turning his back on the hopes of the famous abbé, also attempted to contribute to the construction of that fragile but fertile balance between a republic of citizens and a society of multiple cultures. Yet he remained essentially an opposition republican who only occasionally exercised power: although he was very occupied with the defense of Jewry and the life of its secular and religious institutions, it was too late for him to truly invest in political and administrative life. His friend Lisbonne was, in contrast, a true administrator in local politics, more oriented toward his fellow citizens as a whole, as his duties as *président* of the *conseil général* required. Although they died about the same time, one belonged more to the first part of the nineteenth century, while the other contributed to rooting the Republic in French soil.

The assimilated southern Jews, by the very fact of their assimilation, elicited a very distinct kind of antisemitism, excessive in regard to Crémieux, but discreet with respect to Lisbonne. Gambetta's Republic became for many the very image of the "Jewish Republic," of which Crémieux was the damned soul. And in any case, the explanation was obvious: Gambetta himself must be Jewish! Drumont was among the first to spread that tenacious legend. For the author of *La France juive*, "a Württemberg Jew did business in cafés and engaged in smuggling, married a Jewess of the region and Italianized his name to Gambetta. The son or grandson came to France, established himself in Cahors and gave us a great man."[67] A man who did not disdain surrounding himself with a few Jews in his immediate entourage could only be Jewish himself; and in fact, "with his nose's pronounced curve, he is linked to the tribe of Ephraim."[68] This fable immediately took hold and has found many people credulous enough to share it, even up to the contemporary period. Under those circumstances, Crémieux, Gambetta's friend, could only be his closest accomplice: he was supposedly at the origin of the birth of a true "Jewish Republic." In fact, in 1848, the Fourierist left had itself already brought a similar accusation against Crémieux, when he moved to the Department of Justice: Victor Considérant maintained that "the presence of M. Crémieux at the Ministry of Justice is a grave danger. . . . France has just had a revolution, not a Sabbath."

Following the establishment of the Third Republic, according to Drumont this time, "Crémieux was the important leader of the French democracy, the veritable impresario in the human comedy in France. . . . He incarnated the Masonic revolution in its most complete form."[69] Curiously, the author of *La France juive* saw in him "a Jewish Nazi [*sic*, a misspelling of the Hebrew *nasi*, 'prince']" who "contributed, more than anyone, to confiscating the French Revolution on behalf of Jewry."[70] The strategy of Gambetta, his ally, had led directly to "the establishment of a Jewish Republic in France."[71] In his works, Drumont also attacked David Raynal, Camille Sée, Alfred Naquet, and Joseph Reinach, not forgetting Lisbonne. Political antisemitism was inscribed in the imaginary order: but in its excesses, it still rested on one indisputable fact, the presence of a few Jews, almost all of them from the South, in Gambetta's immediate entourage. They were, however, hardly visible, because so rare: hence, of the one hundred and twenty-seven *préfets* named between 4 September 1870 and 6 February 1871, only two were Jews, and one of them remained at his post for only six weeks! Similarly, in the political staff and in the magistracy, while a few Jews attained posts of authority or saw political mandates entrusted to them, this represented only a few individuals lost in the impressive sea of new *députés* and senators or in the even more imposing corps of magistrates. The "Jewish Republic" that was formed around Gambetta by Jews who, like him, often came from the south of France with its solid republican traditions had reality only in fantasy.

Since the Republic was once more calling into question the social order and overturning elites, who often came from Catholic milieus, it elicited violent reactions; considered artificial, a break with the organic unity of the nation in favor of an abstract citizenship cut off from the land, it provoked a rise in political anti-Protestantism and antisemitism that was more and more vehement, expressing a rejection of individualism and rationalism. To varying degrees, the few southern Jews devoted to the Republic and close to Gambetta would rapidly realize this. Lisbonne and Milhaud in Hérault, the men most integrated into local networks of sociability, were less affected than Crémieux in Chinon or Raynal in Gironde, both of whom had occupied ministerial posts. Unlike Lisbonne, concerned almost exclusively with the affairs of his department, David Raynal, who served as minister several times, was taken up in the whirlwind of the great national disputes and faced a permanent and particularly cruel antisemitic campaign with which almost all the political parties were associated, including the Guesdists, who accused him of all kinds of depravity.[72] All those who attained a national position, who were absorbed in the Franco-French wars and so acquired great public visibility, saw a ferocious antisemitic hatred develop toward them, even in the most welcoming regions in the South:

this observation can also be verified in the case of Alfred Naquet in Vaucluse and Joseph Reinach in Digne.

At the national level, that ostracism become so vast, so inscribed within the framework of the Franco-French wars, that even the south of France, which had in the past proven so tolerant toward the Jews of the region, launched violent antisemitic campaigns. Ironically, these affected the son and grandson of Eugène Lisbonne, for example. In Hérault, a department that was usually peaceful and pluralistic, songs like this one circulated:

> Of the thieving Jew, cursed race
> Let us rid ourselves in all haste
> It's with us, the men of Hérault . . .
> It's with us they'll have to deal.[73]

At the turn of the century and during the interwar period, these republican regions, so open to and respectful of cultural pluralism, experienced antisemitic movements directed in Hérault against the distant successors of Eugène Lisbonne, such as Albert Milhaud, Pierre Masse, and Jules Moch. In this context of profound national dissension, the myth of Gambetta, king of Jews, who was imposing a republic apprehended as artificial, remained intact for decades,[74] becoming under Vichy a finally acknowledged and self-evident fact. That would justify the exclusion measures that were then considered urgent, and which also applied to the distant descendants of these southern Jews who were so attached to building the Republic.[75]

CHAPTER FOURTEEN

Alfred Naquet, Anarchist

Here is a loving portrait of Alfred Naquet as only Léon Daudet could paint it in his best moments of inspiration. These were not a few lines thrown to the wind as was his habit: this time, he did not bristle at the task, but took his time to tell us all the good he thought of the famous senator from Vaucluse.

Hunchbacked as in Arabian tales, eyes shining like a sadistic oriental dancing girl, he takes after the spider and the crab. You see him in a nightmare, descending lopsided from the ceiling, skirting the bed curtains and going to drink from the wash bucket. . . . Of what Sabbath copulations is Alfred Naquet the issue, what witch's cauldron cooked and recooked the elements from which he was formed? Under what ray of the threefold Hecate were the cursed beasts assembled, of which he represents the conglomerate? Tenacity in destruction is one of his traits. . . . Joseph Reinach and he have shared the task they carried out among us: while the first attacked the commonwealth, the second did his deed on the family and showed the relentlessness of a burrowing termite in implementing divorce. Naquet has a taste for ruin, corruption, and death. He haunts the social charnel house, sniffing. This former chemist passionately loves everything that is in a state of decomposition, degradation, putrefaction: a family's tears, national mourning, riots, civil war, all scourges.[1]

Although it is true that Léon Daudet was intimately acquainted with the most violent antisemitic caricatures, this passage nevertheless distinguishes itself in the hatred that animated it, a hatred that perhaps only Léon Blum could have elicited against himself. In certain ways, Naquet and Blum were very similar. Of course, everything separated them: the social success of Léon Blum, his elegance, his time spent in the Conseil d'Etat, his place at the head of a mass party, his role as *président du Conseil*, his central place in the political staff for so many years — all traits that could only overshadow Alfred Naquet. In a slightly provocative manner perhaps, let us nevertheless outline elements of resemblance: assimilated state Jews from two sites par excellence of French Jewry, Alsace and Comtat Venaissin, both intellectuals, antiestablishment, social reformers, concerned at various periods with Spanish revolutions, attentive to the destiny of women, and anxious to please, they incarnated the idea of a critique of the social order, even though they rejected the most rigid collectivist theories. But one shared the road for a time with Boulangism, whereas the other put all his ardor into combating the nationalist and populist right; one saw himself as a freethinker, whereas the other remained a believer. . . . We could multiply the similarities and differences ad infinitum.

The fact remains that, in his time, Alfred Naquet was almost alone among state Jews, normally so attached to the republican order, because he preached social protest; in the interwar period, however, Léon Blum was one of many involved in socialism, modifying a bit the very image of the state Jew within French society. Naquet preceded them on this path and caused a scandal. Witness the fact that, even in 1946, the following text could be written by an author as levelheaded as Adrien Dansette. According to that historian with a sense for nuances,

Naquet was a horrid hunchbacked gnome with a long, ageless face, such as we see among the Ashkenazim who cry in Jerusalem at the Wailing Wall. His wavy and bouffant hair, his dark mustache and beard, framed a large yellow forehead, a large yellow hooked nose, and large yellow teeth; but admirable moist eyes through which passed all the nostalgia of his race illuminated his ghetto face. . . . His intelligence, as Semitic as his face, escaped the intoxication of destructive controversies only to abandon itself to some messianic passion. Seized by the idea of divorce, he became its apostle throughout the region and, thanks to him, the law was voted in by the high assembly in 1884.[2]

Therein lay the cause: in 1914, as in 1946, for the satirist as for the historian, with Alfred Naquet there arose the scandalous question of divorce; it was that question that forever marked the man. Let us thus return to the incident. In 1876, Naquet proposed to the Chamber of Deputies that divorce be reestablished. It had been instituted by the French Revolution and abolished in 1816 at the instigation of Bonald, theorist of the counterrevolution. Naquet's initiative dumbfounded a number of his colleagues; as he himself told it, he was "received with bursts of laughter."[3] Nothing discouraged him: after six years, in 1884, his efforts finally bore fruit, he was victorious, and France renewed its ties to 1792. In the meantime, he had relentlessly covered the countryside and the cities, giving lecture after lecture, receiving threats, becoming the object of personal attacks in one region or another, and becoming a laughingstock for many. He did not deviate from his path, confronted adversity, and little by little elicited general curiosity. Finally, the moment came when everything shifted. The debate that began before the definitive vote in July 1884 also deserves to enter the symbolic pantheon of the minor Franco-French wars. On both sides, matters were clearly articulated.

His most determined opponent was none other than the bishop of Angers, the very conservative Monsignor Freppel. In his view, it was all very simple: "Through the law you are going to vote in," he exclaimed, "you are pronouncing the divorce between the Third Republic and the Catholic Church. Well then, vote for that law! Move, if you wish, to the side of Israel, go to the Jews!" Two years before the publication of *La France juive*, in the Chamber, accompanied by applause from the right, one of the most famous elected officials of the nation, without waiting for Drumont and his follies, by himself constructed the phantasmic model of the "Jewish Republic." Monsignor Freppel hammered it in:

You are going to ravish from this country its moral superiority. . . . And to whose benefit? Certainly not democracy's. For after all, gentlemen, who is asking for divorce? The population of our countryside? Divorce horrifies them! Nor is it the workers in our cities, for, in their praise, I say that the workers in our cities intend to maintain the honor of their wives and children in their homes, however modest, however poor they might be. Who is asking for divorce, gentlemen? A few scatterbrained women, a few novelists. . . . And in this anti-French, anti-Catholic campaign, who have they depended upon? I would not want to hurt anyone, but in the end, you have to call things by their names, you have to say how they have come about, what has led to the law on divorce. They have depended upon a handful of Jews (*exclamations on the left. "Very good" on the right*). . . . The movement that has led to divorce is, in the true sense of the word, a Semitic movement (*interruptions on the left, cries of approval on the right*), a movement that began with M. Crémieux and has ended with M. Naquet, through a whole series of Jewish agitators and promoters of divorce. Elsewhere, in the rest of Europe, antisemitic movements are taking shape, and I hardly need tell you that I do not approve of them in any way. Here, on the contrary, we are witnessing a Semitic movement that will triumph in the question of divorce. . . . I still have enough French honor and Christian pride, in what concerns me, not to lower the walls of Christian civilization before the Jews (*strong marks of approval on the right, interruptions on the left*).[4]

The great antitheses resurfaced: the Republic and the Church; the nation, all social classes combined, and the Jews; the real Catholic identity of

French society and its enemies; health, and the illness that carried decadence and immorality; the civility of mores and debauchery, cosmopolitan licentiousness; the organic community of the Catholic nation and disruptive Jewish individualism, and so on. These oppositions had also emerged during the discussion of the bill on the separation of Church and state elaborated by Camille Dreyfus, the bill dealing with girls' schooling, whose paternity could be traced to Camille Sée, and other bills as well, whose initiative sometimes fell to state Jews elected by the nation. Each time, as the accounts of the debates attest, a large proportion of national representatives ascribed to such oppositions, excluding Jews de facto from the nation. The public's "approval," in the eyes and understanding of everyone, came to legitimate the positions taken, which would otherwise have appeared marginal, caricatured.

Let us turn our attention once more to Monsignor Freppel: divorce was "another step on the way to secularization, which means quite simply the de-Christianization of France." By the same token, it would logically lead to the diminution of marriages and births: "For lack of any other motive, might not reason, that so eminently French and patriotic reason, be enough to lead to a rejection of a bill that is so contrary to the interests of the country?" The accusation became more pointed: It was a defeatist measure bordering on national treason and taken precisely by Jews, cosmopolitans unworthy of trust. If France hoped to recover its past glory, if it wished to remain faithful to its traditions and to regain the lost provinces where the Catholic faith was so marked, it had to reject the republican undertaking of excessive secularization of society. It had to begin by combating divorce, which threatened the Christian family, the ultimate foundation that had until then been spared from attacks by the advocates of freethinking. Monsignor Freppel was unshakable, the first in the 1882 debate to attack the theorists of anticlericalism in the name of "working France, the true France, believing France, the most healthy nation of the people of the cities": he led the assault against Alfred Naquet, not retreating before any argument. In his view, "before importing that foreign production into our country, we should preoccupy ourselves with the national character. . . . It is impossible to admit that Flemish sangfroid, British phlegm, and German patience dominate among men of our race."[5] Even if all these foreigners devoid of physical strength had resigned themselves to divorce, this could not be the case for men of the French race, so alive and passionate! The national character would not tolerate it! What a gamble to want to link gloomy and lifeless Protestants to French Catholics of such a vigorous race!

For fear that this argument might appear inadequate, the bishop of Angers went on: "I can understand how a freethinking Jew like M. Crémieux could have taken the initiative for such a proposal, but you who, for the most part, represent Catholic populations, cannot vote for it without betraying your mandate. . . . Do not touch the French family for, along with religion, it is the last force remaining to you!" From one era to the next, the core of the argument did not vary: it was the Jews who were risking the disintegration and, we might say, "the Protestantization" of France. While the right loudly approved this view, the proposal for which Alfred Naquet had fought for several years was in the end voted in by the Chamber, where *députés* of Catholic origin were in the majority. They had been elected with a republican mandate whose coherence rested solely on secularization. Thus, several hundred *députés* voted in favor of divorce, among them Waldeck-Rousseau, Pelletan, Clemenceau, Casimir-Perier, Cavaignac, and Martin Nadaud. Gambetta also supported the plan and, beside him, all his "men," from Ferdinand Dreyfus to David Raynal, joined by Ferry's Protestant friends such as Steeg and Buisson.

Alfred Naquet had earned himself fame and a fate: there were countless caricatures and drawings portraying him as the executioner of marriage, a bad genie for happy couples, a murderer of fetuses that would never see life. Continually endowed with a markedly Semitic profile, he brought with him unhappiness and desolation, like a threatening demon.[6] The press and cabaret singers wholeheartedly threw themselves into the fray, taking swipes at this torturer of happy couples, whom he was pushing toward adultery. While he was praised to the skies by the proponents of the Republic and of secularism, the portraits that his admirers drew of him were not devoid of all ambiguity. Far from it. Hence this ironic and tender text from *Gil Blas* on 21 November 1888:

Of him I will speak no ill. He was the propagator of divorce, the liberator of the territory, the healer of the conjugal bond. . . . And I know of Catholics who in the evening, before falling asleep, mumble a word asking the Lord to look favorably on this pagan. . . . A curious mug, Hebraic and faun-like, superb in anger, like the august face of a prophet of Israel, sensual in laughter . . . the great hooked and pugnacious nose of the dominating races.[7]

Even among the celebratory, antisemitic clichés flowed from their pens. And when conservative novelists evoked the vote on the law, they did it by outlining radical oppositions, for example, between the France incarnated by Joan of Arc and Naquet with his strange and calculating ways: in a little-known text, Barbey d'Aurevilly rebelled against divorce, "the bluestockingism of the family," and in contrast, saw in "Joan a female archangel who held the sword of God."[8]

For Drumont and the extreme right, the mere name Naquet for many years elicited the worst insults. Numerous passages in *La France juive* denounced his actions: "If you want to see a lovely specimen of a Jewish statesman, take Naquet and study him," proclaimed Drumont, going on to judge, as an indisputable specialist, that "divorce, *guittin*, is an absolutely Jewish idea. A single Catholic orator dared to declare it, Monsignor Freppel. . . . To be sure to have the law required, the one adapted to its own institutions, Israel had the bill prepared by rabbis. It was the former rabbi of Brussels who drafted the provisions of the law and dictated them to the Chamber of Deputies."[9] Naquet — the freethinker who professed a militant atheism and was almost banished from Jewish milieus, the anarchist who shared the anticlericalism of Gambetta and all the republicans and who openly opposed the Synagogue — was thunderstruck: he thought he was acting in the name of Reason, and here he was being linked to Jewish religious traditions and rabbis! The issue was still the Judaizing of the Republic and its secularizing practices, which threw the Catholics into turmoil, they who had come to rally behind Marianne. Even in 1906, *La Libre Parole* attacked "Adonis-Naquet" and rushed to the aid of Paul Bourget against "the old Jew Naquet," whose theses on divorce bore "disorganization and anarchy within them, and [whose] mentality can have no relation to our own." And Drumont's newspaper concluded: "What could it matter to that Hebrew whether France lives or dies?"[10]

Let us cite a few samples from the antisemitic literature that this law on divorce elicited. A famous member of the extreme right, Charles Benoist, presented the man whom he considered solely responsible for the legalization of divorce:

One need only see M. Naquet to immediately think of that horrendous misery of the ghetto. His head, large and heavy, expresses craftiness rather than intelligence. . . . M. Naquet's spine is only the visible image of his twisted spirit. . . . His mind is a public dispensary of poison, where projects of reform are arranged on the shelves and labeled like flasks, the arsenic of revision next to the strychnine of public appeal. . . . He is the providence of bad marriages.[11]

Joseph Santo, an expert in the matter, exclaimed: "You know the Jew Naquet, that hunchback, the inventor of a Macassar oil for the hair and the father of an obscene law on divorce, this nationless, anti-French, internationalist, cosmopolitan Jew, this Bohemian of patriotism, this ghetto escapee fresh from Palestine, with the bloody nerve to develop proposals in a Germano-Talmudic jargon in France."[12] Robert Launay sketched his portrait this way: "A living alchemist dragging his way among the horned animals with his long goat face, the crab walk of a witch, who invented divorce as an ideal means to install anarchy."[13] Léon Daudet hardly changed in his evaluation: in 1902, he judged that "for the Semite Naquet the idea of a nation is an old myth that needs to be discarded. The gnome of divorce with the claw-like hands is squatting on our legend."[14] Thirty years later, he describes him as "a hunchbacked Aramaic, as in oriental tales, a kind of nonassimilated Jew from the ghetto of the Marais whose sexual force and libido" explained the relentlessness with which he set to work on that perverse divorce law.[15]

We could multiply ad infinitum these observations, which evoke the litany of antisemitic insults that later greeted the publication of Léon Blum's book *Du mariage* (On marriage). From this perspective as well, the two men resembled each other: they both wanted to reform the relations between men and women by virtue of a more general conception of human justice and freedom for all. Their rationalist and almost libertarian plan was perceived as a demoniacal threat directed against the Christian family. In 1907, Blum extended Fourier's influence by proposing the sexual emancipation of young single women, a measure that would favor both their present fulfillment and their future commitment in marriage: the sexual freedom of single women was the condition for the "marriage of reason" they would enter into later. The level of general hypocrisy would drop, adultery would recede, conjugal happiness and social stability would be better assured. The reaction was not long in coming, and Blum joined the ranks of Naquet and Camille Sée: he was seeking to pervert young French girls to undermine the social order!

La Croix des Alpes-Maritimes asked, "Who more than the hideous Naquet contributed to destroying the French family? Blum, the evildoer with a pen, sowing corruption and death. The collapse of the family and of society will continue to worsen. The Jew can be happy with his work."[16] According to *Jaune*, "The Jewish high official who wrote and published that filth ought to be spanked like Thalamas and before the assembled people. What do you expect, I think the Hebrew is in his element, his way of being; he is synthesizing in a striking manner immodesty, shamelessness — as Drumont said, the verecundia of his race."[17] The antisemitic tradition linked Naquet and Blum, whom it saw as responsible for the perversion of mores, with Catholic French girls letting themselves be seduced by these appeals to debauchery lavished on them by these Jews of eastern origin, devoid of civilization, still oriented toward the beast and its instincts. From Drumont to Céline, the Jews were apprehended as great Satans transforming France into a vast brothel where they could exercise their perfidious talents. Each critic tried to outdo the others in gibing at these "Don Juans of the synagogue"[18] — Naquet, Blum, Mendès France, and Mandel — who were endlessly mocked for their sexual activities, so damaging for the pure Catholic French girls who succumbed to the charm of the unknown. According to Henri Faugeras, "The entire process of demolishing the family, from Naquet to Blum and Zay, from divorce to sex education, is Jewish."[19]

La Libre Parole, still just as vigilant though no longer edited by Drumont, published long excerpts from *Du mariage*, as did *Je Suis Partout* and *Gringoire*. For Jean-Charles Legrand, Léon Blum, "spiteful as a eunuch and tenacious as a scorpion, is teaching our women complacence in rutting his friends, who are lying in ambush."[20] Léon Daudet, who, as we recall, deployed an unparalleled antisemitic hatred against Alfred Naquet, the profaner of family morals, also displayed the same verve against Léon Blum, "the immoralist entirely foreign to our mores, customs, practices, to common sense as Westerners understand it"; in his view, *Du mariage* inevitably evoked the practices of "Turks or Persians."[21] Paradoxically, André Gide, the great contemplator of Western morality, whose name at the time often symbolized the most fundamental amoralism, unhesitatingly joined the proponents of the extreme right: according to him, *Du mariage* was a "dangerous" book proving that "the Jews have become masters in the art of disintegrating our most venerable institutions, those that are the foundation of our Western civilization, in favor of some unprecedented licentiousness and relaxation in mores, at which, happily, our good sense and our Latin instinct of sociability is repelled."[22] The fact that Gide would come to defend the West and the Latin identity of French society says a great deal about the way that the most assimilated Jews were perceived! The oriental character of Naquet and Blum was thus revealed as the sole source of a sexual perversion threatening the West as a whole. Until Vichy, a few state Jews, sensitive to a certain social reformism that led them to the frontier of something approaching moral anarchy compatible with the multisecular tradition of utopian socialism, came to incarnate the spirit of degeneration responsible for the moral downfall of France and also for its demographic decline. In April 1941, when all was lost and there was a need to find out those responsible, Léon Daudet drew the moral of the defeat in *Action Française*:

A recent statistic shows that, since the passing of the Naquet law, approximately one million couples have split up, which, as it happens, has become the easiest thing in the world for them to do. . . . The separation could have been merely temporary. Divorce is a real barrier, and it has given marriage an exit door. It is a venom introduced into good relations. It is against the preservation of the family.[23]

In reality, beyond the morality of families, Alfred Naquet, even more perhaps than Léon Blum, had also very early attacked all the other sources of conformism and social domination. The Bohemian student in worn black corduroy pants and vest, who came to study medicine in Paris in 1852 and lived in the Montparnasse district, was a rebel.[24] He was involved in drafting a *Travail sur l'affranchissement de la femme* (Study on the liberation of women), which he submitted to Père Enfantin. He went to see Enfantin to express his keen admiration for Saint-Simonism; a real working relationship was established between Naquet and the high priest of the new religion of Humanity, one of whose dogmas consisted precisely in the belief in the absolute necessity of abolishing inheritance. A few years later, in 1867, when he had finished his medical studies, Naquet participated in a congress for peace in Geneva, where, among a great number of delegates, were to be found both Bakunin and Garibaldi: during a meeting, he publicly called for the condemnation of Napoleon I as the individual responsible for modern militarism — but he was not heeded. Upon his return to Paris, he made contact with secret Blanquist societies, went to see Blanqui in Belgium, and with their help, prepared demonstrations against Napoleon III. Arrested in November for having been part of the Société Commune Révolutionnaire des Ouvriers de Paris (revolutionary commune society for Paris workers), he was sentenced to fifteen months in prison.[25]

We need to evoke that dimension of Alfred Naquet's life because it was in prison that he drafted a very important work, *Religion. Propriété. Famille* (Religion. Property. Family), which, soon after his liberation, earned him a new conviction, since it was extremely critical of the established order. Not only did he attempt, as a chemist, to demonstrate the nonexistence of the soul and to refute the very idea of God in the name of materialism, but, in addition, embroidering upon Saint-Simon, he opposed the hereditary transmission of property.[26] Although, in contrast to Proudhon and Marx, he did not dispute the idea of property as such, he rejected the principle of inheritance, thus adhering to the meritocratic vision of Saint-Simon that would later be found in Durkheim and, as a result, in several founders of the Third Republic. In their view, "inheritance is unjust; it perpetuates the inequality of conditions, which are originally just."

What followed was almost logical: since "man and woman render services of the same value to society, they are equivalent. . . . Woman is in no way inferior to man."[27] Well before undertaking his campaign in favor of divorce, Naquet proposed that the father no longer be considered the head of the family and advocated the abolition of marriage, with all children, legitimate or not, born entirely equal before the law. It was thus not a question of demanding the reestablishment of divorce — an intermediate solution for which he would soon fight — but of preventing the conflicts that could lead to it. That radical solution attacked the very foundation of the social order: the end of marriage would be the dawning of a kind of communism that was both egalitarian and libertarian. For Naquet, "to make marriage indissoluble is an attack on freedom of the highest order."[28] It was the very idea of the family that was called into question, in favor of a changing and egalitarian love relationship installing real equality among all children, whether or not they were legitimate. Going much further than

the plan Léon Blum would later defend, and adopting a more radical viewpoint than the simple restoration of divorce for which he fought so hard,
Naquet reached the conclusion that only the abolition of marriage would
make adultery and prostitution disappear: "Marriage is an essentially tyran-
nical institution, essentially an attack on freedom. . . . The family has become one of the causes of the destruction of society. . . . Love is the true
savior of humanity."[29] The work caused a scandal and its author was
charged with outraging public and religious morality, criticizing the family
and property: once more sentenced to prison, he preferred to flee to Spain.

Seven months earlier in that country, a revolution directed at the monarchy had broken out and a junta composed of progressives and democrats
had taken power. Republican propaganda called for direct universal suffrage, the separation of Church and state, the distribution of weapons to
the people, and so on. For Naquet, "the Spanish movement of that era resembled in many ways our 1848 movement. There was generosity, greatness of spirit, and fraternal sentiment."[30] From Madrid to Barcelona, Alfred Naquet plunged into these struggles against authoritarianism, led in
the name of a militant internationalism that denied the idea of a nation-
state. He became close to the revolutionaries and shared their hopes; he
was officially sent by them to Cordova—with an order for insurrection!
When the local authorities refused to take action, he left for Grenada, then
was offered the post of governor of Seville in order to proclaim the Republic there. But he was prevented from doing so, barely avoided being
shot and, in November 1869, taking advantage of an offer of amnesty (like
Delescluze, his libertarian friend), he returned to France.[31] Let us rapidly
note how history once more unexpectedly brought together Alfred Naquet
and Léon Blum, both confronted, at slightly more than sixty years of distance between them, with revolutionary convulsions in Spain, which announced social and political changes that they hoped and feared at the
same time. The historical context was certainly not the same; in particular,
whereas Naquet was simply a free militant in his movements and moods,
Blum, at the head of a great mass party, became *président du Conseil*: the
two protesters against the social order were thus not implicated in the same
way in the Spanish conflict. But for each of them, it represented an essential episode in their political careers.

Naquet joined the camp of those who were fighting the plebiscite
of Napoleon III, participated in numerous meetings beside Jules Ferry,
Charles Floquet, and de Lissagaray, engaged in a polemic with Jules Vallès,
who advocated the immediate implementation of socialist solutions, and
continued to oppose inheritance and a permanent army: "To vote yes on
the plebiscite," he claimed, "is to maintain it is right to enlist working
citizens and send them to massacre other working citizens so that a few

privileged men, members of the Senate, the Conseil d'Etat, or the Conseil Privé, can get rich on the booty." The conclusion followed: "Revolutions are made and succeed only when their program is clear and defined—because only then do the people understand where they are going."[32]

In all these declarations, we easily detect a libertarian and individualist tone: what Naquet was protesting above all was the forming of regiments and brigades, authoritarianism at whatever level of society it manifested itself. And, to succeed in the struggle, men had to understand their history in order to truly commit themselves. Then came the decisive days of the fall of the Empire. In August 1870, the conflict was spreading, the crowd was taking over the streets: at the head of a column of more than five hundred demonstrators, Naquet was moving toward the Bastille. He grabbed a banner demanding that the people of Paris be armed and ran right into the police. Despite that setback, he would once more be present at the decisive moment after the defeat: on 4 September, he was in the heart of the crowd that seized the legislative body and City Hall, where he was "one of the first" to enter.[33] After the victory, he volunteered for the national guard; turned down, he decided to serve Gambetta in the ministry of Place Beauvau. He proved to be very active there, taking on part of the effort of rearming and building factories destined for the army; completely occupied with that urgent military task, he refused a prefecture that the residents of Lot-et-Garonne had undertaken to obtain for him quickly.

All his life, Alfred Naquet incarnated the antiestablishment type, the man who stubbornly refused any kind of political domination that abused the popular will, the man who fled any role of authority. *Député* of Vaucluse in 1871, he kept his distance from the Commune even though a number of his friends participated in it, for he anticipated its failure and feared that it would drag down the Republic as well. He cooled the ardor of the Avignon revolutionaries, who were eager to imitate their Parisian comrades. During a tumultuous discussion at the Place de l'Horloge, he declared:

The red flag has never been the symbol of anarchy, it has had a legal existence only under the 1791 Constitution, and at that time, far from being the symbol of anarchy, it was the reverse, it was the martial flag, the flag of the repression of the uprising. I am for the red flag, and yet I beg you not to fly it. We will fly it on the day when it is recognized as the nation's flag.

As we have already noted, Naquet was so opposed to the Opportunists that he opposed Gambetta himself during a legislative election. He felt that the new political elite that was little by little taking the country's reins was too moderate and too distanced from the people, but he also challenged the recourse to violence. He later defended the Radical Party, which even as it rejected the use of violence, also wished for the coming of a regime "professing the worship of all freedoms . . . freedom of conscience, . . . a national, exclusively secular education."[34]

The rebel was transformed into a specialist in constitutional law, praising the merits of the American constitutional government and the Swiss regime, and wishing to obtain a revision in constitutional laws that would allow the people wider access to the public space. It was a question of making society more free, not of doing violence to it: Naquet distanced himself more and more from all those who advocated resorting to force. "We republicans are the men of law and order," he declared. The anarchistic, the seditious, the men of disorder were those who had sought to suppress the Republic.[35] From then on, he explicitly challenged any anarchism that practiced violence and showed confidence in the Republic's ability to build a society that more or less realized the libertarian ideals through the ballot. Thus, during the discussion of a bill aimed at repressing anarchist acts, he declared: "I feel that this Chamber, the result of universal suffrage, which is the true representative of the national will in France, must reserve the right not to extend it on the day that abominable sect of anarchists we wish to destroy has disappeared."[36] As he repeated ad nauseam, "firing guns does not solve problems."[37] From then on, it fell to the Republic to deal with social questions and to abolish inequalities.

After the Boulangist episode—which, with part of the socialist movement, he believed he had to join—a crucial moment in his life that he later considered a dramatic error that had ended his political career,[38] he would belatedly—in 1890—join the Socialist Party, though without feeling that meant he had accepted either Marxist theory or revolution. "I know that revolutions, which sweep clean in order to suppress a past in decomposition, do not create in and of themselves. . . . I do not believe that socialism can arrive through the 'catastrophist' path."[39] Criticizing the Marxist theory of value and collectivism,[40] he believed it vital to do anything possible to achieve "the blossoming of individual callings." In that sense, socialism was only "a battle against those two eternal enemies of human liberation, the praetorian army and the clergy."[41] That vision of socialism, therefore, had only a distant relation to Marxism, which was in full bloom in France at the end of the century.

What Naquet was fighting above all was power, oppression in its political and ideological dimension: what he feared was the omnipotence of the state, which could only be reinforced with the installation of communism. "Whether we want it or not," he noted, "in a collectivist society, bureaucracy would be destined to replace capitalism, and the cause of inequality would be considerably increased," with, in the end, the formation "of an absolutely despotic authority."[42] He feared the state's takeover of production, the press, education, its control over the right to assemble: "They would need only refuse to citizens whose ideas displeased them the public hall, which the state alone would own." Spontaneously rediscovering an anarchist vein, he evoked his "old friend Élisée Reclus" to reject the state's influence, from which he feared everything, in particular "slavery," by means of which it could reduce the freedom of citizens, a fortiori in a collectivist society. At the end of his life, in the last chapter of the book he considered his "testament," Naquet appealed to Reclus, his "comrade in arms," on several occasions, while writing these pages clearly devoted to "utopia."[43]

His eternal enemy was in fact the state, its armed forces and its mind control. Evoking his years in Spain at the heart of revolutionary events, he once more foreswore any form of nationalism that deified a specific national identity and that still carried within itself torrents of hatred: growing tender at the memory of fraternal and internationalist exaltations, he expressed his hope, as a committed advocate of pacifism, for the end of borders. That would put an end to the brutal worship of force that had taken root in France and in Germany since the 1870 defeat, and to which the brutal speeches of Drumont and Bismarck so obviously attested. He no longer hesitated:

Anarchy! The word has been spoken. Why not? Of course, that great and pure doctrine has had wretched followers who have debased it in the eyes of the world through their criminal acts. . . . Those crimes have had a deadly effect. I myself have suffered their influence. Indignant over the abominable acts and the imbecility of the sectarians, I became associated with the measures of repression taken against them. I refused to add my signature to those of the *députés* who implored the president of the Republic for Vaillant's pardon. . . . I have deeply regretted being associated with such acts of repression. . . . Libertarians, they struck down liberty. But they do not suspect it and they believe they are working for the liberation of their peers. . . . Yet, for two years, we have been watching the spectacle of magistrates, of idolized, pensioned, coddled generals using their intelligence and activity to sacrifice an innocent man and exalt a guilty one. We have seen ministers murder an honest man in the corner of a war council; generals, colonels, majors set in place the most odious, the lowest, the most ignoble procedures to save a criminal in order to perpetuate the torture of an innocent man. . . . In comparison with those who committed that moral monstrosity . . . what is the weight of the crime, I ask, of a bomb thrown into a café or into the parliament building? Placed beside the wretched men who committed all these crimes, what are Etievant, Caserio, Henri the anarchist, Vaillant, Lucheni, and Ravachol himself? Almost saints. . . . The anarchists appear to have finally understood that it is not through murder but rather through the defense of the just and the true that a doctrine is spread and grounded. As a result, we can, without running up against public conscience, adopt anarchy as utopia's guide.[44]

This passage deserves to be cited at length, for it constitutes perhaps the essential piece of this "testament." Alfred Naquet is here taking on an almost prophetic role and is inscribing his thoughts and action within the antiauthoritarian utopian current. The sense he intends to give to his life is, in fact, a refusal of any form of constraint infringing on freedom, and he courageously invokes Reclus and Vaillant's individual rejection of the political order. In so doing, he takes his distance from the political class in power, such as the great mass parties that were being constituted under the banner of a strongly collectivist socialism. He deliberately underscores the compromises and injustices that punctuated the unfolding of the Dreyfus affair. He, Naquet, the most rationalist and freethinking state Jew, the most devoted to revolutionary struggles, came to measure the responsibility of anarchists by the yardstick of the guilt of the persecutors of the famous captain, who held seats within the state, with its pomp and advantages, and were acting with impunity. He had seen the Boulangist troops slip into antisemitism, had often run up against a ferocious hatred of Jews; now he did not hesitate, almost at the end of his long political life, to justify his defense of anarchy by evoking the betrayal of a state apparatus that, without a moment's hesitation, had sacrificed one of its servants, whose only sin was to have been a Jew.[45] Made gangrenous by an antisemitism that had moved into the state itself and into most political groups, including the socialist parties (Naquet explicitly denounced their anti-Jewish attitude), society had to change through and through, not by violence but through the mobilizing force of anarchistic utopia.

In the very last years of his life, Naquet still emphasized his libertarian vision. In 1907, one year before the famous work by Blum, *Du mariage*, he published *Vers l'union libre* (Toward free union), a work in which he repeated and extended his critique of the family, marriage, and even divorce.[46] In 1911, in his final text written just before his death, he persisted, pronouncing himself one last time and more fully in favor of an anarchism of "doctrinal purity," which, disdaining bombs, appealed to education and morality to change society. Rejecting once more revolutionary violence, he drafted a last plea for a secular school system served by instructors devoted to the Republic who wanted to institute true equality among citizens, concerned above all with remaining free and escaping from any kind of illegitimate constraint.[47] Rejecting individualism, a factor in egotism leading both to the predominance of the market and to unacceptable forms of anarchism, he sought to make individual happiness compatible with collective happiness: in a word, and it was the final word, "let us repudiate the simplistic solutions of the socialists and anarchists and reconcile Karl Marx and Bakunin, Jules Guesde and Kropotkin, Elisée Reclus and Jaurès, in the pursuit of the true, which is essentially complex."[48]

CHAPTER FIFTEEN

The Clemencist Tradition

In a small Vendée cemetery at the end of November 1929, a few people were preparing to participate in the Tiger's very private funeral; as one of them would remember, the moment he was put in the ground, the sun began to shine.[1] Only five of them did not belong to the family; two of them were Jewish (Georges Mandel and Georges Wormser).[2] Barely eleven years later, in summer 1940, Minister of the Interior Georges Mandel and the man who had become his closest collaborator, Georges Wormser, were trying desperately to inspire the French administration with the spirit of resistance, as that administration was collapsing on all sides: the German armies were surging onto French soil, the enemies' advances in battle were forcing a rapid withdrawal into Africa where so many forces remained intact. Along with other parliamentarians, Mandel left on the *Massilia* on 21 June and managed to get as far as Morocco: when he reached land, he held the bust of Clemenceau that never left his side firmly in his arms and hurried to the Havas agency to launch an appeal to the Resistance.[3] On 24 June, barely a few hours before the first German motorcyclists entered Hendaye, René Cassin, future *vice-président* of the Conseil d'Etat, at the time legal adviser to Giraudoux, *haut commissaire* at Information, climbed onto the *Ettrick* in the company of several thousand Polish soldiers, French officers, and a disguised Raymond Aron: they headed for Great Britain to continue the battle. Cassin thus responded to the appeal of General de Gaulle, who immediately received him and made him one of his closest collaborators. When Cassin told him he was Jewish, fearing that it might be an obstacle, de Gaulle, the Catholic and conservative military man, held out his arm: all the sons of the nation had to unite to confront the enemy.[4] Other state Jews joined the battles of de Gaulle and Free France: from Pierre Mendès France to Jules Moch, there were many who recognized in General de Gaulle the very symbol of legitimate France and who, at the same time, overlooked their political differences and joined his ranks.

From Clemenceau to de Gaulle, a single conception of the nation was expressed, a nationalism quick to take offense. It was different from the nationalism brandished by the radical right, however, in that it was articulated more in the name of justice and law than in terms of race and blood. Of course, everything separated the great priest hater, the radical who was for a time close to the ideas of the Commune, and the conservative and profoundly Catholic officer. But at the hour of greatest danger, they professed the same unassailable confidence in the destiny of a just and thus finally victorious France. That tradition, which Clemenceau best incarnated, in its concern to integrate the army into the nation and rediscover the ideals of 1789, has traversed contemporary history, each time becoming identified with decisive and charismatic great men: from Gambetta to de Gaulle, and including Poincaré[5] and Clemenceau, beyond the differences in the values proper to each one, the same will was always expressed. Henry Torrès explicitly underscored the reality of that filiation: with complete "veneration" for Clemenceau, which he had learned from his own father, who had known Clemenceau as *chef de cabinet* to the *préfet* of Vendée, Torrès linked up with Mandel, whom he respected because of his great devotion to the "service of the French cause." In 1940, before entering the Resistance, he noted that "a voice was suddenly rising up. . . . Our leader had just emerged, de Gaulle was taking up Clemenceau's task."[6] Grandson of the *préfet* Isaïe Levaillant, a quintessential man of law and order, Henry Torrès perfectly incarnated the Clemencist tradition. He quickly came to take an active part in the Gaullist actions during World War II, before becoming president of the Seine federation of the RPF (Rassemblement du Peuple Français).[7]

Among Gambetta's men and among the close collaborators incarnating the ideal of justice for the nation, we note the presence of a few state Jews, who, in the end, respected one another even though they had long been political adversaries. Their shared struggle brought them together. Hence, on 8 July 1946, in the forest of Fontainebleau, the friends of Georges Mandel unveiled a stele representing him on the site where he had been brought down by the *milice*. The stele was realized by the same artist who had sculpted the statue of Clemenceau located on the roundabout of the

Champs-Élysées. After Paul Reynaud, to whom he was very close, it was Léon Blum who celebrated his memory in that place where everything linked the Tiger to his *directeur de cabinet* from the time of the 1917 perils.[8] Léon Blum the socialist and Georges Mandel, whose forceful ways sometimes found echoes on the extreme right, had both been prisoners in Germany and had almost known the same tragic fate: they had had time to get to know each other; and after violent political confrontations, the moment had come for mutual respect and for confidence founded on a shared concept of the French nation. From his prison, Léon Blum had recognized de Gaulle's mission, and it seems that de Gaulle had not concealed his admiration for Mandel's energy. In June 1965, de Gaulle came to meditate before this monument commemorating Mandel's assassination and in a short speech, emphasized the fact that Mandel was "an activist minister among so many indecisive ones."[9]

The Clemencist tradition thus included all these state Jews, most of whom inclined toward a certain social conservatism rather than the idea of revolution, who once more found themselves near great men who quite simply represented the nation-state. The Tiger was its founder, for Gambetta's men had taken it as their primary mission to help him solidify the Republic: certain of them were, of course, present in 1870, at the time of Défense Nationale, but their role had become more perceptible later, when the Republic had been definitively installed. In contrast, Clemenceau's men truly entered the public scene when Clemenceau finally obtained power, a final recourse in the face of the German army, which was threatening to win the war. In November 1917, the Père la Victoire managed to galvanize French soldiers, sometimes brutally putting an end to internal rifts and doubts, and exercising an almost dictatorial authority to reverse the nation's fate. Georges Mandel indisputably played an essential role in this burst of nationalism by virtually replacing the minister of the interior. For example, the control he exercised over the press and the prefect civil service was quite rigorous.[10] At the time, he appeared as the right-hand man of this new Gambetta, that is, Clemenceau, the unconquerable leader whose coming to power was so feared by the Socialists. In their view, he remained the "strikebreaker" of 1906–9 when, as minister of the interior, he had opposed social movements. Georges Mandel was already at his side, and did not hesitate to resort to the most extreme measures of force. In that sense, the Clemencist tradition, with which a certain number of Jews were associated, permitted the use of force in the national interest, which the various factions on the right could only applaud, and which elicited the anger of the workers' movement and its leaders.

When Clemenceau finally came to power in November 1917, he found the left virtually united against him: the former Radical leader, friend of the Communards, the man who had so harassed the Opportunist majority, which he found too conservative socially, too attached to law and order and to maintaining socioeconomic structures, now ended up declaring: "I want to have a majority and I will have it; if it is not on the left, it will be on the right. And yet . . . I am an old Jacobin." The new appeal for votes on the right and his tactic of winning them over allowed him to counter the opposition of his former socialist friends. Georges Mandel helped him establish the definitive list of his ministers and to make contact with certain Socialist leaders whom he was attempting to bring into the government: at that time, Mandel was his principal aide and led the *président du Conseil*'s civil staff with Georges Wormser and Jean Martet: "This group was going to govern France during a year of war."[11]

A flurry of activity began, for there existed a severe state of emergency: Clemenceau confronted the military problems but, as Georges Wormser observed, "thanks to Mandel, he could set aside daily problems, whether social or political. . . . Day after day, Mandel set up the protective screen behind which the essential efforts were made. . . . The Parliament and the press, the *préfets* and the high officials all went to Mandel."[12] "See Mandel" was endlessly repeated, as if to emphasize the extent of his influence in the administrative apparatus, and in particular among the *préfets*. Having organized an autonomous network of information and propaganda, he participated with Édouard Ignace, another state Jew who had been named undersecretary of state at the Department of Interior, in pursuing defeatists and overseeing arrests. A famous drawing of the time represents an immense playing card, the king of diamonds, bearing the name "Georges." Clemenceau is represented at the top, with the inscription, "See Mandel"; and Mandel, on the bottom, is declaring, "I am the state!"[13]

In the narrow circle of the closest collaborators also figured—in addition to Jules Jeanneney and *préfet* Raux—Ignace, whose actions were decisive in the face of defeatist tendencies and treasonous behavior. Clemenceau proved vigilant in that area, but allowed Ignace to act, since he occupied a central place in implementing the repressive apparatus: he was the one to deal with the most sensitive matters, to mobilize national ardor, and also to face the dramatic events when a trial ended in an execution. Klotz also figured in the government: he was named to Finance and was part of the official five-person delegation during the negotiations that would lead to the Treaty of Versailles. A state Jew with rightist views and a member of the National Republican League after the war, Klotz was the inventor of the slogan: "Germany will pay." Even though Clemenceau does not seem to have held him in great esteem, he had a post in numerous governments, and was even a nationalist and authoritarian minister of the interior at the turn of the century. In 1906, arguing in the Chamber with Jaurès, who supported the right of the working class to refuse to go to war when the forces in power turned aggressive, he declared: "I do not in any case allow disobedience, insubordination, insurrection, or desertion." Violently attacked by Vaillant in the name of the extreme left, he reproved both of them: "We are therefore constrained, as the good patriots that we are, to make every sacrifice required to safeguard our society, in order to pave the way to victory for our soldiers."[14] In 1914, Barrès came to see him to announce his intention to join up, emphasizing that he held him in "profound esteem, and profess[ed] a sincere admiration for his exceptional talent."[15] Throughout his life, Klotz was, however, one of the bêtes noires of the antisemitic tradition: *La Libre Parole* called him "minus habens circumcised" and lashed out against his "Jewish impudence."[16] The *Archives Israélites* can hardly be said to have rushed to his aid, since "he has always lived far outside our community and, every time he has had the opportunity, has felt compelled to proclaim his absolute indifference in the matter of religion."[17]

Certain spokespersons on the radical right respected the supporters of that Clemencist tradition and did not hide their regard for Georges Mandel, in particular. In the interwar period, Léon Daudet, another great attacker of Jews whose antisemitic verve we have often encountered in this book, having heard a speech by Mandel, made a comment that has remained famous: "A tribune's speech. Suetonius touched up by Juvenal," and did not hesitate to applaud him almost to the point of compromising himself. For Daudet, "Mandel is a steadfast and intrepid soul, a man of government. . . . If we had had him as *président du Conseil* instead of all the second-rate men we've had since 1919, the affairs of France would have taken a different turn."[18] On several occasions, Maurras himself did not hide his admiration.

The state Jews surrounding Clemenceau shared his nationalism, which made him lean heavily to the right, until he became, in the aftermath of World War I, the leading figure of the Union Nationale of a sky blue Chamber, the furthest to the right since 1871: it was on that occasion that Mandel, after several electoral defeats, succeeded in becoming a *député* in Gironde. The campaign by the Clemencist Union Républicaine to which he belonged had been conducted under the slogan, "Get the Bolsheviks," openly displaying its obsession with social disturbances. Here was a strange historical coincidence: Georges Mandel became *député* on a rightist platform even as Léon Blum, his future comrade in deportation whom he had so often battled, was himself elected for the first time, but on the Socialists' slate. Later, others would compare Mandel to "a French Disraeli," clearly situating him in the camp of social conservatism. In time, however, this French-style Disraeli would distance himself from the right, which he judged cowardly and defeatist. At the end of the 1930s and even more under Vichy, he would end up moving toward the left, against which he had earlier fought so hard.

As we have just indicated in a general way, a few state Jews flanked Clemenceau throughout his life. For his time, Clemenceau was open to the world and to others: his travels in the United States and then in South America, his interest in other cultures, his sense of justice, and the horror he felt toward all kinds of repression—from that suffered by the Poles to that endured by the Armenians—made him almost a being apart. Clemenceau was Protestant in origin: part of his family became Catholic, but he nevertheless married in a Protestant church. One of his closest friends from his youth was none other than the Protestant senator Scheurer-Kestner, whom he rejoined over the course of the Dreyfus affair. Like the republican leaders during the time of Opportunism, his link to Protestantism brought him close to certain Jews. He frequented—too closely in fact—the speculator Cornelius Herz, the court Jew who precipitated the Panama scandal, and flaunted his friendship with Baron Jacques de Reinach, whose sudden suicide gave a dramatic dimension to the affair. These Jewish businessmen compromised him. He was himself splattered with mud; in fact, he may have compromised himself more than was thought at the time.[19] He was the object of violent attacks, in particular from the unavoidable Drumont, who published this incendiary passage in the first issue of *La Libre Parole*: "Do you know who asked Cornelius Herz to relinquish that list of checks that he held as vouchers from Baron de Reinach? It was Clemenceau."[20]

It was the Dreyfus affair that allowed Clemenceau to reemerge and linked him to state Jews, for he rapidly became one of the essential actors in the Dreyfusard camp: he became friends with Mathieu Dreyfus and Bernard Lazare, and was particularly linked to Joseph Reinach, whom he had long battled as a central figure among the Opportunists. The former secretary general for the Grand Ministère, Gambetta's lifelong friend, now pursued a goal similar to that of Clemenceau; later, in the most difficult moments of the war, Reinach-Polybe once more offered his unreserved support for the Tiger's battle. For the time being, Clemenceau published Zola's famous "J'accuse" in his newspaper *L'Aurore* and participated in all the ups and downs of the Affair until the very end. As we have already noted, he professed a sovereign scorn toward Jews such as Fernand Crémieux, Alfred Naquet, and L.-L. Klotz, who came close to taking the side of the anti-Dreyfusards or who were too discreet. As the privileged target of Drumont, the pope of antisemites, he fended off harsh attacks: "As mayor of Montmartre, you were the accomplice of the Jew Simon Mayer, who assassinated our generals. As *député*, you were the active partner and right-hand man of the Jew Cornelius Herz. And now you defend Captain Dreyfus!" The duel took on a symbolic dimension; slightly earlier, Clemenceau had confronted Déroulède, president of the Ligue des Patriotes, with a pistol. A new confrontation with pistols with the author of *La France juive* definitively sealed his anchorage in the republican camp, which was ferociously hostile to antisemitism. The Clemenceau in large part responsible for Boulanger's fame and who, in his time, had worked with Alfred Naquet, had definitively broken with the movement, which from then on was oriented toward the extreme right: Drumont himself and his contingent joined it. Nationalistic and authoritarian, Clemenceau retained from his radical past an absolute devotion to the Republic.

Clemenceau did not shun biting slogans, which were not devoid of antisemitic stereotyping (he evoked his relations with Mandel with the slogan "I fart and he stinks"). During a conversation with Poincaré, he also evoked Mandel, who, "with his Jew nose does what he likes with people." He was the author of the slogan, "I placed the only Jew who knows nothing of finance in Rue de Rivoli," and agreed that Klotz be named to the government. Even so, his real rejection of antisemitism rested on a solid foundation: the most vehement anticlericalism.[21] Clemenceau had been a Gambettist inasmuch as he wanted to install full secularism, a separation of Church and state, in France; despite sometimes quite marked differences regarding the urgency of social change, Clemenceau remained close to Gambetta. As *président du Conseil* in 1909, he unveiled the statue of Gambetta in Nice; while he fought the Opportunists and strongly stood up to Ferry, he still did not become socialist and revolutionary. Like Gambetta, he attracted to himself a few state Jews who, like Gambetta's men, were of a somewhat more authoritarian or hostile temperament, both to socialism and to the extreme right. The defense of the Republic from one era to the next remained the foundation of their actions, with Clemenceau's men not hesitating to resort to the most repressive measures: let us note, however, that Minister of the Interior David Raynal, ever the Gambettist, out of the interest he continually manifested for police matters, preceded Georges Mandel. Clemenceau entrusted Mandel with surveillance missions; he became minister of the interior in 1940, at the moment of extreme danger. As a result, this Clemencist tradition affected other state Jews: when the Republic was threatened, it placed them on the front lines on several occasions. At different periods, in addition to Raynal, Mandel, and Ignace, Klotz and Schrameck also confronted the same subversive schemes in the leagues and on the extreme left, as ministers of the interior. Can we maintain that, in 1958, when Minister of the Interior Jules Moch, using all the administrative and police means at his disposal, attempted to defend the Republic against the putschist strategy of the Gaullist movement, which was committed to doing anything to put an end to the Fourth Republic, the old militant socialist, the resistance fighter close to the de Gaulle of the Resistance, was, unbeknownst to him, prolonging the Clemencist tradition?

By their presence, the Clemencist state Jews reinforced the myth of the "Jewish Republic" and provoked in turn the most harebrained antisemitic deliria: as the inexorable *La Libre Parole* put it,

Ejected from Parliament, M. Clemenceau could return to public life only through the protection of the Jews he had served with so much zeal and ardor at the time of the Dreyfus affair. He owes the fact that he became minister of the interior and *président du Conseil* to the Hebrews. But as usual, Jewry exacts a high price. It has surrounded M. Clemenceau with three circles of kikes, and more and more the Ministry of the Interior looks like a little ghetto.[22]

In 1921, Joseph Santo, an expert in the matter, was still denouncing "Clemenceau's Jews."

His whole life, Clemenceau was, alas, a man of the Jews and of the English. Before the war, he had as his maleficent Egerias and damned souls Baron Reinach, Joseph Reinach, Herz, Mandel, Klotz, among others, who always kept him from accomplishing his full task for France. He worked especially for Israel and England. During the war, he was kept in the political mire and prevented from using all his worth to the good of France by the Jews Reinach, Klotz, Mandel, Wormser, Ignace, Bokanowski, and the like.[23]

The Drumont tradition thus proved attentive to the presence of these Clemencist state Jews, whose sense of mission in the service of the state it deformed and distorted. According to this tradition, Clemenceau was simply their prisoner.

Who were these state Jews who came to be integrated into Clemenceau's close troops? One of the less well known, who nevertheless played a central role, even taking precedence over Mandel for a long time, was *sous-préfet* Roth, whom Clemenceau brought in from Somme after the strikes in Nord; in 1906, in the first Clemenceau ministry, Roth became *directeur du cabinet* in the Ministry of the Interior, which also drew direct authority from the new *président du Conseil*. Efficient and energetic, he became *préfet* after the fall of the ministry, when he was not yet thirty years old.[24] He died on the battlefield in 1914. Among the collaborators belonging to the most restricted circle surrounding Clemenceau, we also find Georges Wormser: although he was not, strictly speaking, a state Jew inasmuch as he was never a high official or a member of either of the two assemblies, he assumed the duties of Clemenceau's civil staff director in 1919 when Mandel, who had been elected *député*, resigned his position. In 1934, at Mandel's insistent request, he agreed to head the ministry staff of the postal system. He later performed the same role under Mandel in the Ministry of Colonies, and then, in 1940, in the Department of the Interior. A graduate of the École Normale and an *agrégé* in letters, he was an intimate of Clemenceau, who told him shortly before his death: "You're the best." He was also one of the executors of the Tiger's will and could later be found in the company of Georges Mandel, among the tiny group of persons attending the funeral of the old fighter.[25] Faithful among the faithful, he wrote two books on Clemenceau and compiled another work devoted to

Mandel: a Jewish Frenchman par excellence, very active in religious and community institutions, he was part of the Clemencist line, and, more than anyone else, gave it a dimension that identified it as one of the privileged moments of Franco-Judaism.

In that sense, we can link Georges Wormser to Joseph Reinach and even more to his brother Théodore, the faithful of the faithful to the Great Man before Clemenceau, namely, Gambetta. As two of the Opportunist leader's men, they bore witness to their great attachment to Judaism, which was, however, conceptualized in a reformed direction. In the context of crises in legitimacy, it was quite simply the meaning of Franco-Judaism that was being carved out. This was even more true later, when René Cassin, more anchored in tradition, visited Palestine with great emotion in 1930; in 1942, he played an important role in defending the interests of the Alliance Israélite Universelle, when he represented France at numerous international meetings; and through the force of his own personality, he brought the support of a part of the state to de Gaulle in London. Although we shall return to this question, let us note in passing how these ideals, from one phase to the next, seemed to become blurred or lose their systematic character. The Reinachs, for example, were completely devoted to the nascent Republic and involved in the complete renovation of Judaism, which had been transformed into a universal ethics: they manifested absolute opposition to nascent Zionism. In contrast, Georges Wormser, an *"israélite Frenchman"* like them, also anchored only in the cult of the French nation and maintaining all his loyalty toward orthodox Judaism, participated, in Clemenceau's name, in the first great diplomatic maneuvers that would later make possible the birth of Israel.[26] To understand intuitively the entire extent of the metamorphosis of this Franco-Judaism, we need only remember the brutal and dramatic break of the 1970s, probably unimaginable in earlier eras, between de Gaulle and René Cassin concerning precisely Israel, the former head of Free France had called the Jews a people "sure of itself and dominating." The General's old companion definitively distanced himself, and Raymond Aron, with whom he had gone to London, also protested and distanced himself from him. The Reinachs, emblematic personalities of this Franco-Judaism of which René Cassin was the distant heir, could not have behaved in that way, not only because they were far from the Zionist viewpoint but especially because the context itself, completely oriented toward strengthening the Republic, was totally different.

Let us return to the Clemencist tradition itself. It was Joseph Reinach who seems to have introduced Georges Clemenceau to Georges Mandel: when Clemenceau met his future collaborator for the first time in the offices of *L'Aurore*, Mandel handed him a letter of recommendation from

Joseph Reinach. As Émile Buré recounted, "Having said a word or two about Reinach, Clemenceau showed him the door to the editing room and said: 'And now, young man, go through that door and take the place that you certainly deserve among our brilliant editors.'" It is revealing that someone else happened to witness this conversation, Lieutenant Colonel Picquart.[27] Clemenceau, Joseph Reinach, and the lieutenant colonel were the essential protagonists in the Dreyfusard camp: the Affair linked the first two, who came from antagonistic political horizons (Reinach served Gambetta's policy, which Clemenceau had long opposed). Between these periods so removed from each other, the Gambetta years and the Vichy years — when the son of Théodore, Julien Reinach, member of the Conseil d'Etat, was imprisoned in Drancy, and Georges Mandel, Clemenceau's right-hand man, was murdered by the *milice* — there had been the Dreyfus affair, during which Joseph Reinach and Clemenceau became close. Beyond their political differences, they embraced the same values.

A few years earlier, things had not been so cozy, and it is not at all certain whether Joseph Reinach would have written a letter of recommendation for Georges Mandel. A small little-known lampoon attests to this: in 1885, at the time of the most lively antagonism, Joseph Reinach published a malicious book titled *Le ministère Clemenceau* (The Clemenceau ministry). It was a political fairy tale, completely made up: the time was 1885 and the Brisson cabinet had just been defeated in the elections. The Opportunists were finished: "To read and hear the songs of triumph by the victors, you would have thought a band of cannibals had just gotten their hands on a convoy of very fat men."[28] That set the tone. . . . Since, in this story, the extreme left triumphed, President Grévy turned to Clemenceau, "the Robespierre of the Third Republic," to constitute the new government. It was then that every misfortune befell France. With a stroke of the pen, all the posts for *préfets, sous-préfets,* and *trésoriers-payeurs généraux* were assigned to Socialists and Radicals; members of the central committee and of the Commune were granted "high positions, fat sinecures, and officers' braids."[29] A plan for suppressing the Senate was quickly prepared. The Madagascar affair provoked violent incidents in the Chamber, and on top of everything, strikes broke out in Anzin and Le Creusot and riots erupted in Paris. A crowd waving "red rags came down the outer boulevards . . . by way of Rue de Rivoli, the quays, and Boulevard Saint-Germain, and moved into the Luxembourg. . . . The leaders even began to tear up the road and build barricades. Swords were drawn; a charge ensued. A bloody free-for-all followed. There were dead and wounded."[30] While this was going on, the army carried the decisive victory in Madagascar, called for reinforcements and fresh supplies. The political majorities cracked and reversed themselves: Jules Ferry came to the aid of Clemenceau, who had been knocked over by the right! Clemenceau then immediately reported to President Grévy and handed in his resignation with a single phrase: "I have just today returned from a ten-year journey. I come from Utopia."[31] Joseph Reinach had joined the fray to warn against Clemenceau's taking power, which would not actually happen until 1906: the most lugubrious predictions were in order when the intention was to manage France in the name of a utopia, leaving behind the real conditions, which, in contrast, held all the attention of the Opportunists. Gambetta's man didn't pull any punches in barring the route to Clemenceau, who was denounced for his anarchist or socialist tendencies, which had led him to the Boulangist adventure. For a moment, he rejoined Alfred Naquet, whose theories in favor of disarmament he would later combat in the name of the patriotism of 1789.[32] Preferring to defend the Republic, however, the Tiger brutally broke off with Boulanger, to the great satisfaction of Joseph Reinach.[33]

The Dreyfus affair linked adversaries who had also harshly confronted each other in the Chamber in 1891 over the meaning of the Revolution. At Zola's trial, Clemenceau declared: "The principle of civil society is law, goodness, justice; the principle of military society is discipline, procedure, obedience. The battle is between the two. The entire revolutionary tradition of France versus the blind authoritarianism of one caste: that was the whole of the Dreyfus affair."[34] Reinach in *Le Siècle* and *Le Figaro* and Clemenceau in *L'Aurore* pursued the same battle, though differing in their means. Reinach wrote five volumes on the Dreyfus affair, while Clemenceau wrote seven. For Clemenceau, who bluntly attacked certain state Jews hostile to the captain, "M. Reinach, at a time when so many great Jews were hiding in their cellars (they are still hiding), bravely faced the blows and received his share without flinching. Now he has the right to speak, for he has fought." After that, they actively corresponded, forgetting in adversity the quarrels that separated the Opportunists from the Radicals.[35] The encounter with Georges Mandel could only have been facilitated by this.

As editor of *L'Aurore*, Mandel succeeded in following Clemenceau when he became minister of the interior in 1906: he was named *chef de cabinet adjoint* in the Sarrault cabinet, then undersecretary of state at the Department of the Interior, before joining Clemenceau's cabinet itself. From then on, he was an integral part of the political leadership. Even more symbolically, he entered the career under a ministry where General Picquart was named to the War Office, a moment that marked the end of the Dreyfus affair and the coming to power of the captain's defenders. Following various incidents, Mandel lost several legislative elections and went on to edit a Clemencist newspaper in Var; he was installed at the heart of the state apparatus in 1917 when Clemenceau, during this dramatic period, once more became *président du Conseil*. Well acquainted with parliamentary maneuvers, Mandel contributed to forming the government and had his say in determining its composition. From then on, he controlled the state to a very large degree in the Tiger's name and did not hesitate to use the administrative machine in the most authoritarian manner possible. In 1919, the man whom some of the press described as without pity, unscrupulous, and Machiavellian, whom it called "the second cop of France," made life difficult for striking workers, who had been encouraged by the events in Bolshevik Russia. Later, Jules Moch, as minister of the interior, confronted other strikes of national dimension, this time linked to the cold war. But Georges Mandel was a Clemencist whereas Jules Moch acted ruthlessly as a socialist. Clemenceau's man shared his rejection of the socialist movement and joined in condemning Jaurès and Longuet. *L'Humanité* endlessly denounced "the Mandel-Clemenceau regime."

Elected in 1919 on the wave of the Union Nationale that had campaigned on Clemenceau's name, he was carried to the Chamber by the nationalist movement on the right, with which he identified: in his district of Gironde, he harshly attacked "Bolshevist anarchy," and his platform statement (signed "*chef de cabinet* to M. Clemenceau") included war metaphors: "Just because the triumphant nation has put its sword back in its sheath, does that mean there are no more battles to wage?" Against the supporters of Bolshevism who

set themselves outside the national pact . . . we must say on which side of the barricade we are to place ourselves. . . . In order for the internal struggle against pressing difficulties to be as decisive as the struggle against the external enemy, let us continue to form, in the spirit that won us the victory with M. Clemenceau, a solid bundle [*faisceau*] of spirits and hearts.[36]

Mandel let his imagination run riot with nationalist images and expressed himself in a rather equivocal language. Elected on the right, he would do everything he could to take hold, becoming at his own initiative *président* of the *conseil général* of Gironde, a notable who could be believed to be solidly rooted. Renouncing a bit of his anticlerical faith from the time of Clemenceau, he became linked to local Catholics, called for freedom of conscience and even, in his first speech to the Chamber and to general astonishment, pronounced himself in favor of reestablishing the French embassy at the Holy See.

This first speech, on 18 November 1920, elicited an almost unprecedented uproar in a place that had seen and heard a great number of them. As he was advancing toward the podium, a growing tumult could be heard; his voice was drowned out by shouts. Upset, he began with an awkward metaphor: "Gentlemen, I have not climbed the calvary of this podium at the risk of mockery, of which I already have a foretaste. . . . I have not climbed the calvary of this podium to repair the crime of Golgotha." Once more, after sarcasm and invectives, after interruptions that were ever more numerous and noisy, a clearly articulated antisemitism had reappeared. Let us turn to this exchange whose fervor has been forgotten, and which took place outside the context of any Franco-French war, during an ordinary meeting of the Chamber:

> *Georges Mandel*: At a time when the pseudo-champions of old French traditions try to revive the flame of millennial hatred in order to flatter the basest popular instincts . . . (*Interruptions from various benches*).
>
> *Léon Daudet*: It's cowardice plain and simple to interrupt in that way.
>
> *Georges Mandel*: I belong to a race that has been a victim of this regime of inquisition over the past centuries (*Noise from various benches on the extreme left and the left*).
>
> *Georges Mandel*: No bull of excommunication frightens me, gentlemen.
>
> *Jules Uhry*: Jews don't excommunicate.
>
> *Alexandre Varenne*: You are from Frankfurt.
>
> *Georges Mandel*: M. Varenne. . . .
>
> *Alexandre Varenne*: M. de Rothschild? (*Laughter from the extreme left*). Go on, state your name!
>
> *Georges Mandel*: I was born in Chatou, in Seine-et-Oise.
>
> *From the right*: And you, M. Blum, where were you born?
>
> *Léon Blum*: I was born in Paris, Rue Saint-Denis.
>
> *Eugène Lefebvre*: What a shame the pope isn't here. The vicar of Christ would have a good time, he would crucify M. Mandel!
>
> *Georges Mandel*: I'm as much a Frankfurter as my father, who was one of the first founders of the Jules Favre committee. . . .
>
> *A member on the left*: Under what name?
>
> *Georges Mandel*: I tell you my father, who was born in Paris in 1843, was wounded on the battlefield in Buzenval in 1870. It might please you to establish two categories of parliamentarians, but I will not consent to it!
>
> *President*: There are only French *députés* here (*lively applause*).[37]

At one time or another, most Jewish *députés* and senators found themselves confronted with this kind of insinuation coming from the ranks of both the extreme left and the extreme right, often to the great satisfaction of a large number of representatives of the nation, members of various parties who applauded and shouted approval. Within a few moments, Georges Mandel and Léon Blum, elected on fundamentally opposed tickets, found themselves called upon to prove their French nationality. When the time for the Front Populaire came, Blum was denounced almost daily as a Jew and foreigner in the Chamber, in a context of near civil war. In 1920, in the eyes of many, Mandel incarnated the Clemencist tradition owing to which France had just won the war; he was most clearly on the right, on the side of the nationalists. He worshiped the authoritarian and efficient "patron state." He had only disdain for political parties. But none of that mattered. The strong man, "the second cop of France," the Tiger's right-hand man, became once more and in a single blow a little Jewish foreigner rejected as much by the representatives of a Catholic France as by the socialist tradition as a whole. If Mandel fought that tradition beside Clemenceau, it was in the name of a particular conception of the nation: part of the extreme left simply treated him as a Jew. In a way that today may appear odd, Léon Daudet was one of the very few to openly come to his aid! Others on the right also supported him with their applause. The scene was all the more stunning in that the man of law and order was mocked as a Jew. The sacred union of the war had burned out, and antisemitism broke out once more, much earlier than is usually recognized. In fact, hatred and prejudice may have remained latent throughout: in January 1919, in *Hommes du Jour* (Men of the day), a national periodical with wide circulation, we read: "Mandel is only a pseudonym. . . . Georges as well probably—striking signs lead us to believe that His Majesty received, at the time of the circumcision that stood in the place of his baptism, the singularly glorious name of Judas. . . . The word 'circumcision' no doubt tells you the origin of his race."[38]

A detour through the local scene reinforces this feeling. There again, antisemitism, which the Gambettists so often confronted, reared its still vigorous head against state Jews in the Clemencist tradition. No study devoted to Georges Mandel has truly taken into account the antisemitic outbursts of which he was the object. Let us offer a few examples. During the 1919 electoral campaign—at a time when, historians claim, a national union prevailed that relegated the demons of the past to the background for a time—we find *Le Petit Radical* rising up against "the epileptic Mandel, a *métèque* Jew imported to Gironde"; "Mandel-Pasha," this newspaper judged, "is the doormat on which our national Tiger wipes his redoubtable claws, the spittoon into which he expectorates his bad humors and mucus. . . . We wonder how a man of Clemenceau's scope could consent to admit such a wretched individual as a confidant to his plans and thoughts? That's a mystery: gratitude for special services?"[39] That set the tone: Mandel could only be asserting himself through more or less maleficent means, like all *métèques*. It was therefore important to reject his candidacy in spite of his association with Clemenceau. This view was shared by *Les Girondins*, a republican newspaper:

This Mandel is not Mandel. It seems he is called Rothschild. Perhaps he has another name. Why doesn't he show up in Paris where his father is a little merchant on Rue de Trévise? . . . Some want to persuade me that Mandel is Clemenceau. I can't believe it. A *chef de cabinet* is not a minister. He obeys, he does not command. Mandel is an employee and that is all.[40]

Although more covert, the commentary was the same. Since it was almost impossible to attack the Tiger directly, it was important, by means of insinuations, to decry his collaborator. All the more so since Clemenceau was abandoning politics: why wouldn't Mandel do the same, as *Les Girondins* insistently invited him to do? That daily, which spoke in the name of republicans, against all oppression and for maintaining secularism, was not above caricaturing Mandel as "a little old man who, beardless and withered, looks like an old maid from Judaea."[41]

At the local level, all the electoral campaigns of the interwar period were the occasion to go to war once more against the Jew Mandel. In 1928, antisemitism reached heights rarely equaled, which once more belies assertions of a relative consensus supposedly prevailing before the rise of the various fascist movements and the coming to power of the Front Populaire. Day after day, *Le Journal du Médoc* obstinately led a declared antisemitic campaign: Mandel,

the troubadour coming straight from Palestine, is now, according to him, playing various tunes on his mandolin for the Medocans. He is singing:

> Christian, to the suffering traveler
> Hold a glass of water at the door
> I am, I am the wandering Jew
> That a whirlwind carries off.

We no longer want a troubadour coming straight from Palestine. . . . At the eleventh hour, we learn that he is preparing to organize a crusade to the Frankfurt ghetto and from there to Judea. It is Yahweh's will! It is Yahweh's will![42]

As a wandering Jew, Mandel could not seek out the protection of Clemenceau's shadow; the time was past when the Tiger's proximity offered a relative shelter. The press was striking harder and harder. According to *Le Journal du Médoc*, which proved particularly relentless, "M. Clemenceau was a great solon while M. Mandel is only a politician. . . . He is not Jewish for nothing, but displays most of the traits of his race. M. Mandel will never resemble a Médocain." *La Bataille* wrote profusely along the same lines: "The Jew Mandel is originally from the flea-infested ghettos of Germany." "Stop there! Filthy Jew," it cried out, resolutely fighting that "scoundrel," that "revolting larva," aligning itself with *Le Democrate* and *Le Petit Médocain*, which relentlessly spewed a flood of insults against "de gut leedle Chew."[43] Thus, Mandel was attacked from every side, even by people who embraced the Republic and democracy. The Communist Party did not take many more precautions, for it was intent on beating this man on the right who was so firmly set against socialist ideals: in the vocabulary of the time, the Party went to war against Mandel, the man of two hundred families with international and cosmopolitan ramifications. If the explicitly antisemitic comments were rarer in this case, the language was still often ambiguous.[44]

In contrast to the most common interpretations, it was hardly easy to be a Clemencist state Jew with nationalist feelings, openly hostile to socialist values. Mandel claimed to be on the right, but certain of the right's spokespersons distrusted him, wanting to see in him only a foreign Jew; he attacked the left, which, in return, did not spare him. It is true that he also attacked its leaders with great consistency, as Clemenceau had done in the past: In his platform statement for the 1928 legislative elections, he still claimed to be the "Great Frenchman," in order to better attack Marx, Guesde, Jaurès, and Blum, and reasserted that private property was "sacred" to him.[45] Sometimes, he even used more than equivocal arguments against Blum, arguments in vogue on the extreme right: in 1932, during a meeting held in Hourtin, he denounced the way that the son of the Socialist leader had supposedly obtained a job thanks to the attentions of the swindler Oustric. He was also upset that Blum was envisioning "vacations from legality" in order to implement his internationalist theories.[46]

As he became more important, no longer in Clemenceau's shadow but a statesman whose stature made his entry into government probable, the attacks increased. Fifteen years after he left the Clemenceau cabinet, Georges Mandel reached his goal: he became a minister. When in 1934 Pierre-Étienne Flandin named him to the postal ministry, his first gesture was to place a statue of Clemenceau next to him in his ministry office; vigorous as usual, he immediately set to work, imposing his authority over services and deploying considerable energy in improving the workings of his administration. He reformed with all his might, changed the staff leaders, confronted unions, inspected, innovated, intervened relentlessly with the help of Georges Wormser, whom he had recruited. In the company of that coworker, the Clemenceau era reemerged with its methods of expediency, which once more led to success. The minister's vigor impressed most of the political groups and even some on the extreme right: after Léon Daudet, it was now *Gringoire* and *Candide* that endlessly sang his praises. Mandel effected a kind of tour de force, for he moved closer to the left even as he benefited from the personal support of certain leaders among the various factions on the right, including Pierre Taittinger, Philippe Henriot, and Jacques Bainville. Was he a rightist or a leftist?[47] The path to power seemed to be set out before him, for it was obvious to all that "the second cop of France" was setting his sights higher. In December 1935, President Lebrun considered him for a moment for the post of *président du Conseil*—but the plan was aborted.

His rise nevertheless continued. In April 1938, Daladier entrusted the Ministry of Colonies to him. Mandel would have preferred Defense, where there was great urgency; he had to be satisfied with Colonies, but not without first obtaining an institutionalized link with the military, which allowed him access to various information. Mandel put all his energy into preparing the empire to support the effort of national defense. In great haste, he mobilized thoroughly to face war, which he sensed was very close. From then on, he was at the heart of the political system and became, even more than before, one of the privileged targets of antisemitic satirists. The new *Libre Parole* vented its bile, with Georges Mandel and Léon Blum taking the place of Joseph Reinach, Alfred Naquet, and Camille Dreyfus.[48] In 1938, this relatively distant past had not been erased in the slightest: *Je Suis Partout* once more rose up against this possible candidate for *président du Conseil*, who had benefited from "the sponsorship of Joseph Reinach" before "serving as a living card index for Clemenceau." "We have only escaped M. Léon Blum to fall into the hands of M. Georges Mandel!" cried this extreme rightist newspaper. "France, ruined by a Jew, could only be saved by another Jew! Oh, after all! . . . A national France, a Christian France, a corporative France, that France belongs no more to M. Georges Mandel than to M. Léon Blum."[49] In addition, according to Pierre Dominique, Mandel was "hideous. . . . Woe to pregnant women who catch sight of him!" He was a "eunuch"[50] and it was out of the question to entrust France's destiny to him.

Hostile to Munich, Mandel was also the target of all the pacifists, who portrayed him as a relentless warmonger. Things continued on apace: in March 1940, Paul Reynaud constituted a new cabinet that was resolved to go head to head with Germany. Pétain, the victor of Verdun; Weygand, Foch's former right hand; and Georges Mandel, Père la Victoire's strongman, entered the government to galvanize energy, as had earlier been done during World War I. As he had long ago, under equally dramatic circumstances, Mandel returned to the Department of the Interior, this time as minister: he had to act quickly, impose his orders on the *préfets*, combat the signs of defeatism. He pursued communist militants accused of sabotage in airplane factories, turned against the extreme right, and had the chief members of the editorial board of *Je Suis Partout* arrested. Then came the time of the debacle: he ordered civil servants to remain at their posts and to struggle against disorder. Through him, the Clemencist tradition was being expressed: the irony of history is that Mandel and Pétain were charged with incarnating it together.

They had lunch together on 3 June 1940. In Tours, Mandel pushed to keep France in the war, exhorted Reynaud to remain faithful to the British alliance; in Bordeaux, he failed and Reynaud resigned. Pétain succeeded him. As Mandel would say somewhat later, "is it not natural that at three-quarters of a century of distance the collaborator of Clemenceau (who had been beside Gambetta at the Assemblé de Bordeaux) had in turn refused to be associated with a capitulation that was contrary to the honor and interest of France?"[51] A line can be drawn from Gambetta to Vichy, retracing in a remarkable way the destiny of Clemencist state Jews, and in fact, of all Jews. The English proposed he leave for Great Britain to continue the struggle; he had their confidence and could have been the voice of the French nation at war: Churchill nicknamed him "Mandel the Great." But he refused; to General Spears he responded: "I will not leave tomorrow. You are worried about me because I am Jewish. It is precisely because I am Jewish that I will not leave tomorrow."[52] More than he wished, his entire life was, as it were, fashioned by a status that he now fully assumed: he, the solitary soul, who in certain respects, had such a negative image of his own person, the Clemencist who recognized only the nation.[53] But the representatives of the nation disappointed him to such an extent that he rapidly abandoned all the ideas that had long made of him a rightist. The short time remaining of his life would literally overturn his values.

Soon the marshal had the Tiger's right-hand man arrested. Mandel demanded the charges in writing: on the day of his death, he was still carrying the document he had obtained from Pétain. Then came the adventure of the *Massilia* evoked earlier, and once more imprisonment in Vichy jails: The Tiger's son, Michel Clemenceau, tried to come to his aid by interceding with Marshal Pétain, who listened but did not want to know anything about the matter. Turned over a bit later to the Germans, he had a very simple comment: "At least this way it's clear; I'd rather deal with masters than with servants." During that entire period, for four years, he was dragged from one prison to another, then deported to Germany. The Vichy regime demanded his return: turned over to the *milice*, Mandel was assassinated on 7 July 1944 in the forest of Fontainebleau. Laval himself was furious: "He was," he declared, "among the national Jews whom Clemenceau had so well distinguished." Laval may have been wrong: the man elected by the National Bloc, the adversary of the *Cartel des Gauches*, of Blum and of the Communist Party, had moved to the left, which alone was defending the ideas of the nation. Shortly before the defeat, he had linked up with Gabriel Péri; at the time of his incarceration in Germany, he had even earned the confidence of Blum, who like Jules Moch had come to judge that he was "one of the great statesmen of the century."[54]

On his corpse was found a text that bore witness to this overturning of values, which attacked his Clemencist identity, to the point, paradoxically, of perhaps linking him to the early Clemenceau of the Commune:

The working world — the people — at the forefront of Resistance. It was the people who were behind Joan of Arc, whom Henry IV depended upon to refashion a national unity shattered by the religious wars. The people made the Revolution, saved France with the Committee for Public Safety. Founded the Republic against factious undertakings for a half-century. Held fast in the trenches in 1914–18. And who, after a moment of blindness in June 1940, did not delay in discerning the treason of military leaders and rendered through their resistance. . . .[55]

Bloodstains prevent us from reading the end of this final testament, which sounds like a return to the most radical period of Clemencism, the most attentive to the fate of a struggling people.

CHAPTER SIXTEEN

Jaurès's Heirs

It was Sunday 26 December 1920 at the Congress of Tours, and the future of the French workers' movement was being played out. The confrontation between enemy brothers was becoming more violent every day; tension was mounting; interruptions were commonplace; enthusiastic advocates of unconditionally joining the Third International, more or less resolute opponents, and constructors of various allegiances addressed one another. The delegates were taking stock of the internecine wars that were ravaging every federation, and cries of "long live Lenin" and "long live Jaurès" reverberated relentlessly. These cries marked the two main tendencies that were tearing French socialism asunder. That Sunday morning it was the turn of the delegate from Haut-Rhin to present the result of the votes on various motions. Reynaud read the following declaration: "The result, according to the mandate of the committees, is: 36 votes for Cachin-Frossard, only 32 votes for Longuet, and a single vote for Blum. As a result, according to the committees, the Cachin-Frossard motion obtained the majority. . . . In addition, we would like to bring the Congress's attention to the fact that Citizen Salomon Grumbach, until now a pure-blooded chauvinist . . ." Bracke interrupted: "You'd do well to send that to *La Libre Parole*, that would make them happy!" The hall stirred with emotion: for the first time since the beginning of debates, the political struggle between delegates of differing opinions was openly taking an antisemitic turn, which would have overjoyed Drumont.[1] The historic moment when the workers' movement split irrevocably into enemy brothers resembled for a moment a populist meeting where such outbursts were commonplace.

On Monday afternoon, after almost three days of debates, Léon Blum took the floor; along with Longuet and Paul Faure, he steadfastly battled to "save the old house" threatened by the Bolshevik "adventure," whose "military" and centralizing logic, according to him, threatened the freedom of all and anticipated the coming of a dictatorial political order that would push toward the uniformization of society as a whole. For the second time since the beginning of that key event, the Congress of Tours, beyond the cries, the interruptions, and other various outbursts, insults flew, relentlessly punctuating Léon Blum's grave and controlled statement with terms evoking the tradition of Proudhon and Toussenel more than Jaurès. Exhausted at the end of a long exposition interrupted by incessant noise, Léon Blum had hardly taken his seat, resigned in advance to a schism that seemed unavoidable because intolerance was taking over, when a violent altercation once more erupted, between Daniel Renoult, a fierce supporter of joining the Third International, and Salomon Grumbach and Georges Weill, the two *députés* from the east of France, who opposed the idea.[2]

At the very moment when, borne on the nationalist and conservative wave of Union Nationale, Georges Mandel had triumphed in Gironde, prolonging for a time the Clemencist tradition, which was now oriented toward law and order, other state Jews were playing a significant role in the quarrel that ripped apart French socialism in the aftermath of the Bolshevik revolution. In contrast, Mandel and other state Jews—Édouard Ignace, Jean Ehrlich, and André Fribourg—vigilantly fought against socialism by deliberately situating themselves in the camp of the nationalist right. As Ehrlich put it, "The supposed methods of the Bolshevist dictatorship leave all the terrors of the bloodiest periods of the czars far behind. . . . As a socialist and democrat, I want no dictatorship, and that is why I am leaving a party that, in advocating the dictatorship of one class, places itself outside democracy."[3] Ignace and Ehrlich were both elected in 1919 in the company of Barrès: along with the theorist of French-style nationalism, they denounced the "deadly" communist doctrines. For them, it was important to "constitute a common democratic front against the Bolshevist flood. . . . If, by some misfortune, these deadly theories were to take root among us, it would be not only the end of the republican regime but also the suppression of all individual liberty; it would be even more than that, it would be the end of France."[4] It was as if the two Clemencist traditions suddenly found a concomitant resonance among state Jews: on the one hand, the socialist tradition, which for a moment crossed paths with Alfred Naquet, who had joined the Socialist Party in 1900; on the other, the nationalist tradition, which had become irremediably hostile to the working world and its protest demonstrations.

At the Congress of Tours, we note among the delegates, in addition to Léon Blum, Salomon Grumbach, and Georges Weill, the presence of Jules Haïm Uhry, who in the end supported the Blum motion: the son of a teacher of Alsatian origin, he joined Jaurès's Socialist Party and became legal editor at *L'Humanité*. That same year, he defended an astonishing thesis before the Paris law faculty: strikes, he asserted, were only the inevitable consequence of capitalism. "Only the disappearance of class will make it possible to ensure social peace." In support of his thesis, he turned to passages from Feuerbach and Engels to justify the abolition of capitalism.[5] In fact, a more attentive reading of this Marxist and iconoclastic thesis would also reveal numerous references to the ideas of Jaurès, who even wrote the preface for one of Uhry's brochures.[6] Influenced by Marxism, a very active propagandist in the workers' movement, Uhry nevertheless shifted away from Jaurès and toward Blum, and refused to join the new Communist Party.[7] Of course, he was always open to communist ideas and, in his platform statement of 1919, asked voters "not to be taken in by the Bolshevist bugbear. In Russia, the peasants have simply reclaimed the land that the grand dukes stole from them; and that is why, despite all efforts, the counterrevolutionaries are failing and the peasants are supporting their government and ensuring its victory. Whereas in struggling against them, your children, the classes of 1918 and 1919, are sent to their deaths."[8] He nevertheless joined forces with Blum at the moment of decision. Of course, other Jews attentive to Marxism participated in these confrontations; on the front lines were obviously Charles Rappoport, a very active proponent of joining the Third International, who was, however, rejected soon after by the French Communist Party (PCF). Unlike those already mentioned, however, none of these Jews were or would be elected. Let us remark as well that Henry Torrès, grandson of Isaïe Levaillant, whose name we have already encountered on several occasions, was one of the very rare state Jews to sign the Cachin-Frossard motion favoring the Moscow theses: he was, however, rapidly excluded from the Communist Party in 1923, becoming first a Socialist *député*, and then a Gaullist one.[9] In contrast, Léon Blum, Salomon Grumbach, Georges Weill, Jules Uhry, and soon after Jules Moch, elected to the SFIO in Drôme in 1928, all engaged in sociopolitical protests against capitalism and in favor of socialism, but opposed Moscow, claiming instead the inheritance of Jaurès and the French Revolution. In a certain way, they symbolized a faithfulness to the early Clemenceau's radicalism, attentive to the ideals of the Commune and to the values of the people. This means that state Jews who protested the social order usually had to distance themselves from their predecessors, whether these were the Emperor's faithful (Koenigswarter or Javal), Gambetta's men (Joseph Reinach and David Raynal, both fundamentally hostile to socialism), or the advocates of the later Clemencist tradition (Georges Mandel). Alfred Naquet was the one exception: at the end of his life, he was tempted by an anarchism that was more and more compatible with socialist theories.

No doubt social protest was belated and limited among state Jews. To embrace it, they had to transgress a real taboo, their absolute devotion to a republic of citizens. For a long time, in accordance with the ideology of the period, social questions were supposed to be resolved without any recourse to violence, and a fortiori to the socialist perspectives founded on class conflict and confrontation. The Gambettists, as we recall, all manifested to various degrees a solid distrust of revolutionary movements that might shake the foundation of the Republic. Like Gambetta and Jules Ferry, they always considered the division into antagonistic classes a sacrilege that disturbed the unity of citizens. Like the republican leaders as a whole, at the end of the 1880s they looked favorably on the emergence of the solidarist movement through which Léon Bourgeois, but also Ferdinand Buisson, Ernest Lavisse, and Henry Monod set in place a program for social assistance to the poor, openly situating themselves within the tradition founded by the French Revolution.[10] In that sense, the positive state could prolong the Jacobin heritage, reinforcing the cement of the nation-state: the solidarist schema came to mirror a school policy with the same goals, which was conducted by the same agents. Jaurès's heirs could only truly declare themselves with the retreat of that solidarist tradition, with which the Gambettists identified. Let us rapidly evoke that tradition.

Just as they contributed to defining education and civic instruction, Gambettist state Jews were already proving to be active in the social domain thus defined. Far from socialism and in accordance with their conception of a republic of emancipated citizens in all senses of the word, they wanted to vie for the field held by Christian philanthropists, to extend the movement of general secularization to the social field. Solidarism led to social education, which was to liberate citizens from injustice. It was also charged with preventing socialist and revolutionary excesses. When, in November 1886, the directorship of public assistance at the Ministry of the Interior was created, Henry Monod, a Protestant *préfet*, was the first to be named to that post; another Protestant, Jules Siegfried, presided over the great mutualist movement. As in education, some state Jews nevertheless participated side by side with Protestants in implementing that solidarist policy: in the forefront we find a former Gambettist, Paul Strauss, who along with Ferdinand Dreyfus, signed a report in the *Revue Philanthropique* addressed to the Comité Central des Oeuvres d'Assistance par le Travail (central committee on acts of charity through work) in view of establishing a "fraternal society."[11] Strauss also fought for the creation of a ministry of public health capable of undertaking "a sanitary defense of the French Republic," with hygiene replacing the class struggle.[12] Like Ferdinand Dreyfus,[13] he expended endless energy in the "social defense" of the Republic. His preoccupations remained constant and in 1922–24 he became minister of hygiene, assistance, and social precautions in the second Poincaré cabinet, an endpoint and synthesis of the Gambettist and Clemencist traditions regarding the destiny of state Jews. With great energy, he occupied himself with public health, problems of child care, depopulation, public assistance in general, and with labor negotiations and the codification of labor laws. In each instance, it was a question of remedying the flaws in the social order to contribute to its stabilization. In his early youth, Paul Strauss, like others, had been close to Gambetta, though he later advanced Poincaré's determined policy.

This solidarist tradition, attentive to national concord, would take on greater scope with World War I: as Pierre Laroque, a high official linked to the tradition of state Jews, remarked, "The state has completely taken over the economy everywhere. . . . A profound feeling of solidarity has linked all classes, allowing for better mutual understanding and making it possible to realize social progress not through violent conflicts but through the collaboration of all."[14] Pierre Laroque and Paul Cahen-Salvador, directors of workers' and peasants' retirement in 1920, both members of the Conseil d'Etat,[15] were the principal actors in implementing the social security system. Intimately linked to one another, these few *conseillers d'Etat* — and their children, such as Jean Cahen-Salvador — set about accomplishing a single task; it was Paul Cahen-Salvador who, in 1920, was charged with drafting the first bill on social insurance covering the principal risks, which was prepared in the spirit of public interest shared by all classes. For him, "it is in common that risks are shared."[16] This high official, a former Dreyfusard, was later named secretary general to the Conseil National Économique (national economic council), an organization whose works he directed until 1940, simultaneously occupying the post of *président* of the interior committee at the Conseil d'Etat.[17] Concerned with the general interest and with regulations that would limit the temptation to move toward socialism, these state Jews were simply committed to the implementation of a more just social order. To that end, they even imagined a system of representation by various social groups in the state that would favor their integration and cooperation under the control of public power, a kind of neocorporatism that both Paul Cahen-Salvador and Pierre Laroque, in his *Traité des assurances sociales* (Treatise on social insurance, 1937), fervently supported. The logic of collectivity had, at all cost, to take precedence over confrontation.

After Paul Cahen-Salvador, Pierre Laroque became the author of the French social security plan and, in the aftermath of World War II, the first director of the organization responsible for implementing it. As a result, these two state Jews, committed to law and order and wishing to reduce inequality, appear to have played a tangible role in the 1930s in elaborating a philosophy of economic planning and neocorporatism. Paul Cahen-Salvador and Pierre Laroque thus established a link between the solidarist thinking of the turn of the twentieth century and the neocorporatist generation involved in economic planning in the 1930s: for them, the role of ensuring the coordination of private interests, in order to favor the coming into being of a more just social order for all citizens, fell to the republican state. From Durkheim, the father of civic morality — but also the author of a plan creating new corporations where the delegates of all social classes would meet — to Pierre Laroque, a certain continuity seems to be in evidence. Like Durkheim in his famous second preface to the *Division du travail social* (Division of social labor), Pierre Laroque, in *La représentation des intérêts et le service public* (The representation of interests and public service, 1935), maintained that "to channel the union forces, there is no other measure to be taken than the integration of unionism into the state."[18] For a time close to the newspaper *L'Homme Nouveau* (The new man), whose inspiration was Henri de Man, he also shared the ideas of the neosocialists. He was joined by Jewish socialists Max Hymans and Robert Lazurick, who rejected employer authoritarianism but praised the integration of the unions into a "strong state." As Laroque put it,

There is no doubt that a social organization worthy of the name, realizing a harmonious and fruitful collaboration of efforts, requires the intervention and the control of public power. To our thinking, such should be the directing principle of social policy: assistance gives way to collaboration as an instrument for social achievement. Furthermore, it is necessary for that collaboration itself to be organized within the framework of the state.

Published in 1934, this text is obviously situated at the opposite extreme of the social policy of the Front Populaire.

The distance separating Gambetta's men and their distant descendants, Jaurès's heirs, was therefore great. Jaurès's heirs were more open to a socialism that overturned the republican consensus of citizens, who were now also considered social agents. Léon Blum, for example, openly rejected the solidarist vision of social relations and denounced any neocorporatist perspective. The protesters all more or less embraced Marxism and the class struggle, reasoned in terms of confrontation and exploitation, and sometimes displayed reservations toward a republic that had simply taken on the traits of a parliamentary regime and had not installed true political democracy. In that sense, they were more critical than the Gambettists, even though, like all their predecessors, they were careful not to deny the inheritance of 1789, as desirous as they still were to preserve the framework of the emancipatory nation-state while avoiding a fall into dependence on an external internationalist movement that proclaimed its indifference toward the idea of nation. Nevertheless, though situated to the left of the Gambettist tradition, most of them took their place at the Congress of Tours, for example, to the right of their Socialist comrades, who were receptive to Bolshevik ideas. In fact, until the end of the Third Republic, only Georges Lévy (and, briefly, Henry Torrès) joined the Third International at Tours. Lévy was a convinced supporter of the Russian Revolution; at a public meeting organized in November 1919 in Oullin, near Lyon, he denounced "the government and its militarism, praised the Russian Revolution, and criticized the actions of France, which wanted to stifle that spirit of liberty. The working class owed it to itself to tear itself away from the constraints of the agreement."[19] He joined the directing committee of the PCF in 1921 and became a Communist *député* in 1936, after regaining a seat in Lyon. In January 1940, he was defeated in his mandate along with the other Communist *députés* who refused to depart from solidarity with the policy of their group after the conclusion of the German-Soviet pact: arrested, he was incarcerated in Algeria. In reality, at that time, few state Jews took the path leading from protest against capitalist society to communist activism.

They were nevertheless often very combative and resolved to struggle against socioeconomic inequality. Fernand Josué Crémieux, several times *député* and senator of Gard between 1885 and 1928, epitomizes the transition between radical extremism and socialism. Born in Pont-Saint-Esprit, he became a lawyer, and can be considered the heir to that republic of southern Jews identified with Gambetta: in fact, he occupied a middle position between two of his relatives, Gaston Crémieux, a Socialist who was shot in March 1871 after the insurrection at the Marseilles Commune, and Adolphe Crémieux, the great orchestrator of the little group of republican Jews faithful to Gambetta. With the 1885 elections, Fernand Crémieux committed himself in his platform statement to fighting on the side of "working men" to improve their fate. In that way, he ran up against the Church, in particular the priest of Uzès, who supposedly declared from the pulpit: "The kingdom of France cannot perish. Let us pray for the Conservatives." Crémieux did not conceal his convictions: in election meetings, he publicly celebrated the fact that he "belonged to the faction of the Republican party that, as late as yesterday, was considered a bugbear."[20] The newspaper *Le Républicain du Midi* (The Midi Republican) underscored how "Crémieux voted for all the workers' issues."[21] Defeated in the 1898 legislative elections, he ran for senator in 1903 and supported the creation of a newspaper, *Le Franc-Parler*, in order to support his own candidacy: "We know no enemies on the left," he proclaimed from the outset, receiving the enthusiastic support of the Socialist Party, the *Maison du Peuple*, and the Comité Ouvrier Révolutionnaire (revolutionary workers' committee).[22]

Solidly rooted in Gard, Fernand Crémieux thus continued the tradition of southern republican Jews, while at the same time moving it toward the left. He was not the only one to find support in this milieu, which had always been open to republican ideas and had often respected cultural pluralism: Jules Moch was also elected first in Drôme and then in Sète; Léon Blum became *député* of Narbonne; Salomon Grumbach, long *député* of Mulhouse, was elected in Castre in 1936; and Charles Lussy was also *député* of Vaucluse in 1936. Thus, virtually all state Jews who became social protesters found support, at one moment or another in their careers, in these southern regions. Others easily established roots in the eastern provinces, another traditional place of origin for Jews of France, from which Léon Blum's family came: hence, Georges Weill, like Salomon Grumbach and Jules Uhry, canvassed for their fellow citizens' votes in this region, which was no doubt more conservative than the Southeast, but which they succeeded in rallying to the socialist cause. Their profound rootedness in these provinces symbolically attached to the Hexagon could only make them more attentive to the legitimacy of the nation-state. Jean Pierre-Bloch established himself in the adjacent region of Aisne: elected in 1934, he was long its representative. Finally, Robert Lazurick was elected in Cher to be Socialist *député* in the Front Populaire. Max Hymans joined the socialist battle by joining the SFIO: *député* of Châteauroux in 1928, he kept that seat until World War II. On two occasions, he was part of the Chautemps cabinets where Léon Blum also held a seat.

As a result, if there were many who found themselves close to Blum at the Congress of Tours, was it not because, in spite of their common commitment to socialism and often even to Marxism, they still wanted to believe they were the heirs of a nation fashioned by the ideals of 1789? In Strasbourg and Mulhouse, Weill and Grumbach engaged in the polemics internal to the Marxist movement, in particular concerning the fact of nationhood. Hostile to local particularisms with autonomist ambitions, they were also careful not to join the Third International, which intended to suppress allegiance to the nation, this time from above. Georges Weill was born in 1882 to a Jewish family from Strasbourg, which was closely tied to the nation: between loyalty to France, integration into German socialism, and the problem of expressing Alsatian specificity, he found himself forced to make radical choices that distanced him from his German socialist comrades and from certain Alsatian milieus around him. He then set his sights on Paris and there joined a group of collectivist students, frequented the Cercle d'Étude et de Propagande Socialiste (circle for socialist study and propaganda) founded by Péguy, and joined the magazine *Le Mouvement Socialiste* (The socialist movement), directed by Lagardelle. It was also in Paris that he became close to Jaurès. The Dreyfus affair indisputably affected him, awakened his particularist consciousness, linked him for good to Jaurès and the moral combat for the Republic's ideals of justice. Returning to Alsace, he was responsible for organizing the Party and participated actively in the debate on the new Reichsland Constitution: at the Congress of Magdeburg in 1910, he maintained that Alsace should be granted a republican constitution in accordance with the values of '89 and in conformity with "the true national tradition, which is the tradition of the French Revolution and the republican past." His ideas were close to the conception of the nation proposed by Bauer and implied maintaining Alsatian legal and cultural particularism within the German whole: the first socialist elected official in Lorraine in 1912 in Metz, he held a seat in the Reichstag, where he forcefully demanded that Alsace not be annexed by Prussia and that it enjoy a status favoring the growing association between Germany and France. At the time, he was very close to Jaurès, whom he frequently met in Paris as an official correspondent for *L'Humanité*, in the newspaper office or the home of the Socialist leader. He was very attached to France and wrote: "We do not want to renounce our national personality. It would be absurd to confuse socialist internationalism with the annihilation or negation of the national idea. . . . If there is in Alsace-Lorraine a tender memory of France, we owe it to the Great Revolution. . . . The cult of the past and our hopes meet in socialist acts."[23] Sharing Jaurès's values—his pacifism but also his worship of the French Revolution—he took part in numerous international encounters in the company of Jaurès: on the day of the Socialist leader's assassination at the Café du Croissant, he was seated at his table, directly across from him.

Consistent with his commitment to the Republic, he fought in the French army and was sentenced to death by a German war council: in *L'Humanité*, he proclaimed to the Alsace-Lorrainians that "there are no more reservations to our hopes and our patriotic will." The French press underscored this remarkable example of "loyalty to the nation"; the German press, in contrast, saw in that commitment the result of temporary insanity due to the death of Jaurès! After the war, he rejected Bolshevik doctrine, which seemed to him incompatible with the indispensable "national defense"; in particular, he maintained "that it is allowable to be both a convinced internationalist, a good republican, and a good Frenchman." At that point, everything had been said: he pronounced himself in favor of the Blum line at the Congress of Tours and, at the local level, continually opposed the Alsatian communists, who favored an eventual separation of Alsace-Lorraine from France.

At that point, Georges Weill became the bête noire of autonomists of all political leanings and fought for the introduction of the laws of the Republic as a whole, and in particular of secularism,[24] in the recovered provinces. His contributions in this regard were countless: in May 1924, for example, at the Palais des Fêtes in Strasbourg, he declared at a large public meeting: "Particularism is no longer possible today, because we live in a state that is not a confederation; we do not want anything to do with defensive reinforcements against France, and the Republic is united and indivisible. . . . It is indispensable for Alsace and Lorraine to mix more and more with the whole of France and participate in the shared life of the nation."[25] A Marxist, Weill nevertheless displayed profound Jacobin sentiments, praising the qualities of "French national genius" and, at the same time, limiting the pursuit of class confrontation to the framework of the single nation-state. As a result, a strange alliance formed against him, one that united communists and autonomist Catholics: in a communist meeting held in Strasbourg on 26 April 1928, an orator cried out: "Weill, 'the *préfet*'s friend,' is no longer the representative of the workers. We are hardly the allies of the autonomists and clericals, but we support those two parties." The clericals did not bristle at a close alliance with the communists "to avenge the too French attitude of Georges Weill."[26] Conscious of what was at stake, Weill maintained in 1932, before a packed hall, that "it is no longer the Party that is at issue, but the Republic, national unity."[27]

Locally, as we have noted, the two Clemencist traditions almost came to be indistinguishable: a Socialist leader, Georges Weill, showed himself firmly attached to national unity. Beyond fundamental political differences and antagonistic ideological visions, both sides were fierce opponents of any enterprise calling into question the republican nation-state. From this perspective, Salomon Grumbach, elected several times to be *député* at Mulhouse, also presented himself as a diehard Jacobin; opposed to the theses of the Third International at Tours, he fought autonomist tendencies to such an extent that the newspaper *Els*, which was its mouthpiece, amalgamated his name to Wallach's, his opponent on the right, who was also a state Jew; in its view, they were simply "two chauvinists" who were victimizing local autonomism.[28]

Just as Poincaré was accused of coming to the rescue of Georges Weill, Salomon Grumbach was suspected of receiving help from all the advocates of law and order. Grumbach, denounced as "a demagogue who comes to preach his gospel of socialism,"[29] nonetheless incarnated the image of a law-and-order man. This viewpoint was often formulated: according to the autonomist press, "*préfets* and *sous-préfets* help G. Weill and S. Grumbach on the orders of Poincaré, the great Lorrainian who has come to support them against the autonomists." The ambiguity became so intolerable that

Léon Blum himself, during a large meeting held at the Palais des Fêtes in Strasbourg, went over to support his socialist friends and at the same time attacked autonomism, because "the Socialist Party wish[es] the total assimilation of Alsace to France" — and to Poincaré! The communist militants present in the hall, in contrast, proclaimed in high German their attachment to Alsatian autonomism. During the same meeting, Georges Weill, in French and then in Alsatian, declared that "the SFIO is the only bulwark of the French idea in Alsace."[30] As for *Le Temps*, it explicitly emphasized "the national character" of his candidacy.

Like Weill, Grumbach, from a Jewish family in Mulhouse, first became active in the German socialist movement: he believed that Alsace could convert Germany to the Republic and break up class power of a feudal nature. In his view, "The French republican constitution is far superior to the German monarchical system." He was also very close to Jaurès and played an important role in supporting certain of his doctrinal positions concerning the nature of the German socialist party; he also wrote for *L'Humanité* and participated in public meetings beside the French Socialist leader. Like Jaurès, he was against war and actively fought for peace. He found refuge in Switzerland during the conflict as a correspondent for *L'Humanité*. In 1915, he drafted a brochure titled *Le Destin de l'Alsace-Lorraine* (The destiny of Alsace-Lorraine), dedicated to Jaurès.

Also like Georges Weill, he supported Léon Blum at the Congress of Tours: as a member of the administrative and political commission of the SFIO, he stood out as an undisputed leader in the two federations of Haut-Rhin and Bas-Rhin. Locally, he led the same battle as his Socialist colleague in favor of the laws of the Republic; in his platform statement during the 1928 elections in Mulhouse, he expressed the wish that "Alsace be more and more linked to national life" and protested "the hate campaign led by the clerical party . . . against republican and secular France." Also firmly opposed to autonomism, he declared himself an advocate of the separation of Church and state and of secular schools. Quite naturally, when Léon Blum had become head of the government and seemed to be moving in that direction by extending the laws of the Republic to the recovered eastern provinces, Grumbach and Weill were at his side: as we recall, however, all of them had to retreat before the general outcry that manifested itself in those regions.

At the national level, in 1925 he pronounced himself in favor of the Socialists' participation in the government beside the Radicals, but fought against the alliance with the Communists. At the SFIO, he was most often found on the so-called right of issues, like Georges Weill. For example, he rejected the notion of a dictatorship of the proletariat in a long series of articles in *La Vie Socialiste* (Socialist life). Salomon Grumbach presented himself as a socialist who was attached to the nation-state above all else: a resolute opponent of the neosocialists such as Déat and Marquet, he put all his energy into saving the Republic from the Hitlerian enterprise, which was also finding so many echoes in France. He expected much from the state and came to doubt the capacity of the socialist movement to defend democracy. There too, he rejoined the other Clemencist tradition incarnated by Georges Mandel: like him, he placed all his hopes in the force of the state, and asked that France pursue the war overseas. He too left on the *Massilia* and was arrested and imprisoned; unlike Mandel, he managed to escape and joined the Cévennes *maquis*.[31] For his part, Georges Weill succeeded in reaching Algiers and sat on the Comité de la France Combattante: thus, they all participated in the war effort to save the nation.

From the viewpoint of the theory of the nation, these heirs to Jaurès leaned toward the right of socialism and defended the Republic, weapons in hand: they identified with Léon Blum, who in these tragic times, finally saw in Georges Mandel a true defender of the Republic, in spite of the immense political differences that separated the two men. The head of the Front Populaire was both the true heir to Jaurès and the man who had assumed the responsibility for the break at the Congress of Tours, the rejection of the Bolshevik branch. He was also a friend of Jean Jaurès even before the Dreyfus affair and participated in that battle beside him, in the company of Lucien Herr. In 1898, he joined the group Unité Socialiste (socialist unity), fought actively, and returned to Jaurès's French Socialist party in 1902. With Guesde and Vaillant, they founded the SFIO in 1905. Like Weill and Grumbach, he had a regular column in *L'Humanité*. *Maître des requêtes* for the Conseil d'Etat, he was no doubt the first high official who was a state Jew to embrace socialism: it was in this way that he became *chef de cabinet* to Marcel Sembat in 1915, at the Ministry of Public Works. At that time, he quietly stated: "I choose neither Wilson nor Lenin; I choose Jaurès. We remain revolutionary socialists without in any way submitting to the influence of the Bolshevik world."[32] A *député* in 1919, he headed the Socialist parliamentary group and opposed with brio the Bloc National — and therefore Mandel. At the Congress of Tours, as we have seen, he played a capital role: in 1920, he denounced the Bolshevik logic that, according to him, led inevitably to the dictatorship of one man or of one group taking the place of the proletariat. He pronounced his respect for the specificity of historical contexts, marking the difference between the situation prevailing in Russia and that of parliamentary democracies such as France, where universal suffrage and the concept of citizenship had already instituted a minimum of political equality: to triumph, the revolution had to win over minds and modify values in France, appealing to morality and ethics without resorting to the force of a centralized movement that destroyed freedoms. Continually referring to Jaurès, Blum presented himself as his direct heir and underscored the extent to which the great leader saw in the French Revolution the triumph of a moral system and not an event that could be explained simply in terms of the class struggle. Needless to say, he did not reject Marxism and wrote in *Le Populaire*: "In the present state of things, an anti-Marxist socialist would not be a socialist and would quickly become antisocialist. How could we reject socialism's identity with Marxism when our most ferocious enemies hold it against us? . . . Yes, we are Marxists."[33] But he also wanted to see himself as Jaurès's successor, since Jaurès had been an integral part of Marxism: in his pamphlet, *Pour être socialiste* (To be socialist), he maintained, like Jaurès, that socialism grew out of a moral need, and he drew the legal consequences regarding the process of political change. Explicitly drawing inspiration from Jaurès, he maintained that reform in itself had a revolutionary character.

In his view, the socialist had to respect republican laws as much as possible. When Blum became head of the government, he set to work scrupulously to satisfy various constitutional obligations, but avoided transforming the "exercise of power" into a "conquest of power." Presenting his program before the Parliament in 1936, he declared: "We are a government of the public good, which has no other object than the public good; we claim to be a national government in the highest sense of the word, and that is why we are today addressing all Frenchwomen and Frenchmen." Later, he added: "This government must, at every moment and in every circumstance, inspire the twofold conviction that no other government could have done as much for the working class, procured the same satisfactions of its demands, the same improvement in its conditions, and at the same time, that no other government could have managed with more uprightness, vigilance, and courage all the affairs of the nation." Blum made Jaurès's slogan his own: "Aim for the ideal and understand the real," inasmuch as he assumed these two approaches of his teacher once he had taken charge of the government.[34]

Above all, as a state Jew he situated all his actions within the framework of the French nation, challenging Leninist internationalism. In a word, Blum took on the task of accomplishing his "duty as a socialist, a republican, and a Frenchman" all at the same time.[35] Even in 1918, as *maître des requêtes* at the Conseil d'Etat, he became famous for his conclusions regarding the Lemonnier verdict, which significantly extended the responsibility of public service, thus giving the state greater responsibility for protecting its citizens. On several occasions, he maintained a Jacobin-style discourse, which all state Jews, whatever their own political values, had embraced; for example, in *Nouvelles Conversations de Goethe avec Eckermann* (New conversations between Goethe and Eckermann), he maintained that "it is in a centralized, unified, leveled nation that individuals are truly free. The Montagnards of '93 saw this very well against the Girondins, whom Barrès embraces."[36] Joseph Reinach, a Gambettist fiercely opposed to socialism who, as we recall, rejected the heritage of '93 and, to Clemenceau's great anger, retained only that of '89, could not subscribe to such an assertion wholeheartedly, but he shared with Blum a conception of the nation-state as freeing up all particularisms of region and class: in this, he was inspired by Jaurès and by Mandel, Clemenceau's right-hand man. In Blum's view, socialism in France had to be inserted into national political traditions. As he wrote in 1936, "Every time the Republic has been threatened, it has been saved by that union of the bourgeoisie and the republican people, the masses of workers and the peasants."[37] Hence, we understand why the Socialist leader rarely used the notion of class struggle and instead preferred the term "class action" to support workers' movements, which he saw as demands inserted into the framework of the Republic and stemming from the struggles of '89.

At the time of the 1935 elections, to make his candidacy credible, Léon Blum began his platform statement by insisting on "the great body to which he belonged," that is, the Conseil d'Etat. During the 1936 legislative elections, he once more wrote in his platform statement:

We wish the state, or better, the collective will of the nation of which the state must be the instrument, to exercise itself simultaneously on all the nerve centers of economic life in order to increase the mass of revenues, to ensure an equitable remuneration to producers, to reestablish commercial and industrial transactions at their normal rate. Everything is linked together in such an action and it is the nation as a whole that will profit by it.

And he signed it: "*député* of Aude, president of the parliamentary socialist group, editor of *Populaire*, honorary *conseiller d'Etat*."[38] In fact, Blum the socialist, Blum the republican, also presented himself as a high official of the state charged with social action of "solidarist" dimensions: as if, at the moment of making the move, of coming into power, the socialist protester who respected Marxism did not forget the earlier message of the republican reformists hostile to internal confrontation with its uncertain consequences regarding the common good.

The beginnings of social protest by these state Jews loyal to Jean Jaurès, that is, schematically, the synthesis between 1789 and Marx, implied simultaneous membership in the SFIO and a rejection of Leninism, that is, of the constraints exercised by the Comintern on every communist party in the name of a purely internationalist vision of the class struggle, and its indifference to the legitimacy of the nation-state that had resulted from the French Revolution. In that sense, 1936 and the strategy of the Front Populaire were, in fact, an at least tactical recognition of the reality of that context fashioned by a national history that from the outset had emancipated all its citizens, including Protestants and Jews, and was at the time liberating citizens from their sole identity as workers. And, in February 1942 in Riom, before his judges, Léon Blum prided himself on having taught the workers in the Front Populaire once more to sing the *Marseillaise*.

Beside him, Jules Moch performed the duties of secretary general to the government, duties that had been those of Joseph Reinach in Gambetta's Grand Ministère. Jules Moch resembled him in every respect: a graduate of the École Polytechnique, the son and grandson of Polytechnique alumni, he was the very image of the Jewish high official. His socialist membership dated back to 1924. Elected in Drôme, then in Hérault, two southern regions, he became undersecretary of state to the *président du Conseil* in 1937, and then minister of public works in the second Blum government in 1938.[39] In 1924, returning from Russia, he had seen the light: "Poor Marx!" he cried, maintaining that "the Russian dictatorship is unfortunately the negation of freedom."[40] As he told it himself, it was reading Blum that led him to socialism; in his view, 1789 remained the model to follow.[41] In his Hérault electoral campaigns, during incessant meetings where the *Internationale* was sung as often as the *Marseillaise*, he took care to embrace the values of the Republic, calling for the rejections of the "whites," for a mobilization favoring the reinforcement of "fraternity among all citizens." While he was seen in Sète as "the supporting beam of socialism," he intended to install it only within the republican framework.[42]

Needless to say, in the economic domain, he advocated the abolition, or at the very least, a profound transformation of capitalism, which brought with it "injustice and exploitation"; in that sense, he pronounced himself in favor of widespread nationalization of industries, which would also mark the end of monopolies, the only way to get at "the exploitation of poverty."[43] But, like Blum, he thought the Matignon accords sufficient in themselves to "remodel the social order" by strengthening national unity;[44] and throughout his life he remained persuaded that "the communist threat is mortgaging the future of France."[45] In 1948, he put down strikes led by the CGT and the PCF, maintaining quite simply, in a speech to the Chamber, that "a profound divorce between communism and the Republic" was about to come about; he immediately asserted that "Lyautey was right to proclaim that one must show force to avoid using it. The slogan, alas, also goes for the cold war, which is being waged against the nation."[46] Out of his rejection of communism, this state Jew thus came to evoke the authority of Lyautey! Having participated in two world wars, he did not hesitate to use strongarm tactics against the communist strikes, which he considered dangerous for the Republic, but also against the return to power of

General de Gaulle in 1958, whom he judged to be putschist and antirepublican. Like Léon Blum, he was marked by the memory of Boulanger and forcefully rejected the strengthening of the executive branch. This heir to Jaurès proved adept in the methods of Clemenceau.

There were many other state Jews around Léon Blum, often from the eastern provinces, who wanted to reconcile the Republic and socialism. That was the case for Cécile Brunschvicg, whom Léon Blum named undersecretary of state at the office of national education in the Front Populaire government. She actively worked for women's inclusion in the Republic; she wanted to obtain the implementation of a truly universal suffrage, the acquisition of real equality in university exams, such as the *agrégation* for secondary education, and the transformation of the Civil Code in ways favorable to women.[47] There too, she was part of a long tradition of state Jews with diverse public opinions, who from Alfred Naquet to Camille Sée, and including Léon Blum himself, tried to introduce sexual equality into society; that in itself illustrated a kind of synthesis between the republican ideal and a socialist perspective understood primarily in the moral sense of the term.

Many other state Jews participated during that period in the socialist movement. Let us underscore the fact, however, that for the first time, some of them belonged to the prefect civil service, proof if need be of the slow penetration of the values of social protest into an administration of authority where there was a fierce attachment to law and order. Here, things progressed more slowly. Only two examples come to mind: first, that of Henri Elie Dadoun, *sous-préfet* in 1921, whose opinions were clearly oriented toward socialism. In his personnel dossier, his superior noted in 1920 that "he passes for having sympathy for the Parti Indépendente Socialiste (independent socialist party); has at certain times manifested very active sympathies for the CGT [Confédération Générale du Travail]."[48] The second case, that of Albert Gabriel Heumann, is even more revealing of this very slow change of mind that affected a high administration traditionally hostile to socialism: *sous-préfet* in 1918, he became *préfet* in 1934. In his administrative dossier, there figure letters of recommendation from Léon Blum, among others; in 1936, a note from the office of the minister of the interior concisely observes that he was "particularly recommended by the Party."[49] This type of remark probably appears in other dossiers of high officials of the time; but this is the only one we could find among those of state Jews. It attests quite simply to the success of strong integration into the state: outside the anarchist mode or communist strategies, it made possible a protest that remained respectful of the laws of the Republic.

From then on, state Jews could be found both on the left and the right: they even advanced quite far on the side of nationalist values, even as they also identified with socialist ideals, without fear of breaking the republican contract. The anarchist and socialistic faith — a very lonely one — of Alfred Naquet gave way, at the end of the Third Republic, to a commitment within a disciplined party devoted to social struggles and hungry for collective justice, though still rejecting the old Guesdist dream, now incarnated by its communist enemy brother. The era of emancipation, like the slow integration into the public space, which took up the entire nineteenth century, slowly became more distant, authorizing an increasing diversification of political attitudes, as long as they were fundamentally respectful of the republican base. The small social milieu of state Jews, still relatively dense at the turn of the century, became so heterogeneous that it seemed to lose any existence proper: in the process, as a function of the very centralization of political struggles, partisan loyalty took the lead over any other link of sociability. As we have noted, the few Jews present within the political elite during the interwar period confronted one another, even directly, during various electoral contests, much more than they had done earlier. Political ideologies more and more shaped well-defined camps. And yet, as during the time of the Affair, ideological opponents found themselves linked by antisemitism both latent and overt.

Throughout their long careers, the Republic's fools, whether politicians or government appointees, encountered antisemitic hatred, which negated their true integration into the public space. On the left and on the right, even though they might very well be fools for love of the Republic, its values and institutions, they all suffered rejection. We have already noted this, but it is fitting, in conclusion, to deal with its various dimensions. The most striking, the most visible, the best known, that which, for example, emanated from every Franco-French war and was also very much alive in the lulls of everyday life, came from political groups that persisted in rejecting the republican order and attacked its Jewish servants, transforming them into scapegoats; the most hidden, the most surprising, and the most odious inasmuch as it surprises, found its origin this time within the republican state itself. It is true that the construction of the Republic was far from finished and that, in certain ways, the rejection coming from society overall found expression even within a structure that was supposed to be universal and meritocratic. As painful as it is to point out, this second aspect of antisemitic hatred will now hold our attention.

PART V

Political Antisemitism

CHAPTER SEVENTEEN

Jews Without Land: The Debate on Political Representation

In April 1893 in Digne, in the tolerant Southeast, just before the Dreyfus affair erupted, it was easy to see a growing political agitation due to the proximity of the upcoming legislative elections, which were taking place in the still heated context of the Panama scandal. Joseph Reinach, one of its protagonists who, like many others, had been splattered with mud, attempted to start over and regain the confidence of his electorate. "Two peasants" who wouldn't be fooled addressed a long missive to the minister of the interior regarding Reinach, and it was published in the *Journal des Basses-Alpes*. It ended with a vigorous: "He is not from around here." To give all its weight to the protest, the newspaper published an editorial in the same issue, underscoring the fact that "nothing justified the choice of a German candidate of the Jewish religion, who knows nothing . . . of our mores, our habits, our needs." Heedless of such arguments and faithful to the republican ideal that was solidly shared in those regions, the voters made their will known in the first round of elections, renewing their confidence in their *député*, who thanked them for not having acceded to "the furious assault of medieval hatred that has been reawakened."[1] The same year, this time in Bordeaux, David Raynal's opponent, another friend of Gambetta, violently attacked the corrupting influence of Jews and did not hesitate to declare in his official platform statement: "I offer myself to you as the representative of all the interests and all the affections that are attached to French soil.

Coming from a family of French landowners, I have from my birth a love of the soil and an instinctive mistrust of all foreigners. Confronted with the danger of Jewish dominance threatening us, I appeal to all Frenchmen of France."[2]

Three years later, in early 1896, a grave danger seemed to be threatening the somnolent Picard region: it was time to sound the alarm, since "the Semites are venturing to plant their tent in Somme." The time was quickly coming when "the close union of all Picards in heart and in land, the magisterial elimination of the Semitic precursor" would be indispensable. Hennard, the region's native son, the valiant knight who dared to stand up to L.-L. Klotz's parachuting in, did not mince words; he was indisputably "a Picard whose heart beats in unison with all Picards." And he dotted his i's: "That Jew is no Picard. . . . How could he represent us?"[3] He shouted a lively "Picardy for the Picards!" "The Jewish lawyer, a foreigner to the region, indifferent to agricultural questions," was transforming the department into "a Semitic fief" and was rooting himself for the duration in that peaceful province.

The campaign for the 1928 legislature was now at its height: Jean du Médoc was still fuming. In his "peasant's remarks," which he repeated day after day, he thundered against the "wandering Jew" Mandel, who "does not possess an acre of land, in Médoc or anywhere else," and he regularly ended his papers with a vigorous "Médoc for the Médocains!"[4] According to another of his witty opponents, Mandel "wanted to plant two grapevines in his little garden in order to present himself as a wine grower in a region where he one day intends to seek votes. Tartarin himself would have been jealous of that tall tale!" He then went hammer and tongs at the "men of foreign origin who are threatening those of the French race." The speech merits detailed consideration, for it echoes almost to the word a declaration we have already evoked, made thirty years earlier, also in Gironde, against David Raynal. It begins: "I offer myself as the representative of all the interests and all the affections attached to the French soil. Coming from a family of French landowners, I have from my birth a love of the soil," and concludes, "We need a Médocain capable of honorably representing Médocains."[5]

France had just stumbled, a real upheaval had taken place, one that was propitious for all kinds of intolerance. Through what strange phenomenon had the Popular Front carried off the victory, by what aberration had the French been able to identify with this body of doctrine that was so incomprehensible for them, and defended by someone like Léon Blum in the first place? That question took on increased urgency at the local level where French citizens had elected a leader of the SFIO. In fact, to many, such a choice seemed altogether incongruous, all the more so since the citizens of

Narbonne, rather than correcting their earlier vote, inexplicably reaffirmed it. In 1934, *Je Suis Partout* was already shouting itself hoarse:

> The fact that M. Léon Blum is *député* of Narbonne and that, in this capacity, he is allowed to play a role, and what a role, in the French Parliament, now that is something that suggests the level of absurdity and tragedy in the electoral world. M. Léon Blum is neither from the north, nor from the center, for from the east, nor from the west, nor from the Midi of France. What family does he claim as his own? To what land is he attached? Where is his vineyard?[6]

From this perspective, Joseph Caillaux set the tone, emphasizing, first, that Blum, unlike Jaurès, "doesn't have enough French soil on his shoes" to legitimately represent a district. The metaphor would mark the era. In an apocalyptic text, Maurice Bedel portrayed Blum as

> a leader of the International who seems to fear contact with the land; he does not walk about in solid laced boots through paths in the fields. . . . He has never shuddered at the odor of the furrow opened by the iron of the plow rose in his nostrils; he is a stranger to all that is sap, humus, pathways among the hedges, puddles after the downpour, clods, clay, rich earth, the good, friendly earth. Oh, no, he is not someone from around here![7]

In Narbonne, certain people shared that evaluation: *L'Indépendant de l'Aude* (The Aude independent), for example, pushing the logic implied by that argument to its extreme, asked: "When will the yid finally decide to cede his Narbonne seat to a militant of the vineyard?"[8] *Le Courrier de Narbonne* declared that it was appalled "by the grotesque representation of our Languedocan Midi. . . . We must suppose that our populations, which are nevertheless the heirs of Latin good sense, have gone mad."[9] The loss of all reason was all the more certain in that his opponents were, after all, local boys, "authentic wine growers who work with their hands."[10] Persisting in their oblivious behavior, the voters once more acclaimed Léon Blum: "Does the city of Narbonne still belong to France?" asked his opponent Émile Sabatier. "Narbonne has become a corner transplanted from Palestine where the money changers have once again invaded the Temple. . . . Citizens of Narbonne, how can you suffer the tyranny of that man of another race?"[11]

In spite of everything, Blum was reelected in Narbonne; in his footsteps, Jules Moch conducted a difficult campaign in Sète in April 1937. He certainly benefited from the help of the local SFIO and depended on a solid local republican tradition with a taste for banquets, conviviality, and the memory of a past marked by so many passionate struggles for democracy. Like Léon Blum, the high official was parachuted into that district in the name precisely of the universalist dimension both of the Republic and of socialism. In every meeting, the *Marseillaise* and the *Internationale* reverberated, sung by enthusiastic militants and voters. Citizens loitered in front of cafés to meet the man who, in Paris, was doing such a good job of backing up the head of the Front Populaire. In face of the "fascist threat," "France as a whole will have its eyes fixed on the Third of Montpellier," shouted a speaker at a large public meeting held in Sète. "We need to know whether men and women in this country wish to disavow the government of popular assembly." In the neighboring streets, the crowd listened to the speeches, which were retransmitted over loudspeakers, while a little further away other gatherings were held in support of a candidate of the PPF, who claimed to embrace Doriot, "the representative of French Hitlerians." In such a context, that electoral jousting match took on a national and ideological dimension in everyone's eyes. And yet, the newspaper *L'Information* alerted its readers: the debate had to be posed in different terms, for the questions of ideology and political values hardly sufficed to guarantee the local authenticity of a candidacy come from so far off. After all, Jules Moch was not "a child of Sète"; lacking "any attachment to the region," he did not understand very much about the "little nation." The conclusion was obvious. "Our Midi is too discerning not to distinguish between those who represent it and those who do not."[12]

Let us leave these regions of the Southeast, which were, however, reputed to be hospitable, and turn toward Normandy. During the same electoral campaign, on 22 April 1936 in Louviers, Modeste Legouez, the opponent of Pierre Mendès France, exclaimed before three thousand people: "There is not a single Jew among Norman farmers, so why would they choose one to represent them?" He was "the son, the grandson, the great-grandson of farmers" and would better accomplish the task, for he was "a boy of the vineyard."[13] In spite of his qualifications, the voters, deceived once more, repeated their 1934 error: four years earlier, Pierre Mendès France had run against Alexandre Duval, "a native son who has remained faithful to the region and has served it well. . . . Coming from an old family of skilled farmers who, for two hundred years, have worked the same land from father to son."[14] The main newspaper of Louviers had already fervently embraced the cause of candidates opposed to Mendès France and declared:

You, sir, do not know the state of mind of the Normans whose votes you are soliciting. They do not like to give their votes to unknowns. To claim the honor of being chosen as the representative of the people, you must first introduce yourself, especially if you are facing a man such as Alexandre Duval, whose family has farmed the same piece of land in Le Neubourg for two hundred years and who is very much a 'boy of the vineyard.' . . . It's a question of race. The Jewish race, which has remained very pure despite its dispersion, has good qualities and faults that rarely correspond to those of the people of the land such as we are. The great majority of the voters of this region are rural people attached to their land. The Jewish race are wanderers and little inclined to be sedentary. I do not think there are many farmers among them, and around here, we don't know of any. And that creates a spontaneous mistrust of men who are attached to no place.[15]

From one era to the next and in every place, the same litany was repeated: as landless people, lacking any roots in the soil where the peasant soul was fashioned, state Jews had no place within networks of sociability, which included only "boys of the vineyard." People of the city and of the state, these Jews who ran for elections could not claim to represent a population that had remained largely rural: the "end of the soil," in Eugen Weber's expression, was slowly spreading across time and exacerbating a difference that was labeled a handicap. The resistance to the campaigns for national unification made the Republic more fragile and put state Jews in an unstable position, faced with the survival of regional identities. What is striking in this selection of declarations pronounced at the local level is a profound calling into question of the theory of citizenship and even of the public space itself: representation, a concept that recurs in each text, is now situated in the substance of the soil, in the absolute identity between the elected official and his constituents: the first had to be identical in every way to the second, even in his personality and his most deeply held values, as they had developed slowly over centuries of regional history. For state Jews, a specific and particularly vulnerable target, this was simply a denial of the republican ideal: spontaneously rediscovering counterrevolutionary theories, small-time polemicists, who feared the city as much as the state, would later find a following.

With the exception of Léopold Javal, who was himself only partly a farmer, none of the state Jews, whether *députés* or senators, drew their income from working the land. Outside certain parts in Alsace, religious reasons and various kinds of ostracism had excluded Jews as a whole from possessing any land. Fears from the Middle Ages and the uneasiness and hatred provoked by modernization efforts refreshed the peasants' memory, more closely bonding communities, which were fearful of the Other come from the city, and even more, from the state. In fact, their own history also turned many Jews away from agricultural careers, since in the past they had been confined to the ghettos; the construction of their memory was timeless, without reference to a soil, roots, or even regional customs. In France in particular, assimilationist Franco-Judaism had incited them to join the camp of progress and modernization, even while neglecting, in the very name of the positivist Republic, particularist folklore. In that sense, their consciousness as state Jews, a result of the ideals of 1789, rarely linked them to local concerns. In the end, they had hardly listened to the advice proffered them by Abbé Grégoire or by the *Almanach du Bas-Rhin*, which told them in 1799:

Leave behind, yes, leave behind a way of life that has all the outward appearances of idleness: take up the pickax and the hoe; handle the plow, the harrow, become farmers. It is not enough that you become attached to the soil; the soil must also become attached to you. Cooperate with other Frenchmen in fertilizing the land of Liberty, let the dark tint from working the fields fill out the nationality of your faces, may the calluses of work honor your hands! It is only then that you will offer a serious guarantee to the Republic, that you will become worthy of the confidence of your fellow citizens.[16]

Jews, who constituted a highly urbanized population, had every disadvantage in relation to this form of republican ideology: it was turned more toward the land than toward Reason and, oddly enough, made full access to citizenship depend on a return to the fields, which we would expect to find rather in counterrevolutionary discourses. As the nineteenth century unfolded, Jews experienced ever greater rates of migration to the largest urban centers, in particular, Paris, where a large proportion of them had already made their homes by the 1880s; those who refused to remain in the lost eastern provinces after the 1870 defeat quite naturally headed for the capital. In 1872, 94 percent of the Jewish population was urbanized, in contrast to 34 percent of the population as a whole.[17] In the big cities, they encountered fewer difficulties in exercising their professions as lawyers, doctors, teachers, salesmen, or businessmen, socioprofessional categories that especially attracted them. Like many of their colleagues in the Chamber, Jewish politicians were thus obliged to be "parachuted in" to districts where, for the most part, they had no attachments of family or property. As Jews from the city, they represented a perfect target for the attacks of their opponents, few of whom neglected such a godsend in denigrating their competition.

Whether they were Opportunists, Radicals, Conservatives, or Socialists, their rejection took the same form everywhere. Through it, the very notion of representation was perverted, becoming distanced from the classical ideal of the century of Enlightenment to which the French Revolution laid claim. The *députés* were no longer designated as the representatives of the general will beyond the sum of localist and particular interests, but rather as the delegates of each province, of each land, of which they ought to be the mirror image. While the Ligues paraded to cries of "France for the French!" local supporters of this community-based nationalism, turning their backs on republican traditions, echoed with "Médoc for the Médocains," "Picardy for the Picards," or "Normandy for the Normans." . . . And we could multiply ad infinitum the expressions of such localisms, which perverted the very notion of representation in its constitutional dimension.

For the advocates of this French-style nationalism,[18] which found its source in Barrès and his cult of "the land and the dead," every region made an effort to preserve its own personality by delegating a representative drawn from its ranks to go to the Chamber, a delegate shaped by its local traditions and at the same time almost indifferent to the ideologies and various "-isms" prevailing among certain candidates from the capital. In that public space, which was suddenly degenerating into a multiplicity of regions anxious to preserve its own values, it was parliamentarism itself that was under attack. State Jews in particular suffered from it, for they were almost by definition more on the side of the newcomers in every sense of the term than on that of the "heirs." When organic metaphors prevailed over republican rationalism, it was certain that state Jews of all parties would see their own legitimacy collapse, founded as it was on principles for the most part disconnected from any particular rootedness in local customs.

Their integration into the republican state also did damage: when they campaigned for the votes of their fellow citizens, they sometimes appeared as instruments of a state that was rejected in and of itself and that still provoked hostile movements due to its pretension to regulate the entire social space. As state servants, enthusiasts of centrality, they were perceived by various peripheries in a way unavoidably linked to the role they performed in the state's administration. The congruence between landless Jews and the state was striking. What was a severe handicap in conservative and rural society disappeared in an urban world where the predominance of the state was more easily affirmed. Enthusiasts for the law, avid for norms and rights, concerned with institutional legitimacy founded on the idea of a neutral and sovereign public power, they definitively turned their backs on the particularisms of the land. As state Jews, to varying degrees of course, they also found themselves inadvertently linked to the conflict between the state and a society that had remained in its depths solidly Christian and that intended to choose its representatives out of respect for its own religious values.

Let us resume our tour of France. We have noted how our "two peasants" complained to the minister of the interior about being represented by the Jew Joseph Reinach, a stranger to the region. What followed in their missive only takes on greater significance: "Although we are not pillars of the church, we do have our children baptized, we send them to mass and catechism, we have them take their first communion, we marry them in the church, and we bury our dead in blessed ground, with a priest in attendance. We did not like the idea of being represented by a Jew." A Catholic population could not identify with a Jewish *député*: that was the essential conclusion of a letter that, in its own language, developed a discourse identical to that of Barrès. He considered "French nationality closely linked to Catholicism, formed and developed in a Catholic atmosphere. . . . In attempting to destroy, to tear the nation away from that Catholicism, so closely linked to all our manners of feeling, you cannot foresee all that you would tear asunder."[19] The most profound French identity, built on the land over the centuries, would be broken apart by the construction of a re- publican state whose universalist logic was such that it made possible the implantation of Jews into regions where, from time immemorial, the Church had reigned without competition. At the local level, the separation of Church and state had had the most severe consequences, with allegiance to the land, to Catholicism, and to nationalism combining into a homoge- neous whole. According to that logic, only Catholics had the right to the status of citizen, only they could vote, only they could run for office; a strict correspondence was thus established between religion and political representation in the Chamber. Not only did the land reject rootless Jews, but that land, peopled with Catholics, could also not allow a Jewish *député* to speak in its name.

That reasoning, which was to be fatal for state Jews, was repeated with an astonishing consistency from one electoral district to another. When Raynal presented himself to his voters in August 1892, his unlucky oppo- nent, the marquis of Lur-Saluces, thanked those who "courageously did their duty as Catholics and Frenchmen to the end" by voting against him. And in 1896 L.-L. Klotz's opponent congratulated "the true Picards who attempted to fend off an invasion, whether from Germany or Judaea, with royalists and Christians as the first line of defense." The *Chronique Picarde de La Croix* (Picardian chronicle of the cross) mocked the "changeable yid" and hoped that Picardy, like Nord, would have its Abbé Lemire as *député*. Things could not be clearer. The *sous-préfet* of Montdidier was completely aware of this supposed incompatibility: in his *préfet*'s report, he maintained that "many voters of the arrondissement are against him (Klotz), less be- cause of his political program than because of his personality, which is for- eign to the region, and we must add, his religion, which shocks the local population, which is profoundly Catholic."[20] While the Picards wished for the coming of an Abbé Lemire, Catholics in Médoc could not allow them- selves to vote for Georges Mandel in place of his opponent Abbé Bergey: "The Catholic Médocains will never vote for a Jew."[21] To the east this time, in Vosges, Camille Picard presented himself to his voters in 1919 during a by-election. According to a police report, "he is not animated by an antire- ligious spirit"; that did not seem to be enough, since his opponent ap- pealed to "Vosgian good sense," declaring he was certain that "the country of Joan of Arc, the sublime heroine," would bar the route to the "obscene Picard Jew." The *sous-préfet* of Neufchâtel found himself obliged to "signal that there are votes, even republican votes, that will never go to him be- cause he is Jewish."[22] Let us turn once more to Hérault; in 1914, Albert Milhaud ran for the legislature in the second district of Béziers: one of his opponents maintained that "no Catholic could vote for him without being a renegade and a traitor." *La Croix* raised the stakes, calling upon every voter: "If you are a good Catholic, do your duty, and plant your little corner with this bloc to contribute to demolishing him, since he is himself intending to crush religion."[23] The same year, still in that region, in the arrondissement of Lodève, Pierre Masse was denounced as a candidate from "Jew, Crook and Co.," whom Catholics ought to spurn.[24] Closer to our own time, in 1925 in Hautes-Alpes, Maurice de Rothschild encountered a very hostile campaign: one of his opponents pleaded, "as the father of a Catholic family, do not vote for a Jew."[25]

Separated from a Christian land, pushed toward the city, an especially large number of Jews were elected in the capital itself. Several nonetheless succeeded in overcoming their handicap by winning the confidence of rural populations: They were sometimes even seen announcing loud and clear their love for the "little nation" that their district constituted for them. In their platform statements, most of them promised, like David Raynal, to "establish closer and more frequent ties" with their voters, and committed themselves to serving local interests. Joseph Reinach, a personality who was long central to French political life, was on intimate terms with his fellow citizens of Digne: "You have known me for a long time. I have settled here, I live among you; I have become one of you." Théodore Reinach addressed the Savoyards in the following terms: "I am not a passing guest in your land, but an adopted son. This lovely region has won me over for life. . . . I would like to see the ties that unite the two Savoys grow closer: the large nation is now too well cemented to have anything to fear from the development of the little nations."[26] With great conviction, he then launched into a fervent plea for respect for regional identities. On all his election posters, Camille Picard also took care to proclaim: "All Vosgians! Vote for Camille Picard, a child of the region."[27]

In his platform statement, Lazare Weiller also noted that he felt "a filial tenderness for this lovely region of Charente, to which all his childhood memories were attached," then paused to shed light on "the wondrous efforts of the wine growers" who were succeeding in "conserving the vineyards, which are a national glory."[28] Close to Maurice Barrès—whose works he admired without reservation—intoxicated with revenge, and determined to recover the lost lands of Alsace and Lorraine, he considered himself "an Alsatian of old stock." Having emphasized how "delicious the wines of Alsace are," he added: "I have often noted that so curious kinship between my native province and the land of Mistral," a poet who, however, inspired currents on the most radical right.[29] While the theme of land and its worship most often remained absent from speeches by state Jews, external threats led them to refer to it. Some rediscovered such regional accents in order to oppose not the German invader but the Bolshevik threat: hence, Henry Torrès asserted that the French people, "whose patriotism rests on the love of the soil and who, in the patient history of Jacques Bonhomme, have been elevated to freedom through property," were "the living antithesis of Bolshevism."[30] At almost the same period, Maurice Bokanowski, at the time minister of commerce and industry, praised the merits of "French work, agricultural work, industrial work," which were the foundation of "our old French race."[31]

Most often born in the big cities, state Jews were all concerned to be "adopted" in order to blend in with the region and escape local critics, who persisted in seeing them as "foreigners." They even came to sing the praises of the land, even in the absence of any external danger: for example, on 1 May 1933, Pierre Mendès France published a brochure for the department of Eure, where he was serving as *député*, and described in great detail "the Norman countryside," underscoring "the ineffable peacefulness of the French countryside." With emotion, he told of the wealth of "this lovely region of Eure, land of history, of lazy and capricious rivers, of fragrant memories, of delicate and slowly savored food, this land where it is sweet to live among rural labor — this lovely region of Eure, which sums up all of France."[32] Again in 1955, in a speech before the Association des Maires de France (association of mayors of France), he declared in a lovely flight of language: "On several occasions during the travels I have just undertaken, while speaking in the name of our region, my thoughts came back to this corner of France where the mayor of Louvier is to found among the men and women of our region, reestablishing contact with that good and strong base: our homeland."[33] Many of these Jewish politicians were, in fact, born in Paris, far from the remote countryside: at very distant removes, that was the case for Joseph Reinach and David Raynal, for Pierre Mendès France, Léon Blum, and Jules Moch. When Moch tried to settle in Drôme, he acknowledged he was "born in Paris of Parisian parents." But, he added, "did not the Revolution abolish internal borders? They tell you that, not having been born on the banks of the Rhône, I must know men and their needs less well than someone else. Do you believe that the several thousand friends who have already so generously adopted me have not let me know all that a man 'of the land' can know?"[34] "I have become one of you," L.-L. Klotz also emphasized, not beating around the bush, committing himself, like many others, to defending local agriculture.[35] Albert Milhaud "paid a moving tribute to the little nation" and promised to support the interests of the local wine growing industry, praising "the defense of French wines against the competition of exotic wines."[36]

Often elected by southern departments, Gambettists, like Jaurès's heirs, were almost all involved in protecting the wine industry and the privileges of home distillers: when President Doumer, in the wake of Fernand Crémieux's death, retraced his career before the Senate, he insisted on the fact that, "as a representative of a wine growing region, Crémieux took up the defense of this French resource. We heard him plead the cause of wine growers, struck down by a fearful crisis and victim of the watering down of wines, with conviction and eloquence."[37] Like Émile Javal, but completely opposed in his political ideas, Jules Moch admirably held forth on the merits of the local vineyards; in 1937, during an electoral campaign in Hérault, in each community he analyzed the legal regulations on wine and the way they could be improved."[38] Like Fernand Crémieux, many were even members of agricultural and wine growing groups in the Chamber; Pierre Masse, who also belonged to these groups, noted that "in our arrondissement of Lodève, wine industry questions matter above all. As a member of the Confédération Générale Viticole (general wine growing confederation), entirely dedicated to the interests it represents, I want to collaborate closely with it to resolve wine industry actions."[39] Alexandre Israël defended tooth and nail the quality of the champagnes in Aube and urgently called for "the restoration of the rights of home distillers";[40] G. Lévy-Alphandéry in Haute-Marne demanded "in the name of equity, the right of home distillers to freely dispose of the fruits of their properties for their own use."[41] Camille Picard, the *député* of Vosges and "child of the region," never lost the opportunity to recall that he was a member of the national office of the Comité National de Défense des Bouilleurs de Cru (national committee in defense of home distillers) and president of the Société Vosgienne de Viticulture (Vosgian society of wine growers). André Hesse also declared to his voters of La Rochelle: "Not to bedeck myself with the sometimes illusory label of agricultural candidate, I nevertheless bring my most loyal and absolute cooperation to farmers. I will energetically refuse any new tax on natural eaux de vie."[42]

In Gironde this time, Jean du Médoc loudly proclaimed against Georges Mandel, that "stranger to all things relating to wine growing," of whom he was an unrepentant critic: "I am against all those who seek to destroy our wines." He declared he was "the only candidate who owns a vineyard, a wine grower in the great tradition."[43] Clemenceau's right-hand man, attached to national causes, did not neglect any gesture to make known his attachment to the various wines, his desire to "diminish the right to circulate cheap wine and to make the right to produce cheap wine proportionate to the size of the crop." He touted his decision to work "relentlessly for that sacred cause, the prosperity of Médoc and the greatness of France," and his renewed interest in "modifying the provisions of wine laws relating to distillation and the embargo, which should not have been applied to regions with an original trademark . . . thus attacking Médoc and its wealth."[44]

At the other end of the political spectrum, Léon Blum was hardly better off. "Three years ago," he wrote,

people touted my ignorance in matters of wine. Ignoramus that I was, however, I greatly contributed to resolving difficult questions, such as the tax on the business receipts of wine merchants. My actions were crucial in the text of the wine law. The amendment that saved the irrigated vineyards of the Narbonne region bore my signature and was only voted in because of me. . . . Never during my numerous publicity campaigns have I encountered so much warmth, so much devotion, so much affection as among you.[45]

Elected in Narbonne, preoccupied, like Georges Mandel, with the great debates of ideas and international issues, he was also forced, because of the polls, to become the representative of the world of the vineyard, which predominated in his district. Let us note that in 1919, in his first platform statement as candidate in Paris, no localist dimension appeared: he spoke there of the Republic, of socialism, of social classes, of Bolshevism, addressed the "sovereign people," and on the shared ticket signed, "Léon Blum, *maître des requêtes* of the Conseil d'Etat."[46] In 1924, he ran with Théodore Valensi, among others, in the name of the *Cartel des Gauches*, simply invoking "the Republic which, having rescued a threatened civilization with its allies, has refashioned the integrity of the party." "To destroy the National Bloc" represented in Paris by Bokanowski and his slate among others, it was important to "confront the undertakings of the plutocratic, militarist, and clerical reaction";[47] in Narbonne, things were not the same, for this man who praised the Republic and socialism this time had to convince wine growers to vote for a state Jew whom all his detractors cheerfully mocked. Émile Sabatier, a local antisemitic critic, wrote: "To think that the aware and lucid Narbonnais have entrusted the defense of their primordial interests as wine growers to that puppet, that sybarite and satrap, is to shudder in incomprehension. Blum would be able to tell the difference between a white wine and a red only by their color, not their taste."[48] *Le Courrier de Narbonne* urged wine growers to clearly manifest their opposition to the Socialist leader: "Wine growers, merchants who live by the product of the vine, grant your confidence to the candidate who best knows your needs. Blum doesn't give a damn about wine growing. Vote French!"[49] From Paris, the great spokespersons for antisemitism brought their contribution to the local anti-Blum fight: Léon Daudet "wondered what the good wine growers of Narbonne can think of that commie who has as much affinity with them as a Baltic herring has with our roosters." Maurras shouted his anger at "the vagabond, the wanderer, the man without a country, invited to sit in the legislative armchair of Narbonne, even though the Midi as a whole, from Médoc to Var, bore witness to its horror that such a teetotaler has forced his way in with all kinds of secret support — Masonry, Money — on which he founded his power." [50] Again under Vichy, Laurent Viguier became indignant in seeing "that circumcised fellow reign in the southern capital of Gaul, represent the nation of Clovis and Joan of Arc," [51] while the *Cahiers Jaunes*, to indicate the state of abasement of the French people in the Third Republic, underscored the fact, incredible in their view, that "we have seen drinkers of red wine in Narbonne elect that miscarriage of a teetotaler!" [52]

As a result, outside their universalist vision of the Republic or their prejudices in favor of conservatives — or socialists — like many of their colleagues elected in largely rural districts, state Jews took care to come to the aid of all the peasants and wine growers, of whom some of their opponents claimed to the sole spokespersons, owing to their own local roots. Their efforts as "parachuters" to integrate into the world of the vineyard, to become in turn "local boys," men of the soil, unrepentant defenders of local interests, were successful, since most of them were elected by these districts, which were often southern and republican in tradition. Their local antisemitic opponents nevertheless made the argument about their Judaism to attempt to delegitimate their ability to represent the interests and values of the world of land and vine. In the image of their colleagues in the Chamber as a whole, state Jews rarely dared to combat resolutely the misdeeds of alcohol. Although some of them, for example Paul Strauss, participated in philanthropic efforts and came to the aid of the children of alcoholics, few of them openly called into question the privileges of wine growers and home distillers. Along with Ignace and Maurice Bokanowski, *députés* of Paris, Klotz was one of the very rare politicians to attack home distillers directly, raising the ire of *La Libre Parole*, which was astonished at the audacity of "that young Hebrew, who does not deign to encourage the peasants by his presence." [53] Closer to our time, Pierre Mendès France also attracted the anger of wine growers through his campaign in favor of milk; in addition, he tried to end the privileges of home distillery by abolishing their hereditary character. The radical right did not mince words: *Rivarol* made fun of the "supermale of milk" while, for *Fraternité Française*, the organ of Poujadism, "wine, even 'the coarse wine that leaves a stain' is an excellent thing; it is an exclusively French drink. Unless your name is Pierre Mendès France, just try to do without that prestigious vermeil when you visit foreign countries." [54] The audacity of the Radical *président du Conseil* grew when it came to light, since, as *député*, he represented a population strongly attached to its prerogatives in that area: Normandy was alcohol country, and directly attacking home distillers was almost suicidal. The fact was, taking his conception of a single rational state, representative

of the nation, to its logical extreme, disdainful of the particular and corporatist interests, Mendès France, beyond the Gambettists and the heirs to
Jaurès, rediscovered a Clemencist tradition, which Mandel pursued at the
national level, even at the cost of leaving behind his own electoral district
of Médoc.

CHAPTER EIGHTEEN

Hue and Cry over High Officials! The Long Reverberations of the Dreyfus Affair

M. Denis, *député* of Landes, evoking in the Chamber the recent and sudden dismissal of a "Jewish high official," namely, Isaïe Levaillant, *trésorier-payeur général* of Loire and former director of Sûreté Générale, linked it to that "of the wretched traitor Dreyfus," and in a request for an inquiry published in the *Journal Officiel* in February 1895, asked about the "measures that the government intends to take to stop the predominance of Jews in various branches of the French administration." Some time later, on 30 March, the viscount of Hugues, *député* of Sisteron, called for an inquiry "into the dangers of the continual infiltration of the Jewish race into our midst." Very quickly, the direct consequences of the Dreyfus affair were felt even within the Chamber; beyond the person of the captain, state Jews who were high officials as a group found themselves in a difficult position. The storm that would carry away Isaïe Levaillant only took on more importance: he was indisputably at the top of the hierarchy and the man to bring down, since for many he incarnated a despised power, through his successive administrative duties, beginning with the official birth of the Third Republic up until Boulangism.

Let us go back a bit in time: on 22 December 1877, Levaillant wrote the minister of the interior a long letter in support of his candidacy for *sous-préfet*. As a republican journalist in Nevers, member of the *conseil municipal* of that city, he did not neglect to indicate (a very common practice at the

time) a long list of personalities able to speak to his competence and reliability. In addition to the *président* of the civil tribunal of Nevers, the *procureur de la République* in the same city, and its mayor, there also figured on
that list Gambetta, Spuller, Hérold, and Léon Cohn, the *préfet* who was
Hendlé's son-in-law.[1] By clearly situating himself in the Gambettist movement, he thus began a career that quickly carried him to the summit of the
administrative hierarchy. Time passed; it was now October 1910 and Levaillant had just died. Among the persons who followed his funeral procession, we note the presence of the police prefect Lépine, the key man in
maintaining order during the previous years, which had been so troubled,
a man whose iron fist had so effectively protected the institutions of the Republic.[2] From Gambetta to Lépine, Levaillant joined the resolute followers
of the Republic; he was also part of the small group of state Jews in prefectoral careers who found themselves particularly exposed to antisemitism,
since their actions in service of the state encountered the enmity of a nationalist and Catholic political fringe, which was irremediably hostile to
the new regime. Witness the article *Action Française* published on the day
of his death: "The deceased was one of the most representative types of
that Jewry which, coming from Germany or the remote parts of Poland,
brought down France after the 1870 disasters. . . . He was the quintessence
of the squalid, stingy, filthy Jew with a mop of hair."[3] Such a portrait at
that moment says a great deal about the hatred the victim had attracted
throughout his administrative career.

To take stock of it, we need only turn to *La France juive*, where Drumont outdid himself in his antisemitic verve: from the first pages of that incendiary book, Levaillant was called the quintessence of the "torturer of
Christ," who had made clever use of the principles of 1789. "Coming to the
world thirty years earlier, Hendlé, Cohn, Schnerb, and Isaïe Levaillant
would have broken down doors in one of the Hebraic-German gangs that
Maxime Du Camp describes; today they are *préfets*. You will say that does
not change their occupation very much." And the finale: "It happens that,
in Isaïe Levaillant, Jewish atavism emerges in a very particular way; though
in a *préfet*'s uniform, he has remained the 'sordid and bleary-eyed Jew' spoken of by Saint-Victor, whom Rembrandt so often drew in the picturesque
costume of his filthy rags."[4] As always, Drumont boldly combined the true
and the false to make his point; Schnerb, like Vel-Durand and Hérold,
to whom he also returned in great detail, was not Jewish. In addition,
Hendlé, Cohn, and Levaillant figured among the very rare Jewish *préfets* to
actually hold posts at the time. As an expert, as the spokespersons of antisemitism so often are, Drumont — who carefully examined all the sources
of information, including Jewish newspapers — was not ignorant of the fact
that these three *préfets* were quite close to one another; he developed the

thesis of an imaginary plot, on which his argument rested. The *Archives Is-raélites* denounced this fantasy: "To say that, because there have been a few Jewish *préfets* — three or four, no more — therefore the Jews are masters of political administration, is as ludicrous as to claim that art is essentially southern in France because many painters, sculptors, and even musicians are native to Haute Garonne! They want to see in our coreligionists only Jews and not citizens, Frenchmen, which is a sovereign injustice."[5]

Let us now briefly consider the atypical career of Levaillant: along the lines of the *Protocols of the Elders of Zion*, *La Libre Parole*, by analyzing the course of that career, meant to

shed a little light on the invading march of Israel, for we must not forget that the Jews march in troops, following a plan long since come to fruition, on mysterious orders emanating from a power that is all the stronger in that it is hidden. Isaïas [*sic*] Levaillant is but one link in the chain that is strangling us, one of a thousand tentacles of the horrible octopus that has been sucking our blood for many years.[6]

In that spirit, the dazzling ascension of the *préfet* resulted from a predeter-mined plan; he became director of Sûreté Générale and head of all the po-lice, head of intelligence, not to battle the enemies of the Republic but rather to establish in a lasting way the power of "the Jewish Republic" for the greater advantage of those citizens sharing his religious beliefs. For *L'Autorité*, "I. Levaillant was named director of Sûreté Générale. The Jews of France moaned with joy. It was their plan to hold the police of France in their hands, to have informers at their service and to be able to spy on those Christian dogs at their leisure."[7] Among certain satirists, seeing him occupy such a post of authority elicited an exacerbated, phantasmic vision, as the following text illustrates:

Here is a Jew come from who knows where, named who knows what. What do the Opportunists make of him? A director of Sûreté Générale, that is, the repository of all state and individual secrets. If only this were a unique case! But no, there are swarms of Isaïe Levaillants. There are Jews everywhere, in the *préfectures*, the *sous-préfectures*, in all the administrations. . . . Yes, we have come to that: 38 million Frenchmen are governed by a few thousand Jews. At the present time, a single Isaïe Levaillant is more powerful than fifty *députés*.[8]

Isaïe Levaillant was born in April 1845 in Bas-Rhin and his family left Al-sace after the annexation. With little money, he married a coreligionist, Pauline Segal, who bore him four children; the couple lived in poverty. Ac-cording to his administrative dossier, Levaillant was a "vigorous" person with a "marked physiognomy"; his "Alsatian accent is rather pronounced."[9] As he himself emphasized in his application letter for a job in the *préfecture*, "for many years, he defended the liberal and constitutional cause in the

press, if not with finesse and talent, then at least with dignity and energy."
Like most of Gambetta's men, as several police department reports note, he
began by fighting the regime of the Paris Commune: "The liveliness of his
articles against the Commune greatly contributed to the invasion of the
offices of that newspaper by the insurgents."[10] He thus had many points in
common with all those on whom Gambetta would depend: he was hostile
to the Commune and very committed to the Republic. Up to that point,
nothing out of the ordinary.

One event, which reads like something out of a pennydreadful, and
whose origins and outcomes we still know very little about, was to propel
him to the forefront of current events. His activity as a journalist led him to
discover a mysterious letter that would bring about the unseating of a
député whose vote, by itself, could have prevented the definitive installation
of the Republic. What was at issue? In fact, we know very little about this
imbroglio, which the press on the radical right discussed for a long time. It
was this medium in particular that related in great detail the incident
which, confirmed by other newspapers, seems either to have escaped the
vigilance of historians or to have elicited a skepticism so absolute that they
have passed over it in silence. On 6 June 1874, the *député* of Nièvre, Cyprien
Girerd, spoke out at the Assemblé Nationale and provoked an indescrib-
able storm by reading a document that created a stir: accidently found in a
train car, it attested to the existence of a Bonapartist plot destined to overthrow the Republic. This text gravely compromised the Baron de Bourgoing, who was easily unseated as a result. And, as *La Libre Parole* tells it in
its own version of the facts, "Some time later, the constitutional law of 1875
was voted in by a majority of one! Without the unseating of Bourgoing, it
would have been rejected! It was thus wrong to call M. Wallon 'the father
of the Constitution,' for the true father of the Constitution and of the Opportunist Republic was none other than the Jew Isaïe Levaillant!"[11] As the
Action Française of 24 October 1911 recalled, this affair proved the success
of *député* Girard, who, named undersecretary of state at the Ministry of
the Interior, gave the *préfecture* of Nièvre, his own department, to *sous-
préfet* Levaillant. Levaillant supposedly discovered or even — who knows? —
invented that document whose astonishing consequences we have just
seen: he thus deserved something from the Republic in return. . . . That
was the antisemitic thesis continually spread, which believed that therein
lay the truth of the illegitimate character of that famous "Jewish Republic"
it had taken so much trouble to denounce. In this view, the Third Republic
was purely and simply the product of an Opportunist plot constructed out
of whole cloth by unscrupulous Jews for the greater advantage of a corrupt
political clique, which in turn rewarded its protégés with all kinds of administrative sinecures.

Even today, it is almost impossible to know more about this dark, even Machiavellian affair. Let us note that the government press did not deny the facts, but simply refuted the interpretation. Hence, a republican newspaper congratulated Levaillant on his promotion to the post of director of Sûreté Générale and added:

The role of savior is in his temperament and his habits. He already saved the Republic ten years ago by discovering at just the right moment a Bonapartist conspiracy, in the form of a circular in a first-class train car. We have not forgotten that affair that caused such an uproar in its time. It was at the origin of the political fortunes of M. Levaillant. It also assuredly brings him today to Sûreté Générale. M. Brisson, who apparently recognizes that the Republic is once more in great danger, judges that we must resort without delay to men who have so effectively served under difficult circumstances.[12]

We do not know more about this: what is striking in these divergent interpretations is that, on one side, Levaillant is seen as a loyal instrument of the republican cause, while on the other, his supposed intervention is interpreted in a completely different way and is seen as the proof of Jewish maneuvering.

His career was to remain marked by this ambiguity: in this, it even takes on an exemplary dimension. As director of Sûreté Générale, Levaillant delivered severe blows to the Boulangist movement, which all the Opportunists opposed, setting up vigilant police surveillance on the general's slightest comings and goings, and according to some, even ordering that his apartment in London be robbed and his correspondence with Dillon stolen. In fact, a great deal is attributed to him, and his double role as the man responsible for police actions and as a Jew excited the imagination. The robbery did, in fact, take place while he was performing his duties as director of Sûreté Générale; was he directly responsible for it, did he himself order it? All the police, in these periods when so many Franco-French wars threatening the Republic succeeded one another, continually conducted more or less legal operations. Was Levaillant responsible for a robbery that appeared to play a certain role in the undoing of the Boulangist movement? In any case, the scandal erupted and he was forced to resign. For *Le Petit Caporal*, "counterfeiter, murderer, lock picker of drawers, and liar, that is how Levaillant the dirty Jew seems to us. . . . And it is with such scoundrels that the Opportunist Republic staffs its upper echelons![13] As would later occur against Georges Mandel, the legend of an "off the record" Levaillant arose; he was seen as a despot who did not balk at any method to arrive at his ends. *Le Figaro*, like *L'Intransigeant* (which called him the "great spy of Ferryism"), and *La Patrie*, demanded and got his dismissal. *Le Petit Parisien*, more sober, concluded on 15 April 1888:

"In M. Levaillant, the Opportunists are losing one of their most devoted agents." "The procedures of the Moral Order" appeared to *La Lanterne* as "delicate and scrupulous" in comparison to those implemented by such men as Rouvier, Spuller, and Levaillant; "Opportunist policy," added the newspaper, "in the putrid fermentation that is eating away at it, has produced the most deleterious effects on our public mores."[14]

In reality, nothing was simple in that affair, especially since a merciless police war was unfolding offstage, which would be exacerbated a bit later, when the Schwob brothers scandal erupted. Named in 1888 to be *trésorier-payeur général* of Loire, in a department whose *préfet* was none other than his friend Lépine, Levaillant was definitively dismissed in early 1895, only shortly after the beginning of the Dreyfus affair. He was quite simply accused of having intervened with several magistrates to save the Schwob brothers, with whom he had business relations, from certain conviction.[15] Personal letters written by Levaillant to the Schwob brothers were published by the press; they established the reality of his financial participation in their business in Buenos Aires. Others seemed to suggest that he had advised them on the tack to take toward certain magistrates of his acquaintance during different lawsuits taken against them after their bankruptcy. The affair was fairly complex and many ambiguous expressions led to suspicion: above all, as the trial would show, it was a question of delaying tactics allowing Levaillant to remain apart from any direct intervention. The general context further poisoned the matter since the police war seemed to be reaching an unprecedented intensity at that time: the lawyer who denounced Levaillant's behavior during the trial and publicly demanded a guilty verdict was none other than Andrieux himself, former police prefect, who still confessed a solid hatred for the former director of Sûreté Générale.[16]

In a long pamphlet titled *Ma justification*, Levaillant attempted to defend himself by pointing out the incoherence of the accusations, which did not take into account one capital point, namely, that at the time of the acts for which he was criticized, he was no longer a civil servant; he attacked his opponents' imputations of guilt by association and declared he was innocent, wanting to see in these maneuverings nothing more than the ultimate revenge of the enemies of the Republic, to which he had been a "faithful and disciplined servant." "I see," he added, "that my acts have brought hatred and anger down on my head. I have one final cause for complaint against me, the most terrible, the most irremissible of all: I am Jewish and I feel obliged, since the name of Jew has become an epithet of hatred and suspicion, to claim so openly. Was not that reason enough to have me thrown to the wolves?"[17] As early as 1889, *La Libre Parole* wrote: "When we have Isaïas [*sic*] Levaillant at Sûreté with Grumbach at his right hand, and

Dreyfus providing military information flanked by the 'divine Picquart,' France will be well served and 'the first aristocracy of the world' will declare it is satisfied."[18]

Levaillant's *Justification* is a rare document, for it indisputably shows that the backlash caused by the Dreyfus affair extended well beyond the captain's person and touched a number of Jewish high officials. It takes on even more relief in that Levaillant himself would become editor-in-chief of the *Univers Israélite*, the conservative organ of French Jewry. His political articles, written with great rigor, bestowed the role of moral authority on him during those years of trouble. In addition, in 1901 he was one of the founders of the Comité de Défense contre les Antisémites (committee for the defense against antisemites). From every point of view, then, this man was essential. An Opportunist journalist and, like many others — Jews and non-Jews — a high official devoted body and soul to the Republic, whose successive opponents he steadfastly battled, he played a large role as *préfet* in the secularization of his department. That earned him the inexpiable hatred of *La Croix*, which recalled his role against the Church in Haute-Savoie and used every means possible against this "hook-nosed" *préfet*[19] — this state Jew, found innocent during a high profile trial, was nonetheless brutally recompensed by a state that folded under the pressure of an antisemitic press. To better attack him, the press even placed in doubt his French nationality and his name. Like many other state Jews, he was called a "German informer," a "German spy," and was suspected of having changed his name to disguise his origin.[20] This high official with such a rare fate was abandoned by the state in these times of near civil war. He devoted all the energy he had earlier expended to serve the Republic in the service of various Jewish institutions: he was elected 26 June 1905 to the central consistory where he proved to be very active.

Isaïe Levaillant's fate merits our continued attention, for it retraces the history of a state Jew who had reached the summit of republican administrative power and was brutally excluded under external pressure. The *préfets* and, a priori, the successive ministers of the interior were all violently attacked during that particularly troubled period in France's history, when police maneuvering and endless scandals punctuated everyday life, while the enemies of the Republic were mobilizing and, under various pretexts, taking action. The few Jewish *préfets* and *sous-préfets*, like the sole Jewish chief of police, offered still easier targets for their vendetta: the hue and cry over Jewish high officials took hold as a constant. In the violence of those attacks, spokespersons of Jewish institutions were virtually the only ones to come to the aid of their coreligionists, even though they did not always share their political views. They were sometimes joined by a few high officials anxious to help a wounded colleague, as corps solidarity required.

Again from this point of view, the example of Levaillant is intriguing: while the former police prefect Andrieux publicly played the role of accuser during the trial, it was another police prefect — and what a prefect! — Lépine, who delivered Levaillant's eulogy:

I am performing a duty of justice in coming here to pay tribute to Levaillant's remains. We both began our administrative careers on the same day. For some of those who pursue that career today, he is a forebear who has been somewhat forgotten, perhaps even misunderstood. For me, he was a role model, I should even say a teacher, for I greatly admired the wondrous faculties with which he was endowed. I have never encountered a more acute sensibility, a more reliable judgment, a clearer intelligence more fertile in resources, more professional courage: to sum it up in a word, he belonged to the tradition of great administrators. He was one of the civil servants who left his mark on our profession. And yet his career was short. No one else would have had time to show his mettle. His premature retirement was a terrible loss. The honorable chief rabbi and M. Salomon Reinach have said what a precious adviser he was for his coreligionists, how helpful to the humble. You can see the kind of father he was by the despair of his children. For all, friends and adversaries, he was just, impartial, and good. May his ashes rest in peace.

During the same ceremony, *député* Laroche underscored the fact that Levaillant "devoted to the service of France and the Republic all his strength, an inexhaustible devotion, the resources of a talent without equal, and the inspiration of a generous heart." And he added *in fine*:

It is not in vain that one is born Jewish and does not deny one's brothers: does not that amount to offering one's chest as a target for poisoned arrows? Although the authors of his disgrace later suggested they were sorry for it, his successors stopped short of a complete reparation. Waldeck-Rousseau himself had his former collaborator enter into a permanent commission of the ministry to demonstrate that he still held him in esteem.[21]

These speeches say a great deal about the status of state Jews during that terrible period marked by the Dreyfus affair, in which, as we know, Waldeck-Rousseau himself was one of the principal actors. The "teacher" of Lépine, who would become in turn that of *préfet* and future minister of the interior Abraham Schrameck, the man whom that shocking *préfet* of the Third Republic himself called a "great administrator," whose "premature retirement was a terrible loss," was as it were abandoned by the political leaders he served so effectively. Unlike Captain Dreyfus, he never obtained the slightest official "reparation," even though Waldeck-Rousseau continued to hold him in "esteem." At the time of Levaillant's death, the *Archives Israélites* ended their lengthy obituary by emphasizing "that he was honored by the friendship of the leaders of the republican party: Waldeck-

Rousseau, Brisson, and Léon Bourgeois, for example."[22] More exposed than anyone else, this state Jew too closely involved in the obscure operations of the Republic, object of a hatred on a scale with his effectiveness, was forced after his ouster to limit his actions to the struggle against antisemitism, which was also threatening the Republic itself.[23]

Again and again, a single point needs to be emphasized: Catholicism was continually invoked to justify the incompatibility between the identity proper to French society and the Republic, which entrusted Protestants and Jews with positions of authority. Just as the Jewish *députés* constantly encountered a type of argument that delegitimated their roles as representatives, appointed officials also confronted a logic that, beyond their persons, aimed at the republican state itself. Commenting on the Levaillant trial, the newspaper *L'Autorité* declared:

> The current regime has decided to have Catholics persecuted by Jews. In this way, we find out what Jewish *préfets* are capable of. They are persecutors whom the government inflicts on Catholics by sending Jews as their *préfets*. It is impossible for them to be impartial! They are more than sectarian, they are executioners. And God knows there are a lot of Jewish *préfets* and *sous-préfets*!

Drumont, who never lost an opportunity to drive in the nail, added, regarding both Levaillant and his Toulouse colleague Léon Cohn, another of his whipping boys along with the Hendlés: "The Catholics have only to attack themselves."[24] We recall how the *préfets* Hendlé saw anathema poured out on them, reproaches for their role in the secularization of schools and hospitals, at the local level and in the large national press.[25] Without respite, the antisemitic press violently attacked the two "yids" Ernest and Albert Hendlé, "foreign in [their] ancestors and interests to old France, which is on its deathbed."[26] Catholic demonstrations were unfolding in Rouen, Caen, and other locations, protests against the secularization measures decided on by the government and imposed by the *préfets*. Meanwhile, *La Libre Parole* and numerous local newspapers stubbornly attacked the *préfets* Hendlé, throwing them together with *préfets* E. Sée, Léon Cohn, and Levaillant; they linked all of them to Captain Dreyfus, to better underscore the fundamental betrayal of French identity that, they claimed, they were bringing about by abusing their positions.[27]

The example of Léon Cohn alone deserves a separate study. Brother-in-law to Ernest Hendlé, he also belonged to the Gambettist staff, working for the new citizenship and the separation of Church and state. He had a particularly brilliant career. For Lépine, he was indisputably "a great *préfet*."[28] For everyone, he appeared as the convinced republican: for *La Gazette de la Somme*, for instance, "from the first years of the Republic until the fall of the Moral Order, he conducted a republican correspondence designed to fight, and we have all fought the reaction so valiantly that we have overcome it. He is going to Toulouse, the reward for his devotion to the Republic."[29] In the big city, he became such a central figure that *La Dépêche* denounced the power of "the Judaico-pontifical trinity."[30] At the end of his career, he, like Levaillant, was named *trésorier-payeur général* in Ardennes, a fairly frequent end for the careers of high quality *préfets*. His promotion was noted by *La France Libre*, a Lyon newspaper: "We also remember M. Cohn, the Jew from Toulouse, who presided so well over the *préfecture* of that city during the electoral operations of 1889. The minister has just named him *trésorier-payeur général* in Ardennes. Doesn't the introduction of Jews into Finance seem to you to be the last word in government vigilance?"[31] When he ran for the legislature in the district of Saint-Gaudens, a local paper immediately denounced "the Jew," "the stranger," "the protégé of some unknown Dreyfus."

These generalized attacks against Jews who were members of the prefect civil service redoubled in violence when Jews participated in extraordinary operations to maintain order: when he became minister of the interior in 1894, David Raynal provoked antisemitic articles against him (for example in Lyon) that were so insulting that the *procureur général* of the *cour d'appel* court proposed that the *garde des Sceaux* begin legal proceedings.[32] Recall also the boundless hatred poured out on the *préfet* Lambert, who was called a "priestophobe," on *sous-préfet* Isaac in Fourmies, and on *préfet* and later minister of interior Abraham Schrameck. In every case, their denunciation as state Jews was very often founded on the explicit desire to defend the Catholic identity of French society, which was supposedly violated by these republican Jews. Let us select a single quotation for the Isaac case: in the words of *Le Constitutionnel*, "once more, we have noted the low and fierce hatred that animates the sons of Jews against Christian workingmen. . . . The sinister victory of Jews over our race and our religion has been definitively elucidated; the dogs lying about in the Ghetto have in turn put the collar of servitude around our necks."[33]

The prefectoral administration was aware of the force of antisemitic prejudices among certain Catholic populations, whose spokespersons sometimes reacted harshly to the presence of these Jewish *préfets* or *sous-préfets*. In February 1893, for example, in his administrative report on Émile Lion, *sous-préfet* of Pontivy, the *préfet* of Morbihan wrote: "He is an excellent civil servant who deserves in every respect the benevolence of the administration. Unfortunately, he belongs to the Jewish religion, and in a region as religious as Brittany, that is a redhibitory vice in some sense."[34] Similarly, according to his *préfet*, *vice-président de préfecture* Jules Lévi, named in Finistère in 1899, "earned the consideration of all those not blinded by prejudice. His religion created a difficult situation for him in this Catholic environment."[35] This rejection by the public could only confirm the xenophobic theses of advocates on the extreme right: on 5 January 1896, *La Libre Parole*, as was its habit, launched into a violent diatribe against Émile Waltz, *sous-préfet* of Gray. "This little Hebrew thinks he is master in his *sous-préfecture*. . . . The Yid Waltz insults every minister of the Catholic religion."[36] The same newspaper also denounced the attitude of Beaucaire, *sous-préfet* of Arles, who

completely lost his head upon seeing Maillainais women coming out of church, carrying the statuette of the venerated Virgin in a procession, and had these harmless women charged by the gendarmerie. . . . Never has such an incident troubled this lovely procession. To see an obstacle placed before that touching tradition, we had to await the arrival in the region of a Jewish *sous-préfet* who acts like a little tyrant. . . . The Jewish *sous-préfet* Beaucaire must be convinced that Adonai has arrived.[37]

And as *La Libre Parole* put it,

Our good friend Weill, the Jewish *sous-préfet* from Meaux, whose conduct we denounced at the time of the expulsion of the venerable bishop of Meaux, is not content to operate against the prelates, he also does not neglect the modest priests. As soon as that Jew learns that a municipality in his arrondissement wants to leave a priest the use of its presbytery or rent it at a moderate price, he immediately delegates one of his informers or a teacher to propose a higher price.[38]

We could multiply without difficulty this kind of quotation, hostile to Jewish members of the prefect civil service, through which a properly Catholic rejection was being expressed time after time. It is true that on other occasions, this hue and cry over high officials had no need to make use of this cultural dimension. The most traditional antisemitism reemerged in all its forms at the local level. Named *préfet* of Haute-Saône, Eugène Sée received a charming welcome: "Does the ministry wish to transform the department into a synagogue?" asked *Le Réveil de la Haute-Saône*. When the ministry began proceedings against the newspaper, *Le Radical de la Haute-Saône* approved the *préfet*: "We thank the God of Abraham and of Jacob for this proceeding. The honorable *préfet* probably wished to make up for the damage that his interdiction causes us through a *gut liddle* offer on the eve of the elections." Somewhat later, the newspaper became threatening: "The time is near when his bosses will be swept up and the *préfectures* cleaned out. On that day, weeping will be heard throughout all of Jerusalem — Excuse me! Vesoul. As for M. Sée, he will be able to devote his administrative capacities to reconstituting the kingdom of Judaea, promised to the children of the twelve tribes and predicted by the Talmud." With local incidents multiplying, a *député* of the arrondissement wrote to the minister: "I ask with my colleagues of Haute-Saône that the honorable *préfet* Sée be transferred. . . . In any case, do not give us a Jewish *préfet*!"[39]

Le Républicain de l'Est also thundered against Edmond Cahen, the *sous-préfet* of Verdun-sur-Meuse, who "arrived in our city with his hat on his head as in a synagogue; this cosmopolitan Jew did not understand that his place was not in the administration of our border departments." It ended its tirade with the classic slogan, "France for the French."[40] This judgment was undoubtedly shared by *La Libre Parole*, which claimed that the *sous-préfet* had

transformed the offices of the *sous-préfecture* into a ghetto where all the Jews of Verdun came to have tea every Saturday. When his successor replaced him, he was literally obliged to hold his nose when he penetrated the apartments of the hall. We ask that in the future Jews no longer travel in railroad cars or in *sous-préfectures* without a sign attached to their backs that reads: to be disinfected.[41]

The *sous-préfet* had not seen the end of his difficulties: on 2 February 1898, according to *L'Est Républicain*, "during the night, a red poster was posted on the walls of the Verdun *préfecture* where M. Cahen, *sous-préfet*, resides. It bore these words: 'Death to the Jews! Down with Zola! Long live the army!'"[42] And to return finally, though indirectly, to Isaïe Levaillant, *La Libre Parole* systematically pursued *sous-préfet* Fernand Torrès, father of the future *député* Henry Torrès, who was none other than Levaillant's son-in-law. Recounting in detail a conflict opposing this *sous-préfet* named to Blanc in Indre, this newspaper was overjoyed that "the independent French refuse to lie down before a Portuguese Jew. Everywhere departmental supplies are divided in a biased manner. It is the Jews and Freemasons who benefit. That is what the Opportunists call a republican regime."[43]

As functionaries in authority under a Third Republic that was making an effort to remodel society in order to impose its own values, Jewish *préfets* and *sous-préfets* were the first to be exposed; like their non-Jewish colleagues, they received merciless blows from the Republic's opponents of every stripe. Even more than the Protestants, they were in a fragile and precarious position, inasmuch as their particularism provided weapons to the detractors of the new regime. The antisemitic violence that aimed at the Republic's officials at the local level was striking for its systematic character. In addition to the Dreyfus affair, which got the attention, and sometimes because of it, Jewish high officials were quite simply being hunted. Until now, that hunt has rarely held the attention of historians.

In fact, these prefects were not the only civil servants who were victims of almost constant antisemitic denunciations. Judges, officials in authority who were just as involved in society, whose actions and gestures had great visibility, were often also confronted with similar campaigns. There too,

La Libre Parole imposed a vigilant censure: it spoke ironically, for example, of the behavior of *juge d'instruction* Worms, who "as a Hebrew, no doubt judges that unduly keeping a goy woman in prison has no importance, given that goys, male and female, are the offspring of cattle."[44] It sarcastically and pointedly presented the career of "Jew Judge Alphandéry,"[45] and regularly attacked the *procureur général* of Aix-en-Provence, Eliacin Naquet, whose resignation finally allowed "the city of Aix to breathe a little while awaiting total relief from Jewish oppression."[46] Like his brother, *député* Alfred Naquet, Eliacin Naquet was truly persecuted. *La Libre Parole du Midi* railed as follows: "Israel, the days of Babylon have returned, the gentiles are again rearing their heads, here is a new Nebuchadnezzar rising up, a terrible army like a scourge with the anger of the implacable Yahweh, who will plunge you into Gehenna, where you will be annihilated."[47]

La Libre Parole also attacked the *procureur de la République* of Mayenne, "the Jew Weiller," who was accused of acting in a lewd manner toward young women;[48] and "the Jew Worms, *juge d'instruction* in Auxerre," who made a martyr of "a dirty little Frenchman of thirteen, a little goy who stole eight francs."[49] Finally, Drumont's newspaper asked the question, capital in its view, concerning another Judge Worms of Versailles:

Whatever our sloppiness, can we tolerate Frenchmen being arrested as Catholics and because they are Catholics, being judged, that is, ridiculed at the hearing and thrown into prison by a Jew! That is our situation in our press trials; invariably, we are placed in the presence of judges bearing the stigmata of all the tribes; this was the case yesterday in Versailles, where Catholics arrested for defending their faith, their temples, and freedom appeared before the Jew Worms, that synagogue judge.[50]

We can also cite numerous episodes where the effort was made to show the profound incompatibility between Catholic populations and these Jewish judges. In 1872, according to his superior, Judge Isaïe Berr confronted great "difficulties in his position in Besançon, a city that has remained very Catholic."[51] Similarly, in 1885 in Corbeil, a young boy who had broken a cross was brought to justice: Judge Eugène Cahen asked for indulgence. Embittered, the newspaper *Justice* wrote: "A cross, what is that? It represents the faith of a few million men! The cross is the emblem of human redemption. What piercing words for Catholic consciences!" And it added: "The cross is the Catholics' flag."[52] Let us offer another example: in December 1882 in the newspaper *L'Opinion*, we read a denunciation "of the young *substitut* with the un-French name of Anspach. We have been invaded by German soldiers and German Jews. This Judaic gentleman is not one of us either by his race or by his education or by his religion."[53]

Like the Jewish members of the prefect civil service, those who performed the duties of judge ran up against an attempt at delegitimation:
antisemites wished to see not the Republic's functionary but only a Jew
who, by definition, could not exercise any authority over a Catholic. According to that conception, it was no longer citizens who found themselves confronting other citizens in different roles: the public space lost any
universalist dimension and was transformed into a field of confrontation
between antagonistic cultural particularisms. Judge Worms of Versailles,
evoked above, came to occupy a certain place in current events when he
found himself in the somewhat unexpected situation of having appear before him Charles Maurras himself! Emotions were running high on the
side of the extreme right. Through Worms, Maurras went to war "against
the Four Confederate states, the hundred thousand Jews of the Occupation," who deserved to meet Captain Dreyfus's fate.[54] And, as often, Léon
Daudet mounted the ramparts and wrote a vengeful article in *Action Française*, where he denounced

the insolent presumption on the part of Judge Worms to judge antisemitic Frenchmen; does he imagine that the French are definitively reduced to servitude? We will
show them clearly that we are not. The minute he put on the magistrate's robe,
Worms declared he was likely to convict, strike down, any Frenchman who did not
put his head under the Jewish boot. It's the eternal "my race will wreak revenge on
your race" of the traitor Dreyfus to Major Paty de Clam.[55]

Later, following up on his ideas, he returned to that incident: "The Jew
Worms, judge at the Versailles tribunal, has dared to sate his ethnic hatred
on the master of us all, our friend Maurras. . . . In the name of the Ghetto,
the wretched Worms slapped eight months in prison on the man of letters
of French thought—that jailbird in wig and robes, sitting in the name of a
people not his own."[56] Somewhat earlier, Drumont (as always) formalized
in the most systematic manner this interpretation of the role of Jewish
magistrates: holding forth as was his habit against Levaillant, he maintained that "the Jews have Frenchmen sentenced by Jewish magistrates or
those who have been sold to Israel."[57]

Note that in certain of these quotations the Dreyfus affair was very
much present, and incited certain anti-Dreyfusards to attack Jewish judges
generally. These attacks were all concomitant with the unfolding of the Affair or broke out just after it ended. They revealed, like certain antisemitic
attacks launched against Jews in the prefect civil service, the extent to
which the Franco-French war proceeded in waves, penetrating into the
deepest part of French society, with Jewish representatives of the state
being assimilated to the captain who was supposedly a traitor to French
identity. Let us offer a last example that admirably demonstrates the reality

of these small-scale Dreyfus affairs. In Mulhouse in February 1898, Sommer, *procureur de la République*, was the object of a violent antisemitic attack explicitly linked to the captain's trial. *La Moselle*, which took care to officially declare itself "the republican-democratic organ of the arrondissement of Toul" observed: "On the night of Tuesday 2 February, several hand-written posters were posted in different neighborhoods of our city. They bore the words: Down with the Jew! Down with Zola! Long live the army! The home of the Jew Sommer, *procureur de la République*, was not spared. It was studded with inscriptions that were eminently suggestive for the compatriot of Dreyfus."

No mistake: in the view of this republican and democratic newspaper, Dreyfus and Sommer were compatriots, not coreligionists. The antisemitic charge, surprising in such a newspaper, was here openly combined with an appeal to exclude state Jews from French nationality. A little later, an editor commented on the local affair in these words: "It is time for true Frenchmen to open their eyes, to close ranks, to send patriots to the Chamber in order to destroy the Judaico-Opportuno-clerical coalition that drags about in its senile decrepitude. Only then will the reign of Cornelius Herz, Reinach, Dreyfus, and Scheurer-Kestner be completely over. It will be the definitive return of France to the good French."[58] The hue and cry over Jewish officials thus extended to magistrates, who also suffered the consequences of the outcry due to the Dreyfus affair. In the remotest provinces, contrary to many interpretations by historians,[59] the Affair continued to induce feelings of rejection that personally affected a number of state Jews, who were publicly singled out for the vendetta of their constituents. These constituents even came to dispute the legitimacy of the magistrates' administrative role, since they no longer agreed to see them as fellow citizens. The entire political order was disintegrating, and for some, minimal solidarity was no longer an issue. It was important to drive state Jews from the public space, because their particularist origin might pervert the judgments they made as officials.

Let us give in to the temptation to evoke one last example of what appeared to many as a real incompatibility, namely, the fact that a Jew could obtain a post that put him in a position to exercise any authority whatsoever over his non-Jewish fellow citizens. At the end of 1892, a murder was committed in Saint-Pons-la-Calm in Gard: the *juge d'instruction* Abram, had M. de Vaucroze arrested and charged with patricide. Scandal immediately erupted, for the imprisonment of this notable surprised and shocked. The local and national press seized hold of the affair in crazed fashion since, despite the "nonlieu" pronounced regarding M. de Vaucroze, Judge Abram persisted in his convictions. As *L'Autorité* put it,

Whether he is a soldier or a judge, the Jew always acts abnormally. . . . From the beginning of the affair, the Jewish judge Abram showed himself against M. de Vaucroze, especially because he was Catholic and conservative. . . . No opportunity could ever be more favorable for him and his race. . . . The government clique and the Ligue des Droits de l'Homme (league for the rights of man) were on their knees.

From the beginning, a local affair turned into a trial of general interest. As Henri Rochefort harshly explained in his newspaper *L'Intransigeant*,

Abram is openly protected by everything the Dreyfusard and Jewish defense can muster in red and black robes. As the coreligionist of Zadoc-Kahn, he knows very well that everything is permitted him. . . . Jewry reigns more despotically than the Shah of Persia in his country. . . . The autos-da-fé from the Inquisition that we criticize are today organized by the Huguenots and the Hebrews against their politico-religious opponents, with the difference that, with wood become so expensive, they replace burning at the stake with the guillotine.

Rochefort, overjoyed at this godsend, pounded in the nail, accusing "the League for the Rights of the Yid," the "Dreyfusard reporters"; a pessimist, he maintained that Judge Abram "naturally has all the ministry, all the majority, and all of Israel for him."[60]

As we see once more, the slightest local incident putting a state Jew in conflict with certain of his Catholic fellow citizens immediately took on a national dimension and became part of the great drama of the Dreyfus affair where, united and in solidarity, Protestants and Jews were supposedly oppressing an innocent Catholic France, not hesitating to take revenge, as during the time of the Inquisition, and able to depend without difficulty on government power! The agreement on this point was quite broad: for *La Presse*, "the only appearance of force that M. Abram, Jewish and sectarian, has going for him is that he is supported by the government." We should also mention, to better understand the underpinnings of this affair, the report of the special commission: "In these last months," it notes,

an antisemitic campaign had been directed by *La Libre Parole*, *Le Gaulois*, *L'Éclair de Montpellier*, among others, against M. Abram, *juge d'instruction* of Uzès, who is of the Jewish religion. That campaign, to which M. Pascal, *député* of the arrondissement of Uzès and former opponent of M. Crémieux, ex-*député* of the arrondissement, seems to be no stranger, is in no way justified. M. Abram is the second *juge d'instruction* to have been occupied with this matter; the first was M. Penchinat, of the Protestant religion.[61]

Of all the bad luck, a Jewish judge was succeeding a Protestant judge! The opportunity was too beautiful not to mobilize all the stereotypes on the domination of the Huguenots and Jews, who were letting loose at full tilt with a persecution worthy of the Inquisition.

This hue and cry over Jewish high officials also extended beyond members of the prefect civil service and judges to members of the Conseil d'Etat: relentlessly, antisemitic newspapers such as *La Libre Parole* designated for their readers one or another *conseiller d'Etat* — Paul Grunebaum-Ballin, Georges Cahen, and Camille Lyon — as so many inveterate members of the Dreyfusard camp. According to *La Libre Parole*, "the Conseil d'Etat will soon be like the criminal chamber of the Cour de Cassation: it will be all to the devotion of Israel. Unable to people all its courts, all its tribunals, with its creatures, Jewry is taking hold of supreme jurisdictions, those that serve as judgment of last resort, strategic points."[62] The idea of a Jewish plot was becoming clearer by the day: to obtain the liberation of their coreligionist Dreyfus, state Jews were systematically taking over key jurisdictions. That was also the thesis often supported by the official representatives of Catholic France at its most profound level. For the *Semaine Religieuse du Diocèse de Nevers* (Religious weekly of the Nevers diocese), Jews were everywhere.

There are more than thirty *préfets* or *sous-préfets* in the Ministry of the Interior; in the Ministry of Justice, ten *conseillers* at the Paris *cour d'appel* court, nine Jews at the Conseil d'Etat, and countless Jews in all the courts and tribunals of France; at the Ministry of Public Education, thirty Jews, not counting the Jews who people the dependencies of that ministry. . . . Can we then be surprised that the Dreyfus affair is taking on such proportions?[63]

Endlessly linked to the Affair, this systematic denunciation of Jewish high officials nevertheless took on a more general aspect: just as Jewish *députés* could not represent a Christian land without at the same time delegitimating the very notion of national sovereignty, those who held very high posts within the state could not perform the roles that endowed them with great power over their Christian fellow citizens without attacking the legitimacy of the state itself. A single conclusion arose every time: in all urgency, it was important that the political class, like the state as an administrative machine, be once more crafted in the image of the France of Clovis: everything had to be set in place to rapidly accomplish that goal.

CHAPTER NINETEEN

An Antisemitic Republican State?
Obstructed Careers

A major surprise awaits anyone imprudent enough to venture into the jumble of astonishing administrative dossiers that retrace in great detail the ups and downs of the eventful careers of the Republic's high officials. In capital letters, clearly spelled out, undeniably displayed for the information of the highest state authorities, there figures the rubric "religion." This is not an unfortunate comment due to the personal initiative of an obscure bureau chief, or a shameful practice rapidly abandoned, or even a piece of information, certainly regrettable, but nevertheless rendered indispensable by the passing dangers threatening a republic that was experiencing birth pangs at the time. The rubric, neatly printed without evasions, demands a precise and detailed response on the part of the superior who fills it out, whether he is a *préfet*, a *procureur de la République*, or a general. And that response does not remain hidden, reported in quasi-clandestine fashion in the records, devoid of any official character, like the scandal of General André's records. As we recall, that scandal concerned the political activities of Catholic officers, the discovery of which provoked a general outcry, an unequivocal condemnation, inasmuch as such practices seemed to leave a stain on the republican tradition. No, the response in this case was faithfully retranscribed in each of the administrative records that traced the career path of an official of the Republic. As a result, it took on a truly legal dimension.[1]

But in looking more closely, can we maintain that it is really religion that is in question? The dossiers of Catholic *préfets* and *sous-préfets* or judges are, from this point of view, of a fearsome monotony, stripped of any variations. Soberly, without invention or superfluous commentary, the person in charge of the dossier records each time: "Catholic." From time to time, he also adds the same notation next to the spouse's name. Anxious to defend the secular values of the Republic, those responsible sometimes noted simply: "Catholic but not clerical," "born into the Catholic religion but anticlerical," or, more rarely, "freethinking Catholic."[2] The content of these dossiers is nevertheless anodyne, devoid of all prejudice. The official's political opinions are certainly reported; there is an attempt to evaluate his level of devotion to serving the Republic; his relations with the various social groups is observed, but always in a relatively flat, monotonous prose. In general, even when republican France again ran into the resistance of the Church, even when the Franco-French wars were to a great extent turning on that opposition, the immense mass of *sous-préfets* and *préfets* of the Republic, almost all of them designated Catholic in their dossiers, seemed to be altogether sheltered from ostracism during the courses of their careers: no event troubled them, except at times drunkenness, gambling debts, adultery, or other weaknesses in character. Apart from normal career problems affecting the rate of advancement, the numerous dossiers consulted are devoid of all passion. Similarly, a rapid look at the few dossiers of Protestant officials in our sample led to few surprising discoveries; at most, we once found the presence of the same notation, "freethinker."[3]

Things were very different in the case of state Jews. We very quickly perceive that a large variety of possible responses reigned in that case and merit examination: In the eyes of the hierarchy, is one or another state Jew — *préfet* or judge — of the "Jewish" religion, or, more generally and a bit less precisely, in administrative language, "a Jew," "Israelite," "of the Jewish race," "a convert," "a freethinker," "secular"? How to explain the fact that similar expressions were also used regarding spouses, whereas usually the religion of the wives of Catholic and Protestant high officials was ignored? Were these terms more in use at the beginning of the Third Republic or, on the contrary, during its final years? Were they applied indifferently to Jews of Ashkenazic and Sephardic origin? Did they change proportionally from one corps to another? During a period of crisis or a Franco-French war? What use did the administration make of them? The fact that we can even ask such questions can only be surprising in a republic that had legalized the separation of Church and state and wanted only to recognize equal citizens, identical from the perspective of their rights and their careers in an administrative institution that took pride in meritocratic values. It is even

more curious that systematic deformations of the names of state Jews sometimes appeared in these same very full dossiers.[4]

Responding to such inquiries is not a routine matter, for they seem incongruous within a strong and universalist state. On the whole, this republican state exercised Reason and functioned through administering exams;
its respect for secularism was almost its essential foundation; and it worked
to drive religious or "ethnic" considerations from the public space. Nevertheless, this state persisted, up until the eve of World War II — and as a result, until Vichy itself — in distinguishing between its high officials by all
sorts of qualifications. This state was the hope of all the followers of the liberating ideas of Gambetta and Jules Ferry, to whose logic so many Jews devoted themselves body and soul, precisely because it continued the emancipatory ideology of 1789. Could it then turn its back on its raison d'être, the
equality of all citizens whatever their cultural identity, to appropriate, without admitting it to the outside, certain of the prejudices more current, in
fact, among those it was fighting? Did antisemitic feelings, surprisingly,
figure at the very heart of the republican state with which the Jews were
madly in love? This state, almost alone in the world at the time (setting
aside the examples of Italy and Hungary), made possible the political integration of Jews, leading them bit by bit, by means of meritocratic promotion, to the highest careers in the administrative apparatus; did it nonetheless present something like a hidden face? This almost sacrilegious question
needs to be addressed with prudence but without evasion.

The fact that religion figures in the administrative dossiers of officials
long after the end of violent quarrels that accompanied the implementation
of secularism is astonishing, but does not adequately explain the presence
of prejudices. This is especially true because, according to the dominant
values of the time fashioned by Franco-Judaism, there was an impercepti-
ble move in the dossiers from the use of "Jewish" to that of "Israelite."
Hence, at the end of the nineteenth century, the religion rubric of a single
person, for example, Oscar Kinsbourg, a member of the prefect civil service, shifted in a very short time from "Jewish" to "Jew" and then to "Israelite."[5] Similarly, Judge Isaïe Berr was designated as a "Jew" in 1855 and
1857, while in 1869 and 1872 he was presented as an "Israelite."[6] Several
préfets and *sous-préfets*, however, were considered to be of the "Jew" religion
at the beginning of the Third Republic, which differs a bit from the designation "Jewish" that we might expect. As if, beyond religious identity, a
community or ethnic identity was being designated. Therein lay all the ambiguity of that surprising rubric, even more so since, on several occasions,
in the administrative dossier and in confidential notes on many state Jews,
care was taken to underscore the particularist dimension of the official,
even by circling the notation "Israelite" in blue ink.[7]

Let us take the case of Georges Mossé, *sous-préfet* in the 1880s: he was considered to be both of the "Israelite" religion and "a Jew and a Marseillais," while his wife, born Léa Valabrègue, was apprehended as a "Jewess";[8] religious membership was without question expanded to include insertion into a social framework that was broader than a simple cultural designation. Of course, as traditional historiography dealing with the subject indicates,[9] these administrative dossiers were moving from the designation "Jewish" to "Israelite," and it is altogether exceptional to read the term "Jewish" in the final years of the Third Republic. In the religion box in the 1930s, we find, among the members of the prefect civil service and among magistrates, "Israelite" or, fairly often, "freethinking Israelite" or "freethinker of Israelite origin,"[10] as if a particularist origin preserved its residual character, even when an official, on the admission of his superior, had become fundamentally freethinking or even "atheist." Let us also note — an almost unique example — that in 1921, Elisée Pontrémoli, *président de section*, was designated as an "Israelite who has converted,"[11] as if, there again, the administration felt the necessity of retracing the evolution of one of its members instead of simply presenting him as Catholic.

That change from Jew to Israelite over time, assumed to be the normal course, was nonetheless largely inaccurate among the politico-administrative elite: having access to the highest posts in the state apparatus, in fact, these high officials were for the most part already considered "Israelites" from the first years of the Third Republic. That was the case for members of the Conseil d'Etat, whose confidential dossiers included the notation "Israelite" under religion. But this was not systematic, as we discover, for example, in the information records concerning André Spire (in 1892), René Worms (in 1893), and Henri Weill (in 1912).[12] The enlistment papers of Jewish military personnel often contained the notation "Israelite."[13] For some, such as General Sée, the first to reach that rank without converting, it is emphasized without fail every year in his administrative dossier: "He belongs to the Israelite religion, which makes him somewhat aloof in his relations, though very honorable" (1876). The next year, the formula is transformed into: "frequents by preference Israelite society, to which he belongs by religion and marriage." In 1879, "General Sée is Israelite; he lives in Paris, for the most part in the world of his coreligionists; he everywhere enjoys a consideration earned by the very great honorableness of his private life and habits; in the brigade, he is liked and respected."[14] Let us note, however, that the modifier "Israelite" is not necessarily linked to religion: in 1878, in Lucien Lévy's recruitment certificate for his assignment in Nancy, and in 1880, in his records at the École Polytechnique, someone has added that particularist dimension to the "distinguishing marks" rubric, a rubric very imprecise in its meaning.[15]

While certain judges such as Gustave Bédarridès, Eugène Cahen, and Léon Sommer were still perceived as being "of the Jewish religion" in the 1880s, most were already designated as belonging to "the Israelite religion."[16] In 1900, in a confidential account concerning Judge Abraham Albert Alphandéry, for example, we learn that "this magistrate belongs to the Israelite religion, but maintains an extreme reserve in the matter of religious questions, which could facilitate public opinion."[17] This means that, at that particularly delicate time, his cultural practices, to the great satisfaction of the administration, remained extremely discreet. This was also the case for members of the prefect civil service: *sous-préfet* Jules Franck was presented as a "Jew" in 1867 and as "Israelite" in 1870; similarly, whereas *sous-préfet* Isaac was "of Jewish religion" in 1870, he received the more neutral label "freethinking Israelite" in 1888.[18] In certain cases, however, such a metamorphosis, which made things more or less acceptable, took more time: is it because of his conspicuous patronymic that *sous-préfet* Salomon Weill was still presented in 1886 as being of the Jewish religion and that he had to wait until 1901 to be designated as being of the Israelite religion in his administrative dossier?[19] Sometimes reserved for spouses, the designation "Jewish" was thus fairly rapidly effaced in favor of the supposedly more neutral term "Israelite," less likely to evoke the idea of maintaining some sociohistorical dimension incompatible with the republican ideal.

Up to this point, there is nothing very troubling, except that curious desire on the part of the republican administration to scrupulously note distinctions of a religious nature. Particularly concerning Jews — given their own history and that of French society at the time — that designation referred back to a constellation of historical connotations that were more or less ambiguous in certain people's eyes. At this very weak level of the diagnosis, can we not maintain that is was at least careless for a state administration that had long conducted its process of secularization to the utmost, to write the designation "Israelite" in capital letters, even in 1938, when intolerance and practices of exclusion had become so commonplace that anything could happen? Hence, on 21 December 1938, as had occurred every year since 1920, in the administrative dossier of *préfet* Albert Heumann, the notation "Israelite," destined to become extremely defamatory in a short time, still appears under the "religion" rubric.[20] Less than two years later, Vichy would publish its Statut des Juifs. Did the republican state, object of so much passion on the part of state Jews, underestimate the inadvertent consequences of the continued and surprising use of that rubric, which singled out a portion of its agents very differently than it did Catholics? Illegitimate and illegal practices that perhaps had meaning at the time of the confrontation between Church and state could, at the dawn of World War II, have unwitting and fatal consequences, since the difficult exclusion of Catholics from the anticlerical state was now being succeeded by deportation and death.

But, before evoking such tragic outcomes—facilitated perhaps by the republican state's continuing use of a classification it should have long ago repudiated—let us first return to the flagrant and strange slippages that these administrative records too often included. These records, let us emphasize once more, directly influenced the careers of the highest officials. We are sometimes astounded at how the cries and insults existing within society seem at times to be retranscribed within the state itself. It is as if the hue and cry over Jewish officials were now reverberating within the very structures of the state, as if Drumont and his fanatics sometimes found an attentive ear in the high administrative hierarchy, which thus turned away from its ideology of public service. Examples abound of such veering. Let us cite a few of them at random. First, in the army: in 1887 Lieutenant Julien Carvallo elicited the worries of the general commanding the École Polytechnique, since, according to his report the "tall and handsome boy does not appear to have found his niche. Israelite"; this "tall officer of the southern type (Portuguese race) has not the slightest fanaticism, appears soft."[21] Similarly, in the middle of the Dreyfus affair, in 1899, Major Georges Bloch, according to his superior, displayed "both the good qualities and the defects of his race; he is rather common, full of self-confidence, and shows off a bit too much. . . . Appears especially preoccupied with his own interest."[22] Such observations, however, remained extremely rare in military dossiers, either because the army, closed upon itself and very jealous of its unity, succeeded in maintaining the cohesion of the corps, or because it was prudent and made sure that the anodyne character of these dossiers would let little show through of the political opinions or religious values of the generals.

During the same period, the prefect civil service, thrown directly into the political and ideological storms of the moment, may have found less shelter from manifestations of clearly antisemitic resonance. In 1896, the *préfet* of Haute-Saône quite simply observed that Émile Waltz, *sous-préfet* of Saint-Claude "does not have much of the Jewish character."[23] In his administrative report of 1880, Joseph Léon's superior emphasized the fact that his subordinate, at the time *sous-préfet* in Castellane, "is a young man of fairly agreeable physique, very dark, Jewish type."[24] In 1896, Georges Beaucaire, secretary general for Puy-de-Dôme was "excellent, with few religious prejudices," according to the *préfet* of his department.[25] Among the magistrates as well, we easily find similar judgments: in 1880, the superior of Gustave Bédarridès did not hesitate to attract attention to the fact that Bédarridès, at the time first attorney at the Cour de Cassation, had "like all his Jewish coreligionists, a mind for business and a certain smoothness in his behavior." This is surprising when we recall that, a little earlier, a *président de chambre* had underscored the fact that "he belongs to the Israelite religion [but] he has the manners and ideas of Christian society."[26] In 1895, the *procureur général* of the Rouen court judged that Julien Félix, *conseiller* of that court and *doyen* of magistrates, nominated for a position as *président de chambre*, "even though Israelite in origin, does not have the Israelite mind"; in spite of that observation, which, all things considered, was favorable, Félix did not obtain the post he had a right to, and resigned.[27] Soon after, in 1896, the *procureur général* of the Paris court seemed to be looking favorably on the promotion of Judge Paul Lévy, who "has in fact nothing Hebraic in his manner or habits."[28]

Other examples also come to mind that confirm at least the presence of prejudices that, even in these years of tension, should not have existed in a republican state. Hence, in 1872, the superior of Jules Valabrègue, *substitut de la République* in Béziers, wrote on several occasions that his subordinate "belongs to the tribe of Carpentras Israelite businessmen."[29] His career must have suffered, since he eventually abandoned that association. The example of magistrate Alexandre May's dossier is by far the most probing, for here the signs of ostracism clearly appear: under the Empire, his superior certainly recognized that he was "far from any spirit of caste," but nonetheless feared the violence of prejudices in Sarrebourg against "the Jewish race," inasmuch as May "is Jewish and married to a Jewess." He acknowledged that he would be perfectly fitted for a *cour d'assises* "if he weren't Jewish"; even "though he seeks to appear devoid of the prejudices he is assumed to have, it is difficult for him to establish conformity between his values and our mores and ideas." Even though he was, according to some, "persecuted by his superiors" and unlike many others who preferred to give up, Alexandre May become *président de chambre* in Épinal, then *conseiller* in Nancy. His career, which continued under the Third Republic, did not truly suffer as a result of these biases on the part of the administration. And yet, as the *procureur général* of Nancy explicitly emphasized, "M. May is an Israelite. This status presents a real difficulty in this region. It would be incompatible with the judicial function in several arrondissements in my jurisdiction. This circumstance may explain the delay this magistrate has experienced in his advancement."[30] This amounts to admitting that external prejudices succeeded in obstructing internal advancement.

These prejudices, which appeared even within the state, sometimes considerably slowed the careers of state Jews, especially since they sometimes extended to various members of the same court: thus, according to the report of the *procureur général* of the Dijon court, "M. Julien Sée is an Israelite; it is in great part to this circumstance that we must attribute the hostility manifested toward him by a certain number of his colleagues or fellow workers. In our region, the Jews are not in favor."[31] As we have already discerned, some Jews left on their own, though it is not certain that their decision was motivated solely by the context. Others thought seriously about leaving but decided against it. *Sous-préfet* René Brisac, for example, whose Judaism was underscored on several occasions in his administrative dossier, seemed very bitter: in a confidential note dating from 1901, his superior remarked that "without giving in to a discouragement that would paralyze his actions, and even while conscientiously acquitting himself of his duties, M. Brisac is not without some sadness about not having progressed more quickly." [32]

It is true that the Dreyfus affair was not destined to make matters easier: just as it elicited a hue and cry over state Jews on the outside, it also provoked real difficulties in their careers as officials. Thus, within the republican and meritocratic state founded by Gambetta and Jules Ferry in the tradition of 1789, new and unexpected forms of intolerance arose. They slowed the careers of state Jews, who were sometimes considered the bearers of the same sins attributed to the famous captain. On several occasions, we have observed an unleashing of antisemitism both internal and external to the state that was at the very least concomitant with the Affair, and that without a doubt caused delays in careers; the affected parties were, in fact, aware of it. The *conseiller de préfecture* Lucien Aaron, for instance, had the bad luck to be related to Captain Dreyfus: not only did his superiors in 1896 "oppose his naming in Vaucluse," but in addition, as his superior acknowledged in 1901, "he had a difficult time in recent years because he is Israelite. I therefore recommend him very particularly to the benevolence of the *président du Conseil*." [33] In 1894, when the Affair had just broken out, Paul Grunebaum-Ballin was preparing his entrance exam for the Conseil d'Etat as cries were reverberating in the streets of Paris from vendors of *La Libre Parole*, denouncing the alleged treason of the captain; antisemitism became so violent that, ten days before the exam, Grunebaum-Ballin was asked by the *président* of the interior committee of the Conseil d'Etat not to take the exam, acknowledging that nothing could legally prevent him from doing so. [34] According to André Spire, later also a member of the Conseil d'Etat,

For fear of attacks by *La Libre Parole*, *L'Éclair*, and *La Patrie*, the weak minister of justice, Senator Guérin, crossed Paul Grunebaum's name off the list. André Lebon, who had been Grunebaum's and my professor at the École des Sciences Politiques, along with a certain number of French people indignant about any religious and racial discrimination, took active steps. They were supported by the Conseil d'Etat itself and had the prohibition lifted. [35]

While passions and hatred erupted in 1896, Édouard Masse, father of *député* Pierre Masse (who was later deported by Vichy), observed in a letter addressed to his superior, the *procureur général* of Besançon, that he had "more than twenty years of service in the magistracy, of which more than twelve were as *avocat général*, and, in recent years, a certain number of his colleagues, though with clearly less seniority than he, were named to the posts of *procureur général*, *président*, or *membre du parquet* of the Paris court." This unusual delay is all the more astonishing in that, the same year, that superior had considered him "a magistrate of the elite" and added: "He will measure up to the very highest post entrusted to him"; "he has indisputable rights to advancement."[36] Before such an injustice, Masse abruptly left the magistracy, becoming an important leader in the central consistory, to which he brought his commitment and ability.[37]

Matters became altogether intolerable when the person in question had, in addition, the indelicacy to be named Dreyfus. Let us take the case, significant in and of itself, of Eugène Dreyfus, who began his career in 1882, slightly before the beginning of the Affair, and ended it in 1936 at the top of the judicial hierarchy, as *premier président* of the Paris *cour d'appel*. At first glance, nothing in his dossier attracts attention, for this magistrate had a very brilliant career: considered in 1896 and in 1900 an "excellent magistrate" of "an exceptional value, a fine and distinguished mind" — "few magistrates having as developed a sense of the law as he does" — described again in 1905 as "a magistrate worthy by his merits of the most brilliant career, very devoted to his duties," his advancement nevertheless was seemingly obstructed, unfolding very slowly. In a text rare for its frankness, the *procureur général* of the *cour d'appel* in Rouen gave the reason in 1906. In his view, Eugène Dreyfus was a "very firm republican on whom the government can count absolutely; author of several respected legal works. He has been systematically set aside for several years for any post of advancement solely because of his name. Has right to reparation." In addition, he was able to expand on his judgment in reference to an astonishing report from the *premier président* of the *cour d'appel* in Rouen, who took no precautions in his use of language:

When, during the crisis of the Dreyfus Affair, a post of advancement was refused to Eugène Dreyfus because of his name and because he was Jewish, he redoubled his zeal and devotion. Far from launching recriminations against the government, he devoted himself entirely to his duties. He was my most faithful and devoted collaborator. . . . Also, I could never forget the steadfastness he showed in leading public actions when it was a question of applying the 1901 law to monasteries, at a time when jurisprudence, still on shaky ground, could not serve as a guide. M. Dreyfus displays all the traits of the republican magistrate.[38]

This was proved in what followed: to a large degree, Eugène Dreyfus obtained reparation for the wrong done him solely on the basis of his name, while the most violent of the Franco-French wars was unfolding. Within a few years, between 1907 and 1925, he became judge at the Seine tribunal, then *avocat général* in Paris, director of the staff at the Ministry of Justice, and finally *premier président* to the Paris *cour d'appel*, even attaining the rank of grand officer in the Legion of Honor in 1936, a quite rare event. The republican state sometimes knows how to show its generosity and recognize its wrongs.

In the army, signs of antisemitism were patent but, from the outside, little evidence can be gathered. Only two dossiers allow us to pose the question clearly. The first is that of General Sée, who attained that high rank in 1870 and retired in 1888, well before the arrest of the famous captain. As we recall, he was the first to rise to flag rank; and it is also regarding him that, two years earlier, a controversy broke out, to which I should like briefly to return. When this lieutenant colonel was stationed at Rome, his proclaimed Judaism posed a problem and his superior wrote to the minister of war:

In the current situation of the Thirty-fifth, [there is] some disadvantage to placing him at the head of this corps. We go to mass, a demonstration that is much more political than religious. The colonel of the Forty-second used to come to mass with me every Sunday. Lieutenant Colonel Sée, to whom I proposed the same thing, objected for reasons of freedom of conscience, refusing to make such a demonstration, which I consider entirely political. He is an Israelite and believes that as such he could not agree to my request. The Jews are execrated here. . . . The population itself, which has extremely deep-rooted prejudices, would not look kindly on a Jew at the head of the armed forces.

And he went on to cite the names of several generals who approved of this evaluation of the situation. The career of that officer was clearly obstructed: the logic of the corps seemed to adapt openly to the antisemitism of society. Léopold Sée nevertheless became a colonel several months later, and brigadier general attached to the general staff in 1870. The incident was closed, and the logic of the corps was once more functioning.

The second example concerns Colonel Léon Francfort: this time, the incident occurred in the middle of the Dreyfus affair. This case is altogether intriguing because it is truly the only one, among all the dossiers examined, to take into account the deep internal rifts in the corps. We shall not return to the duels, quite high in number, between Jewish officers and antisemitic satirists; rather, we shall describe a tension internal to the institution, directly induced by the Affair. On 5 December 1897, the general and commanding officer of Grenoble transmitted to his superior, General Faure-Biguet, the following information:

The commission of the officers' club of the garrison is called upon to examine a request that has been formulated by a considerable number of officers in the garrison: for them, "the conduct of the newspaper *Le Figaro* in the deplorable Dreyfus Affair has provoked general indignation. The officers ask that the officers' club of Grenoble cease to subscribe to the paper and that its editors be instructed to no longer send it to us, effective immediately." I believe such a demonstration, no matter how legitimate, is prohibited to officer corps by military regulations. We understand the corps is suffering from attacks directed against the army and is impatient to manifest its indignation. But in my view, it is irregular for it to take an initiative in this regard that belongs solely to the head of the army. . . . The fact that a body of five hundred officers informs the newspaper that it refuses to receive it in its officers' club, even before the subscription has expired, has a significance that cannot escape this newspaper or anyone at all.

Faure-Biguet was visibly perplexed by such a decision and understood the reservations of his subordinate. Needless to say, he also approved the decision of the anti-Dreyfusard officers. In a letter addressed to his superior, General Zédé, commanding officer of Lyon, he wrote:

I share the feelings of indignation among the Grenoble garrison and I believe that, in the absence of any law allowing them to put down the scandalous abuses of the press, the means that this officers corps proposes to use are the only ones that allow it to manifest its disapproval. These means are legitimate and I would not hesitate to approve them if isolated officers were in question. But it is rather a collective demonstration, and under those conditions, I can only turn to you for your mediation and beg you to send me your instructions in this regard.

The same day, General Zédé in turn sent these various documents to the minister of war, adding:

These gentlemen want to cancel their subscription with style. I find that they are right and it seems to me that after language as noble and firm as that used by you in Parliament yesterday, there is nothing more to consider, and we have only to follow your example. Under these conditions, unless for particular reasons you do not judge it appropriate for me to act differently, I intend to telegraph day after tomorrow to the commandant of Grenoble, saying I approve of the officers' way of seeing things and authorizing them to cancel their subscription. I will instruct them, however, not to indicate the reasons for that cancellation so as to avoid any later conflict with the press.

Some of the highest military authorities shared, at least in principle, the positions violently hostile to Captain Dreyfus expressed by a corps of five hundred officers. This document, which has remained unpublished, without a doubt takes on extraordinary importance as evidence of the values and feelings of the officers at a time when France was threatening to become involved in what was virtually a civil war. Events rushed along and, ten days later, on 15 December 1897, the same General Zédé wrote another letter to the minister of war:

I have the honor of reporting to you that, on the register of the Grenoble officers' club the following notation was made: "Given the ignoble campaign led in favor of

Jews and traitors by *Le Figaro*, the undersigned officers demand the immediate suppression of that paper." General Chanson, commanding officer of Grenoble and president of the officers' club, ripped the page from the register as soon as he learned of the act. . . . But before the page was ripped out, someone made a copy and communicated it to the newspaper *La Libre Parole*, which reproduced the note in its issue of 5 December.

Lieutenant Colonel Francfort immediately wrote to General Chanson and to one of his comrades in Grenoble to ask him whether, among the signers, there was an officer of his rank, so that he could ask him to answer for the article. General Chanson, instead of settling the matter, thought he ought to write to the colonel indicating that the text was correct and that the officer who had communicated it, whose name he did not in fact know, had been wrong to send that note to the press. General Chanson could not have been more maladroit, for there are in the officers' club secretaries, orderlies, and civil employees, so that the communication could very well have come from someone besides an officer.

Today, Colonel Francfort came to see me to tell me that, since he found no one from whom to seek satisfaction through arms for an insult addressed to a collectivity in which he was included, he wished a communiqué to be sent to the press to deny the act. I responded to the lieutenant colonel that I would not follow the bad example of the military man (if he was one) who entered into communication with the press, to which only the minister had the right to send communiqués. The act, moreover, cannot be denied because, since it is true, that would give rise to a new debate. The best thing might be to communicate nothing at all, having the torn-out incriminating page stand as adequate satisfaction for the claim made by Lieutenant Colonel Francfort. I felt obliged, M. Minister, to report this incident to you because Lieutenant Colonel Francfort told me he had the intention of involving you in it.

We may never know what became of that rather exemplary story, which says a great deal about the feelings that could come to light in an army anxious to let nothing show on the outside, and ready to distort reality to avoid internal conflicts. It identified almost entirely with the anti-Dreyfusard fight but was careful to maintain its own unity, which implied the expression of a minimal solidarity with Jewish officers. Nevertheless, Léon Francfort, whom an administrative report of 1884 already described as "impatient about the situation that his Israelite origin sometimes creates for him," was named colonel in 1901, then brigadier general in 1906 and attached to the general staff of the army.[39] In the end, his career did not suffer from internal ostracism. Within the military institution, things normally remained very discreet, and nothing, or nearly nothing, can be read openly in the dossiers. The careers of Jewish senior officers did not seem to have been disturbed in the least. Within that constrained context, only one of them, Samuel Naquet-Laroque, was named colonel in July 1894 and brigadier general in 1900, in that way crossing the most crucial thresholds of his career right in the middle of the events.[40] Justin Dennery, Mardochée

Valabrègue, and Jules Heymann, like Léon Francfort, were all named colonels in 1902 and generals—in 1905, 1906, and 1909 respectively, that is, in the wake of the Affair, when it was all over. In spite of everything, that awakens the ghost of a suspicion.[41] Alphonse Weiller, a captain at the time, became a general in 1926: his career does not appear to have suffered.[42] As *L'Univers Israélite* emphasized, "The Dreyfus Affair was a grave moral ordeal for many Jewish officers, and though we had to deplore a few shows of weakness, the example given by those who, like General Weiller, refused to deny or dissimulate their Jewish origin at the time, is only all the more remarkable."[43] In the end, how many Jewish officers who remained faithful to their beliefs fell behind in their careers? We cannot make any definite claims because we lack systematic data for that period in the army, the prefect civil service, the magistracy, and the Conseil d'Etat; only such data would make a true comparison of the course of careers possible. Therefore, we cannot enter into a discussion of the question here.

The fact of awarding the Legion of Honor seems, as in the case of President Eugène Dreyfus, a good criterion for measuring the force of certain prejudices proper to the administration at this so troubled end of the nineteenth century. A certain Beloret, for example, sent a long letter to the minister to protest awarding the decoration to Judge Abraham Albert Alphandéry, given the context of the Dreyfus Affair, which was explicitly mentioned.[44] Judge Benjamin Abram—whose identity as an "Israelite" was constantly underscored in his administrative dossier—did not succeed in being awarded that distinction, the mark of respectability and the tangible sign of successful integration. Eliacin Naquet, at the time *procureur général* for the Aix court, was also a victim of antisemitic prejudices; he nevertheless wrote a letter on behalf of Alphandéry in 1897: "The honorable *vice-président* Abram has less seniority than his colleague from Rennes; he can, however, count twenty-seven years of service, and this is the first time that the doyen of the *vice-présidents* of Marseilles has not been decorated. The fact that this is a magistrate of great professional and moral value makes the persistent lack of success of his candidacy even harder to understand."[45] Similarly, letters were sent in 1895 to the minister of the interior to solicit the same decoration for *sous-préfet* Charles Strauss: "In truth," declared one of the correspondents,

I do not see what M. Strauss could be criticized for. Could it be for having been born into a religion he does not practice and may know nothing about? But who, in our time, could formulate such reproaches unless he were of a systematically malevolent spirit? What are they waiting for to recompense a man so worthy, who may yet render the most outstanding services? Why has he not received the rosette of the Legion of Honor like his predecessors, especially since he is, of all the *préfets*, the one with the most seniority?[46]

Did state Jews receive the Legion of Honor by virtue of their merit or their seniority? Did they rise at the same rate as their non-Jewish colleagues in the hierarchy? Did they reach the highest ranks in the same proportions? It is impossible to answer that question here, for comparative data are lacking.[47]

In a context particularly favorable to internal slips of all kinds, it is true that the administration seemed at times to become involved in managing careers in a way that deliberately took into account the specific origin of its Jewish high officials.[48] On several occasions, for example, it hesitated in naming several Jewish magistrates to the same jurisdiction. In 1895, the *procureur général* wondered whether it was acceptable to designate Oscar Dalmbert to head the Le Havre tribunal; to decide the question, he evoked the essential argument: "One objection relates to the religion of M. Dalmbert. M. Dalmbert is Israelite. Is it appropriate to name him to a tribunal that already has one of his coreligionists, a *substitut*, and in a city where the Israelites file suit fairly often? It seems that that situation would be an obstacle for the independence and impartiality of M. Dalmbert." The magistrate — whose work, it is emphasized "is marked by the German genius" — was never promoted and retired in 1916 as *conseiller* of Rouen, a post he occupied beginning in 1884.[49] The *procureur*'s argument rested on two distinct elements, which we will discuss in turn. The first concerned the fact that another Jewish magistrate — whose name, to his great misfortune, was Dreyfus — performed his duties in the same tribunal; the second took into account the Israelite presence in a city where a Jewish judge was already sitting and argued that his "impartiality" was impossible.

Let us examine each of these points in turn. The administration refused to name two Jewish magistrates to the same tribunal, acknowledging by this fact that, beyond the position, the state was consciously taking into consideration the cultural origin of its magistrates. This is rather surprising, even though similar particularist choices in conducting careers, shocking in themselves, were far from unheard of: even in 1871, Charles Berr was not promoted to the position of *avocat général* for the simple and single reason that Charles Alphandéry had already been promoted; to the great dismay of Adolphe Crémieux, who shared his indignation with the minister, "there was a belief that we mustn't have two Israelite judges. A Christian was named and M. Berr was completely abandoned." But, as if in reparation, his career later took him to the heights of the judicial hierarchy: he finally become *doyen* of the members of the Paris *cour d'appel* and *doyen* of *présidents de chambre*. According to the *premier président* of the Paris *cour d'appel*, he had "all the qualifications for promotion to *conseiller* to the Cour de Cassation," but nevertheless did not attain that post, envied above all others: was that the distant consequence of his earlier disgrace?[50] Many other identical situations could be evoked. At the Conseil d'Etat, for example, a real drama erupted: Paul Grunebaum-Ballin and Georges Cahen-Salvador both had claims on a *présidence* of a section, which provoked antisemitism from the surrounding community, only too happy to denounce what appeared to be a near monopoly of Jews over the highest posts of the Conseil d'Etat, a situation favored by the presence of Léon Blum at the head of the government. At the time, Grunebaum-Ballin wrote a letter to his friend Cahen-Salvador withdrawing his candidacy:

Two *présidences de section* are very soon to be filled with new occupants. During a recent interview, we immediately found ourselves in complete agreement in recognizing that serious questions of opportuneness opposed us both being called on the same day by the current government to occupy these two posts, even though high persons, altogether competent, had judged both of us particularly qualified to fill these posts. I have the pleasure of letting you know that I have definitively decided to give up the nomination as *président de section* that was offered me by the government.[51]

There too, the administration, with of course the consent of the parties involved, gave in to external antisemitism, which managed to dictate its policy in conducting the careers of its agents, which it treated according to criteria different from those of meritocracy or seniority. A bit later, matters became even more patent. In 1939, Georges Cahen-Salvador was to be named to the *vice-présidence* of the Conseil d'Etat. As his son Jean, also a member of the Conseil d'Etat, recalled, Paul Reynaud himself declared: "We cannot at this time name a Jew." Pierre Laroque, also a member of that jurisdiction, confirmed that there were "objections because of his origins."[52]

The most frequent situation, however, was rather more complex: very frequently, in assigning its agents, the administration took into consideration the reactions — indifferent, favorable, or hostile — attributed to the populations over which state Jews were to exercise their authority. This management of careers could not be called antisemitism. Even though it may have been justified as a search for public order, a concern shared by all forces in power to avoid throwing oil on the fire by provoking new sources of tension between the republican state and populations that had not always fully accepted its legitimacy, it is still surprising. In wishing to conform and as it were respect prejudices that were nonetheless unacceptable in regard to the ideals of the Republic, it contradicted the equality of treatment of officials with respect to their religious origin and implied that the state's management of agents was prejudicial to some of them. Outside the state, the quarrel concerning the legitimacy of the Jewish political staff, like the demonstrations against officials of Jewish origin, most often rested on a Catholicism of exclusion; frequently serving as a combat ideology to more easily bring down the republican state, which was judged too open to the new elites, the Catholicism of the populations also placed limits on the state's policy toward its Jewish officials. This allows us to understand the extreme reluctance of the state to assign them to regions that had remained faithful to the Church. Needless to say, Jewish high officials sometimes established relationships of great cordiality and ease with the local authorities of the Church and their flocks: hence the manifest astonishment we read in their administrative reports, which underscore, without appearing to understand the reason, the perfect courtesy reigning between, for example, some members of the prefect civil service, the bishop, and the Catholic population of the arrondissement or department. Eugène Lisbonne in Hérault, Ernest Hendlé in Calvados, Léon Cohn in Haute-Garonne, Abraham Pinède in Juras, and still others managed, without difficulty or rejection, to exercise their authority and even to maintain amicable relations with the highest officials of the Church.[53]

Most often, however, things did not work out that way: manifest signs of rejection erupted almost immediately; in this regard, the examples are legion, and we will merely evoke a few of them. Worried about its own legitimacy, the state favored moving its agents quickly. In fact, once it became committed to that logic, there was a great risk that Jews would not find an assignment: managing their careers then became a headache, the perpetual search for a post. Brittany, the Catholic region par excellence, was not always welcoming: *conseiller de préfecture* Lucien Aaron experienced this, since "his religion sometimes made his situation difficult in Morbihan, to such a point that he wished to be named to a department in the East."[54] In 1891, *sous-préfet* Émile Lion "was in no way an appropriate choice for Brittany, where no Israelite, despite his qualifications as an administrator and his efforts, will ever have more than limited influence and authority." As the *préfet* noted, "this good official does not belong in Brittany. . . . He is very keenly opposed by the Catholics and has little influence in the countryside, where the official is judged likable and devoted, but where no one wants to have any relationship with the Israelite." In 1893, the *préfet* of Morbihan became insistent: "He belongs to the Israelite religion, and in a region as religious as Brittany, that is in some sense a redhibitory vice. Were he to remain there, the election of M. Cadoret, *conseiller général*, would be impeded; he has declared that he will not run for the legislative elections unless M. Lion is replaced in Pontivy by a Catholic *sous-préfet*." And, without hesitating, he proposed to name in his place — M. Lenormand.[55] The Republic had real difficulties imposing its universalist order on Brittany, whose population wanted nothing to do with the idea of equality among officials: Jules Lévi, *conseiller de préfecture* in Finistère, would also learn this at his cost. In 1901, his superior wrote,

M. Lévi is a very good coworker and makes the best of a situation created by the religious prejudice here; but he is suffering from it, as is his wife. I have only praise for him and hold him in the highest esteem; I would be happy to contribute toward his obtaining a post of advancement, preferably in the Midi, where he will not continually feel criticized for his religion.[56]

Decidedly, the state hardly had control over the placement of its officials in the West; even at the turn of the century, it had to give in and send only Catholic officials, whom the populations could identify with, to posts of authority. The difficulty was that, to varying degrees, the French population remained largely Catholic, and it was therefore difficult to find posts for these state Jews! Hence, the religion of *sous-préfet* Isaac "was an obstacle to his being sent into a Catholic department like Nord."[57] In his post in Nord, *sous-préfet* Georges Mossé saw "his religion create a great obstacle for him"; it was judged preferable that he be "*préfet* in a department in the Midi."[58] Fortunately, the South was presented as a haven of tolerance, for similar difficulties appeared in many parts of the territory: "The arrondissement of Toul is composed almost exclusively of very religious Catholics," recalled the president of the chamber of agriculture of that city to the minister. "That makes me think that a first magistrate must not be of a dissident religion. No doubt I have nothing to say regarding the conduct of M. Lambert, *sous-préfet*, even though he is Israelite. I do not wish to show prejudice toward him; on the contrary, I wholeheartedly wish him to obtain advancement"[59] — but somewhere else! Not in Haute-Saône in any case, where that type of assignment also appeared undesirable,[60] or in Besançon, where a Jewish judge encountered strong "resistance on the part of a Catholic population,"[61] or in Dijon,[62] or in Bar-le-Duc, where prejudices against the Jewish "race" were so strong that a judge with such an origin was truly "incompatible" with the spirit of the population.[63]

Fortunately, the Republic also had its regions of choice, where people proved to be more tolerant: witness, for example, the report of the *préfet* of Loir-et-Cher in 1876: "M. Saint-Paul is Israelite," he wrote. "This circumstance, which would be difficult in other departments, I consider favorable in a region where people are inclined to call clerical those administrators who do not profess indifference or hostility toward religion."[64] The regions of the South such as Digne or Barcelonette, were also blessed, and a Jewish magistrate was received there with open arms.[65] In certain departments, Catholics and Protestants were in conflict with each other, and a state Jew was welcome: in Castelsarrasin, according to the report of the *préfet* of Tarn-et-Garonne dated 24 November 1876, "M. Mayer, *sous-préfet*, since he belongs to the Jewish religion, remains apart from the often concealed but always persistent rivalries that divide Protestant groups and Catholic groups in this region."[66]

These unexpected refuges were few in number, inasmuch as an even more unacceptable situation, this time clearly designated by the administration itself, could be created when a state Jew was assigned not to a region where Catholicism remained largely predominant, but rather where Jews were relatively numerous! For that reason, it was altogether unimaginable in the view of several officials of the administration to name a Jewish official in Algeria: the governor of Algiers maintained that Édouard Aron could not occupy a post there, where "his status as Israelite would expose him to difficulties";[67] similarly, since *sous-préfet* Isaac was "an Algerian Israelite, there is reason to take these circumstances into account in the choice of the post that might be assigned him."[68] In the Hexagon itself, one frequently ran into this kind of reservation. In Sarrebourg, as we recall, Judge May, "in the presence of a very numerous Jewish population," might elicit the anger "of a discontented plaintiff when he had a Jew as an opponent, attributing the loss of his trial to an unjust preference on the part of the *président*."[69] In Metz, nothing was simple for a Jewish *sous-préfet*: "M. Lévylier," noted the *préfet* of Moselle, "belongs to the Israelite religion, as does his wife. The prejudice attached to that religion entails certain biases, especially in Metz, a city in which there are many Israelites in very humble positions, and seems to me to represent an obstacle to M. Lévylier's taking over the duties he is seeking in the department of Moselle."[70] Similarly, it was unthinkable to name *sous-préfet* Isaïe Valabrègue in Vaucluse, since "sending him to a region where there are a large number of Jews seems contraindicated."[71] A similar misadventure occurred with the *sous-préfet* of Gray, Émile Waltz, who "being an Israelite, could not be sent to a region where there are a large number of Jews."[72] Almost obsessively, that formula was repeated again and again as if, there again, a kind of consensus reigned within the administration. As the *préfet* of Nord explicitly articulated it in 1896, with a good dose of involuntary humor, "the status of Israelite will not allow one to go into posts where questions of antisemitism could be raised with some passion"![73]

State Jews were the only officials to be considered undesirable in that way in numerous regions of the national territory. Other than Jews — and the parallel is worth remarking — the only ones, it seems, who sometimes encountered similar difficulties were — Corsicans! Even though they were all Catholics, they elicited strong prejudices, though these certainly never reached the same violence and did not elicit as broad a rejection in a great number of departments; they nevertheless reveal a similar rejection of all difference. Beyond Catholicism, and as a result, Judaism, there was clearly a return to the condemnation of particularisms felt to be quasi-ethnic, leading back to fantasies that were still very much alive in a republican society supposedly oriented toward Reason. *Sous-préfet* Charles Benedetti had "relations with his compatriots above all and, neither by his expertise nor his bearing is he fit for a department in the North. . . . His tastes and his interests of every nature designate him for a post in the Midi."[74] Similarly, *sous-préfet* Georges Tommasini "has brought to the continent all the passions of Corsica, and his behavior leaves something to be desired. . . . His interests of every kind appear to require he remain in the Midi."[75] Many other examples[76] confirm the redhibitory character of any cultural differences, in particular those fashioned by a menacing South.

Like many state Jews whose sociability remained incompatible with the more austere mores of the French, Corsicans in the prefect civil service were also cordially sent to the Midi, their South, where their own values and "bearing" would shock less. In fact, there too, things were more complicated since the administration also feared assigning them — to Corsica. Just as it feared the presence of state Jews in departments inhabited by Jews, it was also leery of their supposed complicity with their "compatriots": *sous-préfet* Xavier Sialetti could not be assigned to Corsica, where he had "numerous ties,"[77] nor could *sous-préfet* Georges Baroli, "because of his origins."[78] To take stock of the force of these prejudices hostile to the exuberant Southerners, let us finally underscore the fact that officials from the southern part of the Hexagon were suspected of having the same faults: to be born in Uzès was considered such a sin that "it would be preferable to leave *sous-préfet* Jourdan among the southerners, whose mores and style he shares."[79] It was the same for *sous-préfet* Louis Jalabert from Mirepoix-Ariège, who, being "from the South, would be better off in the Midi than elsewhere,"[80] and *sous-préfet* Tourel from Cavaillon, whose "southern exuberance would prevent him from succeeding in Nord; it would be preferable to call him to a post in Languedoc or Provence"![81]

Protestants totally escaped such stereotypical judgments, even when they came from the South.[82] Anti-Protestantism, at times still so virulent on the national ideological scene at the turn of the century, did not affect the careers of Protestant officials; we only very exceptionally find in their administrative dossiers[83] mention of a demonstration of external rejection or of internal ostracism. The Protestant *préfet* Eugène Schmidt was the only one in our sample to provoke passions comparable to those almost always elicited by state Jews: he was criticized for having a Swiss brother and for having been naturalized as a French citizen very late. Hence his response, which so many state Jews could have cosigned: "The Frenchman who so lightly accuses an Alsatian family is three times infamous" (27 March 1887). A little later, in November 1890, at Bar-le-Duc, he even defended his honor in a duel. Of all the dossiers of Protestant *préfets* and *sous-préfets*, his was also the only one to contain an attack from *La Libre Parole*. On 4 August 1904, the newspaper deformed his name from Schmidt to Schmitz;

La Croix des Côtes-du-Nord also accused him, again in November 1911, of spreading the rumor that "people are too pious in Brittany." The rumors and furors of that era undeniably appeared in this atypical dossier.[84]

Aside from that single example of rejecting a Protestant *préfet*, whose career was not organized around particularist criteria by his guiding administration, only state Jews and Corsican officials in authority had their careers managed according to particularist criteria by the republican state. In society's imaginary and in the judgments of the highest administrative authorities, Protestant officials were not perceived as a social group endowed with its own culture and specific "interests": only state Jews and, to a lesser extent, Corsicans, still appeared as groups of "compatriots" whose loyalties were to one another and not as citizens in the full sense of the term, masters of their reason and preoccupied solely with the public interest. This better explains how, as we have noted on several occasions, the consequences of the Dreyfus affair affected the careers of numerous state Jews taken as a whole, independent of their professional merits and their personal competence. We also understand that such a logic could eventually lead to exclusion, when the state itself changed its logic to the point of denying its own ideas and its own laws.

CHAPTER TWENTY

Vichy:
The Betrayal by the State

In the months before and after the end of 1941, a certain number of state Jews wrote to Marshal Pétain: from the remote corners of France where they had been pushed by the debacle and then the Occupation, they drafted long missives, which they sent to the head of state personally. History was accelerating, their professional lives — their lives period — were in danger of ending quickly: they thus solemnly intended to speak up before it was too late. They did so in their own style, that of state Jews who had long been familiar with the administrative jargon, which they had used all during their careers, and which they knew like their native tongue. Yet in these dramatic times, they tended to set aside the anonymous, passionless vocabulary that public servants were mad for; especially when their fates were in the balance. Without consulting one another, they also publicly made known their feelings and as ousted state Jews expressed their despair, their unrequited love, and how their lives had lost all meaning now that the state had turned away from them with no hesitation, had driven them from public life with no great problems of conscience.

Without a doubt, the two Statuts des Juifs enacted by Vichy on 3 October 1940 and 2 June 1941 were decided on voluntarily, not in response to a pressing demand from the German authorities, who were amazed by such speed. In a sense, they marked the end of an incommensurable love. Were the Republic's fools foolish at the time for investing so much passion in the state, which was suddenly turning its back on them, to the point of excluding them without visible remorse or great internal protest? For if Vichy marked the end of the Republic that was so despised by the extreme right of every stripe, strangely, as in a nightmare, almost everything seemed to remain in place: practically all public servants, without great apparent distress, remained at their posts, pursued their daily tasks almost peacefully, satisfied their normal administrative obligations. At this level of the state apparatus, state Jews were virtually the only ones who now ran the risk of experiencing the same fate as the Republic with which they had identified so thoroughly.

These new texts with the power of law enacted by Vichy were mercilessly simple and clear, offering no possible escape:

Article 1. For the application of the present law any person with three grandparents of the Jewish race or with two grandparents of same if his spouse is Jewish is regarded as Jewish.

Article 2. Access to and exercise of the public duties and mandates enumerated below are forbidden to Jews:

1. Head of state, member of the government, Conseil d'Etat, Cour de Cassation, Cour des Comptes, Corps des Ponts et Chaussées, Inspection Générale des Finances, *cours d'appel, tribunaux de première instance....*

2. Agents from the department of foreign affairs, general secretaries in ministerial departments, general directors, directors of central administrations of the ministries, *préfets, sous-préfets,* secretaries general of the *préfectures....*

3. *Résidents généraux, gouverneurs généraux,* governors, and secretaries general of the colonies.

4. Members of the teaching faculty in public education.

5. Officers or noncommissioned officers of the armies of land, sea, and air.[1]

Of course, several possible exceptions were listed: having a combat veteran's card for 1914–18; having been mentioned in dispatches during the 1939–40 campaign; being a member of the Legion of Honor for military reasons; or having received the Médaille Militaire. But they all proved to be illusory. The great majority of state Jews at the end of the Third Republic had, in fact, received these decorations on the battlefield or during their administrative careers. With the stroke of a pen, their entire integration into the state was called into question, the entire process that had begun with the Revolution, and, after various ups and downs, had accelerated with the Second Empire to become truly institutionalized with the birth of the Third Republic. Of course, resistance to the state's integration had not disappeared as if by enchantment, and certain *grands corps* (for example, the Inspection des Finances, the Cour des Comptes, and the Quai d'Orsay) were not greatly affected by these fateful texts, and for good reason, since they had remained almost hermetically sealed to state Jews. It was a very different case, as we have seen, for the Conseil d'Etat, the *préfecture*, the magistracy, and the army: there, the new laws were applied and directly affected a number of state Jews, shaking them in their most solidly anchored certainties.

The Statuts des Juifs in themselves symbolized the end of the state of Gambetta and Jules Ferry, of Clemenceau and Waldeck-Rousseau, the secular state that acknowledged only the equality of merit and talent. Of course, Protestants were not targeted by similar statutes; nevertheless, the laws of October 1940 and June 1941 were something like the expression of ancient hatreds, signifying the triumph of the Drumont tradition and of nationalism "French-style," which was anxious to assume definitively the full identity between the nation and Catholicism. The state had to be Christian: that was the message passed on by the radical — and sometimes even the moderate — right, which was hostile to 1789, to the separation of Church and state, to public education, to the very idea that a citizen could be something other than Catholic.[2]

Xavier Vallat, the commissioner for Jewish questions, consciously justified the Statut des Juifs in 1941: "This is no imitation of the legislation of any totalitarian regime whatever: it is fidelity to a state anti-Jewish tradition that can find precedents both in the historic past of our own nation and in that of Christianity. That legislation was so to say spontaneous, autochthonous." In the imaginary of the age and, beyond it, of those to whom it would harshly apply, the Statut des Juifs ended the dreams of Gambetta and Jules Ferry. At a symbolic level, the voluntary eradication of the Jewish presence in the state, even in the absence of German wishes, meant conferring on Drumont the role of master thinker of the time. By bringing down the "Jewish Republic," it attacked the legitimacy of the state and its order, which supposedly had ignored the true Catholic identity of French society. This was true to such an extent that a certain number of Jewish *députés* were even stripped of their national identity: Léon Meyer, Maurice de Rothschild, Lévy-Alphandéry, Pierre Mendès France, Henry Torrès, and many others lost not only their mandates as *députés* but also their French citzenship.[3]

These brutal measures also put a sudden end to the careers of state Jews. In their administrative dossiers, we read the same fateful sentence, their expulsion from the state, falling on them one after another: General Albert Baumann, for example, was authorized on 12 August 1942 "to be automatically retired by application of the law of 2 June 1941 entitled Statut des Juifs."[4] General Boris met the same fate on 1 April 1942: a similar condemnation, fashioned in exactly the same terms, appeared in his personnel dossier.[5] Many other dossiers of Jewish generals included that notation, each time carefully written by hand.[6] It also figured in the personnel dossiers of

Jewish *conseillers d'Etat*, who were also affected by the two statutes: hence, the same day and in terms identical in every respect, Georges Cahen-Salvador and his son Jean, Paul Grunebaum-Ballin, Jacques Helbronner, Pierre Laroque, and René Mayer were "authorized to take advantage of their right to retirement" beginning 20 December 1940. We learn in a note that this was taking place through application of the law of 3 October 1940, whose name, prudently (at the level of vocabulary), was not recalled.[7] This law affected all state Jews without exception, outside of a few altogether unusual cases involving fewer than twenty persons (including General Bloch, the chief of the artillery squadron, Professors Robert Debré, Louis Halphen, Marc Bloch, and a few others). Pierre Brisac sent a letter to the military authorities in which he refused any special measures that could work to his advantage; dressed in uniform, he went to have his identity card stamped "Jew" and protested in writing against such measures to Marshal Pétain.[8] When numerous state Jews wrote to the head of state to register their indignation at administrative decisions to turn them out of office, they also took care each time to make it clear that they were not soliciting any personal advantage.

Some of them even wrote sarcastically to challenge a nomination that had become scandalous and incomprehensible in that context: hence, in June 1942, Lieutenant Colonel Roger Dreyfuss had the surprise of seeing himself accorded the rank of Chevalier of the Legion of Honor! Great-nephew to Captain Louis Naquet and General Paul Naquet-Laroque, linked as a result to the Generals Brisac, that officer—who took care to recall that he was himself a *Croix de Feu*—took up his pen to write to Pétain. Let us cite once more his letter:

> I have the honor of asking you, Monsieur le Maréchal, to kindly rescind this ministerial order that can only be due to a regrettable error.
>
> In fact, I belong to that category of Frenchmen who have recently been given the label "Jew," which is meant to be pejorative, men whom various laws of the French state have in practice rejected from the French community. . . .
>
> At a time when I am treated in my own country like a suspect foreigner, when a French admiral is threatening me with French prison if I manage to avoid German prison, the secretary of state at the War Office confers the Legion of Honor on me! That is too much for my weak understanding to grasp.
>
> Hence, I would be allowed into the order of the Legion of Honor by a government that at the same time declares me unworthy to be an officer—what am I saying? unworthy to serve France as a soldier, by a government that seems to place the downfall, the despoiling, the humiliation of French Jews at the forefront of the spiritual and moral principles of the "National Revolution.". . . .
>
> No thank you!
>
> I have too clear a conception of honor to accept under such auspices a declaration that, in my view, would remain marked by an indelible stain.

If some day, following in the traditions of my family, I am destined to enter the order of the Legion of Honor, it shall be on a perfectly equal footing with my comrades in war. Before that day, I will have to have become once more a Frenchman among Frenchmen.

To spell it out, I must be able to receive the cross in uniform during a taking of arms.

Please accept, Monsieur le Maréchal, the expression of respect that a former fighter at Verdun feels for your person.[9]

There were very few Jewish high officials who asked for a personal derogation to the measure affecting them, but the archives, which have not yet been mined, do preserve rare instances of such efforts. Hence, in March 1942, Lyon-Caen, *conseiller honoraire* to the Cour de Cassation, "invoked at the Ministry of Justice, in support of his request, the very ancient establishment of his family in Paris and the exceptional services rendered to France, in particular by his father": this request, for once, met with success. A decree made in the name of the marshal of France, head of the French state, declared: "M. Lyon-Caen is exempted from the prohibitions outlined in article 2 of the law of 2 June 1941 concerning the exercise of judicial duties."[10] Similarly, in a decree dated 7 May 1942 from Pétain, Lévy, the former judge at the Château-Thierry tribunal, "from a family established in France for at least five generations and having rendered exceptional service to the French state . . . is exempted from the prohibitions outlined in article 2 of the law of 2 June 1941 concerning the exercise of judicial duties."[11] Others took a similar approach, such as Schwob, former judge in Laon, and Gaston Narboni, retired *président* of the Algiers tribunal. However, it is not possible to know whether they succeeded. In contrast, Jean Laroque, former secretary general of the *présidence* of the Seine tribunal, who solicited the benefit of such a derogation, failed in his undertaking. According to a letter from the *garde des Sceaux* to the general commissioner on Jewish questions, dated 13 May 1942,

M. Laroque declares he comes from a family from Comtat Venaissin that is illustrious in several areas. A highly valued magistrate possessing a strong juridical education, M. Laroque had been singled out in the aptitude exam for judicial duties. Nevertheless, despite his brilliant professional qualities, it does not appear that the qualifications invoked by the interested party have the exceptional character needed to justify a derogation of the law. I have judged that the dossier constituted for that purpose by M. Laroque cannot, under these conditions, be submitted for examination by the Haute Assemblé.[12]

In its harshness, this comment says a great deal about the professional conscience of magistrates who calmly made decisions that could have the most extreme consequences for the destinies of their colleagues. It was all the more tragic since the father of Jean Laroque, Gustave Laroque, himself *président* of the Chambre des Requêtes in the Cour de Cassation, was also eliminated by Vichy even though he already felt "totally foreign" to Judaism.[13]

One case deserves to be examined in more detail, even though the party involved was not himself a state Jew in the limited sense of our definition. This was Major Paul-Louis Weiller, who earned twelve citations during World War I, signed by Joffre or by Pétain himself, in recognition of his heroism: once, he was wounded in the throat by machine gun fire during aerial combat; another time his airplane crashed, causing him a skull fracture; later, he brought down two enemy airplanes during the same flight, and so on. It was Pétain himself who awarded him the Croix de Guerre with palm leaf, and Weiller was promoted to commander in the Legion of Honor. This hero, who later went into business, was none other than the son of *député* Lazare Weiller; his mother was the daughter of Émile Javal, the second *député* in the Javal dynasty. Even though he was not himself a state Jew, his rank as major and his family ties impel us to focus on his dossier, which is, in fact, altogether exceptional.

On 1 November 1940, Paul-Louis Weiller was stripped of his French nationality and interned in Pellevoisin; when liberated, he attempted to have the decision affecting him reversed. In this undertaking, he benefited from the relative support of the *garde des Sceaux*, Joseph Barthélemy himself,[14] and also received the support of his faithful friend, Paul Claudel, who wrote on two occasions on his behalf to Marshal Pétain, "our venerated leader," then to the minister to attempt to save "the unfortunate Paul-Louis Weiller, still suffering civil death, excommunicated from our nation for which he spilled his blood."[15] But nothing was done and the measure was still not reversed. A certain number of war pilots from 1914–18 and 1939–40 then wrote to Marshal Pétain, assuring him of their "deference and devotion to his person and to the work of national recovery he had undertaken" to ask him to intervene in favor of annulling the measure affecting Weiller. They had no more success.

To plead his case, Weiller then drafted a memoir, where we read:

The fact that P.-L. Weiller is considered a Jew has without a doubt carried great weight on the decision that stripped him of his nationality. Yet, if he is Jewish, it is in a very peculiar way. The Weillers are an ancient family of Alsatian stock, French for three hundred years. For more than a century, almost all the Weillers have converted to Catholicism and most of them have married Catholics. While the mother of P.-L. Weiller is Jewish, his father is Catholic, married for the first time in the Catholic Church. The Weiller family is precisely the prototype of those great Alsatian families of Jewish origin who, through their conversions, marriages, and the great services they have rendered to the country, have been completely assimilated into the French nation.

And he goes on to underscore the family's claims to glory, including an ancestor who was Louis XIV's physician; to point out the outstanding actions of Léopold Javal, who planted the French flag on the highest minaret of the city of Médéa during one of the pacification campaigns in Algeria; and so on.[16] It appears that, like identical cases evoked above, the administration remained firm in its position and did not restore Major Weiller's French citizenship. In spite of a remarkable assimilation into French society, numerous conversions to Catholicism in this rather atypical family, and letters from the highest Catholic personalities such as Claudel, the case failed. This case acquires all the more interest in that it elucidates the destiny of one of Javal's heirs, heirs who had become completely discreet about their Judaism, unlike the founder of the dynasty, Léopold. Let us also note that in June 1942 the immense property that Léopold had bought during the previous century on the Bassin d'Arcachon, in order to create a social charity dedicated to raising orphan children, was seized[17] and "de-Judaized," like so many other properties, under the sole authority of the French administration.

What did these state Jews unseated from their posts and deeply wounded in their certainties say in the end? One of the most famous of them, whom we have run across on several occasions,[18] the *préfet* and former minister of the interior Abraham Schrameck, sworn enemy of Action Française, which was now victorious, sent a long letter to Pétain from Lavandou, where he was now assigned to house arrest under close guard:

The question of whether article 1 of the law of 3 October is or is not applicable to me remains essentially doubtful, and to resolve it, it would be necessary to do research in the registry office archives in Saint-Étienne, Issenheim, and perhaps Durmenach (Haute-Alsace), Strasbourg, and in addition Vienna and Prague. . . . For myself, in fact, I am linked to families to varying degrees, and I could not say whether they are Jewish only by religion or perhaps also by race. . . . It seems to me that I would not show myself worthy of my grandparents and parents, or of my marriage, or of my personal career of a half-century devoted to the service of the national interest if the observations I believe I must make solely out of concern for the truth had the goal or even the effect of exempting myself from the undeserved treatment inflicted on French Jews.[19]

In fact, most state Jews whose testimonies are known to us seem to have reacted likewise to the exclusion laws: true to the very logic of integrative Franco-Judaism, they wanted to be French citizens but also acknowledged they were Jews, without any contradiction between the two identities existing in their minds. We have seen how consistently they maintained minimal religious practices, how numerous were the state Jews who participated in collective institutions that assured the longevity of a Jewish culture within the French nation. As agents devoted to the state, they had set everything in place to assure the public interest, but most of them did not deny a certain kind of loyalty to a specific social identity. Although they protested vehemently to Marshal Pétain, it was in the name of an emancipatory France open to the Jewish presence: in their view, the scandal was that a contradiction could be established between these two harmonious dimensions of their own existence.

General Boris perfectly illustrated what was undoubtedly the most common reaction. On 10 November 1940, he addressed Marshal Pétain in the following terms:

Like my coreligionists, I am obliged to admit the material validity of the Statut, but I shall never admit its moral validity. . . . The Statut explicitly entails the decommissioning of all Jewish officers (whose number in all the armed forces is great) on active duty and in the reserves. I know no other example in the history of France of collective sanctions of this sort, or of condemnation of this gravity, pronounced without any defense being heard. I raise a formal protest against the measure, which affects me personally. I am, on the one hand, the most senior member of the highest rank of Jewish officers, and, even though I am no one's representative, I link my protest in my mind to all my comrades in arms who spilled their blood for the nation in 1914–18 and 1939–40. I believe I have the right and the duty to raise this protest. I have the right, because I have belonged to a French family for centuries, one that has given France a number of civil servants and honorable and honored officers. . . . I have the duty, because I am responding to the appeal of my friends and relatives who were killed in action. For I would be dishonored in the eyes of future generations of French Jews who will survive the persecutions that are beginning and who will go on to serve France, if not as officers then at least as soldiers, if I did not at least try to save their honor by not accepting the insult without reacting, however weakly it is possible to do so materially.[20]

While he was at it, General Boris sent a letter to the secretary minister of state at the War Department. It read:

I have the honor . . . of declaring that, according to you, I am a "Jew" and, according to my numerous friends and comrades, my superiors and my equals and my subordinates in the army, a French Jew. . . . I do not claim and do not desire to accept the benefit of article 8 of the Statut des Juifs even though I belong to a French family that is at least two centuries old and that has numbered many honorable and honored officers. That would mean implicitly recognizing that my status as French citizen with the same rights as other Frenchmen was up for discussion, and that is something that my reason and my heart refuse to do.[21]

General Boris, who was among the most active and the most courageous Jewish high officials on the Conseil d'Etat, publicly engaging in a collective action openly hostile to the racist policy of Vichy, also drafted a long protest in mid-1941 with the help of Jacques Meyer, former student of the École Normale Supérieure, in the name of the central consistory, which had withdrawn to Lyon. This little-known text is emblematic of the fate of state Jews. It was signed ex officio by President Jacques Helbronner, *président de section honoraire* of the Conseil d'Etat, commander in the Legion of Honor, Croix de Guerre, honorary colonel; by Secretary William Oualid, professor at the Paris law faculty, officer of the Legion of Honor, war wounded, Croix de Guerre; by General Boris himself, former inspector general of the artillery, commander in the Legion of Honor, Croix de Guerre; by Henry Lévy-Bruhl, former professor of the Paris law faculty, Chevalier of the Legion of Honor for military reasons, Croix de Guerre with palm leaf; by René Mayer, *maître des requêtes* at the Conseil d'Etat, commander in the Legion of Honor, Croix de Guerre; by Léon Weiss, *conseiller honoraire* to the *cour d'appel*, captain in the reserves, war veteran; by Jacques Meyer, former student of the École Normale Supérieure, officer of the Legion of Honor, Croix de Guerre, war amputee, volunteer in 1914 and 1939; by D. Olmer, former professor at the medical school in Marseilles, physician and lieutenant colonel, Chevalier of the Legion of Honor, Croix de Guerre; by Jacques Sée, former student of the École Polytechnique, lieutenant colonel in the reserves, Chevalier of the Legion of Honor, Croix de Guerre; by Georges Wormser, former student of the École Normale Supérieure, *agrégé* at the university, officer of the Legion of Honor, Croix de Guerre, former *directeur du cabinet* to Clemenceau. This text, at the bottom of which are also found the signatures of the chief rabbis, and of numerous industrialists, engineers, and lawyers at the *cour d'appel*, appears as a distant echo of the honor roll of French Jewry that the *Archives Israélites* had been compiling since 1888. Members of the state's *grands corps*, having gone through the various difficult stages of meritocratic recruitment, these state Jews of indisputable patriotism who were also members of the central consistory, protested in terms that we would do well to reproduce here:

The French Jews are by tradition and culture fully French and completely assimilated with other Frenchmen; particularly in Alsace-Lorraine between 1871 and 1918, they were in the front lines, often subjected to the blows of persecution and finding themselves in the midst of the greatest difficulties, contributing toward maintaining French ties and sentiments. This fact has been recognized by the highest authorities of the state, in the first place by President Poincaré in 1918.

Numerous French Jews have honored the army as well as letters, the sciences, the arts, medicine, and industry, in positions they occupied in higher education, at the Collège de France, and at the Sorbonne. Their presence in the *grands corps* of the state such as the Conseil d'Etat is due to qualifications they owe neither to intrigue nor to favor but only to their own merit, as acknowledged by their peers.

Considering that the French Jews for the most part did their duty in 1914–18 and in 1939–40, as the tribute by Maurice Barrès, a man beyond suspicion, attests; . . .

Convinced that the collective measures of exception taken toward French Jews cannot have been approved, even tacitly, by the French government, inasmuch as they are contrary to its earlier declarations to maintain the French nationality of Jews, and given that these measures would have no other result than to submit French Jews to a regime of persecutions comparable to that of the darkest ages of history, namely, the persecutions of the first Christians or of the Protestants of the sixteenth and seventeenth centuries;

Given that, under these conditions, French Jews still wish to believe that the persecutions of which they are the object are entirely imposed on the French state by the occupying authorities and that the representatives of France are making an effort to attenuate their severity as much as possible;

Considering that, in spite of their misfortune, France is their sole nation, to which the memory of their participation in operations over the centuries, operations that have consecrated their greatness, attach them, as they do their Christian compatriots.

French Jews, if they cannot safeguard the future and perhaps even the lives of their children and grandchildren, yet holding above all to the hope of passing honorable names down to them, ask the head of state, who as a great soldier and a fervent Christian, incarnates in their view the nation in all its purity, to grant them this solemn protest, which is the only weapon in their weakness.

French Jews, more than ever attached to their faith, keep intact their hope and their confidence in France and its destiny.[22]

This protest sounds like the last will and testament of Franco-Judaism: it recalls its claims to glory, the formation of so many state Jews, the supreme sacrifice to which even Barrès bore witness, the unconditional love for that nation whose leader was a great Christian soldier; it ends with a desperate act of faith regarding the innocence, however improbable, of the government authorities, supposedly acting only under Nazi constraints. The time of the Franco-French wars had returned, but this time it was no longer a game. It was no longer essentially a boxing match between opposing intellectuals, conflicting and sometimes violent demonstrations in the streets of French cities: a repetition of the St. Bartholomew's Day massacre was taking shape, and even worse, the possible death of all these men and their descendants.

At this crucial moment of their history within the French nation, these Jews, almost all of them from the *grandes écoles* and universities, loaded up with diplomas and Croix de Guerre, took care to make clear, at the end of this dramatic text, this true definitive inventory, that they intended to remain faithful to their Jewish faith. As state Jews and in contrast to others who had distanced themselves, they were steadfastly determined to die if necessary as Jews with conviction, faithful to their own religious tradition. This text, drafted in 1941 and given to Marshal Pétain when the cause was already lost, owed much to the personality of General Boris, who, after his vote, added the brief final comment: "If we do not have the means to oppose the measures taken by the occupying authority or the measures that threaten us, we at least have the right and the means to raise a protest that history will record." Inasmuch as this manifesto has until now remained almost unknown, it is essential to preserve it in our memory, for in itself it symbolizes the final message from certain state Jews at a time of extreme danger.[23] Let us add, however, that in a short note drafted following an appalling report on the Rivesaltes camp, General Boris added: "I am told that, after my departure from the meeting in Lyon on 30 June 1941, a phrase paying tribute to the person of the marshal was added at the end of the solemn protest; if that is correct, I deplore it, for that completely changes its import." What was the appropriate attitude toward Pétain, whose own attitude was the final legitimation of all these illegal measures? That question proved to be key.

Georges Wormser, one of the signers of the text, who had been Clemenceau's *chef du cabinet* and who at the time occupied a seat on the central consistory, also sent a letter to Marshal Pétain, on 1 August 1941:

On 7 December 1792 in Soultz, a small town in Alsace at the foot of Hartmannswiller, my great-grandfather, Abraham Bloch, "representative" of the Jews, as his father and grandfather had been before him, solemnly swore the civic oath in the name of all those he represented, the first mark of emancipation, which they owed to the relentless efforts of Abbé Grégoire. In 1800, he was designated by the provincial authorities as assistant to the mayor.

A century and a half has passed; yesterday, with my wife and four children, I had to submit to the humiliation of making a declaration that distinguished us from the French community. I would be lacking in all dignity if I did not cry out in protest to you. . . . Did not my grandfather, who in 1871 chose France, observe the pact?

Did I myself not observe it when, as a high school teacher, I instilled in my students moral teachings that thirty years later, some of them remembered in the crises of conscience that assaulted them?

— I who, as second lieutenant in the infantry, "vigorously led my company under fire under particularly difficult circumstances, and gravely wounded in several places, kept my command until the complete exhaustion of my forces" (citation to the Order of the Sixth Army)

— I, who in 1935 went to La Seyne to face the second ballot alone and without hope, for the honor of the flag, in the face of communism, before which everyone else was abdicating at the time?

The protest that I raise today, I also formulate in the name of M. Clemenceau, who until the very last honored me with his confidence and friendship. . . . When he attested, "And you, you will remain standing," I understood that oppression had its limit: in the face of everything, our steadfast consciences and family honor remain untouchable.

A defeat does not efface history, a measure of exception can eclipse but cannot abolish our imprescriptible rights and duties, even less our feelings as Frenchmen above all.

Disavowed today, with opprobrium we do not deserve heaped upon us as a group, we appeal to the soldier, the head of state:

Because we reared them in the belief that we received a sacred inheritance, will our innocent children find themselves separated from the only lasting contentment there is, that of serving their nation? [24]

Wormser hammered in the same message to the man who then incarnated the state. State Jews, respectful of the pact of Franco-Judaism that had for so long organized their existence, were one with the nation, had sacrificed themselves for it on the battlefields, had committed themselves body and soul beside its best servants such as Clemenceau, and, with the help of civic education and the anticommunist struggle, relentlessly dedicated themselves to maintaining the republican order threatened by subversions of all kinds. In the very image of the great figures of the Republic, from Gambetta to Poincaré to Clemenceau himself, they challenged without faltering any attack on the republican order. Nothing, however, could prevent them from remaining Jewish, from transmitting their beliefs and maintaining their faith.

When he was abruptly given notice in a circular from the Chamber to declare himself Jewish, Mandel, the other devoted servant of Clemenceau, manifested a similar attitude, even though he was not a believer: he did not hesitate to respond firmly in a letter addressed to Marshal Pétain.

I have just received a letter from the *président* of the Chamber that asks me to let you know whether I fall under the purview of article 2 of the law of 3 October 1940. I hasten to respond in the affirmative. In fact, to more surely merit certain attacks, I insisted on proclaiming my Jewish ancestry in November 1920, when I made my debut before the Chamber in defending the resumption of relations with the Vatican. . . . For more than half a century, I have been the collaborator of Clemenceau, a collaborator who is honored to remain invariably faithful to his policies. It is for that reason in particular, as you know better than anyone, that I have opposed the armistice and that, for no other reason, I am now charged and interned. [25]

Let us listen again to these state Jews whose protests History has rarely heard or retained. In April 1941, a certain number of "Paris Jews," through the intermediary of the chief rabbi of France, remitted a message to Marshal Pétain, signed by, among others, Léon Lyon-Caen, *conseiller honoraire* to the Cour de Cassation; Didier Durand, *vice-président honoraire* at the Seine tribunal; Pierre Masse, lawyer and former *député*; Pontrémoli, member of the Institut; Robert Debré, member of the Academie de Médicine; L.-L. Rheims, brigadier general, and so on. Most of them were state Jews filling preeminent positions in the administration, from old French families whose patronymics had become almost invisible. What did they say when the very meaning of their lives was about to be transformed? Even more than those who held seats on the consistory, they proclaimed both their fidelity to Judaism and their confidence in Marshal Pétain, head of state. That state could not betray them, and its leader was obliged by his duties and in spite of the exceptional circumstances, to act in conformity with its logic:

> The news that in occupied territory the German authorities are in a short time going to force all those whom a recent law has called "Jews" to constitute themselves into a closed group and live outside the French community has elicited the most painful emotions among us.
>
> Jews by religion or descendants of Jews, but almost all from old French families of which many can claim a past that is many centuries old, we insist on declaring that we were born French, that we are French, and that we shall always remain French. We form neither a race nor a people, but an integral part of the nation from which nothing could separate us.
>
> That is why we appeal without hesitation to the venerated leader, in whom today the very idea of the united and indivisible nation is incarnated, and, broken-hearted, ask him to intervene to avoid the tragic consequences of a decision that is cruel above all others. . . .
>
> Frenchmen, not through adoption, but from the beginning, Frenchmen not in name only but with all our hearts and all their ardent convictions, the great majority of the Jews of France, whose feeling we are certain we express, ask you with confidence not to let the gesture that has been announced be carried out and to save once more French unity.[26]

The idea of separating the Jews from the national community and re-grouping them into a specific organization, charged with representing them before the authorities as a particular group, abolished in an instant the entire long process of emancipation, which had led to their integration into the public space, as citizens equal to everyone else. From that time on, they were no longer considered such, and were shut up in a new particularist ghetto. This incredible view, which implicitly linked them to a race and a foreign people camping on national territory, and as a result subject to specific legislation, could, they believed, have germinated only among the German authorities, who were imposing it on the venerated head of state. In each of these texts of protest, even as Vichy's own deliberate commitment was becoming more obvious daily, even when legislation hostile to the Jews as a whole and to state Jews in particular continued to be decided autonomously from high places — responding to the ideology of the extreme right, whose antisemitic violence we have seen — the fidelity to the head of state, the state that Jewish high officials had always zealously served, was striking.

The fact that the marshal had uttered not one word of protest against the measures attacking freedom to which Jews were being subjected, that he did not deliberately oppose their exclusion from the administration, or more generally, condemn the round-ups, violence, arrests, and first deportations, in the end counted for less than the symbolic dimension of his position: Pétain remained for them the guarantor of national unity, the heir to a state tradition that could not collapse in that way. Loyalty to the head of state remained intact, and it is important to underscore the point: it was not a question of incomprehension, of naïveté, of illusory devotion, of social fidelity, of class conspiracy, or of the will to distinguish themselves from foreign Jews (it existed, of course, and we shall return to this point), and as a result to protect their legal status as French citizens that was obtained with the French Revolution. This behavior, which may appear surprising since things had sunk so low, was more in conformity with a juridical heritage: state Jews they were and state Jews they intended to remain. Even though the state's betrayal became clearer every day, it remained incomprehensible within a system of thought formed and as it were molded by the state. Hence, against all the evidence, there arose this desire to attribute the final responsibility to the German occupier, in order to exonerate the French authorities in spite of it all. As Pierre Laroque, member of the Conseil d'Etat, struck down by the Statut des Juifs, also recalled, "at the time, it was thought that it was imposed by the Germans."[27]

Let us give another example, which has also remained lost in the archives until now: on 20 February 1941, Max Hymans, *député* of Indre, who would later play a national role under the Fourth Republic, wrote to the marshal of France, head of the French state:

I have the honor of informing you that "more than two of my grandparents" practiced the Jewish religion. The French law of 3 October 1940 uses a new terminology. What does the word "race"—which it does not define—mean? Is race determined by religion? . . . To respond to the question of the office of the Chamber, I maintain that I am subject to the consequences of that law of exception and that forfeiture must affect me, as it has affected French professors, magistrates, and officers reputed to be "of the Jewish race."

I will bear it without shame, for I am not of the Jewish race, but of the French race, or rather quite simply French and as much as anyone else. . . . How distressed my grandfather would be if he were here to see those of his descendants who were not killed in action and who were all, or almost all, wounded, cited, decorated with the Médaille Militaire or the Legion of Honor, today reduced to second-class Frenchmen.

You knew one of them, Monsieur le Maréchal: General Geismar, who had the honor of serving under your orders and who may have spoken to you of our family traditions.

After 1870, my grandfather, a wine grower in Alsace, led each of his sons to the border when he was thirteen years old to make of him a Frenchman. . . .

I am thus going to be stripped of the mandate of *député*, and later I will have to make my son understand that he is also a Jew, a Frenchman of an inferior race, even though on his mother's side he is a descendant of Buffon and Daubenton, whose names represent chapters in the history of France.

In falling under the blow of the law of 3 October 1940, I must believe it was imposed by the occupying authorities. If this text is a means of external policy destined to lighten the weight of the nation's sacrifices, I am almost proud to offer my moral suffering for the country.

But if this text survives into the future, I would deplore for France an act that can be compared only to the revocation of the Edict of Nantes whose consequences, even after three centuries, are still being calculated.

Please accept, Monsieur le Maréchal, the expression of my respectful devotion.[28]

With the exception of a few details, all these texts of protest resemble one another and say with passion or humor the heartbreak felt by these men stripped of their identity as French citizens. Here, the spirit of sacrifice to the nation is pushed to the point of accepting the installation of iniquitous measures such as the Statut des Juifs, should it happen to correspond to "a means of external policy" that reduced the collective suffering of France. And always there is the near certainty that such measures could only have been imposed by the Germans, for that is how contrary they were to the French tradition, turning their back on the rationalist ideas before and after 1789, returning to the Saint Bartholomew's Day massacre or the Revocation. Again and again, this dramatic reference reappears in the writings of state Jews, for it was truly the only one that anticipated the eventuality of another massacre, especially since, unlike the Protestants of the past who were collectively armed and organized, the Jews were only simple citizens, isolated and defenseless, handed over for prosecution to extremist groups acting with the full support of the German authorities. From then on, everything suggested that this massacre would be limitless if the state abandoned its citizens, a hypothesis that state Jews still refused to believe.

Nevertheless, their letters revealed increasing confusion before the incomprehensible attitude of the head of state. Let us give two final examples. On 25 February 1941, the senator of Haute-Saône, Moïse Lévy, wrote to the head of state:

Out of deference to your person, I am responding to the circular in which my religion is requested. This question was not asked at the Assemblé Nationale when you sought power from me and my colleagues. It was also not asked at the time of the mobilization of the Jews who died for France, in 1940 and in 1914.

My family name and given name have never deceived anyone. My Catholic fellow citizens who have shown confidence in me, particularly in electing me *conseiller municipal* for forty-six years and mayor for twenty-one years, have always respected my convictions, because their religion commanded them to do so and because I always respected theirs.

I raise the most energetic protest against the law of 3 October 1940, which was imported from abroad. In the nation of Liberty, Frenchmen will one day rediscover the liberty of conscience. . . .

Monsieur le Maréchal, you have given away the honor of Frenchmen of the Jewish religion for the sake of the nation of France: history will tell us whether the rigors of the Occupation were softened by that gift.[29]

Like Max Hymans and many others, Moïse Lévy attributed the responsibility for the anti-Jewish laws to the German foreigner who was imposing his pitiless domination on France. Even more critically and ironically, he doubted that the sacrifice of Jews, for which consent was so easily given, would greatly lighten the collective suffering of the nation. The tone is sharper, less deferential, analogous in many respects to the tone used by the *député* and then senator of Hérault Pierre Masse when he wrote to Marshal Pétain:

I have received under the authority of the honorable president of the Senate, the circular in which you ask me to make known whether I am from a Jewish family.

My first inclination was to give no response; there are no "Jews" in the Senate. Only French citizens participate in that assembly, whatever their religion, citizens elected by a French electoral college in conformity with a constitution that has not been abrogated on that point.

My two grandfathers were of the Jewish religion. . . . Their wives belonged to the same.

I raise the most formal protest against the law of 3 October. Of strictly French ancestry in every branch and as far as I can go back, officer of the infantry, awarded citations that were all earned in the French front lines, former chief of military justice at a time when the fifth column was sent to the foxholes of Vincennes, having among my closest relatives four officers killed by the enemy, member of the council of my order, regularly elected senator by my compatriots of Hérault, I do not agree to be treated as a second-class Frenchman.

Believe me that I regret, in addressing you, to have to express myself with such firmness. I do not forget the deference I owe you, nor that I had the honor to sit with you on the war committee of 1917.[30]

We could multiply the passages from letters to the head of state as they become available: with a few variations, they all express the anger and surprise of state Jews, none of whom refused to consider themselves Jewish to a certain degree. They are all the more moving in that they often come from political personalities or those from the *grands corps* of the state who, during their careers, had been led to support Pétain's actions. At the time of the decisive vote of July 1940, for example, by means of which power fell to the marshal, we find without any great surprise that several Jewish parliamentarians did not join the small camp on the "no" side and granted their confidence to the "Christian leader," the old soldier still bathed in his prestige as savior of the nation: Pierre Masse, Moïse Lévy, Léon Meyer, Abraham Schrameck, Max Hymans, Louis-Louis Dreyfus—the authors of a great number of the letters cited above—contributed through their votes to giving a legal cover to the Vichy regime. On the "no" side, we nevertheless find Léon Blum, Jules Moch, and Robert Lazurick; Charles Lussy, for one, chose to abstain. Others did not vote, for they had decided to pursue the battle in North Africa and had left on the *Massilia*: Pierre Mendès France, Salomon Grumbach, and Lévy-Alphandéry. The Communist *député* Lévy was at that moment under arrest in Algeria following the imprisonment of Communist *députés* for approving the German-Soviet pact. And finally, Senator Maurice de Rothschild did not take part in the vote. It is easy to see that, on the whole, it was the conservative Jews who were on the marshal's side at that instant, for they embraced the state order he claimed to incarnate at the time; but Max Hymans was a Socialist *député* who rapidly joined the Resistance.

Beyond these differing attitudes at the time of the vote, there was an almost unanimous reaction, made up entirely of the will to remain French without, however, denying the Jewish dimension of one's personal heritage, though to varying degrees. Few state Jews, it seems—in the current state of research—came to challenge that dimension explicitly. In an almost logical way, Paul Grunebaum-Ballin—making every effort to celebrate the glory of the ideas of Abbé Grégoire and also to attach his name to the complete secularization of society, views that implied in every case the extreme uniformization of the public space—was one of those who best expressed this constant concern. When Vichy promulgated the second Statut des Juifs in June 1941, he drafted the following declaration of his civil status:

Paul, Frédéric, Jean Grunebaum-Ballin, age 70 years and 3 months, French nationality, *président de section honoraire* of the Conseil d'Etat, *président honoraire* of the *conseil de préfecture* Seine, commander in the Legion of Honor, 42 years of civil service, 3½ years of military service during the war of 1914–18 (volunteered for the armed forces on 21 November 1915 and was attached to the eastern army). . . .

We refuse to declare ourselves "Jewish"; we refuse to see ourselves as belonging to the Jewish "race," since, in the opinion of all the scientists, there is no Jewish race. We refuse to see ourselves as belonging to the Jewish religious community, for the only community to which we belong is the French nation. We have always lived as freethinkers, detached from any religious belief.[31]

No matter: against his deepest desire, Grunebaum-Ballin was forced to fill out more questionnaires relating to a Judaism he had rejected. In November 1941, he was obliged to respond to an even more precise document. He then wrote this letter to the *préfet* of Haute-Garonne:

I address myself to the official representative of the government, not to the former colleague of the Conseil d'Etat or to the friend. . . .

Yes, Monsieur le préfet, for any truly French heart, the violations of the principles that have been progressively drawn from the noble multicultural tradition of this country, those that the French Revolution of 1789 proclaimed and spread throughout the world, that the royalist charter of 1815 maintained in their integrity, cause a pain that nothing can assuage. . . .

And the only comfort permitted us is that which is born of the unshakable confidence in the certain return of the true spiritual destiny of that "eternal France," that "torch-bearing" nation in whose defense so many of my family have found captivity or death on the battlefield and which, for my modest part, I served for almost half a century with a passionate love.

In the rigor of the administrative language and beyond the former friendships of the Conseil d'Etat, the immediate response of the *préfet* is of an unavoidable simplicity: "The establishment of the personal declaration that has recently been requested of you was prescribed by a ministerial instruction taken in application of the law of 2 June 1941. It is not possible for you to exempt yourself from that formality."[32]

Positive law was omnipotent, and one could not expect a *préfet*, whatever his ancient solidarity with the corps, to make a personal judgment on the opportuneness of any juridical act, such as the one Grunebaum-Ballin was contesting. Never mind his ancestors, his passionate love for France, his sacrifices on the battlefield, a law was a law and there was to be no discussion: no escape was imaginable, a man had to register as a "Jew" even if he did not personally identify himself with that designation. The people on the Conseil d'Etat continued to do their work undisturbed, according to the rules in force, letting any cumbersome friendship fall by the wayside: they applied texts that were certainly iniquitous but that, in their view, remained endowed with a legal validity sanctioned by the legality of the state.[33] Matters nevertheless rushed headlong: like the Jews in Paris discussed above, Paul Grunebaum-Ballin had a real moment of disgust when the constitution imposed on the state formed a Union Générale des Juifs de France (general union of Jews of France, UGIF) to represent them before the authorities as a community separate from the nation. In a text that has also remained largely unknown, this great jurist so vilified by the extreme right made clear his own interpretation of a question that would divide French Jews:

Having Jewish ancestry, having never dreamed of dissimulating or denying the fact that my ancestors were attached by their beliefs or practices to the Jewish religion, I categorically refuse to consider myself a French Israelite, a French Jew. I am a Frenchman who is not a Jew by race—for there is no Jewish race: all the anthropologists and other scientists who have concerned themselves with these questions have recognized this, among them, notably, Vacher de Lapouge, one of the prima donnas of French antisemitism. It is therefore in an arbitrary manner that the texts calling for legal measures of anti-Jewish persecution, signed by the marshal of France, head of state, have classified me as a "Jew". . . .

There it is, then, "the Jewish people." You tell Frenchmen of the Jewish religion or of Jewish origin: "You believed you were the compatriots of the Bretons and the Parisians, of the Gascons and the Provençaux, of the Lorrainians and the Dauphinois, next to whom you yourself or your relatives have confronted, on two occasions in less than a quarter-century, the dangers of war. . . . Well now! From now on the French state relegates you to a 'people' it has artificially created, along with Austrians, Germans, Poles, Romanians, and Russians residing in France, and for the sole reason that a number of you share the religious beliefs of foreign Jews or that your grandparents shared them."

"We must refuse everything to Jews as a nation and accord everything to Jews as individuals. They must be citizens individually. It is repugnant that there should be a nation within the nation." Such was the truly national language used by Stanislas de Clermont-Tonnerre before the Constitutional Assembly. . . . And little by little, the visions of Clermont-Tonnerre, of Abbé Grégoire, and of their friends were realized; once more, the assimilating genius of France triumphed. The "Jewish nation" of the times of oppression disappeared, vanished; it was melted into the multicultural pot of the French nation.

One hundred and fifty years later, the marshal of France, head of the French state, is making an effort to reconstitute, through the texts he is promulgating, a "Jewish people" isolated from the French nation: French Jews are participating in the application of the edict of excommunication. . . . We shall see even more: those who have shown no fear about becoming the administrators of the Union have already gotten more than one finger caught in the machinery.[34]

We needed to cite at length these declarations by a state Jew challenging any particularist origin, refusing from that time on to consider himself a Jew in any shape or form, whether with respect to cultural practices, solidarity with a people, or a minimal shared memory. The advocate of secularism, who idolized Abbé Grégoire and was committed in his various communications to reviving his work was in this sense a convinced Jacobin who expected and hoped for the end of all particularisms within the French nation of citizens. Drawing the extreme conclusion from his reasoning, he was much more severe toward Marshal Pétain, explicitly accusing him of backing a considerable historical regression, of legitimating a return to a time before the French Revolution, a time when groups and corporations reigned. Harshly condemning Pétain, he was all the more at ease condemning without chance of appeal the Jewish leaders who in the end made possible the implementation of the UGIF, thus legalizing the rebirth of a new Jewish community apart from the French nation, of a "people" no longer having any tie to the French people. In a certain manner, Pierre

Laroque, also a member of the Conseil d'Etat, adopted the same position in returning to the early years of the century, which had seen the secularization of society and the distancing from Judaism flourish. Like his colleague Grunebaum-Ballin, who played an important role in the implementation of this process, Pierre Laroque was uncomprehending when the Statut des Juifs put an end to his brilliant career: "In principle," he noted, "'Jew' is a religion; and therefore I have never been Jewish."[35]

At the opposite extreme, Jacques Helbronner, also a member of the Conseil d'Etat, became an essential figure, next to General Boris, in the resistance of Jewish organizations openly acting as such. Following Isaïe Levaillant and Camille Lyon, the latter also from the Conseil d'Etat, Helbronner joined in an action challenging the Vichy measures in the name of his fidelity to the national juridical order and his Jewish faith, since he had also assumed the duties of president of the central consistory. One could not imagine a greater contrast between these two state Jews, Helbronner and Grunebaum-Ballin, both scandalized by the antisemitic laws of Vichy that brutally separated the French Jews from the national community: one opposed them because they labeled him a "Jew" when he wished to be simply French; the other challenged them just as violently because he believed that the status of Jew and of Frenchman were compatible, in conformity with the ancient model of Franco-Judaism. Grunebaum-Ballin fought to the end the old battle for secularism, even in his private life, wishing to disappear as a Jew; Helbronner proved to be just as attached to the universalist conception of citizenship governing the public space, condemning the representativeness of any collective structure that was particularist in nature, even while wishing to be fully Jewish in the private space, in conformity there too with a separation proper to French history. For both of them, though they began from opposing values, a Jewish "people" or "nation" could not be reconstituted within the French national community.

While the great majority of state Jews now opposed the Vichy regime in the Resistance or beside General de Gaulle, some devoted their energy to rescuing Jews: these included Jacques Helbronner; René Mayer, also of the Conseil d'Etat; General Boris; Robert Lévy, former judge at the Seine tribunal removed from public duty by the Statut des Juifs, and secretary general adjunct to the consistory at the end of 1941; and Léon Meiss, *conseiller* to the *cour d'appel* in Nancy, who succeeded Helbronner in November 1943 as president of the consistory when the latter was arrested on 28 October. Let us note that Georges Wormser himself, the man who, with Georges Mandel, symbolized the Clemencist tradition, had been selected to succeed Helbronner to the presidency of the consistory: we can easily imagine the striking symbolic dimension of such an assignment under these circumstances. The man who had seconded Clemenceau during World War I would now have represented the Jews of France before Marshal Pétain in Vichy and before the German authorities! But Wormser did not wish to be named, and it was Judge Meiss who succeeded Helbronner.[36] No one has ever really underscored the fact that all these men joined in the battle as state Jews already familiar with the arcana of power. They were at the heart of the structures of power: In this, they resembled Isaïe Levaillant, who confronted antisemitism, and Joseph Reinach, who, during the Dreyfus affair, led the Dreyfusard camp by giving it the benefit of his perfect familiarity with the politico-administrative milieus, which he had long frequented through his close association with Gambetta and then Ferry. Both groups were the heirs to the founders of the Republic and its most decisive leaders, from Gambetta to Poincaré to Clemenceau, leaders attentive to the ideals of 1789 whose glorious names they invoked, as we saw in the letters of protest, in this time when Vichy turned its back on the republican ethic.

More precisely, a place in the Conseil d'Etat proved to be crucial: Jacques Helbronner and René Mayer, who occupied seats there, had essential roles at the head of the central consistory in dialogues and negotiations with state authorities, who were almost always represented by other members of the Conseil d'Etat. Jacques Helbronner was one of the key figures of that period: he came from a family of civil servants, and Élie Saint-Paul, his uncle, had himself been a *conseiller d'Etat*.[37] At the UGIF, the rival organization created by Vichy and the German authorities to organize Jewish representation on a quasi ethnic and racial basis, he was called upon to aid imprisoned and soon-to-be deported Jews (distributing funds, aiding children, and so on). Beside Raymond-Raoul Lambert, who was the real leader, there soon figured Pierre Seligman, also a *conseiller d'Etat*, who joined the UGIF in 1942, participated in the dramatic negotiations conducted in its name to save certain Jews from deportation, before resigning for reasons of legal interpretation in July 1943, when everything had collapsed.[38] We know that the relations between the consistory and the UGIF evolved from the frankest hostility, the total refusal of any shared actions, to a certain reciprocal recognition. To what extent was their total disagreement regarding the strategy to adopt toward Vichy explained by an essential difference: the near absence of state Jews at the UGIF and their strong presence within the consistory, where they proved to be fiercely attached to public law and to a conception of the public space entirely incompatible with the recognition of what the forces in power considered to be a representative organization, which grouped all French and foreign Jews together, endowing them with attributes other than religious? The conflictual history of the consistory and the UGIF, the logic proper to the leaders of each organization, their personal modes of action in relation to Vichy leaders is probably also illuminated by that fact.

Opposing them, leading the dance in Vichy's name, several *conseillers d'Etat* were at the forefront of the antisemitic battle. Naturally, we find, in the very first ranks, Raphaël Alibert, who was largely responsible for the anti-Jewish legislation: *chef de cabinet* to Marshal Pétain, he became the regime's first *garde des Sceaux*, a post where he was allowed to apply his Maurassian conceptions. This high official from the Conseil d'Etat was responsible for the first Statut des Juifs; his closest collaborator, his *directeur de cabinet*, was Pierre de Font-Réaulx, *maître des requêtes* for the Conseil d'Etat. Jean-Pierre Ingrand, also *maître des requêtes* and an equally important and dangerous figure, was named in July 1940 as delegate for the minister of the interior at the general delegation of the Vichy government in the occupied territories. He played a capital role in that post as director of the *personnel préfectoral*, signing a portion of the anti-Jewish legislative texts of 1941 and directing in person the execution of hostages.[39] Among the *préfets* named in the place of those that had been purged, we also find several members of the Conseil d'Etat, with *préfets* playing an essential role in the implementation of the arrest and deportation of Jews; they often applied with great zeal the antisemitic measures that unavoidably affected some of their former colleagues.[40] We might also note that in 1941 the Conseil d'Etat instituted a special commission on the Statut des Juifs, presided over by its *vice-président*. On several occasions, the Conseil d'Etat proposed clearly antisemitic legislation and extended the anti-Jewish measures to persons not targeted by the texts it was examining. The service director for legislation and litigation on the Commissariat Générale aux Questions Juives (general commission on Jewish questions) was also a *maître des requêtes*, as was the director of the national police charged with measures of repression targeting Jews among others, including their expulsion or deportation.[41] Other members of this famous corps sat in great number on the staff of Joseph Barthélemy, secretary general of the Ministry of Justice from 1940 to 1944. He was himself a *maître des requêtes*.

In reality, the regular judicial apparatus almost as a whole, which had included several Jews who had now been removed, agreed without balking to take over the application of the antisemitic Vichy legislation that directly affected state Jews,[42] especially since Joseph Barthélemy, *garde des Sceaux*, covered them with his prestige as a distinguished jurist, under the very benevolent gaze of other great professors of law, such as the dean Georges Ripert, dean Roger Bonnard, Achille Mestre, and many others.[43] In that sense, we can maintain without difficulty that "the French judiciary gave its blessing to Marshal Pétain and the National Revolution, including the Statut des Juifs which formed an integral part of that revolution."[44] Vichy broke up corps solidarity: while many members of the Conseil d'Etat competently implemented its policy, four of them, who identified themselves as

Jews or were so labeled, spent time in Drancy under dramatic conditions and wore the yellow star. These were Jacques Helbronner, Jean Cahen-Salvador, Pierre Lévy, and Julien Reinach; two of them, Jacques Helbronner and Pierre Lévy, would die during deportation. Pierre Pontrémoli, also a member of the Conseil d'Etat, died as a Resistance fighter.[45] Certain members of that institution, more rare perhaps, such as Alexandre Parodi, did not hesitate to write to Paul Grunebaum-Ballin on February 1941 to denounce "the embracing of the regime, abominable in its cowardice. . . . But France has nothing in common with all that, and will be swept clean when the time comes."[46] Here we have evidence of something approaching an explosion of the corps, into unequal parts of course!

The key man with whom Jacques Helbronner now established a dialogue to attempt to modify the antisemitic decisions made by the government was none other than André Lavagne, his colleague at the Conseil d'Etat, at present director of Marshal Pétain's civil staff.

As during the time of the Dreyfus affair, given the careers pursued by these state Jews in politics or the high administration, we necessarily find among their immediate associates almost everyone in power during that tragic period, in particular, Pétain himself and the members of his immediate entourage. Beyond its dissimilarities, which would quickly prove tragic, the government and the bureaucracy also formed a totality, where a minimum of solidarity and conviviality reigned. Thus, Jean Cahen-Salvador had lunch in Vichy with members of Pétain's cabinet, among them André Lavagne, who had become its director. Before the war, Cahen-Salvador was also well acquainted with Max Ingrand, whose essential role in antisemitic repression we have already noted: he considered Ingrand "an obscene individual" and cited as proof—an anecdotal side of this tragic story—that, during a contested tennis match with him, Ingrand had cheated![47] René Mayer, *conseiller d'Etat*, who would play an important role under Vichy as consistorial leader, was *chef de cabinet* to Laval in 1925, when Laval held a seat as minister with the *Cartel des Gauches*. In Laval's cabinet, we also find Robert Lazurick, the future Socialist *député*, who would remain close to Laval until Vichy, especially since he was excluded from the SFIO for having joined the neosocialists and Déat along with Max Hymans. Xavier Vallat also passed for a friend of *député* Wallach, who in April 1941, "considered him a fine fellow";[48] let us not forget that Alfred Wallach, *député*, president of the Fédérations des Engagés Volontaires Alsaciens-Lorrainiens (federation of volunteer soldiers from Alsace-Lorraine) during World War I, who also knew Pétain as president of numerous veterans associations, telegraphed him in June 1940 in the name of the Alsatians to ask him not to abandon the struggle. Later entering the Resistance, he was sentenced to death by the German tribunals, but the French police who had come to arrest him allowed him to escape to Switzerland.[49]

Let us give another example of these links, these encounters due to the chance events of careers and passions: Socialist *député* Jean Pierre-Bloch, after his first escape from a camp, happened to run into Philippe Henriot, and a long conversation took place in an empty compartment of a train crossing through Dordogne. At the end of that exchange, making a fist, Henriot declared:

If you need me for anything at all, call me on the phone, I will help you. And in a letter addressed to a third party, Henriot wrote: "We are thinking only of Jews and not of Frenchmen of the Jewish religion. Let me tell you that one of my colleagues from the Chamber who was in the past violently against me is Jewish. He is Pierre-Bloch, *député* of Aisne. I had the joy to find him again the other day. A magnificent soldier, cited, decorated, escaped; can you think for a minute that our campaigns are targeting such men?"[50]

Having received a more than amicable letter from Valentin, head of the Légion Française des Combattants (French legion of war veterans), which said: "Take courage! Relax! We will soon find you again in Nancy, liberated and purified,"[51] Pierre-Bloch decided to go to Vichy. In early 1941, we thus find him cheerfully eating lunch with Valentin in plain view in a large restaurant, in the company of his wife. Before entering the Resistance, he intervened on several occasions, putting to profit his knowledge of administrative milieus, to defend the interests of former foreign Jewish veterans who were refugees in the free zone; with that end in mind, he established contact with ministry directors.[52]

The most symbolic example of this intersecting of careers that were now reaching their end is without a doubt that of Jacques Helbronner, a close associate of Marshal Pétain himself: as military staff director to Minister of War Painlevé, Pétain supposedly favored his naming to the post of commander in chief of the army group of the Center in 1917. Their relations had remained so close that Helbronner was sometimes called "the marshal's Jew" by some of his coreligionists.[53] While numerous state Jews knew Pétain personally during their careers, Jacques Helbronner and Pierre Masse met him under the highly symbolic circumstances of World War I, one serving as minister of war, the other sitting on the Comité de Guerre (war committee) with Pétain himself: both would die in the deportation. And yet, even in 1941, Jacques Helbronner often had dinner with the head of state, who still considered him his "friend" and repeatedly told him so: Helbronner claimed he had met with the marshal twenty-seven times before July 1941.[54] In March 1941, when so many antisemitic measures had been issued and the violence against Jews, even dramatic arrests, were commonplace, he shared with the consistory the "great friendship" that Pétain still manifested for him. Pétain had even proposed that he take advantage of a derogation to avoid the sanctions of the Statut des Juifs. Helbronner "refused in a dignified manner, not wanting to be the only survivor among all his comrades on the Conseil d'Etat," but he continued to use eulogistic terms to describe the marshal and his policy: "likable old man, keen politician, dominating his government from far above, and so on." While this was going on, he even asked and obtained a vote on "a motion of confidence and fidelity" to the marshal![55]

President of the central consistory and former *vice-président de section* at the Conseil d'Etat, he was, like Isaïe Levaillant at the time of the Dreyfus affair, the very prototype of the state Jew who deployed all his efforts to defend the citizenship of French Jews, their legacy of emancipation: in his view, the consistory remained the sole competent organ of French Jewry in religious matters; and for the rest, the citizens of the Jewish religion could not constitute "a community distinct from the national community." The prophetic words of Count de Clermont-Tonnerre had to govern, still and forever, their destiny in a society of equal citizens. Yet Helbronner was confronted with the essential issue: Xavier Vallat, commissioner general for Jewish questions, now intended to impose the creation of an organization bringing together all Jews, whatever their nationality, into a structure endowed with legal prerogatives that applied to all, and that as such was responsible to Vichy, which would choose its leaders. That meant that French Jews would lose their distinction as French citizens in this group constituted by racial criteria: confused with their foreign coreligionists, they would be brutally distanced from their French fellow citizens. The Vichy policy was, from his point of view, true in every respect to the nationalist visions of Drumont, Barrès, and Maurras, for whom French Jews could not be part of the French nation, which founded its identity on Catholicism: putting an end to assimilationist dreams, they all the more harshly shattered the personalities of state Jews.

To symbolize the radical character of this upheaval, Xavier Vallat wanted the president of the consistory himself, the former *président de section* at the Conseil d'Etat, the man who alone could bring together the two dimensions emblematic of Franco-Judaism, to become the president of that new organization, which would regroup all Jews of various nationalities: in that way, its irreversible dimension would be gauged. Already excluded from the state by the Statut des Juifs, state Jews thus had to leave behind national politico-administrative structures and invest themselves in purely Jewish organizations, in the supposedly racial sense of the term, exercising their competence solely within that framework! When the texts creating the UGIF were promulgated by the government, Helbronner immediately made an effort to obtain the support of his former colleague on the Conseil d'Etat, André Lavagne, who headed Pétain's civil staff. In a letter to Helbronner, Lavagne declared he was "stupefied" by the plan.[56] A strange exchange of letters took place between them regarding the conformity of this new organization to administrative law: as good jurists, they agreed that it was indispensable to have the regularity of the law examined before the jurisdiction from which they both had come, the Conseil d'Etat, the supreme institution that would declare legality during that period when chaos was taking over everywhere! Certainly a respectable move, but one that seems to have been aborted.

These discussions, grounded in maintaining personal relations, continued until the publication of the second Statut des Juifs on 15 June 1941. On that date, Helbronner himself declared before the central consistory that he intended "out of his dignity and that of French Jewry as a whole to put an end to the relations he was undertaking with the forces in power," a decision that was unanimously approved. On 1 July, the man who had long maintained personal relations with both Marshal Pétain and his advisers, the man who, through his own professional education, had continually frequented that milieu, protested once more by again writing to the head of state. The time was past for compromise and the tone became less amenable. In its poignancy, this text stands as a real document of the history of state Jews.

You declared in proclamations that you made to the French people: "I hate lies, which have done you so much ill" and "I battle injustice wherever I find it."

Why must these noble words be so brutally belied by acts that constitute the worst of injustices founded on lies? . . .

The law does not target the Jews as Frenchmen or as foreigners, but, in servile imitation of the occupying authority, no longer knows or recognizes anything but a Jewish herd where nationality, even French nationality, is no longer more than an accessory without value or importance. French Jews . . . will try to suppress the all too natural feelings of contempt and hatred toward their foreign and French persecutors.

They will nevertheless conserve their faith in the destiny of eternal France, in order to obtain the just vengeance of the law that has today been violated.[57]

Jewish citizens, so proud of their citizenship, so in love with this Republic that had emancipated them, so passionate to defend its values, reached the end of a romance that was perhaps too idealized: with immense resentment, this *vice-président* of the Conseil d'Etat could only note that he was now being confused with foreign Jews in the same homogeneous "herd": French nationality, devotion to the state, and sacrifices on the battlefield suddenly lost all meaning. So many certainties reduced to nothing. Before such an injustice, even "the marshal's Jew" came to lose patience, to allow himself a minimum of irony, to engage in an acerbic de-nunciation of the head of state's "lies."

Nevertheless, once he had lost all shame, he still had to negotiate, save whatever he could, attempt still and again to avoid the irreparable blow, the constitution of this UGIF, which, following on the Statuts, would definitively separate French Jews from their fellow citizens. In December 1941, Jacques Helbronner, heir to state Jews, once more wrote to Marshal Pétain, a text that has remained famous among the rest:

The cruel and iniquitous regime that the occupying authorities have imposed on us for more than a year strikes more and more unjustly at so many Frenchmen of the Jewish religion that you will excuse me if I come today to address to the head of state, the father of the nation, and to him alone, a pathetic appeal on behalf of many unfortunate persons who have been deprived of their rights as citizens. . . .

Will these persecutions never end? . . . Do you not fear that in imposing on France legislation so contrary to its traditions and genius, our enemies have not in reality extended the humiliation of our nation by inflicting on us, after a military defeat, a true moral defeat?

You are, along with His Eminence, Cardinal Gerlier, in these desolate hours the sole comfort, the sole support I can find, and I ask you urgently to keep for yourself this cry from my anguished heart.

The *Journal Officiel* of 2 December 1941 published a law instituting a Union Générale des Israélites de France. . . . The central consistory judges that a commit-tee named exclusively by a representative of the government is not qualified to rep-resent the whole of the interests of the faithful Jews before public authority and that its members, in fact, are only the representatives of public authority in relation to associations of persons brought together by a kind of fictitious tie, racial and ethnic in character, of foreign inspiration, whose base is insupportable in the French spirit and legislation and in the current state of science. I permit myself to add that this law of 29 November contains expressions that are in formal contradiction with our public law. . . . It is deeply regrettable that such a law, which brings such important derogations to the principles of our legislation, has been promulgated without hav-ing been examined and discussed by the Conseil d'Etat, as I had the honor to very respectfully suggest to you more than a month ago.

Monsieur le Maréchal, I beg of you, stop this campaign of hatred; it is awful, it unjustly increases the sufferings of Frenchmen who are grieving with you over the misfortunes of the nation. These men believe in God, in his eternal justice. Against their persecutors, they confidently await the impartial and merciless judgment of History.

Believe, sir, in my faithful devotion and my persistent and respectful affection.[58]

Like those that preceded it, this text deserves to be cited almost in its en-tirety, for it illustrates so well the impasse at which Jews abruptly found themselves: Jews as a whole, but especially state Jews, whose values ori-ented toward public service were all belied as if by magic by the policy set in place by the very state they had served, apparently without any great pangs of conscience, by a staff of high officials almost always composed of former colleagues and often even of friends. As Helbronner expressed it, the UGIF was incompatible "with our public law," and the Conseil d'Etat would certainly judge so, were the matter to be laid before it. It was December 1941: certain state Jews had already gone to London and others had joined the Resistance; but Jacques Helbronner, like René Mayer and, for the moment, General Boris—the most reserved, the most hostile to the marshal, and who would resign from the central consistory in July 1942 because he found it pusillanimous—were still attached "as good Frenchmen of the Jewish religion" to the normal rules governing a state of law, that of the Third Republic. They could not conceive of the fact that they found themselves set apart from their fellow citizens and confused with a "herd" of foreign Jews in the name of a "foreign" conception of a racist or ethnic nature, which would link them to those other Jews in a "fictitious" manner. Jacques Helbronner forcefully denounced this plan, this "juridical monster," since it would quite simply create a "moral ghetto." [59]

That is the crucial point we need to end with, for it suddenly placed the feelings that state Jews had developed for their state in contradiction with those, imposed upon them, which linked them to foreign Jews. Suddenly, at a time when everything had seemed to be settled through state integration, everything was once more at stake, through this rending of ancient ties perpetrated by other public servants, their own colleagues from the good old days. These state Jews were always disposed toward accentuating their own integration into the nation to make their particularism disappear more and more from the public space: when all was lost, several of them even gravely discussed the indispensable effacement of Jewish-sounding names or regeneration by means of the return to the land! In November 1941, General Boris presented to the central consistory, in the name of "several of the most distinguished coreligionists," "the question of changing one's name as a mark of assimilation for old families." [60] Similarly, Georges Cahen-Salvador, *vice-président* of the Conseil d'Etat, ousted by the Statut des Juifs, came out against Jewish first names. [61] His colleague Paul Grunebaum-Ballin did the same and, in the same vein, drew the most extreme consequences regarding the secularization of the public space, calling for a process of full uniformization among citizens, who would never again be distinguished in any way in terms of particularist origins. In 1941 in fact, he proposed in an unpublished text to make the gallicization of foreigners' names obligatory at the time of their naturalization. To vanquish antisemitism entirely, one had only to make any external trace of membership in Judaism disappear, such as the family name and even, optionally, the first name. . . . [62]

Fiercely attached to deepening the process of integration in all its forms, the central consistory and the state Jews who held seats there even encouraged, during this period when so many threats were accumulating, "the return to the land and the professional reeducation of Jewish youth" within the framework of the "National Revolution." They even went so far as to vote in April 1941 for large sums to facilitate the realization of this plan. On 7 September 1941, General Boris proposed a move by the consistory before the minister of agriculture to favor "the installation of coreligionists as farmers"; in another declaration to the consistory, he admitted that the Jews were in part responsible for their present misfortunes, for some of them had headed political movements when they were not well enough represented in manual professions, agriculture in particular.[63] With passion, this decisive institution of French Jewry also called for keeping former Jewish war veterans in the Légion Française des Combattants, even proposing, again in 1941, that one of its members sit on the directing committee of that Vichyist paramilitary organization, which was manifesting a notorious antisemitism. Supported by General Boris and other members of the central consistory, that idea encountered the opposition of Georges Wormser and other persons who, however, remained in the minority.[64]

As we have seen, when the French state was no longer concealing its betrayal of Jews in general and of state Jews in particular, when it was imposing statutes that eliminated them from the public space and was preparing with determination the birth of a community structure uniting them with foreign Jews, which would make them lose even the benefits of their nationality, part of these state Jews were still struggling inch by inch to remain fully and solely French, by playing on the professional or social ties they had long maintained with the men now holding power. They nevertheless had to make heartrending decisions, for they were rapidly backed into a corner from which they could not escape: should they participate in the UGIF, as Xavier Vallat was urgently inviting them to do, and make definitive their distancing from the French community? If state Jews agreed to sit on that organization representative of all Jews, both French and foreign, this slow process of integration into the state, which we have attempted to retrace in this book, was all over. What a stunning victory for Drumont, what a triumph for Maurras, of which Xavier Vallat and Darquier de Pellepoix (who succeeded him at the head of the Commissariat Générale aux Questions Juives) were both great readers and convinced followers! If, in the name of their principles and their conceptions of the state, they refused, Vallat would have the power to name on the spot, in his own terms, other "rogues" to do this dishonorable work, to take in hand the fate of all Jews, who were threatened with deportation and death.

Consulted by Raymond-Raoul Lambert, a community leader selected by Xavier Vallat to head the UGIF, René Mayer, member of the central consistory and *conseiller d'Etat*, let his indignation erupt in the face of legislation

where French Jews are, through the application of racial principles entirely foreign to the genius of our country, treated by the government of the marshal exactly on the same footing as foreigners or stateless peoples. . . . Frenchmen and foreigners would be intermingled, without the text saying so directly. . . . Now all Jews are obligatorily grouped into one community of public law controlled by the state. . . . The fears inspired in me by a plan that makes no distinction between Frenchmen and foreigners, that may deprive our unfortunate coreligionists of American aid, and that include provisions I consider inapplicable, are such that I cannot imagine the eventuality of my designation to the council of the Association Générale, unless the law undergoes profound modifications.[65]

René Mayer and Jacques Helbronner, the two *conseillers d'Etat* from the central consistory, refused quite simply to participate in the UGIF. This is not the place to retrace the various discussions that took place at the consistory regarding this fundamental decision, concerning which each man went on the record.[66] What matters is to underscore the steadfast refusal on the part of state Jews, which was linked to the combative attitude of General Boris and Georges Wormser, Clemenceau's right-hand man, who both pronounced themselves in favor of a clearer strategy of noncollaboration with authorities they considered illegitimate. As a result, Vallat entrusted the fate of the UGIF to Raymond-Raoul Lambert, an important figure in Jewish milieus, the editor-in-chief of *L'Univers Israélite* between 1935 and 1939, who had frequented political circles, in particular under the Clemenceau and Herriot ministries. Even though he was well acquainted with high administration, he was not himself part of it: he was thus not truly a state Jew, and that was all the difference between him and Helbronner, Mayer, and Boris. The team he would surrounded himself with included no state Jews, with the exception—on the whole fairly insignificant—of *conseiller d'Etat* Pierre Seligman, who in fact held a seat there for only a brief time.

Very quickly, the relations between the consistory and the UGIF became tense, with Jacques Helbronner and his team obstinately refusing the hand offered by Lambert, and accusing him of overstepping his responsibilities. Lambert, on the contrary, continually pestered Helbronner, who according to him, was acting "like a Jesuit priest" and, betraying his deepest thoughts, made a terrible accusation: "The fate of foreigners does not in the slightest move" the president of the consistory, the former *président de section* of the Conseil d'Etat.[67] That is a crucial question, which took on all its significance with the refusal reiterated by French Jews to be confused within the UGIF with foreign Jews, a situation they wished absolutely to avoid, since it would have set them apart from their fellow citizens. The question is all the more tragic and terrible, since with the fall of Vichy, a striking inequality in the intolerable death count would appear: of 76,000 deportees, about 15,000 were French, and all the rest were immigrants. At the Liberation, 10 percent of French Jews and 40 percent of foreign Jews had been killed.

Did the central consistory and certain state Jews at its head attempt solely to defend French Jews, feeling that a tacit understanding could be reached in spite of everything with a government concerned to a certain extent with protecting only French citizens? Was the UGIF, on the contrary, at the forefront of the battle in defense of immigrant Jews, who were often poor and abandoned? The historians of our time do not accept such a presentation of the matter: the UGIF, led by French Jews, turned its priority toward the defense of French Jews without truly succeeding in limiting the deportation of foreign Jews.[68] For its part, the consistory devoted most of its efforts to avoiding any assimilation of French Jews, for which it wished to be the sole religious representative, to foreign Jews, which it had no authority to represent. In its view — this written proposition today makes us shudder because of its implications, unforeseeable at the time — foreign Jews were to be treated in the same way as all foreigners from their home countries. It is undeniable that this preoccupation, of an almost metaphysical nature, produced by the most distant history of state Jews, fools for love of the Republic, did not fail to appear, as we have already noted.

At the same time, Jacques Helbronner wrote to Laval in June 1942: "Will France then know the shame of being a land of pogroms? And will the principles of justice, of freedom of belief and religion, which have so long been the personification of its ideal, now go unrecognized with regard to French or foreign persons united only by religious ties?"[69] On 13 July, Helbronner and the chief rabbi of France again addressed Laval: "You are not unaware that numerous Jews, both French and foreign, are interned in the Drancy camp. More than fifty thousand unfortunate souls have already left this camp for the tragic fate of deportation. . . . We beg you to intervene with the occupation authorities."[70] On 29 July, after the massive round-ups of the sixteenth, which affected primarily foreign Jews, the central consistory once more turned to Laval:

The central consistory has been deeply distressed by the information reaching us from the occupied zone on the situation of French and foreign Jews. New restrictions, very grave and infamous, have been imposed on their freedom. . . . Considering that it is the primordial duty of any civilized state to safeguard the property, freedom, honor, and lives of its citizens and to protect the foreigners who regularly receive hospitality in its territory, the consistory addresses a renewed and even more solemn protest to the French government against persecutions whose scope and cruelty have reached a degree of barbarism that history has rarely equaled; entreats it to attempt again by any means to save thousands of innocent victims to whom no other reproach can be addressed than that of belonging to the Jewish religion.[71]

Finally, on 25 August:

The central consistory of the Jews of France, conscious of the duty of solidarity incumbent upon it, expresses to the head of government the indignation inspired in it by the decision taken by the French government to hand over to the German government thousands of foreigners of various nationalities but all of the Jewish religion, residing in the nonoccupied zone and who had taken refuge in France before the war, to flee the persecutions of which they were the victims. . . . French citizens that we are, we cannot look on without revolt when the French government, for the first time in history, deliberately violates the right to asylum, the respect for which, according to an age-old tradition, has always been considered a sacred principle in our country.[72]

In this case, the consistory took the defense of foreign Jews, recognized the reality of the religious ties that linked French and foreign Jews in this tragic fate, and called more and more urgently on the French authorities, which it made definitively responsible for the exactions being carried out. In the beginning, state Jews had considered these authorities innocent; the ties they had established with those holding authority in the state had inspired enormous confidence, which permitted them to accuse only German authorities. This was no longer the case, however, and this change could only have strong personal implications. Every day Jews had to face the obvious: it was, after all, the French police force that was primarily responsible for the arrests. In January 1943, Helbronner once more protested to Laval against "operations carried out in the city of Marseilles by French police authorities, during which thousands of French citizens of the Jewish religion, who were perfectly in order with all the laws of our country, were arrested"; in May, in a letter to Pétain, he denounced the measures taken in that city and in Avignon, Nîmes, and Carpentras, "unbeknownst to French authorities," against "French citizens and foreigners of the same denomination."[73] Shortly before his own arrest and deportation, in despair, this former *président de section* of the Conseil d'Etat turned, not to the head of state, Pétain, this time, but "to France and its government," entities that had become abstract, and invoked simply his "status as French citizen" to protest against "the tortures inflicted on its soil on unfortunate and defenseless individuals." "It is of the utmost importance," he added in one of his last texts, "that France and its government break ranks completely with these attacks on humanity." Seeing no way out, knowing for a fact the responsibility that lay in the hands of the highest authorities of that state, which had betrayed French Jews as a whole and was actively collaborating in the massacre of foreign Jews, he judged in spite of it all that it was indispensable to maintain this fiction that had in the past given meaning to the lives of all state Jews. As if this were a minor matter, the military staff director to Marshal Pétain responded immediately, very civilly: "The marshal charges me with telling you that he is going to ask the head of government to take urgent measures with the German authorities to try to obtain an improvement in the sad situation you indicate."[74] This "sad situation" was a lovely euphemism for what was the real prelude to the conscious massacre, the open season on Jews that from then on unfolded on national soil, with the active participation of the French police force under the direction of so many *préfets* and under the jurisdictional control of so many magistrates and members of the Conseil d'Etat!

The unlimited confidence of certain state Jews, among the most prestigious of the time, was not reciprocated in kind, despite the renewed marks of a flawless fidelity. It is true that some high officials who held seats on the consistory had declared themselves advocates of a rapid break with the legal, political, and administrative authorities: in June 1941, Lévy-Bruhl, professor at the Paris law faculty, asked during a meeting "whether it is compatible with our dignity as citizens to collaborate with M. Xavier Vallat, given the declaration he made to the press at the time of the Statut; even more, he asked whether, despite the respect that all French Jews felt for the marshal, we must continue to submit our complaints to him." In response, Jacques Helbronner, with the approval of General Boris at the time, invoked "the friendship" that attached him to the head of state and the necessity of "remaining at his disposal."[75] Needless to say, Boris would later recant and would not conceal his great distrust of Marshal Pétain in the following months; like Georges Wormser, he would propose successive measures to break with and distance himself from the institutions of a state that was so disloyal. On 26 October of the same year, Helbronner himself conceded that "the promises the government made to us have unfortunately not been kept, and our policy of collaboration with the marshal that I advocated must now be considered at an end."[76]

In reality, he could never resolve to take such a measure: until the very end, Jacques Helbronner — the man who at the time represented the final incarnation of Franco-Judaism, its most complete realization, the successful alliance of loyalties so long made compatible — could not, in his heart of hearts, resolve to make a complete break. He knew the duplicity of the French authorities; he guessed the complicity of the head of state; he noted every day Pétain's indifference to the suffering imposed by his own administration on French and foreign Jews. As a jurist, he could not, however, break with the legal order of France and engage Jewry in an attitude of civil disobedience, incite it to enter into clandestine activities, or even in the Resistance. Did his attachment to the state order and his old socioprofessional ties, which suggest such complicity and active solidarity in misfortune, finally play a role in the relative inertia of the consistory, its refusal to help the UGIF, its naïveté, blindness, or even indifference toward the fate awaiting foreign Jews? The love of the republican state, which had once turned toward Reason, was now illegitimately shifted to the authoritarian state the Republic had bestowed upon itself and was transformed into a misplaced devotion. It may bear some of the responsibility.

Yet these state Jews were not lacking in courage or force of character. Wounded in their very souls, they had the sheer nerve to publicly protest, to stand up as accusers desirous of personifying, throughout storms and neglect, the true identity of France. In the end, the same tragic fate awaited the leaders of the two great rival Jewish organizations. On 7 December 1943, Raymond-Raoul Lambert was deported to Auschwitz with his wife and four children, where they were all immediately gassed. Jacques Helbronner was arrested on 28 October 1943[77] when he once more went to Vichy to openly express his opposition to the measures of repression and deportation: this man of seventy years old was at once himself imprisoned, deported with his family to Auschwitz, and gassed. Immediately informed of this arrest, Marshal Pétain, Pierre Laval, and the *vice-président* of the Conseil d'Etat, did not flinch: in any case, Helbronner, the man of the political-administrative seraglio par excellence, was abandoned by his friends and peers. On 10 July 1947, Paul Ramadier, head of government, named him to the Order of the Nation:

M. Helbronner, *vice-président honoraire* of the Conseil d'Etat, colonel in the reserves, commander in the Legion of Honor, Croix de Guerre 1914–18, high official, struck down by the racial laws that removed him from the Conseil d'Etat when, after forty-three years of service, he was about to attain the highest posts of public service; proved during a lifetime devoted to the service of the nation, both as a magistrate and as a soldier, the most ardent patriotism and the purest courage. . . . Called in October 1940 to preside over the consistory of the Jews of France, defended and protected to the best of his abilities his persecuted companions and coreligionists.[78]

One cannot imagine a more beautiful epitaph for a state Jew.

Nevertheless, in wishing to preserve at all cost the gains reserved for French Jews, in singing the praises to the very end of the head of state, his actions inevitably raise many suspicions. Did the leaders of French Jews, considering coreligionists from beyond the national borders "brothers and strangers,"[79] truly attempt to preserve above all the Judaism that emerged from 1789, while taking little or no interest in the fate of immigrants from

Poland, Germany, Hungary, and elsewhere? The responsible parties both in the consistory and in the UGIF indisputably favored French Jews and were slow to engage in effective action on behalf of their foreign coreligionists. That matter does not seem open to dispute. No more, in fact, than the very great inequality in the death toll that, at the end of the war, appeared between these two worlds of Judaism present on national soil, which were very much strangers to each other. But, paradoxically, state Jews seem to have been on the front lines, and their fate often proved tragic: to have reached the heights of the state exposed them to the worst. While a large proportion of French Jews as a whole avoided deportation and death, this was apparently not the case for state Jews. The love of the Republic, the limitless devotion to the state, had exposed them. It was as if they were very specifically sacrificed as figures, now become unacceptable, of the Republic of olden days.

At the present time, it is almost impossible to give definitive statistics, for information remains fragmentary and is still classified by the administration. Let us nevertheless evoke a certain number of well-known cases. *Conseillers d'Etat* Jacques Helbronner and Pierre Lévy died in deportation, while their colleague Julien Reinach, imprisoned in Drancy and deported to Bergen Belsen, was liberated in 1945; Pierre Pontrémoli, also on the Conseil d'Etat, was killed as a Resistance fighter. After spending time in Drancy and Compiègne,[80] *député* Pierre Masse was deported to Auschwitz, where he died in October 1942; Georges Mandel, deported to Buchenwald, was released to the *milice*, which assassinated him in the forest of Fontainebleau; the deputy mayor of Le Havre, Léon Meyer, imprisoned in Drancy and deported to Teresienstadt, was liberated by the allies; Léon Blum, imprisoned, was deported to Buchenwald but returned to France alive; *député* André Wallach was sentenced to death by the Germans but avoided arrest. *Députés* Jean Pierre-Bloch, Salomon Grumbach, Max Hymans, and Charles Lussy played very active roles in the armed Resistance: Jean Pierre-Bloch was sentenced to death by Vichy, and Max Hymans was also sentenced to death by a Lyon tribunal; Pierre Mendès France was imprisoned, escaped, went to London, and engaged in the air war. So did the son of Julien Reinach, Fabrice Reinach, future alumnus of the École Nationale d'Administration and later member of the cabinet of Michel Debré when he was prime minister; Jules Moch participated in military resistance operations and then went to London. Among the Jews arrested and interned in August 1941 in camps from which few returned, we find, besides the philosopher Jean Wahl, *député* Théodore Valensi. Magistrates also figured among the first Jews to be imprisoned: in December 1941, Robert Dreyfus, *conseiller* to the Cour de Cassation, and Laemlé, *premier président de chambre*, were rounded up and taken to the camp in Compiègne.[81] Others were placed under house arrest, such as Paul Grunebaum-Ballin and Abraham Schrameck. Colonel Pierre Brisac formed a *maquis* in Grenoble and barely escaped the Gestapo, became deeply involved in clandestine activities as head of staff of the ORA (Organisation de la Resistance Armeé), and was made brigadier general in 1944.[82] This means that, under Vichy, almost all state Jews whose fate we know paid a high price for the savage repression that was beating down Jews in general. What about those who were members of the prefect civil service,[83] or other magistrates and other generals? The archives will tell us later. Let us nevertheless advance a hypothesis on this point: through an unexpected turnabout of history, under these circumstances when the state betrayed those who had placed themselves in its service with so much passion, it seems that those occupying preeminent politico-administrative positions almost inescapably provoked retaliatory measures at the level of their past glory; these measures struck even the heirs of the most ancient state Jews, since one of the sons of Théodore Reinach and several of the children of Doctor Émile Javal also disappeared at Auschwitz. . . .

Conclusion:
The Two Faces of the Republic

Were the Republic's fools truly foolish in the end? Was their absolute confidence in the promises of Marianne actually all that deluded? The contrast is truly immense between Gambetta's, Ferry's, and Clemenceau's commitments and Pétain's disavowals, accepted by most representatives of the nation and set in place by the vast majority of the state's high officials. If Vichy marked the end of the Republic, it nevertheless also constituted the realization of more or less perceptible exclusionist tendencies that, though internal to the administrative machine, also traversed the entire history of the Third Republic, even beyond the famous Franco-French wars. It was as if the republican state had two very distinct faces, concomitant and contradictory: that of a rationalist emancipatory regime, secular and open to all talents, and that of a politico-administrative power receptive to prejudices, turning its back on its own universalist values.

These two faces of the Republic were not equivalent, with one neutralizing the other. The progressivist, egalitarian, and secular side prevailed in a fundamental way over the intolerant side and, true to French exceptionalism, allowed the formation of this category of state Jews, of all these *préfets*, generals, magistrates, and politicians whose history, values, and way of life we have attempted to retrace here. If the intolerant side was manifested within the state, at times independently of the Franco-French wars that incited a radicalizing of attitudes, it was because the republican state was still under construction, because its norms remained fragile, uncertain, at times heeding the hatred being expressed without restraint in a society still attached in many ways, even late in the century, to prejudices or biases that had little respect for differences. The new nationalism was largely responsible for this, inciting social groups to construct an organic, dreamed-up French identity that was largely mythical: throughout the entire Third Republic, it was this nationalism that pushed for the rejection of the Republic, which was perceived as artificial and imposed by the supposed enemies of Catholicism, namely, Protestants and especially Jews. It was also nationalism that took as the privileged target of its demonstrations the republican state and, perhaps even more, the state Jews who claimed to serve it and to identify with it. We now better understand the origin of those innumerable mini-Dreyfus affairs that periodically erupted on the public scene or, on the contrary, remained in the silence of administrative dossiers. The patient analysis begun here sheds a different light both on the real nature of the state and on the external ideological context that weighs upon it.

From the Gambetta years to Vichy, nationalism "French-style," having emerged directly from Drumont's imagination, thus assimilated the Republic to state Jews, in order to better reject Jews even while beating down the despised Republic. Endowed with a real talent for propaganda, Drumont and his innumerable epigones, famous or unknown, attacked the most varied milieus throughout the whole country, even breaking down the sites of republican sociability; each time, in the most remote provinces, they raised the same cry, calling for the rejection of the Jews. In expressing itself with so much ill temper, this constant and violent delegitimation of state Jews unavoidably came to have repercussions, though in a more muffled manner, within the administrative machine: the unlikely and unexpected result was that the republican state itself sometimes let in prejudices and antipathies affecting the course of careers among Jewish high officials. Even outside the Franco-French wars, the professional lives of state Jews, whose superiors often took a dislike to them, were not always peaceful.

This nationalism, both extreme and banal, which carried with it a constant antisemitism, was also accompanied by a permanent feeling of social superiority, which reigned even inside certain *grands corps*, such as the Inspection des Finances, the Cour des Comptes, and the Quai d'Orsay; it led to the most aristocratic and closed recruitment policies, preventing in a lasting manner state Jews from being named to them and from making their careers there. Late in the interwar period, no unconverted state Jew had yet been assigned to one of these three *grands corps*: with a certain astonishment, we thus note that the Republic tolerated within its own administrative apparatus lapses that were properly intolerable, and of an implicitly antisemitic nature. The *Archives Israélites* continually thundered against this inexplicable injustice in a state that had long since adopted the meritocratic and secular republican ideology. In 1925, they once more denounced "the ostracism of the Cour des Comptes that rejected candidates for the *auditorat* for the sole reason that they were Jews." "After thirty years of an egalitarian, democratic Republic," they added, "there are two careers in France obstinately and irrevocably closed to an entire class of citizens who, as chance would have it, were born into the Jewish religion, namely, diplomacy and the Cour des Comptes. . . . To enter them, the status of Jew is a defect, a redhibitory vice." For its part, the Quai d'Orsay appeared as one "of the last fortresses of anti-Jewish prejudices in our administration."[1]

This hidden face of the Republic with its many dimensions should not make us forget the essential: the undeniable success that most state Jews knew despite the ostracism they might have encountered, the delays in their careers, or the difficulties in being assigned because of their cultural origin. Visible in the public space, they were not very numerous, but their presence awakened many fantasies and provocative exaggerations. For what reason, then, did these effaced and devoted high officials, these fundamentally republican politicians, all attached to the idea of implementing the ideals of Marianne, continually remain on the hot seat during the events, the flurry, of one or another Franco-French war? It was as if the republican state too often entrusted them with a role of unblocking certain sectors of society that had remained fearful and reserved with regard to rationalist values that could upset their mental universe. There is a long list of very controversial decisions, long considered scandalous, provocative, and compromising of Catholic identity, or more generally, incompatible with the logic of conservative thought, that were made in part by state Jews. Beginning with the different plans for separating Church and state, and leading to legislative texts upsetting family life (divorce, girls' education, and more recently, the legalization of abortion), and including measures that profoundly modified the social order (paid leaves, social security, and more recently, the abolition of capital punishment), in each case a state Jew was fully invested with the task of reform and, by the same token, found himself or herself thrown into the middle of debate and confrontation. It was as if the state willingly entrusted them with this thankless task of shaking things up even as it assumed the risk of focusing attention on them, cutting out a perfect role as scapegoats for them. This role was extremely useful, since it worked to turn social protest and violence away from the state. Like the king's fools in the past, perhaps?

In the end, did the Republic's fools adequately take stock of the unexpected effects of their devotion? In responding so enthusiastically to the liberating message of the fathers of the Republic, in expecting everything from the state, they certainly experienced exceptional glory, in spite of all the forms of internal resistance before such a new destiny. But as some of them played the most important roles, they literally attracted to themselves the most extreme anxiety and hatred. In taking such risks, were not these fools for the Republic a bit foolish themselves? In the tempest of the Dreyfus Affair, which almost carried them off, some who had become skeptical and bitter believed this was so: for example, Isaïe Levaillant maintained that the Jews of France saw in "the people of Paris a much more effective shield than they did in the steadfastness of the Chambers and the energy of the government."[2] Strangely enough, was not this same paradox repeated under Vichy at the time of their exclusion, with state Jews now finding protection not with the state but rather among simple citizens? It was as if, between the state, perverted at the time and unfaithful to its own values, and its now triumphant enemies from the deepest recesses of a society that was still somewhat intolerant, the people of France revealed themselves as the true depository for the republican norms that rescued Jews.

Appendix

Statistical Construction
of "State Jews"

A word of explanation is in order regarding the method I have followed. Beginning with the *Archives Israélites* and *L'Univers Israélite*, and supplemented for a certain period of time by the *Annuaire des Archives Israélites*, I have reconstituted the complete population of state Jews named under the Third Republic to the highest offices in the army (generals), the magistracy (*substitut, avocat général, procureur*, and *président de chambre* at the *cour d'appel* or the Cour de Cassation), the prefect civil service (*président de conseil de préfecture, sous-préfet, préfet*), and all those who entered the Conseil d'Etat or were elected *députés* or senators, sometimes even becoming ministers. I have not taken into account a few state Jews, *députés* or high officials, who ended their careers before 1870: for example, a magistrate under Napoleon III was not included in our population unless he obtained a high post under the Third Republic that integrated him into our sample. Conversely, a state Jew who obtained a high post only after World War II, even though he may very well have belonged to the interwar administration, does not normally figure in our population.

Even though they were considered Jews by these different sources within Jewish milieus, it remained indispensable to find more sociological evidence of that assertion. The systematic study of administrative dossiers where the notation "religion" explicitly figured nonetheless shows, with very rare exceptions, the quality of the sociological work done by the

Archives de l'Annuaire under the direction of Henri Prague. A few cases escaped him, however, and I was able to reconstitute them through these administrative dossiers, available at the Archives Nationales or the Services Historiques des Armées in Vincennes, where the religion of the wife, the family names and given names of fathers, mothers, mothers-in-law, and fathers-in-law, and their respective professions also appeared; very often, such information was also given concerning the respective grandfathers and grandmothers, but was more rare for the children. I came up with a total of 171 persons (it was thus not a sample), once double careers had been eliminated (the *préfets* who became *députés*, *députés* who become *conseillers d'Etat*, and so on), whose social origins, place of birth, type of marriage and sometimes dowry, type of education, profession, and finally career are known, with the career being, as for all the high officials, traced with great care by their superiors, who gave a careful account of the physical and moral qualities of their subordinates, commenting at length on their political opinions and their various social activities. Evaluations by superiors, letters of recommendation, and very many press clippings, and so on, also figure in these dossiers. Countless pieces of qualitative information could therefore be used, which has rarely been done in the contemporary work dealing with comparable elites. Let us also note that in certain chapters, I also compared dossiers from non-Jewish members of the prefect civil service systematically drawn from all the boxes where the dossiers of the 171 state Jews were found (see in particular Chapter 10).

To complete the information, archives on these same state Jews were analyzed at the *préfecture de police* in Paris, at the Assemblé Nationale, at the Conseil d'Etat, and at numerous provincial *préfectures* where these high officials were assigned. The dossiers from the departmental archives, owing to the numerous police reports and the press clippings they contained, proved to be extremely rich in information on the state of public opinion, the reactions of the local population when confronted with a Jewish official in authority, the various incidents and demonstrations taking place at the local level, linked, for example, to elections or to the implementation of various administrative decisions. I also consulted numerous archival dossiers evoking these local demonstrations at the Archives Nationales, as well as dossiers dealing with lawsuits against a few state Jews. I supplemented this information with an analysis of the very rich archives of the consistory and the Alliance Israélite Universelle, in order to better apprehend their roles in several community institutions. I also consulted family archives and conducted various interviews with state Jews who were part of our population; at times, I also attempted to question their closest descendants. In addition, I systematically read the greatest available number of books, articles, and even hand-written letters, for example, located in the

Bibliothèque Nationale and published by members of the politico-administrative staff. I also consulted the *Journal Officiel* in a consistent manner to follow the parliamentary debates in which they were involved. The platform statements were studied in Barodet and numerous biographical dictionaries were consulted. Certain newspapers, such as *La Libre Parole*, *Action Française*, and *La Croix*, were read in their entirety, year after year, for the entire period in question. The following statistics give details about state Jews.

TABLE I

Professional Origin of Députés *of the Third Republic (before 1914)*

Profession	N	Pct.
Administration		
High officials	0	
Magistrates	2	9.5%
Professors	0	
TOTAL	2	9.5%
Liberal professions		
Journalists	2	9.5%
Doctors	3	14.3
Lawyers	8	38.2
TOTAL	13	62.0%
Business		
Industrialists	2	9.5%
Tradespeople	2	9.5
Engineers	2	9.5
TOTAL	6	28.5%
GRAND TOTAL	21	100.0%

TABLE 2
Professional Origin of Députés *of the Third Republic (after 1914)*

Profession	N	Pct.
Administration		
High officials	2	6.4%
Magistrates	1	3.2
Professors	2	6.4
Other	1	3.2
TOTAL	6	19.2%
Liberal professions		
Journalists	7	22.7%
Magistrates	1	3.2
Lawyers	10	3.2
TOTAL	18	58.1%
Business		
Industrialists	5	16.3%
Tradespeople	1	3.2
Engineers	1	3.2
TOTAL	7	22.7
GRAND TOTAL	31	100.0%

TABLE 3
Geographical Origin of Députés *(1870–1940)*

	Before 1914		After 1914	
Region	N	Pct.	N	Pct.
East	4	19.0%	11	35.5%
Paris	9	42.8	10	35.2
Southeast	5	23.8	2	6.5
Abroad	2	9.5	2	6.5
Other	1	4.9	6	19.3
TOTAL	21	100.0%	31	100.0%

NOTE: East = Bas-Rhin, Haut-Rhin, Vosges, Haut-Saône, Meurthe-et-Moselle, Haut-Marne; Southeast = Gard, Drôme, Var, Bas-Rhône, Vaucluse; Paris = Paris, Seine, Seine-et-Oise.

TABLE 4

Professional Origin of Députés, *Senators, and Ministers from the Third Republic (before 1914)*

Profession	N	Pct.
Administration		
High officials	2	9.1%
Professors	0	0
TOTAL	2	9.1%
Liberal professions		
Journalists	2	9.1%
Doctors	3	13.6
Lawyers	9	40.9
TOTAL	14	63.6%
Business		
Industrialists/ tradespeople	4	18.2%
Engineers	2	9.1
TOTAL	6	27.3%
GRAND TOTAL	22	100.0%

TABLE 5

Professional Origin of Députés, *Senators, and Ministers from the Third Republic (after 1914)*

Profession	N	Pct.
Administration		
High officials	5	13.5%
Professors	2	5.4
Other	1	2.7
TOTAL	8	21.6%
Liberal professions		
Journalists	7	18.9%
Doctors	1	2.7
Lawyers	10	27.0
TOTAL	18	48.6%
Business		
Industrialists/ tradespeople	9	24.4%
Engineers	1	2.7
TOTAL	10	27.1%
No Profession	1	2.7
GRAND TOTAL	37	100.0

TABLE 6

Geographical Origin of Députés, *Senators, and Ministers (1870–1940)*

Region	Before 1914		After 1914	
	N	Pct.	N	Pct.
East	4	18.8%	12	32.4%
Paris	9	40.9	12	32.4
Southeast	6	27.3	3	8.1
Abroad	2	9.4	2	5.4
Other	1	3.6	8	21.7
TOTAL	22	100.0%	37	100.0%

NOTE: East = Bas-Rhin, Haut-Rhin, Vosges, Haut-Saône, Meurthe-et-Moselle, Haut-Marne; Southeast = Gard, Drôme, Var, Bas-Rhône, Vaucluse; Paris = Paris, Seine, Seine-et-Oise.

TABLE 7

Geographical Origin of Generals (1870–1940)

Region	N	Pct.
East	15	60%
Paris	4	16
Southeast	2	8
Southwest	1	4
Abroad	1	4
Other	2	8
TOTAL	25	100%

NOTE: East = Bas-Rhin, Haut-Rhin, Meurthe, Meurthe-et-Moselle, Doubs; Southeast = Vaucluse; Southwest = Pyrénées-Orientales.

TABLE 8

Social Origin of Generals (1870–1940)

Father's Profession	N	Pct.
Administration		
Military men[a]	2	8%
Teachers[b]	2	8
Eng. bridges/roads	2	8
Tax collectors	1	4
TOTAL	7	28%
Business	14	56%
Other[c]	1	4%
Unknown[d]	3	12%
GRAND TOTAL	25	100%

[a] Noncommissioned officers.
[b] Secondary school.
[c] Rabbi.
[d] Dossiers contain no indication of the father's profession.

TABLE 9

Geographical Origin of the Prefect Civil Service
(1870–1940)

Region	N	Pct.
East	10	23.8%
Paris	12	28.6
Southeast	6	14.2
Southwest	3	7.1
Abroad	3	7.1
Other	7	16.8
Unknown[a]	1	2.4
TOTAL	42	100.0%

NOTE: East = Bas-Rhin, Haut-Rhin, Meurthe, Meurthe-et-Moselle; Southeast = Gard, Bas-Rhône, Hérault, Vaucluse; Southwest = Gironde, Dordogne.
[a] Dossier contains no indication of birth place.

TABLE 10

Social Origin of the Prefect Civil Service (1870–1940)

Father's profession	N	Pct.
Administration		
Military men[a]	1	2.4%
Préfectorale	2	4.8
Teachers	1	2.4
TOTAL	4	9.6%
Business	27	64.3
Unknown[b]	11	26.1
GRAND TOTAL	42	100.0%

[a] Noncommissioned officers.
[b] Dossiers contain no indication of the father's profession.

TABLE II

Professional Origin of the Prefect Civil Service (1870–1940)

Profession	N	Pct.
Administration		
Military men[a]	1	2.4%
University instructors	1	2.4
Secondary school instructors	1	2.4
Other	2	4.8
TOTAL	5	12.0%
Liberal professions		
Lawyers	23	54.6%
Journalists	5	12.0
Engineers	1	2.4
TOTAL	29	69.0%
Business		
Tradespeople	3	7.1%
Other	1	2.4
TOTAL	4	9.5%
Unknown[b]	4	9.5%
GRAND TOTAL	42	100.0%

[a] Noncommissioned officer.
[b] Dossiers include no indication of previous profession.

TABLE 12

Educational Background of the Prefect Civil Service (1870–1940)

Degree	N	Pct.
Doctor of law	2	4.8%
Bachelor of law	24	57.1
Bachelor of art	1	2.4
High school diploma	4	9.5
No degree	5	12.0
Unknown[a]	6	14.2
TOTAL	42	100.0%

[a] Dossiers give no indication of university level.

TABLE 13

Geographical Origin of Magistrates (1870–1940)

Region	N	Pct.
East	15	44.1%
Paris	1	3.0
Southeast	12	35.3
Southwest	1	3.0
Abroad	1	3.0
Other	2	5.8
Unknown[a]	2	5.8
TOTAL	34	100.0%

NOTE: East = Bas-Rhin, Haut-Rhin, Meurthe, Meurthe-et-Moselle; Southeast = Bas-Rhône, Vaucluse, Aude, Drôme, Alpes-Maritimes; Southwest = Gironde; Other = Aisne, the colonies, Nord.
[a] Dossiers contain no indication of birthplace.

TABLE 14

Social Origin of Magistrates (1870–1940)

Father's profession	N	Pct.
Administration		
Military men[a]	1	2.9%
Magistrates[b]	3	8.8
TOTAL	4	11.7%
Business	24	70.7%
Other[c]	3	8.8%
Unknown[d]	3	8.8%
GRAND TOTAL	34	100.0%

[a] Noncommissioned officers.
[b] Two judges and one *avocat général*.
[c] Two chief rabbis and one engineer.
[d] Dossiers contain no indication of father's profession.

TABLE 15

Educational Background of Magistrates (1870–1940)

Degree	N	Pct.
Doctor of law	10	29.4%
Bachelor of law	20	58.8
Certificate of competency in law		
Unknown[a]	4	11.8
TOTAL	34	100.0%

[a] Dossiers give no indication of university level.

TABLE 16

Geographical Origin

Region	Political staff (N=54)	Prefect Civil Service (N=42)	Magistracy (N=34)	Military (N=25)	Conseil d'Etat (N=21)
East	29.1%	23.8%	44.1%	60.0%	4.8%
Paris	36.4	28.6	3.0	16.0	57.1
Southeast	16.4	14.2	35.3	8.0	14.3
Southwest	1.8	7.1	3.0	4.0	—
Abroad	3.6	7.1	3.0	4.0	4.8
Other	12.7	16.8	5.8	8.0	19.0
Unknown	—	2.4	5.8	—	—
TOTAL	100.0%	100.0%	100.0%	100.0%	100.0%

TABLE 17

Social Origin

Father's profession	Political staff (N=54)	Prefect Civil Service (N=42)	Magistracy (N=34)	Military (N=25)
Administration				
Military	3.8%	2.4%	2.9%	8.0%
Préfectorale	—	4.8	—	12.0
Magistracy	3.8	—	8.8	—
Primary/sec. education	1.8	2.4	—	8.0
TOTAL	9.4%	9.6%	11.7%	28.0%
Business	59.2%	64.3%	70.7%	56.0%
Other	1.8%	—	8.8%	4.0%
Unknown	29.6%	26.1%	8.8%	12.0%
GRAND TOTAL	100.0%	100.0%	100.0%	100.0%

TABLE 18

Educational Background

Degree	Political staff (N=54)	Prefecture (N=42)	Magistracy (N=34)	Conseil d'Etat (N=21)
Doctor of law/medicine	25.9%	4.8%	29.4%	14.2%
Engineering	9.2			
Bachelor of law	16.6	57.1	58.8	47.6
Bachelor of art		2.4	—	
Polytechnique	—	—	—	9.5
High school diploma	5.5	9.5	—	—
No diploma	5.5	12.0	—	—
Unknown	37.3	14.2	11.8	28.7
TOTAL	100.0%	100.0%	100.0%	100.0%

TABLE 19

Professional Origin

Profession	Political staff	Prefect Civil Service
Administration		
Grands Corps	5.4%	—
Magistracy	3.8	—
Military	—	2.4%
Higher education	3.8	2.4
Secondary education	—	2.4
Other	1.8	4.8
TOTAL	14.8%	12.0%
Liberal professions		
Journalism	12.8%	12.0%
Law	59.2	54.6
Medicine	7.6	—
Engineering	3.8	2.4
TOTAL	83.4%	69.0%
Business	—	9.5%
No profession	1.8%	—
Unknown	—	9.5%
GRAND TOTAL	100.0%	100.0%

Notes

Notes

Introduction

1. Maurice Lever, *Le sceptre et la marotte: Histoire des fous de cour* (Paris, 1983), chaps. 2 and 8.
2. On this distinction, see Pierre Birnbaum, *Antisemitism in France: A Political History from Léon Blum to the Present* (London, 1992), 15 *et seq.*
3. *Annuaire des Archives Israélites*, 1889–90.
4. In the Appendix, I discuss the problems of method linked to the construction of the population of state Jews analyzed in this work. I would like to thank Yves Deloye, whose infinite knowledge of the period under discussion has been precious to me on more than one occasion. He also agreed to read, with all the rigor characteristic of him, a large part of this text.

Chapter One

1. *Journal Officiel*, 30 Jan. 1891.
2. See Chap. 20.
3. Interview by the author with Fabrice Reinach, *vice-président* of the Paris *tribunal administratif*, June 1990.
4. Théodore Reinach, *Ce que nous sommes* (Paris, 1927).
5. *L'Univers Israélite*, 3 Mar. 1899.
6. See Corinne Casset, "Joseph Reinach avant l'Affaire Dreyfus: Un exemple de l'assimilation politique des Juifs de France au début de la IIIe République" (thesis for the École des Chartes, 1982).

7. Perrine Simon, *Contribution à l'étude de la bourgeoisie juive à Paris entre 1870 et 1914* (Paris, 1982), 58ff.

8. Julien Benda, *La jeunesse d'un clerc* (Paris, 1936), 43–44.

9. Joseph Reinach, *La vie politique de Léon Gambetta* (Paris, 1918), 305 and 310.

10. Joseph Reinach, *La foire boulangiste* (Paris, 1889), 67 and 253.

11. See Chap. 9.

12. Joseph Reinach, *Démagogues et socialistes* (Paris, 1896), 39.

13. Ibid., 4–29.

14. Joseph Reinach, *Les commentaires de Polybe* (Paris, 1919), 36 and 153.

15. Jean El Gammal, "Joseph Reinach et la République" (Ph.D. dissertation, Université Paris X-Nanterre, 1982), 1 : 152.

16. Ibid., 223.

17. See Chap. 17.

18. El Gammal, "Joseph Reinach et la République," 1 : 224.

19. Quoted by J. Reinach, in *La République Française*, 26 Nov. 1888.

20. *L'Intransigeant*, 30 Sept. 1887.

21. *La Libre Parole*, 2 Dec. 1892. See the Archives de la Préfecture de Police (hereafter cited as APP), BA 189.

22. See *La Diane*, 30 Nov. and 21 Dec. 1891. See also *Don Quichotte*, for example, 3 Nov. 1888.

23. *La Croix*, 13 Apr. 1888.

24. Ibid., 12 July 1899.

25. See, for example, *Le Pilori* of 25 May; 19, 26, and 27 Oct.; and 13 Sept. 1891.

26. See, for example, *La Croix*, 28 Apr. 1898.

27. See Pierre Pierrard, *Juifs et catholiques français* (Paris, 1970), 104ff. See also Stephen Wilson, *Ideology and Experience: Antisemitism in France at the Time of the Dreyfus Affair* (London, 1982), chap. 4.

28. *La Libre Parole*, 27 Jan. 1899.

29. Joseph Reinach, *Histoire de l'affaire Dreyfus* (Paris, 1904), 3 : 339ff. See Pierre Vidal-Naquet, *Les Juifs, la mémoire et le présent* (Paris, 1991), 2 : 129ff.

30. *Action Française*, 5 July 1908.

31. Léon Daudet, *L'Avant-guerre: études et documents sur l'espionnage juif-allemand en France depuis l'Affaire Dreyfus* (Paris, 1913), 308.

32. Cited in Casset, "Joseph Reinach avant l'Affaire Dreyfus," 278.

33. See André Chouraqui, *L'Alliance israélite universelle et la renaissance juive contemporaine* (Paris, 1965), 422.

34. *Archives Israélites*, 20 Dec. 1888.

35. *L'Univers Israélite*, 22 Apr. 1921.

36. E. Drumont, *La France juive* (Paris, 1886), 1 : 30. Leven was one of the leaders of the *Alliance Israélite Universelle*.

37. Léon Daudet, *L'Entre-deux-guerres* (Paris, 1932), 60. See also his article in *Action Française*, 8 July 1908.

38. Théodore Reinach, *Histoire des Israélites depuis l'époque de leur dispersion jusqu'à nos jours* (Paris, 1885), 7, 325–26, and 342–43.

39. Ibid., 385, 389, and 390.

40. Théodore Reinach, *Beauté et religion* (Paris).

41. Théodore Reinach, *Israël et le prosélytisme* (Paris, 1920), p. 30.

42. Théodore Reinach, speech given at the general assembly of the Société des Études Juives (society for Jewish studies), *Revue des Études Juives,* Apr. 1895, p. 6.

43. Théodore Reinach, "Le judaïsme prophétique," *Revue des Études Juives* 70 (1920):2.

44. Théodore Reinach, *Grande Encyclopédie* (Paris, 1894), s.v. "Juifs."

45. Théodore Reinach, "Actes," *Revue des Études Juives,* 15:132.

46. See Michael Marrus, *The Politics of Assimilation: A Study of the French Jewish Community at the Time of the Dreyfus Affair* (Oxford, 1971), 138ff., and Paula Hyman, *From Dreyfus to Vichy: The Remaking of French Jewry, 1906–1939* (New York, 1979).

47. On this theme, see, for example, Phyllis Cohen Albert, "Ethnicité et solidarité chez les juifs de France au XIXe siècle," *Pardès* 3 (1986): 34ff. The Reinachs' relation to Judaism and their networks of sociability will be analyzed in Chaps. 6 and 7.

Chapter Two

1. Departmental Archives (hereafter cited as AD) of Seine-Maritime, Box 1M371.

2. *Le Figaro,* 9 Feb. 1900.

3. *Le Temps,* 9 Feb. 1900.

4. *La Libre Parole,* 9 Feb. 1900.

5. APP, BA 1114.

6. *La Libre Parole,* 8 Apr. 1893.

7. Ibid., 24 July 1899.

8. Archives of the Conseil d'Etat, Hendlé dossier.

9. Archives Nationales (hereafter cited as AN), F1 B1 784, Henri Hendlé dossier.

10. Ibid.

11. Ibid., F1 B1 166 8, Lambert dossier.

12. Pierre Birnbaum, "L'entrée en République: Le personnel politique juif sous la Troisième République," in *Idéologies, partis politiques et groupes sociaux: Hommage à Georges Lavau,* ed. Y. Mény (Paris, 1989).

13. See Robert Eude, "Les préfets de la Seine-Inférieure," in *Bulletin de la Société libre d'émulation, Rouen* (Paris, 1945), 266o5.

14. *L'Union républicaine de Saône-et-Loire,* 30 May 1882. On Ernest Hendlé, see Charles Louis Foulon, "Les préfets de la République modérée, 1877–1898," in *Administration: Sept études pour servir à l'histoire du corps préfectoral* (Paris, 1986), 145.

15. AD of Seine-Maritime, Box 2M26.

16. See Bernard Le Clere, "La vie quotidienne des préfets au XIXe siècle," in *Les préfets en France, 1800–1940* (Geneva, 1978), 97.

17. Anatole France, *L'Orme du Mail* (Paris, 1986), 67.

18. Ibid., 31–35. See also Jean Levaillant, *Les aventures du scepticisme: Essai sur l'évolution intellectuelle d'Anatole France* (Paris, 1965).

19. Cited in Mona Ozouf, *La classe ininterrompue: Cahiers de la famille Sandre, enseignants, 1780–1960* (Paris, 1979), 264–65.

20. *La Libre Parole*, 20 Nov. 1897.

21. Ibid., 16 Aug. 1894.

22. AD of Seine-Maritime, 4 M 2710 and 4 M 2711.

23. Drumont, *La France juive*, 2:73.

24. *Le Temps*, 3 Sept. 1889. See APP, BA 1114.

25. Jean-Marie Mayeur, "Catholicisme intransigeant, catholicisme social, démocratie chrétienne," *Annales*, Mar.–Apr. 1972.

26. Fénélon Gibon, *Où mène l'école sans Dieu*, 4th ed. (Paris, 1925), 104.

27. *La Libre Parole*, 19 June 1906.

28. *La Vigie de Dieppe*, 6 Nov. 1882, AN, F 19 5657.

29. See Pierre Chevalier, *La séparation de l'église et de l'état* (Paris, 1931). The author underscores the role of E. Hendlé in the removal of crucifixes (380). In contrast, we might observe that his actions were marked by great prudence.

30. Drumont, *La France juive*, 2:419.

31. See the very full dossier in AN, F 17 2551.

32. Ibid., F 17 9125 (9).

33. Ibid., F 195657.

34. Ibid., F 12386.

35. Ibid., F 17 9125 (4).

36. See the doctoral thesis in political science by Yves Deloye, "La citoyenneté au miroir de l'école républicaine et de ses contestations: Politique et religion en France de 1870 à 1914" (Université Paris-I, 1991).

37. AN, F 17 9125.

38. Ibid.

39. *La Libre Parole*, 23 Mar. 1906. See also 15 Sept. 1898, 26 Feb. 1916, and 5 Jan. 1917.

40. See Birnbaum, *Antisemitism*.

41. AN, F1 B1 569, Albert Hendlé dossier.

42. Ibid., F1 B1 784, Henri Hendlé dossier.

43. See Marie-Christine Kessler, *Les Grands Corps de l'état* (Paris, 1986).

44. Pierre Birnbaum, *The Heights of Power* (Chicago, 1982); Christophe Charle, *Les élites de la République* (Paris, 1987).

45. AN, 79 AP, Cohn papers. See also Louis Ariste and Louis Braud, *Histoire populaire de Toulouse* (Toulouse, 1988), 793–97. One of the directors of the municipal library in Toulouse, Mme Lise Cohen, indicated to me the existence of local news reports in which prefect Cohn appeared.

46. AN, 79 AP, Cohn papers.

47. Ibid.

48. Ibid., F1 B1 321, Cohn dossier.

49. Ibid., F 17 12531.

50. Ibid.

51. Drumont, *La France juive*, 1:73.

52. *La Libre Parole*, 29 Sept. 1894.

53. Louis Lépine, *Mes souvenirs* (Paris, 1928), 44.

54. AN, 79 AP, Cohn papers.

55. See Chap. 7.

56. See Michael Graetz, *Les juifs en France au XIXe siècle* (Paris, 1989), 85–86, 139, and 145–47.

Chapter Three

1. Cour de Cassation, opening session, 16 Oct. 1899 (Paris, 1899).
2. Minutes of M. Bédarridès's inauguration as *procureur général impérial*, imperial court of Bastia (Bastia, 1862).
3. Cour de Cassation, opening session, 4 Nov. 1967. Speech given by M. Bédarridès, *avocat général*, Paris, 1867, Bibliothèque nationale (hereafter "BN") LF III 53, pp. 7–8.
4. Ibid., pp. 12, 40, and 58.
5. See M. Rousselet, *Histoire de la magistrature française, des origines à nos jours* (Paris), 1 : 354ff.
6. AN, BB 6 II 26, Bédarridès dossier.
7. See E. Appolis, "Les Israélites de l'Hérault de 1830 à 1870," in *Actes du 84e Congrès national des Sociétés savantes* (Paris, 1960). See also Pierre Burlats-Brun, "Filiations juives à Montpellier de la fin du XVIIe siècle au Second Empire," *Annales de Généalogie et d'Héraldique* 3 (July–Sept. 1985).
8. On the position of Abbé Grégoire regarding Jews' access to positions of authority, see Pierre Birnbaum, "Sur l'étatisation révolutionnaire: L'abbé Grégoire et le destin de l'identité juive," *Le Débat* 53 (Jan.–Feb. 1989).
9. AN, F 11038 and F 19 11048.
10. Archives of the Central Consistory, minutes, No. 61 E 6.
11. AN, F 11 038.
12. See Chouraqui, *L'Alliance israélite universelle*, 418. Drumont underscored his role in the *Alliance Israélite Universelle* in *La France juive*, 2 : 56.
13. AN, BB 6 II 26, Bédarridès dossier.
14. Ibid.
15. Ibid.
16. Ibid.
17. Ibid.
18. See Jean-Pierre Royer, *La société judiciaire depuis le XVIIIe siècle* (Paris, 1979) 280ff.
19. AN, BB 6 II 26, Bédarridès dossier.
20. Ibid.
21. AN, BB 6 II 619, Alphandéry dossier.
22. Ibid.
23. Ibid.
24. AN, BB II 619 (a different dossier with the same classification number).
25. Ibid.
26. *La Libre Parole*, 6 Mar. 1894.
27. AN, BB 6 II 613, Abram dossier.
28. AN, F 7 12926.
29. Ibid.
30. AN, BB 6 II 613, Abram dossier.

31. AN, BB 6 II 613 (a different dossier with the same classification number).
32. AN, BB 6 II 807, Delvaille dossier.
33. AN, BB 6 II 663, Berr dossier.
34. See Chouraqui, *L'Alliance israélite universelle*, 418.
35. AN, BB 6 II 922, Gros dossier.
36. See Rousselet, *Histoire de la magistrature française*, 1: 256ff.
37. Jean-Louis Debré, *La justice au XIXe siècle: Les magistrats* (Paris, 1981), 31.
38. Benjamin Martin, "The Courts, the Magistrature and Promotions in Third Republic France, 1871–1914," *American Historical Review*, Oct. 1982, 986–88.
39. Debré, *La justice au XIXe siècle*, 151.
40. See Chap. 17.
41. AN, BB 6 II 6, Anspach dossier.
42. AN, F 19 11039, Consistory Archives.
43. AN, F 19 11048. See also F 11 038, Consistory Archives. See also Archives of the Central Consistory, minutes, No. 61 E6.
44. Drumont, *La France juive*, 2: 495.
45. *Archives israélites* 20 (1859).
46. AN, BB 6 II 824, Dreyfus dossier.
47. AN, BB 6 II 438, Anspach dossier.
48. AN, BB 6 II 501, Félix dossier.

Chapter Four

1. See William Serman, *Le corps des officiers français sous la Deuxième République et le Second Empire* (Service de reproduction des thèses de Lille-III), 1: 558ff., 1: 634ff., and 1: 1095ff.
2. Service Historique des Armées of Vincennes (hereafter cited as SHA), GB, second series, 4041, Brisac dossier. Note that the man situated today at the farthest point of that long chain, joining the July Monarchy to the Fifth Republic, is General Michel Brisac, who, at the beginning of the 1990s, exercises his command in Strasbourg, the capital of Alsace.
3. Ibid.
4. Ibid., 95 652, Naquet dossier.
5. Ibid., GD, third series, 471, Valabrègue dossier.
6. Ibid., GD, third series, 582, Bloch dossier.
7. Ibid., GD, third series, 386, Naquet-Laroque dossier.
8. Ibid., GD, third series, 471, Valabrègue dossier.
9. Ibid., GD, third series, 582, Bloch dossier.
10. Ibid., administrative archives, 95 652, Naquet dossier.
11. *Le Jaune et le Rouge*, Mar. 1976.
12. We shall analyze examples later on that belie this statement. See Chap. 18.
13. See *La Libre Parole*, 23 May 1892. See also the issues of 26 and 29 May 1892.
14. Ibid., 9 Nov. 1894.
15. Ibid., 24 May 1892.
16. Ibid., 16 July 1903.
17. Ibid.; see also the issues of 1 Feb. 1905 and 20 Sept. 1907.

18. SHA, GD, third series, 582, Bloch dossier.
19. Interview by the author with General Michel Brisac, 1989.
20. See, on this point, Michael Marrus and Robert Paxton, *Vichy France and the Jews* (New York, 1983), 351.
21. See Chap. 20.
22. Archives of the Central Consistory, box 11.
23. AN, BB 6 II 453, Bloch dossier.
24. Archives of the Conseil d'Etat, Valabrègue dossier.
25. Archives of the Central Consistory, minutes, 1906–14.
26. AN, F 19 11046.
27. *L'Univers Israélite*, 1 May 1891.
28. Brisac interview, 1989.
29. Interview by the author with Michel Darmon, general engineer of armaments, 1990.
30. On the career of General Pierre Brisac, see *Le Jaune et le Rouge*, Mar. 1976, and the *Bulletin Trimestriel de l'Association des Amis de l'École Supérieure de Guerre*, first trimester, 1976.

Chapter Five

1. AN, BB 6 II 1144, Pontrémoli dossier. As a result, our study disputes the conclusion of Jonathan Helfand, who claims that the France of the nineteenth century experienced a high rate of conversions. "Passports and Piety: Apostasy in Nineteenth Century France," *Jewish History* (1988) : 3. On the contrary, we share the conclusions of Richard Cohen, "Conversion in Nineteenth Century France: Unusual or Common Practice," *Jewish History* (1991) : 2.
2. On the Foulds, see Frédéric Barbier, *Finance et politique: La dynastie des Fould, XVIIIᵉ–XXᵉ siècle* (Paris, 1991), 283.
3. SHA, GB, third series, 88, Abraham dossier; AN, BB 6 II 6, Anspach dossier; AN, BB 6 II 433, Welhof dossier; AN, F1 B1 166 8, Lambert dossier. We might also note that the father of Deputy Léopold Javal was named Jacob Javal; he gallicized "Jacob" to "Jacques."
4. *Archives Israélites*, 17 July 1889.
5. Ibid., 15 Feb. 1896.
6. *L'Univers Israélite*, 7 Nov. 1902.
7. AN, BB 6 II 1291, Weill dossier.
8. Cited by Brigitte Bergmann, *Paul Grunebaum-Ballin, un siècle au service de la République, 1871–1969* (Paris, 1988), 192–93.
9. Interview by the author with Jean Cahen-Salvador, *conseiller d'Etat*, Paris, 1989.
10. Private Archives of P. Grunebaum-Ballin (under the direction of Brigitte Bergmann).
11. Ibid.
12. For lack of more complete information, it has not been possible to calculate this rate for members of the Conseil d'Etat.
13. It seems that, in the milieu of high officials, the incidence of the abandon-

ment of Jewish given names (first or middle) and of exogamic marriages was clearly lower than in the Jewish bourgeoisie of the better residential areas in general. See Doris Ben Simon-Donath, *Socio-démographie des juifs de France et d'Algérie* (Paris, 1976), 265–69.

14. *Archives Israélites*, 2 Mar. 1905. See also *L'Univers Israélite*, 3 Mar. 1905.

15. On the funeral of Baron Alphonse de Rothschild, see *L'Univers Israélite*, 2 June 1905, and *Archives Israélites*, 1 June 1905. By way of comparison, read the account of the funeral of Achille Fould in 1867 in Frédéric Barbier, *Finance et politique*, 284–85.

16. AN, F1 B1 526, Levaillant.

17. Henry Torrès, *Souvenir, souvenir: Que me veux-tu?* (Paris, 1964), 13. See also, Archives of the Assemblé Nationale, Torrès dossier.

18. AN, F1 B1 166 32, Levylier dossier. Another member of the family, Léon Levylier, became judge at the Seine tribunal. AN, BB 6 II 1024, Levylier dossier.

19. *La Loire Républicaine*, 20 Nov. 1890, AN, F1 B1 526, Levaillant.

20. See the Anspach dossier in AN, BB 6 II 6. See also *Archives Israélites* 20 (1859): 190 and 371–72. On this marriage, see also Graetz, *Les juifs en France au XIXᵉ siècle*, 138.

21. *Archives Israélites*, 36 (1875): 747–48.

22. Ibid., Feb. 1911.

23. *L'Univers Israélite*, 15 Jan. 1915.

24. *Archives Israélites*, 15 Mar. 1896.

25. Ibid., 14 (1884): 18.

26. Cahen-Salvador interview, 1989.

27. *L'Univers Israélite*, 10 Oct. 1902.

28. *Archives Israélites*, 17 Mar. 1904.

29. Ibid., 15 Mar. 1896.

30. Ibid., 61 (1900): 473–74.

31. Zadoc-Kahn, *Souvenirs et regrets, 1868–1898* (Paris, 1989), 38–39.

32. Zadoc-Kahn, *Souvenirs et regrets* 33 (1872): 235–37.

33. Ibid., 52 : 126. On the 1838 marriage of Léopold Javal to Augusta de Laemel, a descendant of Austrian Jewish bankers, see Emmanuel Chadeau, *L'Economie du risque: Les entrepreneurs, 1850–1980* (Paris, 1988), 244.

34. *Archives Israélites*, 57 : 349–50. See also *L'Univers Israélite*, 23 Oct. 1896.

35. *Archives Israélites*, 17 : 166.

36. Zadoc-Kahn, *Souvenirs et regrets*, 201–3.

37. *L'Univers Israélite*, 19 Mar. 1897.

38. *Archives Israélites*, 2 Feb. 1899. On the funeral of Seligmann, *président* of the *chambre civile*, see *Le Temps*, 17 Oct. 1928.

39. On the funeral of Théodore Reinach, see *Le Rayon*, Nov. 1928.

40. The funerals of Adolphe Crémieux, Eugène Lisbonne, and David Raynal, considered to be Gambetta's faithful, are described at length in Chap. 13.

41. *L'Univers Israélite*, 16 Feb. 1891.

42. Georges Wormser, *Georges Mandel: L'homme politique* (Paris, 1967), 16.

43. Interview by the author with *député* Jean Pierre-Bloch, Paris, 1991.

44. *Archives Israélites* 86(29 Jan. 1925): 17. On his career, see the Archives of the

Conseil d'Etat, Bloch dossier, and Emmanuel Chadeau, *Les Inspecteurs des finances au XIXe siècle, 1850–1914* (Paris, 1986), 109. Emmanuel Chadeau and Nathalie Carré de Malberg were kind enough to supply me with this information.

45. Archives of the Assemblée Nationale, Wallach dossier.

Chapter Six

1. Archives of the Central Consistory, minutes, 1905.

2. Certain authors consider the consistory "an appendix of the State." See Eric Smilévitch, "Halakha et Code civil: Questions sur le grand sanhédrin de Napoléon," in *Pardès* 3 (1986). In contrast, we might maintain here that the presence of state Jews within the consistory assured that it had the competence of an administrative staff that was also profoundly religious.

3. See Raymond Lazard, *Michel Goudchaux, son oeuvre et sa vie politique* (Paris, 1907). See also Archives of the Alliance Israélite Universelle (hereafter cited as AIU), Halff collection, MS 586, Goudchaux dossier.

4. Archives of the Central Consistory, minutes, 1906–14.

5. *L'Univers Israélite*, 27 Oct. 1910.

6. Archives of the Central Consistory, minutes, 1906–14.

7. Ibid., nos. 6 1 E 6. The deliberations of the consistories, during which state Jews also intervened, can be found in a wonderful archival collection dealing with the period prior to the passing of laws imposing the separation of Church and state. AN, F 11038, 11029, 11040. The elections of Crémieux, Anspach, Bédarridès, and Camille Lyon, among others, are also documented here. At times, we even find ballots bearing their names. On the consistories for the period prior to the Third Republic, see Phyllis Cohen Albert, *The Modernization of French Jewry: Consistory and Community in the Nineteenth Century* (Hanover, N.H., 1977). The role of Anspach is analyzed there on pages 82–86 and 167–68.

8. See Chap. 20.

9. Archives of the AIU, France, VA 35.

10. *L'Univers Israélite*, 15 Nov. 1896, p. 165. Isaïe Levaillant harshly condemned such an attitude in his role of editor-in-chief of *L'Univers Israélite*, 14 Feb. 1897.

11. See Chouraqui, *L'Alliance israélite universelle*, 417–23. At the death of Léopold Javal, the *Archives Israélites* expressed its regret at the passing of the man who "so honored French Jewry." *Archives Israélites* 33 (1872): 235.

12. On the role of Crémieux as head of the *Alliance*, see S. Posener, *Adolphe Crémieux, 1796–1880* (Paris), 2:146, and Daniel Amson, *Adolphe Crémieux: L'oublié de la gloire* (Paris, 1988), 309ff. On Crémieux, see Chap. 13.

13. *Bulletin Mensuel de l'Alliance Israélite Universelle*, Dec. 1911.

14. Archives of the AIU, France VIII, A 62. For former prefect Eugène Sée, "the *Alliance*, for the benefit of Judaism as a whole, without distinction for religious doctrines or nationalities, has realized its grandiose work so appreciated in the Jewish world. It must remain in Paris, in that center of liberty and progress." *Bulletin de l'Alliance Israélite Universelle*, 17 Dec. 1911.

15. *L'Univers Israélite*, 10 Oct. 1902.

16. Archives of the AIU, Halff collection, MS 586, Geismar dossier. Let us also

note that General Rheims was vice president of the Israelite Loan Office. *L'Univers Israélite*, 24 Jan. 1936.

17. Archives of the Central Consistory, minutes, no. 5.

18. Cited in *L'Univers Israélite*, 15 Jan. 1915. On Camille Lyon, see the Archives of the Council of State, Lyon dossier.

19. *Archives Israélites*, 23 Feb. 1926.

20. Ibid., 2 Feb. 1899.

21. *L'Univers Israélite*, 19 Mar. 1897.

22. Ibid., 18 June 1920.

23. AN, BB 6 II 1305.

24. *Le Monde*, 4 Oct. 1988.

25. Archives of the AIU, France, III A. 11. The various elections to the central committee of the *Alliance* can be followed in the *Bulletin Mensuel de l'Alliance Israélite Universelle*. For example, in March 1902, June 1905, and June 1911, the election or reelection of Isaïe Levaillant, Charles Berr, and Camille Lyon came about all at once.

26. Archives of the AIU, France, IV, A 23.

27. Ibid., France, VIII, A 60.

28. AN, BB 6 II 462, Cahen dossier.

29. Ibid., BB 6 II 1024, Levy dossier.

30. Ibid., BB 6 II 284, Marx dossier.

31. Ibid., F1 B1 166 32, Levylier dossier.

32. *L'Univers Israélite*, 18 July 1875. On Albert Cohn, see the thick dossier in the Archives of the AIU, France, III A 16.

33. Isidore Loeb, *Biographie d'Albert Cohn* (Paris, 1878).

34. That was the case, for example, for subprefect Daniel Weibel, whose father was pastor of Chauray. AN, F1 B1 391. Similarly, the father of Deputy Théodore Steeg was none other than Pastor Jules Steeg.

35. SHA, GB, fourth series, 124.

36. Ibid., GB, third series, 1831.

37. See *L'Univers Israélite*, 1 July 1889, and the article "Nos parlementaires: Leurs accointances synagoges," *Archives Israélites*, 12 June 1920.

38. SHA, GD, third series, 46, Hinstin dossier.

39. Ibid., administrative archives, 95 652, Naquet dossier.

40. Ibid., Colonel Moch dossier.

41. *Archives Israélites*, 6 Sept. 1886. See also, on Naquet and antisemitism, *Archives Israélites*, 22 Mar. 1888.

42. Alfred Naquet, *Temps futurs. Socialisme. Anarchie* (Paris, 1900), 1.

43. See Chap. 14.

44. Naquet, *Temps futurs*, 61–63.

45. See Chap. 9, where we shall take up the incidents of the Banquet of Tours. During that important Boulangist meeting, antisemitic allusions were proffered against Naquet, who was one of the essential leaders of that movement (AN, F 7 12447). On the local level, see for example AD of Vaucluse, 1 n. 309.

46. See Alfred Naquet, *Varia*, BN Lb 57 14019, vol. 1.

47. Alfred Naquet, *L'Éclair*, 7 July 1892, in *Varia*, vol. 4.

48. *Archives Israélites*, 6 June 1895.

49. Chamber of Deputies, session of 27 May 1895.

50. *L'Univers Israélite*, 1 Dec. 1889.

51. AD of Vaucluse, 1 J 32.

52. In its issue of 21 July 1894, *L'Univers Israélite* recounted with amusement the following incident: "If Camille Dreyfus has little faith in his heart, at least he has — or had — a great deal of wine in his cellar. Scoundrels have just ransacked it. . . . Unable to complain to the good Lord, whom he does not know, M. Dreyfus explained his case to the commissioner of Saint-Thomas-d'Aquin."

53. *L'Univers Israélite*, 15 Nov. 1894.

54. Ibid., 15 Nov. 1894.

55. *La République du Gard*, 30 Nov. 1928.

56. *L'Univers Israélite*, 16 Apr. and 1 July 1889.

57. On this exchange, see the *Archives Israélites* 45 (1884). We also find in the personal papers of Ferdinand Dreyfus a very curious sketch for a cantata entitled *David and Goliath*, with main characters "David, tenor, Goliath, bass, and Naomi, the mother of David, soprano." AN, 346 AP/8, Dreyfus papers.

58. *L'Univers Israélite*, 4 Apr. 1902.

59. Ibid., 6 Aug. 1897.

60. Ibid., 30 Apr. 1897.

61. Ibid., 5 Dec. 1902.

62. Jules Moch, *Une si longue vie* (Paris, 1976), 23.

63. *L'Univers Israélite*, 25 May 1906.

64. Isaïe Levaillant, *La genèse de l'antisémitisme sous la Troisième République* (Paris, 1907), 25–26.

65. Jean Pierre-Bloch, *Jusqu'au dernier jour* (Paris, 1983), 24ff. and 254ff.

66. *L'Univers Israélite*, 15 July 1927.

67. *Le Réveil Juif*, 5 Aug. 1925.

68. *L'Univers Israélite*, 7 and 14 Apr. 1933.

69. See the various documents contained in the archives of the Center for Documentation and Vigilance, Alliance Israélite Universelle, dossiers 31 to 57.

70. See Simon Epstein, "Les institutions israélites françaises de 1929 à 1939: Solidarité juive et lutte contre l'antisémitisme" (doctoral thesis, Université de Paris-I, 1990), 154ff. and 168ff.

71. Simon Epstein also links these identical actions, without however underscoring the fact that a large portion of the Jews who leapt into action belonged to the state. See Epstein, "Les institutions israélites françaises," 242.

72. *Archives Israélites*, 8 Mar. 1900 and 10 May 1928.

73. Ibid., 8 Apr. 1898.

74. On the habitual anti-Zionism of French Jews in general, see Catherine Nicault, "La France et le sionisme: 1896–1914" (thesis of the Université Paris-I, 1985), and, by the same author, "La réceptivité au sionisme, de la fin du XIXe siècle à l'aube de la Seconde Guerre mondiale," in Pierre Birnbaum, *Histoire politique des juifs de France* (Paris, 1990).

75. Théodore Reinach, "Le judaïsme français et le sionisme," *Paix et Droit*, Feb. 1927.

76. These articles and the polemic as a whole are analyzed in Michel Abitbol, *Les Deux Terres promises* (Paris, 1989), 126ff.

77. Joseph Reinach, "Sur le sionisme," n.d., BN A 18364.

78. Naquet, *Temps futurs*, 59–60.

79. Alfred Naquet, speech given at the protest banquet of the great Jewish fast of Yom Kippur, 1 Oct. 1903, in *Temps futurs*, 59–60.

80. *L'Univers Israélite*, 3 Sept. 1897.

81. Ibid., 14 Mar. 1902.

82. Ibid., 31 Jan. 1902.

83. Georges Wormser, *Français israélites* (Paris), 164–65; André Wormser, "Comment la France ratifia la déclaration Balfour," *Tribune Juive*, 29 Jan. 1988.

84. André Spire, *Souvenirs à bâtons rompus* (Paris, 1961), 106.

85. *La Terre retrouvée*, Mar. 1930.

86. *La Tribune Juive Strasbourg-Paris*, 9 Dec. 1938.

87. Léon Blum, "Le drame de l'*Exodus*," in *L'Oeuvre de Léon Blum 1947–1950* (Paris, 1958), 391–92.

88. On Blum and Zionism, see Birnbaum, *Antisemitism*, 52 *et seq.*

89. *La Terre Retrouvée*, 25 Jan. 1930.

90. On the role of General Geismar and ex-Councillor of State André Spire in the Zionist movements, see Abitbol, *Les Deux Terres promises*, 150ff.

91. *L'Univers Israélite*, 19 Nov. 1937. Jean Pierre-Bloch recounts his travels in Israel beginning in 1957 in *Jusqu'au dernier jour*, 257ff.

92. Moch, *Une si longue vie*, 252.

93. Jules Moch, *Confrontations* (Paris, 1952), 262.

94. Pierre-Bloch interview, 1991.

Chapter Seven

1. See, for example, Christophe Charle, *Les hauts fonctionnaires en France au XIXe siècle* (Paris, 1980).

2. Here, we are comparing our own data, which can be found arranged into tables in the appendix, with all those that were presented systematically in the book by Christophe Charle, *Les élites de la République*. See in particular the very complete tables regrouping all the available data on the period, pp. 50, 58, 66–67, and uniting all the results also proposed by other earlier surveys of the prefectoral corps, magistrates, and so on, pp. 74 and 85. Let us note, however, that here again the religious variable was not used to compare the different elites. As a general comparative base, one may also consult Mattei Dogan, "Les filières de la carrière politique en France," *Revue Française de Sociologie* 8 (1967), and "How to Become a Cabinet Minister in France: Career Pathways 1870–1978," *Comparative Politics*, Oct. 1979. In Dogan, however, this variable is rarely discriminatory. See also Jean Estèbe, *Les ministres de la République, 1871–1914* (Paris, 1982); William Serman, *Le corps des officiers français* and *Les officiers français dans la nation, 1848–1914* (Paris, 1982); Jeanne Siwek-Pouydesseau, *Le corps préfectoral sous la Troisième et Quatrième République* (Paris, 1969); Vincent Wright, "La réorganisation du Conseil d'état en 1872" (Paris: Conseil d'État, *études et documents*, 1973); Jean-Pierre Royer, Renée Martinage, and Pierre

Lecocq, *Juges et notables au XIXᵉ siècle* (Paris, 1982). See also Roger Berg, "Les juifs dans l'espace politique français," *Pardès* (1991), 14.

3. AN, BB 6 II 392, Seligmann dossier; AN, BB 6 II 1221, Seligmann dossier; AN, BB 6 II 453, Bloch dossiers; Archives of the Council of State, Cahen-Salvador, Laroque, and Weil dossiers; AN, F II B 1 599, Caen dossier; Archives of the National Assembly, Masse dossier; AN, F1 B II 160, 13, Franck dossier; AN, BB 6 II 658, Berr dossier; SHA, GB, third series, 1081, Francfort dossier; F1 B1 784, Heumann dossier; SHA, GD, third series, 582, Bloch dossier; SHA, GD, third series, 692, Heymann dossier. On the recruitment by the École Polytechnique during that period, see William Serman, *Le corps des officiers français*, 1 : 662.

4. AN, BB 6 II 26, Bédarridès dossier; AN, BB 6 II 619, Alphandéry dossier; AN, BB 6 II 1024, Levylier dossier; AN, BB 6 II 619; AN, F1 B1 384, Simon dossier.

5. Chadeau, *L'économie du risque*, 237.

6. AN, F1 B1 523, Sée dossier; AN, BB 6 II 964, Katz dossier.

7. AN, F1 B1 673, Schrameck dossier; AN, F1 B1 358, Levaillant dossier; AN, BB 6 II 305, Job dossier; AN, F1 B1 170 16, Pinède dossier; AN, F1 B1 507, Mossé dossier; AN, F1 B1 297, Aron dossier; AN, BB 6 II 663, Berr dossier. Let us also note that the father of Judge Édouard Bloch, whose son Alphonse was also a judge, was a banker named Moïse. See AN, BB 6 II 453, Bloch dossier.

8. SHA, GD, third series, 386, Naquet-Laroque dossier; SHA, GD, third series, 4571, Valabrègue dossier; SHA, GD, third series, 1081, Francfort; SHA, administrative archives, 95652, Naquet dossier; SHA, GD, third series, 1831, Carvallo dossier. In all, these sums were quite comparable to the dowries received by a number of senior officers. See Serman, *Le corps des officiers français*, 2 : 1664–69.

9. AN, F1 B1 449, Cahen dossier; AN, F1 B1 439, Beaucaire dossier.

10. AN, BB 6 II 619, Alphandéry dossier; AN, BB 6 II 392, Seligmann dossier; AN, BB 6 II 964, Katz dossier.

11. AN, F1 B1 166 26, Léon dossier.

12. AN, BB 6 II 284, Marx dossier.

13. AN, BB 6 II 1024, Levy dossier.

14. AN, F1 B1 526, Torrès dossier. On the origins of Pierre Mendès France in the Southwest, see Birnbaum, *Antisemitism*, chap. 2.

15. AN, BB 6 II 663, Berr dossier.

16. AN, BB 6 II 922, Gros dossier.

17. AN, BB 6 453, Bloch dossier.

18. AN, F1 B1 646, Levi dossier.

19. AN, BB 6 II 613, Abram dossier.

20. AN, F1 B1 581, Aron dossier.

21. AN, F1 B1 608, Crémieux dossier.

22. AN, BB 6 II 419, Valabrègue dossier.

23. AN, F1 B1 528, Valabrègue dossier.

24. AN, F1 B1 297, Aron dossier.

25. AN, BB 6 II 1095, Naquet dossier.

26. AN, BB 6 II 613, Abram dossier. In the same way, Eliacin Naquet also intervened in favor of Judge Édouard Welhof, born in Lorraine but holding a post in Aix at the time, since "he performs his duties with such devotion, zeal, and

conscience that he has attracted the respect and sympathy of all his colleagues." AN, BB 6 I 433, Welhof dossier.

27. AN, F1 B1 305, Berr dossier.

28. See the very rich dossiers of still-unpublished correspondence, AN, Cohn Papiers, 79 AP 1 and 2. See also AN, F1 B1 321, Cohn dossier.

29. AN, BB 6 II 789, Dalmbert dossier.

30. AN, F1 B1 501, Félix dossier.

31. AN, F1 B1 166 26, Léon dossier.

32. AN, F1 B1 749, Dadoun dossier.

33. AN, Dreyfus Papers, 346 AP 7. On Ferdinand Dreyfus's circle of friends, see also Simon, *Contribution à l'étude de la bourgeoisie intellectuelle juive*, 56.

34. This dossier was unique in this respect because of the numerous letters from the chief rabbi of Bordeaux it contained. AN, BB 6 II 1024.

35. AN, F1 B1 350, Kahn dossier.

36. AN, BB 6 II 453, Bloch dossier.

37. AN, F1 B1 449, Cahen dossier.

38. AN, F1 B1 305, Berr dossier.

39. *Archives Israélites*, 3 Apr. 1924. See also the issue of 10 May 1928.

40. Ibid., 15 Sept. 1919.

41. Ibid., 15 May 1924.

42. As the *Archives Israélites* put it, "In general, the *députés* born into Judaism care very little about taking in hand the cause of their coreligionists. . . . There seems to be no need for Jewish representatives in Parliament. In their absence, and on the occasions when an intervention in favor of our rights imposes itself, it often has better chances of succeeding if it emanates from deputies who do not belong to our religion" (14 Mar. 1912).

43. AN, F1 B258, Levaillant dossier; AN, F1 B1 530, Weill dossier; AN, F1 B1 490, Kinsbourg dossier; AN, F1 B1 170, Pinède dossier; AN, BB 6 II 594, Sée dossier.

44. AN, BB 6 II 824, Dreyfus dossier.

Chapter Eight

1. *Archives Israélites*, 16 May 1889.

2. AD of Gironde, 1 M 721, police report.

3. *L'Univers Israélite*, 16 May 1889.

4. *Archives Israélites*, 23 May 1899.

5. *L'Univers Israélite*, 16 May 1889.

6. *La Nation*, 6 May 1889.

7. Ibid., 4 Aug. 1889.

8. *Journal officiel*, session of 10 Mar. 1892.

9. Ibid., 30 Jan. 1891.

10. *Archives Israélites*, 12 Feb. 1891.

11. J. Reinach, *Démagogues et socialistes*, 11.

12. Joseph Reinach, *Essais de politique et d'histoire* (Paris, 1899), 364.

13. Chambre des Députés, session of 29 Oct. 1891, 157.

14. APP, BA 1055, Camille Dreyfus dossier.

15. *Archives Israélites*, 5 Nov. 1891.

16. Ibid., 20 Dec. 1888.

17. Ibid., 5 Apr. 1888, and *L'Univers Israélite*, 16 Apr. 1888.

18. J. Ferry collection, B.M., Saint-Dié, box 18.

19. Émile Poulat, *Liberté, laïcité: La guerre des deux France et le principe de la modernité* (Paris, 1987), 208ff.

20. Cited by Louis Capéran, *L'Invasion laïque* (Paris, 1935), 324–25.

21. Jules Ferry, speech on the law regarding primary education, 23 Dec. 1880. Reproduced in *Discours et opinions de Jules Ferry* (Paris, 1896), 4:127. See Jean-Marie Mayeur, "Laïcité et idée laïque au début de la Troisième République," in *Les Opportunistes: Les débuts de la République aux républicains*, ed. Léo Hamon (Paris, 1991).

22. See Pierre Barral, *Jules Ferry: Une volonté pour la République* (Nancy, 1985); and Jean-Marie Mayeur, "Jules Ferry et la laïcité," in *Jules Ferry, fondateur de la République*, ed. F. Furet (Paris, 1985).

23. Cited by Deloye, *La citoyenneté au miroir de la République*, 248. On this point, see also chap. 5 of the same work. See also Mona Ozouf, *L'École, l'Église, et la République, 1871–1914* (Paris, 1963).

24. See A. Encrevé and M. Richard, eds., transcript of the colloquium *Les protestants dans les débuts de la Troisième République, 1871–1885* (Paris, 1979). See also André Encrevé, "Les protestants et le début du IIIᵉ République," *L'Histoire*, Mar. 1980; Douglas Johnson, "Jules Ferry et les protestants," in *Jules Ferry, fondateur de la République*; and Jean Bauberot, *Le retour des huguenots* (Paris, 1985).

25. Dèsiré Barodet, *Recueil des professions de foi* (Paris, 1881, 1885, 1889). Later Alexandre Israël, deputy of Aude, for example, praised the merits of the school system in the Jules Ferry mode. See his book, *L'école de la République: La grande oeuvre de J. Ferry* (Paris, 1931). On A. Israël, see Annie Rey, "L'école de la République d'Alexandre Israël," *Travaux de l'Académie de Reims*, 161(1987).

26. Françoise Mayeur, *L'Enseignement secondaire des jeunes filles sous la IIIᵉ République* (Paris, 1977), chap. 1.

27. Cited ibid., 76. On the ties between Freemasonry and the secularization of schools, see Françoise Mayeur, "Le positivisme et l'école républicaine," *Romantisme* 21 (1978). On these questions more generally, see Claude Nicolet, *L'Idée républicaine en France* (Paris, 1982).

28. AN, F1 B1 173 12, Sée dossier.

29. Archives of the Conseil d'Etat, Camille Sée dossier.

30. Drumont, *La France juive*, 2:67 and 443.

31. *L'Univers Israélite*, 18 Apr. 1881.

32. *Archives Israélites*, 12 Nov. 1871. Note that, in the 1880s, a few Jews attained the post of inspector general and thus set in place the school policy of the republican state, like their colleagues: that was the case for Eugène Manuel, the Germanist Benjamin Lévy, and the linguist Michel Bréal. See Claude Singer, "L'Université et les juifs: La remise en question de l'intégration en France de 1940 à 1944" (thesis of the Université Paris-I, 1991), 1:81. That was also the case for Inspector Petit, very often taken as a privileged target of Drumont and the antisemitic press.

33. Guy Thuillier, "La situation religieuse en 1879–1881," *Mémoires de la Société académique du Nivernais* 61 (1979):108.

34. According to his administrative dossier, "he has very good relations with the bishopric despite the religion to which he belongs." AN, F1 B1 170 16, Pinède dossier.

35. AN, Cohn papers, 70 AP 1.

36. Cited in C. Darmon, *Abraham Schrameck, administrateur et homme politique de la Troisième République* (Paris, 1878), 25.

37. *La Libre Parole*, 16 Aug. 1894.

38. AN, F 17 9125 (9). See also Jacques Gadille, *La pensée et l'action politique des évêques français au début de la IIIe République* (Paris, 1967), 2:218.

39. AN, F 19 5657.

40. AN, F 17 9125 (4).

41. AN, F 17 12531.

42. *Discours d'E. Hendlé.* Awards ceremony at the Lycée Corneille, BN, 80 R Pièce, 4551–4595.

43. Ernest Hendlé, *La séparation de l'église et l'état* (Paris, 1869). See the reserved commentary of the *Archives Israélites* 30 (15 Apr. 1869):709. See also his book *Questions politiques et sociales* (Paris, 1868), 70, in which he declares that "whereas morality is one, religions are diverse and their diversity imposes absolute indifference and neutrality on the state."

44. Drumont, *La France juive*, 2:419.

45. AN, F1 B1 597, Brisac dossier.

46. *L'Univers Israélite*, 14 Oct. 1895.

47. *Archives Israélites*, 21 July 1904.

48. Ibid., 27 Oct. 1904.

49. Ibid., 16 Mar. 1905.

50. Ibid., 6 July 1905.

51. Ibid., 5 Jan. 1905. In *L'Univers Israélite*, former prefect Isaïe Levaillant, who had become editor-in-chief of the newspaper after his resignation, wrote: "We wonder whether, in legislating with an electoral goal in mind too exclusively for Catholics, in our anxiety to prevent, or at least to weaken, the formidable outcry that the Church had threatened to provoke against the republican government following the repeal of the concordat, we have not lost sight of the rights and interests of dissident sects, whose opposition we have no need to fear, since they joined the regime of separation from the first moment" (14 July 1905). See also the issues of *L'Univers Israélite* from 25 Aug. 1905, 12 Jan., and 9 and 23 Feb. 1906, in which Levaillant worried about this all too unequal treatment and its consequences for Jewish life.

52. Barodet, *Professions de foi*, 1906 and 1910; and AD of Vosges, 3 M 62.

53. Paul Grunebaum-Ballin, *La séparation des églises et de l'état: Étude juridique* (Paris, 1904).

54. See Bergmann, *Paul Grunebaum-Ballin*; and Jean-Marie Mayeur, *La séparation de l'église et de l'état* (Paris, 1966), 46.

55. Cited by Bergmann, *Paul Grunebaum-Ballin*, 67.

56. We could once more take the example of Abraham Schrameck, who will be evoked later on. At the time, he was prefect of Tarn-et-Garonne, and in this role signed numerous legislative texts of application. See AD of Tarn-et-Garonne.

57. Note this presentation of the event by G. Cholvy and Y. Hilaire: "After the

excesses of Combism, the Opportunist republicans of the Bloc, guided by expert jurists—the Protestant Louis Méjan, the Jew Paul Grunebaum-Ballin—the councillors of the reporter of the parliamentary commission, Aristide Briand, wished to make a liberal law of separation." *Histoire religieuse de la France contemporaine* (Privat, 1986), 2:108.

58. Bergmann, *Paul Grunebaum-Ballin*, 179 and 184.

59. Charles Benoist, *Souvenirs* (Paris, 1935), 3:97. Louis Capéran also sees Paul Grunebaum-Ballin as the essential driving force behind the plan. *L'Invasion laïque*, 366, 377, 411.

60. *La Libre Parole*, 12 Jan. 1908.

61. *Action Française*, 30 Sept. 1909.

62. Léon Daudet, *Le Palais de Police* (Paris, 1931), 16.

63. *Action Française*, 7 Jan. 1909.

64. Ibid., 28 Oct. 1909.

65. See for example *La Libre Parole*, 17 Jan. 1919.

66. Monsignor Jouin, "Le péril judéo-maçonnique," *Revue Internationale des Sociétés Secrètes* 5 (1925).

67. Barodet, *Professions de foi*, 1924.

68. *Les Dernières Nouvelles de Strasbourg*, 10 May 1924.

69. AD of Strasbourg, E L 98, 1078 21.

70. Ibid.

71. Ibid., D 307/8, police report.

72. Ibid., A L 98 1076 (2).

73. Ibid., A L 98 1076 (2), police report.

74. Ibid., 98 1076 (1), police report.

75. Ibid., D 307/9; see also AL 1073 (15 a).

76. On the quarrel as a whole, see AD of Strasbourg, E L 98 1079. The quotation is taken from *La Voix d'Alsace*, 3 May 1928. On G. Weill and Salomon Grumbach, see François Igersheim, *L'Alsace des notables, 1870–1914* (Strasbourg, 1980). On G. Weill, see his biography in J. Maitron, *Dictionnaire biographique du mouvement ouvrier français* (Paris, 1977), vol. 15. Finally, see Jean-Claude Richez, Léon Strauss, François Igersheim, and Stéphane Jonas, *Jacques Peirotes et le socialisme en Alsace, 1869–1935* (Strasbourg, 1989).

77. *Action Française*, 25 May 1936.

78. Centre de Documentation et de Vigilance, *Bulletin de l'Alliance Israélite Universelle* 24. For *Tribune Juive*, "as soon as civil equality is allowed, it is also illogical to seek out a politician's social or religious origin. Politically, there are only citizens."

79. *Les Jeunes d'Alsace*, 7 Feb. 1937.

80. *La Nouvelle Voix d'Alsace et de Lorraine*, 17 Apr. 1937.

81. On these events, see Birnbaum, *Antisemitism*, 187 *et seq.*

Chapter Nine

1. See Michel Winock, "Les affaires Dreyfus," *Vingtième Siècle*, Jan.–Mar. 1985.

2. See Pierre Birnbaum, "Haines et préjugés," in *Histoire des droites en France*, ed. Jean-François Sirinelli and Eric Vigne (Paris, 1992).

3. *Archives Israélites*, 11 June 1908.

4. Ibid., 24 Apr. 1902.

5. *L'Univers Israélite*, 15 Oct. 1898.

6. See Chap. 14.

7. Sybil [Charles Benoist], *Croquis parlementaires* (Paris, 1891), 90.

8. Adrien Dansette, *Le Boulangisme* (Paris, 1946), 153.

9. See Odile Rudelle, *La République absolue, 1870–1889* (Paris, 1986), 203.

10. Alfred Naquet, *Varia*, BN Lb57 14019, vol. 2.

11. Zeev Sternhell, *Maurice Barrès et le nationalisme français* (Brussels, 1972), 82. Georges Cahen-Salvador, member of the Conseil d'Etat, later classed him among "the Boulangist phalanx." "Le procès du général Boulanger," *France-Illustration*, 7 Feb. 1953, 20.

12. Sternhell, *Maurice Barrès et le nationalisme français*, 230–31.

13. Cited in Jacques Néré, *Le Boulangisme et la presse* (Paris, 1964), 186.

14. See AN, F 7 12447, Banquet of Tours dossier, telegram, Tours, 17 Mar. 1889, document 96.

15. According to the expression of Jean El Gammal, "Recherches sur le poids du passé dans la vie politique française de 1885 à 1900" (thesis for the *doctorat d'état*, Université de Paris-X, Nanterre, 1990), 2:285.

16. *Archives Israélites*, 28 Mar. 1889.

17. Ibid., 21 Mar. 1889.

18. AN, F 7 12447, Banquet of Tours dossier.

19. Ibid.

20. *Le Mont-Ventoux*, 11 Aug. 1895, in Naquet, *Varia*, vol. 5.

21. *Archives Israélites*, 7 Feb. 1889.

22. See Albert Bataille, *Causes criminelles et mondaines de 1889* (Paris, 1890).

23. A very large number of proclamations signed by Naquet and Déroulède will be found in the collections 1 J 32 and 1 J 35 of the AD of Vaucluse.

24. On these developments, see Zeev Sternhell, *La droite révolutionnaire 1885–1914: Les origines françaises du fascisme* (Paris, 1978), 202ff.

25. *Archives Israélites*, 24 Apr. 1902.

26. Published by *L'Univers Israélite*, 1 Dec. 1889.

27. *L'Univers Israélite*, 6 Nov. 1896.

28. Naquet, *Varia*, vol. 3.

29. Ibid., vol. 4.

30. AD of Vaucluse, 1 J 32.

31. Naquet, *Temps futurs*, 1 and 13.

32. Dansette, *Le Boulangisme*, 113.

33. Arthur Meyer, *Ce que mes yeux ont vu* (Paris, 1911).

34. Cited by Néré, *Le Boulangisme et la presse*, 114.

35. See for example *La Nation*, 27 Jan. 1889.

36. AN, Dreyfus Papers, 346 AP 1.

37. Barodet, *Professions de foi*, elections of 22 Sept.–6 Oct. 1889.

38. *Lettres de Jules Ferry, 1846–1895* (Paris, 1914), 8: 426, 435, 486, 523, and passim.

39. Joseph Reinach, *La foire boulangiste*. See also *Le cheval noir* (Paris, 1889).

40. Édouard Drumont, *La dernière bataille* (Paris, 1890), 188.

41. *La Libre Parole*, 27 Jan. 1899.

42. Ibid., 12 July 1890. See also the issue of 27 June 1899, titled "La journée de Reinach."

43. Jeanne Verdès-Leroux, *Scandale financier et antisémitisme catholique: Le krach de L'Union générale* (Paris, 1969).

44. AD of Gironde, 3 M 239.

45. Jean Bouvier takes apart the mechanism of this "second Panama scandal" in *Les deux scandales de Panama* (Paris), 107–19. See, more recently, Jean-Yves Mollier, *Le scandale de Panama* (Paris, 1991).

46. Édouard Drumont, *De l'or, de la boue et du sang* (Paris, 1896), 40.

47. See for example *L'Intransigeant*, 1 Jan. 1893.

48. *La Croix*, 24 July 1897.

49. Cited by Casset, "Joseph Reinach avant l'Affaire Dreyfus," 256.

50. *La Libre Parole*, 2 Nov. 1894.

51. On Joseph Reinach as a central character in the Dreyfus affair, see El Gammal, "Joseph Reinach et la République," 1:259ff.

52. Cited by Michael Marrus, in *The Politics of Assimilation*, 184–85.

53. J. Reinach, *Histoire de l'affaire Dreyfus*.

54. *L'Aurore*, 29 May 1898.

55. See the positions taken on this incident, *Le Franc-Parler*, Dec. 1902, AD of Gard, 3 M 748.

56. Cited by P. Simon, *Contribution à l'étude de la bourgeoisie juive*, 145.

57. Archives of the Assemblé Nationale, L.-L. Klotz dossier.

58. Léon Blum, in *L'Oeuvre de Léon Blum*, 491.

59. J. Reinach, *Histoire de l'affaire Dreyfus*, 3:333. On the antisemitism unleashed upon Joseph Reinach, see APP, E_A 109, Joseph Reinach dossier.

60. J. Reinach, *Histoire de l'affaire Dreyfus*, 3:339ff. According to Drumont, "It was Reinach who led all the intrigue. . . . Let Mercier be quiet or Reinach will speak. That is the watchword passed around at the Palais-Bourbon and at the Senate. Everyone understood. And Mercier was quiet." *La Libre Parole*, 4 Nov. 1894. See Patrice Boussel, *L'Affaire Dreyfus et la presse* (Paris).

61. *La Libre Parole*, 9 May 1898. See El Gammal, "Joseph Reinach et la République," 1:240ff.

62. See Wilson, *Ideology and Experience*, chap. 5, and Pierrard, *Juifs et catholiques français*, 102–7. On the caricatures of the period, see Norman Kleeblatt, ed., *The Dreyfus Affair: Art, Truth, and Justice* (Berkeley and Los Angeles, 1987).

63. *Archives Israélites*, 21 Apr. 1898.

64. J. Reinach, *Histoire de l'affaire Dreyfus*, 5:107.

65. Charles Péguy, *Notre jeunesse* (Paris, 1961), 635.

66. Chambre des Députés, parliamentary debates, 11 Jan. 1923.

67. Cited by Marc Vichniac, *Léon Blum* (Paris, 1937), 10.

68. Cited in André Blumel, "Léon Blum juif et sioniste," *Revue de la Pensée Juive* 9 (fall 1951):8.

69. See Marc Jarblum, "Léon Blum, le sioniste," *Renaissance* 3 (Oct. 1956).

70. For a more systematic discussion, see Birnbaum, *Antisemitism*.

71. *Candide*, 7 Apr. 1938.
72. *Journal Officiel*, 7 June 1936, p. 1327.
73. *L'Action Française*, 23 Apr. 1937.
74. L.-F. Céline, *Bagatelles pour un massacre* (Paris, 1937), 317; Marcel Jouhandeau, *Le péril juif* (Fernand Sorlot, 1936), 10–12.
75. See for example Henri Béraud, *Popu-Rois* (Paris, 1938), 13–115.

Chapter Ten

1. These rifles had been recently introduced into the French army by none other than General Boulanger!
2. AN, BB XVIII 1848, Lafargue dossier, sub-dossier A 91, Lafargue-Culine dossier.
3. Cited by Alexandre Zévaès, *La fusillade de Fourmies* (Paris, 1936).
4. As *L'Univers Israélite* noted on 1 Aug. 1891, that is, exactly three months after the incident of Fourmies, Lille and its region formed "an environment notoriously hostile to Jews." See in general Danielle Delmaire, *Antisémitisme et catholiques dans le Nord pendant l'affaire Dreyfus* (Lille, 1991).
5. See Jean-Marie Mayeur, *Les débuts de la IIIe République, 1871–1898* (Paris, 1972), 175, 182, 201.
6. Note for example that *National-hebdo* (National weekly), which belongs to the Front National movement, commented on these events in our own time, ending with the following observation: "Fourmies was a hundred years ago and it was yesterday. Fourmies is today" (2 May 1991).
7. The most complete research concerning the acts and close or distant reactions they elicited is that of André Pierrard and Jean-Louis Chappat, *La fusillade de Fourmies* (Pas-de-Calais, 1991). To this day, there exist only a few historical works, which in addition, far from take into account all the available archival evidence. The small commissioned work compiled by Claude Willard, *La fusillade de Fourmies*, is strongly marked by a reductionist economic Marxism (Paris, 1957). See also the small text by Pierre Pierrard, "Le 'complot juif' selon Drumont," *L'Histoire*, Dec. 1985. Note as well to what extent Drumont's problematic unconsciously influenced even the best authors: Pierre Pierrard, a remarkable analyst of Catholic antisemitism, himself considered the *préfet* "Veil-Durand" [*sic*], Isaac's boss, a Jew; this prefect was named Vel-Durand and, even though Drumont sometimes deliberately changed his name, he was not at all Jewish. See his administrative dossier at AN, F1 B1 388, sub-dossier Vel, called Durand Henry, Auguste, Gaspard, which contains his birth certificate; his mother's name was Jeanne Dode. Similarly, Maurice Agulhon, the great historian of the Republic, evokes the Fourmies affair and notes: "The very detailed account he [Drumont] left is still one of the good sources of information today." *La République, 1880 à nos jours* (Paris, 1990), 62. It would be better to follow C. Willard, but only on this point, who judges that it is "a terribly partial book where everything is seen through the lens of antisemitism." Willard, *La fusillade*, 86. Similarly, A. Pierrard and Jean-Louis Chappat, in their book cited above, write, oddly, "Drumont proceeds to a serious inquiry. . . . As a researcher, Drumond brings back from a Fourmies that is still in shock numerous morsels of truth,

and today, without forgetting the ignominy of his thinking, we must include them in the historical debate; otherwise, we would be falling into his own Manichean blunder" (264–66). In fact, it is urgent to analyze in general other historians' entirely unconscious borrowings from antisemitic literature.

8. AN, F1 B1 487, Isaac dossier.

9. Ibid.

10. AD of Nord, Lille, M 6 (12), Isaac dossier.

11. All these evaluations are found in Isaac's administrative dossier, AN, F1 B1 487.

12. AN, F7 12527.

13. AN, F1 B1 507, Georges Mossé dossier.

14. "Le circoncis de Fourmies," *Le Courrier de l'Est*, 2 May 1891.

15. Édouard Drumont, *Le secret de Fourmies* (Paris, 1892).

16. *La Croix*, 5 May 1891.

17. Ibid., 12 May 1891. See Jérôme Grondeux, "L'intervention du curé de Fourmies: lectures d'un acte" (typescript, Fourmies colloquium, 1991).

18. Drumont, *Le secret de Fourmies*, 33.

19. Ibid., 6 and 9.

20. Ibid., 15–17, 69.

21. Ibid., 65.

22. Ibid., 89 and 105.

23. *La Libre Parole* would nevertheless consider him Jewish throughout his long career, with at times a few hesitations; hence, on 29 Mar. 1896, that newspaper wrote: "If he is not really Jewish, he is certainly worthy of being so." In contrast, on 29 Sept. 1894, *La Libre Parole* commented in this way on the secularization that was striking a monastery's primary school: "Fourmies has decidedly no chance with the Opportunist Yids. The Jew Isaac had workers fired on without notice there. The Jew Vel-Durand, from one day to the next, without informing anyone, expelled the sisters esteemed by a whole population."

24. *Archives Israélites*, May 1891.

25. Chambre des Députés, 4 May 1891, 77 and 79.

26. These excerpts were taken from Pierrard and Chappat, *La fusillade de Fourmies*, 295–307.

27. *Le Lillois*, 17 May 1891, Ecomuseum of Fourmies.

28. See the press file contained in dossier F1 B1 487.

29. *Archives Israélites*, 17 Mar. 1892.

30. Léon Daudet, *Panorama de la IIIe République* (Paris, 1936), 93.

31. AN, BB 18 1848, dossier of the Lafargue-Culine trial, subdossier 849 A 91.

32. AN, F1 B1 487, Isaac dossier. For a socialist republican candidate from Bordeaux defeated in the 1893 elections, "it was on an order from Rome that, throughout France, the priests and the rallied troops, united in the blood of Fourmies and the mud of Panama, led a campaign for the Rouviers, the Burdeaux, and the Raynals." *La Petite République du Sud-Ouest* (6 Sept. 1893), AD of Gironde, 3 M 229.

33. AN, F 7 12527.

34. J. Reinach, *Démagogues et socialistes*, 35, 93, 213; Théodore Reinach, platform statement, 1910, Archives of the Assemblé Nationale, T. Reinach dossier.

35. AN, F1 B1 166 8, Lambert dossier.
36. AN, F1 B1 347, Hendlé dossier.
37. AN, F1 B1 384, Simon dossier.
38. AN, F1 B1 507, Mossé dossier.
39. See André Bénac, *Vie et oeuvre politique de David Raynal* (Bordeaux, 1923), p. 18.
40. Lépine, *Mes souvenirs*, 177. For him, Raynal was "the most gallant man, the most attractive Gascon you'd ever see. Physically, the image of Henri IV."
41. *L'Intransigeant*, 19 Feb. 1894.
42. APP, B$_A$ 1237 and E$_A$ 54, D. Raynal dossiers.
43. *La Libre Parole*, 16 Feb. 1895. See the I. Levaillant dossier in APP, B$_A$ 1155.
44. Lépine considered Levaillant his own "master." *Archives Israélites*, 17 Apr. 1909. See also Lépine, *Mes souvenirs*, 89. Collaborator and friend of Raynal, he was also that of Joseph Reinach.
45. The most significant case of this was certainly that of Schnerb, director of Sûreté Générale at the Ministry of the Interior in the Waldeck-Rousseau cabinet of 1884, whose famous circular against monarchist candidates, ordering careful investigations from prefects, was continually denounced. See AN, F 7 12431, Schnerb circular. Drumont considered him the very prototype of the authoritarian Jew tracking down true Frenchmen. See *La France juive*, 2 : 222, 275, and 417. Yet Schnerb was not at all Jewish. See his administrative dossier at F1 B1 383. Drumont nonetheless linked Schnerb to Levaillant to protest the presence of a Jew at the post of director of Sûreté Générale, in *La France juive*, 2 : 421. For a part of the press during the period, as for Drumont, Schnerb's true name was thought to be Simon, and he must therefore be Jewish, just like Jules Simon and Simon Gambetta!
46. See Darmon, *Abraham Schrameck*, 60ff. Among the state Jews who were to assume heavy responsibilities in the social conflicts of national importance, let us also cite, for example, Jules Moch, who did not hesitate to use the most extreme measures in 1953 to struggle with large police forces against very violent strikes organized by the Communist Party and the Confédération Générale du Travail (general confederation for work, CGT). Hence his reputation as a "strikebreaker."
47. AN, F1 B1 673, Schrameck dossier.
48. *Action Française*, 14 May 1925.
49. See, for example, the very rich dossier at AN, F 7 13197.
50. *Action Française*, 9 June 1925. This text, like all those presented in what follows, are contained in dossier AN, F 7 12 197.
51. A little later, Maurras brought together these texts in a book titled *La lettre à Schrameck* (Paris, 1919). See also his book *Ce qu'il faut à la France* (Paris, 1925), 84, in which he maintained that "all the elites of France" were ready to execute Schrameck if the order was given. Léon Daudet again violently attacked Schrameck in his book *Magistrats et policiers* (Paris, 1935), 228.
52. AN, F 7 13 964, death threats dossier.
53. AN, F 7 13964.
54. See, for example, *Au Pilori*, 31 Jan. 1929. Léon Daudet considered Schrameck, minister of the interior, "a comical Jew, hideous and impulsively fearful," in *Paris vécu: Rive droite* (Paris, 1929), 180.

Chapter Eleven

1. *Le Petit Meridional*, 5 Oct. 1876, Archives of the AIU, France IV A 19.

2. Vicky Caron, *Between France and Germany: The Jews of Alsace-Lorraine, 1871–1918* (Stanford, Calif., 1988), 27.

3. Sylvain Halff, *La fidelité française des israélites d'Alsace et de Lorraine, 1871–1918* (Paris, 1921), 1–2.

4. A. Robert and G. Cougny, *Dictionnaire des parlementaires français* (Paris, 1891).

5. See Caron, *Between France and Germany*, 97 and 100.

6. Major Paul-Louis Weiller, "Lazare Weiller," *Annuaire de la Société des Amis de la Bibliothèque de Sélastat*, 1973. We find this brochure in the AD of Strasbourg. On the career of "Lazare Weiller," see also Jules-Albert Jaeger, "Sur la vie de M. Lazare Weiller," *L'Alsace Française*, 26 Aug. 1928, Archives of the AIU, Halff collection, Weiller. This dossier contains other press clippings on Weiller.

7. Édouard Millaud, *Le Soufflet: Devons-nous signer la paix?* (1871), pp. 14 and 27.

8. Camille Dreyfus, *La guerre nécessaire: Réponse d'un Français à M. de Bismarck* (Paris, 1890).

9. APP, BA 1055, C. Dreyfus dossier.

10. Army commission, Chambre des Députés, BN Le 89 26 Bis.

11. Joseph Reinach, *L'Armée toujours prête* (Paris, 1913), 279, 322, 382, and 428.

12. Joseph Reinach, *L'Alsace-Lorraine devant L'Histoire*, BN 80 LK.2 6177.

13. Alfred Naquet, [letters], BN NAF 22864.

14. François Bérarida, "L'armée et la République: Les opinions politiques des officers en 1876–1878," *Revue Historique*, July 1964, 141–55.

15. Raoul Girardet, *La société militaire dans la France contemporaine, 1815–1939* (Paris, 1953), 264. See also David Ralston, *The Army of the Republic: The Place of the Military in the Political Evolution of France, 1871–1914* (Boston, 1967), 83 and 202.

16. Some general empirical data can be found in Serman, *Le corps des officiers*, 2:1095–99.

17. Serman, *Les officiers français dans la nation*, 101ff. On their careers, see Chap. 19.

18. See for example the series of articles in *La Libre Parole* in May 1892, titled "Les juifs de l'armée" (The Jews in the army), where several Jewish officers in particular are denounced.

19. Ferdinand Dreyfus, *Misères sociales et études historiques* (Paris, 1901), 245.

20. On Captain Dreyfus's values, his attitude toward the Prussians who won the war of 1870, see Michael Burns, "Majority Faith: Dreyfus before the Affair," in *From East and West: Jews in a Changing Europe, 1750–1870*, ed. Frances Malino and David Sorkin (Oxford, 1990).

21. *Archives Israélites*, 27 Aug. 1914.

22. Ibid., 21 July 1916. Similarly, on 14 July 1917, according to this newspaper, at the time of the ceremony "there were neither Jews nor Christians nor freethinkers. There were only patriots acclaiming the glorious defenders of immortal rights" (18 July 1917).

23. *Bulletin du Comité de Vigilance*, 24 Nov. 1928, AIU.

24. Philippe Landau, "Les juifs de France et la Grande Guerre" (master's thesis in history, Université de Paris-VII, 1984), 140.

25. SHA, colonel series, Salmon Lévy dossier.

26. SHA, administrative archives, 95652, Louis Naquet.

27. SHA, lieutenant-colonel series, Oscar Kahn dossier.

28. Cited by Philippe Landau, "La patrie en danger," in Birnbaum, ed., *Histoire politique des juifs de France*, 80.

29. "Alfred Wallach, 1882–1961," in *Bulletin de la Société Industrielle de Mulhouse* 1 (1962).

30. *Encyclopédie de l'Alsace* (Strasbourg, 1985), 7706. See also Igersheim, *L'Alsace des notables*.

31. Archives of Seine, D 3 M 2 10.

32. Ibid., D 2 M 1 12. It was pointed out that he "struggled mercilessly against defeatism and treason."

33. J. Reinach, *Les commentaires du Polybe*, nineteenth series, 36 and 153.

34. Barodet, *Profession de foi*, 1914.

35. Moch, *Une si longue vie*, 42.

36. This information was taken either from personnel dossiers kept at the Assemblée Nationale or from the many national and regional dictionaries used.

37. L.-L. Klotz, *L'Armée en 1906* (Paris, 1906), 284 and 289.

38. L.-L. Klotz, *De la guerre à la paix* (Paris, 1924), 11 and 55.

39. André Fribourg, *Les martyrs d'Alsace et de Lorraine* (Paris, 1916), 31 and 172.

40. André Fribourg, *La guerre et le passé* (Paris, 1916).

41. All of Fribourg's books with a dedication to Maurice Barrès can be found in the Barrès collection of the BN.

42. André Fribourg, *La victoire des vaincus* (Paris, 1938), 345.

43. Ibid., 11.

44. AD of Calvados, box M 13, Albert Hendlé dossier.

45. AN, F1 B 569, Albert Hendlé dossier.

46. AN, F1 CIII 1126.

47. See Darmon, *Abraham Schrameck*, 64–69.

48. AN, F1 B1 784, Henri Hendlé dossier. On 16 June 1920, he was listed on the special roll of the Legion of Honor: "Excellent officer, with a modesty equaling his valor. Had very difficult battles with enemy aircraft."

49. AN, F1 B1 581, Pierre Aron dossier.

50. AN, F1 B1 599, André Caen dossier.

51. AN, F1 B1 734, Marc Brisac dossier, and F1 B1 749, Henri Dadoun dossier.

52. See SHA, GB, third series, 1119, Dennery dossier, and GD, third series, 582, Bloch dossier.

53. *Archives Israélites*, 7 Oct. 1915.

54. SHA, GD, fourth series, 1, Alexandre dossier.

55. SHA, GB, fourth series, 124, Lévy dossier.

56. Cited by Halff, *La fidélité française*, 32.

57. SHA, GD, fourth series, 56, Levi dossier. On the armed service of General Camille Lévi, see *Archives Israélites*, 2 Nov. 1916.

58. SHA, GB, fourth series, 173 and 21, Grumbach and Geismar dossiers.

59. SHA, GD, third series, 114, Frank dossier.

60. SHA, GB, third series, 1831, Carvallo dossier.

61. Carvallo family archives, communicated by Mme Sarah Leibovici.

62. SHA, GB, fourth series, 664, Baumann dossier.

63. SHA, GD/4, Boris dossier. See also the Boris collection, 1 K 157.

64. SHA, GB 1534/4, Rheims dossier.

65. SHA, GD 1384/4, Rueff dossier.

66. SHA, GB, fourth series, 1572, Weiller dossier.

67. *La Tribune Juive*, 24 June 1938.

68. See E. Rubin, *140 Jewish Marshals, Generals, and Admirals* (London, 1952).

69. *L'Univers Israélite*, 24 June 1938.

70. Ibid., 2 June 1939.

71. *Revue Hebdomadaire*, 23 Nov. 1935. Maurras's attacks in this direction were very numerous. See, for example, *Action Française*, 8 June 1936.

72. *Action Française*, 2 Sept. 1933.

73. *La Libre Parole* and *Le Porc-épic*, 1 June 1936.

74. See Jean-Noël Jeanneney, *Georges Mandel: L'homme qu'on attendait* (Paris, 1991), 93–94.

75. Pierre Mendès France, *Oeuvres complètes* (Paris).

76. Georges Weill, *Le péril allemand* (Algiers, 1944), 43.

77. Moch, *Une si longue vie*, 157, 169. See also idem, *Rencontres avec Darlan et Eisenhower* (Paris, 1957), 143.

78. See Jean Pierre-Bloch, *Londres, capitale de la Résistance* (Paris), and idem, *Mes jours heureux* (Paris, 1946).

79. This information comes from the personnel dossiers of the Archives of the Assemblée Nationale and from local archives such as, in the case of André Wallach, the biographical notice in the archives of the city of Mulhouse, B 141, or from various brochures such as Georges Godefroy's *Le Havre sous l'occupation, 1940–1944*, n.d.

80. A plaque dedicated to French Jews fallen on the battlefield during the two world wars was fixed in the courtyard of the synagogue on Rue de la Roquette, and had been placed in the honor court of the Hôtel des Invalides.

81. See also Chap. 20, on Vichy.

Chapter Twelve

1. AN, F1 B1 166 8, Lambert dossier.

2. AD of Meurthe-et-Moselle, 2 M 6.

3. In his remarkable book *La promotion des juifs en France à l'époque du Second Empire, 1852–1870*, David Cohen also retraces the history of this exceptional *sous-préfet* (Paris, 1980), 2:391ff.

4. AN, F1 B1 166 8, Lambert dossier.

5. AN, F1 B1 155 (12), Azevedo dossier.

6. Meyer, *Ce que mes yeux ont vu*, 129–30.

7. AN, F1 B1 173 8, Salvador dossier.

8. AN, F1 B1 314, Caen dossier.

9. AN, F1 B1 166 8, Lambert dossier.

10. AN, F1 B1 166 8, Lambert dossier.

11. AN, BB 6 II 6, Anspach dossier. On the marriage of his daughter, see *Archives Israélites*, 15 Nov. 1859 (vol. 20), and Chap. 5 herein.

12. AN, BB 6 II 501, Félix dossier.

13. AN, BB 6 II 392, Seligmann dossier.

14. AN, BB 6 II 26, Bédarridès dossier.

15. AN, BB 6 II 619, Alphandéry dossier.

16. AN, BB 6 II 33, Berr dossier.

17. AN, BB 6 II 453, Bloch dossier.

18. AN, BB 6 II 290, May dossier.

19. Graetz, *Les juifs en France au XIXe siècle*, 71.

20. Serman, *Le corps des officiers*, 1:1099.

21. Cohen, *La promotion des juifs en France*, 2:418ff.

22. His personnel dossier is quite rich in qualitative data, SHA, GD, third series, 31, Lambert dossier.

23. SHA, GD, second series, 1615, Sée dossier.

24. See Rubin, *140 Jewish Marshals*, 89 and 99. The personnel dossiers can also be consulted: on Rottembourg, SHA, GD, second series, 610. On Wolff, SHA, GD, second series, 1123.

25. See Vincent Wright, *Le Conseil d'état sous le Second Empire* (Paris, 1972), 42.

26. Cited by Cohen, *La promotion des juifs en France*, 2:387ff.

27. Jacques Basso, *Les élections législatives dans le département des Alpes-Maritimes de 1860 à 1939* (Paris, 1968), 12.

28. See Cohen, *La promotion des juifs en France*, 2:589ff.

29. See ibid., 2:592–98.

30. *Archives Israélites*, 15 Mar. 1870.

31. See Chadeau, *L'économie du risque*, chap. 9. Chadeau retraces the distant history of the Javal dynasty.

32. *L'Univers Israélite* 8 (1852).

33. AD of Yonne, 2 M 1 150.

34. Chadeau, *L'économie du risque*, 245–46.

35. AD of Yonne, 2 M 1 149.

36. Ibid., 2 M 1 164.

37. Ibid., 2 M 1 157.

38. Ibid.

39. Speech by Léopold Javal to the legislative body on 15 Jan. 1864, BN Le 83 272.

40. Dr. Louis Roché, *Notice sur la vie et les travaux de M. Émile Javal* (Auxerre, 1908). See also Michel Burseaux, "Javal. Sa vie. L'actualité de son oeuvre scientifique" (thesis for the doctorate in medicine, Paris, 1944), BN Th Paris, 1877.

41. *La Croix*, 16 Sept. 1890.

42. AN, C 4608. Only once, in 1885, do we find by his name, "The Jew of the Rue de Vendôme, who is stealing the land of his neighbor to make himself a lovely garden."

43. *L'Univers Israélite*, 1 Sept. 1891.

44. In Louise Weiss, *Souvenirs d'une enfance républicaine* (Paris, 1937), 19. Louise Weiss was thus the granddaughter of Émile Javal. On the Javal family, see also certain documents in the archives of the AIU, Halff collection, MS 586.

45. *La Libre Parole,* 27 July 1913.

Chapter Thirteen

1. Posener, *Adolphe Crémieux,* 2:256ff.

2. Paul Bert, *L'Instruction civique à l'école* (Paris, 1882).

3. Robert and Cougny, *Dictionnaire des parlementaires français.*

4. Édouard Millaud, *Journal d'un parlementaire* (Paris, 1914), 1:5.

5. AN, F1 B1 16634, Édouard Millaud dossier.

6. Émile Pillias, "Alfred Naquet, Autobiographie," *Revue d'Histoire Politique et Constitutionnelle* (1939), 7 and 10. Note that Eliacin Naquet, the brother of Alfred, was named *substitut* in Lyon in 1870. AN, BB 6 II 1095, Naquet dossier.

7. See, for example, letter no. 472 in D. Halévy and E. Pillias, eds., *Lettres de Gambetta, 1868–1882* (Paris, 1938).

8. Pierre-Barthélemy Gheusi, *Gambetta par Gambetta (Lettres intimes et souvenirs de famille)* (Paris, 1909), 233. See Amson, *Adolphe Crémieux: L'oublié de la gloire,* 297ff.

9. Halévy and Pillias, *Lettres de Gambetta,* letter no. 78.

10. Millaud, *Journal d'un parlementaire,* 1:42.

11. André Bénac, *Vie et oeuvre de David Raynal* (Bordeaux, 1923); and Albert Decrois, *Discours prononcé le 1ᵉʳ février sur la tombe de David Raynal* (Bordeaux, 1913).

12. P. Bayaud, "Les préfets des Basses-Pyrénées de 1880 à 1885," *Bulletin de la société des Sciences, Lettres et Arts de Pau* (1970), 180. In 1886, Jules Ferry wrote to him: "I am quite deprived of all news of you." *Lettres de Jules Ferry, 1846–1895,* 3:429. The correspondence between Raynal and Ferry was in fact constant and intimate. See B M Saint-Dié-des-Vosges, Jules Ferry collection, Correspondence, Raynal dossier.

13. *Le Temps,* 2 Feb. 1903; APP, BA 1237, D. Raynal dossier; *Archives Israélites,* 15 Feb. 1903.

14. J.-P. Bury, *Gambetta and the National Defence* (New York, 1970), chap. 2.

15. Raymond Huard, *Le mouvement républicain en Bas-Languedoc, 1848–1881* (Paris, 1982). The author briefly evokes the role played by most state Jews in rooting the republican movement of these southern regions. In a more general way, see Maurice Agulhon, "Conscience nationale et conscience régionale," in Maurice Agulhon, *Histoire vagabonde* (Paris, 1988), vol. 2. The *Archives Israélites* notes that, among the Jews elected to the Senate, "in the early years, the Judeo-meridional element was preeminent" (30 Jan. 1920).

16. The historians of the Third Republic have underscored the presence of these Jewish politicians, born for the most part in the south of France, without, however, giving it any particular significance. See I. Tchernoff, *Le parti républicain au coup d'état et sous le Second Empire* (Paris, 1906), and Georges Weill, *Histoire du parti républicain en France de 1814 à 1870* (Paris, 1900). Carol Iancu also insists on the welcoming nature of a French Midi open to dialogue, finding the explanation in the nonconformism of Midi Jews in relation to those in the East. Carol Iancu,

"Adolphe Crémieux et la défense des droits des juifs au XIX^c siècle," in *Armand Lunel et les juifs du Midi*, ed. Iancu (Montpellier, 1986), 259. See also idem, "Les juifs à Montpellier," in *Bulletin Historique de la Ville de Montpellier*, 7. Jean El Gammal explicitly situates David Raynal in that Girondin tradition, which was particularly strong in Bordeaux, in *Recherches sur le poids du passé dans la vie politique française de 1885 à 1900* (Paris, 1990), 3 : 700ff.

17. In the expression of Odile Rudelle, *La République absolue, 1870–1889* (Paris, 1986), 282.

18. Millaud, *Journal d'un parlementaire*, 1 : 41.

19. Édouard Millaud, *Ronde d'ombres* (Paris, 1908).

20. Cited in Posener, *Adolphe Crémieux*, 2 : 122.

21. *Papiers Crémieux*, AN, 369 AP 1.

22. *La Liberté*, 1 Jan. 1871, AD of Hérault.

23. [My thanks to Thomas R. Hart for his translation of these lines. — trans.]

24. Daudet, *L'Entre-deux-guerres*, 219.

25. See E. Appolis, "Les israélites de l'Hérault de 1830 à 1870," *Actes du quatre-vingtième congrès national des sociétés savantes* (Dijon, 1960), 499; and Gérard Cholvy, "A propos des juifs à Montpellier au XIX^c siècle," in Iancu, ed., *Les juifs à Montpellier et dans le Languedoc*.

26. Who were both part of the population of state Jews.

27. *Archives Israélites*, 19 Feb. 1880. See also, on that funeral, the large, little-known dossier found in the archives of the AIU, France IV A 19.

28. This proposed medal would serve to "immortalize the Great Jew, the great Citizen who had but one thought: to make France glorious and strong, to make Judaism free and honored." The proposal figures in this same dossier of the archives of the AIU, France IV A 19.

29. See *Le Petit Méridional*, 8, 9, and 10 Feb. 1891; and *Archives Israélites* 52 (1891).

30. Philip Nord, "Republicanism and Utopian Vision: French Freemasonry in the 1860s and 1870s," *Journal of Modern History*, June 1991.

31. Pierre Chevalier, *Histoire de la franc-maçonnerie* (Paris, 1975).

32. J.-P. Bury, *Gambetta and the Making of the Third Republic* (London, 1973), 5 and 249.

33. Estèbe, *Les ministres de la République*, 210.

34. Vincent Wright, "Francs-maçons, administration et République: Les préfets du gouvernement de la Défense nationale, 1870–1871," *Revue Administrative* (1989), nos. 240 and 241. On page 519 of his first article, Wright excludes Lisbonne from the list of Freemason *préfets*; we might judge, on the contrary, that he was a Freemason, as indicated above.

35. I. Tchernoff asserts that E. Millaud was a member of Freemasonry in Lyon in 1867. See *Le parti républicain au coup d'état*, 315. On the formation of networks of sociability in that region, where republicans and Freemasons intermingled, see Maurice Agulhon, *Pénitents et francs-maçons de l'ancienne Provence* (Paris, 1984).

36. In his personal papers in the Archives Nationales, we find the different badges symbolizing his position, 369 AP.1, Crémieux Papers.

37. AD of Vosges, 1 J 125, *Compte rendu de la fête offerte le 24 octobre 1878 aux maçons étrangers*, n.d., 9–13.

38. These quotations were excerpted from Gambetta's speeches, published by Pierre Barral in *Les fondateurs de la Troisième République* (Paris, 1968).

39. Pierre Allou and Maurice Chenu, *Grands avocats du siècle* (Paris, 1895), 67.

40. AN, F1 B1 168, Naquet dossier. In 1879, he said, "I take pride in the fact that in less than a year, through a firm, vigilant, and impartial administration, I have cured this department of a shameful Bonapartism."

41. Gustave Naquet, *80 ans en 80 minutes: Conférence historique* (Paris, 1877), AN, F 17/2531.

42. See the description of that event by a resident of Montpellier in *Le Petit Méridional*, 13 Aug. 1925, AD of Hérault, 1 E 12,000.

43. AN, F1 B1 168.34, Lisbonne dossier.

44. These letters were excerpted from the *Archives Israélites* 76 (1875).

45. *Montpellier Notre Ville: Journal d'Information Municipale* 136 (Nov. 1990).

46. See *La Liberté*, 19 and 29 Sept. 1870, 27 Oct. 1870, 6 Nov. 1870, 15 Jan. 1871, and 29 Apr. 1871. All his proclamations as *préfet* are collected in series 1 J 304 of the AD of Hérault. The administrative measures he instituted are included in S 15 M 26 and 27.

47. AN, F1 B1 166.34, Lisbonne dossier.

48. *La Liberté*, 30 Oct. 1871.

49. Ibid., 3 Nov. 1871. On this incident, see Marcel Blancard, "A propos d'un buste de la République (1871), deux lettres inédites de Thiers," *Revue Historique*, Sept.–Dec. 1924.

50. See Maurice Agulhon, *Marianne au pouvoir: L'imagerie et la symbolique républicaines de 1880 à 1914* (Paris, 1989). In this book, Agulhon also briefly recalls this conflict that opposed the prefect and the *conseil général* of Hérault (41).

51. Édouard Lisbonne, *Allocution prononcée par M. Lisbonne, sénateur* (Montpellier, 1890), 12210, pp. 17–18.

52. Édouard Lisbonne, *Allocution prononcée par Me Lisbonne, bâtonnier* (Montpellier, 1867), 12337; and Record of the Deliberations of the Municipal Council of the City of Montpellier, 19 Nov. 1875 and 23 Feb. 1878, AD of Hérault, IJ 307.

53. *Lettre pastorale de Monseigneur l'évêque de Montpellier sur l'instruction obligatoire, gratuite et laïque* (Montpellier, 1872), 5 and 15.

54. See Gérard Cholvy, *Géographie religieuse de l'Hérault contemporain* (Paris, 1968).

55. *Archives Israélites* 37 (1876).

56. Ibid.

57. Édouard Lisbonne, "étude nécrologique sur Israël Bédarride," excerpted from the *Revue Judiciaire des Cours Impériales* (Montpellier, 1870).

58. *L'Univers Israélite*, 16 Feb. 1891.

59. AN, F 19 11046, Consistorial Archives.

60. To his dismay, Crémieux's wife converted to Catholicism, as did his two children; for a long time, Adolphe therefore left the leadership of the consistory.

61. See Michel de Certeau, Dominique Julia, and Jacques Revel, *Une politique de la langue: La Révolution française et les patois* (Paris, 1975).

62. *Archives Israélites*, 6 Mar. 1924.

63. Posener, *Adolphe Crémieux*, 2:149.

64. Ibid., 1:118–21. See also Birnbaum, "Sur l'étatisation révolutionnaire."
65. Dreyfus, *Misères sociales et études historiques*, 221ff. We recall that Ferdinand Dreyfus was also close to Gambetta.
66. See J. Reinach, *La vie politique de Léon Gambetta*, 168.
67. Drumont, *La France juive*, 1:530. Similarly, Rochefort claimed that Gambetta was a "Jew by origin," in *Les aventures de ma vie*, vol. 2. On that legend, see Bury, *Gambetta and the National Defence*, Appendix 3, "Was Gambetta a Jew?" Waldeck-Rousseau was also sometimes accused of being Jewish during that period. See J.-P. Rioux, *Nationalisme et conservatisme: La Ligue de la patrie française* (Paris, 1977), 82.
68. Drumont, *La France juive*, 1:34. According to *La Croix*, 27 Nov. 1887: "We have become vassals of the Jew Crémieux, and never did a feudal lord treat his lieges with so much tyranny and scorn."
69. Drumont, *La France juive*, 2:4.
70. Ibid.
71. Ibid., 2:430.
72. AD of Gironde, 3 M 2 36 and 39. See also 3 M 241.
73. AD of Hérault, 39 M 279.
74. See, for example, Joseph Santo, *La question juive* (Paris, 1921). The author attacks the Jewish Republic of Gambetta, Crémieux, Reinach, Lisbonne, and so on, 112–13. See also Robert Launay, *Figures juives* (Paris, 1921).
75. See, for example, *L'émancipation des juifs en France* (Paris, 1942), 40–41. Gambetta as well as Crémieux and his friends are once more denounced.

Chapter Fourteen

1. Léon Daudet, *Fantômes et vivants* (Paris, 1914), 240–41.
2. Dansette, *Le Boulangisme*, 151–52.
3. Alfred Naquet, *Le divorce* (Paris, 1881), chap. 1.
4. *Débats parlementaires*, 20 July 1884.
5. Ibid., 13 June 1882.
6. For a selection of caricatures, see APP E.A 52, Naquet dossier.
7. Naquet, *Varia*, 2:49.
8. J. Barbey d'Aurevilly, *Dernières polémiques* (Paris, 1891), 237–39.
9. Drumont, *La France juive*, 1:112–14.
10. *La Libre Parole*, 1 Feb., 23 Aug., and 7 Dec. 1906.
11. Sybil [Charles Benoist], *Croquis parlementaires*, 78–82.
12. Santo, *La question juive*, 45.
13. Launay, *Figures juives*, 122.
14. *La Libre Parole*, 22 June 1902.
15. Daudet, *L'Entre-deux-guerres*, 91.
16. *La Croix des Alpes-Maritimes*, 7 July 1907, Léon Blum collection, Fondation Nationale des Sciences Politiques.
17. *Jaune*, 24 Feb. 1909, Léon Blum collection, Fondation Nationale des Sciences Politiques.
18. Count A. de Puységur, *Les maquereaux légitimes: Du coursier des croisades au bidet de Rebecca* (Paris, 1938).

19. Henri Faugeras, *Les juifs, peuple de proie* (Paris, 1943), 61.
20. Jean-Charles Legrand, *Paroles vivantes* (Paris, 1941), 184.
21. *Action Française*, 19 Apr. 1937. On this literature hostile to Léon Blum, see Birnbaum, *Antisemitism*, 157 *et seq.*
22. André Gide, *Corydon* (Paris, 1925), 115.
23. *Action Française*, 17 Apr. 1941.
24. See Alfred Naquet, *Autobiographie*, completed by Émile Pillias (Paris, 1939). We have also drawn inspiration from the remarkable thesis by Ginette André, "Alfred Naquet, adversaire de l'Empire et défenseur de la République radicale, 1867–1884" (doctoral thesis [3e cycle], Faculté des lettres d'Aix-en-Provence, 1972), 71ff.
25. André, "Alfred Naquet," chaps. 8 and 9.
26. Alfred Naquet, *Religion. Propriété. Famille* (Paris, 1869), part 2.
27. Naquet, *Temps futurs*, 192 and 204.
28. Ibid., 231.
29. Ibid., 281–83.
30. Naquet, *Temps futurs*, 327.
31. On this episode, see André, "Alfred Naquet," chap. 10.
32. *Le Rappel*, 13 May 1870, cited by André, "Alfred Naquet," 247.
33. Mario Proth, *Alfred Naquet*, "Célébrités contemporaines" collection, 1883.
34. Alfred Naquet, *La République radicale* (Paris, 1873), 59–66.
35. Ibid., 47.
36. *Débats parlementaires*, 28 July 1894.
37. Lecture by Naquet in Béziers on social questions, 23 Oct. 1878, BN eighth R, document 32.
38. On Naquet's role in the Boulangist movement, see Chap. 9.
39. Naquet, *Temps futurs*, 6.
40. He had early conducted a systematic critique of Marxist political economy in his work *Socialisme collectiviste et socialisme libéral* (Paris, 1890).
41. Naquet, *Temps futurs*, 229 and 333.
42. Ibid., 187.
43. Ibid., 265 and 316.
44. Ibid., 318–22.
45. On Naquet, antisemitism, and Zionism, see Chap. 6.
46. Alfred Naquet, *Vers l'union libre* (Paris, 1907).
47. Alfred Naquet and André Lorulot, *Le socialisme marxiste, l'individualisme anarchique et la Révolution* (Paris, 1911), 10–12.
48. Ibid., 39.

Chapter Fifteen

1. Georges Wormser, *La République de Clemenceau* (Paris, 1961), 472.
2. Jean-Baptiste Duroselle, *Clemenceau* (Paris, 1988), 455.
3. Christiane Rambaud, *L'Affaire de Massilia, été 1940* (Paris, 1984).
4. Marc Agi, *René Cassin, fantassin des Droits de l'homme* (Paris, 1979), 84–100.
5. Ferdinand Dreyfus, for example, was very close to Poincaré. In September 1914, Poincaré entrusted him with the drafting of a plan to reorganize the administration of Alsace-Lorraine. See AN, 346, AP/8, F. Dreyfus papers. Their correspondence

attests to the closeness of their relations. Beginning in 1881, Poincaré returned often to his own hostility toward religion in his letters to F. Dreyfus. These letters have never been published. AN, 346, AP 5/6, F. Dreyfus papers.

6. Henry Torrès, *De Clemenceau à de Gaulle* (Paris, 1958), 236.

7. Archives of the Assemblé Nationale, Torrès dossier.

8. Favreau, *Georges Mandel* (Paris, 1969), 260.

9. *Le Figaro*, 7 July 1984.

10. David R. Watson, *Georges Clemenceau: A Political Biography* (Plymouth, 1974), 278.

11. Duroselle, *Clemenceau*, 635. See also Marie-José Domestici-Met, "Le deuxième gouvernement Clemenceau, 1917–1920," *Revue du Droit Public et de la Science Politique en France et à l'étranger* 4 (1986).

12. Wormser, *Georges Mandel*, 68.

13. Favreau, *Georges Mandel*, 83.

14. Klotz, *L'Armée en 1906*, 284–89.

15. Klotz, *De la guerre à la paix*, 11.

16. *La Libre Parole*, 6 Mar. 1913.

17. *Archives Israélites*, 15 May 1910.

18. Daudet, *Paris vécu: Rive gauche*, 158. In another work, Daudet declared of Mandel: "He is one of the most magnetic personalities I've ever encountered in my life. He is serious. He is a man." *L'Agonie de la régime* (Paris, 1925), 141. In this same book, he is also very kind in his praise of L.-L. Klotz (126).

19. See Jean-Yves Mollier, *Le scandale de Panama* (Paris, 1991), 439.

20. *La Libre Parole*, 15 Dec. 1892.

21. See a little-known article by Barnett Singer, "Clemenceau and the Jews," *Jewish Social Studies* 1 (winter 1981). See also Duroselle, *Clemenceau*, chap. 14.

22. *La Libre Parole*, 20 Apr. 1907.

23. Santo, *La question juive*, 149. We know that Maurice Bokanowski was minister of the navy in the Poincaré government. See the Paris Archives, D 3 M 2 12.

24. On his career, see AN, F1 B1 671. More generally, see Wormser, *Georges Mandel*, 23–25. See also John Sherwood, *Georges Mandel and the Third Republic* (Stanford, Calif., 1970), 10.

25. See René Massigli, "Georges Wormser, 1888–1978," *Revue des Deux Mondes*, Apr. 1979.

26. Wormser, *Français israélites*.

27. Émile Buré, *Georges Clemenceau et Georges Mandel* (Paris, 1946).

28. Joseph Reinach, *Le ministère Clemenceau* (Paris, 1885), 23–24.

29. Ibid., 59.

30. Ibid., 78.

31. Ibid., 101.

32. See the numerous articles by Clemenceau against Naquet's internationalist pacifism, in Naquet, *Varia*, vol. 10.

33. Georges Wormser, *Clemenceau, vu de près* (Paris, 1979), 98–100.

34. Cited by Wormser, *La République de Clemenceau*, 187.

35. Duroselle, *Clemenceau*, chap. 14. For a fairly critical evaluation of both Mandel's and Ignace's actions, see the *Archives Israélites*, 5 Oct. 1922. For example,

the newspaper accused Ignace of pushing, in the name of a false conception of patriotism, for the expulsion of foreigners from France, among them a number of Jews who had fled persecution.

36. Barodet, *Professions de foi* (Gironde, 1919).

37. Cited by Favreau, *Georges Mandel*, 267ff.

38. *Hommes du Jour*, 4 Jan. 1919.

39. *Le Petit Radical*, 12 Nov. 1919, AD of Gironde, 3 M 269.

40. *Les Girondins*, 17 Nov. 1919; AD of Gironde, 3 M 269.

41. *Les Girondins*, 12 Nov. 1919. See also the issue of 31 Oct. 1919, AD of Gironde, 3 M 269.

42. *Le Journal du Médoc*, 19 Feb. 1928; AD of Gironde, 3 M 280.

43. *Le Journal du Médoc*, 5 Feb. 1928; *La Bataille*, 14 Apr. 1928; *Le Démocrate* and *Le Petit Médocain*, 8 Apr. 1928; AD of Gironde, 3 M 280.

44. See the propaganda posters of the PCF from the Bordeaux region in 1932, AD of Gironde, 3 M 287.

45. AD of Gironde, 3 M 280.

46. Report of Sûreté Générale, AD of Gironde, 3 M 285.

47. See Sherwood, *Georges Mandel and the Third Republic*, chap. 11.

48. See, for example, *La Libre Parole-Le Porc Épic*, 13 and 27 June 1935.

49. *Je Suis Partout*, 20 and 27 May 1938.

50. Pierre Dominique, *Monsieur le Parlement* (Paris, 1928), 44–45.

51. Georges Mandel, "Lettre à Édouard Herriot," dated 15 Dec. 1941, published by Michel Soulié, *La vie politique d'Édouard Herriot* (Paris, 1962), 523.

52. Cited in Favreau, *Georges Mandel*, 225.

53. Jeanneney, *Georges Mandel*, chap. 9.

54. Jules Moch, *Rencontres avec Léon Blum* (Paris, 1970), 330.

55. See Favreau, *Georges Mandel*, 262; Wormser, *Georges Mandel*, 299–300.

Chapter Sixteen

1. See Jean Charles, Jacques Girault, Jean-Louis Robert, Danielle Tartakowsky, and Claude Willard, *Le congrès de Tours* (Paris, 1980), 299.

2. Ibid., 410ff.

3. Archives of Seine, D 2 M 2 12.

4. Barodet, *Professions de foi*, 1919. See also the various proclamations to this effect signed the same year by Barrès, Erlich, Ignace, and others. Archives of Seine, D 3 M 2 12.

5. Jules Uhry, "Les grèves en France et leur solution" (doctoral thesis, Paris law school), BN 80 F 16 119.

6. Jules Uhry, *L'Aventurier contre la loi: L'étranglement de la grève des cheminots* (Paris, 1910).

7. "Jules Uhry," in *Dictionnaire biographique du mouvement ouvrier français*, ed. Jean Maitron (Paris, 1977), vol. 15.

8. Barodet, *Professions de foi*, 1919.

9. See Henry Torrès, *Histoire d'un complot* (Paris, 1921). At that time, Torrès was a lawyer defending the members of the Committee of the Third International.

10. J. E. S. Hayward, "The Official Social Philosophy of the French Third Republic: Léon Bourgeois and Solidarism," *International Review of Social History* 6 (1961); and John Weill, "Origins of the French Welfare State: Poor Relief in the Third Republic, 1871–1914," *French Historical Studies* (spring 1983).

11. See Paul Strauss, *Assistance sociale: Pauvres et mendiants* (Paris, 1901).

12. Paul Strauss, *La croisade sanitaire* (Paris, 1902), 322.

13. Dreyfus, *Misères sociales et études historiques*.

14. Pierre Laroque, *Les rapports entre patrons et ouvriers: Leur évolution en France depuis le XVIIIe siècle: Leur organisation contemporaine en France et à l'étranger* (Paris, 1938), 161.

15. Archives of the Conseil d'Etat, Pierre Laroque dossier; interview by the author with *conseiller d'Etat* Pierre Laroque, Nov. 1989.

16. See François-Xavier Merrien, "L'édification des états du 'bien-être.' Une étude comparative France-Grande-Bretagne" (thesis for the *doctorat d'état*, Université de Paris I, 1991), 333ff.

17. Archives of the Conseil d'Etat, P. Cahen-Salvador dossier; interview by the author with *conseiller d'Etat* Jean Cahen-Salvador, Paris, Feb. 1990.

18. Pierre Laroque, *La représentation des intérêts et le service public* (Paris, 1935), 46. See Merrien, "L'édification des états," 390ff.

19. Police department report, AD of Rhône, 3 M 2103.

20. AD of Gard, 3 M 805.

21. Ibid., 3 M 813; *Le Républicain du Midi*, 16 Apr. 1898.

22. AD of Gard, 3 M 291.

23. *L'Humanité*, 1 Apr. 1912.

24. See Igersheim, *L'Alsace des notables*; Jean-Claude Richez, "Georges Weill," *Encyclopédie de l'Alsace* (Strasbourg, 1985); J. Raymond, "Georges Weill," in Maitron, ed., *Dictionnaire biographique du mouvement ouvrier français*, vol. 5.

25. *Les Dernières Nouvelles de Strasbourg*, 10 May 1924, AD of Bas-Rhin, AL 121/50.

26. Police department report, AD of Bas-Rhin, EL 98, 1078.21 (a).

27. AD of Bas-Rhin, EL 98, 1079.

28. Ibid., AL 98, 1076, 2.

29. Ibid., 121/150.

30. Ibid., AL 98, 1076, 1.

31. See Jean-Claude Richez, "Salomon Grumbach," *Encyclopédie de l'Alsace* (Strasbourg, 1985); J. Raymond, "Salomon Grumbach," in Maitron, ed., *Dictionnaire biographique du mouvement ouvrier français*, vol. 30 (1987).

32. *L'Humanité*, 15 Nov. 1918.

33. *Le Populaire*, 14 Aug. 1933.

34. Alain Bergounioux, "Léon Blum, le socialisme et l'idée de République," *Cahiers Léon Blum* 19 (1988); Léo Hamon, "Réforme et pouvoir dans la pensée et la pratique de Léon Blum," *Annali della Fondazione Feltrinelli* (1983); "Jean Jaurès et Léon Blum," *Cahiers Léon Blum* 11 (1982); J. Raymond, "Léon Blum," in Maitron, ed., *Dictionnaire biographique du mouvement ouvrier français*, vol. 9 (1981); Joël Colton, *Léon Blum* (Paris, 1967).

35. Léon Blum, "Mémoires," in *L'Oeuvre de Léon Blum, 1940–1945* (Paris, 1964), 70.

36. Léon Blum, *Nouvelles conversations de Goethe avec Eckermann*, in *L'Oeuvre de Léon Blum 1891–1905* (1954), 220.

37. *L'Oeuvre de Léon Blum, 1934–1937* (1964), 282.

38. Barodet, *Professions de foi*, 1935 and 1936. In his platform statement during the same 1936 elections, Max Hymans also asked for "a reform of the state allowing it to dominate individual interests."

39. Archives of the Assemblée Nationale, Moch dossier, biography of the members of the provisional government, Ministry of Information, Paris, 1944, BN 40 Ln 6 185.

40. Jules Moch, *La Russie des Soviets* (Paris, 1925), 148.

41. Jules Moch, *Socialisme, crise, nationalisation* (Paris, 1932), 7.

42. See the very rich archival dossier on his electoral campaigns. Archives of Hérault, doc. 662.

43. Jules Moch, *Le partie socialiste et la politique financière* (Paris, 1928), 30ff.

44. Moch, *Rencontres avec Léon Blum*, 160. See also, by the same author, *Le Front populaire* (Paris, 1971).

45. Jules Moch, *Le communisme, jamais* (Paris, 1978), 16.

46. Jules Moch, "Le communisme et la France," speech given at the National Assembly, 16 Nov. 1948.

47. Archives of the Assemblée Nationale, Brunschvicg dossier.

48. AN, F1 B1 749, Dadoun dossier.

49. AN, F1 B1 784, Heumann dossier.

Chapter Seventeen

1. *Journal des Basses-Alpes*, 30 Apr. 1893, cited in El Gammal, "Joseph Reinach et la République," 1:222ff.

2. AD of Gironde, 3 M 238.

3. Numerous citations to that effect are in dossiers M 81095 and M 81189 of the AD of Somme.

4. *Journal du Médoc*, 13 Dec. 1927.

5. *Le Nouvelliste*, 8 Aug. 1928. Numerous quotations to that effect are in dossier 3 M 280 of AD of Gironde.

6. *Je Suis Partout*, 27 Oct. 1934.

7. Maurice Bedel, *Bengali* (Paris, 1935), 147.

8. *L'Indépendant de l'Aude*, 7 Mar. 1936.

9. *Le Courrier de Narbonne*, 21 Mar. 1935.

10. *L'Indépendant de l'Aude*, 28 Mar. 1936.

11. *Le Courrier de Narbonne*, 1 Aug. 1936.

12. *L'Information*, 18 Apr. 1937, AD of Hérault, doc. 662.

13. *L'Industriel de Louviers*, 21 and 28 Mar. and 4 Apr. 1936.

14. Ibid., 16 Apr. 1932.

15. Ibid. On these reactions against Blum and Mendès France, see Birnbaum, *Antisemitism*, chap. 6.

16. Cited by Freddy Raphaël and Robert Weyl, *Juifs en Alsace* (Toulouse, 1977), 377.

17. Doris Bensimon and Sergio Della Pergolia, *La population juive de France: Socio-démographie et identité* (Paris, 1986).

18. Birnbaum, "Nationalisme à la française," in Birnbaum, *La France aux français — Histoire des haines nationalistes* (Paris, 1993), chap. 11.

19. Maurice Barrès, *Bulletin Officiel de la Ligue de la Patrie Française*, 1 Jan. 1907.

20. AD of Somme, M 81189.

21. AD of Gironde, 3 M 280.

22. AD of Vosges, 3 M 62 and 13 M 69.

23. AD of Hérault, 15 n 64; *La Croix*, 26 Apr. 1914.

24. AD of Hérault, 15 n 64, *La Dépêche*, 6 Apr. 1914.

25. "Maurice de Rothschild," *Dictionnaire des parlementaires français*. In 1933, the deputy-mayor of Le Havre, Léon Meyer, was the laughingstock of *Je Suis Partout* because of his desire to win over Catholic confidence at all cost. *Je Suis Partout*, 19 Aug. 1933.

26. Barodet, *Professions de foi*, Oct. 1889, May 1906, May 1910.

27. AD of Vosges, 3 M 62.

28. Barodet, *Professions de foi*, May 1914.

29. Lazare Weiller, *Pro Alsatia*, 1930, BN LK 2 7519, pp. 19 and 84.

30. Henry Torrès, *La France trahie: Pierre Laval* (New York, 1943), 286.

31. Maurice Bokanowski, *Pour mieux connaître la France* (Paris, 1928).

32. Mendès France, *Oeuvres complètes*, 1 : 197 and 202.

33. Ibid. (1986), 3 : 417.

34. Barodet, *Professions de foi*, Apr. 1928.

35. AD of Somme, M 8695.

36. AD of Hérault, 15 M 64; and Barodet, *Professions de foi*, May 1924.

37. Jolly, "Fernand Crémieux," *Dictionnaire des parlementaires français*.

38. E. Javal, *Conférence*, 9 May 1889, BN Lb 57 11734. On Jules Moch, see *L'Information méridionale* for the month of Apr. 1937, AD of Hérault, doc. series 662.

39. Barodet, *Professions de foi*, May 1914. See also speeches to this effect in AD of Hérault, 14 n. 16.

40. Barodet, *Professions de foi*, Nov. 1919.

41. Ibid., May 1924.

42. Ibid., May 1910.

43. AD of Gironde, 3 M 280.

44. Barodet, *Professions de foi*, Apr. 1928, May 1932, May 1936.

45. Ibid., May 1932.

46. Archives of Paris, 3 M 2 12.

47. Archives of Paris, D 3 M 2 12.

48. *L'Insurgé*, 13 Apr. 1936.

49. *Le Courrier de Narbonne*, 23 Apr. 1936.

50. Léon Daudet, in *Action française*, 11 Apr. 1929; Charles Maurras, *Dictionnaire politique et critique*, 1 : 199.

51. Laurent Viguier, *Les juifs à travers Léon Blum: Leur incapacité à diriger un état* (Paris, 1940), 17.

52. *Cahiers Jaunes*, Oct. 1943.
53. AD of Somme M 81189; *La Libre Parole*, 27 Sept. 1901.
54. *Rivarol*, 3 Feb. 1955; *Fraternité Française*, 19 May 1956.

Chapter Eighteen

1. AN, F1 B1, 358, Levaillant dossier.
2. *Le Temps*, 26 Oct. 1911; APP, BA 1155, I. Levaillant dossier.
3. *Action Française*, 24 Oct. 1911.
4. Drumont, *La France juive*, 1 : 16 and 73 and 2 : 420.
5. *Archives Israélites*, 31 Mar. 1898.
6. *La Libre Parole*, 16 Feb. 1895.
7. *L'Autorité*, 12 Feb. 1895.
8. *La Libre Parole*, 19 Mar. 1893.
9. AN, F1 B1 358, Levaillant dossier.
10. APP, B A 1155, Levaillant dossier.
11. *La Libre Parole*, 29 Mar. 1893.
12. *Le Pays*, 18 Apr. 1885, in AP of Police, B A 1155, Levaillant dossier.
13. *Le Petit Caporal*, 31 Jan. 1888, AP of Police, B A 1155, Levaillant dossier.
14. *Le Petit Parisien*, 15 Apr. 1888; *La Lanterne*, 12 Apr. 1888.
15. Judge Charles Berr, whose name has often been cited, denied having had contact with Levaillant. AN, F1 B1 663, Berr dossier.
16. On this point, see the works in progress by Jean-Marc Berlière.
17. I. Levaillant, *Ma justification* (Paris, 1895), 7.
18. *La Libre Parole*, 7 Aug. 1889. In a later text, the same newspaper wrote: "By what this Yid confesses he did in the sphere within which he moved, by what Dreyfus of Nantes did, we can judge what Jewry would do if Catholic France lent its ear to the obscene 'pssst! pssst!' of Arthur Meyer and Naquet" (7 Mar. 1895).
19. See, for example, *La Croix*, 12 Feb. 1895.
20. The "true" names attributed to him are legion: from Levy to Volgesmuth, to name just two.
21. Published by the *Archives Israélites*, 12 Nov. 1911.
22. *Archives Israélites*, 28 Oct. 1911.
23. In 1907, I. Levaillant gave a famous speech, *La genèse de l'antisémitisme sous la Troisième République* (Paris, 1907). We shall return to this point.
24. *La Libre Parole*, 29 Sept. 1894.
25. See Chapter 8.
26. *La Libre Parole*, 9 Feb. 1900.
27. Ibid., 16 and 17 Aug. 1894, 20 Nov. 1897.
28. Lépine, *Mes souvenirs*, 44.
29. *La Gazette de la Somme*, 17 Nov. 1886, AN, F1 B1 321, Cohn dossier.
30. See Henri Lerner, *La Dépêche: Journal de la Démocratie* (Toulouse, 1978), 551.
31. *La France Libre*, 10 Feb. 1896, in AN, F1 B1 321, Cohn dossier.
32. AN, BB 18/1973, dossier 1523 A94.
33. See Chap. 10.
34. AN, F1 B1 498, Lion dossier.

35. AN, F1 B1 646, Lévi dossier.

36. *La Libre Parole*, 5 Jan. 1896. See also his administrative dossier F1 B1 530, Waltz dossier.

37. Ibid., 4 Sept. 1904. See other texts of an antisemitic nature in his dossier. AN, F1 B1 439, Beaucaire dossier.

38. Ibid., 13 Feb. 1907.

39. AN, F1 B1 523, Sée dossier.

40. AN, F1 B1 449, Cahen dossier.

41. *La Libre Parole*, 30 Aug. 1898.

42. *L'Est Républicain*, 3 Feb. 1898, AN, BB 6 II 1230. On political antisemitism in the east of France during this period, see William Serman, "The Nationalists of Meurthe-et-Moselle, 1898–1912," in *Nation and Nationalism in France, from Boulangism to the Great War*, ed. Robert Tombs (London, 1991).

43. *La Libre Parole*, 22 Dec. 1893. See Fernand Torrès's administrative dossier, AN, F1 B1 526.

44. *La Libre Parole*, 30 Aug. 1904.

45. Ibid., 3 Mar. 1896. We also find antisemitic attacks in the administrative dossier of Charles Berr, AN, BB 6 II 663.

46. *La Libre Parole*, 15 Mar. 1894 and 23 Mar. 1898. Eliacin Naquet was in fact the object of local antisemitic attacks. See AN, BB 18/900, legal proceedings for defamation of an antisemitic nature toward the *procureur général* of Aix, Eliacin Naquet.

47. *La Libre Parole du Midi*, 28 June 1890, in AN, BB 6 II 1095, E. Naquet dossier.

48. *La Libre Parole du Midi*, 18 June 1895.

49. Ibid., 11 Feb. 1900.

50. Ibid., 10 Feb. 1906.

51. AN, BB 6 II 33, Berr dossier.

52. AN, BB 6 II 462, Cahen dossier.

53. AN, BB 6 II 438, Anspach dossier. See one last letter of denunciation of a Jewish magistrate sent to the minister of justice in AN, BB 6 II 1230, Sommer dossier.

54. *Action Française*, 19 Aug. 1909. We find other antisemitic attacks against Victor Worms, at the time judge in Versailles, in his administrative dossier.

55. *Action Française*, 1 July 1909.

56. Daudet, *Le Palais de Police*, 30.

57. *La Libre Parole*, 9 Feb. 1895.

58. AN, BB 6 II 1230, Sommer dossier. The Dreyfus affair stirred up imaginations everywhere: hence, according to the police superintendent of Angers, the priest of Saint-Martin incited murder by claiming that the *président* judge of the Cour de Cassation, "M. Loew, is Jewish and wants to control the course of the Dreyfus affair." Yet this M. Loew was not at all Jewish, AN, F 19 5613. Simply put, the Affair led to a hunt for all supposed state Jews. Let us also note this astonishing commentary from *La Croix*, 15 Aug. 1893: "M. Bruman, Catholic by birth and even with relations in Normandy, proved to be a sectarian Jew in Nivernais in

relation to its citizens. This *préfet*, Jewish in his heart, has had the pensions of two priests suppressed."

59. Such is the thesis in many ways iconoclastic but also disputable maintained by Eugen Weber, "Reflections on the Jews in France," in *The Jews in Modern France*, ed. Frances Malino and Bernard Wassertain (Hanover, N.H., 1985), 23ff.

60. *L'Autorité*, 18 Dec. 1902; *L'Intransigeant*, 19 Dec. 1902 and 8 Jan. 1903, AN, F 7 12 926. See also the anonymous letters of denunciation, AN, BB 6 II 613, Abram dossier.

61. *La Presse*, 18 Dec. 1902. See also *La Libre Parole*, 19 Dec. 1902.

62. *La Libre Parole*, 28 Dec. 1898. See also *La Libre Parole* of 28 July 1908 and 17 Jan. 1919; and *Action Française* of 25 July 1908 and 28 Oct. 1909.

63. *Semaine Religieuse du Diocèse de Nevers*, 42 (15 Oct. 1898), AN, F 19 5447.

Chapter Nineteen

1. Let us once more underscore the fact that there exists to date no systematic study of the prefect civil service, the magistracy, or the army under the Third Republic. It is therefore not possible to make comparisons here between these general populations and that constituted, in each of the three corps, by state Jews. It is also not a question of undertaking rigorous quantitative analyses on the rate of careers or their duration, since their significance, once more, would have no meaning except in a comparative study with Catholic and Protestant functionaries in each of these sectors of the administration. As a result, we have rather undertaken a qualitative description of the elements playing a role in the course of these careers. Let us note, finally, that the more global problem of purges did not arise during that period, at least after 1877 and that, in any case, nothing comparative could be legitimately undertaken in this matter for lack of adequate information. On this period in general, see Vincent Wright, "Les épurations administratives de 1848 à 1885," in *Les épurations administratives. XIXe et XXe siècles*, ed. Paul Gerbod et al. (Geneva, 1977). In order to be better able to evaluate these administrative dossiers of state Jews, we nevertheless tried to compare them, solely from a qualitative point of view, with those of their non-Jewish colleagues. This work was not conducted in a systematic manner but simply by considering all the dossiers in the same box as the dossiers of Jewish *préfets*, that is, a total of 152 dossiers of Catholic and 11 dossiers of Protestant functionaries from the prefect civil service.

2. We have counted eighteen dossiers bearing this type of notation of "anticlerical Catholic" or "freethinking Catholic" or "nonpracticing Catholic" or "born in the Catholic region. Anticlerical." See, for example AN, F1 B1 449, Buisson dossier; AN, F1 B1 384, Spinosi dossier; AN, F1 B1 425, Lallemand dossier; AN, F1 B1 457, Lamargue dossier; AN, F1 B1 321, Comolet dossier; AN, F1 B1 305, Bernard dossier; AN, F1 B1 526, De Tournefort dossier; AN, F1 B1 487, Huguet dossier; AN, F1 B1 297, Abeille dossier, and so on. The dossier of *sous-préfet* Vaillant, AN, F1 B1 528, even includes the notation, "Catholic, anticlerical republican"; an admirer of Voltaire, he was opposed in Côtes-du-Nord by a priest who preached in Breton. All that nevertheless remained good-natured and rarely elicited local passions of rejection leading directly to a virulent ostracism. A single Catholic from our sample

married a Protestant woman who, moreover, was born in the United States: as a result, for once, a short excerpt from *La Nation* of 22 Apr. 1889 figures in this dossier, accusing him of being "an Opportunist, Joseph Reinach's right-hand man." See AN, F1 B1 250, Jossier dossier.

3. Even when they had somewhat conspicuous patronymics that could have led to confusion in that time of intolerance, Protestant officials did not provoke local rejection or national press campaigns. See, for example, AN, F1 B1 391, Weibel dossier, or AN, F1 B1 530, Zurcher dossier. It was the same for Catholic officials whose names suggested an origin that could be considered foreign. See, for example, AN, F1 B1 391, Zaëpgel dossier; AN, F1 B1 391, Youf dossier; AN, F1 B1 414, Konarski dossier; and AN, F1 B1 437, Koziorossicz dossier. We could extend that idea and note that the few Catholic officials whose names were identical to those of Jewish officials had utterly calm dossiers.

4. Let us give a single example, that of Judge Édouard Bloch. See AN, BB 6 II 453, Bloch dossier.

5. AN, F1 B1 490, Kinsbourg dossier.

6. AN, BB 6 II 33, Berr dossier.

7. See the example of the dossier of *sous-préfet* René Brisac and his administrative reports from 1894 and 1903 where, each time, "Israelite" is underlined in blue, AN, F1 B1 597. At that time, it was the same for the dossier of Judge Benjamin Abram, BB 6 II 613.

8. AN, F1 B1 507, Mossé dossier.

9. See Hyman, *From Dreyfus to Vichy*; Simon Schwartzfuchs, *Du juif à l'israélite* (Paris, 1989).

10. In 1937, therefore, we find the expression "freethinker of Jewish origin" in the dossier of *sous-préfet* Henri Hendlé, while, in those of Pierre Aron (in 1926) and Édouard Aron (in 1923), there figured the notation "Jewish, freethinker" or "Jewish, nonpracticing freethinker." This notation rarely appears among magistrates, who are simply called Jewish, even in the 1930s.

11. AN, BB 6 I 1164, Pontrémoli dossier.

12. See Archives of the Conseil d'Etat, dossiers concerning André Spire, René Worms, and Henri Weill.

13. See the dossier of Paul Grumbach, SHA, GB 21. His enlistment papers date from 1879.

14. SHA, GD, second series, 1615, Sée dossier.

15. SHA, GB, fourth series, 124, Lévy dossier.

16. AN, BB 6 II 26, Bédarridès dossier; AN, BB 6 II 462, Cahen dossier; and AN, BB 6 II 1230, Sommer dossier.

17. AN, BB 6 II 619, Alphandéry dossier.

18. AN, F1 B1 160.13, Franck dossier; and AN, F1 B1 487, Isaac dossier.

19. AN, F1 B1 530, Weill dossier.

20. AN, F1 B1 784, Heumann dossier.

21. SHA, GB, third series, 1831, Carvallo dossier.

22. SHA, GD, third series, 582, Bloch dossier.

23. AN, F1 B1 1530, Waltz dossier.

24. AN, F1 B1 166 26, Léon dossier.

25. AN, F1 B1 439, Beaucaire dossier.

26. AN, BB 6 II 26, Bédarridès dossier.

27. AN, BB 6 II 501, Félix dossier.

28. AN, BB 6 II 1024, Lévy dossier.

29. AN, BB 6 II 419, Valabrègue dossier.

30. AN, BB 6 II 290, May dossier.

31. AN, BB 6 II 594, Sée dossier.

32. AN, F1 B1 597, Brisac dossier.

33. AN, F1 B1 297, Aaron dossier.

34. See Bergmann, *Paul Grunebaum-Ballin*, 24.

35. André Spire, *Bulletin de L'Amitié Charles Péguy*, Aug. 1954, 1.

36. AN, BB 6 II 551, Masse dossier. Others who were the object of antisemitic attacks also complained of the slow rate of their careers, though it is not always possible to strictly link one to the other. See, for example, AN, BB 6 II 1292, Worms dossier.

37. See Chap. 6.

38. AN, BB 6 II, Dreyfus dossier.

39. SHA, GB, third series, 1081, Francfort dossier. The letters cited earlier were all taken from this rather unusual dossier.

40. SHA, GD, third series, 386, Naquet-Laroque dossier.

41. SHA, GB, third series, 1119, Dennery dossier; GD, third series, 471, Valabrègue dossier; and GD, third series, 692, Heymann dossier.

42. SHA, GB, fourth series, 1572, Weiller dossier.

43. *L'Univers Israélite*, 15 July 1927.

44. AN, BB 6 II 619, Alphandéry dossier.

45. AN, BB 6 II 613, Abram dossier.

46. AN, F1 B1 524, Strauss dossier.

47. The Archives Nationales contain dossiers indicating conferral of the Legion of Honor, which would have to be analyzed in a comparative and systematic manner. See, for example, the dossiers of Anspach, LH 41/54; Félix, LH 953/35; Hendlé, LH 1281/133; Levaillant, LH 1623/71; Mossé, LH 1935/41; Sée, LH 2478/35; and Strauss, LH 2554/41.

48. We cannot undertake a comparative analysis with the careers, advancements, and types of promotion of non-Jewish officials for lack of general data. On the problem as it was posed in the nineteenth century, see Guy Thuillier, *Bureaucratie et bureaucrates en France au XIXe siècle* (Geneva, 1980), part 3.

49. AN, BB 6 II 789, Dalmbert dossier.

50. AN, BB 6 II 663, Berr dossier.

51. Cited by Bergmann, *Paul Grunebaum-Ballin*, 140–41.

52. Interviews by the author with *conseillers d'Etat* Jean Cahen-Salvador and Pierre Laroque, Paris, 1989.

53. See AN, F1 B1 166 34, Lisbonne dossier; AN, F1 B1 321, Cohn dossier; AN, F1 B1 347, Hendlé dossier; and AN, F1 B1 170 16, Pinède dossier.

54. AN, F1 B1 297, Aron dossier.

55. AN, F1 B1 498, Lion dossier.

56. AN, F1 B1 646, Lévi dossier.

57. AN, F1 B1 487, Isaac dossier.
58. An, F1 B1 507, Mossé dossier.
59. AN, F1 B1 166 8, Lambert dossier.
60. AN, F1 B1 314, Caen dossier.
61. AN, BB 6 II 33, Berr dossier.
62. AN, BB 6 II 594, Sée dossier.
63. AN, BB 6 II 290, May dossier.
64. AN, F1 B1 173 5, Saint-Paul dossier.
65. AN, BB 6 II 613, Abram dossier.
66. AN, F1 B1 365, Mayer dossier. Similarly, a police report explains the election of David Mossé to the head of the Uzès mayor's office by the equal influence of Catholics and Protestants, which canceled each other out, thus making possible his victory in the local elections. AN, BB 6 II 560, Mossé dossier. His later career as magistrate was not very glorious, however.
67. AN, F1 B1 581, Aron dossier.
68. AN, F1 B1 487, Isaac dossier.
69. AN, B II 290, May dossier.
70. AN, F1 B1 166 32, Lévylier, dossier.
71. AN, F1 B1 528, Valabrègue dossier.
72. AN, F1 B1 530, Waltz dossier.
73. AN, F1 B1 439, Beaucaire dossier.
74. AN, F1 B1 305, Benedetti dossier.
75. AN, F1 B1 526, Tommasini dossier.
76. See AN, F1 B1 530, Zevaco dossier; and AN, F1 B1 626, Sigaudy dossier.
77. AN, F1 B1 748, Sialetti dossier.
78. AN, F B II 439, Baroli dossier.
79. AN, F1 B1 344, Jourdan dossier.
80. AN, F1 B1 312, Jalabert dossier.
81. AN, F1 B1 526, Tourel dossier.
82. See, for example, AN, F1 B1 498, Lombard dossier; this Protestant *sous-préfet* was born in Gard; or AN, F1 B1 528, Verdin-Havard dossier; this *préfet* came from Nîmes.
83. This remark obviously does not apply to all Protestant officials; I am merely evoking here the dossiers of Protestants consulted during this research. See, for example, AN, F1 B1 391, Weibel dossier; AN, F1 B1, Bujeaud dossier; and AN, F1 B1 530, Zurcher dossier.
84. AN, F1 B II 523, Schmidt dossier.

Chapter Twenty

1. See the different texts in *Le Statut des juifs de Vichy: Documentation* (Paris, 1990).
2. Pierre Birnbaum, "Identité catholique et suffrage universel: L'exemple français," *Revue Internationale des Sciences Sociales*, Aug. 1991.
3. Archives of the Assemblé Nationale, Meyer, Rothschild, Lévy-Alphandéry, Mendès France, and Torrès dossiers. Léon Daudet was overjoyed at such measures

(1 Nov. 1940). On the more general problem of the Vichy regime's rescinding of French nationality, which affected Jews for the most part, see Bernard Laguerre, "Les dénaturalisés de Vichy, 1940–1944," *Vingtième Siècle*, Oct.–Dec, 1988, p. 11.

4. SHA, GB, fourth series, 664, Baumann dossier.

5. SHA, GD, 635/4, Boris dossier.

6. See SHA, GD, 1534/4, Rheims dossier; GD, 1384/4, Rueff dossier; and GB, fourth series, 1572, Weiller dossier.

7. See Archives of the Conseil d'Etat for the dossiers concerning Cahen, Salvador, Grunebaum-Ballin, and Pierre Laroque, among others. From this perspective, we cannot cite the administrative dossiers concerning state Jews who were members of the prefect civil service or the magistracy because it is still impossible, given the current state of the law, to consult them. We cannot therefore account for the fate under Vichy of those state Jews of which it has often been a question in this book through their own personnel dossiers. As a result, in the following pages, there is a certain altogether involuntary imbalance.

8. Interview by the author with General Michel Brisac, Paris, 1989. Other derogations were granted, from which, for example, the inspector of finance Jacques Ruef, a few mining engineers, and some others benefited. In reality, quite a few Jewish high officials were excluded through this proceeding: 59 in Justice, 25 in Interior, 1,284 in the armies, 1,111 in National Education, and so on. See Claude Singer, "L'université et les juifs: La remise en question de l'intégration en France de 1940 à 1944" (doctoral thesis in history, Université Paris I, 1991), 302 and 439. On the purge of Jewish *conseillers d'Etat*, see Marie-Christine Kessler, *Le Conseil d'état* (Paris, 1968), 65.

9. Archives of the Central Consistory, box 11.

10. AN, BB 30 1714.

11. Ibid.

12. Ibid. Somewhat later, however, Jean Laroque proposed to the central consistory to work in its service. Archives of the Central Consistory, box 11.

13. Interview by the author with *conseiller d'Etat* Pierre Laroque, brother of Jean Laroque, Paris, 1989.

14. Joseph Barthélemy, *Ministre de la Justice: Vichy, 1941–1943 — Mémoires* (Paris, 1989), 267.

15. AN, BB 30 1711.

16. Ibid.

17. On the Javals, see Chap. 12. On this specific point, see Michel Slitinsky, *Les spoliations à Bordeaux et dans la région, 1940–1944* (Bordeaux, n.d.).

18. See, for example, Chap. 10.

19. Cited by Darmon, *Abraham Schrameck*, 91.

20. Archives of the Central Consistory, box 32.

21. Ibid.

22. Ibid., box 1.

23. Ibid.

24. Wormser, *Français israélite*, 11–14.

25. Cited in Jules Jeanneney, *Journal politique* (Paris, 1952), 475.

26. Archives of the Central Consistory, box 32. Some of these texts, often in

more abridged form, are presented in Adam Rutkowski, *La lutte des juifs de France à l'époque de l'Occupation* (Paris, 1975).

27. Pierre Laroque interview, Paris, 1989.

28. Archives of the Central Consistory, box 49.

29. Ibid., box 9.

30. Cited in Jeanneney, *Journal politique*, 284–85. In another very famous letter, Pierre Masse protested before Pétain against the exclusion of Jews from the Legion of Honor: "I would be very obliged to you to tell me if I must remove the stripes of my brother, second lieutenant of the Thirty-sixth Infantry Regiment, killed in Douaumont in April 1916, or of my son-in-law, second lieutenant of the Fourteenth Motorized Cavalry, killed in Belgium in May 1940, or of my nephew, Jean-Pierre Masse, killed in Rethel in May 1940? May I leave my brother the Médaille Militaire earned in Neuville-Saint-Vaast, with which I buried him? And finally, am I assured that someone will not take back the medal of Sainte-Hélène from my great-grandfather? I want to conform to the laws of my country even when they are dictated by the invader" (*Pierre Masse* [Paris, 1947]).

31. Cited by Bergmann, *Paul Grunebaum-Ballin*, 183–84.

32. These two texts are also cited in ibid., 185–86.

33. On this theme, see Danielle Lochak, "La doctrine sous Vichy ou les mésaventures du positivisme," in Danielle Lochak et al., *Les usages sociaux du droit* (Paris, 1989).

34. Private archives of P. Grunebaum-Ballin (under the direction of Brigitte Bergmann).

35. Pierre Laroque interview, Paris, 1989.

36. See André Blumel, *Un grand juif: Léon Meiss*, postface by Georges Wormser (Paris, 1967).

37. See the Archives of the Conseil d'Etat, Helbronner dossier.

38. On Jacques Helbronner and Pierre Seligman, see Raymond-Raoul Lambert, *Carnet d'un témoin, 1940–1943*, presented by Richard Cohen (Paris, 1985); and Richard Cohen, *The Burden of Conscience: French Jewry's Response to the Holocaust* (Bloomington, Ind., 1987).

39. Pierre Aubert, "Les circulaires de Vichy et de sa délégation générale à Paris," *Administration*, 15 Jan. 1988.

40. Bernard Bergerot, "Le corps préfectoral de 1940 à 1944," *Administration*, Oct. 1987, 9. The example of the Bordeaux *préfecture* where Maurice Sabatier and Maurice Papon efficiently operated is one of the better known. See Michel Slitinsky, *L'Affaire Papon* (Paris, 1983).

41. Marrus and Paxton, *Vichy France and the Jews*, 139, 236, 274.

42. Joseph Billig, *Le commissariat général aux questions juives* (Paris, 1955–60), 3:159. For a more general outline of this question of the role proper to Vichy, see Denis Peschanski, "Exclusion, persécution, répression," in Azéma and Bédarida, eds., *Vichy et les Français*. Some prefects collaborated enthusiastically, others were more prudent, and still others entered the Resistance (some of them were deported). See Sonia Mazey and Vincent Wright, "Les préfets," in Azéma and Bédarida, eds., *Vichy et les Français*.

43. See Barthélemy, *Ministre de la Justice*.

44. Marrus and Paxton, *Vichy France and the Jews*, 138. See also Robert Paxton, *Vichy France* (New York and London, 1972), in particular chap. 5.

45. Cahen-Salvador interview, Paris, 1989. See also Jean Cahen-Salvador, *Le Conseil d'état, 1799–1974* (Paris, 1974), chap. 13, "Le Conseil d'état de 1939 à 1945," 794.

46. Cited by Bergmann, *Paul Grunebaum-Ballin*, 202.

47. Cahen-Salvador interview, Paris, 1989.

48. Archives of the Central Consistory, box 5.

49. Archives of the Assemblé Nationale, Wallach dossier.

50. Jean Pierre-Bloch, *Le temps d'y penser encore* (Paris, 1977), 78–79.

51. Pierre-Bloch, *Mes jours heureux*, 103.

52. Pierre-Bloch, *Jusqu'au dernier jour*, 173 and 185.

53. A. Weil-Curiel, *Le temps de la honte* (Paris, 1947), 3:169.

54. Jacques Adler, *Face à la persécution: Les organisations juives à Paris de 1940 à 1944* (Paris, 1985), 251.

55. Archives of the Central Consistory, box 5.

56. Ibid., box 9.

57. Ibid., box 3.

58. Ibid., box 9.

59. Ibid., box 1.

60. Ibid., box 2.

61. Cahen-Salvador interview, Paris, 1989.

62. Bergmann, *Paul Grunebaum-Ballin*, 192–93.

63. Archives of the Central Consistory, boxes 2, 3, and 5.

64. Ibid., box 2.

65. Ibid., box 44.

66. See Zosa Szajkowski, *Analytical Franco-Jewish Gazetteer, 1939–1945: With an Introduction to Some Problems in Writing the History of the Jews during World War II* (New York, 1966); Adler, *Face à la persécution*, chap. 3; and Cohen, *The Burden of Conscience*, chap. 7.

67. See Lambert, *Carnet d'un témoin*, 151 and 178.

68. Adler, *Face à la persécution*, 156.

69. Archives of the Central Consistory, box 9.

70. Ibid.

71. Ibid.

72. Ibid.

73. Cited by Serge Klarsfeld, *Vichy-Auschwitz: Le rôle de Vichy dans la solution finale de la Question juive en France, 1943–1944* (Paris, 1985), 278.

74. Consistorial Archives, boxes 9 and 11.

75. Ibid., box 9.

76. Ibid., box 1.

77. See Maurice Moch, *L'étoile et la francisque: Les institutions juives sous Vichy* (Paris, 1990), 194ff.

78. Archives of the Central Consistory, box 5.

79. Such was already the dilemma of long standing for German Jews toward all their coreligionists from the East. See the book by Steven Ascheim, *Brothers and Strangers* (Madison, Wis., 1982).

80. On his stay in Compiègne and his deportatiop, see Jean-Jacques Bernard, *Le camp de la mort lente: Compiègne, 1941–1942* (Paris, 1944), 173ff. On his stay in Drancy, Jacques Charpentier, *Au service de la liberté* (Paris, 1949). We know that Pétain supposedly intervened personally to attempt to save Pierre Masse. See Barthélemy, *Ministre de la Justice*, 590.

81. We read an astonishing description of Robert Dreyfus, *conseiller* to the Cour de Cassation, devoured at the Compiègne camp by "lice" in Bernard, *Le camp de la mort lente*, 223.

82. *Le Jaune et le Rouge*, Mar. 1976.

83. It seems that no Jewish *préfet* or *sous-préfet* died under such circumstances; three members of the prefect civil service of lower rank were, however, deported and murdered: Bernard Bernstein, editor of the central administration, Georges Bloch, special senior agent, and Alain Mossé, grandson of a *préfet*, himself *chef de cabinet* to the *préfet* of Savoy. Two others died in battle during acts of resistance: Jacques Cahen, *chef de cabinet* to the *préfet* of Côte-d'Or, and Maurice Lévy, bureau chief. Georges Thomé, "Mémorial des fonctionnaires du corps préfectoral et de l'administration centrales morts pour la France, 1939–1945," *Administration* (15 July 1988).

Conclusion

1. *Archives Israélites*, 27 June 1901, 26 Nov. 1903, 6 Dec. 1906, and 29 Jan. 1925. In its issue of 14 Apr. 1927, this newspaper wrote that only one Jew had managed to enter diplomacy, to be named consul general in China. We recall, in fact, that Maurice Bloch exercised important duties both at the Cour des Comptes and at the Inspections des Finances, but he probably "abjured his native faith." *Archives Israélites*, 28 Feb. 1929. We can only hope that another researcher will come to examine these "fortresses," these three *grands corps*, for that period.

2. *L'Univers Israélite*, 9 Dec. 1898.

Index

Library of Congress Cataloging-in-Publication Data

Birnbaum, Pierre.
  [Fous de la République. English]
  The Jews of the Republic: a political history of state Jews in
France from Gambetta to Vichy / Pierre Birnbaum ; translated by Jane
Marie Todd.
    p. cm. — (Stanford studies in Jewish history and culture)
  Includes bibliographical references.
  ISBN 0-8047-2633-7 (cloth: alk. paper)
  1. Jews in public life — France — Biography.   2. Jews — France —
Biography.   3. Jews — France — History.   4. France — Politics and
government — 1870–1940.   5. France — Ethnic relations.   I. Title.
II. Series.
DS 135. F9B57   1996
994'.004924 — dc20
[B]
96-10603   CIP

Original printing 1996

Last figure below indicates year of this printing:

05 04 03 02 01 00 99 98 97 96